THE MITCHELL BEAZLEY
TRAVELLER'S GUIDES TO ART

ITALY

Helen Langdon

with a major contribution by

Paul Holberton

Mitchell Beazley

Contributors

Ian Chilvers	Biographies
	Glossary
Paul Holberton	North East Italy
	Southern Italy (excluding Naples, Capua and Caserta)
	Sicily
Sarah Hyde	Siena recorded in frescoes
Michael Jacobs	Sardinia
	Venetian palace interiors

Acknowledgments
The author and publishers wish to thank the following for their help in the preparation of this book: Marco Fabio Apolloni, Linda Cole, Joseph Coughlan, Diana Davies, Robert Gibbs, Italian State Tourist Office, Anthony Langdon. They are also grateful to Weidenfeld and Nicolson Ltd. for permission to reprint extracts from *Born Under Saturn* by Rudolf Wittkower (p.125, p.148, p.238).

Jacket picture
Cima da Conegliano, **Madonna of the Orange-tree** *(detail), c.1500, Accademia, Venice. Photograph courtesy of Scala, Florence.*

Editor	Diana Grant
Designer	Nigel O'Gorman
Picture Researcher	Brigitte Arora
Assistant Editor	Catherine Jackson
Editorial Assistants	Barbara Gish
	Alison Hancock
Production	Jean Rigby

Maps and floor plans in two-colour by
Eugene Fleury, Illustra Design Ltd.,
Colin Salmon, Technical Art Services

Edited and designed by
Mitchell Beazley International Limited
87–89 Shaftesbury Avenue
London W1V 7AD

Filmsetting by Vantage Photosetting Co. Ltd.,
Eastleigh, England
Printed and bound by New Inter Litho, Milan,
Italy

CONTENTS

FOREWORD

The intention in researching this guide has been not only to visit the maximum number of museums and galleries with art treasures, but also to bring to light little-known works that deserve recognition, as well as unjustifiably neglected artists. A special feature of the book are the illustrated tours, which concentrate on artists and styles with strong regional connections. In the gazetteer sections, no attempt has been made to compile exhaustive lists of works of art; instead, the approach is critical and selective. The main emphasis is always on fine art, although mention is made of major archaeological and decorative arts collections. Wherever possible, the author and contributors have tried to verify attributions and to look at traditional masterpieces with a fresh eye.

Few guidebooks are without error, and no guidebook can ever be completely up to date. Without any warning, opening times and telephone numbers change, collections are reorganized, and museums and galleries close for restoration. While every effort has been made to ensure that all information is accurate at the time of going to press, the publishers will be glad to receive corrections and suggestions for improvements, which can be incorporated in the next edition.

How this book is organized

The guide is sectioned into areas, each with its own introduction and map, and these sections are arranged alphabetically by town and museum (see pp.8–9 for a map of all the areas). Each area map shows (in black) the towns and villages listed in the section, and all these entries are identified by province, region and map reference.

Names of regions, towns and museums are given in Italian so that you can easily locate them when you are on the spot; a translation is given if the English name is especially familiar; thus Colonna Traiana is translated as Trajan's Column. Churches with saints' names are listed under S, alphabetically by the name of the saint; thus Santa Teresa will appear after Santo Stefano. Church museums and treasuries are generally listed under the appropriate church but larger collections, especially those displayed in separate buildings, have individual entries.

Entries for museums, galleries and churches

Addresses and telephone numbers are given for each entry where applicable. Opening times are provided for museums and galleries and for churches that keep particularly unusual hours. For other churches, the standard hours are roughly 7.30am–12.30pm and 3–6.30pm (4–7.30pm in summer), although these may vary considerably. On Sunday, some churches are open only to those participating in services, or they may be open to sightseers only when services are not in progress. On public holidays, museums and churches generally follow Sunday opening times, but it is always worth checking before visiting. Other practical information is provided in the form of symbols (see right).

Italic type is used for entry details; **bold** type for highlighting sections, rooms or individual works of art; ***bold italic*** for titles of works of art. Single or double stars denote collections and works of art that are, in the authors' opinion, of particular or outstanding importance. For the sake of clarity, no punctuation is added after these stars. Room numbers are given in Arabic or Roman numerals, according to the usage of the museum. The text sometimes refers to coins for operating the lights in churches; 100L coins are sufficient for most machines, but at Spello 1,000L notes are required.

Cross-references
Different typefaces are employed to cross-refer to different parts of the book; thus MUSEO DEL DUOMO refers to another museum within the same town, MASSA MARITTIMA to another town within the same area, and *NORTH CENTRAL ITALY* to another area.

Abbreviations
As far as possible, only standard abbreviations are used. These include Mon, Tues, etc. for days of the week; Jan, Feb, etc. for months; N, S, E, W for points of the compass; C for century; c. for *circa*; m, km, etc. for measurements; mins, hrs, yrs for times. As a general rule, the abbreviation AD is dropped from dates after AD300. Less common abbreviations are b. for born, a. for active and d. for died.

Key to symbols
Symbols used in text

☆   Important collection, not to be missed

☆☆ Outstanding collection, not to be missed

★   Important work of art

★★ Outstanding work of art

▣   Entry free

▩   Entry fee payable

➤   Parking

𝄆   Guided tours available

▮   Guided tours compulsory

▯   Catalogues, guidebooks and other publications on sale

▮   Refreshments available

🏛   Building of architectural interest

☑   Well displayed and pleasant to visit

♣   Garden or courtyard open to the public

▦   Temporary exhibitions worth investigating

▴   Important single artist's collection

Symbols used on maps

⊕   Major art center

O   Minor art center

⦂⦂ Archaeological site

How entries are organized

STRA ————— Red capitals for name of town
Padova, Veneto Map B5 ——— Red italic type for province, region and map reference

A peaceful little town on the banks of the river Brenta, Stra is renowned for its many villas, of which the most famous is the 18thC Villa Pisani.

Villa Pisani ——————— Bold red type for name of museum,
Tel. (049) 502074   church or villa
Open Tues – Sat 9am – 1pm, 3 – 6pm, Sun 9am – 1pm. Park open daily 9am – sunset —— Black italic type for entry details
Villa closed Mon
▩ ▯ 🏛 ☑ ♣ ————————— Symbols providing other practical information

The villa is perhaps now more famous as the site of the first meeting between Hitler and Mussolini than for its architecture, furniture, paintings and especially fine ceiling by Tiepolo, the ***House of the Pisani in Glory*★** ——— Bold italic type for titles of works (1761–62). The **furniture and** —— of art; stars to denote works of **paintings** are all 18thC and 19thC (the particular importance paintings including works by Amigoni, Carriera and Longhi) and there is a   Bold type for emphasis magnificent park.

ART TREASURES
of ITALY

Italy is richer in art treasures than any other country in the world, yet its
towns and cities are not dominated by museums; the frescoes in the churches,
the statues that still stand in so many squares, are easily accessible; art is both
revered and taken for granted, part of everyday life and yet profoundly
moving; our enjoyment is enhanced by the sheer splendour of so many
settings – by the abundance of churches, palaces, fountains and piazzas, which
all create an unbroken sense of design stretching back to Roman antiquity.

The GREAT CITIES

Three great centers – Rome, Florence and Venice – dominate. The Vatican
museums, with the Sistine ceiling and Raphael Stanze, the Florentine
galleries of the Uffizi and Pitti, the festive Piazza San Marco in Venice – are
among the most celebrated tourist attractions in the world. Yet it is
sometimes a pleasure to turn from the crowds to quieter parts of these historic
cities. In Rome, with its exciting mixture of ancient grandeur and Baroque
panache, where the simple brick campanili of early Christian churches stand
out against classical ruins, the other galleries are surprisingly little visited and
almost every church has something to offer; it is still startling to discover
Bernini's **Death of the Blessed Ludovica Albertoni** in a dark, almost
forgotten church in Trastevere. Florence, smaller and more intimate, is given
its distinctive character by a wealth of outdoor Renaissance sculpture; in
Venice, the streets away from the center are wonderfully picturesque, and
many far-flung churches retain spectacular works of art.

A MOVING SENSE *of the* PAST

Throughout Italy, the grandeur of the past mingles vividly with the present.
A Roman temple facade is incorporated into the tiny square at Assisi; little,
red-roofed houses ring the site of a Roman amphitheater at Lucca. Sicily has
plentiful evidence of an even earlier civilization, in impressive Greek ruins
that rival even those of Greece. Etruscan tombs are scattered around the
desolate, rocky countryside N of Rome. The brilliance of Byzantine
civilization lingers on in the glittering mosaics of Ravenna and Venice.
   In Italy, the Middle Ages are never very far away. The medieval hill
towns of Tuscany and Umbria – set in an idyllic countryside, planted with
cypress trees, olive groves and vineyards that have changed little since they
were painted by Renaissance artists – are the very essence of Italy; a 14thC
Italian would still feel at home in the dark, narrow streets of San Gimignano
and Siena, of Gubbio and Spoleto. Even in the industrial North, many cities
retain impressive old centers; both here, and in the southern region of
Apulia, a wealth of Romanesque sculpture attracts the art lover.

ART OUTSIDE *the* GALLERIES

Medieval church sculpture; dusty cathedral treasures with dazzling examples
of the goldsmith's craft; Baroque fountains splashing in lively, festive squares;
these are only some of the attractions outside the galleries. Among the best
loved of all Italy's art treasures are her great Renaissance fresco cycles. Few of
us need directing to the works of Giotto at Padua or Assisi, or of Piero della
Francesca at Arezzo. Yet there is still a sense of discovery in stumbling across
frescoes by Benozzo Gozzoli at tiny Montefalco, or a chapel frescoed by
Pintoricchio in the little town of Spello.

From the 16thC onwards, the more opulent villas were embellished with frescoed decorations; outstanding examples – their beauty often enriched by splendid gardens – are in the Veneto, around Florence and in Lazio. The 16thC also heralded a new era in church decoration; Correggio's frescoes in Parma lead on to the spectacular illusionism and opulence of 17thC Baroque churches in Rome and Naples.

PRINCELY COLLECTIONS MADE PUBLIC

Many of the great Italian collections began life in private hands. The Renaissance prince was a passionate collector, using art to express his own power and glory. Most of the celebrated Gonzaga heritage has now been dispersed, yet one may still sense something of its scale and splendour in the rooms of the ducal palace at Mantua. Further S, at Urbino, the spirit of that learned collector, Federico da Montefeltro, lingers on in the harmonious apartments of his own ducal palace. In Florence, Vasari designed the light and spacious galleries of the Uffizi to house the Medici collections of ancient and modern sculpture; here, too, the opulence of a later age is suggested by the princely collections and frescoes of the Palazzo Pitti.

In Rome, the Vatican museums acquired their treasures through the power and for the prestige of the papacy. Julius II, one of the greatest art patrons of all time, displayed his most celebrated antiquities in the courtyard of the Palazzo Belvedere, where most remain to this day. In the 17thC, the papal nephews competed ruthlessly with one another. The wide-ranging collection of the luxury-loving and powerful Cardinal Scipione Borghese has been preserved virtually intact, its grandeur contrasting with the smaller collection of Cardinal Bernardino Spada. The galleries of the Palazzo Doria Pamphili were designed by the Doria family especially for the pictures that still hang there, gold frame to frame, in gilded splendour.

The PROVINCIAL GALLERIES

Two of the grandest Italian galleries, the Brera in Milan and the Accademia in Venice, were founded by Napoleon in the early 19thC. Other public museums followed, civic consciousness growing with the unification of Italy in 1870. Now, every little town seems to have its local Pinacoteca, often tucked away in the town hall with the library and civic offices. Amid the clutter of centuries, almost all these galleries yield something of interest. Occasionally, the rewards are spectacular; at the little known gallery of Pesaro, for example, is a lovely **Coronation of the Virgin** by Giovanni Bellini. Many of the larger provincial galleries are housed in historic castles and palaces; some, such as the Castello Cinquecentesco at L'Aquila or the Castello Visconteo at Pavia, are lavish and beautiful conversions.

LOCAL ARTISTS REVERED

Some towns preserve the works of local artists in one-man museums. Of these, the Fra Angelico museum in Florence is probably the most celebrated, but there are interesting foundations devoted to Canova at Possagno, to Boldini at Ferrara and to Burri at Città di Castello. The Canova museum is set behind the sculptor's own house, and other artists' houses remain elsewhere. Vasari's, in a quiet Arezzo street, is particularly charming; Mantegna's at Mantua is used for temporary exhibitions; and Urbino zealously preserves the house where Raphael was born. In Florence, the Casa Buonarroti was built as a shrine to the memory of Michelangelo, its most famous son. All these are essential places of pilgrimage for the dedicated art lover.

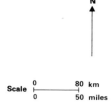

N

Scale

| 0 | 80 km |
| 0 | 50 miles |

VAL
D'AOSTA

LOMBARDIA

Torino (Turin)

Milano (M

Po   Mantov

NORTH & NORTH WES

PIEMONTE

E

Genova (Ge

LIGURIA

P

MARE LIGURE

MARE MEDITTERANEO

SARDINIA
SARDEGNA

This guide groups the regions of Italy into six convenient touring areas, each one corresponding to a separate gazetteer of places with art treasures worth visiting. (Sardinia has relatively little art and is therefore bracketed with Sicily into one area.) This map shows major art centers only; minor centers and other towns appear on the more detailed area maps.

TRENTINO–
ALTO ADIGE

NORTH EAST

FRIULI–
VENEZIA
GIULIA

VENETO

Vicenza

erona
Padova
(Padua)

Venezia
(Venice)

Po

Ferrara

MAGNA

Bologna

Ravenna

Firenze (Florence)

Arezzo

Urbino

MARCHE

ena

NORTH CENTRAL

SCANA

Perugia

Assisi

UMBRIA

Orvieto

MARE ADRIATICO

LAZIO

ABRUZZI

Tevere

Roma (Rome)

SOUTH CENTRAL

MOLISE

MARE TIRRENO

CAMPANIA

Napoli (Naples)

PUGLIA

BASILICATA

SOUTH

CALABRIA

MARE IONIO

Palermo

SICILY

SICILIA

NORTH & NW ITALY

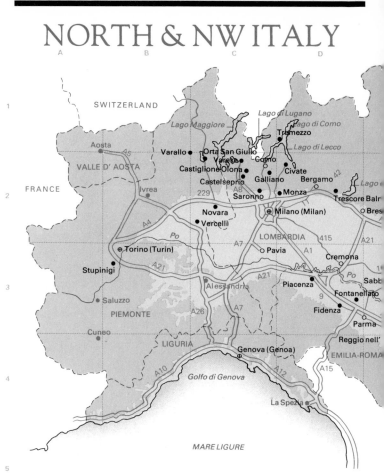

Italy's industrial heartland spreads like a blanket from the foothills of the western Alps, across the plain of Lombardy, towards the Adriatic coast. It preserves ancient centers and a rich and varied artistic heritage. Further N, Alpine valleys, hills and lakes offer scenic views and enchanting towns, whose long histories are reflected in their fine, well-preserved monuments.

PIEMONTE (*Piedmont*) *and* VALLE D'AOSTA

To the N is a pastoral, mountainous region, riven by the dramatic gulf of the Valle d'Aosta and, to the E, Lake Orta, the smallest of the Italian lakes, and the center of a lovely countryside of wooded hills and valleys and pretty Alpine villages; in the S lies the plain of the Po, a flat, monotonous landscape with fields of wheat and rice and flickering poplars.

The area as a whole is rich in Romanesque and Gothic art. The 17thC saw the development of the Sacri Monti – extraordinary ensembles of highly realistic sculptures and paintings – at Varallo and Orta San Giulio, and of the highly idiosyncratic Baroque architecture that makes Turin such an exciting city. In the 18thC, with the dominance of Juvarra, Turin became the center of a sophisticated Rococo style.

LOMBARDIA (*Lombardy*)

The river Po continues its course into Lombardy, etching out the southern boundary of the region between flat, rather dreary stretches of countryside;

further N, in the foothills of the Alps, are the majestic Italian lakes – Maggiore, Como, Varese – now slowly recovering from pollution.

During the 11thC and 12thC Lombardy was alive with artistic activity; there are fascinating Romanesque monuments in Pavia and Milan, Como and Galliano; the masons of Como were celebrated and their exuberant, fantastic style spread through Italy and Europe. The Renaissance saw the development of an ornate, richly decorative style; spectacular examples are the Cappella Colleoni in Bergamo and the Certosa di Pavia.

Later, Leonardo and Bramante brought something of the grandeur of the High Renaissance to Milan. Bergamo and Brescia, both splendid cities

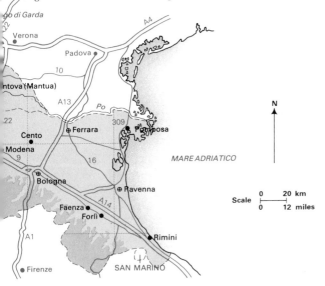

under Venetian influence, developed highly original local schools. The genius of Mantegna made Mantua one of the most creative centers in Europe.

EMILIA-ROMAGNA

The towns of Emilia-Romagna are spread out along the old Via Aemilia, crossing some of the dullest countryside in Italy from the Adriatic to Piacenza. There are Romanesque monuments of outstanding beauty and importance at Modena and Parma; both Parma and Cremona were flourishing centers in the Renaissance, becoming celebrated for the works of Correggio and the Friulian painter Pordenone; Bologna, a splendid university city, prospered in the 17thC with the school of the Carracci. To the E lie Rimini, with fine Roman and Renaissance monuments, and Ravenna, with the most splendid early Christian mosaics in the whole of Italy. Ferrara was in the 15thC distinguished by a highly individual school of painters.

LIGURIA

Liguria is a narrow, curving strip of land, where deep valleys, studded with olives and vines, drop down to a rocky and beautiful coast. Artistically it is dominated by Genoa, a city that enjoyed its Golden Age in the 17thC; here, the palaces and picture galleries give a vivid idea of the past luxury and splendour of the old Genoese trading families.

BERGAMO
Lombardia   Map D2

Bergamo is an ancient city, which from 1428–1797 belonged to Venice. It consists of an old upper town, crowning a steep hill and still circled by the Venetian walls, and a lower, modern city, laid out in the 1920s. The two are linked by funicular, or one may walk up the steep Via Pignolo, lined with Renaissance palaces, or take one of the little pathways that twist upward through gardens and orchards. The Piazza Vecchia is one of the most picturesque squares in Italy; beyond the arches of the Gothic Palazzo della Ragione is an enchanting glimpse of the smaller Piazza del Duomo, with the Romanesque porch of Santa Maria Maggiore, and the glittering, ornate facade of the Cappella Colleoni.

Cappella Colleoni ☆☆
Piazza del Duomo
🏛

This is the memorial chapel of Bartolommeo Colleoni, planned by the famous *condottiere* to dominate the Piazza Vecchia, as his equestrian statue dominates the Campo outside Santi Giovanni e Paolo in Venice (see **NORTH EAST ITALY**); the sacristy of SANTA MARIA MAGGIORE was torn down to make way for it. The flat facade is encrusted with white and coloured marble inlay, and glitters with an abundance of motifs – including friezes of putti, round reliefs of Roman emperors, marble statues of the *Virtues* and reliefs of scenes from Genesis.

The chapel was designed by Amadeo and completed in 1476; its lavish decoration is characteristic of the Lombard Renaissance, and contrasts sharply with the formal purity of Brunelleschi's Cappella Pazzi at Santa Croce in Florence (see **NORTH CENTRAL ITALY**).

Inside, on the wall opposite the entrance, is the **tomb of Colleoni** carved by Amadeo and two assistants. To the left of the entrance is the **tomb of Medea** (Colleoni's daughter). The frescoes in the lunettes of scenes from the *Life of St John the Baptist* ★ are by Tiepolo (1733).

Duomo
Piazza del Duomo
The cathedral was begun in the 15thC; it has an 18thC interior and a modern facade. The apse is decorated with seven altarpieces by distinguished 18thC painters; the finest works are Tiepolo's **Martyrdom of St John the Bishop** (second from left) and Pittoni's *St Esteria* (second from right).

Pinacoteca dell'Accademia Carrara ☆
Piazza Carrara 81a
Tel. (035) 242409
Open Wed–Mon 9.30am–12.30pm, 2.30–5.30pm
Closed Tues
🎭 🛏 ☑

The gallery was founded in 1795 by Count Giacomo Carrara and added to by later gifted connoisseurs – among them, Count Lochis (1859) and Senator Morelli (1891). Its greatest wealth is in Bergamese painting. In the early 16thC Bergamese painters echoed the style of the great painters of the Venetian Renaissance; later, the presence of the melancholy Lotto, whose pictures, though eclectic, are strikingly original and dramatic, encouraged the growth of a more powerful and distinctive style; with Moroni, there developed a careful attention to reality that looked forward to the 18thC, culminating in the portraits of Fra Galgario and the elegant still-lifes of Baschenis.

Yet the gallery also has works of outstandingly high quality from other Renaissance schools – including the Venetian – and is arranged to suggest both the contrasts and connections between them. It is one of the most enjoyable galleries in Italy, quiet and not too large.

The main exhibition is in 15 rooms on the first floor. In **Room I** are 15thC Lombard and Venetian paintings, with works by artists still linked to the courtly style of International Gothic; note especially a *Madonna* by Jacopo Bellini. In **Room II** there is a small group of works by Tuscan and Sienese artists, and a sculpture by Benedetto da Maiano – yet the outstanding work is Pisanello's medallion-like portrait of *Lionello d'Este* ★ probably painted in 1441 at the court of Ferrara, in competition with Jacopo Bellini (Pisanello won). Pesellino's *cassone* panels, the **Story of Griselda**, relate the narrative with courtly grace and charm, influenced by the new space of Lippi and Fra Angelico; in sharp contrast is an exquisitely linear *Madonna* by the Sienese Neroccio de' Landi, which looks back to the highly-wrought beauty of Duccio and Simone Martini.

Room III is the highlight of any tour of the Carrara, with an array of splendid *Madonnas* and portraits by 15thC Venetian painters. Note, especially, a grave *Madonna* ★ by Mantegna; next to it hangs Bellini's *Madonna Lochis* ★ (c.1470), softly modelled yet retaining the gold hatching of an earlier style; opposite is Bellini's lovely, and unusually well preserved, **Madonna of the Pear** ⋆⋆ (1480s) where the Virgin and Child are shown before a landscape that has almost Flemish precision. There is a dreamy, narcissistic **Portrait of a Young Man** by Lotto and Carpaccio's **Birth of the Virgin** (part of a fresco cycle); the painterly quality of the latter is not high, but the still, sunny interior and everyday details look on to Pieter de Hoogh.

In **Room IV** there are paintings by other Renaissance schools, notably the Lombard and Emilian. The warm humanity of Bellini's **Madonnas** are far removed from the sharp colours and cold, unreal grace of Tura's **Madonna** ⋆ once the central panel of a triptych (c.1484).

Beyond, in **Room VI**, is a group of works by Lotto and by artists influenced by him; Lotto was in Bergamo from 1513–26 and left here many complex and highly original works. These include the **Mystic Marriage of St Catherine** ⋆ a curious, slightly disturbing work; the landscape was cut away during the French occupation; the portrait of the patron, Niccolò Bonghi, relaxed and sharply observed, looks forward to the directness of Moroni. The **Portrait of Lucina Brembate** ⋆ (c.1523) is an enigmatic and subtle portrayal of a plain, bejewelled sitter against a mysterious night sky; the picture demonstrates Lotto's fascination with obscure symbolism; the moon is inscribed *CI* to form *LUCINA*. Portraits by Bergamese artists suggest different responses to Venice and to Lotto; Altobello Meloni's **Portrait of a Gentleman**, set against a stormy sky and said to be of Cesare Borgia, has a wayward, romantic melancholy; Cariani's portrait of **Giovanni Benedetto da Caravaggio**, one of his few signed works (c.1515), is a more solid and robust portrayal, slightly stiff despite the breadth of design, and with shimmering colours and a dusky landscape closer to the Brescian artist Savoldo.

Rooms VII and **VIII** show 16thC Italian painting, with an early, Peruginesque **St Sebastian** by Raphael in Room VII. In **Room IX** is an interesting group of works by Moroni. In an age where portraits were generally intended to flatter the rich and powerful, Moroni's gently descriptive, silvery works are almost startlingly direct; he recorded a wider range of society – sculptor, writer, tailor, lawyer – than had previously been portrayed. Note especially the **Old Man in an Arm Chair**, and the pair of full-length portraits of **Bernardo Spini** and **Pace Rivola Spini** (early 1570s). Moroni established a tradition in Bergamo, which was taken up in the 18thC by Fra Galgario (Giuseppe Ghislandi).

Galgario's fresh directness is best appreciated in his **Portrait of a Young Painter** ⋆ which looks on to Greuze; a tougher, more vital realism is manifest in his portrait of **Bertrama Daina de' Valsecchi**; his **Portrait of a Gentleman** is bold and swaggering.

A grave observation of reality inspired the still-life painter Baschenis; his **paintings of musical instruments** ⋆ in Room XII have none of the everyday, untidy charm of Dutch still-life; careful arrangements of form and colour, they are intensely poetic. In **Room XIII** there are a few 17thC Dutch and Flemish pictures; in **Rooms XIV** and **XV**, 18thC Italian paintings, with some good Venetian landscapes including Guardi's **Beggars' Canal**.

San Bartolommeo
Piazza Giacomo Matteotti
The church dates from the 17thC and has a 19thC facade. Over the high altar is a spectacular and grandiose work by Lotto, the **Madonna with Saints** ⋆ (1516); the Madonna is enthroned beneath a coffered vault reminiscent of the architecture of Bramante; yet the cupola is open to the sky, and the picture is full of movement and rich in dramatic contrasts of light and shade.

San Bernardino in Pignolo
Via Pignolo
This 16thC church has another important altarpiece by Lotto, also of the **Madonna with Saints**, but dating from 1521 and more lyrical and relaxed than the work in SAN BARTOLOMMEO.

Santa Maria Maggiore
Piazza del Duomo
🏛
The building, in Romanesque-Lombard style, was begun in 1137; the N and S porches are fine 14thC works by Giovanni da Campione. Within, the entire surface of the church seems covered with an extraordinary variety of decorative schemes from different periods – 14thC frescoes, 16thC stuccoes and Florentine and Flemish tapestries, 16thC and 17thC oil paintings, and an elaborately inlaid wooden **choir** ⋆ (1522–55). The choir is perhaps the finest work in the church; many of the designs are by Lotto. Most interesting among the paintings are frescoes on the vault of the N transept (1665–67) by the Roman Ciro Ferri and, on the end wall of the nave, the **Crossing of the Red Sea** (1681) by Luca Giordano. The monument to Cardinal **Guglielmo Longhi** (d.1319), also in the nave, is by Ugo da Campione.

San Michele al Pozzo Bianco
Via Porta Dipinta
The church dates from the 14thC. In the chapel to the left of the choir, the Cappella della Vergine, are frescoes of the *Life of the Virgin* ★ by Lotto (c.1523); these are remarkably naturalistic works, full of sharply observed domestic detail.

Santo Spirito
Via Torquato Tasso/Via Pignolo
This is an early Renaissance church, designed partly by Pietro Isabello. Within, in the right aisle, there is a luminous *Virgin with Four Saints* ★ (1521) by Lotto.

BOLOGNA
Emilia-Romagna   Map F4

Bologna has an ancient and distinguished history; Felsina under the Etruscans, and Bononia under the Romans, it became in the Middle Ages a celebrated university city and has remained renowned for learning and scholarship. The impressive buildings of the Piazza Maggiore form a fine center; from the corner of the Piazza Nettuno a picturesque composition opens out before you. To the left are the dramatic leaning towers, all that remain of the 200 or more towers that studded the medieval skyline, grim reminders of the rivalries that once plagued the city. Before you is Giovanni Bologna's Fontana del Nettuno and, just beyond it, the unfinished facade of the vast basilica of San Petronio; beneath, in the subway, are traces of Roman Bologna. The city has fine medieval monuments, and Gothic churches that are rich in paintings, sculptures and frescoes – amongst them Santo Stefano, San Domenico, San Francesco and San Petronio. Arcaded streets, many lined with Renaissance and Baroque palaces, give the city its strong character of attractively crumbling and festive grandeur. A local Bolognese school of painting opened with Vitale da Bologna and Simone de' Crocifissi. Later, Costa and Francia developed a pretty, tranquil Renaissance style. In the 17thC, Annibale and Ludovico Carracci made Bologna an art center that challenged Rome in importance.

Collezioni Comunali d'Arte
Palazzo Comunale, Piazza Maggiore
Tel. (051) 267738
Open Mon, Wed – Sat 9am – 2pm, Sun
   9am – 12.30pm
Closed Tues
🎨 🏛

The Collezioni Comunali are tucked away at the top of the Palazzo Comunale, an impressive palace that preserves echoes of its papal governors, and the *Madonna of the Earthquake* (1505) by Francia, showing a view of Bologna.

The far rooms include some notable Trecento works: three sculpted crucifixes, one by Simone de' Crocifissi; a pair of panels by Vitale da Bologna, one showing a pilgrim kneeling before a dramatically papal St Peter; a *Nativity* by Barnaba da Modena; and a colourful *Annunciation* with remarkable perspective by Jacopo di Paolo, which was painted for the Camera degli Atti in the palace itself.

Other pictures include a moving little *Crucifixion* by Francia, *St Mary Magdalen* by Signorelli and an *Old Man* by Tintoretto. But the single most striking aspect of the collection is probably the series of late Baroque works in the idealized classicism of Donato Creti and Gaetano Gandolfi, particularly Creti's *Virtues* ★ and *Deeds of Achilles* ★

Galleria Davia Bargellini e Museo d'Arte Industriale
Palazzo Davia Bargellini, Strada Maggiore
   44
Tel. (051) 236708
Open Mon, Wed – Sat 9am – 2pm, Sun
   9am – 12.30pm
Closed Tues
🎨 🏛 ☑

The palace was built in 1638 – 58 to a design by Bartolommeo Provaglia, but the magnificent staircase is the work of Carlo Dotti (1720). Below it is the entrance to the eight rooms of the gallery and museum, where pictures are displayed alongside furniture and objets d'art.

The Davia collection includes Vitale da Bologna's *Madonna dei Denti* ★ (1345) and a melodramatic *Pietà* ★ by Simone de' Crocifissi – two of the most important Trecento works in the city to survive – also, two works by Cristoforo da Bologna and one by Michele di Matteo. There are *Madonnas* by Antonio and Bartolommeo Vivarini, a *Marriage of St Catherine* by Innocenzo da Imola (a major follower of Raphael) and a series of genre paintings and portraits by Giuseppe Maria Crespi, in his vigorous painterly manner.

Around 1900 a major collection of "industrial" art, essentially the crafts and manufactured goods of the 15thC – 18thC, was compiled from public donations. Packed densely into the rooms, in the manner of the last century, like a miraculous antique shop, are dozens of chairs, tables and chests. Some are arranged by period (the Early Renaissance room), others by function (the collection of religious objects), still others by material (the rooms of ceramics, which include important 15thC pitchers and plates from Bologna and Ferrara). Not to be overlooked are the terra-cotta statuettes and the stamped leather boxes of the Quattrocento, nor the paintings of Samacchini, Procaccini, Franceschini and Canuti.

Museo Civico Archeologico
Via dell' Archiginnasio 2
Tel. (051) 221896
Open Tues – Sat 9am – 2pm, Sun
  9am – 12.30pm
Closed Mon
▣ ✗ ▥

The civic art and archaeological collections have been under reorganization for many years; medieval and Renaissance works are currently being transferred from this building to the Palazzo Ghislandi Fava. Only the Egyptian, Etruscan and Roman sections are open to the public at present; together they form one of the most important archaeological collections in Italy. Works of artistic interest include **bronzes** from Monteguragezza (c. 480BC) and a Roman copy of Phidias' **Athena Lemnia**.

The medieval collection (not at present on view to the public) includes several carved tombs of medieval professors, reflecting Bologna's vigorous university life; and a bronze statue of **Boniface VIII** by Manno da Siena (1301), recalling the papal rule of the city. The Renaissance collection (also closed) has bronzes by Riccio and Vittoria.

Oratorio di Santa Cecilia
Via Zamboni 15
To gain entry, inquire at sacristy of San
  Giacomo Maggiore

This little Renaissance oratory is worth visiting for its very pretty **frescoes ★** (1506) by Lorenzo Costa, a Ferrarese painter who worked in Bologna.

Palazzo Salem
Via Zamboni 20
Tel. (051) 268974
To gain entry, inquire at Credito
Romagnolo
▣ ▥

Formerly the Palazzo Magnani, this fine 16thC palace was built by Domenico Tibaldi (1577–87). The magnificent Salone d'Onore has a frescoed **frieze ★★** (1588–91) on which all three of the Carracci – Agostino, Annibale and Ludovico – worked together; it is the

most impressive of their joint achievements and shows a movement away from the intricate ornament and stylistic complexity that characterizes 16thC Bolognese decoration towards a greater simplicity and emphasis on narrative.

Fourteen scenes illustrating the founding of Rome alternate with ornamental figures in a glowing and festive array of grinning masks, herms and satyrs, bronze youths, feigned marble putti and vivid swags of fruit. Although derived from Mannerist schemes, the frescoes are painted with a new and sensuous beauty; the arrangement is everywhere crystal clear; their charm and vitality seem to involve the spectator in the drama painted in the frieze; the whole looks on to Annibale's great decorations in the Palazzo Farnese in Rome.

Among the individual scenes, the loveliest is perhaps Annibale and Ludovico's **Romulus and Remus Nursed by the She-wolf**, where the poignancy of the melancholy landscape is emphasized by the distant figure of the fleeing servant who has abandoned the twins.

Pinacoteca Nazionale ☆
Via delle Belle Arti 56
Tel. (051) 223774
Open Tues – Sat 9am – 2pm, Sun
  9am – 1pm
Closed Mon
▨ ☑ ▦ ⚲

This is a major Italian gallery, richest in Bolognese works, but with some outstanding paintings from other schools. The display opens with a lively collection of 14thC pictures of the local Bolognese school (**Rooms I – VI**); this is dominated by the dramatic and extravagant paintings of the great Vitale da Bologna, whose anagrammatic signature is implanted on the horse in one of his most exciting pictures, **St George and the Dragon ★** (Room I) – in marked contrast to the discreet signature on Giotto's polyptych in the next room. Vitale's landscapes in his **Stories of St Antony** are also remarkable. Pathos and fury find bold expression in the **polyptych** of Jacopino da Bologna. There are also the mannered but vivid works of Jacopo di Paolo, Pietro Lianori and Michele di Matteo, and a fine **crucifix** by Giovanni da Modena.

Room II has a **polyptych** by Giotto and assistants, dating from Giotto's later years (c. 1330). In Rooms V and VI, Vitale and the prolific Simone de' Crocifissi are represented in fine detached frescoes reconstructed within the gallery together with their *sinopie*.

From here one moves into a series of

small spaces displaying Renaissance pictures. There is a grave **Madonna** by Cima da Conegliano; a large tempera **Madonna with Sts Petronius and John ★** (1474) by the Ferrarese painter Francesco del Cossa – a work in which he moves away from Tura's fantasy towards a new grandeur and remarkable plastic force; and a number of delicate works by Francia – the most significant 16thC Bolognese painter – including a moving **Pietà**.

Yet the outstanding work in this section is Raphael's **St Cecilia with Sts Paul, John the Evangelist, Augustine and Mary Magdalen ★★** (c. 1513–16). This painting was commissioned by Elena Duglioli for a chapel in the church of San Giovanni in Monte, where the lovely original frame, with a copy of the painting, remains. The most striking figure is the Magdalen on the right, whose highly artificial and elegant beauty introduced a new ideal that was to inspire the Mannerist artists of the next generation – and perhaps most deeply Parmigianino, who is represented here by his great and brilliantly patterned **Madonna with St Margaret and other Saints ★** (1528–29), painted when the artist had fled to Bologna after the Sack of Rome in 1527.

Beyond a corridor displaying changing exhibitions of prints and drawings is a series of splendid marble-floored galleries lined with great 16thC and 17thC altarpieces. Whole rooms are devoted to the Carracci family and to Guido Reni.
Carracci family By the 1590s the school of Bologna dominated painting in Emilia; the three Carracci – the brothers Agostino and Annibale, and their cousin Ludovico – had reacted against the tired formulae of late Mannerism and introduced a new, vigorous style, inspired by a renewed study of nature, the glowing colours of Venetian art, and the grandeur and clarity of the High Renaissance. Annibale is the only 17thC Italian artist whose genius bears comparison with Caravaggio; the sheer scale of his drawings, and the exuberance of his style, laid the foundations of the Baroque.

There are major works here by all three artists, illuminating both their similarities and differences. Of the three, Ludovico's style is the most painterly and elegant; his early **Annunciation** (1585) is a sweet, pretty work, with graceful figures and smooth draperies; the mysterious, lyrical beauty of his **Madonna degli Scalzi★** is enhanced by shifting patterns of light and shade and radiant colour. The solid structure and rational space of Annibale's pictures contrast strongly with Ludovico's soft, melting surfaces; the composition of his **Madonna with Six**

Saints ★ (1587–88) is more finely balanced, whilst its soft colouring is indebted to Correggio; in his later **Madonna with Sts John and Catherine ★★** (1593) the solid weight of the figures and the compositional clarity are yet more marked: the painting perfectly illustrates the sources that inspired Annibale's revolt against the irrationality of Mannerism. The pyramidal composition is a return to High Renaissance principles: the Virgin, Child and St John the Baptist are directly based on Raphael's **Madonna of the Goldfinch** (see Galleria degli Uffizi, Florence, **NORTH CENTRAL ITALY**). The brilliant warmth of the colours – sharply opposed to the cold hues of Mannerism – is Venetian.

In Annibale and Ludovico's most violent and dramatic works the contrast remains: Annibale's **Assumption of the Virgin ★** (1592) is strongly classical despite the dramatic Tintorettesque lighting; Ludovico's **Conversion of St Paul** is a passionate, intense drama full of Mannerist confusions; his **Preaching of St John the Baptist ★** (1592) a brilliant, restless display of flickering surfaces.

Agostino is the least interesting of the three, but his **Last Communion of St Jerome** – which inspired Domenichino's far greater painting of the same subject in the Musei Vaticani (see Rome, **SOUTH CENTRAL ITALY**) – shows that he was closer to Annibale than to Ludovico; the composition is lucid, and there is a firm emphasis on precision of gesture and expression.
Guido Reni Originally inspired by the classicizing style of the Carracci, Reni was immensely successful in Rome in the early years of the 17thC, yet in 1622 returned permanently to his native city of Bologna where his vast studio spread his influence throughout the region. His art is distinguished by the subtle beauty of colour – ravishing and bold combinations of pinks and oranges and mauves – and by the grace of his line and form.

The pictures here open with the **Coronation of the Virgin with Four Saints** (1595), close to Annibale. The dramatic **Massacre of the Innocents ★** (1611) is one of the first great works of Baroque classicism, where violent action is controlled by careful symmetry and flowing rhythms; emotion is stylized, caught and frozen, at a moment of passionate intensity. The painting is deeply indebted to Raphael and to classical art, and looks on to Poussin.

From the same year is the strange and haunting **Samson Victorious ★** a picture where hints of Caravaggesque realism – in the desolate battlefield strewn with bloody corpses – are oddly juxtaposed with the elegaic beauty of the dusky landscape and the strange weightless elegance of Samson himself.

Reni's later works are calmer, and reject the Baroque utterly; the **Pietà dei Mendicanti** is a clear, static and symmetrical arrangement of figures. The latest works of all – of which the **St Sebastian** ★ (1640–42) is an outstanding example – are light and silvery, and intensely spiritual.

To the left of this room is a gallery, with smaller rooms opening off it, of 17thC and 18thC paintings. The first outstanding work is Guercino's **St William of Aquitaine** ★ (1620). Guercino was one of the most brilliant and original artists of the early Baroque, initially responsive to the colours and textures of Venetian art and to Ludovico Carracci. This is an intensely poetic work, dominated by bold diagonals and by splashes of light and colour.

Further on is his **St Sebastian Tended by St Irene** ★ The soft chiaroscuro and extraordinary range of plums, blues, dark greys and vivid reds, make this one of his loveliest pictures. Close by are two fascinating portraits – Guido Reni's **Portrait of an Old Woman** ★ (traditionally held to be his mother) and Simone Cantarini's touchingly frail portrait of **Guido Reni** ★

Alessandro Tiarini and Giacomo Cavedoni were the two most significant Bolognese painters associated with the Carracci, and there are fine works by both artists: Tiarini's **Deposition**, an intense, dramatic work, and Cavedoni's masterpiece, the **Madonna in Glory with Sts Aloe and Petronius** ★ (1614), in which the glowing colours and rich fabrics suggest a strong response to Venetian painting as well as to Ludovico Carracci.

At the end of this sequence of rooms there is a group of pictures by Giuseppe Maria Crespi, the most original painter of the late 17thC and early 18thC in Bologna. Crespi rejected the grandeur of 17thC Bolognese art: his most attractive works are startlingly vivid and sketchy genre scenes. **Hamlet**, the **Painter's Family** and the **Girl Defleaing Herself** capture – without satire – domestic, often slightly squalid, scenes of everyday life. Such subjects were almost new in Italian art. Crespi's soft chiaroscuro, which gives his pictures a touch of melancholy, initially derived from the Caravaggesque works of the young Guercino.

On your way out, note the small room with detached 16thC **frescoes** by Niccolò dell'Abate.

San Domenico ☆
Piazza San Domenico
🏛
The interior of this vast Dominican basilica was redesigned in the Baroque style between 1728–32 and contains many works of art but is most celebrated for its magnificent shrine, in the sixth chapel off the right nave.

Arca di San Domenico ★★ The shrine was originally designed by Nicola Pisano (1264) as a rectangular sarcophagus; the sides were decorated with six reliefs by Arnolfo di Cambio and Lapo, showing scenes from the life of the saint; the reliefs by Arnolfo of **St Dominic and his Brethren Fed by Angels** and the **Confirmation of the Dominican Order** are the finest; they are his earliest known works. In 1469 an elaborate canopy was commissioned from Niccolò da Bari, who then took the name Niccolò dell'Arca. At the summit of the canopy is **God the Father**; lower down are extraordinarily vivid and individual statuettes of the **Four Evangelists** and **Saints**; on the front, a **Pietà**.

Niccolò died in 1492, and the Arca was completed by Michelangelo (1495), who carved two Bolognese saints – **St Proculus** and **St Petronius Holding a Model of Bologna** – and an **Angel Holding a Candelabrum** – a soft, translucent work, its breadth of design contrasting with Niccolò's Quattrocento grace. The apse of the chapel is decorated with a fresco of **St Dominic in Glory with Christ, the Madonna and Saints** (1613–15) by Guido Reni.

Other important works in the church are the **Mystic Marriage of St Catherine** (1501) by Filippo Lippi (chapel to right of choir); marquetry choir stalls by Fra Damiano da Bergamo and others (1528–30); a painted wooden **crucifix** by Giunta Pisano (seventh chapel of left aisle); the **Mysteries of the Rosary**, an altarpiece comprising 15 small paintings by Calvaert, Cesi, Ludovico Carracci and Guido Reni (fifth chapel of left aisle); and the Renaissance **tomb of Alessandro Tartagni** (1477) by Francesco di Simone Ferrucci (vestibule of side entrance).

Museo di San Domenico
Entrance through sacristy
📷 𝒳
The most interesting works are a terra-cotta bust of **St Dominic** ★ (1474) by Niccolò dell'Arca and the **Madonna del Velluto** (1395) by Lippo di Dalmasio.

San Francesco
Piazza San Francesco
🏛
One of the most beautiful churches in the city, San Francesco was built between

1236–63. The outstanding work is the large and very spectacular marble **high altar** ★ (1388–93) by the Venetian artists Jacobello and Pierpaolo dalle Masegne.

San Giacomo Maggiore
Piazza Rossini

An important Gothic church, founded in 1267, San Giacomo has an elegant Renaissance loggia running down one side. It is exceptionally rich in works of art from the 14thC–17thC.

In the fourth chapel of the right nave, Ercole Procaccini's **Conversion of St Paul** (1573) is a Mannerist vision of panic and confusion, with strange, distorted poses, irrational, crowded space and a sharp range of acid lemons and pinks. In the sixth chapel, Bartolommeo Passarotti's **Madonna with Saints** (1565) is an oddly unattractive work, clearly inspired by Correggio, yet lacking his gaiety and charm; smiles have stiffened into grimaces, and the drawing and the draperies have become hard and sharp.

In the eighth chapel, there is a **Mystic Marriage of St Catherine** (1536) by Innocenza da Imola and, in the tenth, **St Roch Comforted by Angels** by Ludovico Carracci. Further on is the 16thC **Cappella Poggi** ★ an intricate Mannerist design with stuccoes and frescoes by Pellegrino Tibaldi.

In the second chapel of the ambulatory, there is a **polyptych** ★ (c.1345) by Paolo Veneziano; in the third chapel is a **Coronation of the Virgin with Saints** (1420) by Jacopo di Paolo and, above and hard to see, a large **Crucifixion** ★ (1370) by Simone de' Crocifissi.

The sixth chapel of the ambulatory is the celebrated **Cappella del Bentivoglio** ★ with a high dome and three round-headed arches framing the high altar and side paintings. The high altarpiece, in a lovely 15thC frame, is a **Madonna Enthroned with Saints** ★ (1494) by the leading Bolognese painter of the late 15thC, Francesco Francia; the symmetrical, spacious composition, and sweet, dreamy grace of the figures are indebted to Perugino.

On the left side wall are two frescoes by the Ferrarese painter Lorenzo Costa, of the **Triumph of Death** ★ and **Triumph of Fame** ★ (1490) – strange works, crowded with a bewildering array of allegorical figures. On the right side wall is Costa's **Madonna of Bentivoglio**. Also on this wall there is a high relief of **Annibale Bentivoglio on Horseback**, by an anonymous mid 15thC sculptor.

Against the wall of the apse, facing the entrance to this chapel, is an unusually uninspired work by Jacopo della Quercia, the great Sienese Renaissance sculptor: the **tomb of Anton Galeazzo Bentivoglio**.

Santa Maria dei Servi
Strada Maggiore 41
🏛

This imposing Gothic church was begun in 1346 and completed in the 16thC. The most interesting works of art are in the ambulatory behind the high altar; as you enter from the right, the frescoes on the vault are by Vitale da Bologna, the polyptych is by Lippo di Dalmasio and, in the third chapel, the **Madonna Enthroned** ★ recently restored, is attributed to Cimabue. In the fourth and second chapels of the left nave there are 17thC paintings by Francesco Albani.

Santa Maria della Vita ☆
Via Clavature

The church is late Baroque, with a 19thC cupola. Its outstanding work, to the right of the high altar, is a stunning terra-cotta group, the **Lamentation over the Dead Christ** ★ (c.1485) – perhaps the most violent expression of grief ever sculpted. It is by Niccolò dell' Arca, and the figure of Nicodemus is traditionally described as a self-portrait.

San Martino
Via Oberdan 23

This Carmelite church was founded in 1217 and reworked in the 15thC; it is a fine building despite clumsy restoration and is too often overlooked by the hurried tourist. In the fourth chapel of the right nave is an **altarpiece** ★ by Amico Aspertini, an interesting and eccentric Bolognese painter who had studied under Francia. In the first chapel of the left nave are fresco fragments of a **Nativity** recently discovered and attributed to Uccello or Cossa – the altarpiece is by Francia; in the fourth chapel is a **St Jerome** (1591) by Ludovico Carracci; in the fifth, an **Assumption** (1506) by Costa.

San Petronio ☆
Piazza Maggiore
🏛

This immense basilica was begun in the Gothic style in 1390 from designs by Antonio Vicenzi yet never completed. The lower section of the facade, sheathed in marble and decorated with reliefs of saints designed by Jacopo di Paolo, dates from the late 14thC.

The **central portal** ★ (1425–38) is the major late work of the great Sienese sculptor, Jacopo della Quercia. The original project was extremely ambitious. The door now consists of a tympanum, with a free-standing **Madonna and Child** between **St Petronius** and **St Ambrose** (the latter by another sculptor); in the architrave, five reliefs of scenes from the New Testament; on each of the two pilasters on either side of the door, five reliefs of scenes from the Old Testament, beginning, at the top of the left jamb, with the **Creation of Adam**.

The Old Testament scenes are tense and dramatic; they are worked in a very low relief influenced by Ghiberti and Donatello, and yet the profuse, swelling draperies and elongated, expressive figures look back to northern Gothic art; in their nobility, in their taut, spare compositions, and in their emphasis on the essential features of each episode, they look on to Michelangelo. The most profoundly moving of the reliefs is the **Creation of Eve** where the influence upon Michelangelo's composition on the Sistine ceiling is particularly clear.

Interior
In the right aisle are 15thC frescoes (second chapel); good stained glass by Giacomo da Ulma (1464–66, fourth chapel); more 15thC frescoes and a **Pietà** (1519) by Amico Aspertini (fifth chapel); **St Jerome** by Lorenzo Costa (sixth chapel) and fine inlaid **choir stalls** by Fra Raffaelle da Brescia (1521, eighth chapel).

The most interesting works in the left aisle are two allegorical **frescoes** by Giovanni da Modena (1420, first chapel); a fine early 15thC Venetian Gothic painted and carved **polyptych** with a predella by Jacopo di Paolo (fourth chapel); frescoes of the **Life of St Petronius**, the **Three Kings** and the **Last Judgment** by Giovanni da Modena (1410–15, also in fourth chapel); **St Christopher** by Giovanni da Modena (outside the same chapel); and intarsiaed **choir stalls** by the Marchi brothers (1495, fifth chapel).

Museo di San Petronio
Tel. (051) 226225
Open Mon, Wed, Fri–Sun 10am–noon
Closed Tues, Thurs
▨
The museum contains projects for the facade of the basilica, never carried out, and 15thC–16thC illuminated choir books.

Santo Stefano
Via Santo Stefano 24
This is a group of churches and cloisters of various periods, brought together under the name of Santo Stefano, although none of the individual churches bears this name. The most interesting works of art are in the Chiesa del Crocifisso and Chiesa della Trinità.

Chiesa del Crocifisso   The 11thC church was restructured in the 17thC. Over the high altar is a great **crucifix ★** (c.1380) by Simone de' Crocifissi, a 14thC Bolognese painter; it is remarkable for showing St Francis and the Magdalen grieving and, above, Christ with the Imperial sword and St Peter's keys, representing the two Laws, Civil and Religious, taught in the university.
Chiesa della Trinità   The grave and moving group of carved and painted sculptures, recreating the **Adoration of the Magi ★** in three dimensions, dates from the late 14thC and is sometimes attributed to Simone de' Crocifissi.
Museo di Santo Stefano
Tel. (051) 223256
Open 9am–noon, 3–6pm
▨ ▥
This small but very interesting collection has recently been rehoused in the main, later, cloister of the Santo Stefano complex. It has a fine Romanesque fresco of the **Massacre of the Innocents** attributed to Marco Berlinghieri of Lucca and taken from the church of San Sepolcro. Several panels by Simone de' Crocifissi include two good early works, a **Bishop** and a **Madonna**.

There is also a **triptych** by Jacopo di Paolo and a frescoed polyptych of **St Petronius** by Michele di Matteo. The important **reliquary of St Petronius ★** (1380) by Jacopo Roseto has fine enamels showing the saint's life with Bolognese buildings in the background.

BRESCIA
Lombardia   Map D2

Brescia is an ancient and distinguished city, where the grid plan and ruined Capitoline temple recall its history as a Roman colony. In the 12thC it became a free commune; in the 15thC, part of the Venetian domains. The lovely and spacious Piazza della Loggia at the center is Venetian in feeling; it is flanked by the Palazzo del Comune (begun 1492), richly and beautifully decorated with classical ornament, and by the crisp, linear facade of the Palazzo del Monte di Pietà. The Piazza del Duomo is less homogenous, but the buildings ranged along the E side – the austere Romanesque Rotonda or Duomo Vecchio, the towering Baroque facade of the 18thC Duomo Nuovo, and the severe medieval palace known as the Broletto, movingly express successive stages of history. Brescian art, although dependent on Venice, has a strong individual character, and the churches and art gallery contain many works of the Brescian school.

Museo Civico dell' Età Cristiana   See PINACOTECA TOSIO MARTINENGO.

Museo Civico Romano
Via dei Musei 57
Tel. (030) 46031
Open Tues – Sun 9am – noon, 2 – 5pm
Closed Mon
🎥 🏛

The most important Roman ruin in Brescia is the Capitoline temple erected by Vespasian in AD73. The building has three *cellae*; in the central one is a 2ndC mosaic pavement; in the left one, a good collection of Roman inscriptions; to the right, funerary reliefs and another mosaic pavement.

The museum itself is a modern addition reached from the central *cella*. It is best known for a bronze **Victory** ★ discovered in 1826; the statue was originally conceived – as a Venus in the Augustan era – with a mirror in her hand, and her foot on the helmet of Mars; probably under Vespasian she was transformed into a Victory: the two bronze wings were added, and the mirror replaced by a shield.

There are also six gilded bronze **Roman heads** ★ (3rd – 2ndC BC); among these powerfully characterized works note especially the brilliant spontaneity of the **Septimius Severus**. The fine **Head of an Athlete** is perhaps an original Greek work. There are in addition good collections of Roman glass and coins – the coins from Taranto are particularly vivid.

Pinacoteca Tosio Martinengo
Via Martinengo da Barco 1
Tel. (030) 91473
Open Tues – Sun 9am – noon,
2.30 – 5.30pm
Closed Mon
🎥 🎭 🏛 ♿ ⸬

The Pinacoteca is housed in a 16thC palace, elegantly remodelled in a Neoclassical style; the building is now somewhat forlorn and creaking, with faded remnants of 16thC and Rococo decoration. The gallery is richest in Renaissance and Baroque Brescian painting. Vincenzo Foppa was born in Brescia and worked here from 1489 to the end of his life. The leading 16thC painters were Savoldo, Romanino and Moretto; their work is deeply influenced by Venetian art yet retains the luminous spaciousness of Lombard painting and is gentler and more realistic. In the 17thC the Brescian interest in realism culminated in the coldly objective low-life scenes of Giacomo Ceruti.

At present, the greatest works from the Museo Civico dell' Età Cristiana, closed for restoration, are displayed in **Room I** of the Pinacoteca. These include the **Lipsanotheca casket** ★★ a rare and very beautiful ivory casket, decorated with low reliefs showing scenes from the Old and New Testaments. Another outstanding work is the **Galla Placidia crucifix** ★★ an extraordinary piece of medieval goldsmiths' work which Desiderius, king of the Lombards, gave to the Benedictine monastery in Brescia in the 8thC; it is perhaps the work of Byzantine craftsmen in Ravenna; the heavy cross is studded with cameos, precious stones – amethyst, agate, onyx – and coloured glass and crystal; on the back are vivid and delicately modelled portraits, traditionally said to be of Galla Placidia and her two children. Also from the Museo Civica dell' Età Cristiana is a fine collection of medals, some of which are now displayed in Room VI, others in Room IX.

In **Room II**, there is a polyptych by the 14thC Veneto-Byzantine painter, Paolo Veneziano. **Room IV** has good Limoges enamels and an anonymous 15thC painting of **St George and the Dragon**. Also in this room is Vincenzo Foppa's **Madonna with Saints** ★ a grave, restrained painting, touched with melancholy, its silvery greys and greens looking forward to Moretto and Savoldo; nearby hangs the **Orzinuovi standard** ★ (1514), Foppa's last dated work.

Beyond the medals in **Room VI**, **Room VII** has two small works by Raphael. The lyrical, Peruginesque **Head of an Angel** is a fragment of a very early work, an altarpiece commissioned in 1500 by Andrea di Tommaso Baroncio for his chapel in Sant' Agostino in the Umbrian town of Città di Castello; the painting was damaged in an earthquake in 1789 and the fragments dispersed. The other work, a rather ungainly **Christ Blessing**, is slightly later (c.1506).

In **Room VIII** Venetian and Brescian painting continues with two versions of the **Adoration of the Shepherds** by Lotto ★ and Savoldo; both are intimate, lyrical works, yet Lotto's breadth of design is more assured than Savoldo's wayward composition. Savoldo's subtle, evocative poetry contrasts with the splendour of Venetian painting; his pictures are serious, tenderly observed, yet touched by a mood of unreality conjured up by the effects of night or by artificial light. The moonlit shepherd, framed in a window, is one of his loveliest inventions.

Further on, in **Room IX**, is Moretto's **Portrait of a Gentleman** ★ a romantic, Venetian picture, where the beauty of the light falling on salmon-pink satin is particularly characteristic of this artist. It hangs alongside two acute, sober works by his pupil Morone – the *Portrait of a Magistrate* is a particularly fine blend of dignity with sharp observation.

In **Room X**, there are works by Romanino and Moretto. Note especially Moretto's *Madonna with St Nicholas of Bari*; the composition stems from Titian's *Pesaro Madonna* in the Frari in Venice (see *NORTH EAST ITALY*) yet the quiet mood, gentle realism and cold, silvery tonalities are intensely personal. Through **Room XII**, with a charming Rococo ceiling, you come to **Room XIV** with two aggressively realistic and Riberesque *Philosophers* by Luca Giordano.

Beyond, in **Room XVI**, are works by the Brescian artists Giacomo Ceruti and Antonio Cifrondi, part of a group of artists working in Bergamo and Brescia from the 1640s to the 1740s and known as the "Lombard painters of reality". Ceruti was known as "*il pitocchetto*", the beggar painter, for his depiction of a sordid array of beggars, tramps and cripples. His *Two Wretches* ★ (c.1730–40) is a repulsive, oddly intense image; the *Washerwoman* is a more sympathetic work – although less so than Cifrondi's *Woman Sewing*, a soft painting of a weary-looking girl patiently sewing in bad light. Beyond, in **Room XVIII**, the *Battle Scene* is by the Neapolitan artist Aniello Falcone, who created a new kind of battle genre, devoid of individual heroism.

Rotonda
Piazza del Duomo
🏛
This austerely simple Romanesque building dates from the early 12thC, but has a 15thC choir. Over the high altar is a stiff *Assumption* (1526) by Moretto. In the chapel to the right, three pictures by Moretto include *Elias and the Angel*, with a fantastic nocturnal landscape influenced by Flemish painting. In the S transept is Francesco Maffei's *Procession of the Patron Saints from the Castle to the Cathedral* (17thC).

Sant' Alessandro
Via Moretto
On the first altar on the right of this Renaissance church is a rigidly patterned *Annunciation*, generally attributed to Jacopo Bellini. The second altar on the right has a *Deposition* by Civerchio (signed and dated 1504) where the stiff, frozen quality of the grieving foreground figures contrasts with the brilliant, sketchy vivacity of the soldiers in the distance, dismantling the cross.

San Giovanni Evangelista
Contrada di San Giovanni
The 12thC church was rebuilt in the 15thC and later given a Baroque interior. It is rich in Brescian painting. On the third altar on the right is a *Massacre of the Innocents* (1530) by Moretto.

The **Cappella del Sacramento** (left transept) has a *Deposition* by Zenale and, above it, a *Coronation of the Virgin*, again by Moretto. The paintings on the right wall are by Moretto, and include a Leonardesque *Last Supper*; those on the left wall are by Romanino. More interesting, however, are the *Four Evangelists* (1521–24) on the pilasters, by Moretto and Romanino; their powerful realism looks on to Caravaggio – perhaps most strikingly in Romanino's *St Matthew*, bare-footed and burly, and laboriously writing by the light of a candle held by an angel.

Santi Nazaro e Celso
Corso Matteotti
This 18thC church has a number of works by Moretto: a *Transfiguration* (third chapel on right), *Coronation of the Virgin* (1534, second chapel on left) and *Nativity* (fourth chapel on left).

Over the high altar, disappointingly hard to see, is Titian's *Averoldi altarpiece* ★★ (1519–22). The papal legate, Altobello Averoldi, bishop of Brescia, commissioned this altarpiece in what was by then the rather old-fashioned format of a polyptych; it combines intensely romantic lighting with powerful Michelangelesque figures – compare the pose of the *Risen Christ* with the celebrated antique *Laocoön* in the Musei Vaticani in Rome (see *SOUTH CENTRAL ITALY*).

CASTELSEPRIO
Varese, Lombardia Map C2
Castelseprio is a small village that preserves the remains of an ancient Lombard castrum. Close by is the tiny pilgrimage chapel of Santa Maria Foris Portas.

Santa Maria Foris Portas
This rough brick chapel contains part of a celebrated cycle of frescoes of the *Infancy of Christ*. The precise date of the frescoes remains controversial (7thC–9thC), but their outstanding quality suggests that they are the work of a Byzantine master. Only discovered in 1944, they refuted the belief that no good painting was created in Lombardy in this period. Some of the frescoes are now in the Musei Civici at VARESE.

Alpine pilgrimage churches

The mountain sanctuaries of Piedmont and Lombardy are extraordinary manifestations of popular religious art. Their art owes much to the rough realism of the medieval mystery play, which flourished in the Alps as a bulwark of Catholicism against the dark threat from the North. There is nothing remotely like these sanctuaries elsewhere in Italy; their startling super-Realist shine and violence should appeal to contemporary taste.

This tour takes one right out of the gallery and into the loveliest countryside in northern Italy. It begins with the Sacro Monte at VARESE, near Como, which was patronized by Federico Borromeo. The first chapel may be reached by road; from here, climb the grassy track that leads up the mountainside, linking the 14 chapels – each decorated with sculptures and frescoes illustrating the *Mysteries of the Rosary* – and culminating in the church of Santa Maria del Monte, a celebrated pilgrimage site. Near the summit, pause to enjoy a glimpse of the romantic garden and exuberant architecture of the Museo Lodovico Pogliaghi; beyond, the track opens out to yield lovely views of the distant lakes and snow-capped Alps.

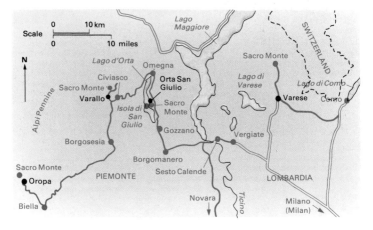

From Varese, take the *autostrada* to Vergiate and continue W to Sesto Calende and Borgomanero, then turn N to Gozzano and ORTA SAN GIULIO. Orta is a pretty town on the shores of one of the loveliest Italian lakes. From the tiny yet grand Piazza Motta, an elegant road climbs the hill – past fine palaces of different dates, with traces of painted decoration – to the chapels of the Sacro Monte. These have terra-cotta and frescoed decorations, illustrating scenes from the *Life of St Francis*. The site has a tranquil, pastoral charm; the earliest of the chapels line a terrace overlooking flower-filled meadows, dotted with goats and sloping down to the lake. Later chapels are scattered amongst gently wooded hills and their classical grace is enhanced by the Arcadian setting.

From Orta, turn N to Omegna, from where VARALLO is well sign-posted; the road leads through the spectacular pass of Colma di Varallo and offers wonderful and varied views – first back to the lake and then, while descending from Civiasco, of the strange, thrusting spurs of rock that majestically ring Varallo; note, at the junction with the road to Borgosesia, the prettily decorated little church of the **Madonna di Loreto**.

The sanctuary lies on a mountain spur that juts out over Varallo; it is the first, most vigorous and elaborate of them all and has a pleasantly festive

*A detail of the early 17thC **Ecce Homo** chapel on the Sacro Monte at Varallo.*

atmosphere, crowded with Italian families enjoying the many open-air cafés. You can go there by car, but it is worth following in the steps of the 17thC pilgrim and climbing the very steep track that leads from the church of Santa Maria delle Grazie. Beyond, the path twists and turns up and down little hills between the chapels, opening out into squares, and culminating in the Piazza della Basilica, flanked by elegant arcades.

The 44 chapels have frescoes and sculptures illustrating scenes from the *Life of Christ*. The spectator peers through grilles in the door of each chapel, and is thus thrust startlingly close to the realism of the drama within. The scenes of the *Road to Calvary* and the *Crucifixion* (nos. **36** and **38**) are overwhelmingly violent, with much emphasis on repulsive realistic detail – battered teeth, glassy eyes, goitrous growths. Others are gentler, and the *Last Supper* (no. **20**) bears a touching resemblance to Beatrix Potter's *Tale of Two Bad Mice*.

From Varallo, turn S to Biella – across some dullish, flat countryside. Yet from Biella the road climbs steadily to the sanctuary of **Oropa**, dramatically isolated in wild scenery, ringed by snow-capped peaks and by waterfalls cascading down the wooded mountainsides. Oropa is very much more majestic than the other sanctuaries; it is a famous pilgrimage site, where a series of vast courtyards, crowded with shops and restaurants, forms a splendid prelude to a grandiose and gloomy Baroque church. The simple, white-washed chapels of the Sacro Monte are scattered somewhat randomly down the banks of a grassy slope to one side; they lack the elegance of Varese, or the panache of Varallo, but have a charmingly fresh, naïve appeal.

CASTIGLIONE OLONA
Varese, Lombardia   Map C2

Castiglione Olona was rebuilt between 1421–44 by Cardinal Branda Castiglione who wished to bring to his little native town the new style of the Florentine Renaissance. In the 1420s he commissioned the Collegiata and baptistry; in the 1430s, the family *palazzo* and the Chiesa di Villa. The result is an idiosyncratic blend of the new architecture of Brunelleschi with the lingering traditions of north Italian Gothic – and of the graceful International Gothic style of his favourite painter, Masolino, with the cruder style of Lombard sculptors. It is one of the oddest places in Lombardy: a sleepy, almost creepily quiet medieval town, touched by the Tuscan Renaissance yet set among the flourishing industries of the Olona valley N of Milan; the hum of factories mingles with the sound of waterfalls as you climb from the rather forlorn main piazza up the hillside that leads to the Collegiata.

Battistero ☆
Via Cardinale Branda
Open Tues–Fri 10am–noon, 3–6pm
  (summer 3–7pm), Sat, Sun
  10am–12.30pm, 2.30–6pm (summer
  2.30–7pm)
Closed Mon
◙

The baptistry stands beside the COLLEGIATA. Its walls are covered with frescoes of the **Life of St John the Baptist ★★** perhaps the greatest surviving work of Masolino. There is considerable controversy as to whether these frescoes are earlier or later than the dated works in the Collegiata.

One of the loveliest scenes is the **Baptism of Christ** in the lunette above the window facing the door; an elegant Christ stands in the delicate, luminous waves of the Jordan, attended by three angels whose sweet Gothic beauty recalls Masolino's earlier style; on the other side, the group of men undressing is livelier, more vigorously realistic.

On the right wall, the famous scene of **Herod's Banquet** is a more complex composition; the episodes are set beneath the diminishing columns of a Renaissance loggia, a reminder of Masolino's interest in perspective. The slim elegance of the figures suggests the style of the great International Gothic artist – Gentile da Fabriano; Masolino's lack of interest in drama is clearly displayed in the graceful Herodias, who impassively receives the macabre gift of the Baptist's head, and in the unconvincing horror of the attendants.

Chiesa di Villa
Piazza Garibaldi
▥

This square building, surmounted by a semi-circular dome, is a wayward derivation from Brunelleschi's Old Sacristy in San Lorenzo in Florence (see **NORTH CENTRAL ITALY**). On either side of the Renaissance doorway – perhaps designed by Masolino although executed by a Lombard sculptor – are colossal statues, in a naïve Renaissance style, of **St Antony Abbot** and **St Christopher**. Within is the **Castiglione tomb** by a follower of Amadeo.

Collegiata
Via Cardinale Branda
For entry details, see Battistero above
In the vault of the choir of this Gothic church are scenes from the **Life of the Virgin ★** (1435) by Masolino. At this date Masolino was aware of the innovations of Masaccio; yet these are decorative International Gothic works, framed by elaborate canopies which are subtly attuned to the slender Gothic divisions of the vault. The soft grace of line, clear, delicate colours and frail, elongated, sweetly idealized figures contrast with the sturdier, more pedestrian narratives on the side walls, the **Life of St Lawrence** by Paolo Schiavo and **Life of St Stephen** by Lorenzo Vecchietta. On the left wall is the **tomb of Cardinal Branda Castiglione** by a Venetian-Lombard sculptor.

CENTO
Ferrara, Emilia-Romagna   Map F3

Cento is a little agricultural and industrial center on the left bank of the Reno. It is famous as the birthplace of Giovanni Francesco Barbieri, known as Guercino, one of the most original of Italian Baroque painters. Guercino's early work is intensely dramatic and glows with brilliant colour and shifting patterns of light and shade; in his later years he aspired to the classical style of Reni and his work became duller.

Pinacoteca Civica
Palazzo del Monte di Pietà, Via Matteotti
Tel. (051) 903640
Open Tues–Sat 9.30am–12.30pm, Sun
  10am–12.30pm
Closed Mon
◙ ⚞ ⚟
The gallery has several paintings by Guercino and one great altarpiece by

Ludovico Carracci, by whom he was influenced. Ludovico's *Holy Family with St Francis* ★★ (1591) looks on to the art of the Baroque in its lovely, flickering patterns of light and shade, its zig-zagging movement and blend of fantasy and passionate feeling; Guercino deeply loved this painting, and it reaches beyond him to Preti and Crespi.

Among the works by Guercino are some very early **frescoes** detached from the Casa Panini (1615) – unexpectedly spontaneous and freshly observed scenes of country life. An important early altarpiece, *St Bernard in Prayer before the Madonna of Loreto* (1618), is influenced by the vibrant touch of Ludovico and shows Guercino moving towards the sweeping diagonals, rich painterly surfaces and dusky light that were to distinguish his mature style. By contrast, *Christ Appearing in Triumph to his Mother* is a later and rather dull work (1630); by this time Guercino was more interested in monumental, classical forms and severe, lucid compositions.

CIVATE
Como, Lombardia Map D2

Civate is a small town of medieval origin. It is best known for the church of San Pietro al Monte, which stands on the slopes of Monte Cornizzolo, overlooking the lake of Oggiono.

San Pietro al Monte
After San Vincenzo at GALLIANO, this church has the most important cycle of Romanesque wall painting in Lombardy. The cycle probably dates from the end of the 11thC, and it is likely that several artists worked on the frescoes over a longish period. The most interesting compositions are the *Archangels of the Apocalypse* ★ (interior wall of facade) and the *Heavenly Jerusalem* ★ (first vault of vestibule).

COMO
Lombardia Map C2

Como lies in a site of romantic beauty – on the shores of a lake, ringed by hills that stretch towards the Lombard plain and with a distant view of the majestic peaks of the Alps. It is a lively modern city with flourishing textile industries and an attractively busy waterfront – yet its long history is reflected in fine Romanesque and Renaissance monuments, rich in the monstrous and exuberant imagery that distinguished the local style.

Duomo
Piazza del Duomo
🏛
The cathedral is one of the outstanding Renaissance buildings in northern Italy. The Gothic nave dates from 1396, the Gothic-Renaissance facade of white marble from 1487–1526. Much of the decorative sculpture on the portals and around the apse was added in the early 16thC by the Rodari brothers. Over the splendid W portal is a relief of the *Adoration of the Magi*, also small statues in niches; on either side are 15thC statues of the *Plinys* (who were born in Como), currently under restoration. Note, too, the lavishly ornamental N portal, the Porta della Rana.

Inside, along the central nave, hangs a series of outstanding 16thC **tapestries** ★ – Ferrarese, Florentine and Flemish. In the third bay of the right aisle, two early 16thC paintings – a *Flight into Egypt* by Gaudenzio Ferrari and an *Epiphany* by Bernardino Luini, the most prominent of Leonardo's followers – flank an elaborate wooden **altar** (1514), which is decorated with reliefs influenced by Florentine Renaissance art. The fourth bay has a *Madonna and Saints* by Luini. In the *Sagrestia dei Mansionari* to the right of the presbytery there is a ceiling fresco of the *Coronation of the Virgin* (1611–12) by Morazzone – a brilliant, flickering pattern of light and shade framed by elegant stucco.

In the left aisle, fourth bay, is a *Deposition* (1498) by Tommaso Rodari and, in the third bay, an *Adoration of the Shepherds* by Luini and a *Betrothal of the Virgin* by Ferrari.

Sant' Abbondio
Via Sant' Abbondio
🏛
An outstanding Romanesque church with two fine campanili, Sant' Abbondio was consecrated in 1095. In the apse and organ loft is a vast cycle of mid 14thC **frescoes** by local Lombard artists.

San Fedele
Via Vittorio Emanuele
This 12thC church is worth visiting for the bold and fantastic Romanesque **carvings** of fabulous animals on either side of the portal.

CREMONA
Lombardia Map D3

Situated on the left bank of the river Po, Cremona is a distinguished city with fine Romanesque and Renaissance buildings. At its center is the splendid Piazza del

Comune, where monuments of different eras create an unusually balanced and harmonious composition. The dramatically high Romanesque belltower known as the Torrazzo is linked to the lovely facade of the cathedral by a refined Renaissance loggia; close by are the baptistry and two Gothic palaces – the Palazzo del Comune and the Loggia dei Militi.

Duomo
Piazza del Comune
🏛

This exceptionally beautiful, largely Romanesque basilica was begun in 1107; the W front is a peculiarly satisfying blend of Romanesque, Gothic and Renaissance styles. The rose window dates from 1274; the portal rests on two large stone *Lions* by Giambonino Bissone (1285); the frieze of the *Labours of the Months* above it is by a sculptor associated with Benedetto Antelami (best known for his work at PARMA).

Within, the dark interior glows with rich decoration; the heavy pillars are wrapped around with 17thC Flemish tapestries; the walls are lavishly frescoed by artists of the Cremonese school.

The frescoes above the first four arches of the **left wall** show eight scenes from the *Life of the Virgin* by Boccaccino; the *Birth of the Virgin* ★ is distinguished by its idiosyncratic, steep perspective and strong, realistic detail. On the **right wall**, the vigorous dramatic frescoes above the fourth and fifth arches are by the Brescian artist, Romanino. The frescoes of scenes from the *Crucifixion* ★★ above the first three arches are the most celebrated surviving works of Pordenone, who worked mainly in the Veneto; they are crowded compositions, full of wild movement, startling foreshortenings, and somewhat contrived illusionistic effects.

Note also the two **pulpits** with reliefs by the Lombard Renaissance sculptor Amadeo and, in the crypt, the **sarcophagus of Sts Marcellinus and Peter** (1507) by Benedetto Briosco.

Museo Civico
Via Dati 4
Tel. (0372) 29349
Open Tues – Sat: summer 10am – 12.15pm,
*   3 – 6pm, winter 10am – noon, 2 – 5pm;*
*   Sun 9am – noon*
Closed Mon
📷 🛏

The museum has an archaeological section, with mosaic floors, bronzes, Greek vases and a collection of sculpture and decorative arts. The Pinacoteca, on the first floor, is more interesting; it is a rather dingy although well-documented collection, mainly of Cremonese art of the 15thC – 17thC, but also including a somewhat random group of Dutch and Flemish paintings of the 17thC and 18thC.

Two vast and striking works stand out. In **Room VII**, Giambattista Crespi's *Madonna Guiding St Dominic to Victory over the Albigensians* is a startlingly proto-Romantic work of wild and visionary intensity, left unfinished in his studio at his death in 1632; in **Room X**, Procaccini's powerful and dramatic *Death of the Virgin* ★ (c.1616) would alone make a visit to the gallery worthwhile.

Note also a *Portrait of a Woman* by the Cremonese artist Sofonisba Anguissola (**Room VIII**) and a *Holy Family* by Strozzi (**Room IX**).

Sant' Agostino
Via Plasio
The church dates from the 14thC; the rose windows of its early 15thC facade were inspired by the DUOMO. The interior is richly decorated with 16thC stuccoes and marble. In the third chapel on the right are frescoed profile portraits of *Francesco Sforza* and *Bianca Maria Visconti* by Bonifacio Bembo; on the fifth altar on the right is a *Madonna and Saints* by Perugino.

San Sigismondo
Piazza Bianca Maria Visconti
2.5km (1¼ miles) outside the city center,
*   towards Casalmaggiore*
The church was founded in 1463 by Francesco Sforza and Bianca Maria Visconti, to replace the humble little church in which they had married. Their portraits appear in Giulio Campi's *Madonna in Glory* (1540) over the high altar and in stucco busts in the **frieze** above. The wonderfully festive decoration is by leading 16thC Cremonese artists and the church is a gallery of their work.

Note on the vault of the nave the *Ascension of Christ* by Bernardino Gatti and the *Pentecost* by Giulio Campi. In the third chapel of the left nave, *Sts Cecilia and Catherine* by Bernardino Campi (Giulio's cousin) is an elegant yet odd Mannerist piece; the fifth chapel has a fresco by Antonio Campi (Giulio's brother) depicting *Supper in the House of Simon* – a strikingly personal mixture of a very formal style with strangely realistic detail; in the sixth chapel, the *Nativity* by Gervasio Gatti (Bernardino's nephew) is a bold experiment with effects of light and dark that looks on to Caravaggio.

FAENZA
Ravenna, Emilia-Romagna Map F4

Faenza is a pleasant town, its grid of streets prettily lined with flowering chestnuts, and the buildings predominantly Renaissance. It has been known since the 12thC for ceramics, and touches of *faïence* decoration brighten doorways and window surrounds.

Cattedrale
Piazza della Libertà
🏛

Giuliano da Maiano designed this fine Renaissance church in 1474. The most interesting works of art are the 15thC **Arca di San Terenzio** (fifth chapel off right nave), by an unknown Tuscan sculptor, and the **Arca di San Savino ★** (1471–72, in chapel to left of high altar), the earliest surviving work of Benedetto da Maiano, an important Florentine sculptor – its lovely reliefs are close in style to Antonio Rossellino.

Museo delle Ceramiche
Viale Baccarini
Tel. (0546) 21240
Open Tues–Sat: summer 9.30am–1pm, 3.30–6.30pm, winter 9.30am–1pm, 2.30–5.30pm; Sun 9am–1pm
Closed Mon
🚻 📷

This is a very large collection of ceramics. It opens, on the first floor, with a display that traces the history of ceramics in Faenza; continues with works from other important Italian centers, and with Eastern, African and American examples; and ends with archaeological fragments from sites around Faenza.

In the basement is an extensive display, far more informative than beautiful, of contemporary ceramics from all over the world. The display opens with dullish works by big names – Matisse, Picasso, Rouault – and grows increasingly depressing.

Pinacoteca e Museo Civico
Via Santa Maria dell' Angelo 1
Tel. (0546) 28376
Open Mon–Fri 9.30am–12.30pm, 2.30–4.30pm; Sat 9.30am–12.30pm
Closed Sun
🚻

The Pinacoteca has a good collection of paintings from Faenza with interesting works from other schools. In **Room II**, the **Madonna Enthroned between Sts Michael and James** (c.1498) is by Marco Palmezzano of **FORLÌ**; the picture's lucid space and simple volumes derive from Melozzo da Forlì but are softened by a

hint of the lyrical poetry of Cima and Bellini. Also in this room are a 16thC **polyptych** by the local artist Giambattista Bertucci and a polychrome wooden statue of *St Jerome* (c.1457) – mentioned by Vasari as by Donatello, and probably by Donatello and assistants.

In **Room IV**, the fine early Renaissance bust of *St John the Baptist* is now attributed to Antonio Rossellino. **Room VII** contains a late 17thC *Portrait of a Magistrate* by an unknown artist – a powerful meditative work that has something of the gravity of Philippe de Champaigne. Further on, in **Room XI**, are some Arcadian landscapes – perhaps by Locatelli – and a flower painting attributed to Guardi.

FERRARA
Emilia-Romagna Map F3

At the exact center of Ferrara towers the vast and gloomy Castello Estense, still circled by a 14thC moat and approached by a drawbridge. The castle symbolizes both the past grandeur of the city and the power of the Este family, who in the 15thC turned the dull little town surrounded by unhealthy marshes into one of the liveliest and most elegant centers of the Renaissance in northern Italy. Under Leonello d'Este the court became a renowned center of humanist learning; his brother, Borso d'Este, introduced a new gaiety and magnificence that banished the darkness of the Middle Ages. Between 1430–50 the court welcomed such celebrated artists as Pisanello and Jacopo Bellini; in 1449 the great Flemish painter Rogier van der Weyden worked here, and Piero della Francesca, on his way to Rimini, decorated rooms in Borso's palace, now destroyed. A highly original Ferrarese school of painting opened with the fantastic and intricately detailed pictures of Cosimo Tura and reached new heights of brilliance and splendour in the frescoes of Francesco del Cossa and Ercole de' Roberti in the Palazzo Schiffanoia (now the Museo Civico d'Arte Antica). The principal Ferrarese artist of the 16thC was Dosso Dossi, whose most imaginative works are magically lit, fantastic landscapes, peopled by exotic figures. Ferrara was later the home of Ariosto and Tasso, of Copernicus and Calvin. It is now a lively modern town, just recovering from a long decline, yet a sense of the past remains dominant. The Renaissance spaces of Ferrara fascinated the Surrealist painter Giorgio de Chirico; it was here, in 1917, that he founded Metaphysical painting with Carlo Carrà.

Castello Estense
Piazza della Repubblica
Open Tues – Sun: June – Sept
    9.30am – 12.30pm, 3 – 6pm, Oct – May
    9.30am – 12.30pm, 2 – 5pm
Closed Mon
🏛 🚻 ♿ 🏛

This vast fortress, dating from 1385, is of architectural and historical rather than artistic interest, but some of the rooms retain decorations by early Ferrarese painters; the Salone dei Giochi, Saletta dei Giochi and Camerina dei Bacchanali are all worth visiting.

Cattedrale
Piazza della Cattedrale
🏛

The cathedral is an important mid 12thC Romanesque building with a fine W front. The **main portal** ★ (1135) is a signed work by Niccolò, a sculptor who later worked at Verona.

Inside, in the right transept, is a **Martyrdom of St Lawrence** (1629) by Guercino. The monumental **Altar of the Calvary**, at the end of the right nave, was composed in 1678 by Carlo Pasetti from large 15thC bronzes. These include the **Virgin** and **St John** by Niccolò Baroncelli, a Florentine sculptor who brought the new art of the Renaissance to Ferrara; his style is deeply influenced by Donatello. The **St George** and **St Maurelius** were finished by his pupil Domenico di Paris. In the apse, the **Last Judgment** (1580) is by Bastianino.

See also MUSEO DEL DUOMO.

Museo Archeologico di Spina
Palazzo di Ludovico il Moro, Via XX
    Settembre 124
Tel. (0532) 33869
Open Tues – Sat: May – Sept 9am – 1pm,
    3.30 – 7pm, Oct – Apr 9am – 2pm; Sun
    9am – 2pm
Closed Mon
🏛 ♿ 🏛 ☑ ♨

The museum is housed in a palace built from 1495 – 1503 by the great Ferrarese architect, Biagio Rossetti. On the ground floor, the **Sala del Tesoro** has a ceiling fresco by Benvenuto Tisi da Garofalo, in which elegant men and women look over a fictive balcony to the room below – a variant of the Camera degli Sposi by Mantegna in the Palazzo Ducale at MANTOVA.

On the first floor is a large display of material discovered in the archaeological zone of Spina; Spina was an important Etruscan center, deeply influenced by Greece, and recent excavations have unearthed more than 4,000 tombs. The grave goods here displayed consist mainly of fine **red figure vases** ★ but there are also some interesting bronzes and goldsmiths' work.

Museo Boldini   See PALAZZO MASSARI.

Museo Civico d'Arte Antica ☆☆
Palazzo Schiffanoia, Via Scandiana 23
Tel. (0532) 62038
Open 9am – 7pm
🏛 ♿ ☑

The Palazzo Schiffanoia was used by Borso d'Este as a summer retreat. Only the fine Renaissance doorway prepares one for the inside, where the **Sala dei Mesi** ★★ or Room of the Months has one of the most charming of all Renaissance fresco cycles, by Francesco del Cossa and Ercole de' Roberti with assistants.

These frescoes are, however, very badly damaged; they represent the months, but **January, February** and **November** are missing, and very little remains of **December**; they can be something of a disappointment to those well acquainted with the much reproduced and enchantingly pretty details. Each month is shown in a compartment of three tiers: uppermost, the triumphal car of the god of antiquity who presided over the month; below, the sign of the Zodiac; beneath, appropriate rural tasks and vivid scenes of everyday life at the court of Borso d'Este, who appears in every scene.

The scenes by Cossa (over the entrance door) – **March, April** and part of **May** – dominate the series; they are distinguished by their original sense of space and by the monumentality of the figures, whose grave, sturdy beauty sometimes recalls Piero della Francesca. Yet the frescoes' greatest appeal is that they so exuberantly evoke the atmosphere of court life at Ferrara; the courtiers are precisely characterized, their costumes magnificent; the splendid architecture celebrates Renaissance Ferrara; the landscape is enlivened by sharp details – dogs, monkeys, birds.

The Palazzo Schiffanoia also houses a fine collection of coins, bronzes (works by Riccio and Giambologna) and ceramics (especially Ferrarese pieces of the 15thC and 16thC). A group of Ferrarese paintings and sculptures includes a 15thC polychrome wooden **Madonna** by Domenico di Paris and 17thC pictures by Scarsellino Bonone and Bambini.

Museo Civico d'Arte Moderna   See PALAZZO MASSARI.

Museo Documentario della Metafisica   See PALAZZO MASSARI.

Museo del Duomo ☆
Cattedrale, Piazza della Cattedrale
Open Mon–Sat: June–Sept 10am–noon,
4–6pm, Oct–May 10am–noon,
3–5pm
Closed Sun
📷 💷

This is a small museum, in a rather dark and gloomy room (the stairs are to the left of the atrium) yet with works of outstanding quality. These include 12 vigorous and charming late 12thC marble reliefs of the **Months** ★ once on the left portal of the S side of the CATTEDRALE.

The **organ shutters** ★★ (1469) with, on one side, *St George and the Dragon* and, on the other, the *Annunciation*, are seminal works by Cosimo Tura, the first major artist of the Ferrarese school. Both paintings reveal an intensely personal vision; the *Annunciation* is set beneath a vast Renaissance arch, and the space is lucid, yet the almost menacing figures on the side panels, the feverish, animated drapery, and the craggy spurs in the background, create a strange and disturbing mood; the taut, nervous rhythms of the *St George* are heightened by the fantasy of the background and the dark, unreal colour.

Note too a lovely marble **Madonna** ★ (1408) by the Sienese sculptor Jacopo della Quercia, intended for a side altar in the cathedral; this is a restrained, austere work that looks back to Nicola Pisano, yet it has a soft delicacy and sensuousness that are wholly Renaissance.

Palazzina di Marfisa
Corso Giovecca 170
Tel. (0532) 36923
Open Tues–Sat: Mar–Sept
9am–12.30pm, 3–6pm, Oct–Feb
9am–12.30pm, 2–5pm; Sun
9am–12.30pm
Closed Mon
📷 🏛 ☑ �€™

The 16thC palace, for many years the home of Marfisa d'Este, was restored in 1938; it is an elegant Renaissance building, with grotesque decoration, fine period furniture, tapestries and bronzes.

Palazzo Massari
Corso Porta Mare 7–9
Tel. (0532) 37816
Open May–Sept 9am–1pm, 2–7pm;
Oct–Apr 9.30am–1pm, 3–6.30pm
📷 💷 🏛 ☑ � ⁚⁚⁚

This fine 16thC palace has recently been restored and converted into a center devoted to 19thC and 20thC art. It contains a photographers' gallery and three specialist museums; these are not self-contained and, in places, the displays overlap:

Museo Boldini
The museum has works to illustrate the artist's entire career. Boldini was born in Ferrara and moved to Florence in 1862 where he came under the influence of the Macchiaioli and developed an interest in brilliant colour and a free, rapid touch. The **Laskaraki Sisters** (1867) is one of the most attractive of his early portraits; the sense of catching the sitter unaware in a relaxed and informal – even ungainly – moment has something in common with Degas' portraits of the same period.

In 1872, Boldini settled in Paris where he painted a series of celebrated society portraits, in an increasingly flashy and superficial style. Yet some works stand out, especially the powerfully conveyed **Gardener of Veil-Picard** ★ and above all his **Self-portrait** ★ (1911), a work with an almost aggressive immediacy that contrasts strongly with the fantasies of pallid nymphs that filled his final years.

Museo Civico d'Arte Moderna
The most interesting feature of this rather depressing collection is a group of works by Filippo de Pisis.

Museo Documentario della Metafisica
The museum uses large colour transparencies to trace in fascinating detail the sources and development of de Chirico's and Carrà's styles and explores the work of those artists briefly associated with Metaphysical painting.

Palazzo Schiffanoia See MUSEO CIVICO D'ARTE ANTICA.

Pinacoteca Nazionale ★
Palazzo dei Diamanti, Corso Ercole I d'Este 21
Tel. (0532) 21831
Open Tues–Sat 9am–2pm; Sun
9am–1pm
Closed Mon
📷 🏛 ☑ �

The gallery is mainly devoted to Ferrarese painters, but also has some interesting works by artists of other schools. In the 14thC and early 15thC, Ferrara had not yet produced an original style; this period is represented by detached frescoes by unknown painters and some small 14thC panels by the Bolognese artists Cristoforo da Bologna and Simone de' Crocifissi.

Towards 1440 Ferrara became an important artistic center, dominated by the strange and disturbing genius of Cosimo Tura – yet there are disappointingly few works here of this later period. Two **tondi** ★ by Tura, in a harsh, angular style closely related to the organ shutters in the MUSEO DEL DUOMO, are all that survive from an altarpiece once in the cathedral; they show the

Seizing of St Maurelius and *Martyrdom of St Maurelius*.

Ferrarese painting declined in the late 15thC, but revived in the early 16thC, enriched by contacts with both the evocative poetry of Giorgione and the grandeur of Roman classicism; Vasari wrote that Garofalo was a friend of Giorgione and his *Nativity*, an early work, is a gentle, sweet rendering of a Giorgionesque theme; his later *Massacre of the Innocents* is a rather uneasy blend of the powerful, dramatic movements of late Raphael with a romantic, Titianesque landscape. Dosso Dossi, early influenced by Garofalo, recalls the intense lyricism of the early Ferrarese school; his *Rest on the Flight into Egypt* is framed within a magically evocative landscape. The large polyptych, a *Madonna and Saints*, was begun by Garofalo and finished by Dossi.

The golden age of Ferrarese painting was over by 1600 and the 17thC saw the emergence of only two gifted painters – Scarsellino and Carlo Bonone. The art of Bonone was closely linked to the Bolognese school and his *Guardian Angel* ★ has something of Guido Reni in its cold, silvery tones. The delicacy and lyricism of Guercino's small *St Bruno Kneeling before the Virgin* (1616–17) suggest his early response to Scarsellino.

FIDENZA
Parma, Emilia-Romagna Map D3

Fidenza is a little industrial town of Roman origin, famous for its cathedral.

Duomo
Piazza del Duomo

Fidenza cathedral is best known for its unfinished **facade** ★ The three deep portals, their slender columns supported by crouching lions, are characteristic of north Italian Romanesque. The friezes – which reflect the influence of the Romanesque style in Provence – are attributed to Antelami, the most distinguished Italian Romanesque sculptor, and his workshop. The three-dimensional statues of *David* and *Ezekiel*, set into niches on either side of the central portal, are an unusual feature; they look on to the Renaissance and are attributed to Antelami.

FONTANELLATO
Parma, Emilia-Romagna Map D3

Fontanellato is a small agricultural center, medieval in parts. It was once ruled by the Sanvitale family.

La Rocca
Tel. (0521) 877188
Open Tues–Sun: Feb–May
*   9.30am–12.30pm, 3–6pm; June–Nov*
*   9.30am–noon, 3.30–7pm*
Closed Dec–Jan, Mon
🎭 🚻 🏛 ⚓

The castle was the seat of the Sanvitale from the 13thC and is now occupied by the town council. It is a picturesque building that still retains its water-filled moat. The main attraction is the **Saletta di Diana e Atteone** ★ the boudoir of Paola Gonzaga, wife of Galeazzo Sanvitale, which has exquisite decorations by Parmigianino. These frescoes are an almost immediate homage to Correggio's Camera di San Paolo in PARMA; a painted pergola opens the vault of the room to the sky and in the openings are the mythological scenes.

FORLI
Emilia-Romagna Map F4

Forlì, a busy provincial capital, lies on the right bank of the river Montone. The most famous artist associated with the city is Melozzo da Forlì, whose sense of space was influenced by Piero della Francesca. None of his work survives in his native town but the gallery has good pictures by Marco Palmezzano, his assistant.

Pinacoteca e Musei Comunali
Corso della Repubblica 72
Tel. (0543) 32771
Open Sept–July: Mon–Fri 9am–1.30pm,
*   Sun 10am–1pm*
Closed Aug; Sat
📷 ✗ 🛍 🚻

The Pinacoteca is on the first floor. The first room has Antonio and Bernardo Rossellino's **tomb of Marcolino Amanni** (1485) and Canova's *Ebe* and a series of large 17thC and 18thC paintings. The paintings include two of the most successful of Guercino's late works, *St John the Baptist Preaching* and the *Annunciation*, painted when Guercino was eliminating the painterly drama of his early Baroque works and moving towards the classic monumentality and academic draughtsmanship of Guido Reni. The stiff composition of the *St John* is enlivened by some lovely touches – note the beauty of the ivy twisting around the tree trunk – while the *Annunciation* has an almost Pre-Raphaelite quality, oddly reminiscent of Sassoferrato.

Two vast paintings by Guido Cagnacci, the *Apotheosis of St Mercury* and *Apotheosis of St Valerian* (1642), were originally intended for the cathedral. Cagnacci was a pupil of Guido Reni and his work has a charming, festive gaiety that reminds one of Venice – yet in the upper half of the *St Valerian* are some coyly appealing nudes, aimlessly dotted about, that point to the later development of his art – as a painter of rather unimaginatively provocative nudes. There is also a *Madonna with St Francis de Sales*, an exceptionally fine Baroque picture by Maratta.

In the rooms to the left, there are paintings by 16thC local artists and by artists of various other schools, among them Ludovico Carracci. Of the three rooms to the right, the first, dedicated to Marco Palmezzano, is the most interesting. Marco's *Annunciation* was once attributed to Melozzo da Forlì, his master, and it is easy to see why. Melozzo's influence is apparent in the lucid, even goemetric, organization of the deep space and the boldly simplified forms. The lovely poise and gravity of this picture is lost in the *Communion of the Apostles*, a later, more magniloquent work.

Room X has some of the most famous works in the collection, by 15thC Florentine artists: a *Portrait of a Young Woman* by Lorenzo di Credi and two small panels, the *Nativity* ★ – a magically evocative night scene – and the *Agony in the Garden*, by Fra Angelico.

GALLIANO
Como, Lombardia Map C2

Galliano is a village just outside Cantù, important for its Romanesque art.

San Vincenzo

The church was reconstructed in 1007. It has an important cycle of **wall paintings** ★ deeply influenced by Ottonian art. In the apse, **Christ in Majesty** is shown enthroned between the Archangels and the Prophets Jeremiah and Ezekiel; the figures are solemn and majestic, yet drawn with energy and passion. Beneath are four smaller scenes depicting vivid, concisely told episodes from the **Life of St Vincent**. The paintings on the walls of the nave are poorly preserved; they are not as fine and may have been done by another artist.

GENOVA (*GENOA*)
Liguria Map C4

Genoa's long history stretches back to the 5thC BC, when it was already a busy trading center, and it remains an important Mediterranean port. It is a vivid and dramatic city, alive with the intense activity of the port, full of sharp contrasts, and entirely lacking any museum atmosphere. The Porta Soprana and Porta dei Vacca survive from the 12thC walls that enclose the medieval town; the dark and dramatically narrow alleys of the old center, lined with high buildings, crowded and slightly sinister, twist up steep hills; Pisan-inspired black and white striped facades can be seen on houses as well as churches – notably on the houses of the Doria, now sadly dilapidated. North of the medieval area the narrow streets suddenly open into the 16thC grandeur of the Via Garibaldi; this is lined with palaces that exploit to the full the dramatic potential of the steeply rising ground of Genoa; they have airy loggias, and long vistas through lovely courtyards to spectacular staircases. In the 17thC another grand street, with the magnificent university building, was opened. The palaces of this new quarter were richly decorated with frescoes by leading Genoese artists and adorned with opulent sculpture and furniture by Parodi and Schiaffino. Rubens and van Dyck both visited the city during this period, inspiring local artists to attain a glowing colour and dazzling splendour that perfectly satisfied the taste of the great 17thC Genoese trading families.

Cattedrale di San Lorenzo
Piazza San Lorenzo
🏛

The cathedral was consecrated in 1118; its striped Romanesque facade is enriched by three 13thC Gothic portals.

In the right aisle, in the chapel to the right of the apse, there is a *Vision of St Sebastian* ★ by Barocci (1596). In the left aisle, to the left of the apse, the 16thC **Cappella Lercari** has vault frescoes by Bernardo Castello and, on the walls, frescoes and canvases – the *Nativity* and the *Adoration of the Magi* – by Luca Cambiaso.

At the end of the left nave is the **Cappella di San Giovanni Battista**; its marble **screen** ★ is one of the most important early Renaissance works in Genoa. It was designed by Domenico Gaggini, the most distinguished of a family of Lombard sculptors who dominated sculpture in Genoa in the second half of the 15thC. Some of the rather flat reliefs are by Elia Gaggini. The grace and delicacy of Domenico's *Angel of the Annunciation* suggest a response to Ghiberti, whose works he had seen in Florence. The statues in the niches are by Matteo Civitale, a sculptor from Lucca; the *Madonna* and *St John the Baptist* are by Andrea Sansovino.

See also MUSEO DEL TESORO DI SAN LORENZO.

Gesù
Piazza Matteotti
Also known as the Church of Santi Ambrogio e Andrea, this is a fine Baroque building, richly decorated with coloured marbles and gilt stucco and with a number of outstanding works of art.

On the vault and grand cupola there are 17thC **frescoes** by Giovanni and Giambattista Carlone. In the right aisle, second bay, is an altarpiece of the **Crucifixion** (1621–22) by the French Caravaggesque painter Simon Vouet and, beneath, a sculptured **Nativity** by Tommaso Carlone. In the third bay, the **Assumption** is a broadly handled dramatic masterpiece by Guido Reni. The altarpiece in the fourth bay is an **Immaculate Conception** by Andrea Pozzo (17thC).

Over the high altar, there is a **Circumcision** (1605) by Rubens. In the left aisle, in the chapel to the left of the apse, the three canvases on the vault are by Valerio Castello (17thC); on the side walls, the two canvases showing episodes from the **Life of St Francis Xavier** are attributed to Domenico Fiasella. In the fourth bay of the left aisle, the **Stoning of St Stephen** is by Giambattista Paggi (17thC). The altarpiece in the third bay is by Rubens and shows the **Miracles of St Ignatius** (1610) – the clarity and balance of this work contrast with the Tintorettesque drama of the high altarpiece. The first bay has a late 17thC altarpiece by Andrea Pozzo.

Museo d'Arte Orientale Chiossone
Villetta di Negro, Via Piaggio
Tel. (010) 53285
Open Tues–Sat 9.30–11.45am, 2–5.15pm
Closed Sun, Mon
🏛 ☑ ⚘ ⛶
The museum has a particularly lovely site: it stands in a hilly park, looking down over the city and harbour. The building is a long, low, modern pavilion, and the emphasis on crisp geometric form and clean line is beautifully adapted to the display of Oriental art.

There is a small prehistoric collection of Japanese objects; large sculptures from China, Japan and Siam; an outstanding collection of Japanese arms and armour; Japanese Kakemono paintings from the 11thC–19thC; enamels, ceramics and porcelain; bronzes and theatrical masks; and a good collection of 17thC–19thC Japanese prints with examples of Utamaro, Toyo-Kuni and Hiroshige.

Museo del Tesoro di San Lorenzo
Cattedrale di San Lorenzo, Piazza San Lorenzo
Tel. (010) 296695
Open Tues–Sat 9.30–11.45am, 3–5.45pm
Closed Sun, Mon
🕿 📖 🏛 ☑
This is one of the most striking and successful modern museum designs in Italy; from the central space, one's eye is drawn to the brilliant golds and jewels of the precious objects, shining within the dark interiors of circular spaces opening from it; the design emphasizes the rarity and beauty of each object, enclosing the spectator within a small space where nothing distracts from their contemplation.

The works of art are spectacular. Note especially, in the center, a brilliant Baroque statue, the **Virgin of the Immaculate Conception** (1747) by the Genoese sculptor Francesco Schiaffino; in the second space, the Byzantine **Zaccaria cross ★** dating from the 10thC but reworked in the 13thC, and the **reliquary of the arm of St Anne**. The third space has objects associated with St John the Baptist: a **silver casket ★** (1438–45) by Teramo Daniele and Simone Caldera – note the lovely intricacy and variety of the Gothic tracery, and the vivid realism of the little scenes; and a 1stC BC **chalcedony plate** – the **Head of St John the Baptist**, which gives this work an oddly 19thC macabre quality, was added in the 15thC. In the last space, there is a good display of 19thC and 20thC goldsmiths' work.

Palazzo Bianco ☆
Via Garibaldi II
Tel. (010) 291803
Open Tues–Sat 9am–7pm, Sun 9am–12.30pm
Closed Mon
🕿 ✗ *by prior arrangement at tourist office*
📖 🏛 ☑
The palace houses a distinguished collection of Genoese paintings from the 14thC–17thC, enriched by a group of works by Dutch and Flemish artists whose influence on the Genoese school is made fascinatingly evident. Genoa responded more warmly to the art of the Netherlands than any other Italian city; in the 15thC Genoese merchants commissioned works from Dutch and Flemish artists, and in the 17thC the visits of van Dyck and Rubens left a lasting mark.

The Genoese school opens with the 16thC painter, Luca Cambiaso, most celebrated for his unusual and poetic nocturnes, of which the **Madonna of the**

Candle in **Room 2** is an outstanding example. The most interesting work in **Room 3** is Pontormo's *Portrait of a Florentine*. **Room 4** has Dutch and . Flemish works including Jan Provost's *Annunciation*; crowded with the tiny, realistic detail that·fascinated Flemish artists, this work is in sharp contrast to the austerity of Hugo van der Goes' *Christ* ⋆ and to the severity and intensity of Gerard David's *Crucifixion*.

In **Room 5**, works by Jan Massys include a powerful portrait of *Andrea Doria* ⋆ The Mannerist sophistication of his and Jan van Scorel's works contrasts with the dignified realism of Aertsen's *Cook* – a new kind of serious genre that attracted 17thC Genoese artists.

The outstanding work in **Room 6** is an unexpectedly passionate *Crucifixion* by Veronese. Paintings by and after van Dyck in **Room 7** include van Dyck's *Tribute Money* and *Portrait of a Genoese Woman* ⋆ – the latter a powerfully characterized work. Among the Dutch and Flemish pictures in **Rooms 8** and **9**, *David with the Head of Goliath* by the French painter Vouet shows this artist moving away from Caravaggio towards Bolognese classicism.

In **Room 11** a group of works by Zurbarán, unusual in Italy, is dominated by the *Last Communion of St Bonaventure*. **Room 12** has a fine collection of pictures by Strozzi, the most brilliant artist of the Genoese Baroque; these range from the powerful Caravaggesque realism of *Isaac and Jacob* to the spiritual intensity of the *Penitent Magdalen*. **Room 13** has an attractive group of still-lifes, winter scenes and rustic genre works by Genoese artists close to Flemish realism; Vassallo's *Animals and Still-life* has a directness that looks on to Chardin; Sinbaldo Scorza's *Circe and Ulysses* is full of gay, decorative detail reminiscent of Jan Brueghel. The powerful, dramatic realism of pictures by Gioacchino Assereto in **Room 15** strikes quite a different note.

Rooms 17–19 move on to the late Baroque and Rococo; works by Ferrari, Gaulli and Valerio Castello lead on to the lighter colours and flickering movement of 18thC art; notice especially the almost Rococo charm of Castello's small, sketchy *Miracle of St Zita* in Room 19. **Room 20** has a *Crucifixion* by Castiglione, close to the emotional fervour of late Bernini. Castiglione's brilliant freedom and drama look on to Magnasco, a strange artist well represented by characteristically bizarre and sinister subjects and stormy landscapes; his greatest work is perhaps

the large *Figures on a Terrace at Albaro*, a morbid vision of decaying aristocratic society.

Palazzo Reale
Via Balbi 10
Tel. (010) 206881
Open Tues, Thurs 10am–1pm, Sun
9am–noon
Closed Mon, Wed, Fri, Sat
📷 🏛 ♨

A splendid 17thC palace, completed in 1705, the Palazzo Reale has a finely sited garden, opening out towards the sea. The depressingly empty rooms, beautifully frescoed and with good pictures, are a somewhat ghostly reminder of old Genoese magnificence. None of the pictures is labelled, with the result that visitors tend to wander around rather forlornly.

Room 3 has 17thC pictures by Castiglione. **Room 5** is a richly decorated salon, with a copy of a Veronese. **Room 6**, a magnificent gallery, glittering with mirrors, has **sculptures** along the walls by Filippo Parodi, Genoa's greatest Baroque sculptor; Parodi's work reflects that of Bernini, with whom he had studied in Rome; he brought to the Genoese palaces a richly expressive decorative style that satisfied the Genoese taste for magnificence. Francesco Schiaffino was his pupil; he, too, studied in Rome, with Rusconi, and his famous *Pluto and Persephone* ⋆ at the end of the gallery is executed from a model by Rusconi and is of course an echo of Bernini's great work in the Galleria Borghese (see Rome, *SOUTH CENTRAL ITALY*).

Room 7, the **Sala del Castello** ⋆ is the most beautifully decorated room in the palace. The light and flickering, almost Rococo *Allegory of Fame* – framed in a weighty *quadratura* setting by Mariani – is by Valerio Castello, who had studied with Correggio at Parma. Through this room is the **Camera del Duca di Genova** (**Room 8**), with a *Sibyl* by Guercino. Later on, in **Room 12**, there is a *Portrait of a Woman* by van Dyck, and in **Room 18**, a powerfully realistic work by Strozzi, *St Lawrence Giving the Treasures of the Church to the Poor*.

Palazzo Rosso
Via Garibaldi 18
Tel. (010) 282641
Open Tues–Sat 9.30am–7pm, Sun
9am–12.30pm
Closed Mon
📷 ♨ 🏛 ☑

The palace is of princely magnificence, its brilliantly festive decoration and the remains of its splendid family collection evoking the tastes and glittering aspirations of the great Genoese trading families. The palace was built for the Brignole family between 1672–76.

First floor

Venetian pictures in **Rooms 2** and **3** include Veronese's unusually gory *Judith*. In **Room 4**, the *Ecce Homo* was only recently attributed to Caravaggio: 17thC sources state that Monsignor Massimi commissioned rival paintings on this theme from Caravaggio, Cigoli and Passignano; he retained the painting by Cigoli (now in the Palazzo Pitti in Florence – see *NORTH CENTRAL ITALY*). Caravaggio's influence is here revealed at its best in dramatic works by Mattia Preti. **Room 5** has 17thC Lombard, Bolognese and Roman works, including a repulsive *St Francis* by Giambattista Crespi.

Rooms 6, 7 and **8** are devoted to the Genoese school, and vividly suggest the Genoese collectors' interest in the Flemish manner – in still-life, genre and landscapes with animals. The collection ranges from paintings by Luca Cambiaso, founder of the Genoese school – whose *St Jerome* illustrates his interest in poetic night scenes – to Sinibaldo Scorza, who introduced the charming detail of Flemish naturalism into Genoese art. It culminates in the richly coloured and textured works of Bernardo Strozzi, whose response to Flemish painting is evident in the powerful genre scenes of the *Cook* ★ and *Piper*. In **Room 9**, a characteristic work by Castiglione, the *Journey of Abraham*, piled high with animals and pots and pans, continues this Genoese love of Flemish realism.

Second floor

A series of apartments frescoed by the most celebrated Genoese artists opens with Ferrari's glowing, exuberantly decorative ceilings, *Spring* and *Summer* ★ (**Rooms 13** and **14**). The **family portraits** ★ in these rooms, by van Dyck (painted on a visit to Genoa in 1625), introduced a new kind of Baroque court portrait – aloof, graceful and overwhelmingly magnificent – which seems to capture the essence of aristocracy. Rubens, on an earlier visit to Genoa, had introduced the idea of a portrait on a terrace; yet in van Dyck's portrait of *Paolino Adorno Brignole* the architecture and the Baroque props of curtain and columns ennoble the elegant sitter in a new way. Similarly, Rubens had introduced the Baroque equestrian portrait; yet van Dyck's portrait of *Anton Giulio Brignole Sale* has a refined and melancholy air that contrasts with Rubens' panache.

Rooms 15 and **16** are frescoed by Domenico Piola with scenes of *Autumn* and *Winter* and display some

uninteresting Flemish pictures; the loggia looks out over rooftops to the striped tower of the cathedral and is decorated with a playful illusion of crumbling architecture by Paolo Piola. **Rooms 18** and **19** have sculptures by the Genoese Baroque sculptor Filippo Parodi.

Palazzo Spinola
Piazza Pellicceria 1
Tel. (010) 294661
Open Tues – Sun 9am – 1pm
Closed Mon
🖸 💷 🏛

Overlooking a narrow square hemmed in by dark alleyways, this palace was begun by the Grimaldi family in the second half of the 16thC; it passed to the Spinola in the 18thC. The gloomy, faded rooms, with relics of rich furniture, hint at the princely magnificence in which the old patrician families once lived.

First floor

Rooms 1 and **2** are decorated with stiff 16thC frescoes celebrating the deeds of the Grimaldi family. Note in the first room a brilliantly vivid sketch by Gaulli for a *Nativity*; in the second, an elegantly classical *Madonna* by Vouet. In **Room 3**, a small room beyond, are three outstanding works: a statue of *Justice* by Giovanni Pisano; an *Ecce Homo* by Antonello da Messina – a poorly preserved but fine work by the greatest southern Italian painter of the 15thC; and a magnificent triptych of the *Adoration of the Magi* ★ by Joos van Cleve (15thC Netherlandish).

Second floor

Room 6 has feigned architectural settings, created in the 18thC to frame 17thC pictures; these include Castiglione's huge and dramatic *Journey of Abraham*, packed with pots and pans, and a fine example of the kind of subject for which the artist was famous; an ugly Luca Giordano, *Mars and Venus*; and a powerfully realistic Strozzi, the *Blessing of Jacob*. **Rooms 7** and **8** have charming frescoed ceilings; in Room 8 note an elegant small study of the *Betrothal of the Virgin* by Valerio Castello (17thC Genoese), painted with a lively, flickering touch. **Room 9**, the **Salotto Verde**, has a sketch by Procaccini for the *Last Supper* in SANTISSIMA ANNUNZIATA. The charming Rococo gallery was added in the 18thC; beyond, in **Rooms 11** and **12**, are Guido Reni's *Sacred and Profane Love* and paintings of the *Four Evangelists* by van Dyck.

Santissima Annunziata
Piazza della Nunziata
Originally a Gothic church, later transformed by a galaxy of the most

celebrated Genoese artists, this has one of the richest and most characteristic Genoese Baroque interiors; it was badly damaged in World War II.

The frescoes on the vault are by the Carlone brothers, with the exception of **St Peter Healing the Lame Man**, by Gioacchino Assereto. On the interior wall of the facade, the **Last Supper** by Procaccini is a late work perhaps executed with studio assistance. The sixth chapel of the right aisle has an altarpiece of the **Annunciation** by Domenico Piola.

Santa Maria Assunta di Carignano
Piazza di Carignano
This is a 16thC centrally-planned church, set dramatically high on a hill, with lovely views over Genoa. In the two niches of the right-hand crossing piers are statues by the French sculptor Puget of **St Sebastian** and the **Blessed Alessandro Sauli** – works close to the emotional fervour of the Italian Baroque.

Over the second altar on the right is the **Martyrdom of St Biagio**, an unusually brilliantly coloured and dramatically Baroque work by Maratta. To the right of the high altar is Francesco Vanni's **Last Communion of the Magdalen** (c. 1600). In the left aisle are, over the first altar, a rather feeble **St Francis** by Guercino and, over the second altar, Procaccini's **Madonna and Saints**.

MANTOVA (MANTUA)
Lombardia Map E3

Mantua is famous above all as the city of the Gonzaga, whose brilliant patronage made this small, unhealthy town in the marshes into one of the most renowned Renaissance centers in northern Italy. Mantua lies in the dull, featureless countryside of the Lombard plain, now transformed into rich agricultural land; it is surrounded on three sides by lakes – once an effective defence – but they are melancholy and swampy rather than picturesque. Historic Mantua remains dominated by the great Gonzaga monuments, which have become major tourist attractions and are unpleasantly crowded. At the center is the spacious, cobbled Piazza Sordello, now gaily decked with tubs of flowers and pavement cafés – yet the gloomy facade of the Palazzo Reggio is a reminder of a grimmer past. To the S of the city is the Palazzo del Tè, a festive, elegant palace in a particularly scruffy and depressing area of the town. Mantua has been the home of many renowned poets and artists; it

was the birthplace of Virgil; Mantegna's house is still here and can be visited, as can his lovely funerary chapel in Sant' Andrea; and in Via Poma, one can see the exceptionally refined and elegant facade of the house that the celebrated Mannerist architect and sculptor, Giulio Romano, designed for himself.

Casa di Andrea Mantegna
Via Acerbi 47
Tel. (0376) 326685, 360506
Open Mon, Thurs 8am–1pm, 3–6pm;
Tues, Wed, Fri, Sat 8am–1pm
Closed Sun
◧ ⋔ ⚏
Mantegna may have designed this house himself. The most striking architectural feature is the round courtyard – perhaps inspired by Francesco di Giorgio's reconstructions of Roman houses. The house is now used mainly for temporary exhibitions.

Museo Diocesano
Piazza Virgiliano 55
Tel. (0376) 322051
Open Mar–Nov: Tues, Thurs, Sat, Sun
9.30am–12.30pm, 3–5.30pm
Closed Dec–Feb, and days not given above
◧ ⋔ ⋔ ⚏ ⚏
The cloisters of the convent of Sant' Agnese are generally run-down, weed-ridden and neglected. Yet a series of light and elegant rooms has been built within them to house a display of religious art from the churches of Mantua and its province, from the Middle Ages to the end of the 18thC. The museum has only recently opened; it is rapidly expanding and more rooms will soon be open; at present the most interesting exhibits are a late 15thC gilded silver **Madonna** from the cathedral; a **crucifix** by Tacca; some damaged but interesting pictures by the 18thC Mantuan painter Bazzani; and a spectacular set of 15thC armour.

Palazzo d'Arco
Piazza d'Arco 1
Tel. (0376) 322242
Open Mar–Oct: Tues, Wed, Fri
9am–noon, Thurs, Sat, Sun
9am–noon, 3–5pm; Nov–Feb: Thurs
9am–noon, Sat, Sun 9am–noon,
2.30–4pm
Closed Mar–Oct Mon; Nov–Feb
Mon–Wed, Fri
▨ ⋔ ⋔ ☑ ⚏
The palace with its fine Palladian facade was built from 1784 by the Neoclassical architect Antonio Colonna, for a branch of the d'Arco family. It is now open as a museum but still preserves the atmosphere of a family house: there are many family portraits, some good

antiques, and a number of musical instruments. The decorations of the 19thC drawing room are especially fine. The most interesting pictures are the eight scenes from the *Life of Alexander the Great* by the 18thC Mantuan painter Giuseppe Bazzani.

In the garden is a fragment of an earlier, 15thC palace. On the ground floor are two small rooms with a chapel and, above, the **Sala dello Zodiaco** ★ with frescoes by the Veronese painter Falconetto (c.1520); these illustrate the legends associated with the signs of the Zodiac, and their backgrounds are fascinatingly crowded with famous buildings – the Colosseum, San Vitale at Ravenna – from many different cities.

Palazzo Ducale ☆☆
Piazza Sordello
Tel. (0376) 320283, 320586
Open Tues – Sat 9am – 2pm, Sun
  9am – 1pm
Closed Mon
▨ ▦ ▥ ⚐

One needs a vivid historical imagination to enjoy a visit to the Palazzo Ducale; little remains of the great art collections of the Gonzaga; the palace is immensely crowded and noisy; the guided tour, although of reasonable quality, allows no lingering; the time spent in the Camera degli Sposi is all too short – although with a little skill one can hang around and merge with a later group. Nevertheless it is a great building, recording some 300yrs of Gonzaga patronage; and, luckily, it both opens and closes with outstanding works – Pisanello's frescoes and Mantegna's Camera degli Sposi. The palace consists of three main parts: the Corte Vecchia (dating from the end of the 13thC), the 14thC – 15thC Castello or castle, and the 16thC Corte Nuova (designed mainly by Giulio Romano). Tours do not always follow the same pattern and rooms are often closed, but this account suggests some of the most interesting things to look out for.

Near the beginning, note Domenico Morone's *Expulsion of the Bonacolsi*; this is not a high quality work, but it is of exceptional historical and topographical interest. The picture records the beginning of Gonzaga rule in Mantua, when Luigi Gonzaga and his sons defeated the Bonacolsi family in battle in 1328; fighting took place in the main square, and Luigi killed Rinaldo Bonacolsi, afterwards having his body mummified for good luck. The painting shows what the piazza looked like in the 1490s.

Next is the **sarcophagus of Margherita Malatesta** by the Venetian late Gothic sculptors Jacobello and Pierpaolo dalle Masegne. Further on, Pisanello's frescoes and brilliantly free *sinopie* (c.1436) recently uncovered in the Sala dei Principi – now the **Sala del Pisanello** ★★ – are one of the most spectacular of recent art discoveries. Around the three walls of the room there unfolds the vast scene of a battle tournament set against a panoramic landscape (best seen in the *sinopie*) where the skyline is a dazzling, picturesque array of little towers, castles and fantastic spires. The subject of the frescoes has not yet been satisfactorily explained, but their slightly melancholy mood suggests the fading of the courtly world of Gothic romance.

Beyond lies the **Appartamento degli Arazzi**, designed in the Neoclassical style by Paolo Pozzo, and with exceptionally fine **tapestries** ★ after Raphael's cartoons of the *Acts of the Apostles* in the Victoria and Albert Museum, London. The **Salone dei Fiumi** with Rococo decorations by Anselmi is the most attractive of the late 18thC interiors. The ceiling of the **Sala dello Zodiaco** has frescoes by Lorenzo Costa (1580). In the **Corridoio dei Mori** are pictures on slate by Domenico Fetti, a 17thC Venetian artist; Ferdinando Gonzaga's patronage of Fetti, Albani and Saraceni represents the last brief sparkle of Gonzaga patronage.

The **Salone degli Arcieri** has a *Nativity* by Tintoretto, and Rubens' vast early work, the *Gonzaga Family Adoring the Holy Trinity* ★ (1604–5), which has been reconstructed after being cut into fragments; in this painting, Rubens reveals his deep response to the brilliant, painterly splendour of Venetian art. The **Appartamento dei Nani** or Apartment of the Dwarfs (1626–27) is an extraordinary series of miniature rooms, complete with chapel and staircase.

Further on, the **Galleria della Mostra**, one of the most spectacular of all the interiors, is where Duke Vincenzo displayed his art treasures. The walls are divided into three tiers: originally, large antiques were ranged along the lowest tier; in the middle were pictures; and along the topmost tier were the busts of Roman emperors that still look down on the visitor today. From the gallery there is a fine view of the late 16thC Corte della Cavallerizza. Beyond is a series of rooms with stuccoes and frescoes by Giulio Romano and Primaticcio.
Camera degli Sposi ★★
The highlight of this long tour is a square audience chamber in the castle itself. It was frescoed by Mantegna between 1465 – 74 and is a masterpiece of

perspectival illusionism. The most novel part of the decoration is the ceiling, where Mantegna painted a *trompe l'oeil* oculus: over the steeply foreshortened balcony, ladies of the Gonzaga court peer down into the room below; a basket of fruit balances precariously on the parapet; a peacock looks over. It is a witty, charming scene, a playful blend of fantasy and reality; the ladies mingle with winged putti, one of whom poises an apple above the spectator's head. Around the oculus runs a festive swag of fruits and flowers and beneath are roundels of Roman emperors.

On the walls, the finest scenes are the *Gonzaga Court* (right wall) and the *Meeting* (left wall). The first impresses with a sense of the startling physical presence of the Gonzaga family, their courtiers and dwarf. Painted architecture blends with real architecture to create a powerful illusionistic effect. A curtain is looped back to reveal the terrace to the spectator; figures stand, apparently in real space, before painted pilasters. We also respond to the warmth and humanity with which Mantegna portrays this relaxed moment in the life of the court; Ludovico turns away from the group to receive a letter from a messenger; a little dog sits under his chair; the poses are informal.

The *Meeting* shows Cardinal Francesco Gonzaga returning to his family; in the background is a landscape dotted with classical monuments. The figures hold themselves more stiffly than in the *Court* scene, but the fresco still succeeds in creating a sense of the closeness of the family, as the children take each others' hands and the eldest child solemnly clasps the hand of the returning Cardinal. On the pilaster to the left of the scene, Mantegna included a tiny self-portrait.

Palazzo del Tè ☆☆
Viale Tè
Tel. (0376) 323266
Open Mon–Sat: Apr–Sept
9.30am–12.30pm, 3–6.30pm,
Oct–Mar 9.30am–12.30pm,
2.30–5pm; Sun 9am–1pm
🎫 👑 🏛 ✿ 🦌

The Palazzo del Tè is an elegant, witty, festive building, designed by Giulio Romano for Isabella Boschetti, mistress of the handsome Federico Gonzaga. It was built on an island, with stables for breeding horses, and facilities for lavish entertainments. The architecture is refined and subtle with, in the courtyard, a sophisticated play on forms; the slipped triglyphs are famous. The effect of the suite of rooms within depends on

surprise, variety and extravagant contrast. The palace has now lost its air of aristocratic refinement; it stands in a rather scruffy part of Mantua, surrounded by souvenir stalls and fairgrounds, and attracts so many coach tours that you may have to queue to get in.

Among the most interesting of the rooms decorated by Giulio Romano are the **Sala dei Cavalli** – a large, grand room where, before feigned windows with a view of a painted landscape, are portraits of Federico's horses, one of his greatest passions; the **Sala di Psyche ★** with lecherous pagan scenes from the *Story of Psyche*; the **Sala di Fetonte**, with a fresco of the *Fall of Phaeton*; and the **Sala degli Stucchi** and **Sala di Cesare** – both later rooms, their increased seriousness and formality perhaps encouraged by Charles V's visit to Mantua in 1530 when Federico was raised to the title of Duke; the stuccoes in the **Sala degli Stucchi** are extremely elegant and classical, and were designed by Primaticcio.

The climax of any tour is Giulio's **Sala dei Giganti ★★** the most startling and exuberant of all the rooms; from the vault, Jupiter hurls a thunderbolt at the rebellious giants; around the spectator, the very walls of the room seem to collapse; the massive giants are dramatically buried in a chaos of crashing columns, crumbling walls and hurtling boulders.

One wing of the palace houses the **Galleria d'Arte Moderna**, now closed for restoration, with an unexciting collection of pictures by artists such as Giorgi, Zandomenghi and Giudi.

Sant' Andrea ☆
Piazza Mantegna
🏛

This is an important Renaissance church, its grand facade reminiscent of a Roman triumphal arch. It was designed by Alberti and executed by Luca Francelli (1472–94); the dome was added by Juvarra.

The first chapel on the left is the **funerary chapel ★** of Mantegna. The lovely decoration was designed by Mantegna himself; the mural paintings were probably executed by his sons, although it has been suggested that Correggio had some part in them. The bronze bust of *Mantegna* is a grim, melancholy portrayal, showing the artist in a classical pose, crowned with laurel; the origins of the bust have been the subject of considerable controversy, but it seems likely that this too is by Mantegna. The chapel is perhaps the most ambitious funerary chapel of any Renaissance artist.

MILAN (*MILANO*)
Lombardia   Map C2

Milan is an important industrial city which, since the early years of this century, has been the cultural and intellectual center of Italy. It was badly damaged by bombs in World War II yet retains important monuments from its long history. It began life as a powerful Roman city and became one of the key cities in the Lombard kingdom and, later, the Lombard league; through the Renaissance it was ruled by the luxury-loving and powerful Visconti and Sforza families.

In the S of the city the great Romanesque churches – Sant' Ambrogio, Sant' Eustorgio and San Lorenzo Maggiore – are surrounded by busy traffic and desolate patches of wasteland and seem sadly out of context. And yet they are worth the effort of visiting them; Sant' Ambrogio, with its celebrated gold and silver altar, is one of the major Italian Romanesque churches.

The Piazza del Duomo remains the lively center of Milan. The vast and sumptuous cathedral suggests the Lombard love of lavish ornament; a walk on its rooftop, amid the almost fairytale exuberance of Gothic pinnacles and spires, is enjoyed even by children and gives one a good idea of the layout of the modern city below. The piazza is flanked by 19thC buildings, including the somewhat gloomy and grandiose Galleria Vittorio Emanuele II.

The cathedral was begun in the late 14thC by Gian Galeazzo Visconti, whose magnificent court was unrivalled anywhere in Europe; it faces the vast Castello Sforzesco, which bears witness to the splendour and power of the succeeding Sforza family. This backs onto a stately park and has been converted into an exceptionally beautiful museum of painting and sculpture. A wide modern road links the two monuments, but the historic center of the city also has plenty of narrow old streets that make pleasant walking; many, such as the Via Puccini, still yield glimpses of beautiful Renaissance courtyards. To the N of the Piazza del Duomo, past the Scala opera house, is the Via Manzoni, a wide street lined with elegant shops and art galleries and opulent Neoclassical mansions.

In the Renaissance, Milan was one of the great art centers of Italy and it remains famous for its wealth of artistic treasures. The Sforza alliance with the Medici is symbolized by the Cappella Portinari in Sant' Eustorgio, a memorial to the Medici banker Pigello Portinari; architecturally it echoes the formal purity of the Tuscan Renaissance whilst Foppa's frescoes suggest a response to Masaccio. In the late 15thC the learned and generous patronage of Lodovico il Moro attracted Leonardo and Bramante, who brought something of the brilliance of the High Renaissance to Milan; Leonardo's **Last Supper** in the refectory of Santa Maria delle Grazie – a splendid church enlarged by Bramante – attracts millions of visitors every year.

The art museums of Milan are overwhelmingly rich; the Museo del Duomo is a vast and lavishly documented display of Lombard sculpture; the Musei del Castello Sforzesco have a late and moving work by Michelangelo; and the Pinacoteca di Brera is a major and magnificent Italian gallery. Yet the smaller and more personal collections should not be overlooked – the Pinacoteca Ambrosiana, with Leonardo's **Portrait of a Musician**, and the charmingly eclectic Museo Poldi Pezzoli. In the 20thC the Futurists brought modern art to Milan; the city's main collection of 20thC art is currently undergoing extensive reorganization, but a number of important modern works may be seen in the Brera.

Brera See PINACOTECA DI BRERA.

Civica Galleria d'Arte Moderna
Via Palestro 16
Tel. (02) 702819
Closed for restoration
This large gallery of 19thC and 20thC art is at present closed for restoration and the future of some sections is uncertain. The 19thC collection includes works by Neoclassical and Romantic artists and by the Macchiaioli and school of Posillipo. There is also a group of paintings by 19thC and 20thC French artists. A special section is devoted to Marino Marini, the internationally celebrated Italian sculptor and painter, best known for his many variations on the **Horse and Rider** theme. Opposite the gallery is the **Padiglione d'Arte Contemporanea** which at present shows temporary exhibitions.

Civiche Raccolte Archeologiche
Corso Magenta 15
Tel. (02) 806598
Open Wed–Mon 9.30am–12.30pm
Closed Tues
🖾 ⑭ 血 ☑
This museum is located in the converted buildings of an ancient Benedictine monastery beside the Renaissance church of San Maurizio. Much of its charm depends on the setting; the small arcaded courtyard is strewn with Roman capitals and sarcophagi; the austere rooms of the ground floor frame a view of the overgrown, leafy garden beyond, encircled by a small cloister, and of the crumbling brick walls, half covered with ivy, of a polygonal Roman tower.

The ground floor rooms display a collection of Greek and Italiot vases and Roman sculpture and mosaics. Beneath, the basement rooms have more Roman art, as well as Etruscan and Greek sections. The Roman art is displayed against the backdrop of an excavated Roman wall and includes floor mosaics and a lovely collection of glass and small lamps. The two outstanding works are a 4thC **silver patera** ★ from Parabagio and the **Trivulzio cup** ★ (4thC or 5thC). The Etruscan section includes vases, urns, bronzes and a sarcophagus from Tarquinia, showing a reclining woman. The Greek room is presently being restored.

Duomo ☆
Piazza del Duomo
血
Milan cathedral is a vast and fantastic Gothic building, adorned with a forest of pinnacles and spires and over two thousand statues. It was founded in 1386 by Gian Galeazzo Visconti and has a long and complex building history.

The facade is a somewhat unsatisfactory mixture of Baroque, Neo-Gothic and Neoclassical styles. The bronze doors are 20thC; the most successful is the central portal, designed by Lodovico Pogliaghi in 1906, in a Neo-Gothic style touched by the flowing line of Art Nouveau. The five **low reliefs** in the tympani of the doorways were designed by Giambattista Crespi in 1629 and executed by various sculptors. Most of the sculpture decorating the facade is early 19thC. The sculpture along the side walls is mainly earlier (14thC–16thC); statues stand beneath canopies; above are exuberantly fanciful waterpipes in the shape of dragons, sea horses and serpents – upheld by wild giants – or sculptured knights, pilgrims and artisans.

The oldest part of the cathedral is the apse, where the three lovely rose windows were designed by Filippino da Modena. The pavement of coloured marble mosaic was designed by Pellegrino Tibaldi in the 16thC.

In the right aisle, the most striking monuments are the **tomb of Archbishop Aribert** (d.1045) with, above, an 11thC gilded **crucifix**; in the second bay, the **monuments to Ottone Visconti** (d.1295) and **Giovanni Visconti** (d.1354); and, in the third bay, the Gothic **tomb of Marco Carelli** (d.1394). Against the W wall of the right transept is the **tomb of Gian Giacomo Medici** (1560) with bronze figures by Leone Leoni; the **altar of the Presentation in the Temple**, an elegant Renaissance work by Agostino Busti, known as Bambaia, is on the E wall; next to it is the ugly and notorious statue of **St Bartholomew** (1562) by Marco d'Agrate with the amusing inscription "Non Me Praxiteles sed Marcus Finxit Agrates" ("I was made by Marco d'Agrate, not by Praxiteles").

The lunette over the door leading to the S sacristy is decorated in the Gothic style by Hans di Fernach (1393). In the ambulatory is the **monument to Pope Martin V** (1424) by Jacopino da Tradate and, further on, Bambaia's **tomb of Cardinal Mario Caracciolo** (d.1538). The door to the N sacristy is decorated by Giacomo da Campione. In the presbytery, the **high altar** dates from the late 16thC; the magnificent late 16thC **choir stalls** are by Pellegrino Tibaldi, Camillo Procaccini and others. In the left transept stands the celebrated **Trivulzio candelabrum** ★ a Gothic candelabrum, possibly of French workmanship.

See also MUSEO DEL DUOMO and MUSEO DEL TESORO DEL DUOMO.

Musei del Castello Sforzesco ☆☆
Piazza Castello
Tel. (02) 6236 ext. 3947
Open Tues–Sun 9.30am–noon,
  2.30–5.30pm
Closed Mon
🎨📷🏛☑🦯🏺

An imposing fortress built by Francesco Sforza from 1451–66, the Castello Sforzesco was heavily restored after bomb damage in World War II and now houses an outstanding museum complex. Spacious rooms, many decorated with Renaissance frescoes, contain one of the most beautifully arranged displays of painting and sculpture in Italy.

The visitor enters the castle under the restored Torre di Filarete, originally built by Filarete in 1452. Beyond the vast Piazza d'Armi lies the Corte Ducale; on the right is the entrance to the **Civiche Raccolte d'Arte Antica**, which comprise sculpture, decorative arts and a picture gallery; in the basement of the Rocchetta wing is the **Museo Archeologico**, with interesting collections of prehistoric and Egyptian art.

Sculpture
This collection is arranged on the ground floor; it starts with works from the late Roman Empire and extends through to the 18thC. **Room 1** has works from the early Christian to Romanesque eras. The outstanding works are the 4thC **Lambrate sarcophagus**, distinguished by the directness and freshness of the early Christian symbolism; and, from a more courtly world, a highly sophisticated 6thC **marble head** ★ which has been identified as a portrait of the Byzantine Empress Theodora because of its similarities with the mosaics in San Vitale in RAVENNA. The same room has some lovely decorative fragments from the 12thC church of Santa Maria d'Aurona.

Further on, the Gothic sculptures in **Room 2** include the solemn and majestic **tomb and monument of Bernabò Visconti** ★ attributed to the great Lombard sculptor Bonino Campione. **Rooms 3–5** display works of Lombard Gothic sculpture of the 14thC and 15thC; **Room 6** returns to an earlier period with the rough and vigorous reliefs of the dismantled Porta Romana, of greater historical than artistic interest; this monument was erected after 1171 when the Milanese re-entered the city, repairing the ravages wrought by the German emperor Barbarossa. **Room 7** has a fine painted ceiling and tapestries (17thC).

The decorations in **Room 8**, the **Sala delle Asse**, are, with the *Last Supper*, the only documented works by Leonardo

da Vinci in Milan. They have been restored almost out of existence, but one may still catch something of the beauty of Leonardo's concept – the interweaving branches of 16 trees form a leafy canopy against the sky; on one of the walls, two monochrome fragments, discovered in the 1950s, have been attributed to Leonardo. In the rooms beyond are Renaissance sculptures; note in **Room 10** Agostino di Duccio's marble **low relief** from the Tempio Malatestiano in RIMINI.

Room 15 has the most celebrated works in the collection; these are the effigy from the early 16thC **tomb of Gaston de Foix** ★ by Bambaia – fragments of the tomb are scattered amongst collections in Milan and Turin – and Michelangelo's ***Rondanini Pietà*** ★★ This is Michelangelo's last work; Daniele da Volterra wrote that he was struggling with it six days before his death in his eighty-ninth year; unfinished, mutilated, awkwardly composed and strangely Gothic in feeling, it remains profoundly moving, a poignant expression of the fears of death and age.

Decorative arts (1)
On the floor above, the visitor passes through rooms displaying a large collection of Piedmontese and Lombard furniture of the 15thC and 16thC, also fresco fragments, tapestries, and the famous early 17thC **Passalacqua cabinet**, richly decorated with ivory and bronze and with paintings by Morazzone.

Pinacoteca
Here the main emphasis is on Lombard painting, but in the first room (**Room 20**) there are some good Tuscan and Venetian Renaissance pictures. These include Filippo Lippi's ***Madonna and Saints*** – an early, somewhat awkward work, striving to emulate the plastic force of Donatello and Masaccio; an early Bellini ***Madonna***, exhibited next to a dark, frail ***Madonna*** by Montagnana, clearly influenced by Bellini; and, the outstanding work of this section, Mantegna's ***Madonna in Glory between Angels and Saints*** ★ (1497).

Room 21 has works of the Lombard Renaissance including frescoes and a small, early ***Madonna*** by Vincenzo Foppa. A group of Leonardesque works suggests Leonardo's influence on other painters; there is a copy of the ***Virgin of the Rocks*** by Marco d'Oggioni; a smirking ***Madonna*** by Giampietrino; and a vividly coloured ***Madonna*** by Luini, where only the head is close to Leonardo. **Rooms 22–25** have changing exhibitions of 16thC and 17thC Italian and Flemish paintings, sometimes featuring Lotto and Correggio.

Room 26 contains an interesting

group of 17thC and 18thC pictures, mainly Lombard but with some works from other schools. There is a robust and dramatic **Still-life with Skulls** by the Genoese painter Castiglione and an elegant **David and Abigail** by the Neapolitan Cavallino. The more intense, morbid streak that runs through Lombard Seicento painting is evident in the sickly greens and purples of Morazzone's **Head of St John the Baptist** and in the hysteria of Francesco del Cairo's **St Francis in Ecstasy** and **Agony in the Garden**. The most moving Lombard work is a sketch by Daniele Crespi for his great painting of **St Charles Borromeus Fasting** in SANTA MARIA DELLA PASSIONE.

Decorative arts (2)
The decorative arts continue with fine collections of ceramics (**Room 30**), porcelain (**Room 31**), and gold, ivories and bronzes (**Room 32**); the most famous of the ivories are the 5thC **Marys at the Sepulchre** and a single panel from the 6thC **Consul Magnus diptych**.

Prehistoric and Egyptian art
In the basement of the Rocchetta wing, the collections open with a section devoted to prehistoric cultures; the most interesting works artistically are the bronzes from the **soldier's tomb** at Sesto Calende (6thC BC). The small but interesting Egyptian section is divided into two parts: one illustrates funerary rites, with sarcophagi, *stelae* and papyri; the other is devoted to daily life, with jewellery and small bronzes.

Museo del Duomo
Piazza del Duomo
Tel. (02) 860358
Open Tues, Wed, Fri–Sun
  10.30am–12.30pm, 3–6pm; Thurs
  11am–12.30pm, 3–5.30pm
Closed Mon
🕿 ⛽ ☑

This is a large and very informative museum, which documents in considerable detail the different phases of the long history of the cathedral – with architectural models, drawings and plans, accompanied by lucid notes – and displays many of the finest works of art created for it. The collection of Lombard sculpture from the 14thC–20thC is outstanding and includes a great many terra-cotta *modelli* and *bozzetti*; but there are also some lovely stained-glass windows from the 15thC and 16thC, tapestries, paintings and drawings.

From the earliest, Gothic period note especially a fantastically bearded Nordic **Giant** bearing a water-spout. Renaissance sculptures include a somewhat stocky **St George** (1404) by

Giorgio Solari; a robust figure of **St Paul the Hermit** (late 15thC); and a statue described as **Galeazzo Maria Sforza**, perhaps by Amadeo, the most distinguished of the Lombard Renaissance sculptors.

In the late 16thC and early 17thC the patronage of Archbishop Federico Borromeo opened a new phase in the cathedral's history; a small room displays drawings by the most celebrated Milanese artists of the period – including Giambattista Crespi and Giulio Cesare Procaccini – for a cycle of paintings to honour St Charles Borromeo.

Further on is a series of large chiaroscuro **tempere** (1628) by Giambattista Crespi for the low reliefs on the facade of the cathedral, accompanied by terra-cotta *modelli* by Gaspare Vismara; note especially the **Judith and Holofernes**. In the showcases between the pillars of this room are many terra-cotta *modelli* by 17thC and 18thC sculptors, including opulent and elaborate works by Angelo de Marinis and more passionate and intense sculptures by Dionigi Bussola.

Museo Nazionale della Scienza e della Tecnica "Leonardo da Vinci"
Via San Vittore 21
Tel. (02) 462709
Open Tues–Sun 9am–5.30pm
Closed Mon
🕿 ⛽ 🏛

The museum occupies parts of a former monastery, dating from the 16thC and with two lovely cloisters. For the art lover, it has two interesting features. On the first floor, the **Galleria di Leonardo da Vinci** concentrates on Leonardo as an inventor and displays a number of models of machinery invented by him. On the top floor, there is a reasonably good collection of **19thC Italian painting**, with works by Fattori and Lega.

Museo Poldi Pezzoli
Via Manzoni 12
Tel. (02) 794889
Open Tues, Wed 9am–12.30pm,
  2.30–6pm, Thurs 9.30am–12.30pm,
  2.30–5.30pm and 9–11pm (except
  Aug), Fri–Sun 9.30am–12.30pm,
  2.30–5.30pm
Closed Mon
🕿 ⛽ 🏛 ☑

This charming little palace once belonged to Gian Giacomo Poldi Pezzoli, a gifted 19thC collector, who lavishly and romantically decorated its rooms in a variety of styles – Renaissance, Rococo, and Neo-Gothic – as a setting for his wonderfully varied art collection. The museum was severely bombed in 1943, yet echoes of its original decoration may still be glimpsed beneath the cool severity of 20thC remodelling. The lovely Rococo **staircase**, curving around a fountain, its walls inset with large canvases by Magnasco, was comparatively little damaged; the **Saletta di Dante**, a little Neo-Gothic chamber, has been carefully restored. The setting, and the very high quality of the small and fascinatingly varied collections – armour, porcelain, clocks, bronzes, Renaissance pictures, jewellery, arbitrarily juxtaposed – create an unusually private and attractive atmosphere.

On the ground floor, the **Salone dell' Affresco** has an 18thC ceiling fresco by Carlone. (The sketch for the ceiling is exhibited in the same room.)

On the first floor, to the left of the staircase, are three small rooms, the **Salette dei Lombardi**, with Lombard pictures of the 15thC and 16thC. These include a fine **portrait** by Vincenzo Foppa and a particularly attractive group of small works by followers of Leonardo – *Madonnas* by Boltraffio and Cesare da Sesto and a *Rest on the Flight into Egypt* by Andrea Solario.

Opposite the stairs, the **Sala degli Stranieri** has some pretty Flemish and German works, including two tiny landscapes by Jan Breughel. Beyond the **Saletta degli Stucchi** – with delicate Rococo decoration and a collection of porcelain from Capodimonte, Sèvres and Saxony – is the **Salone Dorato**, once a gilded Renaissance room with coffered ceiling and 16thC fireplace, and still displaying the greatest of the Renaissance works.

On the floor is a spectacular **Persian carpet** ★ dated 1523. The pictures are of exceptional quality; note especially Pollaiuolo's *Portrait of a Woman* ★ and Piero della Francesca's *St Nicholas of Tolentino* ★ There are three very different treatments of the theme of the Madonna and Child: Vivarini's regal *Madonna Enthroned*; Mantegna's *Madonna and Child* ★ a warm, grave work, where the Madonna caresses the sleeping Child – although her melancholy looks to the future; and Botticelli's *Madonna del Libro* ★ The last is an intimate, charming work – and yet the Christ Child poignantly holds the nails of the Cross, and a gold crown of thorns encircles his wrist. The naturalism of this work contrasts with the expressive mood of the later *Lamentation* (1490s) – the second and rather weaker version of a theme that Botticelli painted twice in this period (the more powerful work is in Munich). A stranger in this company is Guardi's *Grey Lagoon* ★ a small,

startlingly impressionistic view of Venice that almost looks like a Whistler.

Beyond are rooms containing the **Emilio Visconti Venosti collection** and a collection of **portraits**. The first group of works includes an exquisitely poised 15thC *Madonna* ★ by Neroccio de' Landi; the second, Vittorio Ghislandi's sensually decadent *Portrait of a Gentleman* ★ (18thC). A small room beyond contains clocks and scientific instruments.

Back through the **Salone Dorata** is the **Sala Nera** – note the elaborate doors remaining from the original decoration – and beyond, through a small room with a collection of glass, the extravagantly Gothic **Saletta di Dante** ★ A further sequence of rooms displays 15thC pictures, including some exceptionally fine small works by Crivelli; Venetian 18thC pictures including sketches by Tiepolo; and a collection of bronzes, mainly of the 16thC.

Museo del Tesoro del Duomo
Piazza del Duomo
Tel. (02) 808229
Closed for restoration

Among a rich collection of ivories, silver and goldsmiths' work two pieces are outstanding: the extraordinarily elaborate **evangelistary cover of Archbishop Ariberto** ★ encrusted with gems and rich in filigree work – suggestive of the early Lombard taste for rich pattern, although the figurative elements are Byzantine; and a small **ivory bucket** ★ of the 10thC.

Palazzo Clerici
Via Clerici 5
Tel. (02) 860564
Closed for restoration

This 18thC palace has a salon with a fine **ceiling fresco** ★ by Tiepolo, his last work in Milan (1740).

Pinacoteca Ambrosiana ☆
Piazza Pio XI 2
Tel. (02) 800146
Open Sun – Fri 9.30am – 5pm
Closed Sat
🎨 ⛪ 🚻 ☑ ♿

This gallery was founded in 1618 by Cardinal Federico Borromeo, a learned patron of the arts, to complement the celebrated Ambrosiana library, and to provide a study collection for the Accademia delle Belle Arti (founded in 1620). The Cardinal was most attracted by 16thC painting – by Leonardo, and by Titian, whose *Adoration of the Magi* he valued most highly amongst his possessions – and by the intricate decorative detail and Mannerist fantasy of contemporary Flemish painters; in Rome from 1581–1601 he developed a lasting friendship with Jan Brueghel.

The Renaissance paintings in **Room I** include works by Botticelli and Ghirlandaio and a small *Madonna* by the 15thC Dutch painter Geertgen tot Sint Jans.

Jan Brueghel The son of the more famous Pieter Bruegel, Jan Brueghel was in his own day even more celebrated than his father; his works are distinguished by their exquisite delicacy and detail. In **Room V**, note two miniatures from a series of the *Four Elements* painted for Cardinal Federico Borromeo. In **Room VI** is a collection of small landscapes, flower pieces and allegorical scenes. It includes two groups of small copper panels, which suggest the grace and charm of his art. His range was wide; the Mannerist love of startling vistas and bizarre detail in the *Hellish Scene* contrasts with the close, loving observation of the *Winter Scene* – directly developed from a work by his father – and the *Forest Glade* – a dense, mysterious woodland setting that was wholly new in landscape art. Note also the careful delicacy of Jan's study from nature entitled *Mouse and Rose*.

In **Room VII** the Lombard Renaissance is introduced by a strange, melancholy *Adoration of the Shepherds* by Bramantino, the most fascinating of the Lombard early 16thC painters. **Room VIII** moves to the High Renaissance and is dominated by Leonardo da Vinci's *Portrait of a Musician* ★★ the only portrait by Leonardo now in Italy; the *Portrait of a Young Woman* is now attributed to Ambrogio da Predis. **Room X**, a large room used for concerts, is devoted to Raphael's cartoon for the *School of Athens* in the Musei Vaticani in Rome (see *SOUTH CENTRAL ITALY*).

Room XII displays 17thC pictures; there is a lovely, romantically lit *Nativity* by Barocci and Caravaggio's *Basket of Fruit*. This work, Caravaggio's only independent still-life painting, raised Italian still-life to a new level of seriousness. Its *trompe l'oeil* immediacy and the suggestion of transience – bloom lies on the fruit, the leaves are withering, the apples worm-eaten – contrast with the artificiality and ideal beauty of Jan Brueghel's flower pieces. Caravaggio's doctrine of truth to nature was provocative, and he is said to have remarked that "it required as much skill to paint a good picture of flowers as one of figures".

Further on, in **Room XIII**, Titian's *Adoration of the Magi* is outstanding amongst some good Venetian pictures.

Pinacoteca di Brera ★★
Via Brera 28
Tel. (02) 808387
Open Tues–Sat 9am–2pm, Sun
*   9am–1pm*
Closed Mon
🅿 💟 💷 🏛 ☑ ⚒

The Brera was founded in the late 18thC with a specifically educational purpose, born of Napoleon's cultural policies. The original collection consisted mainly of church and altar paintings that were seized after the suppression of the religious orders from 1796–99. Although in recent years it has become very much more varied, the grandeur of the religious paintings of the Lombard and Venetian schools – great altarpieces by Savoldo, Bellini, Tintoretto and Veronese – still dominates.

The gallery is housed in a fine Neoclassical palace – approached through a courtyard with, in the center, a monumental bronze statue of *Napoleon* (1809) by Canova; a splendid double staircase leads to the collections on the *piano nobile*; the over-riding impression is of space and magnificence, although recently some smaller rooms have been created for the 20thC collection, and the atmosphere is agreeably lively.

The collections have recently been reorganized and rearranged; even now, pictures are frequently shifted – thus some of these room numbers may no longer be accurate. Large sections are often closed due to lack of staff – the Lombard pictures seem to suffer most – so telephone first if there is a specific picture that you wish to see. The important rooms highlighted here are described in order of viewing rather than in numerical order.

Room 1 The display opens, perhaps symbolically, with the Futurist painter Boccioni's *Self-portrait* (1908). This shows the artist tense before an industrial landscape, suggesting his commitment to modern urban reality – it was painted when Milan was rapidly becoming the economic and cultural center of Italy.

A series of stormy Baroque landscapes opens with Rosa's *Landscape with St Paul the Hermit* (mid 1660s). Rosa was the greatest Italian landscape painter of the 17thC; he created a new category of landscape – wild and savage, with towering rocks and jagged, moss-laden trees – which anticipated Romanticism. The grandeur of this painting looks back to Titian, yet Rosa's work has a new expressive intensity, created by the flickering surfaces and strange flashes of stormy light. By contrast, Dughet's *Landscape with St John the Baptist* is quieter and more lyrical.

A group of landscapes by the Genoese painter Magnasco are yet more violent; Magnasco's handling of paint is astonishingly loose and expressive, and his bizarre subjects – anguished processions of monks, desolately wandering in vast stormy landscapes, are a recurring theme – create a profound sense of psychological unease. In a small room to the side (**Room 2**), detached frescoes from the **Cappella di Santa Caterina in Mocchirolo** attributed to Giovanni da Milano suggest that an awareness of Tuscan art had begun to infiltrate northern Italian painting in the 14thC. Beyond (back in **Room 1**) is a vivid group of artists' self-portraits – note the bizarre picture by Lomazzo – and thence one enters the main gallery.

Room 3 The splendour of Venetian painting is introduced by Veronese's *Baptism of Christ* ★ and by Paris Bordone's rendering of the same subject, both distinguished by the beauty of their landscapes. A lovely, shimmering **altarpiece** ★ by the Brescian painter Savoldo unites the gentle luminosity of the Lombard tradition with the warmer colours of Venice.

Room 4 Here one may compare the strongly contrasting styles of the three great 16thC Venetian Mannerists. Veronese's *Sts Antony, Cornelius and Cipriano* ★ is a rich and sumptuous work. Jacopo Bassano's *St Roch* is a quiet, warm picture; unusually for an altarpiece, its subject matter is largely drawn from everyday reality; gesture and expression are precise and careful; the delicacy of the brushwork seems to reflect the delicacy of the emotion.

By contrast, Tintoretto's *Finding of the Body of St Mark* ★★ explodes with a tense, violent drama. The subject is macabre: St Mark, on the left, halts the tomb robbers who have discovered his body; the agitated, kneeling figure in the center is the donor; on the right are a possessed man and woman. The strange, hallucinatory quality is created by the startling effects of space, the weird light and flickering brushwork, and the expressive power of the contorted, Michelangelesque figures.

Room 5 This reverts to an earlier period, with a vast canvas of the *Preaching of St Mark*, begun by Gentile Bellini and finished by his brother Giovanni; it shows the city of Alexandria as a fantastic variation on the Piazza San Marco in Venice.

Rooms 6 and 7 The frescoes of *Armed Men* ★ (c.1480–85) are the only certain surviving paintings of the celebrated High Renaissance architect, Bramante; the cycle came from the house of the

Panigarola family; the armed men were intended to be seen from below, their vast, heroic figures standing out sharply from their architectural frames; the overriding emphasis on solid form and depth is close to Melozzo da Forlì. The monumental and sharply modelled *Christ at the Column* – a slightly disturbing, unpleasant picture – is attributed to Bramante.

Room 8 This small room glows with the golds and delicate patterns of the International Gothic, in sharp contrast to Bramante's monumental forms. In Gentile da Fabriano's richly decorative **polyptych**, the weight of the figures is denied by the twisting gold hems of sinuous draperies; in Ambrogio Lorenzetti's *Madonna* ★ (1340–45), Sienese grace is tempered by a Florentine sense of space, and the tenderness between mother and child is touchingly conveyed.

Rooms 39–46 In Room 39 and a series of small rooms leading off it is displayed the **Jesi-Jucker collection** of 20thC Italian art. The Futurist fascination with the violence and energy of modern life is evident in Boccioni's *Brawl in the Milan Galleria* – painted in the Divisionist technique of early Futurist works, and with something of the macabre, nightmare quality of German Expressionism – and in the spiralling forms of his *Elasticity*; Severini's *Dancer* and Balla's studies of movement are lighter and more decorative.

The strange poetry of Metaphysical painting touches Carrà's enigmatic paintings of mannequins, dice and maps, and the two still-lifes dating from Giorgio Morandi's brief association with the movement (Room 41); something of their haunting stillness lingers on in Morandi's later, contemplative still-lifes (Room 42) and in Filippo de Pisis' magical *Still-life with Eggs* (1924) (Room 39). You should now return through Room 8 and continue with Room 7.

Rooms 7–17 These rooms display Lombard pictures of the Renaissance and 16thC. The highlights are, in Room 7, Bonifacio Bembo's portraits of *Francesco Sforza* and *Bianca Maria Sforza* – bejewelled, courtly pictures in the tradition of Pisanello, yet with a startling hint of realism in the strongly characterized profiles; in Room 13, Ambrogio da Predis' *Portrait of a Young Man* – derived from Leonardo da Vinci's *Portrait of a Musician* in the PINACOTECA AMBROSIANA, yet coarser and obsessively polished; and in Room 17, Vincenzo Foppa's resplendent **altarpiece** ★ (1476) from the church of SANTA MARIA DELLE GRAZIE.

Room 18 The group of paintings by Crivelli is one of the high points of the Brera. Crivelli's works are distinguished by their rich decorative beauty and elaborate detail; such works startle and amaze with their virtuosity – note the *trompe l'oeil* tricks in the foreground of the *Madonna of the Candle* ★ The later *Coronation of the Virgin* is an almost suffocatingly rich work, lacking the hint of melancholy that lightens the earlier painting.

Mantegna's *Dead Christ* ★★ in the same room is a startling contrast; this is no glimpse of the court of heaven, but dramatic foreshortening draws the spectator disturbingly close to the brutal realism of the dead body of Christ – his heavy feet, torn by holes, thrust out towards us – and to the ugly grief of the women. Mantegna was fascinated by the new Renaissance sciences of perspective and anatomy, and uses both in this austere, tragic work.

Room 19 The sharp precision of Mantegna's style influenced Giovanni Bellini's *Pietà* ★★ a profoundly moving work where the grief of the figures is echoed in the desolate beauty of the pallid sky and landscape. This room also has two Bellini *Madonnas* ★ One is an archaic early work which is nevertheless touched by melancholy; the other, a late work set against a soft Giorgionesque landscape.

Room 20 This has a *Madonna* ★ by Mantegna and the side panels of a triptych, *St Peter* ★ and *St John the Baptist* ★ by Francesco Cossa, a Ferrarese Renaissance artist; the latter is distinguished by the sharp, bright clarity of the space and the crystalline precision of the details.

Room 22 Here are the most celebrated works in the gallery: Piero della Francesca's grave *Madonna with Saints and Angels, Adored by Federico da Montefeltro* ★★ in which the architecture is of outstanding beauty; and an early Raphael, the *Betrothal of the Virgin* ★★ where the lovely balance of the composition and the poetic sense of space are indebted to Perugino, yet the draughtsmanship attains a new delicacy.

Rooms 28–30 The collection of Italian 17thC painting is dominated by Caravaggio's restrained and subtle *Supper at Emmaus* ★ the second version of a more theatrical painting in the National Gallery, London. Gentileschi's *Sts Valerian, Tiburtius and Cecilia* suggests his response to the smooth draperies and elegance of Caravaggio's early works, while the intensity of Caracciolo's *Samaritan at the Well*

derives from the spirituality of Caravaggio's later works. Room 30 has a lovely *Immaculate Conception* ★ by the graceful, lyrical Neapolitan painter Bernardo Cavallino; Guido Cagnacci's *Death of Cleopatra* is a somewhat stolid attempt at sensuality, lacking both the ravishing allure of Reni and the disturbing eroticism of Furini.

Rooms 31–33 These rooms display the Dutch and Flemish collection, with works by Rubens and Rembrandt, and a startling, powerful study of the *Head of a Bull* by Paulus Potter.

Rooms 34–36 Italian 18thC paintings include works by Tiepolo, Canaletto and Guardi; outstanding is Piazzetta's *Rebecca at the Well* ★ (c.1740).

Room 37 The 19thC Italian collection has good works by the Macchiaioli, and Hayez's *The Kiss*, perhaps the most famous Italian Romantic painting.

Sant' Ambrogio
Piazza Sant' Ambrogio
🏛

Founded by St Ambrose in 386, this church was restructured in the 9thC and 11thC and is of seminal importance in the development of the Romanesque style in Lombardy. Parts of the church, including Bramante's **Portico della Canonica** (1495), were badly bombed during World War II and have since been restored.

The most important works inside the church are the **mosaics** in the apse, mainly of the 11thC; and the celebrated gold and silver **high altar** ★★ (835), with its 12thC **ciborium**. The altar, richly decorated with filigree and enamels and with outstanding narrative reliefs, is signed and dated by Wolvinus, an artist perhaps from the court of Charlemagne. The **pulpit** (c.1200) is reassembled from fragments.

Museo di Sant' Ambrogio
Piazza Sant' Ambrogio 15
Tel. (02) 872059
Open Mon, Wed–Fri 10am–noon,
3–5pm; Tues, Sat, Sun 3–5pm
📷 📖 ☑ 🔽
Entrance under Portico della Canonica
This is a small collection of paintings, frescoes, fragments of sculpture and architecture, ecclesiastical vestments, photographs and records that suggest the long and illustrious history of the basilica. Note especially a 4thC Oriental **damask** with hunting scenes.

Sant' Eustorgio ☆
Piazza Sant' Eustorgio
🏛

A vast Dominican basilica, founded in the 4thC and rebuilt in the 9thC and

13thC, Sant' Eustorgio has outstanding
sepulchral monuments and a charming
Renaissance chapel, the Cappella
Portinari. Note, in the first chapel to the
right, the **tomb of Giacomo Brivio**
(1484) by Tommaso Cazzaniga; in the
fourth chapel, the **tomb of Stefano
Visconti** (c. 1337). At the end of the
right aisle, in the **Cappella dei Magi**, is a
Romanesque sarcophagus which, legend
relates, contained the relics of the Three
Kings before they were presented to the
city of Cologne by Frederick Barbarossa
in 1162.

Cappella Portinari ★
📷

*Opens from the chancel; if locked, look for
the sacristan*
Designed by Michelozzo (1462–68) for
the Medici banker Pigello Portinari, the
chapel derives from Brunelleschi's
Cappella Pazzi (in Santa Croce) and his
Old Sacristy (in San Lorenzo) – see
Florence, **NORTH CENTRAL ITALY**.
Around the dome dance a charming
frieze of angels, probably by Foppa; the
frescoes by Foppa of scenes from the *Life
of St Peter Martyr* ★ are distinguished by
their grave realism and clear
compositions.

In the center of the chapel is the **tomb
of St Peter Martyr** ★ (1339) by Giovanni
di Balduccio of Pisa and assistants. This
monument was inspired by the Arca di
San Domenico in San Domenico,
BOLOGNA; it consists of a sarcophagus
surmounted by a tabernacle and
supported by eight caryatids representing
the *Virtues*; these are the loveliest part of
the ensemble and were probably worked
by Giovanni di Balduccio himself.
Around the sarcophagus are eight
crowded scenes from the *Life of St Peter
Martyr*, to which various Lombard
sculptors contributed; at the base of the
tabernacle are figures of the *Madonna*
with *St Dominic* and *St Peter Martyr*.

Santa Maria delle Grazie ☆☆
Corso Magenta
🏛 ♥ 🎨

The 15thC church has a tribune, dome
and cloister by Bramante. In the
adjoining refectory is Leonardo da Vinci's
Last Supper.
Cenacolo Vinciano
Piazza Santa Maria delle Grazie
Tel. (02) 4987588
*Open Tues – Sat 9am – 1.30pm,
2 – 6.30pm, Sun 9am – 3pm*
Closed Mon
📷

Leonardo's *Last Supper*, the most famous
painting in the Western tradition, was
painted between 1495–98; it began to
deteriorate almost immediately, and has

suffered many restorations, the last of
which is now in progress. Yet the power
and beauty of the composition and of
expression and gesture speak through the
damage.

Leonardo has chosen the moment
when Christ says "Verily I say unto you,
One of you which eateth with me shall
betray me" (Mark 14:18). The Apostles,
arranged in groups of three – Judas, subtly
isolated, shrinks back from Christ – react
vividly to his words, their agitation
contrasting with his stillness at the
center, where the perspective of the
architecture converges; the dramatic
composition transformed the quieter,
more commemorative renderings of
Andrea del Castagno and Ghirlandaio.
(See Cenacolo di Sant' Apollonia and
Ognissanti, Florence, **NORTH CENTRAL
ITALY**.)

Santa Maria della Passione
Via Conservatorio
🎨

This is a 15thC church, with so many
pictures by Daniele Crespi – the most
brilliant Lombard painter of the early
17thC – that it has been called a Crespi
museum. Along the pillars of the nave
there is a series of powerfully realistic,
half-length saints by Crespi. The
outstanding work, Crespi's *St Charles
Borromeus Fasting* ★ is in the first chapel
of the left aisle. This is the most
celebrated of all 17thC Milanese
paintings – a strong, austere work, which
movingly expresses the piety of the
Counter-Reformation. The organ
shutters are painted within and without
by Crespi.

In the left transept, the *Last Supper* is
by Gaudenzio Ferrari (16thC). In the
right transept are works by Luini (16thC)
and Bergognone (15thC).

Santa Maria presso San Celso
Corso Italia
🏛

The church was begun in 1490 and has a
fine late 16thC facade by Alessi. The side
aisles are decorated with Mannerist
stuccoes and frescoes by two of the
leading Milanese artists of the early
17thC, Giulio Cesare Procaccini and
Giambattista Crespi. There are also
interesting paintings by both artists,
including, in the fourth bay to the right,
Procaccini's *Martyrdoms of Sts Nazarius
and Celsus* (1606), a violent, expressive
work which influenced Crespi's
Martyrdom of St Catherine (1609) in
the second bay to the left.

Other interesting works are, in the
right transept, Paris Bordone's *Holy
Family with St Jerome*; in the

ambulatory, Gaudenzio Ferrari's *Baptism of Christ* and Moretto's *Conversion of St Paul*; and, at the beginning of the left aisle, Bergognone's *Madonna and Saints*.

MODENA
Emilia-Romagna   Map E4

An ancient city, inhabited since Etruscan times, conquered by the Romans, and later governed by the dukes of Este, Modena now has a quiet provincial atmosphere. A wide avenue, replacing the old walls, rings the old part of the city; the historic Via Emilia cuts through its center. Several of the churches have late 15thC and early 16thC terra-cotta groups by the Modenese sculptors Guido Mazzoni and Antonio Begarelli; Mazzoni's straightforward realism was developed by Begarelli into a more dramatic style.

Duomo ☆
Piazza Grande
🏛

The cathedral was begun by the Lombard architect Lanfranco in 1099 and completed in the 13thC. In terms of both architecture and sculpture, it is one of the masterpieces of the Italian Romanesque. A tablet on the facade, held up by the prophets *Enoch* and *Elias*, praises the sculptor, Wiligelmo da Modena (12thC), who thus emerges as the first distinct artistic personality in the history of Italian sculpture.

Wiligelmo's works include four **relief panels** * of scenes from Genesis, one on either side of the main portal and one over each of the side portals; the finest, the *Creation and Fall of Adam and Eve* ** (over the left portal) is distinguished by the dramatic power of Wiligelmo's sturdy expressive figures. The jambs of the main portal, and the two *Genii Holding Torches* are also attributed to Wiligelmo.

The **Porta dei Principi** on the right flank of the cathedral has sculptures by the school of Wiligelmo showing the *Life of St Gimignano*. Further along the right flank is the 13thC **Porta Regia** and, in the last bay, a low **relief** by Agostino di Duccio (1442). The **Porta della Peschiera** on the left flank is by a follower of Wiligelmo (c.1120–30) and has, in the architrave, a charming scene from the Arthurian legend.

The outstanding feature of the interior is the **tribune** * with reliefs attributed to Anselmo da Campione and his workshop (late 12thC). Anselmo was associated with the cathedral as both sculptor and architect; he was one of the founders of a large workshop of Lombard sculptors and builders which flourished from the 12thC to the 14thC, now known as the Campionesi. The pulpit and altar, and the capitals in the crypt, are all by the Campionesi, as is the **Porta Regia** (see above).

Galleria Estense ☆
Palazzo dei Musei, Via Emilia
Tel. (059) 222145
Open Tues–Sat 9am–2pm, Sun
*   9am–1pm*
Closed Mon
🖼 🔊 ☑

This is an attractively varied and elegant gallery, where groups of pictures alternate with showcases of small bronzes, majolicas, ivories, coins and medals. The display culminates in four big rooms, grandly hung with works of the 16thC Venetian and 17thC Italian schools.

Immediately opposite the entrance, beyond cases of small Etruscan and Greek bronzes, is Bernini's heroic bust of *Francesco I d'Este, Duke of Modena* * (1650–51), commemorating the man who created the collection. To the right is the long gallery, where the display opens with 14thC pictures by Barnaba da Modena and the Bolognese artist Simone de' Crocifissi. Cosimo Tura's *St Antony of Padua* * is a late work, disturbing and intensely melancholy. Beyond are some fine Renaissance bronzes, including Bertoldo di Giovanni's *Hercules* * and busts by L'Antico and Tullio Lombardo.

A small group of Dutch and Flemish pictures is followed by terra-cotta sculptures – a speciality of Modenese artists; the outstanding work here is the pretty *Madonna del Latte* * (c.1540) by Antonio Begarelli, an artist better known for his dramatic *Lamentations* – yet this vivid, almost Rococo work, is more appealing. Close by hangs a large **carving** by Grinling Gibbons, presented by James II to the relatives of his wife, Mary of Modena; it consists of a small, self-portrait medallion hanging from a skull, a grim *memento mori* amid symbols of human achievement.

At the end of this gallery is Correggio's *Campori Madonna* * a work of c.1518 which brings his earliest period to a close; it is an intimate close-up, exceptional for its blond, delicate colours. A series of small rooms beyond has mainly 16thC pictures, including some dark, disturbing works by Lelio Orsi and others, more decorative, by Niccolò dell' Abate.

Next comes the grand display of the 16thC Venetian and 17thC Italian schools. The Venetian paintings include works by Veronese, Tintoretto and Palma

Giovane. The 17thC collection is richest in works by Bolognese artists, including a **Venus** by Annibale Carracci and a **Crucifixion** by Guido Reni. Guercino is fascinatingly represented by works which make startlingly clear the dramatic contrast between his late and early styles. The early **Martyrdom of St Peter** ★ is a passionate, brutally realistic work, glowing with rich Venetian colour and painterly textures. Later Guercino moved towards the cool classicism of Guido Reni; his **Hamon and Tamar** is a somewhat stiff and posturing work; yet the **Marriage of St Catherine** ★ is one of the most convincingly majestic and measured of these often vapid late works.

A group of Caravaggesque pictures includes works by Manfredi; a candlelit **Judith with the Head of Holofernes** by Saraceni; and the **Fortune Teller**, a poetic treatment of a Caravaggesque theme, unexpectedly attributed to the Milanese painter Francesco del Cairo.

The two early works by Salvator Rosa are his only securely datable landscapes, painted in 1640 for the Duke of Modena. The bucolic and pastoral mood of the **Landscape with Erminia**, with a sunlit vista on the right, and the lovely effects of flickering light on the tree trunks on the left, is unexpectedly close to Claude. The **Harbour Scene** is a more Baroque work, full of the artist's delight in the drama of masts pitched over and crossed at steep angles and in the patterns made by ribs and planks; it is a development of the kind of composition that had been introduced to Rome by the Flemish artist Paul Bril.

Biblioteca Estense

Open Sun–Fri: summer 9am–2pm, winter 9am–8pm; Sat 9am–2pm

🔲

The library has an important display of illuminated books, most celebrated of which is the 15thC **Bible of Borso d'Este**, illuminated by Taddeo Crivelli and Franco Rossi.

San Giovanni Battista
Piazza Matteotti

This elegant, centrally planned Baroque church contains a powerfully realistic **Deposition** ★ (1480) by Mazzoni.

San Pietro
Via San Pietro

A graceful Renaissance church dating from 1476–1506, San Pietro is richly endowed with works of art. The most interesting are the six statues attributed to Begarelli that stand against the piers of the central nave.

The second chapel of the right nave has an **Assumption of the Virgin** by Dosso Dossi. The **Madonna in Glory with Saints** in the right transept is the last work of Begarelli. The chapel to the right of the choir has a **Pietà** by Begarelli. In the left nave, note especially the seventh chapel, with a **Madonna and Saints** by Dossi, and the second chapel, with **St Peter Reviving Tabitha** by Giacinto Brandi.

MONZA
Milano, Lombardia Map D2

Monza is a city of Roman origin, but was most powerful under the Lombards in the 7thC. It is now a busy industrial center, famous for motor racing.

Civica Galleria d'Arte
Villa Reale
Tel. (039) 386984
Open Apr–Sept, Tues–Sun 3–6pm
Closed Oct–Mar; Mon
🔲 🏛

The gallery is housed in one wing of a spectacular Neoclassical villa. It has a group of works by rather minor 17thC painters, many of them of uncertain attribution; the most interesting is Daniele Crespi's **Martyrdom of St Lawrence** – a curious blend of grave realism with dramatic foreshortening, startling lighting and mannered body poses. There is a larger 19thC collection, with many dullish works in a Neo-Impressionist style – yet some stand out: a poignant **Portrait of an Old Woman** by Pompeo Mariani, and an exceptionally horrid **Leda and the Swan** by Arturo Martini. Twentieth century works include Marino Marini's **St George and the Dragon**, a very early treatment of a theme that was to obsess him.

Duomo
Piazza del Duomo
🏛

The original church was founded in the 6thC by Theodolinda, Queen of Lombardy, and many times rebuilt. Its lovely green and white marble facade is by Matteo da Campione and dates from 1396; the 18thC campanile was added by Pellegrini.

In the nave, there is a fine **cantoria** (singing gallery) by Matteo da Campione. To the left of the presbytery, the **Cappella di Teodolinda** has frescoes of scenes from the **Life of Queen Theodolinda** (1444) by the Zavattari. These frescoes are the most important Milanese paintings of the early 15thC; they are a pretty, gentle version of the courtly style of Pisanello – with gorgeous costumes, elegantly caparisoned steeds, little palaces and turrets perched fantastically on rocky hills. The chapel also preserves the **Corona del Ferro** or Iron Crown of Lombardy, but this can only be viewed from the adjacent MUSEO SERPERO.

Museo Serpero (Tesoro del Duomo) ☆
Piazza del Duomo
Tel. (039) 22392
Open Tues–Sun 9am–noon, 3–5pm
Closed Mon
🔲 ✗ ⚜ 🏛 ☑

The cathedral treasury is spectacular; the minor or decorative arts flourished more brilliantly than painting in medieval Lombardy, and the treasury preserves goldsmiths' work, jewellery and ivories from the late Roman period to the Renaissance; the collection was enriched by exceptionally important gifts from Queen Theodolinda.

The splendid examples of ancient Lombard art include a **gilded silver hen with seven chickens** ★ studded with ruby eyes; an overwhelmingly ornate **reliquary**, decorated with precious stones, for the tooth of St John; and a 9thC–10thC ivory diptych of *King David and St Gregory* ★

The most famous work – although not the most beautiful – is the **Corona del Ferro** or Iron Crown of Lombardy, which dates from the beginning of the Carolingian age (5thC–8thC). The name derives from the band of iron – said to be from one of the nails of the True Cross – that runs around the rim; the crown itself is made of gold, and inlaid with enamels and jewels.

NOVARA
Piemonte Map C2

Novara is a modern industrial city, rather drab and depressing, set on a featureless plain. Reminders of earlier periods linger on in the decaying grandeur of the Broletto, a court of medieval buildings in the city center, and in the vast and gloomy Neoclassical cathedral and extraordinarily elongated cupola of San Gaudenzio, both by Antonelli.

Duomo
Piazza della Repubblica
The vast Neoclassical building preserves remnants of an earlier cathedral in the presbytery. On the second altar on the right is a **Betrothal of St Catherine** by Gaudenzio Ferrari (16thC). The adjacent baptistry dates back to the 4thC but has been restored many times; it has Romanesque **frescoes** of the 11thC.

Museo Civico
Palazzo del Broletto, Via Fratelli Rosselli
Tel. (0321) 23021
Open Tues–Sat: summer 10am–noon,
3.30–6.30pm, winter 9am–noon,
3–5.30pm; Sun 9am–noon
Closed Mon
🔲 ✗ ⚜ 🏛

This museum has a collection of local archaeological finds, some interesting 15thC–18thC Lombard pictures – including Tanzio da Varallo's sketch for the **Battle of Sennacherib** in SAN GAUDENZIO – and a section devoted to modern art.

San Gaudenzio
Via San Gaudenzio
The church dates from 1577 but has a 19thC campanile and dome. In the first chapel on the right are 17thC frescoes by Morazzone – note especially his **Last Judgment**. The first chapel on the left contains a vast canvas of the **Battle of Sennacherib** ★ (1629) by Tanzio da Varallo – a dark mixture of fantasy and brutal realism by the most gifted Lombard Caravaggesque painter.

ORTA SAN GIULIO
Novara, Piemonte Map C2

Orta is an enchanting lakeside town with a pretty 16thC town hall decorated with fading frescoes. The main square frames a view of the Isola di San Giulio, crowned by a cluster of villas and the Romanesque campanile of the church. The narrow streets of the town are lined with elegant 17thC and 18thC houses – many with fine Rococo ironwork – that blend picturesquely with the medieval buildings.

Sacro Monte
10 mins' uphill walk from main square
🔲 ⚜ 📷 🏛 🅿

The Sacro Monte of Orta, overlooking the lake, is one of the most beautiful mountain sanctuaries in northern Italy. It consists of 20 chapels dedicated to St Francis, each decorated with *tableaux vivants* of life-size terra-cotta statues and with frescoes of scenes from his life. The chapels were begun in 1592, by the Capuchin architect Padre Cleto; his designs are lucid and elegant variations on Renaissance themes.

Notice especially the lovely simplicity of **Chapel 6** which echoes many churches in the Orta region; and the more ambitious **Chapel 15** with strong overtones of Bramante and Raphael. The most important sculptors associated with the project were the Milanese Cristoforo

Prestinari and the Lombard Dionigi Bussola – best represented in **Chapels 4** and **7** respectively. The outstanding frescoes are those by Morazzone in **Chapel 11**, but unfortunately this is often closed.

San Giulio
Isola di San Giulio
The island can be reached by a 20min boat journey

The Romanesque church was richly decorated in the Baroque era. Its **pulpit ★** is one of the most celebrated works of medieval sculpture in northern Italy, decorated with powerful, almost flamboyant symbols of the Evangelists and with monsters and foliage. This taste for fabulous imagery is characteristic of the sculptural style that spread from Como; yet here the figures have a strikingly mysterious and moving solemnity, and it has been suggested that the sculptor also worked in Germany.

PARMA
Emilia-Romagna   Map E3

Parma is an ancient city with a history stretching back to Roman times – yet it is mainly modern in appearance, with wide streets and squares laid out in the 19thC in the French manner. It is a substantial and busy provincial capital, with a harmonious and impressive old center around the Romanesque cathedral and pink marble baptistry. Historic monuments outside this area have a somewhat gloomy and neglected air; the vast and dour Palazzo della Pilotta, surrounded by a depressing area of wasteland – half car park, half bomb site – houses the city's principal art collections. Two periods are outstanding in the history of Parma's art: the Romanesque, when the powerful artistic personality of Benedetto Antelami emerged; and the Renaissance, which witnessed not only the building of such splendid churches as the Madonna della Steccata but also the art of Correggio transforming the city into a brilliant and influential artistic center. Parma remains the best place to see Correggio's pictures and frescoes, and there are good works by artists whom he influenced, notably Parmigianino.

Battistero ★★
Piazza del Duomo
Tel. (0521) 35886
Closed for restoration
🏛

Both the construction and the **sculptural decoration ★★** of the baptistry – an octagonal building, with a gravely Romanesque exterior, yet within dominated by the soaring Gothic lines of the ribbed dome – are attributed to Benedetto Antelami, the most significant Italian sculptor before Nicola Pisano; on both counts, architectural and sculptural, the baptistry is without doubt the greatest and most original work of the Italian Romanesque.

The N portal (1196–1200), W portal (1200–4) and S portal (c. 1204–8) are richly decorated with reliefs and solemn sculptured figures; they are linked by a frieze of plaques decorated with flowers, animals and more figures. Among the interior sculptures, by Antelami and assistants, in the central part of the first gallery are personifications of the **Months** and **Seasons**, which suggest the influence of French Gothic. The 13thC frescoes with their darkly outlined figures and strikingly vivid colours are influenced by Byzantine art.

Camera di San Paolo ★
Via Melloni
Tel. (0521) 33309
Open Tues – Sat 9am – 2pm, Sun 9am – 1pm
Closed Mon
◧

The Camera was one of the rooms in the apartments of the learned and independent-minded Abbess of San Paolo, a noble lady called Giovanna da Piacenza. From the windows of the rooms on the ground floor, the cloisters of the Benedictine convent, long suppressed, can also be seen.

The decoration of the Camera was Correggio's first work in Parma (1518); above the fireplace is a representation of **Diana**, goddess of chastity, hunting and the moon – she is shown here riding a chariot. The vault of the room is a pergola with oval openings in the lush green foliage that reveal the sky beyond, and a cavorting hunt of putti. Below, in the lunettes, are classical scenes, mostly adapted from Roman coins, and painted to imitate stone reliefs. They are divided by grinning rams' heads, and are all more or less obscurely related in subject matter to Diana.

Despite the erudite subject matter, the whole effect is one of pagan lightness and good humour, and there is not a trace of piety. The perspective skill is indebted to Mantegna, yet the wit and charm of Correggio's approach to antiquity seem closer to Raphael's **Cupid and Psyche** cycle in the Villa Farnesina in Rome (see *SOUTH CENTRAL ITALY*). You have only to look at the pedantic classicism of the ceiling in the adjoining room, frescoed by

Alessandro Araldi, a Parmese painter of the previous generation, to see why Correggio was such a success.

Duomo ☆☆
Piazza del Duomo
🏛

The cathedral is a fine 12thC Romanesque building, with a slender Gothic campanile that dates from 1284. The interior is exceptionally dark and gloomy, and it is important to take plenty of coins for the light machines. Against the right wall of the right transept is a **Deposition** ★★ signed and dated by Benedetto Antelami (1178) and the earliest of his known works. The relief retains faint echoes of Byzantine stylization; yet the austere, simple figures convey deep emotion in a way that was entirely new in northern Italian sculpture.

Dome ★★ Against the sober background of the cathedral's Romanesque interior, Correggio's frescoed dome stands apart, but at the same time gives the building a commanding focus. This was Correggio's last fresco, commissioned as early as 1524 in the wake of the success of the dome of SAN GIOVANNI EVANGELISTA, but not completed until 1530. It comprises an elaborate depiction of the **Assumption of the Virgin**, circled below by the **Apostles** and with the four **Patron Saints of Parma** in the pendentives. Incorporating the real windows at the base of the octagon into his design, Correggio depicts the wonder of the Apostles as the Virgin rises in a glory of light towards heaven. Above their heads, almost submerged in a flood of angels, she makes her ascent through a ring of Old Testament figures such as Adam and Eve towards a solitary angel (often said to represent Christ) who descends to greet her.

The work reveals Correggio at his most teasing and ecstatic and remains a triumph of illusionism: the skill of the foreshortening on an irregularly-shaped surface has not been surpassed. Following a recent restoration, it is again possible to see the detail as well as the whole.

The fresco was not well received at the time – a canon of the cathedral described it as a "stew of frogs' legs" – but it was nevertheless immensely influential, as a comparison with the dome of the MADONNA DELLA STECCATA amply demonstrates. It was a lasting source of inspiration to 17thC painters, and echoes of it reverberate through the great Baroque ceiling decorations of Rome.

In the presbytery, usually inaccessible, are a carved 12thC altar of red Veronese marble and an **episcopal throne** ★ by Antelami.

Galleria Nazionale ☆
Palazzo della Pilotta, Piazzale Marconi
Tel. (0521) 33309
Open Tues – Sat 9am – 2pm, Sun
* 9am – 1pm*
Closed Mon
🚻 🚏 🏛 ♿

The gallery is housed in a massive, rather bleak Renaissance palace, built by the Farnese family between 1583 and 1622. It is one of Italy's major galleries – yet in a creaking and dusty state, awaiting a long-overdue restoration; the paintings themselves are undergoing some reorganization and room numbers are likely to change.

In the first part of the gallery are 14thC and 15thC pictures; art in Parma during this period was rather unexciting and the influence of other schools predominated; the Tuscan, Sienese and Bolognese pictures are more interesting, with a **triptych** by Simone de' Crocifissi and a **Madonna** attributed to Fra Angelico. Further on is a **Head of a Girl** ★ a *bozzetto* attributed to Leonardo da Vinci.

Correggio   Rooms VII–IX are devoted to an outstanding group of works by Correggio. First, in **Room VII**, are detached frescoes of the mid 1520s – the **Madonna of the Stairs** and an **Annunciation** – and an altarpiece, the **Madonna with St Jerome** ★★ (1527–28). The altarpiece is one of Correggio's happiest pictures, with St Jerome and St Mary Magdalen crowding contentedly around the absorbed Virgin and jolly Child. It is related to the fresco in the DUOMO on which Correggio was then working, both in the grandeur of St Jerome – recalling the Apostles – and in the arrangement of the receding figures and the golden light (the picture is also known as *Il Giorno*).

Room VIII has two works from the Cappella del Bono in SAN GIOVANNI EVANGELISTA, the **Martyrdom of Sts Placidus and Flavia** and the **Lamentation at the Foot of the Cross**, both of which were meant to be seen at a sharp angle from the body of the church. They are dramatic, violently emotional and luridly coloured.

Room IX has Correggio's **Madonna della Scodella** ★ (1530), still in its original frame; based on sweeping diagonals, this picture depicts a miracle in Christ's infancy when a palm tree bowed its branches to provide the holy family with food and a spring grew up to give them water. The picture is named after the bowl ("scodella") with which the Virgin scoops up the water.

The main collection continues with two fine pictures by Parmigianino in

Room X. In **Room XII**, among a series of northern pictures that includes a good van Dyck, is a fine group of works by the Venetian painter Cima da Conegliano. The ***Madonna with St Michael the Archangel and St Andrew*** ★ (c. 1502–5) is a strange, poignant work; a ruined classical wall leads diagonally into the composition; against it is the brightly lit group of the Madonna and Child. On one side stands an elegant, Peruginesque St Michael; the Madonna and Child are turned – the Virgin's hand raised in a hesitant gesture of protection – towards a gaunt St Andrew bearing the Cross. The light is sharp; the forms crisp and clear; and the details almost Pre-Raphaelite in their intensity. By contrast, the probably later **Sacra Conversazione** is a more conventional composition, with softer light and atmosphere.

Cima's small, circular painting of **Endymion** ★ is a lyrical, magical work; Endymion lies on a grassy bank, with the Moon (Diana) casting a lovely golden light over distant fields; the picture, a response to Giorgione's poetry, is full of delicately observed details.

Room XIII is at present crowded with a vast array of 16thC, 17thC and 18thC pictures. There are works by El Greco and Bronzino and a ***Pietà with Saints*** ★ (1585) by Annibale Carracci. This painting clearly expresses Annibale's response to Correggio, both in the delicacy and beauty of the colour, and in the angels, which derive from Correggio's pendentives in the DUOMO; the swooning Madonna recalls Correggio's **Lamentation** in Room VIII. Yet Annibale's is a warmer, more human picture than Correggio's melancholy and heightened drama; the saints in the foreground gently invite the spectator to share their grief. The painting has the direct emotional appeal and lively naturalism of the early Baroque. There is also a small, Correggiesque **Self-portrait** by Annibale (1593).

Amongst the 17thC works, note some good pictures by Lanfranco, who came from Parma, and by Bartolommeo Schedoni, who came from Modena but entered the service of the duke in 1607. Schedoni's two large works, the **Three Marys at the Tomb** and the **Entombment**, reveal a highly original talent; light falls with startling intensity on the smooth, sharp surfaces of strangely coloured fabrics; the mood of each is oddly disquieting. A good collection of 18thC pictures includes works by Sebastiano Ricci and Piazzetta.

Across the courtyard, under the arches, a new gallery of 18thC art has just opened, featuring landscape and genre.

Madonna della Steccata
Via Garibaldi
🏛

The church was begun in 1521, and is in the form of a Greek cross, with semi-circular apses and four small chapels in the angles of the cross. The cupola is frescoed with an ***Assumption of the Virgin*** by Bernardo Gatti (16thC), deriving from Correggio's work in the DUOMO. In the vault is a fresco decoration begun by Parmigianino in 1530; neurotic and restless, Parmigianino made little headway with this work and in 1535 abandoned it to other artists, soon afterwards fleeing to Casalmaggiore to avoid legal troubles. The grave and elegant figures of the ***Wise and Foolish Virgins*** ★ on the right and left walls look back to the classical style of Raphael and Giulio Romano and suggest Parmigianino's endless aspiration towards an abstract perfection of form.

Museo Civico Glauco Lombardo
Palazzo di Riserva, Via Garibaldi 15
Tel. (0521) 33727
Open Tues–Sat: May–Sept
*   9.30am–12.30pm, 4–6pm, Oct–Apr*
*   9.30am–12.30pm, 3–5pm; Sun*
*   9.30am–1pm*
Closed Mon
📷 ☑

Housed in the elegant rooms of a Neoclassical palace, this is a collection of Napoleonic curios and mementoes that belonged to the Duchess Marie Louise of Austria, ex-Empress of France; it is a low-key but attractive and varied display, with some good French 18thC drawings and watercolours.

Museo Nazionale d'Antichità ☆
Palazzo della Pilotta, Piazzale Marconi
Tel. (0521) 33309
Open Tues–Sat 9am–2pm, Sun
*   9am–1pm*
Closed Mon
📷 �︎ 🏛

One of the most interesting archaeological museums in northern Italy, this collection is especially rich in works discovered at Velleia. In **Room I** are Roman marbles from the Gonzaga and Farnese collections. Further on, in **Room V**, 12 large marble statues of members of the Giulio-Claudian family are ranged around the walls; they include portraits of **Drusilla, Agrippina** and **Livia**. **Room VI** has the loveliest work in the collection, a bronze **Head of a Girl** ★ from the end of the 1stC BC; this is an exceptionally delicate, naturalistic work. Note also in this room some small and lively bronzes – including a paunchy **Silenus**, vivid and full of energy.

Pinacoteca Stuard
Via Cavestro 14
Tel. (0521) 22680
Open Sun – Fri 9.30am – noon, 3 – 5pm
Closed Sat
🔯

This is a dusty, ill-labelled collection, badly in need of rearrangement. There are a few Tuscan pictures, notably works by Paolo di Giovanni Fei and Bernardo Daddi; also, a great many, mainly dull, 17thC works – most interesting among them are a Lanfranco and a Schedoni.

San Giovanni Evangelista ☆
Piazzale San Giovanni
🏛

The most important Renaissance church in Parma forms part of an ancient Benedictine foundation. Correggio worked here from 1520 and his frescoes dominate the church.

In the lunette of the **left transept** is a fresco of **St John the Evangelist**, the church's patron saint. The fresco in the **cupola ★★** is a complex scene of Christ descending to John (at the base of the dome, and only visible from the altar steps), ringed by heroic, Michelangelesque Apostles. On the intrados of the arches of the cupola, Correggio later added eight monochrome figures from the Old Testament. The **apse** was frescoed with the **Coronation of the Virgin**, destroyed in 1587 when the choir was extended, and replaced by a copy by Cesare Aretusi.

Correggio also frescoed the first cross vault of the **choir** with a grotesque decoration in grisaille and completed his contribution to the church with a frieze of **Pagan and Hebrew Sacrifices** (1532 – 34) along the full length of the nave. The presence of assistants is evident here, as it is in his only work for private patrons in San Giovanni, the decoration of the **Cappella del Bono**, the fifth to the right of the nave. The entrance arch of the chapel is frescoed with the coats-of-arms of the patron and his wife, and with a dramatic **Conversion of St Paul** and a more sedate **Sts Peter and John Healing**. These frescoes were supplemented by two lateral canvases, now in the GALLERIA NAZIONALE.

San Giovanni is the perfect place to compare Correggio with his immediate followers: other chapels are adorned with frescoes and altarpieces by Parmigianino, Anselmi and Mazzola Bedoli. Notice especially, in the first, second and fourth chapels to the left, the earliest **frescoes ★** of Parmigianino, where borrowings from the Cappella del Bono blend with the influence of the powerful compositions

of Anselmi and Pordenone. In the right transept, there are two terra cottas by Begarelli.

PAVIA
Lombardia Map C3

Pavia was already an important city in Roman times. From 572 – 774 it was capital of the Lombard kingdom and, in the 12thC and 13thC, an independent commune. The Roman city plan is still discernible and many medieval towers and outstandingly beautiful Romanesque churches give the city a distinctive flavour; at the center is the Piazza Vittoria, a picturesque composition with an attractive crumbling charm. Close to Pavia is a celebrated Carthusian monastery, the Certosa di Pavia – the most spectacular achievement of the Lombard Renaissance.

Certosa di Pavia
10km (6 miles) N of Pavia
Tel. (0382) 925613
Open Tues – Sun: Mar, Apr, Sept
    9 – 11.30am, 2.30 – 5pm; May – Aug
    9 – 11.30am, 2.30 – 6pm; Oct – Feb
    9 – 11.30am, 2.30 – 4.30pm
Closed Mon
🔯 *but donation appreciated* 🗡 🎪 🏛 🔱 ⌖

This sumptuously decorated Carthusian monastery was begun in 1396 by Gian Galeazzo Visconti as a mausoleum for his dynasty. The design of the church itself remains essentially Gothic, yet on the facade the Gothic elements are overlaid by an overwhelmingly rich and intricate display of Lombard Renaissance sculpture; the exuberant classicism of this local style contrasts sharply with the lucid proportions and simplicity of the Florentine Renaissance architecture.

The most important sculptors involved in the decoration of the Certosa were Gianantonio Amadeo, whose works are delicate and refined, and the Mantagazza brothers, distinguished by a tauter and more expressive line. The most notable painter was the Milanese artist Ambrogio Bergognone, a follower of Foppa, who painted in a sweet, grave style. The Certosa now has an attractively festive air and is a favourite Sunday outing for Italian families.

Facade
The facade of the church falls into two halves: the lower half, thickly encrusted with an abundance of sculptures, and the unfinished upper half, in the broader, High Renaissance style of Cristoforo Lombardo. Around the base of the facade runs a **frieze** of marble medallions with Roman emperors and Eastern monarchs,

including many by Amadeo. Above are 18 low reliefs with scenes from the *Life of Christ* interspersed with **statuettes** – some of the reliefs by Amadeo, others by the Mantagazza brothers; the statuettes are also by the Mantagazza. The four exceptionally beautiful **windows** ★ decorated with a wonderfully rich variety of motifs, were designed by Amadeo (1494–96).

The **central portal**, with simple classical forms (influenced by Bramante) far removed from Amadeo's exuberance, is by Benedetto Briosco (1501); beside the entrance are four **reliefs** illustrating scenes from the *History of the Carthusian Order*.

Interior
The outstanding works in the **left transept**, the effigies of *Lodovico il Moro* and *Beatrice d'Este*, are all that remain from a larger tomb by Cristoforo Solari that once stood in Santa Maria delle Grazie in Milan, commissioned shortly after 1474, and brought here in 1564. The bold rhythms of the draperies set off the highly finished detail and the impressively solid realism of the heads.

The **door** ★ to the **Old Sacristy**, with a frieze of medallions by Benedetto Briosco, was designed by Amadeo (c. 1477); within, the early 15thC **ivory polyptych** ★ is from the workshop of the Florentine artist Baldassare degli Embriachi: it is an extraordinarily elaborate piece with 66 low reliefs and 99 little statuettes illustrating the *Life of the Virgin* and the *Life of Christ*.

The **tomb of Gian Galeazzo Visconti** in the **right transept** was designed by Gian Cristoforo Romano (1483–97); it introduced a more restrained classical style to Pavia. The effigy is by Galeazzo Alessi and the *Madonna* by Benedetto Briosco. Beyond the transept, moving down the right nave, the **first chapel** has, over the doorway, a *Madonna* by Bergognone, and the **fourth chapel** a *Crucifixion* by the same artist.

Cloisters
Both the small and great cloisters have intricate terra-cotta decoration by Amadeo and by the Cremonese sculptor Rinaldo de Stauris.

Musei Civici
Castello Visconteo, Piazza Castello
Tel. (0382) 33853
Open Tues–Sun 10am–noon, 3–5pm
Closed Mon
📷 🗺 🏛 ☑ ♨

The castle of the Visconti was built by Gian Galeazzo Visconti between 1360–64. Once a celebrated building with frescoes by Pisanello, visited by both Petrarch and Leonardo, it now has an air of decaying grandeur, the vast courtyard surrounded by crumbling arches and overgrown with ivy and grass. Yet, within, many of the rooms retain fragments of their original decorations and have become a beautiful setting for the civic collections. These are mainly concerned with the history of Pavia and its monuments and are grouped into three distinct sections: archaeology (Rooms I–VI), sculpture (Rooms VII–XIV) and painting (the Pinacoteca Malaspina on the second floor).

The **archaeological section** has inscriptions, columns and other fragments and a particularly good collection of Roman glass.

The **sculpture display** opens with early Christian and medieval works; the most beautiful are the crisply carved **sarcophagi**, one of them decorated with peacocks and the Tree of Life between winged dragons. Further on is an outstanding collection of Romanesque sculpture, mainly from destroyed Pavian churches. The most splendid monument of the Pavian Romanesque was San Giovanni in Borgo; in **Room X** there is a selection of capitals from this church which suggest the Pavian taste for fabulous, even monstrous imagery.

There is also a good and varied collection of mosaic pavements; in **Room XI** pavements from the right nave of Santa Maria del Popolo show lively narratives from the *Life of St Eustace*.

Room XIV is a large room known as the **Sala dei Mantagazza**; Amadeo, and Antonio and Cristoforo Mantagazza were the most distinguished sculptors of the Lombard Renaissance. Works either by or closely related to them include a poignant, powerful *Pietà* by one of the Mantagazza brothers and a series of ten reliefs from Genesis and the New Testament attributed to Amadeo and his circle; the most effective of these are the *Creation of Eve* and *Cain and Abel* – with startlingly fresh and boldly simplified forms.

The **Pinacoteca Malaspina** on the second floor is a beautiful gallery with fragments of original decoration. Yet the paintings themselves are somewhat disappointing and many are by anonymous and unexciting Lombard masters. The interesting works are Vincenzo Foppa's *Madonna with Saints* (a much disputed attribution); a sketchy, spontaneous *Holy Family* by Correggio; and a little panel by Simone de' Crocifissi. Among the Lombard pictures, note a pretty *Portrait of a Woman* attributed to Boltraffio, a follower of Leonardo.

San Pietro in Ciel d'Oro ☆
🏛

This celebrated Romanesque church, with its finely carved **portal** and majestic interior, was consecrated in 1132. Over the high altar is the elaborate, late 14thC Gothic **tomb of St Augustine ★★** one of the four great Fathers of the Church; crowded with many little figures, and delicate, intricate detail, it is probably the work of Lombard craftsmen and is related to the **tomb of St Peter Martyr** in Sant' Eustorgio, Milan.

PIACENZA
Emilia-Romagna Map D3

Piacenza is now a busy agricultural and industrial center, but its long history stretches back to Etruscan times, when it was an important fortified city; its power and prosperity lasted throughout the Middle Ages, and from 1556–1731 it was dominated by the Farnese family. In the city center, the Piazza dei Cavalli recalls successive stages of Piacenza's history. In front of the late 13thC Palazzo del Comune, with its splendid marble arcade and battlemented roof – proud symbol of medieval independence – stand two equestrian statues of the Farnese.

Duomo
Piazza del Duomo
🏛

The cathedral is Romanesque (1122–1233), with good sculpture on the three portals of the facade, and a 14thC campanile. Inside, a large *Assumption of the Virgin* by Camillo Procaccini decorates the vault of the main apse. The fine cupola frescoes, recently restored, were begun by Morazzone and, following his death, continued by Guercino. The *Isaiah* and *David* (1625–26) are by Morazzone; the *Annunciation to the Shepherds, Nativity, Circumcision* and *Return from Egypt* are all by Guercino, as are the lovely *Sibyls* in the lunettes.

Galleria d'Arte Moderna Ricci-Oddi ☆
Via San Siro 13
Tel. (0523) 20742
Open Tues–Sun: Mar–Apr 10am–noon,
* 3–5pm, May–Sept 10am–noon,*
* 3–6pm, Oct–Feb 10am–noon, 2–4pm*
Closed Mon
📷 🍴 ♿ ☑

Founded by Giuseppe Ricci-Oddi, a Piacentine nobleman and collector, and donated to the city in 1924, this is one of the most important collections of modern art in Italy. It is housed in a purpose-built gallery, designed by Giulio Arata (1931),

and traces the development of modern painting from Romanticism through to 1930.

The Macchiaioli are especially well represented (among them, Signorini, Fattori, Lega) as is Metaphysical painting (Carrà, de Chirico, de Pisis). Note also the *Portrait of the Artist's Mother* by the Futurist painter Boccioni, and sculptures by Rosso, Wildt, Canonica and Gemito.

Madonna di Campagna
Via Campagna
🏛

Inside this fine Renaissance church, built on a Greek cross plan 1522–28 by the local architect Alessio Tramello, are dramatic **frescoes** by Pordenone that prefigure the Baroque. The *St Augustine* (1525) to the left of the entrance is his earliest work in Piacenza. The elaborate decoration of the cupola is mainly by Pordenone but was completed by Bernardino Gatti. Also by Pordenone are the frescoes in the **Cappella di Santa Caterina** and **Cappella dei Magi**, the two chapels in the left-hand angles of the Greek cross.

The chapel in the furthest right-hand angle of the cross has an **altarpiece** by Procaccini. A frieze of canvases runs around the entire church, enhancing the richly decorative effect of the interior; it includes works by Guercino, Daniele Crespi and Alessandro Tiarini.

Museo Civico
Palazzo Farnese, Piazza Cittadella
Tel. (0523) 20643
Closed for reorganization
🏛

The museum was moved in 1979 to the ducal palace – an imposing late 16thC building – and has still not reopened in its new premises; to date, there are no immediate plans for its reopening.

The collections include important archaeological material as well as Roman statuary and mosaics. Among the pictures are a tondo of the *Madonna with St John the Baptist* (c. 1480) attributed to Botticelli and *Christ and the Centurion* by Mattia Preti. A cycle of paintings celebrating the *Deeds of Paolo Farnese III* (1680–1720) includes a number of works by Sebastiano Ricci.

Piazza dei Cavalli

Outside the Palazzo del Comune stand the **Farnese statues ★★** These equestrian monuments are the most celebrated works of the Baroque sculptor Francesco Mochi. The one on the right, of *Ranuccio I Farnese* (1612–20), was the first of the pair, and is more conservative in style. The one on the left, representing **Alessandro Farnese** (1625), broke dramatically with the tradition of the equestrian statue established by Giovanni Bologna; taut with energy, it is a fiery, dramatic image, with windswept, billowing draperies – perhaps the most successful of all such Baroque sculptures. Note too the fine reliefs on the base of each monument.

Pinacoteca del Collegio Alberoni
Collegio Alberoni, Via Emilia Parmense 77
Tel. (0523) 63198
Open Mar–June, Oct: Sun 3–6pm, other
*   days by request*
Closed July–Sept, Nov–Feb
▢ ✗ ▢ ▣ ✇
2.5km (1¼ miles) SE of city center, towards
Parma
Cardinal Giulio Alberoni founded this historic collection in 1732. Outstanding is a fine group of **Flemish tapestries**, including 15thC and 16thC examples. The most important picture is a much-imitated **Ecce Homo** (1473) by Antonello da Messina.

Otherwise, the main strength of the gallery lies in its 17thC and 18thC paintings; artists represented include Luca Giordano and Giambattista Gatti (17thC) and Francesco Solimena and Gianpaolo Panini (18thC). A small group of Netherlandish Renaissance pictures includes a **Madonna Enthroned** by Jan Provost.

POMPOSA
Ferrara, Emilia-Romagna   Map G3
Pomposa is a small agricultural town, named after its abbey, which stands in slightly melancholy isolation at the end of the Via Romea.

Abbazia di Pomposa
Tel. (0533) 96160
Open 9am–noon, 2–6pm
▢ ✗ ▢ ▣ ▥ ✇
The Benedictine abbey was built in the 6thC and 7thC and flourished throughout the Middle Ages as an important center of learning.
Basilica
The original building was strongly influenced by churches at nearby Ravenna. In the early 11thC it was enlarged by a colourful, richly textured porch, where sculptures of fantastic animals alternate with majolica discs, accompanied by beautifully patterned Romanesque friezes. The campanile was designed by Deusdedit in 1063.

The interior has many 14thC frescoes. The vault of the apse was decorated by Vitale da Bologna and assistants with a monumental image of **Christ in Majesty** (1351) and, beneath, the **Evangelists**, the **Doctors of the Church** and scenes from the **Life of St Eustace**. The walls of the nave are covered with lively, realistic, crowded illustrations from the Old and New Testaments; on the interior wall of the facade is a stiff **Last Judgment**.
Monastero
The most interesting parts of the monastery are the vast chapter hall and the refectory. The frescoes in the **chapter hall**, dominated by a crowded and confused **Crucifixion**, have led to much controversy both over date and attribution, but it seems likely that they date from the early 14thC. The frescoes in the **refectory ✷** are the most outstanding of all the paintings at Pomposa and have been attributed to Pietro da Rimini (14thC). Note especially the **Last Supper** and the **Miracle of St Guido** – both elegant, refined works, yet with an interest in gesture and expression that suggests a lively response to Giotto at Padua.

RAVENNA
Emilia-Romagna   Map G4
Ravenna's history reaches back many centuries. Tradition relates that it was inhabited by the Umbrians and the Etruscans; by the 2ndC BC, it had become a Roman municipality and the Roman city plan may still be glimpsed today. The Emperor Augustus built the powerful and strategically important port of Classis here. In 402 the Emperor Honorius made Ravenna the capital of the Western Empire; his sister, Galla Placidia, added fine monuments to the city; under the rule of the Ostrogoth kings Odoacer (476–93) and Theodoric (493–526) the city continued to expand and to flourish artistically and the basilica of Sant' Apollinare Nuovo was built. In 540 Ravenna fell to the Byzantine general Belisarius and became part of the Eastern Empire; the brilliance and splendour of the court of Justinian and his Empress Theodora are shown in the mosaics in San Vitale and Sant' Apollinare in Classe. For two centuries the traditions of Byzantine art survived, but in the 8thC the city fell to the Longobards and began to decline. In the 15thC it came under Venetian rule, only to be taken over by the papacy in the 16thC. Yet this long period of decline has meant that the unrivalled monuments of Byzantine architecture, together with their mosaics, have remained extraordinarily well preserved.

Battistero degli Ariani
Via degli Ariani
Open 8.30am – 12.30pm, 2 – 6.30pm
The Baptistry of the Arians lies in a quiet square opposite the Renaissance facade of the church of Santo Spirito; it is a modest octagonal building with four apses, and was probably built during the reign of Theodoric, c. 500.

The design of the mosaics in the dome clearly derives from the BATTISTERO NEONIANO; the subject is the same, with a central medallion showing the *Baptism of Christ* and, in a circle around, a procession of *Apostles*. And yet the composition lacks the wonderful richness and exuberance of the earlier work; the Apostles no longer sweep grandly forward, but stand rather rigidly; their faces are more schematic, and the colours less glowing.

Battistero Neoniano ☆
Via Battistero
Open 9am – noon, 2.30 – 6.30pm
The cathedral baptistry is generally referred to as the Neonian Baptistry in honour of Bishop Neon who, in the mid 5thC, commissioned the decoration; the building dates from 50yrs earlier.

In the lower part of the interior, heavy acanthus scrolls twist and curve, gold on blue mosaic, in the spandrels; above are elegant stucco reliefs, once coloured.

The dome itself is covered with **mosaics ★★** arranged in three decorative zones, culminating in the central medallion, the *Baptism of Christ*. This mosaic was heavily restored in the 19thC, yet it retains lovely naturalistic touches in the fragile flowers that blossom on the rocky banks of the Jordan, and in the sharply modelled river god, who rises from the water bearing a robe with which to dry the body of Christ.

In the band beneath, the *Apostles*, led by Sts Peter and Paul, proceed in triumph around Christ, each bearing a crown, symbol of celestial glory. The Apostles' movements are firm and vigorous, and their Roman heads sharply characterized; this, and the ornate, festive quality of the whole, clearly distinguish this work, still within the classical tradition, from the more rigid, symbolic procession in SANT' APOLLINARE NUOVO and from the greater simplicity of the BATTISTERO DEGLI ARIANI.

Beneath, in the outer band of decoration, is an enigmatic decorative scheme which has been variously interpreted; a throne and cross alternate with an altar and open book, flanked either by plants or empty chairs.

The mosaics are close in date to those in the MAUSOLEO DI GALLA PLACIDIA, and

yet they are quite different in style – exuberant, gay, and with brilliantly intense contrasts of colour.

Duomo
Piazza del Duomo
The present cathedral, an unexciting 18thC rebuilding by Gianfrancesco Buonamici of Rimini, represents an almost complete remodelling of the 5thC Basilica Ursiana. Its most interesting features are the **pulpit**, retained from the ancient basilica and decorated with square panels enclosing animals, and the **Cappella del Sacramento**, with frescoes by Guido Reni and assistants.

Mausoleo di Galla Placidia ☆☆
Via San Vitale
Opening times as for San Vitale
The mausoleum of Galla Placidia, a simple brick building in the form of a cross, preserves the oldest **mosaics ★★** in Ravenna. The chapel is small and low and it can be difficult to enjoy the mosaics among the vast crowds that now throng into it.

The mausoleum is traditionally described as the burial place of Galla Placidia – with whom the three sarcophagi within are associated – although it is more likely that she was buried in Rome where she died in 450. There is a startling contrast between the plain brick exterior and the rich mosaics within; the visitor is drawn into and enclosed by the magical, glowing darkness; light filters through thin alabaster panels to catch the uneven surface of glittering cubes of stone and coloured glass.

In the center of the small cupola the *Triumph of the Christian Faith* is radiantly expressed in the gold cross, whence a myriad of gold stars shimmer and swirl across the deep blue ground to the *Symbols of the Evangelists*, spreading the word of God. In the four large lunettes below are eight *Apostles* in pairs, on either side of narrow windows, pointing to the cross; at their feet, doves drink from the fountain of true faith. In the lunettes of the cross-arms, two pairs of *Stags* drink from the fountain of everlasting life.

The lunette at the E end, opposite the entrance, shows the Roman martyr, *Lawrence*, eagerly seeking his martyrdom on the fiery grid; opposite, above the entrance, *Christ as the Good Shepherd* – the crook replaced by a cross – watches over his sheep in an idyllically pastoral landscape.

The mosaics of the mausoleum remain within the traditions of classical art and precede the rigid stylizations of the

Byzantines; the colours are subtle and
varied; in many passages, the figures are
modelled with contrasts of light and dark
tesserae.

Museo Arcivescovile
Arcivescovado, Piazza Arcivescovado 1
Tel. (0544) 30323
Open Mon, Wed – Sat 9am – noon,
2.30 – 6pm, Sun 9am – 1pm
Closed Tues
🔯

The Arcivescovado or archbishops'
palace now yields only a hint of its
ancient splendour; yet it is well worth a
visit for the celebrated **throne of
Maximian** ★★ (546 – c. 556). Maximian
was bishop of Ravenna during Justinian's
reign, and his throne was a gift from the
Emperor; a portrait of Maximian appears,
beside Justinian, in the apse mosaics of
SAN VITALE.

The origin of the throne is
controversial, but it seems probable that
it was brought from some celebrated
workshop in Constantinople. It is made
of ivory panels, in which three distinct
styles may be discerned. On the base at
the front are *St John the Baptist* and the
Four Evangelists; these austere, grand
figures are framed by a wonderfully rich
and inventive **frieze** ★ where, among the
curving scrolls of a vine, little animals,
vividly observed, nibble the fruit. The
panels showing scenes from the *Life of
Christ* are by another hand and less
interesting. The side panels, however,
feature ten sharply carved and lively
incidents from the Old Testament,
including scenes from the *Life of Joseph*.
Scholars have suggested that these panels
were carved in Alexandria: the story of
Joseph was popular in Egypt and some of
the details look Egyptian.

The small **Oratorio di Sant' Andrea**
within the palace has very heavily
restored 5thC and 6thC mosaics. The
vault of the chapel with four *Angels* and
the *Symbols of the Evangelists* is of
reasonable quality; the vault of the
vestibule is charmingly decorated with
birds and lilies.

Museo Nazionale
Via San Vitale 17
Tel. (0544) 28317
Open Tues – Sun 8.30am – 1.30pm
Closed Mon
🔯 🏛 ☑ ♥ 🔲

This large and well-displayed collection
of Roman and early Christian art is
enhanced by the cool beauty of its setting
in the three cloisters (two Renaissance,
one Baroque) of an ex-Benedictine
monastery built around SAN VITALE.

In the first two cloisters, there are

classical, early Christian and Byzantine
sculptures. Note especially the superb
decorative detail of the **marble fragments**
from Porta Aurea; a funerary *stela* of
Publius Longidenus showing the
deceased, a naval carpenter, building a
boat; and a 1stC BC relief of the
Apotheosis of Augustus.

On the second floor a series of rooms
leads through the collections of ceramics,
bronzes, glass, coins and Creto-Venetian
icons, passing fascinating *sinopie* from
SANT' APOLLINARE IN CLASSE – showing a
different decorative scheme from that
executed.

Room X contains an outstanding
collection of ivories, including a late
5thC or early 6thC Coptic ivory of
Apollo and Daphne ★ – probably carved
at Alexandria, where classical themes
remained popular well into the Christian
era – and, of roughly the same period, the
Murano Diptych ★★ In the center of the
diptych, a beardless *Christ* – a type
derived from Apollo – is enthroned
between *Sts Peter and Paul*; on either
side are vivid scenes from the New
Testament. The panel beneath is a
charmingly lively illustration, filled with
little spiky figures, of *Jonah and the
Whale*; Jonah relaxes on the left beneath
a gourd tree, in the company of an oddly
canine whale; on the right, sailors toss
Jonah into a fishy sea, before the
snapping jaws of the whale.

Pinacoteca Comunale ✩
Loggetta Lombardesca, Via di Roma 13
Tel. (0544) 35625
Open Tues – Sun 9am – 1pm,
2.30 – 5.30pm
Closed Mon
📷 ➡ 🏛 ☑ ♥ 🔲

The gallery is housed in a graceful
Renaissance structure, its internal
courtyard given an oddly exotic touch
by the presence of peacocks and tortoises.
The collection consists mainly of
Renaissance paintings from Ravenna; the
most significant local artists were Niccolò
Rondinelli – whose pretty, slightly
wistful *Madonna and Saints* (15thC) is
characteristic of his dependence on
Giovanni Bellini – and Francesco
Zaganelli da Cotignola.

There are also some Venetian
paintings, including a *Crucifixion* by
Antonio Vivarini. The 17thC section
has a number of pictures by well-known
artists – but most of these are rather dull;
the exception is Sebastiano Mazzoni's
spectacular *Apollo and Daphne* ★
Mazzoni was a Florentine who worked in
Venice; his paintings are distinctive for
the extraordinary bravura freedom of
their brushwork and for their morbid,

decadent quality; here, the pursuit of Daphne by Apollo has almost become a rape scene.

Yet all these works pale before the beauty of Tullio Lombardo's effigy of *Guidarello Guidarelli* ★ (c.1531) which is the main reason for visiting this museum. The young warrior, brutally cut down in the flower of youth, lies, fully armoured, in the sleep of death. His face is soft, intensely beautiful, yet, in the mouth and eyes, poignantly touched by the rigidity of death. It is worth asking the attendant to turn out the electric light, for the delicacy of the shadows on the polished surfaces of marble is finer by natural light. Tullio, generally a rather coldly classical sculptor, here created a work that deeply moved Romantic writers and poets.

Sant' Apollinare in Classe ☆☆
5km (3 miles) SE of Ravenna
Open 8am – noon, 2 – 6.30pm
🏛

Sant' Apollinare in Classe, consecrated in 549, stands some way outside Ravenna, in the middle of a vast and desolate plain, reclaimed from the marshes and once the site of the famous port of Classis. Despite the dreariness of the countryside, there is something intensely moving about this majestic and deserted relic of past grandeur, with its imposing 10thC campanile. Behind the bleak exterior is an exceptionally light and beautiful Christian basilica, with an array of lovely marble columns, surmounted by capitals decorated with soft, luxuriant acanthus leaves. One's eye is immediately drawn to the magical beauty of the mosaics ★★ that fill the apse and the arch before it.

At the center of the arch is an image of *Christ the Judge*; on either side, *Symbols of the Evangelists*; advancing towards the center, 12 *Lambs* are shown leaving the towns of *Jerusalem* and *Bethlehem* – symbols of the churches of the Jews and the Gentiles.

This arch frames the mosaics of the apse where at the center stands the majestic figure of *St Apollinaire*, bishop of Ravenna; he is flanked on either side by six *Holy Lambs*, symbols of the faithful whom St Apollinaire, as the Good Shepherd, cared for and led to everlasting life. Above this is a symbolic representation of the *Transfiguration of Christ*, with Elijah and Moses on either side of a medallion with a great cross; below, the three lambs represent the three Apostles present at the Transfiguration; they gaze in ecstasy at the cross, symbol of Christ.

A description of the Christian symbolism of this mosaic gives little idea of its beauty; the symbols are set within an enchanting green landscape, blossoming with flowers, dotted with trees and rocks, alive with many kinds of little birds; each detail is fresh and direct, and there is a lovely balance between realism and abstraction.

On the side walls of the apse are two big panels showing *Constantine IV Conceding Privileges to the Church of Ravenna* (left wall) and the *Sacrifice of Abel, Abraham and Melchizedek* (right wall). These perhaps date from the 7thC, and are of markedly lower quality than the earlier mosaics.

Sant' Apollinare Nuovo ☆☆
Via di Roma
Open 8am – noon, 2 – 6.30pm
🏛

The basilica was built in the early 6thC by Theodoric and has a typical round campanile but its marble portico dates from the 16thC. The side walls of the nave are covered with mosaics ★ in three horizontal bands. The highest band shows scenes from the *Miracles of Christ* (left wall), beginning with the *Marriage at Cana* and ending with the *Healing of the Paralytic*, and scenes from the *Passion of Christ* (right wall), beginning with the *Last Supper* and ending with *Doubting Thomas*. Beneath, a row of majestic, white-robed *Prophets* stand against a gold background; and below them, the lowest band shows the *Procession of Virgins* (left wall) and *Procession of Martyrs* (right wall).

These mosaics date from different periods; the narrative scenes and the *Prophets*, from the time of Theodoric, still retain hints of the naturalistic Hellenistic and Roman tradition, while the *Processions* are slightly later (c.561) and Byzantine in style.
Miracles of Christ   Christ is the long-haired, beardless young man of early Christian art. The *Calling of Peter and Andrew* is delightfully free and spirited; Christ stands majestically on the edge of the sea of Galilee; the two disciples in the boat – burly, vigorous figures, each strongly characterized – pause in their work to look at him, startled and doubtful; Peter's net wriggles with fish and a charming little dolphin swims by, tossed in the waves of the sea. The next panel, the *Miracle of the Loaves and Fishes*, shows the beginnings of a stiffer, more ceremonial style; the composition is symmetrical, and the figures are shown from a strictly frontal viewpoint; the artist stresses the solemnity and symbolic meaning of the story, rather than creating a vivid and lively narrative.

Passion of Christ   These scenes are less simple and less direct; they depict more figures, and many are intensely dramatic and poignant; Christ is an older, bearded figure. The deep restraint and gravity with which the artist portrays the **Betrayal of Christ** is particularly moving; Christ submits to Judas' kiss with solemn fear; the disciples are sunk in grief and despair; with anguish, Peter prepares to draw his sword. The naturalism of these scenes – the figures solid, their gestures and expressions often lively and free, sometimes even awkward – could not contrast more strongly with the idealized grace and unworldly beauty of the mosaics in the lowest band.

Processions   The Virgins on the left, preceded by the Three Kings in exotic Eastern dress, glide towards the Madonna and Child; rhythm and flowing line predominate; the figures are almost identical in gesture and expression, and yet the composition is enlivened by lovely and subtle differences – in the greens of the palms, in the crowns the Virgins bear, and in the variety of sumptuous jewels and gems and intricate patterns that enrich their gold robes and elaborately dressed hair. On the right, the procession of the Martyrs is led by St Martin and moves towards the figure of Christ.

At the beginning of the nave walls are two compositions showing the **Port of Classis** (left wall) and **Theodoric's Palace** (right wall). The port is lively and vivid, with battlemented walls, and three ships in its harbour. Theodoric's palace is an ornate, festive building that gives some idea of the grandeur of his capital.

San Vitale
Via San Vitale
Open 8.30am – 6.30pm
🏛

Completed in 547, San Vitale is one of the grandest churches built under Justinian; it has a highly sophisticated plan, with a central octagon ringed by two ambulatories, which creates both a lilting rhythm of complex curves and a subtle contrast of light and dark areas. The sense of a magical, mysterious space is enhanced by the solemn, weightless figures poised in the shimmering gold **mosaics** ★★ of the chancel and by the extraordinarily beautiful **capitals** ★★ carved with crisp, filigree patterns that seem to dissolve the solid structure beneath. The mosaics show a clear progression from an interest in movement and expression to the majesty of Byzantine art.

The underside of the arch leading to the chancel is covered with 15 medallions: **Christ the Redeemer** in the center, between the 12 **Apostles** and **St Gervasius** and **St Protasius**. Beyond, the cross-ribs of the chancel vault, like a leafy pergola, blossom with fruits and flowers; at the center is a medallion with the **Mystic Lamb**, symbol of Christ the Redeemer, held aloft by four angels rising from blue globes; between the ribs, acanthus leaves spiral delicately around an enchanting array of little birds, animals and rosettes.

Beneath the vault, the most important mosaics are the two large lunettes over the arches; these show Old Testament **Sacrifices** that prefigure the Crucifixion and the Eucharist. On the left wall are **Angels Announcing the Birth of Isaac** and the **Sacrifice of Isaac**; on the right wall, the **Sacrifice of Abel** and the **Offering of Melchizedek**. The first two scenes are particularly fresh and naturalistic. Sarah, at the door of her house, watches with wifely concern as Abraham offers the roasted calf; the softly modelled angels charmingly enjoy an open-air meal, their gestures lively and relaxed, their poses varied. In the adjacent scene, depth is suggested by the rocks and violet clouds; Abraham's despair is movingly conveyed.

Above the lunettes are the **Four Evangelists**, shown looking up, awaiting divine inspiration, and accompanied by their emblems; the snarling lion of St Mark is one of the most splendidly realistic details in the mosaic. Above, on the arch of the triforium gallery, doves perch around a large urn, from which trails a vine – symbolizing the Eucharist.

On the arch leading to the apse are symbolic representations of the cities of **Jerusalem** and **Bethlehem**. The half dome of the apse is covered with a large mosaic showing a youthful **Christ in Glory** presenting the martyr's crown to **St Vitalis**, whose hands are protected by a ceremonial robe; on the right is **Bishop Ecclesius**, founder of the church, appropriately holding a model of it.

This mosaic differs sharply from those in the lunettes; the scene is no longer set in a sunny landscape, but against a celestial blaze of gold; the flowers are those of Paradise, and beneath Christ's feet flow the four Mystic Rivers; the figures are stiff and severe, shown in strictly frontal poses and the composition hints at those rhythmic processions that characterize SANT' APOLLINARE NUOVO. There is no longer an interest in lively realism, but in solemn symbols of spiritual truth. The mosaic clearly looks forward to the art of Byzantium and to the two large mosaics that face one another across the lower part of the apse.

These show the **Emperor Justinian and his Court** (left wall) and the **Empress Theodora and her Court** (right wall), both works brilliantly conveying the power and magnificence of Imperial Ravenna. Justinian is shown with the dignitaries of Church and State, carrying the requirement for Mass. The austere figures are shown in severely frontal poses; the strength of the composition depends on the bold arrangement of flat areas of colour. The Empress Theodora, her tiny face hung with a galaxy of jewels, her body adorned with rich draperies, is a symbol of power and courtly splendour.

And yet, despite the clear tendency towards abstraction, some of the heads are strikingly realistic portraits; the Emperor and Empress are finely characterized; to the right of Justinian, the ascetic, gaunt features of Bishop Maximian are strongly individual.

REGGIO NELL' EMILIA
Emilia-Romagna Map E3

Built on the Via Aemilia in the 2ndC AD, Reggio was an important Roman town; later, in the Middle Ages, it flourished as a free commune. In 1489 the city passed into the hands of the Este family. It is now a thriving industrial center, which has developed at the expense of many of its historic monuments; a few fine Renaissance and Baroque buildings have, however, survived.

Duomo
Piazza Vittorio Emanuele
The cathedral was founded in the 9thC and rebuilt in the 13thC. The facade has an extremely odd appearance; in the early 16thC, a plan to remodel it was only partially put into effect, resulting only in the strange, Mannerist recasing of the lower part – the statues over the portal, by Prospero Spani (1577), are clumsily derived from Michelangelo's Medici tombs in Florence. The whole is dominated by a truncated octagonal tower, near the top of which is a **Madonna and Child** in copper by Bartolommeo Spani, the most distinguished Renaissance artist working in Reggio.

Within, in the third chapel on the right, is the **tomb of Valerio Malaguzzi** (d. 1498) by Bartolommeo Spani; and in the chapel to the right of the choir, the **monument to Bishop Ugo Rangone** (1556) by Prospero Spani.

Madonna della Ghiara
Corso Garibaldi
The church, in the form of a Greek cross,

was begun in 1597 by Alessandro Balbi, and the dome added in 1619 by Francesco Pecchioni. The severe exterior yields to the most splendid and richly decorated interior in Reggio; the frescoes, dating from the early 17thC and enriched by elegant and intricate stucco decoration touched with gilt, follow a complex iconographical programme honouring the Virgin and culminate, in the vault of the apse, with the **Assumption of the Virgin** (1628) by the Bolognese painter, Alessandro Tiarini.

The dome, and the vault of the right transept, are frescoed by the Caravaggesque painter Lionello Spada. The vault of the arm of the cross that leads to the presbytery has stories from the Old Testament by Tiarini.

In the left transept is the outstanding work in the church, Guercino's **Crucifixion ★** (1625). This is a dramatically lit, powerful picture, with strong overtones of Caravaggesque realism, yet it also looks towards the austere classicism of Guido Reni.

San Giovanni Evangelista
Piazza San Giovanni
The finest work in this small 16thC church is Sisto Badalocchio's fresco in the cupola, of **Christ in Glory**, a startlingly original, early 17thC reworking of Correggio's celebrated dome in San Giovanni Evangelista, PARMA; Badalocchio came from Parma but also worked in Rome.

RIMINI
Forlì, Emilia-Romagna Map G5

Once an important Adriatic port, Rimini is now a vast and sprawling modern seaside resort, where the old distinction between Rimini Città and Rimini Marina has sunk beneath the latest urban development. Yet the city has a distinguished history, stretching back to the Etruscans, and the Arco d'Augusto and ruined amphitheater recall its importance during the Roman era. Rimini reached the height of its power and splendour in the 15thC, under the rule of Sigismondo Malatesta (1417–68).

Arco d'Augusto (*Arch of Augustus*)
Corso di Augusto
The arch was erected in 27BC and is the oldest of all surviving Roman arches. It was built to mark the junction of the ancient Via Flaminia and Via Aemilia. The strangely incongruous crenellation along the top was added in the Middle Ages.

Sant' Agostino
Via Cairoli

The church was begun in 1247, but altered many times, most radically in the Baroque era. The apse is decorated with an important cycle of Riminese **frescoes** dating from the first decades of the 14thC and strongly influenced by Giotto; three different artists worked on them.

San Giuliano
Via San Giuliano

This church was built in the mid 16thC, on the site of an ancient Benedictine abbey; it contains, over the high altar, a splendid painting by Veronese: the *Martyrdom of St Julian* (c.1580). Note also, over the third altar on the left, a **polyptych** by Bittino da Faenza, showing scenes from the *Life of St Julian* (1409).

Tempio Malatestiano ☆☆
Via Quattro Novembre
🏛

The notorious Sigismondo Malatesta has long been considered the archetype of the corrupt Renaissance despot, whose cruelty and depravity vied with his gifts as poet and scholar, and with his inspired patronage of artists and men of letters. Modern scholars have watered down this vivid picture, but the Tempio Malatestiano – the most romantic of his achievements, and a memorial both to his Renaissance pride and to his passion for Isotta degli Atti – remains.

Sigismondo's implacable enemy, Pius II, who took the novel step of canonizing Sigismondo to hell, described the Tempio as "a splendid church dedicated to St Francis, although he filled it so full of pagan works of art that it seems less a Christian sanctuary than a temple of heathen devils". The imagery of the Tempio has never been fully explained; yet it is clearly pagan, and reliefs by the Florentine sculptor, Agostino di Duccio, recreate with extraordinary freshness and originality the beauty of classical art.

The reconstruction of the Gothic church of San Francesco began in 1447, with a chapel dedicated to St Sigismondo; by 1450 the project had become very much more ambitious, involving the distinguished Renaissance architect Alberti and the medallist Matteo de' Pasti; the nave was to be encased in white marble, the eastern part of the church crowned with a cupola, and the side chapels decorated with sculpture. The project was never completed, however; the cupola was never built and the main facade was left unfinished – although an arcade of niches was created, on this and the side facades, to house the sarcophagi of eminent Riminese scholars and artists.

Inside, the nave is encased in white marble, as planned, and the side chapels are filled with a variety of extraordinarily beautiful sculptural decoration – wholly or in large part by the Florentine sculptor Agostino di Duccio and assistants. (Some scholars have seen here two distinct styles and attributed some of the chapels to Matteo de' Pasti.) The intertwined initials of *S* and *I* appear throughout the decoration; and everywhere are the arms and emblems of the Malatesta.

To the right of the entrance is the **tomb of Sigismondo Malatesta**, attributed to Bernardo Ciuffagni and Francesco di Simone Ferrucci. The first chapel on the right is the **Cappella di San Sigismondo**, with sculpture of very high quality; note the two splendid **Angels** by Agostino, and his fully modelled figures of *Virtues*, seated in niches on the pilasters. Next is the small **Cappella delle Reliquie**, formerly the sacristy of the Cappella di San Sigismondo. Above the door is a damaged but once brilliantly decorative fresco of *Sigismondo Malatesta Kneeling before his Patron Saint* ★ by Piero della Francesca (1451); it shows a view of the Rocca di Rimini.

The second main chapel is the **Cappella d' Isotta** with, on the left wall, the **tomb of Isotta degli Atti** ★ Isotta was Sigismondo's mistress; he married her in 1456, after the death of his second wife, and later built for her this magnificent marble tomb, inscribing it in pagan fashion: "Sacred to the deified Isotta".

A new and delicate low-relief style appears in the sculptural decoration of the tomb; the pilasters are decorated with reliefs of angelic, music-making children, exquisitely modelled, and animated by the lovely grace of transparent drapery. The *Crucifixion* (c.1310) on the right wall of the chapel has been attributed to Giotto.

Third is the **Cappella dei Pianeti**, with the most iconographically complex, personal and attractive of Agostino's **linear reliefs ★★** These seem to look forward to Botticelli's romantic mythologies in their wayward, attic grace.

In the left nave – beginning again from the door – the first chapel, the **Cappella degli Antenati**, was planned to balance the Cappella di San Sigismondo opposite. The **Arca degli Antenati** or Tomb of the Ancestors is by Agostino; his reliefs of *Prophets* and *Sibyls*, in niches on the pilasters, are flatter than his earlier *Virtues*.

The second chapel is the **Cappella dei Giochi Infantili** where the reliefs are more crudely carved than those in the chapel opposite, but are nevertheless brilliantly original and charming inventions. Finally, the **Cappella delle Arti Liberali** has reliefs carved in a very different style, quite without Agostino's flowing line; it has been suggested that they are by his brother Ottaviano.

SABBIONETA
Mantova, Lombardia Map E3

Sabbioneta was the dream of Duke Vespasiano Gonzaga (1532–91), the most distinguished member of a cadet branch of the Gonzaga family. Vespasiano was a brilliant patron of the arts, deeply learned in military architecture and in town planning; he created here a miniature, ideal Renaissance city, with lucid and harmonious proportions and a grid-like plan that looks back to the cities of antiquity. Sabbioneta lies in a particularly unattractive and dreary stretch of flat countryside SW of Mantua; the massive, star-shaped walls yield no hint of what lies within; in a sense this heightens the silent, even ghostly beauty of the elegant city. Sabbioneta is now firmly on the tourist map; yet even coachloads of visitors do not destroy its poignant, melancholy air of desertion and decay; the empty palaces and theater create a mood very different from that of Pienza or Urbino.

Chiesa dell' Incoronata
Via Prato Raineri
The octagonal church was built in 1588 and is decorated with scenographic 18thC frescoes. Its chief monument is the **tomb of Vespasiano Gonzaga** (1592), which has a bronze statue by Leone Leoni showing the duke in fine antique armour – clearly inspired by Michelangelo's effigies of the Medici princes in the Medici chapel in Florence.

Palazzo Ducale
Piazza Garibaldi
Tel. (0375) 3375, 52039
Guided tours taking in Palazzo Ducale, Palazzo del Giardino and Teatro Olimpico available Mon–Sat: summer 10am–noon, 3–6pm, winter 2–5pm; Sun 9.30am–noon, 3–7pm. Apply to local tourist office in Via Gonzaga
▨ ▮ ▥
The elegant 16thC building is distinguished by a fine series of magnificent wooden ceilings. The **Sala delle Aquile** on the first floor is notable for the four remaining **equestrian statues** from a series of 12 statues carved in wood for Duke Vespasiano by an unknown

artist. The series showed Vespasiano's antecedents, and culminated in a statue of the Duke himself. This statue has survived and shows the Duke wearing the insignia of the Golden Fleece, granted to him in 1585 by Philip II of Spain. The **Sala degli Antenati** contains a series of stucco portraits of the Gonzaga.

Palazzo del Giardino
Piazza Castello
See Palazzo Ducale for entry details
This summer palace was built in 1584 and many of its rooms have pleasantly decorative frescoes; the most attractive are the hunting scenes by Bernardino Campi in the **Sala degli Specchi**.

Adjacent to the palace and dating from the same period is the **Galleria degli Antichi** (now facing an excessively ugly school building). This long gallery – its length made yet more startling by illusionistic frescoes – was designed to display the Duke's art collection and is the earliest building to have been designed solely for such a purpose.

Teatro Olimpico
Via Gonzaga
See Palazzo Ducale for entry details
▥
Scamozzi's lovely theater (1588) was inspired by Palladio's theater at Vicenza and is decorated with contemporary Venetian frescoes.

SARONNO
Varese, Lombardia Map C2

Saronno is an unattractive industrial suburb N of Milan, with a celebrated pilgrimage church.

Madonna dei Miracoli
Piazza Santuario 1
The church was begun in 1498 by Amadeo and has a Baroque facade by Pellegrini. The vast dome was inspired by Bramante's dome at Santa Maria delle Grazie in MILAN; it was decorated with painting and sculpture by Gaudenzio Ferrari in the 1530s.

The theme of the dome is the **Assumption of the Virgin ★** Over the choir arch is a statue of the **Virgin**; around the drum are statues of saints in niches; from the center of the dome, a bust of **God the Father** looks down towards the ascending **Virgin**. The entire surface of the dome is covered with a frescoed choir of angels, singing and playing music, each one highly finished and detailed, and the different types of musical instrument carefully observed.

The dome forms an interesting prelude to the flickering surfaces and illusionism of Correggio's domes at PARMA.

The church also has many frescoes by Bernardo Luini, Leonardo's most significant follower; in the passage leading to the choir are the *Marriage of the Virgin* and *Christ among the Doctors*; in the choir, the *Adoration of the Magi* and the *Presentation in the Temple*; above, in the lunettes, *Sibyls, Evangelists* and *Fathers of the Church*.

STUPINIGI
Torino, Piemonte Map B3

Stupinigi is famous for the Villa Reale, a vast hunting lodge commissioned by Vittorio Amedeo II from Juvarra in 1729.

Villa Reale
Tel. (011) 3581220
Open Tues – Thurs, Sat, Sun
  10am – 12.30pm, 2 – 5pm
Closed Mon, Fri
🔲 🚹 ⛪ 🏛

The villa is a spectacular, scenographic design, based on a St Andrew's cross, with arms extended to enclose a hexagonal courtyard; for the interior, Juvarra directed a gifted team of artists from many countries – among them, the Venetian Valeriani brothers and Giambattista Crosato and the French painter, Carle van Loo, who had worked with Boucher at Rome. The theatrical decorations capture the vivacious atmosphere of the court of Turin in the 18thC – yet the brilliance of the hunt now seems sadly remote, for this festive building now stands, like a great white elephant, at the busy junction of a motorway system.

The villa has been turned into a museum of furniture and is visited only on a guided tour; the building is very large, and one tends to be whisked through at a brisk pace, with only a passing glance at the furniture displayed in rather bleak rooms – but it is important to be ready to wake up for the frescoes in the **Appartamento della Regina**.

The tour opens with the gloomy **Galleria dei Ritratti**, hung with many dull 18thC portraits by the painter Dupra. Further on, in the **Appartamento di Levante**, many of the rooms have pretty Rococo ceilings – notice especially the **Anticamera (Room 7)** with a ceiling by Gaetano Perego, and **Room 10**, with lovely Oriental-style decoration by Giovanni Pietro Pozzo. Among the furniture, the outstanding works are: in the **Camera da Letto (Room 9)**, pieces by the celebrated cabinet-maker Pietro

Piffetti (c. 1770); and in the **Sala del Bonzanigo (Room 12)**, a celebrated *secrétaire* by the cabinet-maker Giuseppe Maria Bonzanigo (1780s). In the **Sala da Pranzo (Room 17)** note two pastel portraits by the Swiss artist Liotard.

The lovely white marble bath in **Room 19** was installed by Pauline Bonaparte during her stay at Stupinigi. The **Sala degli Scudieri (Room 22)** has a charming ceiling fresco by Crosato and Colonna and, on the walls, hunting scenes by Cignaroli – pleasantly decorative pictures where oddly doll-like figures enjoy the elegance of the hunt.

The oval **Salone** at the center of the St Andrew's cross is one of Juvarra's most theatrical creations, decorated by the Venetian Valeriani brothers with mythological scenes of Diana (the goddess of hunting) and with hunting horns, trophies and garlands of flowers; the overall effect is splendidly festive but both handling and colour are heavy.

On the right of the Salone, the **Appartamento della Regina** has the finest of the frescoed ceilings. **Room 29** was frescoed by the Venetian scenographer, Giambattista Crosato, with the *Sacrifice of Iphigenia* ★ a work of dazzling pageantry and brilliant colour that bears comparison with Tiepolo. **Room 30** was frescoed by the French painter Carle van Loo with *Diana Bathing* ★ – although it has suffered from overpainting, this work still suggests the brilliant freedom and airy lightness of van Loo's style.

TORINO (*TURIN*)
Piemonte Map B3

Turin is quite unlike any other great Italian city. Its history stretches back to 29BC when the Romans founded here a military colony – yet very little remains from the Middle Ages, and the Renaissance more or less passed Piedmont by. A great surge of building activity took place in the 17thC and 18thC, and it was then that Turin gained its distinctive beauty and elegance – with wide, tree-lined streets, and elegant squares and parks, all symmetrically laid out. The Piazza San Carlo at the center is one of the loveliest squares in Italy; its echoing arcades haunted the imagination of the Surrealist painter de Chirico. To the N, the Piazza Castello is flanked by buildings by the greatest of Turin's architects, who gave the city its strong individual flavour: on its N side is the austere, gloomy, 17thC facade of the Palazzo Reale by Amedeo di Castellamonte; to the W, the dome of

San Lorenzo, by Guarino Guarini, whose brilliantly original Baroque style has left its mark on many Turinese monuments; to the E, the Palazzo Madama, a refined and elegant work by Filippo Juvarra. Juvarra was perhaps the most distinguished Italian architect of the 18thC; he made Turin a center of Rococo art that could rank with any court in Europe; the interiors of the Palazzo Reale and of the Villa Reale at nearby Stupinigi are both lovely examples of this style. Turin is comparatively little visited by the tourist, but it has good and slightly unusual art museums; there is an unexpectedly fine Egyptian museum and the Galleria Sabauda has a very attractive group of Netherlandish pictures, rarely found in an Italian gallery. The city is now a flourishing industrial center yet retains an air of gloomy, oppressive grandeur.

Cappella dei Banchieri e Mercanti
Via Garibaldi
This small chapel stands next to the church of Santi Martiri. It has one of the most attractive late Baroque decorative schemes in Turin; the theme is **Christmas**, and the Christmas star occurs throughout. The story is told in large canvases by late 17thC artists, richly framed with black Belgian marble embellished by heavy bronze-flowered scrolls; perhaps the loveliest scene is Andrea Pozzo's **Flight into Egypt** to the left of the high altar; the **Adoration of the Magi**, above the altar, is also by Pozzo.

Duomo
Via XX Settembre
The cathedral is a Renaissance building – rare in Turin – begun in 1490 by the Florentine architect Meo del Caprina. The polyptych in the second bay on the right includes 18 little panels of stories from the **Lives of Sts Crispin and Crispinian** and is attributed to either Defendente Ferrari or Martino Spanzotti. In the second bay on the left, the altarpiece of **St Honoratus** is a 17thC work by Claudio Dauphin. From the end of the nave, steep stairs lead up to the **Cappella della Santa Sindone** or Chapel of the Holy Shroud, guardian of the celebrated relic; the chapel is an extraordinary Baroque design by Guarino Guarini.

Galleria Civica d'Arte Moderna
Via Magenta 31
Tel. (011) 516416
Closed for reorganization
This is an important collection of 19thC and 20thC, mainly Italian, art. The 19thC section is dominated by the Piedmontese, with an especially good group of works by Antonio Fontanesi (whose bold, expressive brushwork looks on to the 20thC). There are fine pictures by the Macchiaioli and, among 20thC works, an outstanding group of oils and watercolours by Filippo de Pisis. The most recent and adventurous trends in Italian painting and sculpture are well represented.

Galleria Sabauda ☆
Palazzo dell' Accademia delle Scienze, Via Accademia delle Scienze 6
Tel. (011) 530501
Open Tues – Sat 9am – 2pm, Sun 9am – 1pm
Closed Mon
🎨 ⛪ 🏛 ☑ ▥
This is a major Italian gallery, with an attractively varied, high quality collection of Italian painting – Piedmontese and Venetian artists, the Caravaggisti and Lombard Mannerists are particularly well represented – and with an unusually rich group of Dutch and Flemish pictures. The gallery is housed on the second and third floors of a grand Baroque palace by Guarino Guarini.
Second floor
This floor is divided into three sections, which may be visited separately.
Italian painting   A sequence of rooms displays an important group of Florentine paintings, including an early 14thC **Coronation of the Virgin** by Bernardo Daddi, a Fra Angelico **Madonna** (a late work, c. 1450) and a late 15thC **Tobias and the Angel** by Antonio and Piero Pollaiuolo, showing Tobias as a charmingly dressed Florentine youth, tripping daintily before a sweeping Tuscan landscape.

Two fine pictures by the Brescian artist Savoldo include an **Adoration of the Shepherds**. This is an intensely personal and poetic interpretation of a Giorgionesque theme; the lovely effects of bright light shimmering on silvery satins suggest his response to Flemish art.
Dutch and Flemish painting   A series of modest rooms leading on from the previous section displays a collection of small and intimate works, grouped according to provenance, all recently restored, and many in their original frames. The first rooms show works collected by Prince Eugene of Savoy, whose tastes lay in exquisite little landscapes, crowded with gay, decorative detail, by Paul Bril, Jan Breughel and Jan Griffier, and in highly polished and minutely observed works by the Dutch genre painters Dou and Frans van Mieris.

Later rooms are less homogeneous; Jan

van Eyck's *St Francis Receiving the Stigmata* is an interesting work; the odd treatment of the feet and the curiously hunched-up pose of St Francis' companion have led to doubts over its attribution.

Piedmontese painting   Rooms I–IV to the right of the main entrance display paintings by Piedmontese masters. In **Room I** an exquisitely refined **triptych** by Jacques Iverney suggests the contacts between Piedmont and the school of Avignon in the 14thC; 15thC painters in **Room II** include Spanzotti and his pupil Defendente Ferrari; **Room III** has important works by Gaudenzio Ferrari, the greatest Piedmontese painter of the 16thC – his rich, dramatic compositions suggest a knowledge of late Raphael; in **Room IV**, Pietro Grammorseo's **Madonna with St Peter** has an eerie landscape, dripping with moss, that echoes both Leonardo and Dürer.

Third floor
In **Room XIII** are vast studio works by Veronese and Bassano, with one outstanding Veronese, the **Supper at the House of Simon** ★ **Room XIV** has works by 17thC Bolognese artists, ranging from Guercino's passionate and dramatic **Prodigal Son** ★ to Francesco Albani's lyrical tondi of the **Four Elements** (1626–28) which look forward to the frivolous charm of Boucher. The classicism of Bolognese artists deeply influenced Nicolas Poussin, whose **St Margaret** shows this great classical painter ill at ease with Baroque vision and ecstasy.

Works by the Italian Caravaggisti in **Room XV** include an elegant, poetic **Annunciation** ★ by Orazio Gentileschi, where only the beauty of the light on smooth fabrics suggests his link with Caravaggio. The Caravaggesque obsession with darkness and violence was, however, taken up by Francesco del Cairo, culminating in the hysteria of his morbid, erotic **Herodias**.

Room XVI returns to Venetian painting and, in pictures by Ricci and Tiepolo, to the pageantry of Veronese. Yet the outstanding work here is of an entirely different nature: Giambattista Crespi's startlingly direct and intimate **Queen of Bohemia Confessing to St John Nepomuc** ★ (1743).

The grand **Salone** (subdivided into three sections) is now being reorganized; it shows works which demonstrate the links between Dutch and Italian art and, at the far end, the most regal of the 17thC Flemish pictures. The latter include van Dyck's portrait of the **Three Children of Charles I** ★ their size suggested by the large dog, and their

lively charm for a moment suppressed by courtly splendour.

Seven smaller rooms display the Gualino Collection, formed by the Turin lawyer Ricardo Gualino and presented to the museum in 1928. It is shown as a private collection or *casa-museo* with the paintings hung amongst an array of Egyptian fragments, Chinese art, jewels, small bronzes and fine furniture. The outstanding works are a small **Mars and Venus** by Veronese; a Bronzino portrait; and a **Venus** by Botticelli. This section is worth a separate visit – it is hard to take in all its varied attractions after the relatively lucid organization of the other galleries.

Museo Civico di Arte Antica
Palazzo Madama, Piazza Castello
Tel. (011) 510350
Open Tues–Sat 9am–7pm, Sun 10am–1pm, 2–7pm
Closed Mon
🚫 📼 🏛 ☑ 🖽

The museum is beautifully housed in the Palazzo Madama, a mixture of medieval buildings and Roman remains transformed in the 18thC by Juvarra, who designed the superb staircase hall which sweeps across the entire width of the facade.

In the medieval rooms of the **ground floor** there is a varied collection of medieval and Renaissance art. Two small rooms of Romanesque and Gothic sculpture lead into a magically evocative chamber, crowded with Gothic furniture and carvings, and with shutters inset with medieval stained glass. Beyond the Roman tower, with its 16thC wooden **Pietà**, is a larger room with elaborate Gothic **choir stalls** ★ from Staffarda.

The great hall is the showpiece of the museum; works include a banner by Pontormo and Antonello da Messina's powerful yet minutely detailed **Portrait of an Unknown Man** ★ (1476). In the Gothic tower, to the left of the great hall, are some small paintings by Defendente and Gaudenzio Ferrari, including Defendente's poetic night rendering of the **Adoration**. Here also are reproductions of the most famous works in the possession of the museum, six pages from the **Turin Hours**, attributed to the great Flemish painter, Jan van Eyck; and a 14thC **Madonna** by Tino di Camaino.

The state apartments on the **first floor** have light, Rococo frescoed ceilings and paintings by Lombard Mannerists and by followers of Caravaggio. On the **second floor** there is a large and important collection of decorative arts, with glass, ivories, enamels, ceramics and porcelain.

Museo Egizio ☆
Palazzo dell' Accademia delle Scienze, Via
  Accademia delle Scienze 6
Tel. *(011)* 537581
Open Tues–Sun 9am–2pm
Closed Mon
🔾 🏃 👺 🏛 ☑

Arranged on the ground and first floors of
the same building that houses the
GALLERIA SABAUDA, this is one of the
finest Egyptian collections in Europe,
and so popular with school parties that it
is hard to find a quiet time – around lunch
is most hopeful. The museum provides an
audio-visual display and an extremely
informative (and free) guide.

The outstanding works in this very
large collection are on the ground floor: a
famous statue of *King Rameses II
Enthroned* ★ (c. 1200BC); statues of the
pharaohs *Amenhotep II* and *Haremhab*;
and, in a separate room, a small
reconstructed **temple from Nuba** ★
dedicated by Thutmosis II to Ellesija, and
presented to Turin by the Egyptian
government in 1969.

The galleries on the first floor show
objects grouped to illustrate different
aspects of Egyptian civilization – for
example, religion, arts and crafts,
writing, death – giving a full and
fascinating picture of daily life and
culture in ancient Egypt. Here, the works
of highest artistic quality are the *stelae*
and small statues in the first room.

Palazzo Reale ☆
Piazza Castello
Tel. *(011)* 546731
Open Tues–Sat 9am–2pm, Sun
  9am–1pm
Closed Mon
🔾 🏃 🏛 ☙

The Palazzo Reale is an extraordinarily
gloomy, barrack-like building
overlooking the melancholy remains of a
formal garden designed by Le Nôtre. Yet
within is a series of sumptuous rooms,
created when the court of Turin was one
of the most brilliant and original centers
of the Rococo style.

The architect Juvarra designed the
grand staircase, one of the loveliest of his
spatial effects, and many of the rooms;
the Turinese painter Claudio Beaumont
established here a highly elegant,
polished Rococo style, a blend of French
and Italian elements; superb pieces were
contributed by the celebrated cabinet-
makers Luigi Pinotto and Pietro Piffetti;
the royal factory, directed by Beaumont,
produced decorative tapestries. With the
French occupation of 1799 this artistic
activity ceased, to be resumed in the
19thC under the direction of the
Bolognese architect Pelagio Pelagi,

whose heavy, cold Neoclassical style and
gilded magnificence stifled the lightness
found in the earlier, Rococo rooms.

The most interesting rooms are the
Sala del Trono, an ambitiously splendid
room of the mid 17thC; the massive
gilded ceiling overwhelms the somewhat
vapidly classical painting in the center by
the Dutch artist Jan Miel. Further on, a
little room to the right known as the
Gabinetto Cinese was designed by
Juvarra; it has lovely Oriental
lacquerwork, and a light and airy ceiling
fresco by Beaumont. Later comes the **Sala
della Colazione**, opening into an elegant
Rococo alcove. The state rooms resume
with the **Galleria del Daniele** decorated
in 1690 by the painter Daniele Seyter.

Next comes a series of little Rococo
rooms known as the **Appartamento della
Regina Maria Terese** ★ The little study
and dressing room are exquisitely
decorated with frescoes by Beaumont and
furnishings by Piffetti; in the dressing
room, the **cupboard** ★ and **mirror** ★ are
among Piffetti's loveliest works,
elaborately inlaid with ivory and mother-
of-pearl and with splendid ormolu
mounts. The chapel has a small
Madonna by Carlo Maratta. The series of
formal rooms beyond is in the laboured
Neoclassical style of Pelagio Pelagi.

Santa Teresa
Via Santa Teresa
The church dates from the 17thC and is
richly decorated with polychrome
marble. The fourth chapel on the right
has an 18thC altarpiece by Sebastiano
Conca. The fourth chapel on the left was
designed by Juvarra, and makes
spectacular use of a concealed light
source; the frescoes and canvases are by
Corrado Giaquinto (18thC).

<hr>

TREMEZZO
Como, Lombardia Map D1

Tremezzo is a pretty lakeside town, worth
visiting for its fine 18thC villa.

Villa Carlotta
N of Tremezzo, towards Cadenabbia
Tel. *(0344)* 40405
Open Mar–Nov 8.30am–6.30pm
Closed Dec–Feb
🔾 👺 ☙ 🎴

The villa is beautifully situated on the
shores of the lake and has spectacular
formal gardens. On the ground floor is a
collection of sculpture and painting,
mainly Neoclassical and Romantic; there
are works by Canova and Thorwaldsen,
and Hayez's **Last Kiss of Romeo and
Juliet**.

TRESCORE BALNEARIO
Bergamo, Lombardia   Map D2

Trescore is a pleasant mountain resort, famous for its thermal springs.

Villa Suardi
Tel. (035) 940010
Villa closed to public; chapel may be visited
by request
🔲 *chapel*
The chapel in the grounds of this villa, the **Cappella di Santa Barbara**, contains frescoes by Lorenzo Lotto. A number of scenes cover the windowless N wall; in the center is the vast figure of **Christ**. Incidents from the *Life of St Barbara* are shown below; these are astonishingly free and lively works, full of vivid genre detail. It seems likely that Lotto was influenced by the popular realism of Gaudenzio Ferrari's chapels for the Sacro Monte at VARALLO.

VARALLO
Vercelli, Piemonte   Map B2

A small, quiet town, Varallo is encircled by pleasantly wooded hills and dominated by the sanctuary of the Sacro Monte.

Pinacoteca
Palazzo dei Musei, Via Don Giuseppe Maio 25
Tel. (0163) 51424
Open June–Oct Sat–Thurs 10am–noon,
3–6pm
Closed Nov–May; Fri
📷 🔲 ☑
This is a small but grand museum, justly proud of its works by Varallo's most celebrated painters – Gaudenzio Ferrari and Tanzio da Varallo – and of its sculptures by Tanzio's brother, Giovanni d'Enrico. Tanzio was the most strikingly original painter of the early Lombard Seicento; his two *Davids*, wielding vast and shining swords, and with sickeningly repulsive heads of Goliath, are a highly personal variant of Caravaggism, while his *St Roch Interceding on Behalf of the People of Camasco* remains a moving reminder of the plague of 1629–30.

Sacro Monte
20 mins' walk from town center
🔲 ⚓ 🔲 🅿
The Sacro Monte at Varallo is one of the most astonishing ensembles of popular religious art in Italy. It was planned by a Franciscan friar, Bernardino Caimi, who had been guardian of the Holy Sepulchre in Jerusalem in 1477; his intention was to turn the entire mountainside above

Varallo into a reconstruction of the holy places of Palestine.

Within the 44 chapels of the sanctuary, *tableaux vivants* reconstruct scenes from the *Life of Christ* with truly astounding realism; life-size sculptures, naturalistically painted, with real hair and glass eyes, enact their passionate, often horrific, dramas before frescoed walls. Distinguished artists – notably Gaudenzio Ferrari – worked on the project in Caimi's lifetime. Later, in the 17thC, the project was revived by St Charles Borromeo, Archbishop of Milan; this was a particularly brilliant period, when the painters Morazzone and Tanzio da Varallo and the sculptors Giovanni d'Enrico and Giovanni Tabacchetti worked here.

The most spectacular of the early chapels is Gaudenzio Ferrari's great *Crucifixion* chapel (no. 38). In 1602 Morazzone was commissioned to decorate the *Road to Calvary* chapel (36) with frescoes that would imitate the dramatic realism of Gaudenzio Ferrari – this he did with great panache, especially in the sweeping grandeur of the horsemen; the violently expressive sculptures are by Giovanni Tabacchetti. The *Ecce Homo* chapel (33) is also frescoed by Morazzone; it is the most unified and ambitiously illusionistic of all the chapels. Painted figures blend with and continue the action of the sculptures.

Three of the chapels have particularly fine frescoes by Tanzio da Varallo with sculptures by his brother, Giovanni d'Enrico; these represent *Christ before Pilate* (27), *Pilate Washing his Hands* (34) and *Christ before Herod* (28).

Besides the chapels, there is the **church of the Assunta** (1641–1728). Its most startling feature is the decoration of the dome, where architecture, painting and sculpture unite in a vast scene showing the *Glorification of the Virgin*; the hundreds of frescoed figures are by the Montaldi brothers; the 142 modelled figures by Dionigi Bussola.

Santa Maria delle Grazie
Piazza G. Ferrari, on the way to the Sacro Monte
This has celebrated frescoes of the *Life of Christ* ★ (1513) by Gaudenzio Ferrari, his first significant work, full of echoes of the Quattrocento and of Perugino.

VARESE
Lombardia   Map C2

Varese is a pleasant modern resort, rich in villas and gardens that spread down the slopes from the Sacro Monte.

Musei Civici
Villa Mirabello, Piazza della Motta 4
Tel. (0332) 281590
Open Tues – Sat 9am – 12.30pm,
2.30 – 5.30pm, Sun 2 – 5pm
Closed Mon
📷 🎞 🌿
The museum is housed in an attractive
18thC – 19thC villa, surrounded by
gardens. There are fragments of frescoes
taken from the church of Santa Maria
Foris Portas at **CASTELSEPRIO** and a
scattering of Lombard Seicento works,
including a dramatic **Deposition** by
Morazzone.

Museo Lodovico Pogliaghi
Villa Pogliaghi, near Santa Maria del Monte
Tel. (0332) 226040
Open Apr – Sept Tues – Sun 10am – noon,
2.30 – 5.30pm
Closed Oct – Mar, Mon
📷 ✗ ☑ 🌿
The museum – an exotic blend of
architectural styles – lies on the way to
the village of Santa Maria del Monte,
which clusters around the sanctuary of
Santa Maria on the summit of the SACRO
MONTE. It displays a wonderfully eclectic
collection that includes a terra-cotta
bozzetto of **St Bibiana** by Bernini and
Pogliaghi's model for the central doors of
the Duomo at MILAN.

Sacro Monte
8km (5 miles) N of Varese
📷 🚠 🎞 💲
Fourteen chapels, begun in 1604, line a
steep grassy path that leads up the
mountainside to the sanctuary of Santa
Maria and the tiny village that has grown
up around it. Within each chapel – and in
sharp contrast to the elegant, restrained
classicism of the architecture – are
startlingly realistic *tableaux vivants*
illustrating the **Mysteries of the Rosary**.
Note especially **Chapel 7**, with paintings
by Morazzone and sculptures by Martino
Reccio.

Museo Baroffio
Adjoining sanctuary of Santa Maria
Tel. (0332) 225593
For entry, apply to custodian of Sacro Monte
📷
The museum has works of art and
architectural fragments associated with
the Sacro Monte, and some Dutch and
Flemish pictures.

San Vittore
Piazza San Vittore
This is an early Baroque church, designed
by Pellegrini. The facade is Neoclassical.
Inside are good 17thC paintings, of
which the most interesting is Morazzone's

St Mary Magdalen (1615 – 16) in the
Cappella del Rosario, with an unusual
predella panel, **Noli Me Tangere**.

VERCELLI
Piemonte Map C2
Vercelli lies in the valley of the Po,
surrounded by spreading fields of rice. It
has fine medieval monuments and is an
important center of Piedmontese art.

Museo Borgogna
Via Borgogna 8
Tel. (0161) 62576
Open Tues, Thurs 3 – 5pm; Sun
10am – noon; other days by request
📷 🎞 ☑
The collection, displayed in light rooms
overlooking a pretty courtyard, was
founded by the lawyer, Antonio
Borgogna, who was first attracted by the
Venetians and Flemings, but later built
up one of the finest collections of
Piedmontese painting outside Turin.
    Interesting works on the **ground floor**
include, in **Room V**, an intriguing
Aeneas at the Court of Dido by a
follower of Bramantino, the Lombard
Renaissance painter; in **Room VI**, a
Sacra Conversazione by Palma Vecchio;
and in **Room XI**, an outstanding group of
works by Defendente Ferrari, the most
distinguished Piedmontese Renaissance
artist. There are some 17thC pictures in
Room XII and, further on, a group of
idyllic 18thC landscapes by Locatelli,
Vernet and van Bloemen.
    On the **first floor**, in **Room IV**, is the
most beautiful picture in the collection:
Hans Baldung Grien's **Madonna with
Angels** ★ Beyond, in **Rooms V** and **VI**, is
a pleasant group of Dutch and Flemish
works, with attractive Poelenburghs, and
two lovely flower pieces by Jan Davidsz de
Heem and Ambrosius Bosschaert.

Sant' Andrea
Via Ferrari
This is an important Romanesque church
with some exceptionally early elements
of Cistercian Gothic (1219 – 27). In the
lunettes of the three deeply moulded
portals are famous Romanesque
sculptures; the central one, the
Martyrdom of St Andrew, is
convincingly attributed to Antelami.

San Cristoforo
Via San Cristoforo
An early 16thC church, San Cristoforo is
famous for a series of **frescoes** (1530) by
Gaudenzio Ferrari in the choir and
transept; their grandeur and dramatic
power look forward to the Baroque.

NORTH EAST ITALY

Venice, an island glittering almost magically in the lagoon, can seem far removed from the real world. But it was and is the functioning capital of an enormous area: the vast flat fertile plain of the Veneto, the foothills of the eastern Alps and of the Dolomites, and the sometimes bleaker plains of the Friuli. Originally the Venetian sphere of influence extended down past Trieste all along the coast of Yugoslavia and Albania into Greece. To the w, the Lion of St Mark held sway past Verona, past the present limits of the Veneto into Lombardy, even ruling the key cities of Brescia and Bergamo.

TRENTINO-ALTO ADIGE

Venetian influence never penetrated far N of Verona. The valley of the Adige, flowing from the Brenner Pass that marks the present border with Austria, and supporting the cities of Bressanone (Brixen), Bolzano (Bosen) and Trento, is culturally a distinct region. The upper parts, N of Trento, are part of the South Tyrol and are Germanic, in a way that Pieve di Cadore (Titian's birthplace) and other cities of the Dolomites, although equally far N, are not. Trento itself is best known for its lavishly frescoed Castello del Buon Consiglio; the Alto Adige for its characteristic painted wooden sculpture

VENETO

The Veneto plain is absolutely featureless and completely flat, although crossed and recrossed by hundreds of rivers, streams and canals bearing down from the mountains. The foothills, however, such as the Colli Euganei to the S and E of Padua, the Colli Asolani between Bassano and Castelfranco and the Montello behind Conegliano, offer some of the most serene and picturesque landscape to be found in Europe – farms quietly nestling beneath gentle slopes, compact vineyards bathed by gentle breezes. There is also much in the Veneto for the art lover, however difficult it may be to tear yourself away from the magnet of Venice.

The area immediately N of Venice – Treviso, Castelfranco, Bassano, Feltre, Belluno, Conegliano – was artistically in constant osmosis with the capital during the Renaissance. Artists of talent soon made their way to the metropolis and, once established there, exported their art back into the countryside. To this only the town of Bassano is an exception; here, the da Ponte family, nicknamed Bassano, continued in residence, although Jacopo Bassano established a Venetian practice and international reputation in the second half of the 16thC.

To the w, Padua had local traditions and a university of international renown too strong to succumb to the ruling city's influence, at least during the 15thC and 16thC. Verona also maintained an artistic independence, bolstered by the rich Roman inheritance still in evidence today; but the art of Paolo Caliari, called Veronese, is entirely Venetian in colour, and there is little of his work to be seen in his native city. Vicenza, too, stands apart, as the city transformed by the genius of Palladio.

FRIULI-VENEZIA GIULIA

By comparison with the Veneto, art in the Friuli, like the landscape, is rather bleaker. The area is richest in Roman remains: Aquileia, for example, has the largest Roman mosaic in Europe. But local Renaissance art eschews the Venetian delight in colour. There are nevertheless some charming little towns in the region, such as Spilimbergo and Cividale del Friuli (with outstanding 8thC Lombard remains). The Friuli was devastated by an earthquake in 1976, and in some places has still not quite returned to normal.

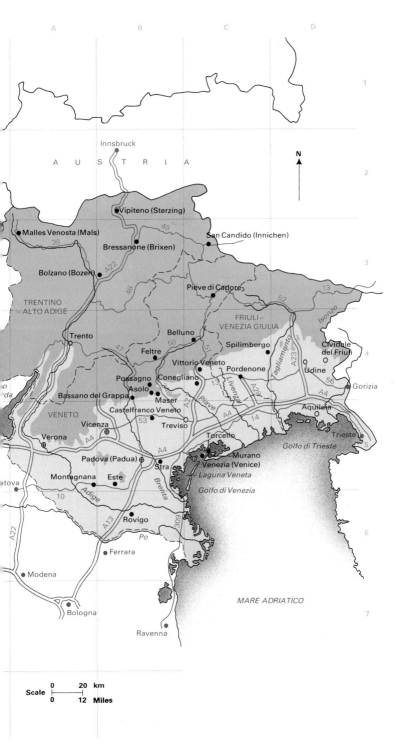

AQUILEIA
Udine, Friuli-Venezia Giulia Map D5

Founded as a military outpost in the 2ndC BC, Aquileia became the Roman capital of the Veneto and, later, its early Christian metropolis. During the early Middle Ages the patriarchate was disputed and divided, and in 1420 Venice expropriated the remnants of its temporal power and ecclesiastical importance. The present town is rather smaller than the old Roman port, but its antique and early Christian monuments are remarkably well preserved.

Basilica
Piazza Capitolo
Open Apr – Sept 9am – noon, 3 – 7pm,
Oct – Mar 9am – noon, 3 – 6pm. Cripta
degli Scavi open Tues – Sat 9am – 2pm,
Sun 9am – 1pm
Cripta degli Scavi closed Mon
🎫 *Cripta degli Scavi (ticket also gives entry*
to Museo Archeologico) 📑 🏛 ☙
The basilica is a Romanesque rebuilding by Patriarch Poppo (1019 – 42), but its magnificent **mosaic floor ★** uncovered in 1909 – 12 and undulating like a venerable carpet up and across the entire nave, is early 4thC. In the **Cripta degli Scavi** (on the immediate left of the entrance) are more mosaics, also featuring animals – notably some vigorous goats.

In the apse of the right transept are fine 9thC Lombard **relief panels**. In the crypt (ask the sacristan to let you in) a 12thC cycle of **frescoes** extends over walls, lunettes and ceiling, heavily Byzantine in its stylization. In the choir are two beautifully carved 15thC **altar tabernacles** by Bernardino da Bissone.

Museo Archeologico
Via Roma
Tel. (0431) 91016
Open Tues – Sat 9am – 2pm, Sun
9am – 1pm
Closed Mon
🎫 *Ticket also gives entry to Cripta degli*
Scavi of basilica 📑
The finest works of art in the museum are the early Imperial statues in **Room II** (ground floor); there are also interesting examples of minor arts, such as a set of gold ornamental flies for a shawl in **Room V** (first floor).

Museo Paleocristiano
Piazza Pirano
Tel. (0431) 92131
Open Tues – Sat 9am – 2pm, Sun
9am – 1pm
Closed Mon
🔲

The museum can be reached on foot from behind the basilica, along the Via degli Scavi, past the remains of the Roman port
The museum encloses an extensive 5thC **mosaic floor** (although neither so extensive nor so fine as that of the basilica); also, mostly crude but occasionally surprisingly refined stone votive reliefs.

ASOLO
Treviso, Veneto Map B4

Most famous as the retreat of the cultured High Renaissance court of Caterina Cornaro (1454 – 1510), ex-Queen of Cyprus, and of the 19thC English poet, Robert Browning, Asolo is a particularly beautiful and unspoiled hill town.

Duomo
Piazza del Duomo
The church is a mainly 18thC rebuilding. Over the second altar on the left is an important early **Assumption** (1506) by Lorenzo Lotto, with a remarkably deep, solid landscape.

Museo Civico
Loggia del Capitano, Via Regina Cornaro
Open Tues – Sat 9.30am – noon, 4 – 7pm,
Sun 9.30am – noon
Closed Mon
🎫 📑
Behind the attractively frescoed facade of the 16thC Loggia del Capitano, the museum contains archaeological material, paintings and sculpture, but nothing outstanding.

BASSANO DEL GRAPPA
Vicenza, Veneto Map B4

More rugged than many of its hill-town neighbours, Bassano is famous for its grape brandy, known as *grappa*, and for the da Ponte family of painters, commonly known as Bassano.

Museo Civico ☆
Piazza Garibaldi
Tel. (0424) 22235
Open Tues – Sat 10am – 12.30pm,
2.30 – 6.30pm, Sun 10am – 12.30pm
Closed Mon
🎫 📑 ⚒
Almost everything worth seeing in Bassano is now in the museum, which also includes an outstanding library and a large collection of prints and drawings. The ground floor is given over to archaeology and features an unusual number of Greek vases. The picture gallery opens out from the octagonal

room at the top of the stairs.

Bassano family In the octagon and a large room to the right are the multitudinous productions of the Bassano family, Francesco (d.1539), his son Jacopo (d.1592) and Jacopo's four sons, who continued his mature style.

On the right wall of the main room, a collaborative *Deposition* by Francesco and Jacopo shows Jacopo's starting point. Opposite, Jacopo's early, still almost clumsy – yet ravishingly elegaic – *Flight into Egypt* ★ clearly reveals the influence of Titian.

Behind this display, a reclining *St Jerome* is typical of Jacopo's more sophisticated, mature style. To the left of this, his *Adoration of the Shepherds* ★ (1568) is another mature work, scintillating with silvery colours and painted with a wonderfully affectionate touch. Nearby is his vast and newly detached **fresco** ★ that once fronted a house on the piazza; it is the finest preserved house front in the Veneto. Opposite are the three earliest works by Jacopo to have survived: scenes exemplifying *Justice* from the Palazzo Pubblico (1538).

Other works A corridor to the right of the main Bassano room leads to the **Sala Parolini**, with important 14thC and 15thC works, notably a bold 14thC **crucifix** by Guariento and a lovely 15thC *Madonna* by Giambono (on the right wall).

Returning to the octagon, in the room straight ahead of the stairs, the 18thC collection includes two storm scenes by Marco Ricci, also works by Tiepolo, Longhi, Zuccarelli and Zais.

BELLUNO
Veneto Map C4

Belluno is an ancient settlement set on a cliff between the confluence of two rivers. The main piazza is dominated by the enormous, early 16thC Palazzo dei Rettori.

Museo Civico
Piazza del Duomo
Tel. (0437) 24836
Open Tues–Sun 10am–noon, 1.30–6pm
Closed Mon
🗺

Above the archaeological collection (ground floor) and a section on the Risorgimento (first floor), the second-floor art gallery is of only moderate interest. It includes late 17thC and early 18thC paintings by Luca Giordano and Sebastiano and Marco Ricci; also, a collection of Renaissance bronze reliefs.

San Pietro
Vicolo San Pietro
If closed, inquire at Seminario Gregoriano next door

Above the entrance is one of Andrea Schiavone's most important works, a lovely mid 16thC **Annunciation**, originally organ shutters. The speed of the arriving angel is conveyed by energetic streaks of brushwork in a kind of effervescent rush of pink. On the high altar is an early 18thC **Madonna and Saints** by Sebastiano Ricci, with a grand setting borrowed from Veronese.

BOLZANO (*BOZEN*)
Trentino-Alto Adige Map B3

Bolzano is a city overlapping two worlds, Italy and Austria. Long fought over by the prince-bishops of Trent and the counts of Tyrol, it became Hapsburg in the 14thC, and remained Austrian (with brief Napoleonic interruption) until World War I.

Castel Roncolo (*Schloss Runkelstein*)
Via Sant'Antonio
Tel. (0471) 2608
Open Mar–Nov, Tues–Sun 10am–noon, 3–7pm (or earlier in bad light)
Closed Dec–Feb; Mon
🗺 🏛 ♿

To reach the castle from Museo Civico: on foot, 20mins' walk N along river bank through park; or by car, cross river at Ponte Talvera, turn right down Via Cadorna, recross river and turn left

The castle dates from the 13thC, but was partly rebuilt in the 19thC. It is one of the most splendid in the region. Inside are secular **frescoes** of the early 15thC, fairly crude in style, but interesting for their portrayal of courtly life. Note especially the **Sala del Torneo** or Room of the Tournament.

Chiesa dei Domenicani
Piazza dei Domenicani

In the **Cappella di San Giovanni**, to the right of the choir, is a 14thC fresco cycle of pure Italian style, showing the influence of Tommaso da Modena and the Paduan school. In the **cloister** are fragments of 15thC frescoes of the style and kind that survive much better at BRESSANONE (Duomo).

Chiesa dei Francescani
Via dei Francescani

In the **cloister** are fresco fragments similar to those of the CHIESA DEI DOMENICANI; in the chapel to the left of the choir, a glowing, charming wooden **altarpiece** by Hans Klocker (1500).

Museo Civico
Via Cassa di Risparmio 14
Tel. (0471) 39212
Open Tues – Fri 9.30am – noon,
3.30 – 6.30pm, Sat, Sun 10am – noon,
4 – 6.30pm
Closed Mon
▨ ▯

The pride of the museum is a rich and entirely Germanic collection of **painted wooden sculpture**. It begins on the first floor, above the usual archaeological collection. Of special interest are **Room VI** with 15thC Swabian works, and **Rooms VIII** and **XI** with painted relief panels from local churches (late 15thC and 16thC); **Room XI** has in particular a fine panel of *St Peter* (c.1480) by the Master of Uttenheim.

On the second floor, Baroque wooden sculpture continues the tradition with only slight change of rhythm. The picture collection (leading name, Paul Troger) shows how close the Austrian and northern Italian idioms became in the 18thC.

Parrocchiale, Gries
Via Knoller, Gries
Open Mon – Fri 10am – noon
Closed Sat, Sun

The **altarpiece ★** (1471 – 75) by Michael Pacher is, with the Multscher altarpiece at VIPITENO, the most important of its kind in Italy; representing the *Coronation of the Virgin*, it is earlier than Pacher's Austrian masterpiece, *St Wolfgang*, and a little stiffer and less energetic; it has a sweet Madonna and a splendid St Michael.

BRESSANONE (*BRIXEN*)
Bolzano, Trentino-Alto Adige
Map B3

Once an independent but disputed bishopric controlling the Val di Pusteria and the way up to the Brenner Pass, Bressanone only became Italian after World War I and is still culturally and visually part of the Tyrol. It is a small, pretty town with two charming porticoed streets.

Abbazia di Novacella (*Neustift*)
Open Mon – Sat 8am – noon, 2 – 6pm
Closed Sun
✗ ▣
Take the road out of Bressanone towards
Vipiteno and the Brenner Pass, then first
turning on right

A vast and sumptuous Baroque monument, dating from the 12thC to the 18thC. The **cloister** preserves important 15thC frescoes by Giovanni da Brunico

and the school of Michael Pacher.

Duomo
Piazza del Duomo
▥

The 18thC Baroque rebuilding is a magnificent ensemble, with two uplifting frescoes in sugar-cake colours by Paul Troger in the vault, and altarpieces around the walls not otherwise distinguished but fitting marvellously with the setting.

The **cloister** has frescoes on three sides, painted piecemeal from the 14thC to the 16thC, including works by Leonardo da Bressanone (mid 15thC) and some particularly fine, softly modelled Evangelist symbols by Giovanni da Brunico in the last bay before the S corner (early 15thC). The frescoes are liberally accompanied by textual explanations and are well preserved – a fine example of the kind of Biblia Pauperum or poor man's bible that once adorned hundreds of churches.

Museo Diocesano
Palazzo dei Principi Vescovi
Open mid-Mar to Oct, Tues – Sat
10am – 5pm
Closed Nov to mid-Mar; Sun, Mon
▨ ☑

This is a general museum rather than an art gallery, but it contains some Tyrolean paintings and wood sculpture. Ranged around the courtyard is a splendid series of **terra-cotta figures** (1600) by Giovanni Reichle, representing the ancestors of Cardinal Andrew of Austria.

CASTELFRANCO VENETO
Treviso, Veneto Map B5

This small, sleepy walled town was the birthplace of Giorgione and preserves a famous picture by him in the cathedral.

Casa di Giorgione
Piazza del Duomo
Generally open Tues – Sun 9am – noon,
3 – 5.30pm
Closed Mon
▨
If closed, inquire at Teatro Accademico, Via
Garibaldi

This so-called house of Giorgione has a frieze (c.1500) attributed to the town's most famous son: a series of still-lifes symbolizing the liberal and mechanical arts.

Duomo
Piazza del Duomo
Giorgione's *"Castelfranco" Madonna ★* (c.1504) is behind bars in the chapel to

the right of the choir. The odd arrangement of the Madonna, so high between Sts Liberale and Francis, creates a powerful effect of spatial recession. Much is overpainted, and the face of the soldier-saint in particular jars; but the Madonna has a lovely, cool purity and the landscape to her right is highly evocative.

CIVIDALE DEL FRIULI
Udine, Friuli-Venezia Giulia Map D4

The importance of Cividale in the early Middle Ages almost surpassed that of AQUILEIA, and the main interest of the city remains its extremely rich collection of Lombard monuments.

Duomo
Piazza del Duomo
This grand, early 16thC church is by Pietro and Tullio Lombardo. The **Museo Cristiano** is through the first door on the right of the nave. (If locked, seek the sacristan.) It contains the so-called **Baptistry of Callixtus** and **Altar of Ratchis**, both outstanding works of Lombard stone relief sculpture of the 8thC.

Museo Archeologico
Piazza del Duomo
Tel. (0432) 731119
Open Tues – Sat 9am – 1.45pm, Sun
*   9am – 12.45pm*
Closed Mon
🖂 🗺
The collection is predominantly archaeological (ground floor), but the first floor has two works by Pellegrino da San Daniele (c.1500 and c.1520), which clearly reveal Pordenone's influence in the region: the lame, almost wooden formula of the first contrasting with the over-insistent monumentality of the second. Pordenone himself is represented by a *Noli Me Tangere* (1524), taken from the DUOMO.

Tempietto Longobardo
Inquire at caretaker's house, Via Monastero
*   Maggiore 17*
Open Tues – Sat 9am – noon, 2 – 5pm, Sun
*   9am – 1pm*
Closed Mon
🖂 *but gratuity appreciated* 🗝 🏛 ☑
Go down steps behind Duomo, turn left,
*   continue until you reach the caretaker's*
*   house*
A spectacular frieze of 8thC **stucco figures** ★ lines the original entrance wall of this little building. The figures are almost three-quarters life size, and amazingly well preserved.

CONEGLIANO
Treviso, Veneto Map C4

A typical but undistinguished town of the Veneto, Conegliano was the birthplace of Cima da Conegliano (c.1459–1518).

Duomo
Via XX Settembre
The only work by Cima da Conegliano in his native town is on the high altar, a *Madonna and Saints* (1493) that shows his less austere version of Giovanni Bellini's style. Upstairs, in the **Sala dei Battuti**, are frescoes by minor 16thC artists.

Museo Civico del Castello
Piazzale del Castelvecchio
Tel. (0438) 22871
Open Tues – Sun 9am – noon,
*   2.30 – 5.30pm*
Closed Mon
🗺
Set in the remaining tower of the medieval fortress, the museum offers fine views over the beautiful wine-bearing hills behind the town. Its best piece is a detached fresco on the ground floor: an early *Madonna and Saints* (1514) by Pordenone, teetering already on the edge of the bombastic.

ESTE
Padova, Veneto Map B5

Este is a pretty town to the S of the Colli Euganei. The well-preserved walls of its 14thC castle now enclose a public park.

Duomo
Piazza Santa Tecla
Over the main altar, Tiepolo's famous canvas of *St Thecla Interceding to Rescue the City from the Plague* ★ (1759) is in poor condition and badly lit, but remains stupendous: almost operatically tragic in some of its details but with a definite grandeur of composition and rapturous colours.

Museo Atestino
Via Negri
Tel. (0429) 2085
Closed for restoration
The museum occupies a 16thC palace built into the castle walls and has one of the most important archaeological collections in northern Italy. Pre-Roman exhibits include some fine incised **bronzes** ★ from the Benvenuti and other tombs (6th – 2ndC BC). There is also a large Roman section, and a *Madonna* (1504) by Cima da Conegliano.

Villas of the Veneto

The idea of the villa as a haven – a retreat and refuge from the cares of the world – was immensely strong in Italy from medieval times (for instance, in Boccaccio's *Decameron*) through the Renaissance and into the 18thC. In the *Decameron* the villa runs itself, an earthly paradise where everyday practicalities are ignored; in real life, the villa was a veneer laid over the pressing reality of running a farm.

The history of the villa begins when it became safe to move down from the hill-top castle to the plain. It starts therefore in the Veneto with the accession of the region to firm and tranquil Venetian rule in the 15thC. An early example (of which only a frescoed fragment, now used as a barn, survives) was the Barco della Regina Cornaro, the villa built by Caterina Cornaro, ex-Queen of Cyprus, near Altivole on the plain below the beautiful hill town of Asolo: it was here, in the early 16thC, that Pietro Bembo set his famous, elegant discussion of High Renaissance love, *Gli Asolani*.

During the same period, important architects such as Sanmichele, Falconetto and Sansovino were developing the design of the villa. But it was Palladio who, in the middle and late 16thC, gathered up and codified their various ideas, setting the standard for all villas to come until the late 18thC. Naturally, his works will be the main attraction of a tour of the Veneto villas, but they are not the only ones, and others must be visited if not for their architecture then for their setting and contents.

The Veneto is a vast area, but the most important villas can be reached in day trips by car from three centers: Vicenza, Padua (the villas of the Brenta) and Castelfranco Veneto. Opening times for the villas change frequently so, before starting out, check the information given here with Ente Ville Venete (*Piazza San Marco 63, Venice. Tel. (041) 35606*).

SOUTH *of* VICENZA

The finest houses are within walking distance of VICENZA, off the road leading S towards Este: the **Villa Valmarana dei Nani**, with 18thC frescoes by Giambattista Tiepolo and his son Giandomenico, and the mid 16thC **Villa Rotonda** by Palladio, famous for its temple fronts on all four sides, and with fine views.

For a day out in a car, the drive S and W through the Monti Berici is beautiful in itself. Just beyond the village of San Germano dei Berici, high up outside the town of Lonigo, is Scamozzi's **Villa Pisani**, also known as La Rocca (The Fortress). It was built in 1578 and is closely modelled on Palladio's Villa Rotonda. If you have time to spare, you can go on to Lonigo and Palladio's early 16thC **Villa Pisani** on the river at Bagnolo. (*Both villas are open Wed and Sat, 10am–noon, 3–5pm.*)

Now continue S through Poiana Maggiore, pausing to look at the facade of the **Villa Poiana**, another early 16thC building by Palladio. You next come to MONTAGNANA, a good place to break for lunch. Just outside the spectacular medieval walls of this enchanting town is yet another **Villa Pisani**, an uncompleted and later modified design of Palladio's (c.1560). The villa is closed to the public, but you can still admire the grand exterior.

From Montagnana the road towards Padua leads to ESTE and Monselice, skirting the Colli Euganei. At Monselice, a narrow road climbs N and W to the village of Valsanzibio, where the late 17thC **Villa Barberigo** has marvellous gardens with fountains that include *giochi d'acqua*, or hidden sprays that can be suddenly launched by secret taps. (*The gardens are open Mar–Nov, 9am–noon, 3–7pm.*) Now continue on to Padua and back to Vicenza.

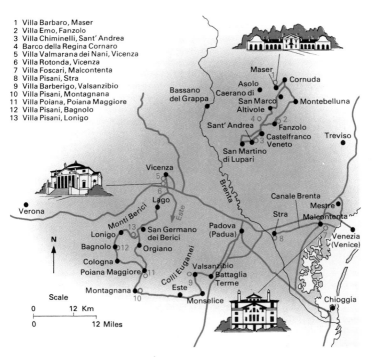

1 Villa Barbaro, Maser
2 Villa Emo, Fanzolo
3 Villa Chiminelli, Sant' Andrea
4 Barco della Regina Cornaro
5 Villa Valmarana dei Nani, Vicenza
6 Villa Rotonda, Vicenza
7 Villa Foscari, Malcontenta
8 Villa Pisani, Stra
9 Villa Barberigo, Valsanzibio
10 Villa Pisani, Montagnana
11 Villa Poiana, Poiana Maggiore
12 Villa Pisani, Bagnolo
13 Villa Pisani, Lonigo

The BRENTA CANAL

During the summer months (May–Sept) a boat should be running between
Padua and Venice on what was once the main route between the two cities.
(*Inquire at the Ente Provinciale di Turismo at the stations in Padua or Venice, or at
reputable travel agents.*) The canal is flanked, like a grand residential avenue,
by the villas of the well-to-do. These include the most famous **Villa Pisani** of
all, that at STRA, with 18thC frescoes by Tiepolo and a magnificent park, and
Palladio's **Villa Foscari** at Malcontenta, with late 16thC frescoes by Zelotti
and Battista Franco, contemporaries of Veronese. The boat stops at both
villas to allow time to look round, and includes a stop for lunch as well. Both
may also of course be visited by car. (*The Villa Foscari is open May–Nov, Tues,
Sat and first Sun of month, 10am–noon.*)

AROUND CASTELFRANCO

For an afternoon visit (*on a Tues, Sat, Sun or public holiday*), the most
beautiful and famous villa of them all, Palladio's **Villa Barbaro** at MASER, with
matchless frescoes by Veronese, is not to be missed. On the way there, near
Altivole, you can visit the remains of the **Barco della Regina Cornaro**, now
overrun by pigs and other farm animals (see above) and, on the way back,
Palladio's mid 16thC **Villa Emo** at Fanzolo, which has fine stucco decorations
by Alessandro Vittoria and frescoes by Zelotti. (*The Villa Emo is open Sat, Sun
and public holidays, Apr–Sept 3–6pm, Oct–Mar 2–5pm.*) In the opposite
direction, but only 4km (2½ miles) S of Castelfranco, is the **Villa Chiminelli**
at Sant' Andrea, a 16thC building with frescoes by followers of Veronese.
This, again, is open only during the afternoon (*May–Sept, Tues and Sat,
3–6pm*) and will probably be too much of a rush to fit in.

FELTRE
Belluno, Veneto Map B4

The old town features some well-preserved 16thC painted facades, notably on the Casa Torro at the lower end of the Via Mezzaterra.

Museo Civico
Via Lorenzo Luzzo
Tel. (0439) 80264
Open Tues – Thurs 9am – noon, Fri
10am – noon, Sat 9am – noon, 4 – 6pm,
Sun 10am – noon, 4 – 6pm
Closed Mon
🎭 🏛

A municipal museum that is charmingly typical of its kind: not much visited, and housing antique furniture as well as the occasionally interesting picture. Above the archaeological section, the first floor offers a late 15thC Gentile Bellini portrait, a contemporary **Madonna** by Cima da Conegliano, and an early 16thC **Madonna and Saints** by the native Morto da Feltre, an assistant of Giorgione.

Ognissanti
Borgo Ruga
The early 16thC fresco of the **Transfiguration** by Morto da Feltre, in the sacristy, is perhaps a better work than his **Madonna and Saints** in the MUSEO CIVICO.

MALLES VENOSTA (*MALS*)
Bolzano, Trentino-Alto Adige
Map A3

Malles is a small ski resort on the Swiss border, preserving some attractive medieval towers and belfries.

San Benedetto (*Sankt Benedikt*)
Open Mon – Fri 9am – noon, 3 – 6pm
Closed Sat, Sun
🎭

This 9thC church contains some of the most important **Carolingian frescoes ★** in Europe: full-length figures between and in niches, painted forcefully although schematically, and including a famous image of a donor-priest offering the church.

MASER
Treviso, Veneto Map B4

Maser itself is only a small farming village, at the foot of the Colli Asolani. But it is famous for the Villa Barbaro, one of the greatest civilized delights of all Europe.

Villa Barbaro ☆ ☆
Tel. (0423) 565002
Open Tues, Sat, Sun, public holidays:
June – Sept 3 – 6pm, Oct – May 2 – 5pm
Closed Mon, Wed – Fri
🎭 🚗 🚽 🏛 ☑ ♨ 🚶

The surrounding countryside is delectable, the villa is by Palladio, the **frescoes ★★** are by Veronese. All in all, the charms of the Villa Barbaro cannot be equalled.

The Veronese frescoes (1566 – 68) are beautifully painted, in ravishing colours – colours that would rekindle the most despairing soul; but also they are so witty, it is almost like entering a magical pleasure-garden. Courtiers come and go, peeping out illusionistically from behind pillars: one can almost hear the giggling in the bower. Up above, not exactly more seriously, but in Olympian dress, there is endless rustle of silk and shaking of fans, a bevy of smirks and straight faces, tut-tuts and learned moral expositions.

For explanations of the stories and allegories, cards (in four languages) are provided.

MONTAGNANA
Padova, Veneto Map A5

Montagnana is justly famous for its magnificent medieval walls and gates, the most perfectly preserved in the Veneto. Its large central square is dominated by the fine late 15thC Duomo.

Duomo
Piazza del Duomo
🏛 🏛

Veronese's **Transfiguration** (1555) on the high altar is rather dirty, which slightly spoils the play of colours, but it is a strikingly monumental work. The early 16thC frescoes of the **Assumption** in the choir apse are by Marescalco; they do not really adjust to the large area they have to cover, as do the frescoes of a similar subject in VERONA (Duomo), designed only a few years later by Giulio Romano.

The **Cappella del Rosario**, off the left of the nave, is unusual for its bold astrological frescoes, dating from the late 15thC.

MURANO
Venezia, Veneto Map C5

This ancient settlement and privileged suburb of Venice is famous chiefly for its glass industry (moved here from the city to limit fire risks) and glass museum; but its churches also have their riches.

Museo dell' Arte Vetraria (*Glass Museum*)
Fondamenta Giustinian
Tel. (041) 739586
Open Mon, Tues, Thurs – Sat 10am – 4pm,
Sun 9am – 12.30pm
Closed Wed
🖅 ⅓ ⏍ ☑ ✸

The oldest and most famous piece in the museum is the 15thC **glass wedding cup** by Angelo Barovier (Room II). But it was not this kind of enamelwork that made Murano's reputation. The crystal-clear vessels to be seen in the neighbouring cases are what caused Venetian glass to become part of the furniture of every princely apartment in 16thC Europe. Glass of such clarity and delicacy just could not be made anywhere else until the 17thC – the period when Venetian glass became irremediably frilly and utterly unusable.

Santa Maria degli Angeli
Fondamenta Sebastiano Venier

Pordenone's **Annunciation** (c. 1540) on the high altar was a crucial work, executed in rivalry with Titian; the latter asked for a larger fee than the nuns of the convent would pay, and his canvas eventually went to Spain. Pordenone's design is full of vigour, but it lacks the colours with which Titian seduced as well as impressed.

Santi Maria e Donato
Campo San Donato
🏛

The 12thC Romanesque church with its elegant colonnaded apse has an impressive 13thC **mosaic** and an early 14thC **altarpiece** by Paolo Veneziano (on left of nave, near entrance). The magnificent **mosaic pavement** ★ is one of the finest Romanesque examples surviving.

San Pietro Martire
Fondamenta dei Vereri
🏛

Giovanni Bellini's **Madonna with Doge Mocenigo** has now been moved to the VENICE Accademia. His **Assumption** (1510 – 13) remains (right wall), but it is clearly by his workshop. On the opposite side of the church, the **St Jerome** (1566) by Veronese is a splendid and imposing work; his **St Peter in Prison** in the sacristy is less interesting, and probably workshop.

PADOVA (*PADUA*)
Veneto Map B5

The second oldest university town in Europe, Padua enjoyed a prestigious cultural position from the 13thC until the late 16thC. Its pre-eminence was not only scholarly and scientific but also artistic (even though Giotto and Donatello, who left their greatest surviving works here, both came from Florence). Padua was only briefly a commune, being ruled by despots, last of them the Carrara, until ceding to Venice in 1405.

Cappella degli Scrovegni (*Arena Chapel*) ✰ ✰
Corso Garibaldi
Tel. (049) 650845
Open summer 9am – 12.30pm,
2.30 – 5.30pm; winter Mon – Sat
9.30am – 12.30pm, 1.30 – 4.30pm
Closed Sun in winter
🖅 ⏍ ✸ ⚒

It is extraordinary how so famous a monument never disappoints. The condition of Giotto's frescoes is wonderful; the clarity, pointedness and humanity of his narrative is always fresh, yet always profoundly dignified. Giotto was the first artist since antiquity to be recognized in his own lifetime as a genius, and was even the friend of princes (although all his secular decoration has since been lost). But Scrovegni was no prince – merely immensely rich, chiefly thanks to his father, for whose soul the chapel was built and painted.

The frescoes ★★ (1303 – 5) Holding the church, Scrovegni senior can be counted among the Blessed in the **Last Judgment** painted on the entrance wall; above the arch over the altar is the **Annunciation**, while around the walls, in three layers, reading from top far right around to top far left, then down to the next layer, is the **Life of Mary** leading into the **Life of Christ** and the **Passion**. (Details of each scene are given in a leaflet available in the chapel.)

Giotto is never spare, although one of his great virtues is economy; he exemplified in painting what in the Renaissance was called decorum, that is, putting in what was appropriate and leaving out what was not. In the first scene, the **Expulsion of Joachim**, the number of figures is reduced to a minimum, the temple is stark, the mood sorrowful; in the **Marriage at Cana**, the scene is jolly, there are more figures, and the servants and great wine-jars amount to a touch of genre. In the harrowing **Deposition**, gestures are emphatic, angels create movement in the sky above, grief cries out.

On the altar is a **Madonna and Two Angels** ★ by the brilliant contemporary sculptor Giovanni Pisano, fluid and seductive in style, in sharp contrast to Giotto's prudent, firm, demonstrative figures.

Chiesa degli Eremitani
Piazza degli Eremitani
Visiting the **Mantegna frescoes** (1454–57) in the Eremitani is rather like paying your respects to a grave in a well-kept cemetery – everything is in pristine order, but there is disappointingly little to see. Only half of the fresco of the **Martyrdom of St Christopher**, together with a contemporary altarpiece by Pizzolo, survived the World War II bombing.

Pizzolo, an assistant of Donatello, was a bright young artist like Mantegna (only 17 when he began work here); if he had not got himself killed in a brawl shortly afterwards he might have gone far. His altarpiece shows the influence of Donatello's SANTO altar rather more obviously than Mantegna's frescoes; these were important not only for their virtuoso mastery of perspective (learnt from Donatello) but also for their uniquely disciplined and precise linear style.

Ammanati's impressive **Benavides monument** (1546) is on the left of the nave, and there are badly damaged 14thC frescoes by Guariento in the choir.

Duomo
Piazza del Duomo
Baptistry closed for restoration
The Duomo and treasury contain works of only minor interest; but the baptistry preserves an important **fresco cycle ★** by Giusto de' Menabuoni. This was painted 1376–78, more or less contemporaneously with the frescoes by Altichiero and Avanzo in the SANTO. In the Tuscan Giusto, the influence of Giotto is stronger; or there is at least nothing of the svelte of Altichiero and Avanzo, which preludes the refinement of International Gothic.

Museo Civico
Piazza del Santo 10
Tel. (049) 23106, 23713
Open Tues – Sat 9am – 1.30pm, Sun 9.30am – 1pm
Closed Mon
▨
The picture gallery (above the archaeological section on the ground floor) is stronger in curiosities than in great masterpieces and can be disappointing for the non-specialist.
Room I The 14thC and early 15thC collection begins with a **crucifix ★** by Giotto from the CAPPELLA DEGLI SCROVEGNI. This is of a very common

type that Giotto made no attempt to change; only when compared with others of the kind does its depth of expression emerge. There follows a series of 25 fine, sprightly **Angels** by the Paduan painter, Guariento; a small **Crucifixion** by Jacobello del Fiore and, beside it, a moving **Dead Christ**, falsely signed Mantegna.

The polyptych of **St Jerome** by Squarcione, teacher and adoptive father of Mantegna, is almost his only surviving work and should be crucial; in fact it is damaged, the forms are rubbery and unprepossessing and it tells us little about Mantegna's early influences – possibly it confirms the view that Squarcione was more of a pundit than an artist.
Room II The 15thC and early 16thC works include an **Anchorite** by Jacopo Bellini; the **Argonauts**, a small, colourful panel attributed to Lorenzo Costa; a ravishing **Portrait of a Youth ★** inscribed *NON ALITER* (*"not otherwise"*) by Giovanni Bellini; and a number of contemporary **Madonnas**. About half way down the room, a vapid, posturing work by Francesco Torbido of a man wearing an over-large wreath apes Giorgione's portrait style; next to it, two long, horizontal scenes from Ovid's *Metamorphoses* are attributed – perhaps optimistically – to Titian.
Room III (to the left) has workshop paintings by later 16thC masters. Passing on through **Rooms IV**, **V** and **VI** (the last with the remains of a late 15thC life-size terra-cotta tableau of the **Deposition** by Guido Mazzoni), you turn right into Room VII.
Room VII The main 16thC collection begins, on the immediate left of the door, with **St Justine** by Veronese; it is strikingly sharp in colour, while his **Sts Primus and Felician** on the opposite wall is bigger, grander and blander. Bronzes in the first half of the room include a **Satyr** by the native Riccio and Jacopo Sansovino's **Peace**.

Passing into the second half of the room, you are confronted by Romanino's fine **Madonna and Saints** (1513), with its tender portrayal of three massacred innocents in a roundel beneath; on the right is a fiercely energetic **Crucifixion** by Tintoretto – and on the spur wall, his **Last Supper**; on the left, a **Last Supper** by Romanino, more intense than the Tintoretto but much less energetic.
Room VIII (reached by passing back through Room VI) Opposite an overblown swashbuckling portrait by the 17thC Baroque painter Sebastiano Mazzoni is Piazzetta's intensely modelled **Supper at Emmaus ★** (early 18thC).
Rooms IX and **X** have more 18thC

Venetian works, including Tiepolo's exhilarating *St Paulinus Exorcising a Devil* (Room X).

Back at the top of the stairs, the **Emo Capodilista collection** contains only third-rate paintings.

Santo (*Sant'Antonio*) ☆ ☆
Piazza del Santo
Scuola del Santo open 9am – noon,
2.30 – 6.30pm. If closed during these
hours, ask a sacristan to let you in

📖

In front of this famous Romanesque-Gothic church stands one of the most significant statements of the early Renaissance, the Gattamelata monument by Donatello.

Gattamelata ★ (1453) The monument commemorates a Venetian *condottiere* or captain whose real name was Erasmo da Narni. The most striking fact about it is that it revives a classical type, the Imperial equestrian statue, and retains its classical form (unlike medieval revivals); and yet, on close inspection, it is very different from the best known example, the statue of Marcus Aurelius outside the Musei Capitolini in Rome (see *SOUTH CENTRAL ITALY*).

Marcus Aurelius moves freely, with a gesture of greeting, in the real world; the Gattamelata is a closed, silent image, hoisted above the real world on an odd, tomb-like structure (Erasmo's real tomb is in the second chapel on the right of the church). The Gattamelata may also be compared with Verrocchio's equestrian statue of Colleoni outside Santi Giovanni e Paolo in VENICE.

Oratorio di San Giorgio, Scuola del Santo On the right of the piazza before the church are the **Oratorio di San Giorgio**, with frescoes by Altichiero and Avanzo, the same team who produced the magnificent series in the Santo itself (see below), and the **Scuola del Santo**, with early 16thC frescoes by a number of artists, including three by the young Titian (1510 – 11).

Titian does not show more than a glimmering of his real power until the episode of the *Jealous Husband*, where he may have borrowed the pose of the murdered wife from Michelangelo's Sistine ceiling. The landscape here is also justly famous. The story told is of the *Miracles of St Antony*, which feature again in the left transept of the church proper and in the reliefs of Donatello's altar.

Basilica This is one of the most richly decorated churches in Italy, and is still very much a pilgrimage center. In the right transept is the earliest of its great masterpieces: the fresco cycle of the

Passion ★ and the *Life of St James* ★ by Altichiero and Avanzo (1372 – 77).

This work is obviously indebted to Giotto but, instead of being a pale or trivializing imitation, in several respects advances beyond him: the colours are softer, more suggestive and more luminous; the expression is more refined, and at a higher pitch; the settings are much more sophisticated.

Opposite, in the left transept, is the **Arca del Santo** (Shrine of St Antony), where masses are said almost continuously. The costly white **marble reliefs** on the walls surrounding the Arca include works by Tullio Lombardo (1525) and Jacopo Sansovino (1563). The signed Lombardo relief is perhaps the finest of all his works – perfect finish and proportion, with more than usual expression.

In the left nave is the **Roselli monument ★** (1464 – 67) by Tullio's father, Pietro Lombardo – the first example in northern Italy of the Tuscan "humanist" tomb.

High altar, Easter candlestick The glory of the church is Donatello's **high altar ★★** (1443 – 50) with, to its left, Andrea Riccio's **Easter candlestick ★** (1507 – 15) (ask a sacristan to let you through the gates). It is perhaps better to look at Riccio's candlestick first, since this mini-Babel of classical allusion and learned allegory looks cold and pedantic after Donatello, although Riccio was an equally great master of technique.

Donatello's high altar has been dismantled and reassembled quite wrongly. Originally the figures were placed together in a box-like frame, so that they formed a closely knit *sacra conversazione*. Only the majesty and tension of the Madonna now remain; the gestures of the saints make no sense. The crucifix that hangs much too low over her was an entirely separate commission.

The most astonishing elements are now the bronze reliefs of the *Life of St Antony*. It is not difficult to see that the *Mule Adoring the Eucharist* was the first: the scale of the figures is inconsistent; the background is much plainer, without the stupendous effects of space and texture achieved in subsequent scenes.

Between these reliefs are symbols of the Evangelists and putti – brothers of the dancing putti on the Cantoria in the museum of the Duomo in Florence (see *NORTH CENTRAL ITALY*). These fat squirmy children populate northern Italian painting until superseded by the exquisitely fleshy ones that Titian introduced in the *Assumption* in the Frari in VENICE.

Perhaps the greatest piece of all in this exceedingly costly and ambitious work is the grey stone relief of the *Deposition*, now behind the altar in the center. The uninhibited grief of mourning – those hollow eyes and distorted, agonized limbs – all this, in 1450, is outright Expressionism.

Santa Giustina
Prato della Valle
This enormous church, rebuilt in the 16thC, contains Veronese's colossal but underpowered *Martyrdom of St Justine* (c.1575). Baroque works include two by Luca Giordano and one by Sebastiano Ricci. The 14thC **Shrine of St Luke** (in the left transept) and 5thC **Shrine of St Prosdocimus** (off the right transept) attest to the church's long history.

San Tommaso dei Filippini
Via San Tommaso
There is a charming mid 15thC *Madonna* by Antonio Vivarini in the sacristy; in the church itself, the 17thC *Mysteries of the Rosary* by Francesco Maffei and others.

Environs
Abbazia di Praglia
Near Abano, 13km (8 miles) SW of Padua
Open Tues – Sun 3.30 – 5.30pm
Closed Mon
📷 *but gratuity appreciated* 🚹 💷 🏛
Leave Padua on the road to Noventa
Vicentina and Vo, passing Abano
Terme. The monastery is on the left, just
past the settlement of San Biagio
This famous Benedictine monastery is worth visiting for its peaceful complex of Renaissance buildings and fine views as well as its late 16thC refectory paintings by Zelotti, a follower of Veronese.

PIEVE DI CADORE
Belluno, Veneto Map C3
The birthplace of Titian, Pieve di Cadore is now a winter sports center.

Casa di Tiziano
Via Arsenale
Tel. (0435) 4195
Open 9am – 12.30pm, 4 – 7pm
📷
The house where Titian was born is worth visiting for its assorted memorabilia and a collection of prints by and after the artist.

Parrocchiale
Piazza Tiziano
The *Madonna and Saints* (c.1560, third altar on left) is a second-rate Titian, showing the artist himself as donor.

PORDENONE
Friuli-Venezia Giulia Map C4
The old town, dating from the 14thC to the 17thC, has remained virtually intact at the center of a large modern development. It was the birthplace of Giovanni Antonio de' Sacchis (1483 – 1539), known as Pordenone, the most important painter in the Fruili in the Renaissance period.

Duomo
Piazza del Duomo
In the first chapel on the right is an important work by Pordenone: the *Madonna with Sts Joseph and Christopher*. It shows his vivid, sometimes violent, didacticism taking form, but the landscape is wholly Giorgionesque. The *St Roch* (last pier on right before crossing) is also by Pordenone, as is the unfinished main altarpiece (begun 1533), which heralds the whipped-up rapid style of the Santo Stefano frescoes in VENICE (see Ca' d'Oro).

In the chapel off the right transept and the chapel to the right of the choir are **frescoes** by Dario Cerdonis da Pordenone, an accomplished but obscure early 15thC painter who deserves greater recognition.

Museo Civico
Corso Vittorio Emanuele 51
Tel. (0434) 255507
Open Tues – Sun 9.30am – 12.30pm,
3 – 6.30pm
Closed Mon
📷 💷 ☑
At the bottom of the porticoed Corso Vittorio Emanuele, the museum preserves early 15thC fresco fragments of courtly scenes (first floor) and 18thC frescoed allegories (second floor) as well as a collection of pictures.

On the **ground floor** the towering painted wooden altarpiece (1509) by Domenico and Giovanni da Tolmezzo is an important example of early 16thC Friuli taste. On the **first floor**, at the top of the stairs, *Sts Gothard, Roch and Sebastian* by Pordenone is a good example of the bombastic style that succeeded it. Round to the right, a smaller room houses a *Finding of the Cross*, again by Pordenone. Across the Salone are two early 18thC portraits by Gianantonio Guardi, rather awkward and wooden but endearingly fresh. These are a temporary allocation.

The **second floor** is devoted to 19thC works, mostly by Grigoletti, another local painter.

POSSAGNO
Treviso, Veneto Map B4

This tiny village was the birthplace and home of the greatest Neoclassical sculptor, Antonio Canova (1757–1822).

Gipsoteca e Casa Natale di Canova
(*Sculpture Gallery and House of Canova*)
Tel. (0423) 54323
Open May–Sept Tues–Sat 9am–noon, 3–6pm, Sun 9am–noon, 3–7pm; Oct–Apr Tues–Sun 9am–noon, 2–7pm
Closed Mon
🎫 🛍 ☑ ⛏

Behind the house, which has mostly prints after Canova's work, but also a portrait of the artist by Sir Thomas Lawrence and some of Canova's own paintings, is the *gipsoteca* or sculpture gallery: an extraordinary Neoclassical barn, all white, in which are located the gesso models for, or copies after, almost all Canova's works – these too in purest Neoclassical white.

The colossal **Hercules and Lichas** (1796), silhouetted against the far end of the hall, shows that Canova did not necessarily discard Baroque sense of scale and theater when he adopted Neoclassical theory. For the most part, however, his works are exquisitely chiselled and delicate, frittering away any inner life in the prettiness of the surface.

Tempio di Canova (*Temple of Canova*)
🏛

Straight up a ramp from the sculpture gallery (a typically regimented Neoclassical vista) rises what is in fact the parish church of the village: a short, domed cylinder set in a star-burst of alternating black and white pebbles.

Inside, Canova's utterly unsuccessful painting of the **Deposition** (1797–99) is on the main altar. More impressive are his bronze **Pietà** (1821) and his own **tomb** (designed by Canova, originally intended for another, and including a marvellous self-portrait).

ROVIGO
Veneto Map B6

Rovigo is an unpicturesque, mainly modern town, with a disproportionately interesting art gallery.

Accademia dei Concordi ☆
Piazza Vittorio Emanuele 14
Tel. (0425) 21654

Open Mon–Fri, Sun 9am–12.30pm, 3.30–6.30pm, Sat 9am–12.30pm
🎫 🛍 ☑

The collection was formed through a series of bequests from local landowners, making the gallery a monument to the discreet prosperity of the region, as well as to its pride and taste. The gallery has recently been modernized and recatalogued.

Renaissance treasures on the ground floor include, in **Room I**, an exquisite early 15thC **Coronation of the Virgin** by Niccolò di Pietro; a superb early **Madonna ★** by Giovanni Bellini (c.1470); and **Christ Carrying the Cross**, also by Bellini and currently being restored.

Room II has early 16thC works, including two large altarpieces by Palma Vecchio, a **Flagellation** and **Madonna and Saints**; a fine **Portrait of a Man Reading**, attributed to Lotto; and a tiny portrait attributed optimistically to Titian.

Room III, also early 16thC, has one of the finest Flemish paintings in all Italy: the **Venus ★** by Mabuse; also a monumental **Madonna and Saints** by Dossi.

Upstairs, in **Rooms IV** and **V**, the 17thC and 18thC collection is even better, although not always featuring well known names. Works include Sebastiano Mazzoni's sensational **Death of Cleopatra ★** (mid 17thC), Girolamo Forabosco's **Joseph Refusing Potiphar** (c.1666–74), a **Marine View** (1712–14) by Luca Carlevaris – a rare example of this forerunner of Canaletto – and a **Nativity** by Pittoni (also early 18thC).

In **Room VI**, the excellent collection of **18thC portraits** includes two by Piazzetta; a dramatic oval by Tiepolo; also works by Pittoni, Alessandro Longhi and Rosalba Carriera.

Madonna del Soccorso
Piazza XX Settembre

The walls of this early 17thC church are covered in three tiers by pictures representing the **Life of Mary**, by Veneto Baroque artists, notably Francesco Maffei. It is all highly representative of contemporary taste.

SAN CANDIDO (*INNICHEN*)
Bolzano, Trentino-Alto Adige Map C3

San Candido is a popular ski resort, near the Austrian border. It takes its name from a Benedictine monastery that was founded here in the 8thC, of which now only the 13thC church remains.

Collegiata

🏛

This outstanding example of early
Romanesque architecture contains
15thC **frescoes** attributed to Michael
Pacher, Leonardo da Bressanone and
their schools; also a fine 13thC **crucifix**.

SPILIMBERGO
*Pordenone, Friuli-Venezia Giulia
Map C4*

The charming Gothic Duomo has just
emerged from restoration after the
disastrous 1976 earthquake; work is still
proceeding in the Castello. Both stand
rather isolated from this predominantly
agricultural town of ancient foundation.

Duomo
Piazza del Duomo
🏛

The most important work is Pordenone's
masterpiece, his **organ shutters** (1525)
depicting the **Fall of Simon Magus**, the
Conversion of St Paul and the
Assumption; unfortunately, the smaller
panels with the **Life of the Virgin** are
ruined. It was for this kind of overblown
aerial scrimmage that Pordenone was
famous, and seen in its original setting, in
its full scale, it is undeniably impressive.

STRA
Padova, Veneto Map B5

A peaceful little town on the banks of the
river Brenta, Stra is renowned for its
many villas, of which the most famous is
the 18thC Villa Pisani.

Villa Pisani
Tel. (049) 502074
*Open Tues – Sat 9am – 1pm, 3 – 6pm, Sun
9am – 1pm. Park open daily 9am – sunset
Villa closed Mon*
🕎 ⛄ 🏛 ☑ ☙

The villa is perhaps now more famous as
the site of the first meeting between
Hitler and Mussolini than for its
architecture, furniture, paintings and
especially fine ceiling by Tiepolo,
depicting the **House of the Pisani in
Glory** ★ (1761–62). The furniture and
paintings are all 18thC and 19thC (the
paintings including works by Amigoni,
Carriera and Longhi) and there is a
magnificent park.

TORCELLO
Venezia, Veneto Map C5

It is hard to believe that the isolated

complex of the Duomo, its baptistry, and
the Palazzo dell' Archivio and Palazzo del
Consiglio opposite, were once the center
of a flourishing town, larger than nearby
Burano. Overtaken by the rise of Venice
itself, and plagued by malaria, Torcello
declined from the 14thC onward.

Duomo
🏛

On the interior facade of this exquisite
and pure example of Veneto-Byzantine
architecture (dating mainly from the
11thC) is a high-quality 13thC mosaic
representing, in tiers, the **Last Judgment**,
including a **Descent into Limbo** – a
Byzantine subject. Fronting the choir, an
iconostasis or screen incorporates fine
marble low reliefs of lions and peacocks
(10thC–11thC). But the glory of the
church is the 13thC **apse mosaic** ★ in
which the slender, august form of the
Madonna gains tremendous effect by its
isolation amid a mirage of gold; beneath
are **Apostles**, lining up in support.

TRENTO
Trentino-Alto Adige Map A4

A prince-bishopric of ancient
foundation, with a fine 13thC Duomo,
Trento was transformed by the energy
and vision of one man – Cardinal
Bernardo Clesio (or Cles), bishop
1514–39. His great monument is the
Palazzo Magno in the so-called Castello
del Buon Consiglio, newly sparkling
under ongoing restoration and, in its
decoration, second only to the Palazzo del
Tè in Mantua (see Mantova, **NORTH AND
NORTH WEST ITALY**).

Castello del Buon Consiglio ☆
Via Bernardo Clesio 5
Tel. (0461) 21324, 35112, 980060
*Open Tues – Sun: Apr – Sept 9am – noon,
2 – 6pm; Oct – Mar 9am – noon,
2 – 4.30pm*
Closed Mon
🕎 ⛇ ⛄ 🏛 ☑ ☙
*Because of continuing restorations, all rooms
except ground floor I – IV may be subject
to closure*

Entrance is into the **Palazzo Magno**,
either through a long **corridor** ★
decorated with posturing putti, heads in
roundels, classical vignettes, a central
flying figure and a magnificent
Prometheus in a lunette at one end
(unfortunately the other end is almost
totally destroyed); or up a flight of **stairs** ★
decorated with music-making and other
irreverent figures, and great standing
colossi. Both approaches are by the
Brescian painter, Girolamo Romanino

(c.1484–after 1559), and both give on to the loggia.

Loggia ★★ The frescoes are among the finest works of Romanino, who here earns his place beside Correggio. In the center is *Phaethon in the Chariot of the Sun*, a stupendous vision with magnificent horses displaying great underbellies; surrounding it are the *Four Seasons*; beneath it, a series of figures without attributes – perhaps *Winds* – who perform typically Mannerist aerobics with a northern Italian lusciousness of paint.

Ground floor In the series of rooms leading off the loggia, ceilings and lunettes alternate fresco and stucco in the manner of the Palazzo del Tè.

Room I has frescoes of Roman emperors by Marcello Fogolino; **Room II**, fine **stuccoes** ★ by Zaccaria Zacchi; **Room III**, the audience hall, frescoes of recent emperors, including Charles V, also *Cardinal Clesio* ★ by Romanino; **Room IV**, frescoed *Virtues* ★ by Dossi and further stuccoes.

Room V, the old refectory, has landscape lunettes with tiny representations of Aesop's *Fables*, again by Dossi – but rather damaged. **Room VIII**, the passage outside the refectory, has Dossi *Deities*.

First floor Up the stairs from the loggia, through the **Sala Grande**, with lunette frescoes by Dossi of putti carrying initials referring to Clesio, you come to the **Stua Grande**, with two Romanino canvases; and the **Camera degli Scarlatti**, with a Giorgionesque fresco over the fireplace and busts of emperors in the lunettes, again all by Dossi.

Either from here, or from the ground floor through Room VIII, there is access from Clesio's Palazzo Magno to the earlier parts of the Castello.

The **Castelvecchio** to the N preserves numerous early 15thC fresco fragments. More interesting, however, on the other side of the Palazzo Magno, are the frescoed *Activities of the Months* in the **Torre dell' Aquila**: access is through a long corridor running along the back of the building.

TREVISO
Veneto Map C5

Famous in the Middle Ages for its chivalric culture, Treviso remained an independent center even after ceding to Venice in the early 15thC. Some four centuries later, it was the last Venetian center of resistance to Napoleon. Still the proud capital of a prosperous province, Treviso is a pleasant city, with numerous streams cutting across its Renaissance streets.

Duomo
Piazza del Duomo

The most important works are in the chapel to the right of the choir, where **frescoes** by Pordenone (1520) surround Titian's altarpiece of the *Annunciation* ★ (also 1520).

It is extraordinary how Titian's lucent colour and strong design sing out against Pordenone's rather yellowed, bombastic frescoes. A bomb destroyed Pordenone's dome, where God the Father despatched the Spirit to Titian's Virgin, but the *Adoration of the Magi* on the left indicates clearly enough his heavyweight style. The apparent spatial oddities of Titian's altarpiece seem to be byproducts of his search for dramatic illusionistic effects. The work is best viewed from a considerable distance.

Also worth seeking out are the slightly later *Adoration of the Shepherds* by Paris Bordone, a follower of Titian (second altar on right of nave); *St Justine and Saints* by Francesco Bissolo, a contemporary local master (third altar on left of nave); and late 15thC **marble decorative sculpture** by Pietro and Tullio Lombardo (in the choir).

Monte di Pietà
Piazza del Monte di Pietà
Open 9am–noon, 3–6pm
🔟 *but gratuity appreciated*
Ring bell for caretaker

The building has a charming, small-scale biblical cycle of late 16thC pictures by Pozzoferrato.

Museo Civico
Borgo Cavour 22
Tel. (0422) 51337
Open Tues–Sat 9am–noon, 2–5pm, Sun 9am–noon
Closed Mon
🔟

This is a disappointing museum for such an important city.

Room VIII is the start of the 16thC collection, with several *Madonnas* of the early 16thC Venetian school, including one by the local master Girolamo da Treviso, but neither the Giovanni Bellini nor the Cima da Conegliano are outstanding.

Room IX has a good *Portrait of a Dominican* by Lotto; also a portrait of *Sperone Speroni* by Titian, somewhat lacking in vitality. In **Room X** are representative works by Paris Bordone; in **Room XI**, second-class works by the Bassano family.

The Baroque collection ranges down

to the awful; but the 18thC section in **Room XXI** picks up with a landscape by Guardi, a good portrait by Longhi, and works by Tiepolo and Rosalba Carriera.

Santa Caterina
Via Santa Caterina
Inquire at Museo Civico for entry
The detached fresco cycle of *St Ursula* ★ (1350s) by Tommaso da Modena is displayed in the nave of the deconsecrated church. Tommaso achieved unprecedented movement in these scenes, but the colours and surface are rather dull compared to the SAN NICCOLÒ works, perhaps through damage.

San Niccolò
Via San Niccolò
🏛
This austere and impressive 13thC–14thC church offers a marvellous *St Jerome* ★ by Tommaso da Modena on the second pier on the left from the entrance – a prelude to the glowing forms and psychological credibility of the frescoes in the adjoining seminary.

The early 16thC **Onigo monument** on the left of the main chapel was sculpted by Antonio Rizzo, with surrounding frescoes by Lotto; it displays a classicism very similar to that of the Vendramin monument in Santi Giovanni e Paolo in VENICE.

In the chapter house of the adjacent seminary (ask the sacristan to take you there), one wall is filled with **Dominican portraits** ★ signed and dated 1352 by Tommaso da Modena, all of the same format, but with a humanity and realism that rank Tommaso beside Altichiero in northern Italian art of the late 14thC.

UDINE
Friuli-Venezia Giulia Map D4
Udine is a medieval town, in an area rich in Roman remains. It became important in the 14thC and was involved in disputes between the patriarch of Aquileia, the Holy Roman Emperor and the counts of Gorizia until its cession to Venice in 1420.

Duomo
Piazza del Duomo
This much reworked 14thC building contains a number of works by Tiepolo. On the first altar on the right is his *Holy Trinity* (1738), with a haunting landscape; it is perhaps more interesting than his *Sts Ermagoras and Fortunatus* (1737) on the second altar, but not as

affecting as his *Resurrection*, a small panel on the fourth altar (the exquisite chiaroscuro *Angels* on the walls of the same chapel are also by him, 1726).

In the first chapel to the left of the choir there survive remains of a spirited fresco cycle by Vitale da Bologna, the *Life of St Nicholas* (1340s).

For access to the **Oratorio della Purità** across the street to the right of the Duomo, find the sacristan. On the ceiling is Tiepolo's *Assumption* (1757), typically ethereal, and lighter in tone than his frescoes in the PALAZZO ARCIVESCOVILE. The altarpiece is also by Tiepolo. On the walls are some fine biblical scenes in a silvery chiaroscuro by his son, Giandomenico (1759).

Museo Civico, Galleria d'Arte Antica e Moderna
Castello
Tel. (0432) 207089
Closed indefinitely for restoration
Still being restored after the 1976 earthquake, the museum is rich in archaeological and particularly numismatic treasures, while the picture gallery holds a number of works by Friuli masters such as Pordenone, Domenico da Tolmezzo and Pellegrino da San Daniele; it also has the *Blood of Christ* by Carpaccio, who exported quite widely to this region.

In the Baroque period, there are works by Francesco Maffei, Bernardo Strozzi and Luca Giordano. The strongest area is the 18thC, with allegories by Tiepolo, a landscape by Sebastiano Ricci, and several altarpieces by Niccolò Grassi.

The modern art collection includes works by Chirico and Marini.

Palazzo Arcivescovile
Piazza del Patriarcato 1
Tel. (0432) 206314
Open Mon–Fri 9am–noon
Closed Sat, Sun
🗖 🔳
You climb the stairs beneath a *Fall of Rebel Angels*, painted by Tiepolo as a prelude to his more famous works in the Galleria and Sala Rossa (1726–28).

On the walls of the **Galleria** are *Abraham and the Angels*, *Rachel Hiding the Idols* and the *Angel Appearing to Sarah*; on the ceiling, *Agar in the Desert*, the *Dream of Jacob* and the *Sacrifice of Abraham*; on the ceiling of the **Sala Rossa**, the *Judgment of Solomon*.

These are youthful works by Tiepolo and, for all their gorgeousness, amusing touches of genre and bold design, the colours are heavy and unsubtle compared with those of his later works.

VENICE (*VENEZIA*)
Veneto Map C5

Horses were banned in Venice in 1392, and since that time it has been not merely a city on the sea, but one in which access and thoroughfare and even assembly are by water or on water. In a way that has never been quite true of any other city, all Venetian streets are back alleys, even though the Austrians filled in some canals and created a few wider streets in the 19thC. In fact, Venice is not nearly such a warren if you travel by boat – which is, ideally, how its architectural wonders should be seen.

For the first-time visitor, the city can nevertheless be utterly confusing. It is a good idea to start where Venice started, with the glittering arches and shimmering, dark interior of San Marco. This is the main monument of the medieval Republic, with its potpourri of stone carvings, magnificent mosaics and bejewelled Pala d'Oro or golden altarpiece. The Palazzo Ducale beside it is a monument of the later Middle Ages and of the Renaissance, with clusters of late Gothic and early Renaissance sculpture on the outside and in the courtyard and, within, pictures by Tintoretto and Veronese. The Piazza was the religious and political center of historic Venice; it is still the tourist magnet of the modern city.

To the N of the Piazza a maze of crooked, crowded streets leads to the Rialto bridge, the commercial center of both ancient and modern Venice. To the W is the road to the Accademia galleries, with masterpieces by Bellini, Titian, Tintoretto, Veronese and Tiepolo. Nowhere else in the world is the lasting Venetian flirtation with radiant colour and light more extensively displayed.

The Piazza, Rialto and Accademia constitute a triangle around which the rest of the city sprawls. And skirting this triangle, passing under the Rialto and Accademia bridges, snakes the Grand Canal. At some point you should take the slow boat down this famous waterway and revel in the leisurely unwinding of its great scroll of palace fronts. These date from the 13thC to the 18thC and run through a unique range of Byzantine, Gothic, Renaissance and Baroque styles. On foot, the routes between the main sights are clearly marked, and include signposted walks to two of the city's most famous churches – the Frari, with treasures by Titian and Bellini, and Santi Giovanni e Paolo, the pantheon of Venice, with its rich if dusty collection of ducal tombs.

Outside these limits, wise tourists should arm themselves with a good map, bought from any stall. Here begins Venice the city of unexpected views, of narrow backwaters and gently lapping tides, of beautiful altarpieces discovered unexpectedly in lesser known churches, and of spectacular picture cycles still in their original settings in the ancient Venetian *scuole* or confraternities.

It was Thomas Mann in his famous novel about the tourist unable to leave, *Death in Venice*, who noted that, as in no other city, pullulating, crowded thoroughfares can turn in a moment to deserted, eerie streets. It is nevertheless advisable to avoid the high season from late July to early September: at this time of year the main monuments can become impossibly crowded and the weather unbearably humid, and it may be hard to find a hotel. Enormous, although very lively, crowds also gather during the two weeks of Carnival in February. At other times the city is relatively quiet but, although its streets are narrow and badly lit, they are perhaps the safest in the world.

Accademia ☆☆
Campo della Carità, Dorsoduro
Tel. (041) 22247
Open Tues, Wed, Fri, Sat 9am–2pm,
*   Thurs 9am–4pm, Sun 9am–1pm*
Closed Mon
🚫 *but* 🎫 *every first and fourth Sat, first and*
*   third Sun of month* ☑ ⠿

The present Accademia delle Belle Arti was originally the Scuola Grande della Carità, and it still contains two pictures belonging to the Scuola, Titian's monumental **Presentation of the Virgin** and Antonio Vivarini's almost equally large **Madonna and Saints**.

The Academy itself was founded in 1750, but transferred here in 1807 and its collection enlarged with pictures from suppressed churches. The process continues: two works by Giovanni Bellini in Room III are recent arrivals. The only Venetian painters not outstandingly well represented here are Titian (despite three fine works), Bassano and Canaletto; paintings by non-Venetian artists are few.

The Accademia is an attractive gallery, although Rooms IV and V with the small Bellinis and the Giorgiones are often impossibly crowded.

Room I The old assembly hall: Gothic and International Gothic works. The **Coronation of the Virgin** ★ by Paolo Veneziano is a crucial work by the founder of the Venetian school. Its use of gold is lavish even for the mid 14thC, and sets the picture in a timeless, never-never world. The love of surface and colour would be something to which the Venetian school would return, after tending, with Lorenzo Veneziano, towards the harder, more solid style of the mainland: two **Annunciations** by Lorenzo clearly show this mainland influence; the first is dated 1357, the second 1371.

Niccolò di Pietro was the eldest of the Venetian painters touched by International Gothic; his little **Madonna** ★ (1394) has a sweet, open naïveté typical of the style. Slightly younger was Jacobello del Fiore, whose **Justice** triptych ★ (1421) shows rather more energy than is usually associated with the style, particularly in the figure of St Michael.

Also attributed to Jacobello, probably incorrectly, is the vast **Coronation of the Virgin** (1438) at the far end on the right; this is one of several surviving pictures reflecting the elaborate staging of Guariento's fresco in the PALAZZO DUCALE; another is the much softer and more luminous version of the same subject ★ by Giambono, directly opposite on the left. Close by, an enchanting early

15thC altarpiece by Michele di Matteo, the **Virgin Adoring the Child with Angels and Saints** ★ shows clearly the influence of Gentile da Fabriano, who also painted in the Palazzo Ducale.

Moving out of the conventions of International Gothic, Antonio Vivarini painted the exquisite mid 15thC **Madonna** ★ – on an easel beside the second display on the left – recalling the contemporary works of the Florentine Filippo Lippi.

Room II The classic picture in the room is Giovanni Bellini's **San Giobbe altarpiece** ★ (c.1485), the figures seen from below in distinct foreshortening. It is famous for continuing into the picture the scale and details, and so the illusion, of the architecture of the church in which it once hung.

Around it hang rivals of similar size and format – notably Cima da Conegliano's **Incredulity of St Thomas** ★ (c.1510), a touch too sweet for some tastes, and Carpaccio's **Presentation in the Temple** ★ (1510), perhaps rather too hard except for the marvellous, music-making angel in the center.

Room III This contains Giovanni Bellini's **Madonna with Doge Mocenigo** ★ (1488), with a landscape in the artist's late style; the painting as a whole is much more colourful than his San Giobbe altarpiece (see above). On the opposite wall is his **San Francesco della Vigna Madonna** (1507), with a landscape that shows more than any other by him the influence of the young Giorgione's style on the aged artist; but it may be a workshop picture. On an easel is an early **Madonna** (c.1506) by Giorgione's assistant, Sebastiano Veneziano (later known as del Piombo), rather charmingly hesitant.

Room IV 15thC pictures by non-Venetians include Mantegna's **St George**, Cosimo Tura's **Madonna**, Memlinc's **Young Man**, Piero della Francesca's terribly damaged **St Jerome**. Jacopo Bellini's **Red Madonna** ★ is also damaged, but his decorative and yet sculptural style of curling, overlapping folds shows through.

The supreme masterpiece in the room is Giovanni Bellini's **Madonna with St Catherine and the Magdalen** ★★ which is not only a moving devotional work but a human document of virginity (St Catherine), young motherhood and ever so slightly peevish matronliness (the Magdalen).

Room V Giorgione's **Tempesta** ★★ has to be behind glass: most people peer into its details to find a clue to its mystery; many even look behind the partition. In fact, the message is probably straightforward:

the naked woman, who is a gypsy, warns the spectator of the storm, but the besotted soldier who stares at her is unaware of it, and unaware of the ruins behind him which, again, symbolize his doom. The magic of the picture lies in the unknown quantity that is the gypsy, and in the dramatic moment in which her stare holds us.

On the right of the *Tempesta*, the theme of Giorgione's *La Vecchia*, the Old Woman, requires no reflection: I grow old, I grow old, she piercingly cries. On the left, the little picture of *Fortune* set above the four *Allegories* ★ by Giovanni Bellini probably does not belong; the Bellinis represent, from left to right: Virtue refusing Drunkenness (and hence Sloth); the ship of Fortune with souls struggling to stay afloat; Fame in her temple; and peasants under the weight of the conch of Venus.

Next on the left is a Giovanni Bellini *Madonna* ★ of great beauty, a little later than his *Madonna of the Alberetti* ★ (Little Trees) beside it, of 1487. On the central partition, a *Pietà* by Bellini appears damaged and looks rather awkward to eyes used to Michelangelo's Vatican *Pietà* (1499), although it was painted a few years after Michelangelo sculpted his group. Next to this, another Bellini, a *Madonna and Saints* ★ (c.1505) with a harbour scene of ravishing beauty – a marvellous, proto-Poussin, proto-Cézanne landscape.
Room VI This moves forward into the new confidence and harmony of the 16thC, and is dominated by the magnificent form of Titian's *St John the Baptist* ★ (c.1530). The other pictures are by Tintoretto and by lesser artists of the first half of the century: Bonifacio's *Feast of Lazarus* (c.1540) shows the influence of central Italian Mannerism, especially in the dramatic perspective.

The side **Rooms VII**, **VIII** and **IX** are notable chiefly for an early 16thC Savoldo altarpiece and Lotto's elegant yet didactic *Portrait of a Young Man in his Study* (c.1525) (VII), a nice Palma Vecchio *Madonna* (c.1520) (VIII), and the early Titian *Tobias and the Angel* (1507) (IX).
Room X On the right, Veronese's recently restored *Feast in the House of Levi* ★★ (1573) now takes up more than the whole wall, because a few inches of turned-over canvas were revealed on each side; the flanking walls were therefore cut away. For this picture Veronese was prosecuted by the Inquisition, who claimed that it was much too worldly for a *Last Supper* (the intended subject). He escaped the charge by changing the title. Now glowing

anew, the painting's colours and pomp draw the spectator into a dazzling theatrical spectacle.

Tintoretto's *Miracle of St Mark Freeing a Slave* ★ (1548) also created an enormous impact when it was unveiled. For the first time a Venetian had made something of the influence of Michelangelo, although its real achievement is not so much in the drawing of the figures as in the design and colour harnessed to dramatic effect.

On the opposite wall hangs Titian's late *Pietà* ★ (1576), finished but not significantly altered by Palma Giovane – full of tragic anguish and, again, drawing on Michelangelo for the figures. Very much last horse in is one of Pordenone's most important works, *San Lorenzo Giustiniani and Saints* (1532), didactic and pietistic.
Room XI Some of the Veronese *Madonnas* are quite breathtaking – marvellous symphonies of echoing colour. Tintoretto's series for the Scuola della Trinità make their effect through vigour and posture and design instead. These stand out against the late 16thC *Resurrection of Lazarus* by Leandro Bassano, against the huge, rather plodding, early 17thC *Supper at Emmaus* by Bernardo Strozzi, and even against the fragments of Tiepolo's **ceiling from the Scalzi church** ★ (1743–44), bombed in 1915.
Room XII Quite a different key is struck with these idyllic 18thC landscapes by Marco Ricci, Zais, Zuccarelli and others. None of the 16thC works in **Room XIII** is the equal of those seen in previous rooms, not even the recently loaned Titian portrait. **Room XIV** has mainly biblical scenes from the 17thC. In **Rooms XV** and **XVI**, the most important Venetian painters of the 18thC are represented: Pittoni, Pellegrini, Tiepolo (a mythological series in XVI). **Room XVIA** has Piazzetta's *Gypsy* ★ (1740), distinctive for its disturbing, imploding light.
Room XVII More 18thC works include portraits by Rosalba Carriera, genre scenes by Pietro Longhi, some good **landscapes** ★ by Guardi and Tiepolo's **sketch for the Scalzi ceiling** ★

After more 18thC landscapes in **Room XVIII** (a corridor), we are suddenly back in the late 15thC and early 16thC: **Rooms XIX** to **XXII** have mostly second class works, but include the famous **views of Venice** ★ by Gentile Bellini and others, from the Scuola di Santa Croce (XX), and Carpaccio's *St Ursula* cycle ★ most of which is currently in restoration (XXI). Its pageantry and occasional moments of intimacy (as in the *Dream of St Ursula*) should emerge with new brightness.

Room XXIII This is the upper part of the original church of the Carità. It also has mostly second class paintings, but there are important late 15thC works by Bartolommeo and Alvise Vivarini and Gentile Bellini. The room is also used for temporary exhibitions and is subject to periodic rearrangement.

Room XXIV The old Albergo or council room: a fitting climax to your tour, Titian's *Presentation of the Virgin* ★ (1534–38) hangs where it has always hung (although originally there was only one doorway cut through it). Against a stupendous landscape and a crowd of onlookers in a sort of visual buzz of conversation, the diminutive Virgin on the steps still holds the focus of attention.

On the right, the *Madonna and Saints* ★ (1446) by Antonio Vivarini and Giovanni d'Alemagna was the first unified *sacra conversazione* to be painted in Venice. The Giovanni Bellini *Annunciation* (c.1490, on either side of the door leading from Room XXII) came from SANTA MARIA DEI MIRACOLI and has an appropriately hard, shiny quality, almost like marble.

ACCADEMIA TOP TEN

If you are visiting the gallery with only an hour or so to spare, use this list to make sure you don't miss the star attractions. (These are numbered in touring sequence, not in order of importance.)

1 Paolo Veneziano: *Coronation of the Virgin*
2 Giovanni Bellini: *San Giobbe altarpiece*
3 Giovanni Bellini: *Madonna with St Catherine and the Magdalen*
4 Giorgione: *Tempesta*
5 Veronese: *Feast in the House of Levi*
6 Tintoretto: *Miracle of St Mark Freeing a Slave*
7 Piazzetta: *Gypsy*
8 Gentile Bellini and others: *Views of Venice*
9 Carpaccio: *St Ursula cycle*
10 Titian: *Presentation of the Virgin*

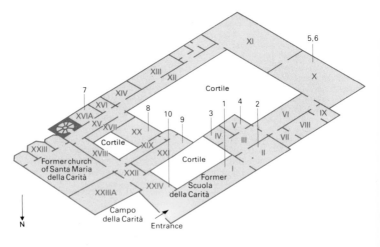

Ca' d'Oro (*Galleria Franchetti*)
Canal Grande, Cannaregio
Due to reopen Sept 1983
🏛

One of the finest architectural examples of International Gothic in Venice, the Ca d'Oro is fronted by intricate tracery and carved marble (originally gilded, hence the name of "Golden House"),

and was once equally well appointed within. The courtyard still has a magnificent **wellhead** by Bartolommeo Bon (1427). The palace was acquired by Baron Franchetti in 1895 and given to the State in 1915. His private art collection now constitutes the Galleria Franchetti.

The pictures are headed by

Mantegna's over-lifesize *St Sebastian* ★ a highly expressive work that was still in the artist's studio when he died in 1506. The surviving frescoes (1508–9) by Giorgione and Titian for the Fondaco dei Tedeschi are here; also one by Pordenone for the cloister of Santo Stefano, an important work of the 1530s.

There are also paintings by Giambono, Signorelli, Pontormo, Titian (a good-quality workshop *Venus*), Tintoretto, Tiepolo, and 17thC Dutch artists. Late 15thC and early 16thC sculpture includes busts by the Lombardo family and plaques by Riccio.

Ca' Pesaro (*Galleria d'Arte Moderna, Museo Orientale*)
Canal Grande, Santa Croce
Tel. (041) 24127 (Galleria) 27681
  (Museo)
Open Tues–Sat 10am–4pm (Galleria)
  9am–2pm (Museo), Sun
  9.30am–12.30pm (Galleria)
  9am–1pm (Museo)
Closed Mon
📷 🏛
The building is stupendous – a grand Baroque palace by Longhena dating from 1652 – with vast rooms in which the modern and oriental art collections look faintly incongruous. Although it boasts names like Rodin, Rosso, Klimt and Nicholson, the modern art gallery is for the most part undistinguished. The oriental museum is of even less interest.

Ca' Rezzonico (*Museo del Settecento Veneziano*) ☆
Canal Grande, Dorsoduro
Tel. (041) 24543
Open Mon–Thurs, Sat 10am–4pm, Sun
  9am–noon
Closed Fri
📷 🏛
The most important palace in Venice by Longhena, dating from 1660, is now the Museum of the Venetian Eighteenth Century. Some of its treasures are an integral part of the structure, such as the *Allegories* ★ by Tiepolo on the first floor (**Rooms II** and **VI**); the one in **Room VIII** came from elsewhere.

The first floor also has portraits by Rosalba Carriera and Alessandro Longhi and two almost kitsch scenes of female domination (*Hercules and Omphale*, *Orpheus and the Bacchantes*) by Lazzarini.

The finest works are on the second floor. In the large Portego or hall, beside pretty landscapes by Marco Ricci and others, the *Death of Darius* ★ is a monumental work by Piazzetta and the portrait by Gianantonio Guardi is

representative and charming.

In **Room XIV** is the most important single collection of genre works by **Pietro Longhi**, well handled, neat, even witty, but relentlessly lightweight. Tiepolo's *Triumph of Zephyr and Flora* ★ on the ceiling is also lightweight, indeed defies gravity. It makes an interesting comparison with the fresco next door (**Room XV**) by Gianantonio Guardi, the *Triumph of Diana* ★ **Room XVI** has more Guardi frescoes, these taken from elsewhere.

On the opposite side of the Portego, in a series of rooms at the back of the palace, are **frescoes** ★ by Giandomenico Tiepolo, perhaps the best work he ever did. They are from the Tiepolo villa at Zianigo. Note especially the melancholy *Clowns*.

Carmini (*Santa Maria dei Carmini*)
Campo Carmini, Dorsoduro
Amid the mostly 17thC and 18thC run-of-the-mill pictures in this dark church there are some good, but not great, 16thC pictures. The *Adoration of the Shepherds* ★ (c. 1510) by Cima da Conegliano is a fine work in the artist's sweet, late manner (second altar on right); Lorenzo Lotto's *St Nicholas* ★ (1529) features a beautiful landscape with a spirited St George slaying the dragon (second altar on left). The panels of the **singing galleries** at the entrance to the choir are fine examples of Andrea Schiavone's bold impasto style.

Doges' Palace See PALAZZO DUCALE.

Frari (*Santa Maria Gloriosa dei Frari*) ☆
Campo dei Frari, San Polo
Open Mon–Sat 9.30am–noon,
  2.30–6pm, Sun 2.30–6pm
📷 🏛
This rosy-pink Gothic church, the Franciscan rival of SANTI GIOVANNI E PAOLO, may well indeed be properly called Santa Maria Gloriosa. It contains among its treasures two of the finest monuments of Venetian art, Titian's *Assumption* ★★ (1516–19) on the high altar, which dominates its huge church as no other altarpiece in the world quite does; and Giovanni Bellini's *Madonna with Sts Nicholas, Peter, Benedict and Mark* ★★ (1488) in the sacristy; both of them painted for the positions they still occupy.

Just how much of a sensation the **Titian altarpiece** caused when unveiled in 1519 can be imagined if you compare it with Raphael's *Transfiguration* in the Musei Vaticani (see Rome, SOUTH CENTRAL ITALY), painted by Raphael at the height of his fame just before his death. Although Raphael's handling of figure and detail is consummate, Titian's work is grander by far, yet displays full mastery of classical form, integrated composition and stupendous colouring. The putti deserve special mention: they are perhaps the finest in all Italian painting, and have been emulated by painters from Poussin to Tiepolo.

The **Bellini altarpiece** (off the right transept) is, in complete contrast, quiet, still, almost neat. These saints, especially the severe St Benedict who confronts your gaze, made such an impression on Dürer that he recalled them in his late *Four Apostles* altarpiece. If the day is fine, study the infinitely soft circulation of light from left across the picture, just as Bellini intended it to be seen, without the distorting electric light.

Through the sacristy, in the chapter house, is a lunette of *Doge Francesco Dandolo and His Wife Being Presented to the Virgin* (c.1339) by Paolo Veneziano, the earliest surviving such dedication picture. In the first chapel to the right of the main altar, the altarpiece of the *Madonna with Sts Peter, Paul, Andrew and Nicholas* ★ (c.1480) is one of Bartolommeo Vivarini's finest works. The wooden *St John the Baptist* (c.1434) by Donatello, in the next chapel, hardly deserves its customary high rating.

In the main chapel, the **monument to Doge Niccolò Tron** ★ (d.1473) on the left, with its tiers recalling the facade of SAN ZACCARIA, is by Antonio Rizzo.

In the left aisle, between the late Renaissance choir screen (possibly by the Lombardo family) and the entrance, hangs Titian's *Pesaro Madonna* ★ (1526). The design is important because it was the first time that the Madonna was placed off-center, something that became virtually standard in Baroque altarpieces. The debate still rages as to why Titian arranged his composition thus, but it may be because the natural light source demanded an oblique viewpoint. It is a work of Titian's early maturity, rich and confident in colour, brilliantly naturalistic in its portraiture.

Opposite, in the right aisle, is a 16thC marble statue of *St Jerome*, a good work by Alessandro Vittoria. Returning to the left aisle, further on down the nave, the **monument to Canova** (1827) was executed by Canova's pupils on the basis of his own design (1794) for a monument to Titian that was never realized.

Gesuati (*Santa Maria del Rosario*)
Fondamenta delle Zattere, Dorsoduro
Open 8am–noon, 5–7pm
This is an entirely 18thC church,

although an old Dominican foundation. The **vault** (1739) is by Tiepolo, glorifying the institution of the rosary, to which the church is dedicated. Also by Tiepolo, on the first altar on the right, is a brilliant *Madonna with St Catherine of Siena, St Rose and St Agnes* ★ (before 1740).

The second and third chapels on the right house altarpieces by Piazzetta of the same period, showing his much more intense modelling and more troubled light. In the third chapel on the left is a Tintoretto *Crucifixion* (c.1560), typically surging and dynamic. There is 18thC sculpture by Morlaiter to go with it all.

Gesuiti
Campo dei Gesuiti, Cannaregio
Open 10am–noon, 5–7pm
The sumptuous facade and interior are 18thC, but the contemporary art in the church is not nearly so distinguished as that of the GESUATI.

Over the first altar on the left, however, is one of Titian's greatest works, the *Martyrdom of St Lawrence* ★★ (c.1557). Through thick and sinister darkness, and twisting desperately on his grill, the saint lifts his head to gaze at the putti in a burst of light a very long way away at the top of the picture. There is violent movement and violent paintwork in the straining of the executioners, and the dramatic effect of flares of light searing through the night is brilliantly achieved.

Guggenheim Collection See
RACCOLTA PEGGY GUGGENHEIM

Madonna dell'Orto
Campo Madonna dell'Orto, Cannaregio
🏛
Featuring one of the finest and most characteristic Gothic facades in the city, the church also contains (over the first altar of the right aisle) a beautiful **altarpiece** by Cima da Conegliano, in his later, sweeter style (c.1510); a small *Madonna* (c.1475) by Giovanni Bellini (in a chapel off the beginning of the left aisle); and important works by Tintoretto.

The most attractive of the Tintorettos is the *Presentation of the Virgin* ★ (c.1552, far end of right aisle), with a heady perspective set off by turning figures. On either side of the main altar are the *Adoration of the Golden Calf* and the *Last Judgment* (c.1560), enormous *tours de force* of falling bodies anticipating Rubens. In the Cappella Contarini (off the left aisle), is *St Agnes Raising the Son of the Roman Prefect* (c.1579).

Museo Correr ☆
Piazza San Marco, San Marco
Tel. (041) 25625, 22185, 29006
Open Mon, Wed – Sat 10am – 4pm, Sun
  9am - 12.30pm
Closed Tues
🚫 🏛 📷 ☑ ⊡

The museum was founded in 1830 by
Teodoro Correr, a wealthy Venetian.
Since 1922 it has been housed in
Scamozzi's late 16thC Procuratorie
Nuove, but entrance is up the stairs of the
Ala Napoleonica, the edifice erected by
Napoleon to close off the Piazza in
Neoclassical harmony.

The rooms straight ahead from the
stairs are given over to temporary
exhibitions. The rest of the **first floor** is
taken up by the historical collections; in
the first section is a graceful early work by
Canova, *Daedalus and Icarus* (1779).
The picture gallery is on the **second floor**.
Its most precious possessions are pre- and
early Renaissance, newly laid out and
introduced by texts in each room.

From Veneto-Byzantine works (**Room
I**), we move to the 14thC and to Paolo
Veneziano (**Room II**), who can be
compared with anonymous
contemporaries who remained
unchangingly in the Byzantine mould.
Room III is devoted to Paolo's younger
contemporary, Lorenzo Veneziano. In
Room IV is a marvellous statuette of
Doge Antonio Venier ★ by Jacobello
dalle Masegne (c. 1400) and other Gothic
sculpture. **Room V** has late 14thC works.

Room VI introduces International
Gothic, with Stefano da Verona's
Angels ★ and works by Giambono and
Jacobello del Fiore. **Room VII** has a late
15thC Cosimo Tura *Madonna* ★ **Room
VIII** has examples of the Ferrarese school
to which Cosimo belonged, also – an
interesting comparison – works by the
Venetian Bartolommeo Vivarini, who
has more affinity with the harder, more
linear Ferrarese works than is ever
achieved by the Bellini. **Room IX** has
wooden sculpture and a fine mid 16thC
relief of the *Madonna* by Jacopo
Sansovino.

The 15thC Flemish paintings in
Room X are, as usual in Italy, a mediocre
bunch; but **Room XI** has a good Bouts
Madonna ★ also a *Crucifixion* that may
be by Hugo van der Goes, and an
impressive *Christ Supported by Angels* ★
by Antonello da Messina – his new oil-
paint style is properly discernible only in
the occasional detail. There follow
(**Room XII**) more indifferent Flemings
and Germans of the 16thC.

In **Room XIII** are four works by the
Bellini, two of them important and two,
quite simply, stupendous. Important are

the late Jacopo Bellini *Crucifixion*
(c. 1460, to right of entrance) in which
Giovanni may also have had a hand; and
Gentile Bellini's charming *Head of Doge
Giovanni Mocenigo* (1478 – 85).

Stupendous are Giovanni Bellini's
Crucifixion ★ (c. 1460), with a
composition reflecting the influence of
van Eyck, and his *Transfiguration* ★
(c. 1465), with forms obviously based on
Mantegna but with light and colour
stating clearly for the first time the
principles of the Renaissance Venetian
school.

Room XIV has some good, sharp
works by Alvise Vivarini. **Room XV**
holds the famous Carpaccio *Two
Courtesans* (c. 1500); the name has
stuck, although there is no reason why
the subject should not be two perfectly
respectable married women taking the air
on an *altana* or patio mounted on the roof
of their *palazzo*.

Museo di Icone dell' Istituto
Ellenico (*Museum of Icons of the
Hellenic Institute*)
Scuoletta di San Niccolò dei Greci, Calle dei
  Greci, Castello
Tel. (041) 26281
Open Mon – Sat 9am – 12.30pm,
  3.30 – 6pm, Sun 9am – noon
🚫

The museum is annexed to the church of
San Giorgio dei Greci. It contains
precious icons – none of medieval origin,
but works by Madonnieri, Greek artists
working in the Venetian Empire, who
kept the Byzantine tradition alive into
the 17thC.

Palazzo Ducale (*Doges' Palace*) ☆☆
Piazzetta San Marco, San Marco
Tel. (041) 24951
Open Apr to mid-Oct, Mon – Sat
  8.30am – 6pm, Sun 9am – 1pm; mid-Oct
  to Mar, Mon – Sat 9am – 4pm, Sun
  9am – 1pm
🚫 🏛 ♿ ⊡

The Palazzo Ducale is primarily a
historical monument, not a picture
gallery. Once it contained highly
important works by Gentile da Fabriano,
Pisanello, Giovanni Bellini and Titian,
to mention only some of the artists who
painted scenes from Venetian history in
the Sala del Maggior Consiglio. But these
were all destroyed by fire in 1577, and the
Tintoretto and Veronese school
replacements are no substitute.

Despite the date of the building itself
(14thC and early 15thC), the interior of
the Palazzo Ducale has much more the
feel of Venice in decline than of Venice
in her heyday in the Middle Ages and
Renaissance.

Exterior This still has some important early 15thC sculpture. The sheer workmanship of the **capitals** of the ground floor arcades is worth studying; on the first floor, at the three corners, are the famous *Adam and Eve*, *Drunkenness of Noah* and *Judgment of Solomon*, partly attributed to the immigrant Florentine Lamberti, and transitional between the International Gothic and early Renaissance styles.

The **Porta della Carta** or ceremonial gateway is about 20yrs later (1438–42) and largely the work of Bartolommeo Bon.

Courtyard The **Arco Foscari** (c.1470) has a profusion of sculpture, the most important being the statues of *Adam*, *Eve* and a *Roman Hero* by Antonio Rizzo – the originals of which are housed inside the palace (see below). At the top of the **Scala dei Giganti** are the famous statues of *Neptune* and *Mars* (1554) by Jacopo Sansovino.

Interior On the first floor, in the doges' **private apartments**, are pictures by the workshop of Giovanni Bellini, by Carpaccio and, most interestingly, Bosch; a fresco decoration by Titian of *St Christopher* (1524) is the only remaining example of his work in the palace. But all these are only visible when the apartments are opened for temporary exhibitions.

Following the directed route, on the second floor, at the top of the stairs, are ceiling paintings by Tintoretto in the **Atrio Quadrato**, with the *Doge Visited by Justice* (1559–67) in the center. In the **Anticollegio** are the best pictures at present in the palace: four **mythological scenes** ★ (1577) by Tintoretto (*Vulcan*; *Mercury and the Graces*; *Bacchus*; *Minerva*); the *Return of Jacob* ★ (c.1580), a fine and representative Bassano; and a scintillating *Rape of Europa* ★ (1580) by Veronese; Veronese again on the ceiling.

In the **Collegio**, *Venice Enthroned* (c.1577) and other allegorical figures are by Veronese; around the walls are doges with saints and allegorical figures by Tintoretto's workshop. The **Senato** has paintings by the same workshop and by Palma Giovane. In the **Consiglio dei Dieci**, three of the ceiling compartments are by Veronese; the central compartment is a copy of the original, now in the Louvre.

Circulating through the armoury, you descend again – to the **Andito del Maggior Consiglio**. Off the Andito, to the left, one room contains the detached *sinopia* or underdrawing of Guariento's *Coronation of the Virgin* (1365–67), once on the throne wall of the Sala del Maggior Consiglio. The importation of the Paduan artist was significant and novel: his elaborate but convincingly constructed architecture and boldly articulated figures made a great impression. Next door, a second room contains the rather dusty and dirty statues of *Adam*, *Eve* and a *Roman Hero* by Antonio Rizzo from the Arco Foscari (see above).

In the **Sala del Maggior Consiglio**, the place of Guariento's fresco is taken by Tintoretto's vast and fiery *Paradise*, a late work (1588) at present being restored. The historical paintings on the remaining walls are merely depressing. The ceiling paintings, however, include Veronese's famous *Apotheosis of Venice* ★ (c.1583) a vast oval of palatial illusionism (near the throne wall).

Palazzo Labia ☆
Campo San Geremia, Cannaregio
Tel. (041) 716666
Visits Mon–Fri 3pm, unless official function
   being held: telephone first to check
🔲 👤 🏛

The Palazzo Labia **fresco cycle** ★★ (c.1757) is justly one of Tiepolo's most famous works. There is a gorgeously refreshing *Flora* on the ceiling of the dining room, but the glory is the Salone, frescoed from floor to ceiling, fictive architecture brilliantly interwoven with real, and the *Meeting of Antony and Cleopatra* presented, like a royal wedding, with exquisite pomp and circumstance. Neoclassicists might well have complained that the whole thing was highly anachronistic, and nothing but vanity and parade.

Palazzo Querini-Stampalia
Campiello Querini, Castello
Tel. (041) 25235
Open Tues–Sun 10am–3pm
Closed Mon
🔲 👜 ☑

This early 16thC palace was the residence of the patriarchs of Venice from 1807–50. It was then acquired by Count Querini, who bequeathed it to the city, with his library and art collection, in 1869.

The most important works are the *Conversion of St Paul* ★ (c.1540–45) by Andrea Schiavone, a wonderful picture-sketch full of movement and energy (**Room V**); the late 15thC *Presentation in the Temple* by the workshop of Giovanni Bellini, an important early example of the half-length devotional picture (**Room VIII**); two unfinished portraits, of *Francesco Querini* and his bride *Paola Priuli* (1528), by Palma Vecchio (also **Room VIII**); *Judith* by

Vincenzo Catena, a copy of a lost work by his friend Giorgione (**Room IX**); 18thC genre works by Pietro Longhi; and a striking full-length portrait by Tiepolo (**Room XVIII**).

Raccolta Peggy Guggenheim ☆ (*Guggenheim Collection*)
Palazzo Venier dei Leoni, Canal Grande, Dorsoduro
Tel. (041) 29347
Open Apr–Oct, Mon, Wed–Sun 2–6pm
Closed Nov–Mar; Tues
🎧 🎪 🏛 ☑ ♨

In the sumptuous apartments of the late Peggy Guggenheim, this is a stunning collection of modern art. Everybody who was anybody met Peggy Guggenheim, and everybody who was anybody has a picture here – from Picasso to Pollock and post-War, taking in Malevich and Kandinsky, Mondrian and Magritte, Bacon and Basaldella.

The pictures are put into store each winter and so may be subject to rearrangement. But you can expect to find several Picassos, including a Cubist *Poet* (1911); Marcel Duchamp's *Sad Young Man in a Train* (1911); a Braque *Still Life* (1912); a Juan Gris *Bottle of Rum* (1914). Cubism is therefore well represented. Of the native Futurism there is less: a *Dynamic Construction* (1913) by Boccioni; *Car and Noise* (1912) by Balla. There are interesting examples of De Stijl: a 1912 and a 1939 Mondrian; two van Doesburgs. Also, three Kandinskys and a Delaunay.

Equally strong is the Surrealist collection: Max Ernst, to whom Peggy Guggenheim was once married, is represented by numerous works; Dali, Magritte, Tanguy, Delvaux, Masson and Miró are also present, with Chagall, Chirico, Picabia and Schwitters among them. Particularly refreshing is the sculpture adorning house and garden: besides African and Oceanic carvings, there are first-class works by Calder, Brancusi, Duchamp-Villon, Arp, Pevsner, Giacometti.

Peggy Guggenheim is most famous for her promotion of Jackson Pollock and the first generation of Abstract Expressionists, and they are all here: Pollock, Tobey, Gorky, Still, Rothko, Motherwell, Baziotes, De Kooning. These works are seasoned with their European equivalents – Dubuffet, Appel and others, as well as Bacon, Mirko Basaldella (perhaps the leading post-War artist of the Veneto), Vasarély, Paolozzi, and others whose work is not easily slotted into any particular school.

There is very little in the collection later than 1960.

Salute (*Santa Maria della Salute*)
Campo della Salute, Dorsoduro
Open 8am–noon, 3–6pm
🏛

It has been nicely remarked that what was not already Rococo in this most famous work by Longhena (begun 1631) soon became so in the hands of 18thC viewpainters such as Canaletto.

Titian's *Pentecost* on the left of the nave has an interesting history. It was commissioned in 1529, but for some reason began to fall to pieces after delivery; Titian therefore repainted it some time in the 1540s.

Also in the nave (on the right) are three altarpieces by the Neapolitan painter, Luca Giordano, a *Birth*, *Presentation* and *Assumption* of the Virgin (1670s), imports which mark the absence of local talent and were influential in its revival.

In the sacristy (ask the sacristan to let you in), the ceiling paintings by Titian (c.1542) – the *Sacrifice of Isaac*, *David and Goliath*, *Cain and Abel* – show him demonstrating to Mannerist foreigners such as Vasari and Salviati, recently arrived, that he too could do contrived foreshortenings; his early altarpiece of *St Mark Enthroned between Saints* (c.1510) should emerge relucent from its current restoration. A splendid vista the equal of anything Mannerist is also achieved by Tintoretto in his *Marriage at Cana* (1561), to the right of the altar.

San Giorgio Maggiore ☆
Isola di San Giorgio Maggiore
Open 9am–12.30pm, 2–7pm
🏛

Palladio's glorious church (1565–76) contains stupendous works by Tintoretto, beginning with the *Fall of Manna* and the *Last Supper* ⋆ (both 1594), on either side of the choir. The latter was the last of Tintoretto's many workings of the same theme: Christ and the Apostles glow in a kind of mystic phosphorus; it is a haunting and unforgettable picture. To the right of the choir is the Cappella dei Morti, with another late work, the hyper-dynamic, centrifugal *Deposition* ⋆ (1592–94).

Ask one of the monks to take you upstairs from here to the Coro Invernale or Winter Choir, where you can compare Carpaccio's *St George and the Dragon* (1516) with the superior version in the SCUOLA DI SAN GIORGIO DEGLI SCHIAVONI.

Returning to the choir, note how the **high altar** and its statuary (1593) by Girolamo Campagnola are carefully organized to blend with the architectural vistas. To the right of the altar is a

Madonna with Nine Saints (1708) by
Sebastiano Ricci. This altarpiece was
much admired in the 18thC and shows
Ricci's blatant dependence on Veronese
for design and mood, if not colour.

Further down the church (first altar of
right aisle) is Jacopo Bassano's night
Nativity (1582), featuring typically
robust peasants.

San Giovanni in Bragora
Campo Bandiera e Moro, Castello
Open 8am–noon, 5.30–7pm
🏛

The high altar of this late 15thC Gothic
church has a fine **Baptism of Christ**
(c. 1494–96) by Cima da Conegliano,
perhaps the inspiration for Giovanni
Bellini's in Santa Corona in VICENZA.

To the right of the choir is the
Resurrected Christ (1498) by Alvise
Vivarini, anticipating the movement and
vigour of Titian. Compare it with the
Gothic altarpiece by Bartolommeo
Vivarini (1478), in the chapel to the left
of the choir.

San Giovanni Crisostomo
Campo San Giovanni Crisostomo,
Cannaregio
🏛

Mauro Codussi's last church
(1497–1504) has three important works.
Sebastiano del Piombo's **St John
Chrysostom ★** (1508–10) on the high
altar is remarkable for its suffused,
Giorgionesque lighting. On the first altar
of the right aisle is a late work by
Giovanni Bellini, **St Jerome with St
Louis of Toulouse and St Christopher**
(1513), while on the second altar of the
left aisle, the high relief altarpiece of the
Coronation of the Virgin ★ (1502) is one
of Tullio Lombardo's finest works,
typically precise and delicate.

Santi Giovanni e Paolo ☆
Campo Santi Giovanni e Paolo, Castello
🏛

This great Gothic edifice is the
Dominican church of Venice, the rival of
the FRARI and, with its rich array of ducal
tombs, the pantheon of the Republic.
Outside stands Verrocchio's famous
Colleoni monument, one of the most
important equestrian statues in northern
Italy.

In addition to its tombs, the church
once also contained Titian's most
celebrated altarpiece, the **Death of St
Peter Martyr**, of which a copy occupies
the original frame (second altar on left of
nave); and an important **Madonna and
Saints** by Giovanni Bellini, which
anticipated the design of his San Giobbe
altarpiece now in the ACCADEMIA. Both

paintings were burned in a fire in the
19thC.

Paintings Still preserved (second altar on
right) is Giovanni Bellini's much earlier
St Vincent Ferrer altarpiece (1469), in
which wiry line predominates. Again on
the right, the third chapel contains an
important and rare ceiling fresco by
Piazzetta, the **Glory of St Dominic**
(1727); this small but vertiginous work
was highly influential in the
development of Venetian 18thC ceiling
painting.

In the right transept, **Christ Carrying
the Cross** is a good early work by Alvise
Vivarini (1474); Lorenzo Lotto's **St
Antonio Pieruzzi, Archbishop of
Florence, Giving Alms** (1542) is rather
dull, like all his Venetian altarpieces.
The Cappella del Rosario to the left of
the nave has three ceiling paintings by
Veronese, transferred here from
elsewhere, including a superb
Annunciation ★ set between illusionistic
twisting columns.

Tombs On the interior of the facade, the
entire wall is given over to the
glorification of the Mocenigo family –
the **monument to Doge Alvise** (d. 1577)
and his wife embraces the doorway; to
the right is the **monument to Doge
Pietro ★** (c. 1476) by Pietro Lombardo; to
the left, the **monument to Doge
Giovanni** (d. 1485) by Tullio Lombardo.
Pietro Mocenigo was one of the great
warrior heroes of the Republic – hence so
much Roman soldiery on his tomb, two
reliefs illustrating his best campaigns, and
even two **Labours of Hercules**. The
tomb of the milder Giovanni is,
appropriately, more discreet.

The monuments on the left side of the
church are more important than those on
the right. On the first altar on the left is a
powerful work by Alessandro Vittoria, **St
Jerome** (1576); Vittoria was the
successor of Sansovino, much as
Tintoretto succeeded Titian, and prized
Tintoretto's kind of vigour. The
monument to Doge Niccolò Marcello
(d. 1474) is only a fragment of the
original by Pietro Lombardo, transferred
from elsewhere. Next to it is the
monument to Doge Tommaso Mocenigo
(d. 1423) by Pietro Lamberti the
Florentine and showing, if superficially,
the influence of Donatello; it set the
pattern for ducal tombs in the 15thC.

Just before the sacristy, the
monument to Doge Pasquale Malipiero
(d. 1462) is an early work by Pietro
Lombardo. In the left transept, the
monument to Doge Antonio Venier
(d. 1400) is by the Masegne brothers,
the leading sculptors of the early
International Gothic in Venice: the

smooth, graceful, rather featureless figures are typical of this style.

In the main chapel, even earlier, is a mid 14thC *Madonna and Saints* by the influential Tuscan sculptor, Nino Pisano. This is just to the left of Tullio Lombardo's magnificent **monument to Doge Andrea Vendramin** ★ (d. 1478), which takes the classicism of Pietro Mocenigo's tomb several steps further. The figures combine precision and smoothness of finish with a slight woodenness of articulation; a long way from the virile, expressive classicism of the Florentines.

A prime example of the new Florentine art, Verrocchio's **monument to Bartolommeo Colleoni** ★★ (1481–88) stands just outside the church, on an elaborately worked base, newly cleaned and restored. Although the best way to see it is from a gondola passing in front, Verrocchio's conception (it was completed after his death) is stirring from any angle and, so far as movement is concerned, certainly outdoes Donatello's Gattamelata monument at the Santo in PADUA.

San Marco ☆☆
Piazza San Marco, San Marco
Open Mon – Sat 9.30am – 5.30pm, Sun
2 – 5.30pm
🔳 *but* 🔳 *Pala d'Oro, Tesoro, Museo* 📱 🏛

The basilica of San Marco was the doges' private chapel and came to be both the church of the Venetian state and the centre of civic consciousness. The outside is a palimpsest of medieval sculpture, disposed around the building as if it were the jewels on a ducal hat. Some of it – such as the early 4thC **bronze horses**, newly restored to their gilt-bronze sheen, over the central front portal, or the porphyry *Tetrarchs*, also 4thC, built into a corner towards the PALAZZO DUCALE – was carried out within the lifetime of the Roman Empire. Most was conceived in the knowledge and emulation of the classical past, but the overall impression is distinctly medieval. Under that umbrella, the number of styles or cross-currents of style is immense, ranging from what we would nowadays recognize as classical, to Byzantine in its various moments, to Romanesque, to a Venetian and unique synthesis of several of these.

Exterior mosaics and sculpture Over the far left arch, the 13thC mosaic of the *Translation of the Body of St Mark* shows the saint being carried in front of a replica of San Marco itself, as it looked in 1260 – 70. It is usual to deplore or ignore the rest of the mosaics on the outside (all 19thC) and those of the inside that post-

date the 15thC; but in fact the mosaic tradition continued more successfully in Venice than anywhere else in Italy, and the 16thC and later mosaics often provide a truly brilliant equivalent to the effects achieved by contemporary painters in oil paint.

Also on the outside of the basilica, around the central arch, note the 13thC carvings of the *Labours of the Month* and *Occupations of Life* – in lumpy but fluent stone, an example of distinctively Venetian workmanship.

Interior mosaics In the portico, the biblical scenes in the vaults (reading from right to left, from *Genesis* on) show a narrative quality that is wholly Western; they are native workmanship of the early 13thC. The walls include 16thC mosaics, notably a *St Mark* (central bay) designed by Titian.

Among the mosaics in the main body of the basilica, some of the oldest (mid 12thC) adorn the central cupola of the nave; the *Ascension* in the central cupola of the crossing is 13thC. Some of the finest mosaics of all are the standing figures lining the walls of the nave side aisles, *Christ, Madonna* and *Prophets* ★ (c.1230); the subtlety of colour and the remote but seductive monumentality of these figures are unsurpassed.

Not only are the domes, arches and walls richly decorated but also, not least, the venerable, uneven floor; every inch of surface is precious; the experience of San Marco was intended to be total.

Other works of art A turnstile to the right of the choir gives access to the famous **Pala d'Oro** ★ or golden altarpiece (10thC – 12thC), impressive chiefly for its enamels – of different dates, styles and workmanship, but including some of the finest examples of this quintessentially medieval art to have survived anywhere in the world. The **cover** ★ painted for the Pala d'Oro by Paolo Veneziano in 1345 is now in the **Museo di San Marco** (showing otherwise chiefly tapestries) at gallery level.

Most other important medieval furniture in the basilica is kept in the **Tesoro** or treasury, entered from the right transept. There are some first-rate icons among the loot from the Sack of Constantinople, notably a 10thC **St Michael** ★ that is all gold, enamel and jewels; there are also sculptural and other fragments that far surpass the usual collection of reliquaries in cathedral treasuries.

From the 15thC, two important works should be noted in the basilica itself: the **iconostasis** ★ or choir screen by the Masegne brothers, with its fluid but slightly dwarfish and constrained bronze figures forming a shimmering line along the top; and the **Cappella dei Mascoli** ★ in the left transept (if it is open) with its marble altarpiece by an unknown sculptor and, on the left, mosaics by Giambono (1430s).

Santa Maria della Fava
Campo Santa Maria della Fava, San Marco
This small 18thC church has a number of important contemporary works. Over the second altar on the left, Piazzetta's **Madonna with St Philip Neri** (1725–27) is stark and firm in colouring and design. In contrast is the early Tiepolo over the first altar on the right, the **Education of the Virgin** (1732), which tends towards dissolution and romance. Note also the Amigoni **Visitation** (second altar on the right).

Santa Maria Formosa
Campo Santa Maria Formosa, Castello
🏛
Begun by Mauro Codussi in 1492, this is one of the prettiest churches in Venice. It contains the **Martyrdom of St Barbara** (c.1520), a fine work by Palma Vecchio that has unfortunately been dismembered and reframed (in right transept); also, a bright but airless triptych of the **Madonna of Mercy** (1473) by Bartolommeo Vivarini (first chapel on right).

Santa Maria dei Miracoli
Campo Santa Maria dei Miracoli, Castello
🏛
Sheathed in marble like a precious casket, this late 15thC Renaissance church has some of Tullio Lombardo's most perfect and delicate **decorative sculpture** ★ (in the marble choir railings).

San Niccolò da Tolentino
Campo dei Tolentini, Santa Croce
This grand, early 17thC church with 18thC columned portico has (right wall of choir) a boldly worked **Annunciation** by the late 17thC Neapolitan painter, Luca Giordano; and (on left of choir arch) a **St Jerome** by the German painter Johann Liss, one of the best and most influential talents operating in early 17thC Venice.

San Polo (*San Paolo*)
Campo San Polo, San Polo
A heavily restored Gothic church containing works by Tintoretto (entrance wall and first altar on right) and Veronese (in chapel to left of main chapel) but its greatest paintings are by the Tiepolo family.
   Giambattista Tiepolo's altarpiece of the **Virgin Appearing to St Julian Nepomuk** (1754, second altar on left) is

rich with ethereal colours, but perhaps even more interesting are the **Stations of the Cross** ★ (1747) by his son Giandomenico (in the atrium at the beginning of the nave). Here, Giandomenico's colours have more life than usual, the compositions are sometimes dramatic, the treatment almost moving.

San Rocco
Campo San Rocco, San Polo
Tintoretto painted dynamic pictures not only for the SCUOLA DI SAN ROCCO but also for the church opposite. **St Roch Healing the Plague-Stricken** (1549, right wall of choir) and the **Pool of Bethesda** (1577–86, right wall of nave) are classic examples.

San Salvatore
Campo San Salvador, San Marco
This largely Renaissance (early 16thC) church contains two important works by Titian: a **Transfiguration** (c.1560) over the high altar – dirty, difficult to see and so difficult to appreciate – and (over the third altar on the right) another late work, a spirited **Annunciation** (1566).
   In the chapel to the left of the choir, the **Supper at Emmaus** is a copy of a late 15thC original by Giovanni Bellini. On the right of the nave, the **monument to Doge Francesco Venier** (1556–61) is by Jacopo Sansovino.

San Sebastiano ☆
Campo San Sebastiano, Dorsoduro
Although rather out of the way, San Sebastiano is a not-to-be-missed delight, an ecclesiastical equivalent to Veronese's frescoes in the Villa Barbaro at MASER.
   The late Titian **St Nicholas** (c.1570, first chapel on right) and Andrea Schiavone's **Christ on the Road to Emmaus** (c.1557, first chapel on left) pale into insignificance beside this joyous, gaudy, exuberant, pageant of colour. Veronese is on the altars, on the walls, on both sides of the organ doors, on the ceiling and even in the monks' gallery above the nave (the sacristan will show the way). As a typical witty detail, note that in the frescoes furthest up the nave, archers on one side shoot across the church at St Sebastian on the other.

San Stae (*Sant'Eustachio*)
Campo San Stae, Santa Croce
Open 10am–1pm
A fine church facing on to the Grand Canal. In the choir, a series of **Twelve Apostles** introduces the leading lights of the new 18thC Venetian school. On the left is the **Martyrdom of St James** by Piazzetta and the **Liberation of St Peter**

by Sebastiano Ricci; on the right, Tiepolo's ***Martyrdom of St Bartholomew***. Piazzetta's intensely solid paintwork and Caravaggesque lighting emerge most memorably.

San Zaccaria
Campo San Zaccaria, Castello
Open 10am–noon, 4–6pm
🏛

Inside Mauro Codussi's late 15thC church, the famous **San Zaccaria altarpiece** ★ (1505) by Giovanni Bellini dominates the left wall in its newly cleaned, astonishingly bright condition. Mellow and full of light, it is one of the finest statements of his late style.

Off to the right, in the apse vault of the attached **Cappella di San Tarasio**, there are frescoes by the Florentine painter, Andrea del Castagno (1442) that announced in Venice the new regime of Donatello – without any immediate effect, however. The Gothic altarpieces on either side of the altar, by Antonio Vivarini and Giovanni d'Alemagna, are in fact slightly later than Castagno's frescoes.

Scuola dei Carmini ☆
Campo Carmini, Dorsoduro
Tel. (041) 26553
Open Mon–Sat 8.30am–noon, 2–5pm,
Sun 8.30am–noon
📷 👓

Longhena's late 17thC building once housed the headquarters of the Carmelite *scuola* or confraternity. Its chief glory is the ceiling of the **Salone Superiore** (1739–44) frescoed by Tiepolo.

In the center, the ***Virgin Delivering a Scapula to St Simon Stock*** ★★ is one of the artist's greatest works. The subject is indeed extraordinary (the scapula is the insignia of the Carmelite order) but Tiepolo handles it in a gorgeously fanciful spirit. Some of the finest figures are the ***Virtues*** at the outer corners, who seem almost more like chorus-girls, reclining in opulent splendour. Among the subordinate scenes there is the rescue by an angel of a mason falling from a scaffold. What better subject than this for Tiepolo to transform into an ethereal vision?

Scuola di San Giorgio degli Schiavoni ☆
Calle Furlani, Castello
Tel. (041) 28828
Open Mon–Sat 10am–12.30pm,
3.30–6pm, Sun 10am–noon
📷 👓 ♿

The *scuola* was built in the 16thC by a confraternity of Slavs. It is famous for its sequence of charmingly meticulous paintings by Carpaccio. These were executed between 1502 and 1511, but not as a single programme.

The justly celebrated scenes are those of ***St George and the Dragon***, revelling in a well-stocked and orderly world subordinate to the demands of perspective and Christianity; ***St Triphon before the Emperor Gordianus***; and, best of all, scenes from the ***Legend of St Jerome*** ★ which include the famous picture of ***St Augustine in His Study*** ★★

Scuola di San Rocco ☆
Campo San Rocco, San Polo
Tel. (041) 34864
Open Mon–Fri 10am–1pm, Sat, Sun
10am–1pm, 3–6pm
📷 👓 ♿

The story goes that Tintoretto won the commission to decorate the *scuola* of the confraternity of St Roch because, instead of the sketch the competitors were asked to produce, he finished and installed an entire ceiling roundel. (This is the one you can see in the center of the Albergo or committee room.)

The first works (1564–66), and in some respects the finest, are all in the **Albergo** (reached through the vast upper hall). Here are the ***Crucifixion*** ★★ with a Cross that seems to lean forward out of the picture with almost 3D-cinema illusionism and (on the opposite wall) the ***Road to Calvary*** ★ with its compelling upward zigzag.

Also in this room (on easels) are a ***Dead Christ*** (c.1500) of doubtful origin and ***Christ Carrying the Cross*** (1508–9), which is disputed between Giorgione and Titian, but is clearly by Giorgione.

The scenes in the **upper hall** (1576–81) are the most dynamic of all. On the walls are New Testament subjects; on the ceiling, Old Testament. Notice especially the exquisitely seductive ***Temptation in the Garden*** and, with its convenient excuse for dramatic airborne effects, the ***Ascension***. The relentless, phosphorescent dynamism of these works may eventually begin to tire. Before leaving the upper hall, note the early Tiepolo ***Abraham and the Angel*** (c.1720) by the altar, its heavy modelling and murky background showing the influence of Piazzetta.

Some of the paintings in the **lower hall** (1583–87) are less frenetic than those above. ***St Mary of Egypt*** and ***St Mary Magdalen***, facing each other, are set in almost swampily vegetal, eerie landscapes; nearby, the ***Flight into Egypt*** ★ has a tender, lyrical quality not often found in Tintoretto.

Venetian palace interiors

Visitors to Venice must frequently be curious as to what lies behind the innumerable palace facades that line the city's canals. Four of the most magnificent of these palaces – the PALAZZO DUCALE, CA' D'ORO, CA' PESARO and CA' REZZONICO – will be seen in the course of any standard tour of the city; yet the vast majority are not officially open to the public, are rarely described in guidebooks and – unlike the city's churches – have no plaques outside them to indicate the treasures contained within. All this should not deter the interested tourist: these palaces now house mainly offices and institutions, and can simply be visited by seeking the assistance of the porter.

A tour of this little known side to Venice can begin with a part of the Palazzo Ducale now divided off from the main building and called the **Palazzo Patriarcale**; it is entered from the Calle Canonica. Once inside you should ask to see the Sala dei Banchetti. This is a massive 18thC banqueting hall, with a ceiling completely frescoed in 1760 by Jacopo Guarana, a follower of Tiepolo, in collaboration with the ornamentalist Francesco Zanchi. The frescoes, representing allegories of **Virtues**, were the last major artistic commission of the Republic; their unveiling was one of the most celebrated events of the Venetian 18thC.

A short walk to the N of the Palazzo Patriarcale, along the Calle Specchieri and Merceria San Zulian, brings you to the **Palazzo Dandalo**, known in the second half of the 18thC for its notorious gambling hall, the Ridotto Venier. Only aristocrats or those wearing masks were allowed to enter the Ridotto; it was closed down by the Republic in 1774, in an effort to prevent the nobility from losing all their money to foreigners. The interior is as intimate as the Sala dei Banchetti is grand, and comprises a series of tiny rooms with walls and ceilings covered with some of the finest and most fantastic Rococo stuccoes in the city.

Going W from here, through the Campo Manin, you eventually reach the **Palazzo Sandi Porto** at Calle dell' Albero 3870. The interior of this rather dark and sinister building is now divided into a series of private apartments. The main room on the first floor contains one of Tiepolo's earliest ceiling frescoes. No one now lives in this part of the palace, and it can be difficult to find a porter who will let you in. Those who persevere will be rewarded by the sight of a fresco of quite astonishing power, the **Triumph of Eloquence** (1724–25). It is a dark and melodramatic work, with figures disposed around the rim of the ceiling as if by some centrifugal force.

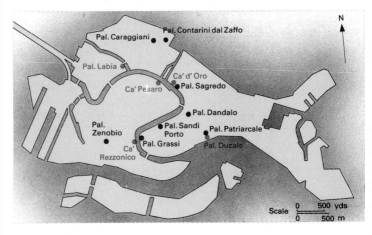

The staircase of the Palazzo Grassi, frescoed by an unknown 18thC artist.

The Salizzada San Samuele and Calle delle Carrozze, to the W of the Palazzo Sandi, lead to the Campo San Samuele, dominated on the N side by the 18thC **Palazzo Grassi**. This is one of the masterpieces of Giorgio Massari, the 18thC Venetian architect who built the Ca' Rezzonico just across the Grand Canal. The Palazzo Grassi houses the Centro delle Arti e del Costume, which puts on exhibitions devoted mainly to folklore and costume. It has a grand marble staircase with charming mid 18thC frescoes featuring figures in contemporary costume staring down at the spectator from behind a fictive balcony. The artist is unknown.

Just to the W of the Ca' Rezzonico, at Fondamenta Foscarini 2597, is the late 17thC **Palazzo Zenobio**. The enormous ground floor Salone has walls covered with mirrors and exuberant Baroque stuccowork, and a frescoed ceiling by the leading Venetian decorator of the late Baroque, Ludovico Dorigny.

One of the least visited and in many ways most enchanting parts of the city is the northern district known as Cannaregio. On the S edge of this is the PALAZZO LABIA, famous for its gloriously ethereal Tiepolo frescoes, perhaps the very finest of this artist's mature works. Two of Cannaregio's long parallel thoroughfares have palaces frescoed by his son, Giandomenico. The **Palazzo Contarini dal Zaffo** at Fondamenta Gaspare Contarini 3539 has a ceiling fresco by Giandomenico (1784) in the first floor Salone. The room is now the sitting room of an old people's home but occasional visitors who are prepared to make themselves pleasant to staff and residents provide a welcome distraction.

The interior of the **Palazzo Caraggiani** at Fondamenta della Sensa 3336 is so small that it seems almost like that of a dolls' house. There are two rooms here with frescoes by Giandomenico (1790–95). The exceptionally delicate and simple style of these works – in one case, just a few birds against a clear white background – is strikingly different from the grand allegorical manner displayed by the artist in the Palazzo Contarini. Such simplicity indicates the changing attitudes towards decoration at the very end of the 18thC.

Making your way back to the Piazza San Marco, you may like to have a brief look at the staircase vestibule of the **Palazzo Sagredo** on the Strada Nuova. On one of its enormous walls is portrayed the *Fall of the Giants* (1734). The effect the artist aimed for was of the whole building collapsing around the spectator; unfortunately his technical abilities were not up to it. These truly abysmal frescoes are by none other than Pietro Longhi, the well known specialist in intimate genre scenes of 18thC Venetian life. Looking at the Palazzo Sagredo frescoes, one can only sympathize with the artist in his subsequent decision to abandon a Baroque manner and work on a small scale.

VERONA
Veneto Map A5

On a broad bend of the river Adige, at a crossroads of routes N and S, E and W, Verona today is still one of the most prosperous cities in Italy. Its long, straight streets (with slightly tilting buildings) link pleasant squares and some remarkable Roman, medieval and Renaissance monuments.

Arche Scaligere ☆
Via delle Arche Scaligere
Open Tues – Sun 9am – noon,
2.30 – 5.30pm
Closed Mon
🔟

These are the grandest medieval tombs in all Italy, erected by members of the della Scala dynasty that ruled Verona from 1260 until toppled by the Visconti of Milan in 1387. Their peculiar form is partly explained by the fact that they are really church tombs, loaded with secular imagery derived from the classical past.

The earliest canopied tomb is the **tomb of Cangrande I** (d.1329), host of Dante and patron of Giotto; the most lavish, but not the best sculpted, is the **tomb of Cansignorio** (d.1375). The original of Cangrande's equestrian statue is now in the MUSEO CIVICO D'ARTE.

Duomo
Piazza del Duomo
🏛

Despite the Romanesque portal, the Duomo is a 15thC and 16thC rebuilding. The first three altars on each side of the nave have enormous early 16thC **fresco surrounds** by Falconetto – highly festive exercises in imaginary triumphal architecture. On the first altar on the left is a gloriously vigorous *Assumption* (1530 – 32) by Titian.

The apse of the choir is also frescoed (1534), by Francesco Torbido, a local artist, to designs by Giulio Romano.

Museo Archeologico
Rigaste del Redentore
Tel. (045) 25360
Open Tues – Sun 9am – noon,
2.30 – 5.30pm
Closed Mon
🔟 🏛 ☑

The museum is located beside the Roman theater, with fine views across the river Adige towards the city center. Its local finds include a few mosaics and some good-quality bronzes.

Museo Civico d'Arte ☆
Castelvecchio, Corso Castelvecchio

Tel. (045) 28817, 594734
Open Tues – Sun 8.30am – 7pm
Closed Mon
🔟 🏛 ☑ ☟

The Castelvecchio was the seat of della Scala power but was much damaged in the 19thC and in World War II. It has now been rebuilt as an attractive modern gallery.

Ground floor Flanking the river Adige, these rooms hold mainly Roman and medieval relics of browsing interest. But, towards the end of the range, **Room XI** has a unique collection of **International Gothic pictures** ★ dating from the late 14thC and early 15thC. The *Madonna of the Rose Garden*, attributed to Stefano da Verona, is set in a world of distant fantasy, yet crammed with realistic detail, while the *Madonna of the Quail* by Pisanello, supposedly trained by Stefano, shows greater discipline, but is still sugary-sweet. There are also three works by Pisanello's rival, Jacopo Bellini, father-figure of Venetian Renaissance painting: despite being damaged, the *St Jerome* shows his interest in light and has a landscape layout that was advanced for its time.

Upper floor The collection now moves firmly into the Renaissance, with late 15thC and early 16thC works: a *Madonna* by Mantegna, another by Giovanni Bellini, and an important collection of local Renaissance masters such as Liberale da Verona, Girolamo dai Libri and Francesco Morone.

Half way along the room sequence is the **equestrian statue of Cangrande** from the ARCHE SCALIGERE. Moving on into the later 16thC (**Room XXIII**), there is a fine *Deposition* ★ by Veronese, with wonderful density of colour, and several good works by Tintoretto and Jacopo Bassano; also a Lotto portrait.

Passing through the main 17thC rooms, you come to some fine late 17thC and 18thC works (**Rooms XXVI** and **XXVII**), including two bold, colourful paintings by Luca Giordano, *Bacchus and Ariadne* ★ and *Diana and Endymion* ★ also a nice little Guardi landscape, a *bozzetto* or sketch for a ceiling by Tiepolo, and works by Sebastiano Ricci and Pietro Longhi.

Sant' Anastasia
Piazza Sant' Anastasia
🏛

Two unusual stone **gobbi** or hunchbacks, carved in the 16thC, greet you as you enter the church. This is a richly decorated Gothic edifice, with only one important work: *St George and the Princess* ★ (c.1436) by Pisanello.

This fresco was originally located

above the arch of the first chapel to the right of the choir, but is now in the Cappella Giusti off the left transept. It is a classic statement of International Gothic gorgeousness, but incorporates Pisanello's particular brand of sometimes gruesome realism.

San Fermo Maggiore
Stradone San Fermo
🏛

The interesting works of art are in the upper church – fragments of **frescoes** by Stefano da Verona (early 15thC, right wall of nave) and by Lorenzo Veneziano (mid 14thC, beside the arch leading into the choir). On the left of the nave is the remarkable **Brenzoni monument** (c.1427–39) by Nanni di Bartolo, a Florentine associate of Donatello; besides a life-size tableau of the *Resurrection*, it features a beautiful frescoed *Annunciation* ⋆ by Pisanello.

San Giorgio in Braida
Via Sant' Alessio
🏛

This grand Renaissance church, enriched in particular by Sanmichele, is also known as San Giorgio Maggiore. On the high altar is one of Veronese's finest works – certainly his greatest in his native city – the *Martyrdom of St George* ⋆ (c.1566). The painting is in magnificent condition, the colours still heightening the grandeur of the scene and uplifting the spectator into a world of heroic pageantry.

There are also interesting works by Romanino, notably his organ shutters of *St George before the Judge* (1540), in the right transept, and a confident *Madonna and Saints* by Moretto of the same date, on the left of the choir.

San Giovanni in Valle
Via San Giovanni in Valle
🏛

This picturesque late 12thC Romanesque church, more or less unaltered, contains a notable **4thC sarcophagus** that mingles Christian with pagan imagery.

San Paolo
Via degli Artiglieri
The church contains a classic Veronese *Madonna* (c.1565), in which the Virgin looks down from off-center to a crowd of excited saints around the steps below.

San Zeno Maggiore ✩ ✩
Piazza San Zeno
🏛

San Zeno is one of the masterpieces of northern Italian Romanesque architecture. The facade bears a charming and typical hodgepodge of relief sculpture, surrounding the celebrated bronze doors of the portal.
Bronze doors ⋆ Two styles can be seen in the plaques nailed on to the door compartments: one of about 1140, the other of the late 12thC or early 13thC (and slightly inferior); the subjects are episodes from the Old and New Testaments and from the life of St Zeno.

These doors have nothing of the classicism or fluency of the bronze doors of Hildesheim, cast each in one piece more than 100yrs earlier, but they do have a narrative immediacy recalling the Bayeux Tapestry and their naïveté is quite compelling.
San Zeno triptych ⋆⋆ (1457–59) Mantegna's masterpiece is one of the most important statements of the early Renaissance in all Italy. Unfortunately, subsequent rearrangements have covered the window that was specially cut to light it; the lighting in the panels was precisely coordinated with the light from the window to create the maximum possible illusionism. But the figures still stand like animated statues, urging the spectator to devotion by their powerful presence.

The fictive framework must have closely resembled the real framework of Donatello's high altar in the Santo in PADUA, but the classicism is of Mantegna's own brand. To complete this triptych, he delayed taking up his appointment with the Gonzaga in Mantua, where he remained for the rest of his life. The predella panels are copies of the originals.

VICENZA
Veneto Map B5

The city of Palladio was a notable but never powerful medieval city; its golden age was indeed the 16thC. Not only is it magnificently adorned with Palladio's architecture (the city had suffered badly in the Wars of Cambrai and was ripe for redevelopment) but it is also one of the pleasantest cities to visit in all Italy.

Basilica di Monte Berico
Viale X Giugno
The basilica is to the S of the city, high up on a hill behind the railway station
In the refectory off the cloister of this rather overblown 17thC Baroque monument, the **Banquet of Gregory the Great** (1572) by Veronese once rivalled his *Feast in the House of Levi* in the VENICE Accademia, but suffered appalling damage; it is still a glorious work, in scale and richness if not in every detail and spark of colour.

Duomo
Piazza del Duomo
Behind its fine Gothic facade, the
Duomo houses one important work: a
richly glittering Lorenzo Veneziano
polyptych (1356), in the fifth chapel on
the right.

Museo Civico
Palazzo Chiericati, Piazza Matteotti
Tel. (0444) 39534
Open Tues–Sun 9.30am–noon,
   2.30–5pm
Closed Mon
🖼 🏛

The Palazzo Chiericati in which the
museum is housed is a particularly
satisfying Palladio creation, just opposite
his Teatro Olimpico in the old Castello.
The usual archaeological collection
(including Lombard finds) on the ground
floor is enhanced by a ceiling fresco, the
Council of the Gods, by Zelotti. The
picture gallery is upstairs.
Gothic and Early Renaissance The
collection begins with the *Death of the
Virgin* and *Sts Antony and Francis* from
an important dated polyptych by Paolo
Veneziano (1333). The late 15thC
Crucifixion by Memlinc is also very fine.
There follows a large number of religious
works by Bartolommeo Montagna, who,
with Giovanni Buonconsiglio il
Marescalco, was the leading local artist of
the late 15thC/early 16thC; his style
most obviously relates to Giovanni
Bellini, but there is a mainland vigour in
the line. The 1489 *Madonna* by Cima da
Conegliano is by contrast softer, more
waxy.
High Renaissance The *Madonna and
Saints* (c.1550) by Veronese is an
unusual work for this artist, with bold,
charged forms rivalling Tintoretto but in
his own luscious colours. *St Augustine
Healing the Spastics* is a fine Tintoretto,
the figures brilliantly placed in deep space
to maximum effect.
Baroque There are several works by the
Veronese master Francesco Maffei,
including a copy after Titian's lost *St
Peter Martyr* in Santi Giovanni e Paolo
in VENICE; the sketch by Johan Liss for
his *St Jerome* in San Niccolò da
Tolentino (also in Venice) is equally
interesting. The *Three Ages of Man* is a
rare van Dyck, sometimes overrated on
this account. Four history paintings by
Luca Giordano are typical, generously
formed works.
Eighteenth Century The collection
includes two mythologies by Pittoni;
Time Discovering Truth, a work of
consummately elegant lechery by
Tiepolo; and a powerful, sombre *St
Francis* by Piazzetta.

Santa Corona ☆
Contrà Santa Corona
🏛

The church is an important example of
Dominican Gothic with mostly
Renaissance fitments, notably the late
15thC intarsia (inlaid) choir stalls and the
extremely elaborate early 16thC altar
frame for Giovanni Bellini's *Baptism of
Christ* ★★ (last on the left before the
transept). Dated 1500, this is one of the
finest statements of Giovanni's late style.
The strength and boldness of the colours
are remarkable, but even more
astonishing is the enormous landscape, in
which form seems almost to shimmer
between something tactile on the surface
and something optical in depth.
   The *Adoration of the Magi* (1573) by
Veronese (middle chapel on the right) is
perhaps spoiled by over-varnishing.

San Niccolò da Tolentino
Contrà Ponte San Michele
For those particularly interested in the
Baroque, this 17thC oratory is a rich,
complete period piece to rival the
Madonna del Soccorso in ROVIGO; it
again features paintings by Francesco
Maffei.

Santo Stefano
Contrà Santo Stefano
In the left transept is a particularly fine
and representative Palma Vecchio, the
Madonna Enthroned with Saints
(c.1525), grand, confident, still solidly
High Renaissance, with not a hint of the
affectations of Mannerism.

Villa Valmarana dei Nani ☆
Via dei Nani
Tel. (0444) 21803
Open mid-Mar to mid-Nov: Mon–Fri
   3–5.30pm, Sat 10am–noon,
   3–5.30pm, Sun 10am–noon
Closed mid-Nov to mid-Mar
🖼 🛏 🍴

*The villa lies to the S of the city, E of Monte
   Berico, off the road to Este*
The villa is unimportant architecturally,
but it has two series of extremely
important **frescoes** ★ (begun 1757): those
by Giambattista Tiepolo assisted by his
son Giandomenico in the main house,
and those by Giandomenico alone in the
foresteria or guesthouse.
Villa The father's touch is always evident
– he painted in broad, unusually free
strokes, and with such matchless,
heavenly colours. The subject matter is
indeed out of this world: operatic scenes
from chivalric romance, machinations of
the classical gods, mythological visions of
a wholly fantastic epic past. Nowhere else
did Tiepolo offer richer fuel to

Neoclassicist complaint. The meaning of
the stories can be discovered from cards
made available.
Foresteria Beside his father's,
Giandomenico's brushwork seems tame.
Although most of his genre scenes are
artificial, comparable for instance with
Boucher's landscapes, others feature
landaus and black tailored suits, giving a
foretaste of 19thC Realism.

A short walk down the narrow path
opposite the gate leads to Palladio's
famous **Villa Rotonda** (**◪** *Grounds only
open 9am–noon, 3–7pm*), lacking
frescoes to match the architecture.

VIPITENO (*STERZING*)
*Bolzano, Trentino-Alto Adige
Map B2*
This picturesque little town beneath the
Brenner Pass looks and feels entirely
Austrian. It became part of Italy for the
first time only after World War I.

Museo Civico
*Piazza Città 3
Open Mon–Sat 9–11am, 3–5pm
Closed Sun*
◪
The museum contains the **shutters** ★
(1456–58) representing the *Life of Mary*
and the *Passion of Christ* from the
altarpiece by Hans Multscher, of which
the remaining extant parts are still in the
local church. Multscher's style is one
generation from the International
Gothic: a sweet, rather plodding
expression predominates, in slightly
bolder, more simplified forms.

Parrocchiale
Via dell' Ospedale
The main altar incorporates five statues
from the original Multscher altarpiece
(see MUSEO CIVICO, above).

VITTORIO VENETO
Treviso, Veneto Map C4
The modern town consists of a couple of
very long streets linking two ancient and
once distinct settlements, Ceneda and
Serravalle.

Museo del Cenedese
*Piazza Flaminio, Serravalle
Open Tues–Sun 10am–noon, 4–6.30pm
Closed Mon*
◪ ▥ 🏛
The museum is housed in an attractive
building, the late 15thC Loggia
Serravallese. Most interesting are the
murals (c.1515) on the end walls of the
ground and first floors. By Francesco da
Milano, they express ideals of Venetian
rule.

Sant' Andrea di Bigonzo
*Via Sant' Andrea/Via Antonello da
Serravalle, Serravalle*
This is an interesting 14thC church, with
odd tabernacles at the corners of the
aisleless nave instead of side chapels.
These are richly decorated, like the walls
between them, with frescoes dating from
the 14thC to the 16thC.

San Giovanni Battista
Via Mazzini, Serravalle
A series of mid 15thC frescoes in the first
chapel on the right is transitional in style
between International Gothic and early
Renaissance. In the second chapel on the
right are slightly later frescoes, by
Antonio Zago.

Santa Giustina
Via Marconi, Serravalle
The **tomb of Riccardo VI da Camino**
(d.1335) survives in a side chapel. By an
unknown Venetian sculptor, it consists
of a Gothic sarcophagus supported by six
magnificent **Romanesque warriors** ★
stolen from another monument.

San Lorenzo
*Piazza Tiziano, Serravalle
Apply to Museo del Cenedese for entry*
The frescoes all round the church are
similar in date to those in SAN GIOVANNI
BATTISTA, but not by the same hand.
They have only recently been discovered.

Santa Maria del Meschio
Piazza Meschio, Ceneda
The *Annunciation* (1514) by Andrea
Previtali, on the main altar, has a
beautiful landscape that reproduces the
profile of the hill behind Ceneda.

NORTH CENTRAL ITALY

The north-central regions have some of the loveliest of all Italian countryside and are overwhelmingly rich in works of art, above all in masterpieces of the early Renaissance.

TOSCANA (*Tuscany*)

The magically evocative landscape of Tuscany, dotted with flickering vines and the darker greens of cypresses, is for many people the very essence of Italy. At its center is Florence; to the W is a chain of cities – Prato, Pistoia, Lucca, Pisa – celebrated for the colourful beauty of their Romanesque architecture and sculpture and for some fine Renaissance monuments. Close to Florence, the glamour of the Medici lingers on in a series of lovely villas at Artimino and Castello. To the E are the ancient Etruscan cities of Cortona and Arezzo; the frescoes by Piero della Francesca at Arezzo are perhaps the most deeply moving of all Renaissance works. To the S lies the lovely medieval city of Siena, rich in works by celebrated artists – Duccio, Simone Martini, Ambrogio Lorenzetti and Jacopo della Quercia; still further S, in a strange, rugged landscape riven with gullies, are the tiny ideal Renaissance cities of Pienza and Montepulciano.

UMBRIA

Umbria is less open than Tuscany; its deep valleys are ringed by wooded mountains; the towns perch dramatically on rocky hills. Umbria's history in the Middle Ages was particularly bloody, and these are defiant, grim towns, their strength symbolized by the austere palaces that flank their main squares – as at Perugia, Todi and Gubbio. Streets tend to be steep alleyways and crooked staircase lanes, criss-crossed by bridges and arches – as at Spoleto, Trevi and Assisi.

In the 13thC, the beauty of Umbria inspired St Francis' *Canticle of the Sun* and art flourished here as never before; celebrated painters and sculptors from all over Italy were called to decorate the basilica at Assisi and the

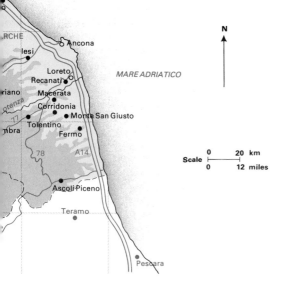

glittering marble cathedral of Orvieto. These centers stand out, yet many small towns retain fading frescoes – perhaps the best are at Montefalco and tiny Spello. In the 16thC Perugino dominated Umbrian art and fine works by him remain at Perugia.

MARCHE (*Marches*)

The Marches are generally less well known to the art traveller; their unspoilt, mountainous landscape is perhaps the most beautiful in all Italy, and there is a real sense of discovery in coming across a splendid Bellini altarpiece in the Pinacoteca at Pesaro. The area was too remote to produce a great artistic tradition, yet Allegretto Nuzi at Fabriano painted in a colourful decorative style that looks forward to Gentile da Fabriano; Crivelli spent many years in the Marches and left important works at Ascoli Piceno; later, Lorenzo Lotto worked here, leaving particularly good collections of his pictures at Iesi, Recanati and Loreto. The two outstanding artistic centers are Urbino, where Federico da Montefeltro's inspired patronage produced one of the most lucid and harmonious of all Renaissance palaces; and Loreto, which attracted many celebrated artists to work on the Santuario della Santa Casa.

ANCONA
Marche Map F3

A flourishing port in Roman times, Ancona was prey to many invading forces during the Dark Ages and suffered a number of humiliating defeats before regaining its importance in medieval times. The new town is busy and bustling as befits the capital of the region while the old town, although badly damaged in the two World Wars and by an earthquake in 1972, retains its ancient charm. The Arco di Traiano, or Arch of Trajan, was erected in AD115 in honour of the Emperor, who extended and developed the port.

Museo Diocesano
Via Giovanni XXIII
Closed for restoration
The museum is on the left of the Duomo – an important Romanesque cathedral, built on the site of a temple of Venus, with a 13thC facade and cupola. It is chiefly noted for its archaeological collection, which includes the 4thC **sarcophagus of Flavius Gorgonius**, decorated with some of the earliest illustrations of scenes from the New Testament.

Museo Nazionale delle Marche
Palazzo Ferretti
Closed for restoration
This museum has a large collection of antiquities illustrating the ancient civilization of Picenum. Perhaps the most fascinating of the archaic Picene works – and a rare example of large-scale sculpture – is the head of a **Warrior** ★ from Numana, with its disconcerting bulging eyes and severely simplified shapes. There are some fine **bronzes** ★ among the Etruscan exhibits. Among the Roman works, note especially the **mosaics** and fragments of a gilded bronze **equestrian statue** from Cartoceto di Pergola.

Pinacoteca Civica e Galleria d'Arte Moderna
Palazzo Bosdari, Via Pizzecolli 17
Tel. (071) 56342, 204262
Open Tues–Sat 9am–7pm, Sun
  9am–1pm
Closed Mon
▨ ▨ ▨
Housed in the 16thC Palazzo Bosdari, the Pinacoteca boasts an exquisite **Madonna** (c.1480) by Crivelli and an important early Titian, the **Madonna with St Francis, St Louis of Toulouse and Alvise Gozzi** ★ (1520).

The Titian is a luminous work with, in the distance, a poignant view of Venice seen across the lagoon. The composition is closely related to Raphael's **Madonna of Foligno** in the Musei Vaticani (see Rome, *SOUTH CENTRAL ITALY*) but where Raphael's work is tranquil and carefully balanced, Titian's glowing picture is full of passionate feeling and movement; the towering figures and the bare branches of the tree are boldly silhouetted against a twilight sky; dramatic gestures and expression link the saints and donor in the foreground with the Madonna and Child. The picture was originally in the church of SAN FRANCESCO DELLE SCALE and is Titian's first dated work.

Also of interest are a **Madonna and Saints** (1546) by Lotto, an **Immaculate Conception** by Guercino, and works by the Ancona-born painter Andrea Lilli (1555–1610).

The gallery of modern art has contemporary graphics, sculpture and paintings, mainly by artists from the Marches.

San Domenico
Piazza del Plebiscito
This undistinguished church is worth a visit for the moving and dramatic **Crucifixion** ★ (1557) by Titian in the apse, and for the Baroque **Annunciation** by Guercino on the first altar on the left of the nave.

San Francesco delle Scale
Piazza San Francesco
The Gothic **portal** has statues and reliefs by Giorgio Orsini (1454). Inside there is an early 16thC **Assumption** by Lotto, who came from Venice to paint it, intending to stay only a few months in the Marches. In fact, he never returned to his native city and ended his days in LORETO.

Santa Maria della Piazza
Piazza Santa Maria
🏛
Built in the 13thC on the remains of two earlier churches, Santa Maria has a Romanesque facade decorated with **sculptures** by Maestro Filippo (1210). The interior has some interesting early **mosaics** dating from the 5thC and a 16thC wooden **crucifix**.

AREZZO
Toscana Map D3

The ancient city of Arezzo was a powerful member of the Etruscan federation, and retained its importance under the Romans. The city is set on a gentle slope, with a backdrop of mountains, and is mainly medieval in appearance. There are quiet squares, and steep alleys twisting down the hill from the cathedral and from the sloping, irregular Piazza Grande – one of the loveliest squares in Italy. On the flat land around, a new town is spreading.

Casa di Giorgio Vasari
Via XX Settembre 55
Tel. (0575) 20295
Open Tues – Sat 9am – 2pm, Sun
  9am – 1pm
Closed Mon
🔟 🏛

Vasari's own house was designed and decorated by the great biographer, painter and architect between 1540–48. Here he wore his immense erudition lightly, and the charming Mannerist decorations are enlivened by *trompe l'oeil* jokes and by sophisticated yet playful allusions to his life.

Duomo
Piazza del Duomo
This impressive Gothic building was begun in 1277, but has an early 20thC facade. The fine stained-glass windows are mainly by Guillaume de Marcillat and date from the early 16thC.

In the second bay of the right aisle is the Gothic **tomb of Gregory X** (d. 1276); over the high altar, the 14thC **tomb of St Donatus**, decorated with reliefs showing scenes from the *Life of St Donatus* and the *Life of St Gregory*, by Aretine and Florentine artists.

At the bottom of the left aisle is Piero della Francesca's *St Mary Magdalen* ★ (after 1446). Beside it is the elaborate **tomb of Bishop Guido Tarlati** (1330) by Agostino di Giovanni and Agnolo di Ventura; the design has been ascribed to Giotto; the tomb is decorated with scenes showing the life of the warlike Bishop.

In the **Cappella della Madonna** there are outstanding 15thC **terra cottas** ★ by Andrea della Robbia and his school; in the sacristy, a detached fresco of *St Jerome* by Bartolommeo della Gatta, an Aretine artist.

Museo Archeologico Mecenate
Via Margaritone 10
Tel. (0575) 20882
Open Tues – Sat 9am – 2pm, Sun
  9am – 1pm
Closed Mon
🔟 ☑

The museum is housed in a 16thC monastery built over the ruins of an old Roman amphitheater. It displays Roman and Etruscan objects found in the city and some fine bronzes, metalwork and

urns from **CHIUSI**. The highlight is the celebrated collection of **coralline vases** ★ in Room VII; these dark red, terra-cotta vases, decorated with reliefs of gods and goddesses and flowers, were made from the end of the 1stC BC to the middle of the 1stC AD.

Museo Statale d'Arte Medioevale e Moderna
Via San Lorentino
Tel. (0575) 23868
Open Tues – Sat 9am – 2pm, Sun
  9am – 1pm
Closed Mon
🔟 🏛 ☑ 🐾

This collection traces the development of painting in Arezzo from the 13thC to the 16thC; it is imaginatively and informatively displayed in an elegant 15thC palace – the courtyard perhaps by Bernardo Rossellino.

The display opens with works by the 13thC painter, Margaritone d'Arezzo. The graceful, late Gothic works of Spinello Aretino and Parri di Spinelli (note especially his delicately patterned *Madonna della Misericordia*) are followed by the tense and highly personal realism of two pictures of *St Roch* by the Renaissance painter, Bartolommeo della Gatta – with faithful views of 15thC Arezzo.

On the second floor, from the 16thC, there are vast, turgid works by Giorgio Vasari; and, from the 17thC, a haphazard collection including works by Cigoli and Caroselli. The pictures are shown among the decorative and minor arts; there are some charming medieval ivories; and, in Rooms VI – VIII, an outstanding display of **majolica**.

San Domenico
Piazza Fossombroni
This 13thC Gothic church has frescoes by Aretine artists dating from the 15thC and 16thC and, over the high altar, a powerful *Crucifixion* (1260–65), an early work by Cimabue.

San Francesco ☆ ☆
Piazza San Francesco
🐾

In the choir of this Gothic, 13thC–14thC church, are **frescoes** ★★ (1453–64) by Piero della Francesca, perhaps the most beautiful of all Renaissance fresco cycles. Their subject, the *Story of the True Cross*, is from the *Legenda Aurea* of Jacopo Voragine. The frescoes are hauntingly still and grave; their beauty depends on the masterly arrangement of geometric shapes and cool tones; on the austere majesty of the figures; and on the dramatic power of expression and gesture. The story unfolds in the following order:

Right wall, lunette On the right, Adam announces his approaching death; on the left, Seth places in the mouth of the dead Adam a twig from the tree of Good and Evil, which becomes the wood of the True Cross. The bodies of the aged Adam and Eve are shown with moving dignity; the sense of an archaic, primitive simplicity contrasts dramatically with the rich retinue of figures that surround the Queen of Sheba in the next scene.

Central section The left half shows the Queen of Sheba many centuries later, recognizing that a bridge over the River Siloam is made from the wood of the tree; she kneels to worship it. In the right half, the Queen tells King Solomon of the tree and its destiny as the Cross on which Christ will be crucified. These are perhaps the loveliest of the scenes, where the ceremonial grandeur of the figures and the careful symmetry of the compositions are particularly striking.

Window wall, right of center The wood is buried on the order of Solomon; the scene looks forward to Christ carrying the Cross to Calvary. **Bottom right** The *Dream of Constantine:* an angel appears to Constantine and tells him to trust in the sign of the Cross to bring victory in the coming battle. Here the story is told with moving directness. Constantine is tucked up in his camp bed; in the moonlight, the tents of his army stretch into the distance. Brilliant light from the angel fills the foreground; the light creates both the illusion of depth and the strange atmosphere of this vision in the silent watches of the night, which presages so great a turning point in history.

Right wall, lowest section After this night scene comes "the most perfect morning light in all Renaissance painting" (Kenneth Clark). The forces of the Emperor Maxentius flee before the sign of the Cross.

Window wall, left of center Judas is tortured to reveal the whereabouts of the True Cross. This scene seems to have been executed mainly by pupils. Beneath it is an *Annunciation*, whose inclusion in the narrative has puzzled scholars; it has been suggested, and widely accepted, that it in fact shows an angel telling St Helena of her mission to find the Cross.

Left wall, central section In the left half, three crosses are discovered; in the right half, the True Cross is revealed when it brings to life a dead youth. **Lowest section** This shows the victory of Heraclius over Chosroes. The Cross was taken to Persia by King Chosroes; here it is recaptured by Heraclius, the Greek

Emperor, and Chosroes is beheaded. The violence of this battle contrasts with the way in which Maxentius' forces melt away before the tiny Cross. Yet the section on the right is quieter and gestures attain symbolic power: Chosroes' son is stabbed at the very base of the Cross; Chosroes himself awaits execution with stoic resignation.

ARTIMINO
Firenze, Toscana Map B2

Artimino is a walled medieval village, overlooking olive groves. Here Ferdinand I, while out hunting with Buontalenti, was so struck by the beauty of the views towards Florence that he commissioned the ageing architect to build him a hunting lodge (1594).

Villa Medicea dell'Artimino
Carmignano
Tel. (055) 8718072
Open Wed: summer 8am–noon, 2–7pm,
*   winter 8am–noon, 2–5pm*
Closed Thurs–Tues
📷 🅿 🏛 ♨

This is one of the loveliest of the Medici villas, an idyllic country retreat with frescoes attributed to Poccetti and Passignano. In the lunettes of the Salone there used to be topographical pictures of the Medici villas by the Flemish painter Justus Utens; these have now been moved to the Museo di Firenze com' era in Florence.

ASCIANO
Siena, Tuscany Map C3

This is a pleasant medieval hill town, encircled by 14thC walls, and surrounded by vineyards and olive groves.

Museo di Arte Sacra
Piazza Sant'Agate
Tel. (577) 718207
Open 8am–noon, 3–7pm
📷 ✗

This houses an unexpectedly good collection of 14thC and 15thC Sienese painting. The highlights are a dramatic *St Michael and the Dragon* by Ambrogio Lorenzetti; an *Assumption* by Giovanni di Paolo; a *Nativity of the Virgin* by the Maestro dell'Osservanza – delicately patterned, with lovingly observed details of everyday life and a child-like charm characteristic of Sienese painting; and a polychrome wooden group of the *Annunciation* by Francesco di Valdambrino – one of his freshest, prettiest works.

ASCOLI PICENO
Marche Map F4

Ancient Asculum was the capital of Picenum and the city still preserves traces of its early past although it is most renowned today for its medieval buildings. Lying on a green plain, ringed by mountains, and at first sight rather sombre, Ascoli has an attractive medieval quarter, with twisting alleys and fine *palazzi*; at its center is the Piazza del Popolo, flanked by the austere 13thC Palazzo dei Capitani del Popolo and by the soaring Gothic lines of San Francesco. Carlo Crivelli spent many years in the Marches after his expulsion from his native Venice in 1457; he left many polyptychs here.

Duomo
Piazza Arringo
🏛

Reconstructed in the late 15thC, with a fine (but unfinished) facade attributed to Cola dell' Amatrice (1532–39), the cathedral has wooden **doors** decorated by Francesco di Giovanni (c.1496).

Inside, in the **Cappella del Sacramento** on the right, is a polyptych by Crivelli of the ***Madonna and Child Enthroned, Christ, the Apostles and Saints*** ★★ (1473). This large altarpiece, with its three rows still intact, is the masterpiece of Crivelli's full maturity; the gold background and elaborate structure remain Gothic, yet there is a clear understanding of perspective; its beauty depends on the sharp precision of the line, the refinement of gesture and expression, and the richness and delicacy of the decorative detail.

Pinacoteca Civica
Palazzo Comunale, Piazza Arringo
Tel. (0736) 64346
Open May – Oct 9am – 7pm, Nov – Apr
*   9am – 1pm*
📷 ✎

The collection is a large and rather haphazard mixture of styles and eras. There are two **triptychs** by Crivelli and works by local painters that suggest his influence. There is also a large number of lesser known works by celebrated artists – including a damaged *St Francis* (1561) by Titian and an early 17thC *Annunciation* by Guido Reni.

A random group of 18thC pictures includes a stormy *St Jerome* by Magnasco and the *Grand Canal* by Bellotto (Canaletto's nephew and pupil). There is also a very fine 13thC **cope** ★ which belonged to Nicholas IV, born in Ascoli around 1230.

ASSISI
Perugia, Umbria Map E4

A tiny medieval town, spread across the slopes of Monte Subasio, Assisi is entirely dominated by the great basilica of San Francesco – one of the most famous pilgrimage centers in the world; the church's massive tiered foundations are built into the hillside, and it towers dramatically over the surrounding Umbrian plain. Beyond it, winding streets and staircase lanes twist up the hill, past fountains and the graceful Roman temple incorporated into the Gothic buildings of the main square.

Duomo
Piazza San Rufino
🏛

The cathedral is a fascinating mixture of Roman remains and Romanesque architecture. Beneath the church is a Roman cistern; and, in the crypt, a Roman **sarcophagus** with a relief of ***Diana and Endymion***, the first tomb of St Rufino.

Museo del Duomo
Piazza San Rufino
Open Tues – Sat: summer
*   9.30am – 12.30pm, 4 – 7pm, winter*
*   9am – 12.30pm, 3 – 6pm; Sun*
*   9am – 12.30pm*
Closed Mon
📷 ℹ

The tiny museum, reached from the right nave of the church along a corridor lined with Roman capitals, has a splendid ***Madonna and Four Saints*** ★ (1470) by Niccolò Alunno; notice especially the charming predella panels featuring the legends of St Rufino.

Pinacoteca Comunale
Piazza del Comune
Tel. (075) 812219
Open Apr – Dec: Tues – Sat, summer
*   9am – 12.30pm, 4 – 7pm, winter*
*   9am – 12.30pm, 3 – 6pm; Sun*
*   9am – 12.30pm*
Closed Jan – Mar, Mon
📷

This is a small collection of paintings, detached frescoes, Deruta ceramics and architectural fragments; it includes works by Niccolò Alunno, Ottaviano Nelli and Matteo da Gualdo.

Santa Chiara
Piazza Santa Chiara
🏛

Fired by the teachings of St Francis, St Clare (1194–1253) renounced the wealth of her family and founded the

Poor Clares, a Franciscan order of nuns; her tomb is in the crypt of this Gothic church (begun 1257), which was inspired by the upper church of San Francesco.

Among many interesting works of art notice the **Crucifixion** in the apse and the *St Clare* with eight small scenes from her life in the right transept, both attributed to the Maestro di Santa Chiara. Off the right nave are the Cappella del Crocifisso, with the **crucifix** which is supposed to have spoken to St Francis, and the Cappella del Sacramento with, on the left wall, a fresco of the *Madonna Enthroned with Saints* now attributed to Puccio Capanna, an Umbrian follower of Giotto.

San Francesco ☆ ☆
Piazza Inferiore di San Francesco
Tel. (075) 812238
Open summer Mon–Sat 6am–7pm, Sun
6am–7.30pm; winter Mon–Sat
6.30am–noon, 2–6pm, Sun
6.30am–7pm
📷 ⛵ 🖊 ♿ 🏛 🔧

The church was founded in 1228, two years after St Francis' death; it was from the beginning planned as two buildings, a lower and an upper church. Celebrated artists from all over Italy were called to decorate the church; and Assisi witnessed the birth of a new kind of naturalistic art, deeply nourished by the Franciscan spirit. The most famous artist associated with Assisi is Giotto, whose precise role here is the most hotly debated issue in the history of Italian art. Throughout this century it has often been argued that Giotto was never at Assisi; more recently, Italian scholars have been confidently reattributing to him an increasing number of the frescoes.
Lower church
The church was built as a crypt to contain St Francis' tomb. The dark, mysterious interior glows richly with the vivid colours of the frescoes that cover the entire surface and pattern the low Romanesque arches. Do not hurry through the gloom to the more celebrated upper church; the paintings here are as fine, and more unexpected. Remember, also, to take plenty of coins for the lights.
Nave The walls to left and right are decorated by the Maestro di San Francesco; note especially on the left wall *St Francis Talking to the Birds* ★
Third chapel on right The frescoes are by Giotto and his assistants; the most convincing attributions to Giotto are the **Resurrection** and the *Noli Me Tangere*.
Right transept The frescoes, by Giotto and his assistants, feature the *Life of Christ* and the *Miracles of St Francis*.

Recent scholars have rightly emphasized the high quality of these works and suggested Giotto's direct participation: the works are close to those of the Cappella degli Scrovegni in Padua (see *NORTH EAST ITALY*), although less austere; the *Visitation* ★ is especially tender and subtle. On the right wall is Cimabue's *Madonna with St Francis* ★ (c.1290), the most famous portrait of St Francis; on the end wall, Simone Martini's *Five Saints*.
Left transept On the upper walls and vaults are 11 scenes of the *Passion* cycle, the last five by Pietro Lorenzetti. The cycle is dominated by the overwhelming scale and dramatic power of the *Crucifixion* ★ with its vast and vividly observed crowd, and by the intense pathos of the *Descent from the Cross* ★ Lorenzetti combines powerful, Giottesque figures with flowing Sienese rhythms.
First chapel on left Richly glowing with marble and stained glass, this chapel is decorated with courtly, elegant frescoes featuring the *Life of St Martin* ★ by Simone Martini (c.1317).
Upper church
The contrast between the dimness of the lower church and the brightness and clarity of the upper church is startling.
Transepts These have damaged frescoes by Cimabue, the grand remnants of a more spiritual age (1270s); note especially the *Crucifixion* ★ in the left transept.
Upper walls of nave There are two cycles of frescoes: on the N wall, scenes from the Old Testament; on the S wall, scenes from the New Testament. These are usually attributed to painters of the Roman school, followers of Cimabue, and, in the last two bays, to the young Giotto (late 1280s).
Lower walls of nave These feature 28 scenes from the *Life of St Francis* ★★ as told by St Bonaventure, and attributed mainly to Giotto.

The finest frescoes are on the N wall, where the stories are told simply and colourfully, with a new emphasis on space and on the expression of warm and tender emotion. Yet even here there are those contrasts of style that have fed the Giotto controversy; the elegant figures and delicate architecture of the *Man Paying Homage to St Francis* (the first fresco) contrast with the robuster, grander style of the second fresco, the *Incident of the Cloak*. *St Francis Renouncing his Worldly Possessions* ★ (fifth fresco) is a particularly dramatic scene; in the *Devils Driven from Arezzo* ★ (tenth fresco), the grand gesture of St Francis is echoed in the lilting lines of the radiantly coloured roofs and towers.

The **E wall** has two of the most delightful and best loved scenes. The powerful naturalism of the man drinking in the **Miracle of the Spring ★** was first praised by Vasari. On the right, **St Francis Preaching to the Birds ★★** is touchingly direct and vivid.

The paintings on the **S wall** are increasingly crowded, and most scholars agree that they reveal less and less direct intervention on Giotto's part. The first three are the finest, and it has been plausibly suggested that they form a coherent stylistic group, quite distinct from Giotto.

In the **Death of the Cavaliere di Celano ★** (sixteenth fresco) the artist creates a dramatic contrast between the crowd of mourners and the solitary friar at the table; **St Francis Preaching before Honorius III** (seventeenth fresco) is rich in sharply observed expression and gesture. The most successful of these late scenes, and the closest to Giotto, is the **Apparition to Gregory IX** (twenty-fifth fresco). The last four frescoes are not by Giotto.

Tesoro della Basilica di San Francesco
Basilica di San Francesco
Tel. as San Francesco, above
Open summer Tues–Sun
9.30am–12.30pm, 3–6.30pm; winter Sat, Sun 9.30am–noon, 2.30–5pm
Closed summer: Mon; winter: Mon–Fri
The treasury contains paintings, tapestries, *sinopie*, and sacred objects made with precious materials. The Perkins Collection of paintings includes works by Lorenzetti, Taddeo di Bartolo, Fra Angelico, Masolino and Signorelli.

BETTONA
Perugia, Umbria Map D4

Bettona is a picturesque little hill town, with remnants of Etruscan walls.

Pinacoteca Comunale
Palazzo del Podestà, Piazza Cavour
Tel. (075) 828120
Open Tues–Sat 10am–noon, 4–6pm, Sun 10am–noon
Closed Mon
This is a small collection, mainly of historical bric-à-brac: archaeological finds, letters and documents. The best paintings are Perugino's **Madonna and Saints** and Dono Doni's mid 16thC **Adoration of the Shepherds.**

CARMIGNANO
Firenze, Toscana Map B2

Carmignano is a small town, set on the slopes of a hill among olive groves and vineyards.

San Michele
Piazza Santi Francesco e Michele
On the second altar on the right of this Gothic church is Pontormo's **Visitation ★** (1530) – a startling, intensely dramatic treatment of the theme; the swelling forms of the two pregnant women fill the foreground, their contact heightened by the steep perspective and the nervous rhythms of the drapery.

CASTELLO
Firenze, Toscana Map C2

Castello is a suburb of Florence, famous for its three Medici villas.

Villa Medicea di Careggi
Viale G. Pieraccini
Visits by appointment only; inquire at hospital of Santa Maria Nuova, Via Bufalini, Firenze
This is one of the oldest of the villas around Florence, still with hints of medieval fortification, yet enlarged and remodelled for Cosimo de' Medici by Michelozzo in the 1430s. Pontormo and Bronzino were employed here in the 1530s; their work was interrupted by the assassination of Alessandro de' Medici in 1536. The villa is now used as a nurses' home by the hospital of Santa Maria Nuova.

Villa Medicea di Castello
Via di Castello 40
Gardens only open 9am–6.30pm or sunset
This villa has the oldest of the great Medici gardens; Duke Cosimo I commissioned from Tribolo in 1537 an immensely intricate design of statues, fountains and grottoes glorifying the deeds of the Medici. The **Fountain of Hercules and Anteus**, designed by Tribolo, has bronze statues by Ammanati. The **grotto**, created by Giambologna, is a sophisticated interweaving of nature and art; encrusted with stalactites of tufa and pumice, it glitters with shells and mother of pearl. The 16thC visitor would have been soaked by *giochi d'acqua* or secret jets of water, a well-worn Mannerist joke. Above the garden, in the park, is a statue of **January** by Ammanati.

Villa Medicea della Petraia
Via della Petraia
Tel. (055) 451208
Open Tues–Sun: summer 9am–6.30pm,
winter 9am–4.30pm
Closed Mon
📷 🚻 🏛 ✿

The 14thC castle, its ancient tower
surmounting the refined proportions of a
Renaissance facade, was transformed by
Buontalenti from around 1575–79 for
Cardinal Ferdinando de' Medici. In the
courtyard (converted into a ballroom by
Victor Emanuel II) are **frescoes** by
Volterrano celebrating the history of the
Medici; in the garden is a **fountain**
designed by Tribolo, crowned by a bronze
Venus by Giambologna.

CHIUSI
Siena, Toscana Map D4

Chiusi stands on a hill, amid land rich in
corn and olives. An ancient town, it was
once one of the most powerful of the 12
Etruscan federated cities (traces of the
massive walls remain); the modern street
plan recalls the later Roman settlement,
Clusium.

Museo Nazionale Etrusco ☆
Piazza del Duomo
Tel. (0578) 20177
Open Tues–Sat 8.30am–2pm, Sun
9am–1pm
Closed Mon
📷

One of the very finest small Etruscan
museums, this collection traces the
fascinating development of the Etruscan
civilization in Chiusi. The display opens
with **biconical urns** with lids from the
Villanovan period; there follow good
examples of the later **Canopic vases**
(from the 6thC BC onwards) in which the
lids take the form of human heads – a type
characteristic of Chiusi; and a related
type of urn (late 7thC and early 6thC BC)
with figures and animals standing on the
lid – a particularly striking example, the
Gualandi casket, is decorated with a
large female figure, griffins' heads, and
small attendants. The collection also
includes outstanding examples of the
heavy **bucchero ware** produced only in
Chiusi.

Necropoli
Inquire at Museo Nazionale Etrusco, above,
for a guide to show the way
📷 🚻

The most interesting Etruscan tombs are
to the N and E of the town. To the N, the
Tomba della Scimmia, or Tomb of the
Ape, has several rooms – two with fine

wall paintings (5thC BC); to the E, the
Tomba Bonci Casuccini has wall
paintings of the same period and an
authentic Etruscan doorway.

CITTÀ DI CASTELLO
Perugia, Umbria Map D3

Città di Castello was an ancient Umbrian
settlement. During the Renaissance it
was ruled by the Vitelli, and celebrated
artists worked here – among them,
Raphael, Signorelli and Vasari; Raphael's
Betrothal of the Virgin once graced the
church of San Francesco (it is now in the
Pinacoteca di Brera – see Milan, *NORTH
& NORTH WEST ITALY*). The city has
now dwindled to a busy provincial town,
with hints of faded grandeur.

Museo Burri
Palazzo Albizzini, Piazza Garibaldi
Tel. (075) 853049
Open Tues–Sun: summer 10am–noon,
4–6pm; winter 9.30am–noon,
3.30–5.30pm
Closed Mon
📷 🚗 🚻 ✿ 🔲 🍴

Alberto Burri was born in Città di
Castello and is perhaps the most
internationally famous Italian abstract
artist. His works are created from odd bits
of sacking and canvas soaked in paint.
The museum has about 80 pieces, dating
from 1948–81.

Museo del Tesoro del Duomo
Duomo, Piazza Gabriotti

The outstanding works here are a 14thC
silver and gold **altar frontal**, presented by
Pope Celestine II, and some splendid
early Christian (5thC) **church silver**,
from Canoscio.

Pinacoteca Comunale
Palazzo Vitelli alla Cannoniera, Via della
Cannoniera 22
Tel. (075) 852402
Open Mon–Sat 9.30am–12.30pm,
3.30–6.30pm; Sun 10am–12.30pm,
3.30–6pm
📷 🚗 🕈 🏛 ✿ 🔲

The collection is housed in a faded,
rather melancholy 16thC palace; the
garden facade, with magnificent graffiti
by Vasari, looks out over a scruffy patch
of grass.

The display opens with 15thC
paintings by Neri di Bicci and Spinello
Aretino. In Room II are works by Luca
Signorelli; his **Martyrdom of St
Sebastian ★** (1493) suggests his interest in
Pollaiuolo's wiry figures. In Room III are
two fascinating early works by Raphael: a
standard, recently restored, with on one

side the **Crucifixion** and on the other side the **Madonna della Misericordia**; and the badly damaged **Trinity standard** ✱ (1499) with on one side the **Holy Trinity with Sts Sebastian and Roch** and on the reverse the **Creation of Eve**. The second standard, painted on a narrow rectangle of cloth, was commissioned by the Confraternity of the Holy Trinity of Città di Castello; the presence of the plague saints, Sebastian and Roch, suggests that it was associated with the plague of 1499. Such standards were carried in procession, or displayed beside the high altar.

Further on, the loggia has **terra cottas** by Luca della Robbia; later rooms are less interesting, with some dullish 16thC and 17thC paintings – but Room X has a lively **frieze** by Cola d'Amatrice, commemorating battles fought by the Vitelli.

CITTÀ DELLA PIEVE
Perugia, Umbria Map D4

Città della Pieve is an unusual, red-brick hill town, with little medieval houses clustering around a 14thC castle; it is famous as the birthplace of Perugino, Umbria's most distinguished painter.

Santa Maria dei Bianchi
Via Vanucci
In the oratory adjoining the church is Perugino's **Adoration of the Magi** (1504). This is a late work, painted when Perugino's art had begun to lose something of its vitality and to depend very much on the repetition of figures from earlier compositions. And yet the painting still has something of the lovely tranquillity and harmony that typify his art; the Madonna in the foreground, the wise men kneeling with their gifts, are still, poised figures in an Umbrian landscape of great beauty – hills run down to the shores of the lake from either side, trees delicately mark the skyline; in the middle distance is a peaceful group of travellers and women drawing water from a well.

This painting is the largest and most elaborate version of a favourite composition; elements of it recur in the **Nativities** at MONTEFALCO, PERUGIA and elsewhere.

CORRIDONIA
Macerata, Marche Map F3

Once known by the more picturesque name of Monte dell' Olmo but renamed in honour of the early 20thC trade

unionist, Filippo Corridoni, the town is set on a steep hillside and enjoys fine views of the countryside below.

Pinacoteca
Canonica dei Santi Pietro e Paolo, Via Cavour 54
Tel. (0733) 431832, 54128
📷 ⬛ ✗
The masterpiece of this little museum is Crivelli's early **Madonna**. The severe look of the Virgin is in sharp contrast to the tender handling of the Child. Other works include a **Madonna** by Pomerancio, a **polyptych** by Antonio Vivarini and a **St Francis**, possibly by Sassetta.

CORTONA
Arezzo, Toscana Map D3

Cortona is an ancient city which retained its power through successive stages of history – Etruscan, Roman and medieval. The old town, ringed by forbidding medieval walls – long stretches incorporating massive blocks of Etruscan masonry – spreads up the olive-clad slopes of Monte Sant' Egidio, to the medieval castle at its summit; it offers spectacular views of the valley and distant plain. The atmosphere is harshly medieval, with dark, narrow streets and, at the center, the irregular Piazza della Repubblica, dourly enclosed by medieval palaces. In the 15thC, Fra Angelico brought the art of the Renaissance to Cortona; it was the birthplace of Signorelli, of the Baroque painter Pietro da Cortona, and of the Futurist Severini.

Museo dell'Accademia Etrusca
Palazzo Pretorio, Piazza Signorelli
Tel. (0575) 63677
Open Tues – Sun: summer 10am – 1pm, 4 – 7pm; winter 9am – 1pm, 3 – 5pm
Closed Mon
🚇 🏛
Housed in the 14thC Palazzo Pretorio, this museum is a dark and weird jumble of Etruscan and Egyptian art, paintings, costumes, coins, porcelain and Futurist paintings.

The highlight is the **Etruscan section**, which has one of the most extraordinary of all Etruscan bronzes, a 5thC BC **candelabrum** ✱✱ with intricate and obscene decoration arranged in concentric bands around a gorgon's head. First, there are fabulous, wild beasts; then, waves and dolphins; finally, eight phallic satyrs between eight sirens.

There is also a fine collection of **coins** ✱ Among the medieval works is a delightful series of decorative fragments from early 15thC **ivory coffers**.

Pictures include a *Madonna and Saints* ★ by Pietro da Cortona and works by Piazzetta and Severini. Of the Italian Futurists, Severini was the most deeply influenced by French Cubism; a small room devoted to his works shows his development from the early *Maternity* (1916) through a series of colour lithographs – decorative works based on Synthetic Cubism – to a series of collages dating from 1964.

Museo Diocesano
Piazza Trento Trieste
Tel. (0575) 62830
Open summer 9am – 1pm, 3 – 6.30pm; winter 9am – 1pm, 3 – 5pm
▨

This is an outstanding small collection, currently in the throes of extensive reorganization. The highlights are two works by Fra Angelico: a triptych of the *Madonna and Saints* ★ (note especially the fine predella panels) and the *Annunciation* ★★ (1433) which set the pattern for many later variants of this theme.

The latter is one of Fra Angelico's earliest paintings, full of the decorative detail of International Gothic, and yet firmly constructed; the angel appears to Mary in a small Renaissance loggia, within a magical enclosed garden; beyond are the desolate figures of Adam and Eve, driven from Paradise. Among the predella panels of this altarpiece, notice especially the *Visitation* ★ with a view of Lake Trasimeno in the distance and a woman slowly climbing the hill.

Pictures by Luca Signorelli include the *Communion of the Apostles* ★ and the *Deposition* ★ There is also a *Madonna and Saints* by Sassetta and a *Madonna and Angels* by Pietro Lorenzetti. Other attractions include a 2ndC AD **Roman sarcophagus** and the 15thC **Vagnucci reliquary** ★ by Giusto da Firenze.

DERUTA
Perugia, Umbria Map D4

This small agricultural town has been well known since the 14thC for majolica.

Pinacoteca Comunale e Museo delle Maioliche
Piazza dei Consoli
Tel. (075) 9711143
Open Mon – Sat 9am – 1pm
Closed Sun
▨

This has Etruscan vases, Derutan majolicas and 18thC chasubles; among the 15thC pictures are a double-sided

processional banner by Niccolò Alunno and a collection of 18thC paintings that once belonged to Leone Pascoli, the biographer.

EMPOLI
Firenze, Toscana Map B2

A town of Roman origin, Empoli developed in the 12thC around the collegiate church of Sant'Andrea. Despite many alterations, the church still preserves part of a lovely Romanesque facade that is reminiscent of San Miniato al Monte in **FLORENCE**. The town is now surrounded by urban sprawl.

Museo della Collegiata ☆
Piazza della Propositura
Tel. (0571) 72220
Open Tues – Sun 10am – noon
Closed Mon
▨ ▥

The museum has a small group of works of outstandingly high quality. On the first floor, in Room VI, there is Lorenzo Monaco's *Madonna Enthroned with Saints* ★ (1404) and Pontormo's *St John the Evangelist* ★ and *St Michael Archangel* ★ (both 1519) – daring experiments with spiralling poses and contorted forms. The *St Sebastian* ★★ (1460s), sculpted by Antonio Rossellino, stands out as perhaps the most perfect Renaissance nude created in the second half of the century.

Further on, in Room VII, the grace of Bernardo Rossellino's *Angel of the Annunciation* ★ (begun 1444) suggests the influence of Ghiberti; the *Virgin* is a stockier figure, perhaps due to the intervention of an assistant. Room VIII shows a *Pietà* ★ by Masolino (c. 1425) and fragments of frescoes by the rare early 15thC artist Gherardo Starnina. Room IX contains terra cottas from the della Robbia workshops.

Santo Stefano
Via Santo Stefano
In the lunette over the door to the sacristy of this 14thC church is a *Madonna and Two Angels* by Masolino (1424); in the **Cappella di Sant'Andrea** (off the right nave) are the remains of frescoes of the *Story of the True Cross* (1424), also by Masolino.

FABRIANO
Ancona, Marche Map E3

An expanding industrial town, long famous for the manufacture of paper, Fabriano retains a rather dour medieval

center. In the 14thC, influenced by
nearby Assisi, the town was already
buzzing with artistic activity; the work of
local painters – among them, Allegretto
Nuzi – heralded the decorative style of
Gentile da Fabriano, the greatest
Italian exponent of International
Gothic.

Duomo
Piazza Umberto I
This is a 13thC church, rebuilt in the
17thC. In a chapel to the right of the
choir, there are lively frescoes by Nuzi of
the **Life of St Lawrence** (c.1365). In the
fourth chapel of the left aisle are a
Crucifixion and frescoes by Orazio
Gentileschi.

Pinacoteca Comunale
Piazza Umberto I
Open Tues – Sat 9.30am – 12.30pm, Sun
   10.30am – 12.30pm
Closed Mon
This is a good collection, featuring
mainly local painters. It includes a group
of 14thC works by Allegretto Nuzi, a
charming, lively illustrator – notice
especially the **Three Saints**, where the
interest in patterned fabrics leads on to
Gentile da Fabriano; also, works by
Antonio da Fabriano (15thC) and
Simone de Magistris (16thC), and an
important detached fresco of the
Crucifixion ★ (13thC).

FANO
Pesaro e Urbino, Marche   Map E2
Fano is a small, slightly run down but
pleasant seaside resort. It retains traces of
its importance, first under Augustus and
later, during the Renaissance, under the
dukes of Malatesta. There is a fine central
piazza, with an elegant 16thC fountain,
and a mixture of grand, crumbling
palaces – the Romanesque-Gothic
Palazzo della Ragione and, across the
courtyard to the left, the Renaissance
Palazzo Malatesta, which houses the art
museum.

Duomo
Via Arco d'Augusto
The church dates from the 12thC, but
has been much altered. The third chapel
in the right aisle is frescoed with scenes
from the **Life of the Virgin** (1618–19) by
Domenichino; the frescoes are now in
poor condition, but preserve a sweet piety
and simplicity that look back to the early
Renaissance – they are somewhat at odds
with the rich stucco decoration, between
Mannerism and Baroque, of the chapel.

Museo Civico e Pinacoteca
Palazzo Malatesta, Piazza XX Settembre
Tel. (0721) 876362
Open Tues – Sat 10am – noon, 4 – 7pm,
   Sun 10am – noon
Closed Mon
The museum has an interesting
archaeological section, with mosaics,
fragments of statues, and funerary cippi.
There follow outstanding collections of
coins ★ – Roman and medieval – and of
Malatestian medals ★ by Matteo de Pastis
(15thC).
   Among the paintings, there is a
polyptych (c.1420) by Michele
Giambono, a pupil of Gentile Bellini;
and some reasonable 17thC pictures
including a **Guardian Angel** by Guercino
– a late, rather saccharine work – and a
David with the Head of Goliath by
Domenichino.

San Francesco
Off Via Garibaldi
In the portico of the deconsecrated
remains of this Gothic church are the
Arche Malatestiane ★ – two monumental
tombs of the Malatesta. On the right is
the Renaissance **tomb of Pandolfo II**
(1460), perhaps designed by Alberti; on
the left, the late Gothic **tomb of Paola
Bianca** (1416–21), by a follower of the
Venetian sculptor, Pierpaolo dalle
Masegne.

Santa Maria Nuova
Via Bonaccorsi
The church dates from the 16thC, with
18thC stuccoes. On the third altar on the
right is Perugino's **Madonna and Saints** ★
The authorship of the predella panels
showing the **Life of the Virgin** ★ is
controversial; some authorities attribute
them to Raphael, others to Perugino. On
the second altar on the left is an
Annunciation ★ (1498), also by
Perugino.

San Pietro
Via Nolfi
This 17thC church has one of the richest
Baroque interiors in the Marches and, in
the first chapel on the left, an
Annunciation by Guido Reni.

FERMO
Ascoli Piceno, Marche   Map F4
An ancient city, already famous in
classical times, Fermo is now
predominantly medieval in appearance,
with many fine churches and palaces; a
steep road climbs up the hill to the
cathedral, which dominates the town.

Duomo
Piazzale del Girfalco

This ancient church was built on the site
of a pagan temple; it was rebuilt in the
Gothic style in 1227, and finished in the
late 18thC by Cosimo Morelli. The
church is full of fascinating remains from
earlier buildings – archaeological
fragments, Roman sarcophagi and, near
the presbytery, the remains of a 5thC
mosaic pavement. In the crypt there is an
early Christian **sarcophagus** (4thC or
5thC) with scenes from the **Life of St
Peter**. On the right of the atrium, against
the entrance wall, is a **monument to
Giovanni Visconti** (1366).

Pinacoteca Civica ☆
Piazza del Popolo
Tel. (0734) 371167
Open summer Mon 5 – 7.30pm, Tues - Sun
8.30am – 12.30pm; winter Mon
4.30 – 7.30pm, Tues – Sun
8.30am – 12.30pm, 4.30 – 7.30pm
Closed Mon morning
🖼 ➤ 🏛 ⛩ 🎭 ▦

The gallery houses a small, interesting
collection of pictures by Venetian and
local artists. The outstanding works are
eight little **panels** ★ by the early 15thC
Venetian painter, Jacobello del Fiore,
who worked in the International Gothic
style and was influenced by Gentile da
Fabriano. In the **Martyrdom of St Lucy**,
the surface is delicately patterned with
little leaves and flowers, fabrics and
decorative flames.

Other highlights of the collection
include a **polyptych** (1369) by Andrea da
Bologna; works by Francescuccio Ghissi
da Fabriano, Giacomo da Recanati and
other local painters; and an **Adoration of
the Shepherds** ★ (1608) by Rubens.

The Rubens is an important early
work, commissioned at the end of the
artist's visit to Italy; it is influenced both
by Venetian painting and by Correggio's
Adoration of the Shepherds (c.1530),
now in Dresden. The painting is of a
night scene, lit by the incandescent glow
from the Christ Child; the effects of
bright light on the faces of the shepherds
– one of whom shields his eyes with his
hands – are beautifully observed.

FIESOLE
Firenze, Toscana Map C2

Fiesole, an Etruscan city far more ancient
than Florence, lies on a lovely hillside;
from the Roman amphitheater, the dark
greens of cypress groves stand out
poignantly against the blue haze of
distant valleys. Fiesole has long been a
favourite summer retreat and behind the

mossy walls that line the narrow road
winding up from the plain are glimpses of
magnificent villas and gardens, most of
them belonging to wealthy Florentines.

Duomo
Piazza Mino da Fiesole

This Romanesque building was enlarged
in the 13thC and 14thC and restored in
the 19thC. The high altar has a triptych
(c.1450) by Bicci di Lorenzo. To the right
is the **Cappella Salutati**, with frescoes by
Cosimo Rosselli and sculptures by Mino
da Fiesole.

Museo Bandini
Via Dupre 1
Tel. (055) 59061
Open Tues – Sun: Mar – Apr, Oct
10am – 12.30pm, 2.30 – 6pm; Nov – Feb
9.30am – 12.30pm, 2 – 5pm; May – Sept
10am – noon, 3 – 7pm
Closed Mon
🖼

This small museum has no great
masterpieces, but a pleasant array of
Byzantine ivories, majolica, 14thC and
15thC Florentine and Sienese pictures –
most charming is the late 15thC **Three
Triumphs of Petrarch** attributed to
Jacopo del Sellaio – della Robbia terra
cottas and minor Renaissance sculpture.

Museo Fiesolano
Via Portigiani 1
Tel. (055) 59477
Open Tues – Sun: May – Sept 10am – noon,
3 – 7pm; Mar, Apr, Oct
10am – 12.30pm, 2.30 – 6pm; Nov – Feb
9.30am – 12.30pm, 2 – 5pm
Closed Mon
🖼

The museum houses a display of
antiquities found in the district; there are
examples of the carved funerary **stelae**
and **cippi** from the archaic period for
which Fiesole is well known; also, some
interesting **cinerary urns** and **Roman
portrait busts**.

San Domenico
Via Giuseppe Mantellini
🏛

The church of San Domenico, founded
in 1406, and remodelled in the late
15thC and 16thC, forms the center of a
hamlet on the road between Fiesole and
Florence. Inside the church, on the first
altar on the left, is an altarpiece of the
Madonna and Saints (c.1428) by Fra
Angelico – the background repainted by
Lorenzo di Credi (c.1501). In the chapter
house, to the right of the portico, is Fra
Angelico's fresco of the **Crucifixion**
(c.1430) and his detached fresco of the
Madonna from the cloister.

FLORENCE *(FIRENZE)*
Toscana Map C2

The most glamorous period in the history of art is the Renaissance and at its very center is Florence, the prosperous merchant city that in the early 15thC became the intellectual and artistic capital of Europe. Many of the most celebrated men in the history of art – Giotto and Ghiberti, Donatello, Brunelleschi and Masaccio, Michelangelo and Leonardo – were Florentines; looking back to the grandeur of Rome, they created an artistic tradition that was to last until the late 19thC.

Florence remains a small and beautiful city where narrow streets and squares are flanked by medieval and Renaissance buildings; much of its attraction lies in the combination of this intimacy and charm with the overwhelming fame of its monuments. The most moving way to begin a visit is to climb to the terrace before the Romanesque church of San Miniato and survey the city spread out against the encircling hills; Brunelleschi's great cupola dominates the view, rising over the red rooftops and contrasting with Giotto's campanile and the slender tower of the Palazzo Vecchio.

From here, across the picturesque Ponte Vecchio – lined with elegant jewellers – past the bank of the Arno where Dante met Beatrice, one reaches the center of Florence, the Piazza della Signoria. Before the massive Palazzo Vecchio stands a copy of Michelangelo's ***David***, whose tense grandeur contrasts with Cellini's languorous and dreamy ***Perseus*** among the sculptures beneath the arches of the Loggia dei Lanzi. Close by, on Orsanmichele, majestic figures of saints look down from their niches with the new confidence and authority of the Renaissance. Further on are the great bronze doors of the baptistry (Battistero) – the delicate grace and beauty of Ghiberti's later set caused Michelangelo to call them the Gates of Paradise. All these sculptures do much to create that sense of closeness to the past that is so characteristic of Florence.

The city was dominated by the Medici and their presence is everywhere – in the little chapel in the Palazzo Medici-Riccardi designed by Michelozzo and frescoed by Benozzo Gozzoli with a festive procession of the Medici family; in the convent of San Marco (Museo dell' Angelico) where Cosimo de' Medici reserved for himself a couple of cells, charmingly frescoed by Fra Angelico and assistants; and in the disturbing melancholy of Michelangelo's Medici Chapel in San Lorenzo. A new note is sounded in the 16thC when, with Cosimo I, the Medici became hereditary dukes; their power and authority are felt in Cellini's vibrant bust of ***Cosimo I*** (Museo del Bargello) and in Bronzino's coldly polished portraits.

The collections of the Medici fill the museums of Florence; the Galleria degli Uffizi has the most celebrated collection of Renaissance art in the world; the Galleria dell' Accademia boasts Michelangelo's ***David***; the Palazzo Pitti across the Arno evokes the splendour of the princely collections of the Medici grand dukes. Other areas away from the immediate center have a quiet charm and character of their own – Santa Croce, with frescoes by Giotto and the graceful early Renaissance Pazzi Chapel, and Santa Maria del Carmine, with crucially important frescoes by Masaccio and Masolino.

The best time to visit Florence is in late spring or early autumn, either before or after the main onslaught of summer tourists and while the weather is sunny, warm and breezy. From June to August the narrow, congested streets and world-famous galleries become almost impossibly crowded, and noise and heat may deter even the most determined sightseers.

The Medici in Florence

The Medici name has a strong fascination, so closely is it associated with that brilliant period of Florentine history when the city shone as the intellectual center of Europe; the spirit of this famous family lingers on in the still small and still recognizably 15thC town. The Medici were originally a banking family, whose fortunes were laid by **Giovanni di Bicci** (1360–1429); his son, **Cosimo il Vecchio** (1389–1464), returning triumphantly from a period of exile, subtly and warily established Medici domination over the government of the Republic. Cosimo's grandson, **Lorenzo the Magnificent** ("il Magnifico") (1449–92), a celebrated patron of poets and scholars, was his most glamorous successor. Two great popes, **Leo X** (1475–1521) and **Clement VII** (1478–1534), sprang from the Medici family. After a period of strife, a second era of Medici fame opened with **Cosimo I** (1519–74), who became Duke of Florence in 1537 and Grand Duke in 1570. A series of grand dukes wielded absolute power over an increasingly gloomy and bigoted court, until the melancholy death of **Gian Gastone** in 1737.

Start your tour with the PALAZZO MEDICI-RICCARDI, which makes brilliantly clear the contrast between two periods of Medici history. The palace was built for Cosimo il Vecchio by Michelozzo, an architect whose restrained brand of classicism particularly appealed to Cosimo's Republican modesty. The austere, arcaded courtyard is decorated only with tondi enclosing the Medici arms and with severely classical, cameo-like scenes from mythology. Here once stood Donatello's *David* and *Judith and Holofernes*.

Within, the small chapel decorated with the *Adoration of the Magi* by Benozzo Gozzoli is perhaps the best loved memorial to Medicean taste. It was commissioned by Cosimo's son, **Piero the Gouty** ("il Gottoso") (1416–69); the horseman leading the retinue of kings has been identified as a portrait of Piero, and the old man beside him as Cosimo; the youth on the outside may be Lorenzo. This is a courtly, aristocratic art but its fresh gaiety and touches of shrewdness contrast with the overwhelming hyperbole of the frescoed gallery across the courtyard. The palace was acquired and enlarged by Marchese Francesco Riccardi in 1659; he commissioned Luca Giordano to decorate his new gallery with an allegory of human life and of the Medici family. The artist created an exalted panegyric to the power of a waning dynasty; at its center is the *Apotheosis of the Medici*, with the ruling duke, **Cosimo III** (1642–1723), and his two sons, Ferdinando (right) and Gian Gastone (left), shown as Castor and Pollux before the throne of Jupiter.

From here go to nearby SAN LORENZO; in the piazza is Bandinelli's stiff statue of the *condottiere*, **Giovanni delle Bande Nere**, father of Cosimo I. The monuments of the Medici church sum up three centuries of their taste, opening with the pure simplicity of Brunelleschi's **Old Sacristy**, commissioned by Giovanni di Bicci in 1421. In 1520 Michelangelo was asked by Cardinal Giulio de' Medici (later Clement VII) to create the **New Sacristy**, a profoundly disturbing reflection of a troubled age; his bizarre, highly idiosyncratic staircase to the library of the church was commissioned in 1524. A new and grander family mausoleum, the so-called **Cappella dei Principi**, was planned by Cosimo I from c.1570 and built from 1602; encrusted with polychrome marble in the reign of Grand Duke Cosimo III (1642–1723), it is a final flowering of the twilight Medicean taste for overwhelming splendour and richness.

In 1540 the tyrant Cosimo I moved from the palace of Republican Cosimo il Vecchio to the **Palazzo della Signoria** (later the PALAZZO VECCHIO), where his ancestor had been imprisoned. Giambologna's equestrian statue of *Cosimo I* in the PIAZZA DELLA SIGNORIA outside was intended to give the approach to the palace an air of imperial grandeur, and Vasari transformed the palace itself into a princely residence extolling the absolute power of the Medici. Vasari's frescoes are stiff and dull, but their imagery provides fascinating evidence of the Medici story.

Only 10yrs later, in 1550, Cosimo once more shifted his residence, this time to the PALAZZO PITTI across the Arno. The decorative programme at the Signoria – now renamed the Palazzo Vecchio – meanwhile continued, but the Pitti was to remain the seat of the later grand-ducal court. Here, the splendour of the sequence of rooms decorated by Pietro da Cortona speaks a new language that looks on to Versailles; the imagery celebrates the education and achievements of the ideal prince. In the first room, the **Sala di Venere**, note the lively stucco portraits of the Medici. In the third, the **Sala di Marte**, Pietro's allegory and illusion are at their most dazzling. In the **Sala dell' Iliade**, below, a grimmer reality is indicated by Susterman's portraits of the decadent, declining family.

If time permits, you may now recross the Arno via Ponte Santa Trinità to view Ghirlandaio's frescoes in the **Cappella Sassetti** in SANTA TRINITÀ. Here, the scenes from the ***Life of St Francis*** include the finest portrait ever painted of Lorenzo the Magnificent.

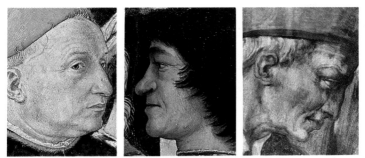

From left to right: Cosimo il Vecchio, Lorenzo the Magnificent and Cosimo I. Details from frescoes by Benozzo Gozzoli (Palazzo Medici-Riccardi), Ghirlandaio (Santa Trinità) and Vasari (Palazzo Vecchio).

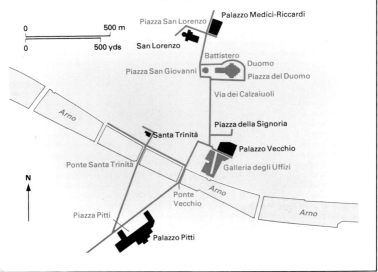

Accademia See GALLERIA DELL' ACCADEMIA.

Badia Fiorentina
Via del Proconsolo/Via Dante Alighieri
🏛

This 10thC Benedictine church was altered in the 13thC and rebuilt in the Baroque period. To the left of the entrance is Filippino Lippi's **St Bernard's Vision of the Madonna ★** (c.1485), which shows the influence of his teacher Botticelli in its expressive line and sweet grace. Works by Mino da Fiesole include the **monument to Bernardo Giugni** (d.1460) and the **monument to Count Ugo** (d.1001) (1469–81), the latter deriving from Desiderio's **tomb of Carlo Marsuppini** in SANTA CROCE.

Bargello See MUSEO DEL BARGELLO.

Battistero *(Baptistry)* ★★
Piazzo del Duomo
Open Mon–Fri noon–5.30pm, Sat, Sun 9am–5.30pm
🏛

In the early Renaissance the octagonal baptistry was believed to have been the Roman temple of Mars, and it profoundly influenced Florentine architects. The date remains controversial; it perhaps goes back to the 5thC or 4thC AD. The building was given its green and white marble revetment in the 12thC, and its rectangular attic in the 13thC. It is most celebrated for its gilded bronze doors. Such bronze doors had not been cast since Roman antiquity; although the wax models for the first (S) set were completed in three months, it took 6yrs to achieve a successful casting.
S doors ★ (1330) by Andrea Pisano. The eight lower panels show the Cardinal and Theological Virtues; the 20 upper panels illustrate the **Life of St John the Baptist**, and relate to the iconography of the mosaics within the baptistry. The panels unite the grace of French Gothic with the vigorous style of Giotto; notice especially the powerful **Interrogation of the Baptist in Prison**. Over the doors, the statues of the **Baptist**, **Salome** and the **Executioner** are by Vincenzo Danti (1571).
N doors ★ (1403–24) by Lorenzo Ghiberti. A famous competition for the commission of these doors was held in 1401; it brought sudden fame and fortune to the young Lorenzo Ghiberti; his winning panel is shown with the defeated Brunelleschi's in the MUSEO DEL BARGELLO. The doors follow the overall design of Andrea Pisano's; the two lowest rows show the four Evangelists and the four Doctors of the Church; above, scenes from the New Testament begin

with the **Annunciation** in the lower left and finish, in the upper right, with the **Pentecost**. The gilded figures, in high relief, shine against the dark bronze background; the panels show a development from the graceful Gothic rhythms of the earlier scenes (the **Annunciation**, the **Nativity**) to the more classical symmetry of the later ones (the **Scourging**, the **Resurrection**).
E doors ★★ (1424–52) by Lorenzo Ghiberti. Michelangelo named these doors the Gates of Paradise. Ten panels showing scenes from the Old Testament – each including more than one episode – are surrounded by a framework of portrait heads in classical roundels and 24 statues of **Prophets** and **Sibyls** – these last, exquisitely finished, an early example of the Renaissance love for the small bronze statuette. One of the portrait heads (left door, inner frame) is an attractively genial self-portrait. An outer frame shows delightful motifs in very high relief – a squirrel nibbling nuts, birds nestling amongst pine cones, flowers and fruits – full of Ghiberti's love of nature.

The reliefs themselves move away from the Gothic tradition towards a new, richly pictorial style; space is created by the gradation from high relief to the most delicate shading of the surface, and by the application of the newly discovered laws of mathematical perspective. The latest scenes (the **Story of Isaac**, the **Story of Joseph**) are unified by architectural perspectives. Yet the landscape scenes (such as the **Creation**, where the eye is invited to wander over a variety of exquisite detail) are perhaps the most magically enchanting. Above the doors is the **Baptism of Christ** (1502) by Andrea Sansovino.
Interior The baptismal font is 14thC and the marble pavement around it, showing signs of the zodiac, 13thC. The vault is decorated with 13thC **mosaics** executed from cartoons by Cimabue and other Florentine artists. The **tomb of Cardinal Baldassare Coscia ★** (d.1419) by Donatello and Michelozzo introduced a new kind of Renaissance wall tomb: Michelozzo was responsible for the austerely classical figures; the powerfully realistic portrait is by Donatello.

Casa Buonarroti *(Michelangelo Museum)*
Via Ghibellina 70
Tel. (055) 287630
Open Wed–Mon 9am–1pm
Closed Tues
📷 🛏 🏛

The house was built on a site bought by Michelangelo for his nephew Leonardo.

In the 17thC it was decorated by leading Florentine artists (Furini, Vignali, Matteo Rosselli) to honour his memory; the programme was devised by Michelangelo's great-nephew, the poet Michelangelo Buonarroti the Younger. The house is now a museum.

The museum has two early works by Michelangelo, the **Madonna della Scala** (1490–92) and the **Battle of the Centaurs** (1492). Although very different from one another, they both look forward to Michelangelo's later development. In the first, the grave Madonna ponders the tragic destiny of the sleeping Child; in the second, the expressive power of the male nude is tentatively explored. A wooden **crucifix**, discovered in the 1960s in Santo Spirito, is perhaps an early work by Michelangelo.

Cenacolo di Sant'Apollonia
Via XXVII Aprile 1
Tel. (055) 2870774
Closed for restoration
The refectory of the former convent of Sant' Apollonia has powerful frescoes by Andrea del Castagno, one of the leading early Renaissance artists after Masaccio.

In the **Last Supper ★★** (1450), grave figures of the Apostles are silhouetted against the geometric planes of a strange, elaborate, marble room. The dark tones and hard surfaces create a heavy, threatening mood; the composition, with Judas isolated on this side of the long table, is traditional – yet no earlier artist had so powerfully contrasted the sinister Judas with Christ, who looks with tender regret at his sleeping disciple, John.

Above this are three scenes from the *Passion*, painted between 1445–50 and found beneath whitewash in 1890. The triumphant Christ looks forward to Piero della Francesca's great work at SANSEPOLCRO.

Cenacolo di San Salvi
Via San Salvi 16
Tel. (055) 677570
In the refectory of the former abbey of San Salvi is an outstanding *Last Supper* ★ (1519) by Andrea del Sarto. Harmony of both colour and composition make this one of the masterpieces of the Florentine High Renaissance.

Chiostro dello Scalzo
Via Cavour 69
Tel. (055) 484808
Closed for restoration
The early 16thC cloister is decorated with splendid grisaille frescoes of the *Life of St John the Baptist* ★ (1511–24) by

Andrea del Sarto. The work was interrupted by Andrea's visit to France (1518–19), and later frescoes – the *Dance of Salome*, (1521–22), the *Feast of Herod* (1523) – are more restrained in style and composition.

Duomo ☆ ☆
Piazza del Duomo
Open 7.30am–noon, 3.30–6pm
The building was begun in 1296 by Arnolfo di Cambio, continued from 1334 under the direction of Giotto and elaborated from 1357 by Francesco Talenti and Lapo Ghini; the great dome which dominates Florence is by Brunelleschi (1436). On the exterior, notice especially the Renaissance **Porta della Mandorla** (on the N side) with, in the pediment, a relief of the *Assumption of the Virgin* ★ – a late, unexpectedly Gothic work by Nanni di Banco (1414–21). The interior is austere, even bleak.
Nave The internal facade has early 15thC stained glass by Ghiberti. To the right of the entrance is Tino di Camaino's **monument to Bishop d'Orso** ★ (1321), distinguished by the beauty of the simplified forms of the face.
Right aisle The bust of *Giotto* is by Benedetto da Maiano (1490).
Left aisle This has two celebrated monuments to *condottieri* or mercenary captains: equestrian, *trompe l'oeil* frescoes (now on canvas) that imitate marble statues. The first, Uccello's **monument to Sir John Hawkwood** ★ (1436), is a complex demonstration of different viewpoints; the second, Andrea del Castagno's **monument to Niccolò da Tolentino** ★ (1456), was inspired by Donatello's famous equestrian statue at Padua (see *NORTH EAST ITALY*). Next is a curious panel painting of *Dante Explaining the Divine Comedy* (1465) by Domenico di Michelino.
Crossing The cupola is frescoed (late 16thC) by Vasari and Federico Zuccaro; the stained glass is from designs by Ghiberti, Andrea del Castagno, Donatello and Uccello. The octagonal, marble **choir enclosure** (1555) is by Bandinelli; its reliefs are among the most successful works of this much-derided sculptor. Over the high altar is a **crucifix** by Benedetto da Maiano (1495–97).
Sacristies Above the door of the New Sacristy is a lunette of the *Resurrection* (1442) by Luca della Robbia; opposite, over the door of the Old Sacristy, is a paired lunette of the **Ascension** (1446–51). The **bronze doors** ★ of the New Sacristy are also by Luca della

Robbia, and their simple designs contrast sharply with the vividness of Donatello's doors for the Old Sacristy at SAN LORENZO.

See also BATTISTERO and MUSEO DELL' OPERA DEL DUOMO.

Galleria dell'Accademia ☆☆
Via Ricasoli 60
Tel. (055) 214375
Open Tues – Sat 9am – 2pm, Sun
9am – 1pm
Closed Mon
📞 💷 ☑ ♨

The Accademia is most celebrated for its Michelangelo sculptures, but it also has important paintings and other works of art. From the 12thC and 13thC, there are works by Taddeo Gaddi and Andrea Orcagna; from the 15thC, paintings by Baldovinetti and Botticelli, and the **Adimari Cassone ★** (1440–45), by an unknown artist and full of delightful genre detail; from the 16thC, good works by Fra Bartolommeo and Perugino – Fra Bartolommeo's **Vision of St Bernard** (1504) is one of his most subtly coloured early paintings.

Michelangelo Collection (Room II) The four unfinished **Slaves ★★** (c.1519–36) are set against a backdrop of splendid 16thC tapestries. They were originally intended as architectural figures for Pope Julius II's ill-fated tomb in St Peter's (see San Pietro in Vincoli, Rome, *SOUTH CENTRAL ITALY*). They yield a fascinating glimpse of Michelangelo's working methods; Romantic writers saw in their heavy, contorted figures, movingly imprisoned within the marble, a sense of profound despair and oppression. Michelangelo's **David★★** (1501–4) was carved from a large, awkwardly proportioned block of marble, which had been previously worked and abandoned by Agostino di Duccio in the 1460s. His **David** is no longer the lithe, victorious youth portrayed by Donatello and Verrocchio in the MUSEO DEL BARGELLO but a gigantic figure, shown in a moment of balance and tense concentration before the contest; the formal beauty of classical sculpture is united with a sense of the vigour and power of man. The **David** was originally set in the PIAZZA DELLA SIGNORIA, in front of the Palazzo Vecchio, seat of government, with Donatello's **Judith and Holofernes**; both symbolize a courageous defence of freedom against the rule of tyranny.

Other works by Michelangelo include the curiously awkward **Palestrina Pietà** and the **St Matthew ★** In 1503 Michelangelo had been commissioned to carve 12 **Apostles** for the DUOMO; the **St Matthew**, an unfinished, yet passionate and dramatic work, is the only one that he began.

Galleria d'Arte Moderna See
PALAZZO PITTI.

Galleria degli Uffizi ☆☆
Piazzale degli Uffizi 6
Tel. (055) 218341
Open Tues – Sat 9am – 7.30pm, Sun
9am – 1pm
Closed Mon
📞 💷 ⬛ 🏛 ☑ ▦

The Uffizi gallery contains the most celebrated collection of Florentine Renaissance art in the world, enriched by fine classical sculptures – once more famous than the pictures – a collection of self-portraits, and important paintings by Venetian and Flemish artists. The narrow galleries on the second floor of Vasari's palace, lined with antique sculpture, 16thC tapestries, and lively grotesques, create a magnificent, colourful setting for the works of art; a long corridor links the Uffizi to the PALAZZO PITTI – offering, as it leads across the Ponte Vecchio and through the little church of SANTA FELICITÀ, spectacular views over Florence.

In winter, the Uffizi is one of the pleasantest of all galleries, with its comparatively small, often beautiful rooms, and the logical arrangement of the pictures, lucidly demonstrating the stylistic development of Florentine art. Yet in summer it is almost intolerably crowded and noisy throughout the day; the lunch hour and late evening are perhaps the most promising times. This tour takes in rooms of major interest only.

On the ground floor, Andrea del Castagno's detached frescoes of **Famous Men and Women** are now displayed; opposite the lift there is a fine **Annunciation** (1481) by Botticelli. The prints and drawings room, on the mezzanine floor, often has good temporary exhibitions.

Room 2 The display opens resoundingly with three vast altarpieces of the **Maestà ★★** which mark a turning point in Renaissance painting; every text book on Italian art opens with a comparison between them. Their relationship is complex; Cimabue's majestic painting (c.1280), while still linked to Byzantine art, has the beginnings of a sense of space that leads on to Giotto. In Giotto's picture, the solid figures are modelled by light and shade; the angels no longer pattern the surface, but recede into depth. Duccio's picture is close to Cimabue's, but the emphasis on a brilliant patterning of the surface is still more marked; the hem of the Virgin's gown twists and flutters with sinuous grace; mother and child are tenderly observed.

Room 3 Sienese Painting. In Siena, painters responded to Giotto's achievements yet retained a predilection for linear grace, delicate detail and lyrical mood. Simone Martini was the principal heir to Duccio's exquisitely-wrought paintings; his *Annunciation* ★★ (1333) with its elegant line, blaze of gold and marble, and lovely patterns of fabrics, flowers and wings, rejects Giotto's austerity. Pietro Lorenzetti's *Madonna in Glory* (1340) draws closer to Giotto's solid forms. The last panel of Ambrogio Lorenzetti's *Story of St Nicholas* ★ (c.1330) has a real sense of depth; lively touches of fresh observation blend charmingly with the fantastic shapes of rocks and sails.

Room 4 This room has dullish paintings by followers of Giotto.

Rooms 5 and 6 The last blaze of Gothic painting, stemming from 14thC Sienese art, is represented by Lorenzo Monaco's radiant, vividly coloured and patterned *Coronation of the Virgin* ★ (1413). His *Adoration of the Magi* ★ (c.1420) – calmer, even melancholy – moves towards International Gothic, a style which finds its most sumptuous expression in Gentile da Fabriano's *Adoration of the Magi* ★★ (1423). This painting is crowded with lively naturalistic detail – note the beauty of the light in the landscapes of the predella panels, and the vivid charm of the Christ Child, his toes curling, and his hand outstretched to the old king's bald head – yet it has the rich decorative beauty of a tapestry, with a joyful, festive crowd wending its way through a fairy-tale landscape to Bethlehem.

Room 7 This has paintings by Masaccio and by artists who developed his great innovations in space, perspective and anatomy. The *Madonna with St Anne* (1424) is by Masolino and Masaccio: Masaccio painted the dignified, solidly modelled Madonna and Child. Fra Angelico's *Coronation of the Virgin* ★ (1430) retains something of Gentile's decorative beauty, yet the clarity of the space and the dignity of the figures suggest an awareness of Masaccio.

The tranquil **St Lucy altarpiece** ★ (1445–48) is a signed work by the rare artist Domenico Veneziano, remarkable for the beauty of the cool light and delicately coloured architecture. Domenico taught Piero della Francesca, whose portraits of *Federico da Montefeltro* ★★ and *Battista Sforza* ★★ (c.1460) are shown in strict perspective –

derived from antique medals – against the rivers and valleys of their spreading domains. The delicate detail and the beauty of the light suggest Piero's interest in Flemish painting. On the reverse of the diptych the Duke and Duchess, shown proudly enthroned on triumphal chariots, are the center of small allegorical scenes; yet again it is the soft, hazy beauty of rounded hills and water that captures the attention.

With Paolo Uccello, a passionate interest in perspective became an obsession; Vasari wrote that "he left a wife who used to relate that Paolo would spend a whole night at his drawing board trying to find the rules of perspective, and when she called him to come to bed, he would answer: 'Oh, how sweet is this perspective!'" The *Battle of San Romano* ★ (1456) is one of three panels that originally hung in the great hall of the PALAZZO MEDICI-RICCARDI. The interest in foreshortening and orthogonals is very evident, but the real battle (of 1432) is transformed into a scene of pageantry from Gothic romance, enriched by fanciful, decorative detail.

Room 8 The main interest of this room lies in paintings by Fra Filippo Lippi, who slowly moved away from the influence of Masaccio towards a more decorative style; his *Coronation of the Virgin* ★ (1441) combines the rather squat, solid forms of his earlier paintings with a highly wrought, ornamental surface beauty: his later, sweetly pious *Adoration of the Child with the Young St John and St Romuald* revives the magic of Gothic landscape; this new sweetness and tenderness is characteristic of Florentine art in the 1460s and 1470s.

Room 9 This has paintings by Antonio and Piero Pollaiuolo. Antonio was passionately interested in anatomy, and the tiny panels (in the case beneath the window) of the *Feats of Hercules* ★ are fine examples of the taut, wiry energy of his figures. His influence is evident in Botticelli's vivid, intense *Finding of the Body of Holofernes* ★ but the *Return of Judith*, in the same series, is an altogether gentler painting, touched by Lippi's melancholy grace.

Rooms 10–14 This celebrated collection of works by Botticelli is the highlight of any tour of the Uffizi. The two great allegories, the *Primavera* ★★ (c.1480) and the *Birth of Venus* ★★ (c.1485), are perhaps the most famous pictures in the gallery.

The *Primavera* is one of the loveliest and most enchanting of all paintings of classical myth; it has inspired very many recondite interpretations; Vasari described the subject simply, as "Venus, whom the Graces deck with flowers, denoting spring". The painting shows none of the Early Renaissance interest in perspective and anatomy, but looks back to the grace of International Gothic; the figures, linked by subtle linear rhythms, are spread out before a dark, tapestry-like background, glowing exotically with fruits and flowers.

The **Birth of Venus** shows the goddess, born of the foam of the sea, being wafted to the shore by two winds; an attendant waits with a billowing, flowery cloak. The extraordinary beauty of Botticelli's line here finds its supreme expression, as it flows through swelling draperies and entangled limbs, and weaves through the elaborate, heavy mass of golden hair. The same rhythms animate Botticelli's lovely **Madonna of the Magnificat** ★★ (1482), their abstract beauty enhanced by the tondo form.

Botticelli's **Adoration of the Magi** was originally in SANTA MARIA NOVELLA. Vasari described the three kings as members of the Medici family; the eldest is Cosimo il Vecchio (d. 1464); the second, Piero il Gottoso; and the third, perhaps Giuliano, who had been murdered in the Pazzi conspiracy. The figure in a yellow cloak on the right was said by Vasari to be a self-portrait.

The **Young Man with a Medal**, one of Botticelli's finest portraits, shares a quality of dreamy, melancholy grace with Filippino Lippi's **Self-portrait**. Close by, the **Calumny of Apelles** is a good example of the more turbulent, intensely dramatic quality of Botticelli's late style.

Opposite the ideal beauty of Botticelli's **Birth of Venus**, and presenting a startling contrast to it, is Hugo van der Goes' **Adoration of the Shepherds** ★★ the great masterpiece of Northern realism, also known as the **Portinari altarpiece**. On the outer panels, the donors are presented by huge, looming saints outlined against a lovely wintry landscape with, in the distance, little scenes from the Nativity. In the center, the tiny Christ Child is strikingly isolated – an effect enhanced by the contrasts in scale and by the rough passion of the shepherds, whose startling realism made them instantly famous. Indeed, both they and the fresh beauty of the still-life had a profound impact upon Italian art.

The cross-currents between North and South are also manifest in Rogier van der Weyden's **Deposition** ★ where the symmetry of the composition, based on a painting by Fra Angelico, is Italian, yet the perspective and the spiky, bony bodies and wrinkled faces remain profoundly Northern.

Around these Flemish works in the center of the room hang pictures by Italian artists who responded to their achievements. Ghirlandaio's **Madonna Enthroned with Saints** has a Flemish emphasis on texture and surface, on the fall of light, and on lovely still-life details. The glimpse of an arid landscape in Filippino Lippi's **Adoration of the Magi** (1496) is indebted to the Portinari altarpiece; its crowded, agitated, intense quality contrasts sharply with the clarity and charming festivity of Ghirlandaio's **Adoration** (1487) and was perhaps a response to Leonardo, whose treatment of the same subject, in the next room, introduced a profoundly new vision. **Room 15** Leonardo's **Adoration of the Magi** ★★ (1481) is the outstanding work here; the colourful charm of the Quattrocento – the angels and shepherds, the stable with its ox and ass – have vanished; instead, Leonardo surrounds the Virgin and Child with a crowd of intense, yearning, passionate worshippers, awed by the importance of the event.

The profound change that Leonardo brought about is intimated in two other pictures in the room. He added an angel to Verrocchio's clearly drawn and structured **Baptism of Christ** ★ and its grace contrasts sharply with Verrocchio's fresh Florentine boy. The soft, mysterious landscape glimpsed in Leonardo's **Annunciation** ★ (c. 1475) introduced a new, subtle poetry, very different from the poised Quattrocento clarity of the **Annunciation** by Lorenzo di Credi (1485). (The Leonardo **Annunciation** is a much disputed work.) **Room 18** The **Tribuna** ★ (1584) glowing with precious materials, was designed by Buontalenti and was once the center of the gallery, where the most celebrated works were displayed. The **Medici Venus** ★ a Roman copy of a Greek original, once moved Romantic poets and writers to endless rapture; today her reputation has fallen as dramatically as that of the **Apollo Belvedere** in the Musei Vaticani (see Rome, *SOUTH CENTRAL ITALY*).

The highlights now are a group of portraits by Bronzino. The portraits of **Eleonora of Toledo** ★ and **Lucrezia Panciatichi** ★ are cold, remote, exquisitely polished; the children are more lively, and range from the round, jolly charm of **Giovanni de' Medici** ★ (1475) – not yet two years old and his two front teeth showing – to the touching poise of **Isabella de' Medici** (1472) and the watchful, sensual **Portrait of a Girl with a Book** ★
Room 17 This room opens from the

UFFIZI TOP TEN

The Uffizi collections are of outstanding quality. First-time visitors to the gallery may find it helpful to refer to this summary, which highlights some of the most famous masterpieces.

1 Giotto: **Maestà**
2 Simone Martini: **Annunciation**
3 Gentile da Fabriano: **Adoration of the Magi**
4 Botticelli: **Primavera**
5 Hugo van der Goes: **Portinari Altarpiece**
6 Leonardo da Vinci: **Adoration of the Magi**
7 Michelangelo: **Doni Tondo**
8 Raphael: **Portrait of Leo X**
9 Titian: **Venus of Urbino**
10 Parmigianino: **Madonna of the Long Neck**

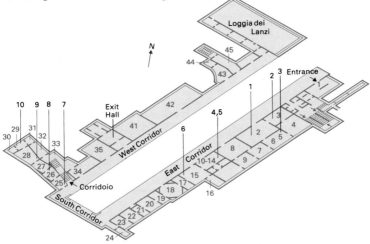

Tribuna and has important paintings by Mantegna: the **Adoration** (1466–67) and the **Madonna of the Stonecutters** (1488–89).

Room 19 The gravity and monumentality of Signorelli's tondo of the **Holy Family** (1491) look forward to Michelangelo's Doni tondo in Room 25. Perugino's portrait of **Francesco delle Opere** (1494) is one of his most powerful works, a blend of almost Northern realism with the soft poetry of an Umbrian landscape.

Room 20 German painting. The intense, visionary character of German Renaissance art contrasts sharply with the bright clarity of the Florentine Quattrocento. In Cranach's **St George**, the tiny figures are dwarfed by a sinister, Nordic forest. Yet Dürer was an artist fascinated by Italian discoveries, and his **Adoration of the Magi** (1504) is a display of sculptural forms and complex perspectives and a balance of profiles and frontal presentations; the Moor is framed

by two sharply foreshortened arches.

Room 21 Venice first developed an artistic tradition worthy to challenge Florence with Giovanni Bellini, whose paintings depend on the beauty of colour and tone rather than line; the geometric clarity and warm, mellow atmosphere of his **Sacred Allegory ★** (c. 1400) create a still, dreamy mood.

Room 22 Holbein's **Portrait of Sir Richard Southwell** (1536) is painted with the flawless, hair-by-hair precision of his second English period. There are also two romantic pictures by Altdorfer, the **Departure** and the **Martyrdom of St Florian** (c. 1527).

Room 23 This has Correggio's **Rest on the Flight into Egypt** (after 1515) and Boltraffio's slightly earlier **Narcissus**.

Room 25 Michelangelo's **Doni tondo ★★** uses painting to imitate sculpture; the extraordinary, unnatural beauty of the Virgin's pose, and the strange, cold colours, lead onto Mannerism – to the weird, irrelevant complexities and disturbing expressions of Rosso Fiorentino's **Moses and the Daughters of Jethro** (1523–24).

Room 26 The pyramidal composition of Raphael's **Madonna of the Goldfinch** ★★ derives from Leonardo; the painting's warmth and humanity, and the softness of the landscape, contrast with the stony strangeness of the Doni tondo; John the Baptist offers Christ a goldfinch, symbol of the Passion. Yet Raphael, the painter of sweet Madonnas, also created the sinister, oppressively powerful **Portrait of Leo X** ★★ (1518–19); the overwhelming, painterly splendour of this work suggests the influence of Venetian and Flemish art; Vasari commented on how, on the back of the chair, "there is a ball of burnished gold, which, such is the brightness, reflects the Pope's shoulder and the division of the opposite window".

Room 27 This has Pontormo's intensely spiritual **Supper at Emmaus** ★ (1540) and Bronzino's **Holy Family** ★ (c.1528).

Room 28 Titian's glowing **Venus of Urbino** ★★ delights with "that perfect face of pleasure, open where Leonardo's was secret, warm where his was pale, its large eyes lustrously dark and the mouth dark too, a ripe stain of promise" (Michael Levey). His **Flora** ★ (c.1515) is a lovely and subtly erotic work; by contrast, his portrait of the Duchess of Urbino, **Eleanora Gonzaga della Rovere** ★ rich, aristocratic, yet warmly human, is strongly characterized.

Room 29 The extraordinary elongations and spatial ambiguities of the **Madonna of the Long Neck** ★★ (c.1535) by Parmigianino epitomize the Mannerist style.

Next door to Room 34 is the entrance to Vasari's **Corridoio**: a collection of artists' self-portraits which vividly suggest the varying aspirations and status of the artist from the 16thC to the 19thC. Look out for a lyrical portrait of the young Raphael; the melancholy Carlo Dolci; Rubens, worldly and self-assured; a flashy, exuberant portrait of Solimena. The portrait of Ingres, solid and severe, contrasts with the fiery, romantic Delacroix.

Room 35 Paintings include works by Tintoretto and El Greco; and Barocci's stormy, windswept **Noli Me Tangere** (1590).

Room 41 Among the paintings by Rubens and van Dyck note a darkly glowing Rubens portrait of **Isabella Brant** ★

Room 42 A collection of 20thC self-portraits oddly confronts 4thC Roman sculptures of **Niobe and her Children**, for which this room was designed. The self-

portraits include works by Annigoni, Emilio Greco, Morandi, and the Americans Sam Francis, Olitski and Rauschenberg.

Room 43 In the early 17thC, artists tired of the frigid abstractions of Mannerism and turned again to nature. Caravaggio's **Head of Medusa** (c.1596) is inspired by an interest in violent expression and emotion. His **Young Bacchus** ★ is a provocatively naturalistic work – an earthy, lazily sensual Greek god, with a sparkling still-life – while Annibale Carracci's **Young Man with a Monkey** has a totally new vividness and spontaneity.

A renewed interest in nature stimulated the development of landscape as an independent genre. Guercino's **Summer Diversion** ★ is a lovely Giorgionesque idyll; the French artist, Claude Lorraine, brought the beauty of the setting sun into landscape art in his **Seaport with the Villa Medici** (1637) – its effect is intensely theatrical and glamorous.

Room 44 The Dutch paintings here are dominated by Rembrandt, but note also the wild grandeur and desolation of Hercules Seghers' early 17thC **Landscape**, which Rembrandt admired.

Room 45 This has 18thC Venetian, French and Spanish paintings. There are characteristic works by Canaletto and Guardi; a Tiepolo ceiling; Jeanne Etienne Liotard's **Portrait of Princess Marie Adelaide**; and Chardin's grave and touching **Girl with a Shuttlecock**.

On the way out, in the small exit hall, the **Wild Boar** is a Roman copy of a 3rdC BC Hellenistic original.

Medici Chapels See SAN LORENZO.

Museo dell'Angelico *(Museo di San Marco)* ☆
Piazza San Marco
Tel. (055) 210741
Open Tues – Sat 9am – 2pm, Sun 9am – 1pm
Closed Mon
🏛 ♿

The site of the Silvestrine convent of San Marco was handed over to the Dominican monks of Fiesole by Cosimo de' Medici in 1436. The grave and elegant buildings were designed by Michelozzo; the corridors, the chapter house, and the small, austere cells on the first floor have simple, tender frescoes by Fra Angelico; the whole movingly conveys a sense of the calm, ordered and scholarly life of the religious community. Today Fra Angelico's most celebrated paintings from the churches and galleries of Florence have been brought here to create a museum especially devoted to him.

The vestibule leads into Michelozzo's Chiostro di Sant'Antonio, tranquilly shaded by a large cedar. In the Ospizio dei Pellegrini, to the right of the entrance, are housed 20 of Fra Angelico's panel paintings.

The **Madonna of the Linen Guild** ★★ (1433) is at once majestic and charmingly decorative; the marble tabernacle was designed by Ghiberti and the imposing saints on the wing panels are reminiscent of his monumental sculptures. In the **Descent from the Cross** ★★ Fra Angelico reveals a true understanding of Renaissance perspective; the solemn figures are placed in a landscape clearly structured around a balance of horizontal and vertical accents.

The predella panels tend to be more spontaneous – note the lucidity and bright colour of the scene featuring **Sts Cosmas and Damian** on the high altarpiece of San Marco, and the charming, vivid humanity of the **Naming of St John the Baptist** ★

In the Sala Capitolare is Fra Angelico's austere **Crucifixion** ★ In the refectory, Ghirlandaio's **Last Supper** ★ is a variant of the painting in the OGNISSANTI.

On the first floor, at the top of the stairs, is Fra Angelico's celebrated **Annunciation** ★★ Monks' cells line both sides of the corridor; these were frescoed by Fra Angelico and assistants between 1439 and 1445. Fra Angelico was most directly concerned with the frescoes on the left side of the corridor. These are radiant, direct paintings, in which form is severely simplified, and narrative reduced; intended as aids to contemplation, they dominate the small, bare, cells.

Notice especially the **Noli Me Tangere** ★ (cell 1); the touchingly simple **Annunciation** ★ (cell 3); the majestic **Transfiguration** ★ (cell 6); and the **Mocking of Christ** (cell 7), in which the concentration on essentials leads to an emblematic representation. Between cells 42 and 43 is Michelozzo's graceful library; cells 38 and 39 were reserved for Cosimo de' Medici.

Museo dell'Antica Casa Fiorentina
Palazzo Davanzati, Via Porta Rossa 13
Tel. (055) 21658
Open Tues – Sat 9am – 2pm, Sun
9am – 1pm
Closed Mon
▨ 🏛 ☑

The Palazzo Davanzati is a splendid example of a mid 14thC palace: the severe three-storey tower is crowned by a Renaissance loggia, showing the need for fortification yielding to a pleasanter way of life. The interior has been skilfully restored and arranged as a museum; a rich array of furniture, tapestries, majolica, sculptures and paintings creates a vivid picture of the way life must have been in a wealthy nobleman's house in 14thC – 16thC Florence.

The museum is all atmosphere – little rooms open into each other at odd angles; there are steep, hooded chimneys and heavy wooden shutters; a collection of marriage chests captures the poetry of Gothic romance.

Especially fine wall decorations include the Sala dei Pappagalli decorated with painted wall hangings and, in the feigned loggia above, with trees filled with birds and little vases perched on the cornice.

On the second floor, a bedroom is decorated with scenes illustrating the medieval French poem, the *Châtelaine of Vergi*.

Museo Archeologico ☆
Via della Colonna 36
Tel. (055) 215270
Open Tues – Sat 9am – 2pm, Sun
9am – 1pm
Closed Mon
▨ 🏛 ⬚

The museum was badly damaged in the flood of 1966, and much of the most important material is still undergoing restoration. At present there is a sharp contrast between the beginnings of a superbly documented and luxurious modern display on the ground floor, and the dusty confusing jumble of the upper floors.

On the ground floor, note especially the **François Vase** ★ (c. 570BC) a signed work of Kleitias and Ergotimus; the monumental, awesome **Mother** ★ from Chianciano (c. 400BC), which has been called a "gloomy ancestress of Michelangelo's sadly prophetic Madonna at Bruges"; also two very fine Greek kouroi; and a small room which is dedicated to the taste and collection of Luigi Adriani Milani, the first director of the museum.

The first floor has an important **Egyptian collection** ★ and outstanding Greek, Roman and Etruscan bronzes. The celebrated **Wounded Chimera** ★ from Arezzo (c. 480BC) – a monster from Greek fable, deeply influenced by Greek art – was found in 1554 and restored by Benvenuto Cellini. The **Orator** ★ (c. 90 – 50BC) is a late Etruscan life-size statue that looks forward to the vigorous realism of Roman sculpture; inscribed on his toga is his name, Avile Metelis, son of Vel and Vesi.

The second floor has a prehistoric section; a large collection of Greek vases; and sarcophagi and cinerary urns from several Etruscan cities, including Sovana, Tuscania, Orvieto and Arezzo. Among the sarcophagi, notice especially the polychrome terra-cotta **sarcophagus of Larthia Seianti** (3rd–2ndCBC), showing all the little toilet articles of the deceased.

At present, a covered walkway leads to the small area for temporary exhibitions, through the garden where Etruscan tombs from Orvieto, Populonia and Volterra have been romantically reconstructed among the roses and pretty gravel walks.

Museo degli Argenti See PALAZZO PITTI.

Museo Bardini
Piazza de' Mozzi 1
Open Mon, Tues, Thurs–Sat 9am–2pm,
Sun 8am–1pm
Closed Wed
🖾 🏛 ☑

An extraordinarily varied array of antiquities, sculptures, paintings, tapestries, oriental rugs and decorative arts, this collection was brought together by the gifted connoisseur and wealthy art dealer Stefano Bardini (1836–1922).

Bardini destroyed the 13thC church of San Gregorio della Pace to build the palace for his collection, framing the windows on the facade with fragments from a Pistoian altar; he boldly put together parts of earlier buildings – chimney pieces, carved wooden ceilings, delicate Renaissance doorways – to create a sequence of rich compositions.

The rooms now have a dusty, little visited air, rewarding the spectator with a sense of discovery that is comparatively rare among the well-photographed museums of Florence.

On the **ground floor**, classical, Renaissance and Baroque sculptures include works by Tino di Camaino and Andrea Sansovino; a small vaulted crypt displays a fascinating collection of tomb slabs and sepulchral monuments, and a terra cotta by Andrea della Robbia. On the **second floor**, an outstanding collection of wooden and terra-cotta sculptures by Tuscan and Sienese artists includes an exquisite, touchingly hesitant **Annunciate Virgin** (Sienese, 15thC). Among the pictures, note especially works by Antonio Pollaiuolo; good portraits by Francesco Salviati; and some interesting 17thC Florentine paintings.

Museo del Bargello *(Museo Nazionale)* ☆☆
Palazzo del Podestà, Via del Proconsolo 4
Open Tues–Sat 9am–2pm, Sun
  9am–1pm
Closed Mon
🖾 🏛 ☑ 🔧

This unrivalled collection of Florentine Renaissance sculpture is housed in the grim 14thC Palazzo del Podestà.
Ground floor The ground floor rooms are entered through the picturesque courtyard, with 14thC loggia and external staircase; across the courtyard, Room III has 14thC Tuscan sculptures, including Tino di Camaino's **Madonna**.

A door to the right of the entrance leads into Room I, a new sculpture gallery, with an exceptionally well-documented and informative display of 16thC sculpture, emphasizing the impact of various masters on each other. Celebrated sculptures by Michelangelo and Cellini dominate the room, but there is also an attempt to revalue the works of such late 16thC masters as Ammanati, Bandinelli and Vincenzo Danti, who worked in the shadow of their greatness.

Works by Michelangelo include the **Pitti tondo** ★ (c. 1504), **Brutus** ★ (1540) and **Bacchus** ★★ (c.1497). The **Bacchus** was his first large, free-standing figure; the unheroic god, drunkenly swaying, eyes glazed, is set against Jacopo Sansovino's more ecstatic, idealized **Bacchus** ★ which was carved as a challenge to Michelangelo.

Exquisitely refined works by the Mannerist sculptor and goldsmith, Cellini, include the **bronze model** ★ for the **Perseus** in the Loggia dei Lanzi (PIAZZA DELLA SIGNORIA); the works that once decorated its base – the relief of **Perseus and Andromeda** ★ and four ingeniously posed **bronze statuettes** ★ – are now also displayed here.

Although it is sad to see works of art vanish from their original sites, the present arrangement recalls Cellini's description in his *Autobiography* of how, when the bronzes were finished, he arranged them "in a row, raised somewhat above the line of vision, so that they produced a magnificent effect"; Cosimo I and Eleanor, his Duchess, took seats before them, the Duchess exclaiming: "I do not like to let those exquisite figures be wasted on the pedestal down there in the piazza, where they will run the risk of being injured." Cellini braved her anger and soldered them into their niches in secret.

The extreme artifice of Cellini's **Narcissus** was caused by a flaw found in the block of marble. His glittering, vibrant bust of **Cosimo 1** ★ (finished

1547) was executed in competition with Bandinelli, whose more dully classical work (across the room) was preferred by the Medici Grand Duke.

First floor The internal staircase leads to Room VI, with polychrome wooden statues of the 14thC and 15thC and ivories. Rooms VII and VIII have goldsmiths' ware, jewellery and majolica. The Loggia has Giambologna's **Mercury** ★ the most celebrated work of this Mannerist sculptor, the pose brilliantly suggesting the lightness of flight; also, a collection of his bronze animals and birds, a speciality of this Flemish-born sculptor.

Beyond the Loggia is the large Salone del Consiglio Generale. Against the wall, the two bronze panels by Brunelleschi and Ghiberti of the **Sacrifice of Isaac** ★ were entries for the famous competition of 1401 to decide on the artist for the second (N) doors of the baptistry (see BATTISTERO).

Brunelleschi's panel, full of sharp, angular movements and violent expression, shows the dramatic moment when the angel seizes Abraham's arm as he brutally lays bare the throat of his son. Ghiberti's less realistic composition is more unified; the figure of Isaac, which was made separately, attains the ideal beauty of classical art.

Against the end wall is Donatello's intensely realistic **St George** ★★ (1416), originally on the facade of ORSANMICHELE. Most celebrated among the free-standing sculptures is Donatello's **David** ★★ (1430) which brought back to Renaissance art the physical beauty of antique sculpture. The young boy's dreamy grace is emphasized by the startling sensuousness with which the crisp feathers of Goliath's helmet curve upwards against the softness of David's thigh.

Yet Donatello also created the astonishing pagan vitality of his **Amor Atys** – in sharp contrast to the fragile tenderness of his marble **St John**. In the second half of the 15thC, after Donatello moved to Padua (1443), a sweeter, more lyrical sculptural style predominated in Florence, suggested here by Desiderio da Settignano's lovely **Pensive Girl** ★ Other important works around the walls are by Luca della Robbia and Agostino di Duccio.

Second floor Room I has a terra cotta by Giovanni della Robbia; Cellini's **Ganymede**; and Bernini's vividly sensual bust of **Costanza Bonarelli**. Room II has terra cottas by Andrea della Robbia. Around the walls of Room III, the Sala di Verrocchio, is a series of famous Renaissance portrait busts. The bust of

Piero de' Medici (1456) by Mino da Fiesole (right of the door), somewhat stiff and rigid, is the first dated work to revive the Roman portrait bust; the development of this type may be seen in the more confident bust of **Matteo Palmieri** (1468) by Antonio Rossellino and in works by Antonio Pollaiuolo and Benedetto da Maiano. The female bust was less indebted to classical antiquity: the warm, dignified beauty of Verrocchio's **Lady with a Bunch of Flowers** ★ contrasts with the exquisite stylization of Francesco Laurana's bust of **Battista Sforza** ★★ In the center of the room is Verrocchio's **David** (1476), whose brisk, martial air was perhaps a criticism of Donatello's languorous nude; also, Pollaiuolo's **Hercules and Antaeus** ★ which shows the artist's interest in violent movement and emotion.

Room VI has an outstanding collection of **bronzes** ★ with fine works by Riccio and Giambologna.

Museo Horne
Via dei Benci 6
Tel. (055) 244261
Open Mon–Fri, first and second Sun of
*   month 9am–1pm*
Closed Sat, third, fourth and fifth Sun of
*   month*
📷 🏛 ☑
This is a fascinating example of the kind of collection that could still be made by a gifted connoisseur, of limited means, at the turn of this century. Herbert Percy Horne was an English art historian, a friend of Pater, associated with Pre-Raphaelite circles, and a pupil of Selwyn Image, with whom he published a fine art journal, *The Hobby Horse*. He came to Florence to write a book on Botticelli, and remained here for the rest of his life.

His collection, housed in a small, late 15thC palace which he scrupulously restored and furnished in period style, includes some attractive early Renaissance works (Gaddi, Daddi, Pietro Lorenzetti, Filippo Lippi), Mannerist pictures by Beccafumi and Dosso Dossi, and two works by Francesco Furini; also, ceramics and decorative arts.

Museo dell'Opera del Duomo ✩
Piazza del Duomo 9
Tel. (055) 213229
Open Mon–Sat 9.30am–1pm,
*   3–5.30pm, Sun 10am–1pm*
📷 🗤 🏛
The museum has a rich collection of Florentine sculptures that once decorated the Duomo, baptistry and campanile.
Ground floor The now destroyed 14thC

facade for the Duomo was designed by the Pisan sculptor, Arnolfo di Cambio, who also worked on the sculptures for it; his *Virgin of the Nativity* ★ is an austere, solid work and was originally in the lunette over the side door. Two small rooms are devoted to Brunelleschi, exhibiting a death mask and the wooden model for the dome.

Mezzanine floor Here stands Michelangelo's *Pietà* ★★ from the Duomo; Michelangelo intended the work for his own tomb, and gave his own features to Nicodemus. He grew dissatisfied with his achievement, and attempted to break the sculpture up; it was later finished by someone else. Yet it remains a powerful, tragic work, and the moving contrast between the highly finished, beautiful body of Christ and the roughly blocked-out figure of Mary particularly appeals to 20thC taste.

First floor The **Sala delle Cantorie** has the famous **Cantorie**★★ (Singing Galleries) by Luca della Robbia and Donatello. In Luca's work, the serious, charming concentration and innocent gaiety of the young musicians is delicately poised; by contrast, the putti dance across Donatello's gallery with wild, Dionysiac abandon – beneath them is his horrifying *St Mary Magdalen* ★

In the next room are 16 statues that once stood in the niches of Giotto's campanile. The series by Donatello culminates in the harsh, expressive *Habakkuk* ★ (1434–36).

The **Sala delle Formelle** contains **relief panels** ★ designed for the campanile. The earliest are by Andrea Pisano, showing the influence of Giotto; the later ones are by Luca della Robbia. The reliefs illustrate stories from Genesis, the sciences and the Liberal arts.

The **Sala dell'Altare** has a **silver altar** ★ from the baptistry, begun in 1366 and finished over the next century by celebrated artists and craftsmen; notice especially Verrocchio's violent *Execution of St John*.

Ognissanti
Piazza d' Ognissanti
Tel. (055) 296802
Open 9am–12.30pm, 4–6pm
🏛

This late 13thC church was rebuilt and decorated in the Baroque period. In the lunette above the second altar on the right is Ghirlandaio's damaged fresco, the *Madonna of Mercy Protecting the Vespucci Family* (c.1472); the boy to the right of the Madonna is probably a portrait of Amerigo Vespucci, the Florentine discoverer of America. In the sacristy, the fresco of the *Crucifixion* is

by Taddeo Gaddi; the painted **crucifix** is by a follower of Giotto.

The **refectory** (entrance from the cloister) has Ghirlandaio's *Last Supper* ★ (1480), the traditional refectory subject. This fresco is influenced by Andrea del Castagno's earlier work (CENACOLO DI SANT'APOLLONIA), but it is gentler and full of charming descriptive detail. The clear silvery light seems to fall from the actual window at the side and the painted space subtly incorporates the central corbel.

On the left wall, Ghirlandaio's straightforward *St Jerome* yields to Botticelli's more profoundly spiritual *St Augustine* on the right wall (both 1480).

Orsanmichele ★★
Via dei Calzaiuoli
🏛

Originally built as a grain market (1337), this ornate Gothic building was turned into a church in 1380. The decoration of the outside was entrusted to the fiercely competitive guilds, who commissioned statues of their patron saints to stand in the niches; the church became an arena where, in the first quarter of the 15thC, the old Gothic style was vanquished by the new, vigorous realism of Renaissance sculpture.

Start on the E side (Via dei Calzaiuoli) where the statue on the right is an old-fashioned, Gothic *St Luke* by Niccolò di Pietro Lamberti, who was driven to Venice by Donatello's rivalry. In the center is Verrocchio's *Christ and St Thomas* ★ (1466–83) the latest work on the facade. On the left is Ghiberti's bronze *St John the Baptist* ★ (1412). Technically, Ghiberti's statue was an extraordinary achievement: an overlife-size, free-standing figure in bronze which, for the first time in the Renaissance, rivalled the achievements of classical antiquity. Stylistically, with its elegant loops of drapery, elaborately wrought curls of hair and goatskin, it is one of the most brilliant works of International Gothic sculpture, in marked contrast to the classicizing tendency that characterizes many of the sculptures on this facade.

Round the corner, on the S side (Via dei Lamberti) past some dullish Gothic works, the fourth statue is Donatello's *St Mark* (1411–12), with drapery and pose inspired by classical models. On the W side (Via dell' Arte della Lana) is an austere *St Eligius* by Nanni di Banco; also two statues by Ghiberti, *St Stephen* (1428) and *St Matthew* ★ (1419–21) – the *St Matthew* is a less decorative work than his *St John the Baptist* and shows how Ghiberti, after a visit to Rome, participated in the contemporary passion for classical art.

On the N side (Via Orsanmichele) there once stood the most excitingly new work of the whole ensemble, Donatello's **St George** ★★ (now replaced by a copy; the original is in the MUSEO DEL BARGELLO). This work is startlingly realistic; the figure is not bound by the niche, but seems poised for dramatic action; the sense of psychological tension is entirely new. The predella of **St George and the Dragon** ★ (temporarily replaced by a copy) was the first relief to use linear and atmospheric perspective (1417). Beyond are Nanni di Banco's **Four Crowned Saints** ★ (c.1411–13), a severely classical work, very clearly derived from Roman models.

The interior of the church houses Orcagna's richly decorated **tabernacle** (1348–59), his most celebrated sculptural work; it frames a painting of the **Virgin** by Daddi.

Palazzo Medici-Riccardi ☆
Via Cavour 1
Tel. (055) 2760
Open Mon, Tues, Thurs–Sat, Sun
  9am–noon
Closed Wed
📷 ⛪ 🏛

This fine Renaissance palace was built by Michelozzo and is famous for its tiny chapel, richly decorated with **frescoes** ★ by Benozzo Gozzoli. Around the walls, a festive, carefree procession of the Magi (many of them portraits of the Medici and their noble friends) twists and turns, past orange trees and cypresses, along the rocky terraces of an enchanting landscape; this leads to the altarpiece of the **Madonna**, an early copy of Filippo Lippi's original work. Gozzoli's Renaissance skill in the foreshortening of forms is evident, but it is subordinated to his love of an ornamental, almost tapestry-like richness.

From the courtyard, the second staircase leads to a lovely Rococo interior, frescoed by Luca Giordano in 1683. The ceiling shows the progress of human life, from birth to death, from dawn to night, and from spring to winter, all grandly culminating in the **Apotheosis of the Medici**.

Palazzo Pitti ☆☆
Piazza Pitti
Tel. (055) 287096
Open Tues–Sat 9am–2pm, Sun
  9am–1pm
Closed Mon
🚊 🍴 ⛪ 🏛 ♿

The Palazzo Pitti was built in the 1450s by Luca Pitti, the bitter rival of Cosimo de'

Medici, and passed into Medici hands in 1549. It is the spirit of the later Medici that is evoked by the splendour of the princely collection, hung three deep, gold frame to frame, and by Pietro da Cortona's opulent decorations, a brilliant celebration of the power of the Medici princes.

Galleria Palatina
Sala di Venere This has the first of Pietro da Cortona's cycles of frescoed allegories, which continue through the next four rooms. Paintings by Titian include the **Concert**, an early work (c.1510–13) once attributed to Giorgione; **La Bella** ★ a seductive painting of a sitter who appears more blatantly, clad only in a fur cloak, in a picture in Vienna; and a portrait of **Pietro Aretino** ★ poet and friend of Titian – a powerful work distinguished by the bold simplicity of the composition and by the brilliant freedom with which Titian suggests the rich glow of the fabrics.

The Baroque drama of Rubens' **Landscape with the Wreck of Ulysses** (c.1625) contrasts with the intensely romantic radiance and lovingly observed detail of his later **Peasants Returning from the Fields** ★ (c.1637), the latter influenced by Pieter Bruegel's cosmic landscapes. There are two vast harbour scenes by the greatest Baroque landscape artist, Salvator Rosa, who worked as court painter to the Medici; the clear structure and setting sun of his **Harbour View** suggest his response to Claude.
Sala di Apollo On the ceiling, the young prince converses with Apollo – the scene framed by wonderfully varied stucco figures against a gilt ground. There are paintings by Titian; a large altarpiece of 1522 by Rosso Fiorentino; and a late Guido Reni, **Cleopatra**, in a daring range of icy blues and mauves.
Sala di Marte This richly decorated room was once the equivalent of the Tribuna in the Uffizi, where the most treasured works were hung. The ceiling (1645–47) is painted as a vast, airy space open to the sky, with Mars swooping down to crown the valiant Medici prince. The paintings include Rubens' intensely human allegory of the **Consequences of War** ★ (1638); his **Four Philosophers**, full of the young artist's passion for classical antiquity; a glittering, vivacious van Dyck portrait of **Cardinal Bentivoglio** ★ (c.1623) with an unusually Baroque emphasis on spontaneity of expression and gesture yet retaining a Flemish delight in qualities of surface and texture; and Tintoretto's exceptionally fine portrait of **Luigi Cornaro** ★
Sala di Giove Originally the audience chamber, this room has frescoes in the

lunettes that portray the "good government" of the prince; the lunette of *Diana Sleeping* is particularly lovely. Outstanding among the paintings is Raphael's portrait of a woman known as *La Velata* ★★ where the rich, ornate swirls of gold and white in the sleeves are a foil to the classical grace of the head and the subtly withdrawn expression. There are also important works by Fra Bartolommeo and Andrea del Sarto. Against the window wall, and hard to see, is Lanfranco's *Vision of St Margaret of Cortona* ★ (1618–19) – an astonishingly early Baroque rendering of saintly ecstasy through dramatic contrasts of light and dark, fluttering draperies and intensely physical imagery.

Sala di Saturno This is the last room of Cortona's cycle, executed largely by his assistant, Ciro Ferri. It contains the most celebrated picture in the gallery, Raphael's *Madonna della Seggiola* ★★ – a triumph of complex design, yet tender and direct, it hangs opposite the earlier, touchingly simple and modest *Madonna del Granduca* ★ (1505–6). The room also has grand altarpieces by Perugino and Fra Bartolommeo, others by Raphael, and a group of Raphael portraits – including his portraits of *Agnolo Doni* and *Maddalena Doni* (c.1505–6). The pose of Maddalena Doni was inspired by the Mona Lisa; the portrait is a lovely study of texture and fabric, yet has a stolid, prim air that contrasts with the more powerful Agnolo Doni. His was a common portrait type in the period, as is shown by the intriguingly melancholy *Portrait of a Young Man* by Ridolfo Ghirlandaio which hangs nearby.

Sala dell' Iliade This contains a more random collection of pictures. The flavour is mainly determined by a series of stiff royal portraits which capture the fleshy decadence of the declining Medici. Yet there is also Raphael's portrait of *La Gravida* ★ two altarpieces by Andrea del Sarto, and Artemesia Gentileschi's gory *Judith*.

Sala dell' Educazione di Giove The hothouse sophistication of the Florentine Seicento opens with Cristofano Allori's ravishing, erotic *Judith* ★ The head of Holofernes is a portrait of the painter, and Judith is a portrait of his mistress.

Sala della Stufa This has enchanting frescoes of the *Four Ages of Man* ★ by Pietro da Cortona.

Sala di Ulisse Cigoli's *Ecce Homo* is one of the most famous 17thC Florentine pictures.

Sala di Promoteo A sudden change from the Baroque, the collection of early Renaissance tondi includes Filippo Lippi's *Madonna and Child* ★ The sweet

charm of the tondi contrasts with the Mannerist sophistication of Bachiacca's *Magdalen* ★ an ambiguous, alluring portrayal of the penitent saint.

Off this room, the **Corridoio delle Colonne** has a collection of small cabinet pictures by Dutch and Flemish artists, including Jan Brueghel and Paul Bril; also, an outstanding collection of works by the Dutch artist Poelenburgh, including many paintings of the Roman Campagna, where a melancholy sense of past grandeur is created by vast, crumbling Roman ruins and soft, melting distances. The Corridoio leads into rooms containing a fine Titian portrait and Dutch and Flemish landscapes and still-lifes.

Sala del Poccetti This has some good 17thC works including paintings of the parables shown as scenes from everyday life, by the Venetian Domenico Fetti, and Francesco Furini's *Hylas and the Nymphs* (c.1637). Furini is one of the most intriguing painters of the Florentine Seicento; the smoky colouring, voluptuous yet slender nudes and slightly morbid, cloying eroticism of this picture are characteristic of the Florentine Baroque and explain much of its appeal to 20thC taste.

Volterrano wing The rooms in this wing have pictures by 17thC and 18thC Florentine artists including Bilivert, Cigoli, Furini, Giovanni da San Giovanni and Salvator Rosa. A small room is entirely devoted to Rosa, who worked for the Medici between 1640 and 1649; paintings include *Landscape with a Bridge* and a *Harbour Scene with a Tower*, where crumbling, broken outlines and stormy light create an intensely Romantic mood, and an unusual series of informal works in brown ink and wash on wood.

Museo degli Argenti

The museum displays a beautiful and varied collection of vases, jewels, ivories, cameos, gems, silverware and goldsmiths' work, either collected or commissioned by the Medici family from the beginning of the 15thC up until the 18thC.

The ground floor apartments were decorated in the 17thC. The airy frescoes in the Sala di San Giovanni, begun by Giovanni da San Giovanni, are a witty, irreverent celebration of Lorenzo the Magnificent. The next three rooms were frescoed between 1636 and 1641 with theatrical illusionistic architecture by Mitelli and Colonna, Bolognese *quadratura* specialists. The highlights of the collection are Lorenzo the Magnificent's **antique vases** ★ Made from sardonyx, amethyst, jasper and agate, these were praised by Vasari; many have elegant early Renaissance mounts and are inscribed *LAUR MED*. Note, too, German silverware and goldsmiths' work from the Silberkammer at Salzburg; and the jewels of the Electress Palatine, which amusingly transform groups of pearls into charming little figures of soldiers and shoemakers.

Galleria d'Arte Moderna
This collection of 18thC to 20thC Italian painting, predominantly Tuscan, is displayed in the cool, Neoclassical rooms on the second floor of the palace. The display opens with Neoclassical and Romantic art (Canova, Boguet, Hayez, Ussi); it includes works by Alberto Magnelli (d. 1971), one of the earliest Italian artists to respond to Cubism and Futurism; yet the highlights are works by the Macchiaioli, late 19thC artists who, like the French Impressionists, were interested in *plein-air* painting; they caught effects of light by painting in *macchie*, or patches, of colour.

The landscapes in Room 14 (Palizzi, Murke) reveal the influence of the Barbizon school and Dutch landscape, and look forward to the realism of the Macchiaioli. In Room 15, Cristiano Banti's **Three Peasants** are close to Corot. Room 16 contains the collection of Diego Martelli, champion of the Macchiaioli and the first Italian to write on the French Impressionists. The effects of filtered light in paintings by Fattori and Lega, the principal exponents of the Macchiaiolo style, are close to French Impressionism; these works hang alongside two paintings by Camille Pissarro. A portrait of **Martelli** ★ by Boldini reveals the attractive informality of this artist's early style, before he became a glittering society portraitist; Zandomenghi's **portrait** ★ of the same sitter is brilliantly relaxed.

In Rooms 23 and 24 are many small, spontaneous landscape sketches, which show the Macchiaioli at their best; notice especially, in Room 23, Fattori's brilliantly lit **Palmeri Rotonda** ★ (1866) and the lively street scenes of Telemaco Signorini.

Palazzo Vecchio *(Palazzo della Signoria)* ☆
Piazza della Signoria
Open Mon – Fri 9am – 7pm, Sun 8am – 1pm
Closed Sat
🎫 👁 🏛

The core of the original fortress-palace was built between 1298 and 1314, probably to designs by Arnolfo di Cambio. It was used by the Signoria – the elected ministers of the Republican government – but from 1540 Cosimo I and his son Francesco lived here, giving it

the rich decoration that befitted a ducal palace; ten years later the Medici moved to the PALAZZO PITTI and the Signoria became known as the Palazzo Vecchio (the old palace).

The palace is a monument to the energy and boundless erudition of Giorgio Vasari, who supervised the elaborate decorative schemes that transformed the entire interior. It is well worth a visit just for the works by Michelangelo and Donatello, but the endless empty rooms, frescoed with complex, obscure allegories celebrating the deeds of long forgotten Medici, are tiring and it is best to concentrate on the following sections.

Courtyard Here, Michelozzo's severe design is transformed into light Mannerist elegance by the gilt stucco and grotesque decoration that was commissioned to celebrate the wedding of Francesco de' Medici to Joanna of Austria in 1565. On the fountain in the center is a copy of Verrocchio's bronze **putto** (the original is in the Cancelleria, see below).

First floor The **Salone dei Cinquecento** was designed for assemblies of the Consiglio Generale del Popolo. The ceiling is heavily coffered and, with the walls, is frescoed with ugly pictures by Vasari extolling Florentine victories in battle. In a niche in the center of the long wall is Michelangelo's **Victory** ★★ placed here in 1565; its elegant, spiralling pose sings out against Vincenzo de Rossi's **Labours of Hercules** around the walls, ludicrous parodies of Michelangelesque power. Opposite the Michelangelo, deliberately complementing its pose, is Giambologna's **Virtue Overcoming Vice**.

To the right of the door is the **Studiolo of Francesco I** ★★ a dark, secret room, where the melancholy prince, obsessed by alchemy, stored his antiquities and natural curiosities. The Studiolo is one of Vasari's most perfect achievements; within the tiny space there is an exquisite variety of paintings, elegant bronzes, and precious and intricate ornament, to which the most celebrated Mannerist artists contributed. The portraits at either end, of **Cosimo I** and his wife **Eleanor of Toledo**, are by Bronzino.

Second floor To the right of the stairs are the **Apartments of Eleanor of Toledo**, the five rooms used by Cosimo's wife. These include the **Sala Verde**, with grotesque decoration by Ridolfo Ghirlandaio, and the **Cappella di Eleonora** ★ frescoed by Bronzino. Further on, the **Cappella della Signoria** has an **Annunciation** by Ridolfo Ghirlandaio (1514).

The **Sala dell' Udienza** is frescoed by Francesco Salviati and has a splendid ceiling by Giuliano da Maiano. It contains Donatello's *Judith and Holofernes* ★★ originally a fountain in the PALAZZO MEDICI–RICCARDI and one of the first Renaissance sculptures intended to be seen from multiple views. It is a harsh, tragic work, in which humility overcomes pride and sensuality. After the expulsion of the Medici in1494, the group was displayed before the Palazzo Vecchio as a grim reminder to aspiring tyrants. It was not taken inside the palace until 1980.

The **Sala dei Gigli** is the most harmoniously decorated room in the palace. It was designed by Benedetto da Maiano, with frescoes by Domenico Ghirlandaio and assistants (1481–85). The fine marble doorway and statue of *St John the Baptist* are by Benedetto da Maiano. In the **Cancelleria** is the original of Verrocchio's bronze **putto** ★ (1476). **Mezzanine floor** The **Charles Loeser Collection** includes Bronzino's portrait of *Laura Battiferri* ★ and Memlinc's *Portrait of a Man*.

Piazza della Signoria ★★

The most important statues in the square are, from N to S, Giambologna's equestrian statue of *Cosimo I* (1594); Ammanati's **Neptune Fountain** ★ (1563–75) – the stiff marble statue of the sea god surrounded by graceful bronze figures in elegantly contrasting poses; Bandinelli's much derided, grimacing *Hercules and Cacus* (1553), which the sculptor rashly paired with Michelangelo's *David* (now in the GALLERIA DELL'ACCADEMIA and replaced by a copy).

The **Loggia dei Lanzi** was designed as a setting for the public ceremonies of the Signoria by Benci di Cione and Simone Talenti (1376–81). It still has celebrated sculptures, including Cellini's elegant *Perseus* ★★ (1545–54) with its wonderful, intricately decorated base (the reliefs and four statuettes are now in the MUSEO DEL BARGELLO); Giambologna's *Rape of the Sabine Women* ★ (1583) with a virtuoso, spiralling composition; and *Hercules Slaying the Centaur* (1599), also by Giambologna.

Cellini, in his *Autobiography*, gives an enthralling account of the technical problems involved in the casting of the *Perseus*; at one point all his pewter cups and platters had to be thrown into the alloy – "which no one else, I think, had ever done before"; he told Duke Cosimo that the right foot would not come out, and describes his mingled irritation and satisfaction when this prophecy was fulfilled.

Raccolta Alberto della Ragione
Piazza della Signoria 5
Open Mon, Wed–Sat 9am–2pm, Sun 8am–1pm
Closed Tues
🗃 📖 ☑

This modern art collection was presented to the city by Alberto della Ragione; it is housed in the center of Renaissance Florence. The main emphasis is on works by comparatively traditional Italian artists who were reaching maturity between 1930–45.

The dominant impression is created by the shadowy portraits of Felice Casorati, the gentle landscapes and still-lifes of Mario Mafai, and the mysterious, empty streets of Rosai and Donghi; theirs is a pallid, misty, introspective art, hovering on the edges of Surrealism. More vigorous are the works by Guttoso.

Santissima Annunziata ☆
Piazza Santissima Annunziata
🏛

The 13thC church was rebuilt by Michelozzo between 1444–81. The atrium, known as the **Chiostro dei Voti**, was frescoed by leading 16thC painters. On the right portico wall are the *Visitation* (1516) by Pontormo and the *Assumption* (1517) by Rosso Fiorentino. At the end of the right wall, Andrea del Sarto's *Birth of the Virgin* (1514) is shown in the splendid setting of a contemporary Florentine house; this picture marks a return to the clear narratives of the Early Renaissance – although the grandeur of the figures is indebted to Michelangelo, and the subtle modelling to Leonardo. Left of the nave entrance, Alessio Baldovinetti's best-known work, the *Nativity* ★ (1460–62), is one of the earliest realistic landscapes in Italian art.

The interior of the church is lavishly Baroque. On the left of the entrance, Michelozzo's marble **tempietto** houses a sacred image of the *Virgin*. The first chapel on the left, the Baroque **Cappella Feroni** by Foggini, has the remains of Andrea del Castagno's *Vision of St Julian* ★ (c.1455). The second chapel on the left has Castagno's *Trinity* (1454–55), a harsh, passionate work, which recalls the expressive, linear style of Donatello. In the fifth chapel on the right is Bernardo Rossellino's **monument to Orlando de' Medici** (1456).

The **Chiostro dei Morti**, to the left of the church, has Andrea del Sarto's *Madonna del Sacco* (1525), a seminal work of the Florentine High Renaissance;

its lucid composition and cool colours look forward to Poussin.

Santa Croce ☆
Piazza Santa Croce
🏛

This important Gothic church was begun in the late 13thC but has a 19thC facade. It is famous for its fine series of Renaissance sculptures and for its 14thC frescoes, much damaged, by Giotto and his followers.

On the right of the nave is a late 15thC marble **pulpit** by Benedetto da Maiano, with reliefs showing scenes from the *Life of St Francis* and, below, the figures of *Faith*, *Hope*, *Love*, *Fortitude* and *Justice*.

In the right aisle, against the first pilaster, is Antonio Rossellino's *Madonna del Latte* (1478). Opposite it is Vasari's **tomb of Michelangelo** (1570). Further on, Donatello's *Annunciation* ★ (c.1435) evokes, with new psychological awareness, a tender and intimate mood. The **tomb of Leonardo Bruni** ★ (1444) by Bernardo Rossellino created a new type of humanist tomb; its grandeur contrasts with Desiderio da Settignano's more lyrical and decorative **tomb of Carlo Marsuppini** ★ (1453) in the opposite aisle, which was inspired by it.

In the right transept, the **Cappella Castellani** has late 14thC frescoes by Agnolo Gaddi. The adjacent **Cappella Baroncelli** has early 14thC frescoes by Taddeo Gaddi, Giotto's most important follower; the scenes from the *Life of the Virgin* ★ are his finest achievement, more richly descriptive than Giotto's austere works, and experimenting with startling effects of light and space.

The two chapels to the right of the chancel, the **Cappella Peruzzi** and **Cappella Bardi**, have damaged frescoes by Giotto. In the left transept, a second Cappella Bardi contains a wooden **crucifix** attributed to Donatello.
Cappella Pazzi
Brunelleschi's Pazzi Chapel is a jewel of early Renaissance art, symmetrical, lucid and beautifully proportioned, and decorated with blue and white terra-cotta tondi by Luca della Robbia. In the spandrels are tondi of the *Evangelists*, perhaps by Brunelleschi.
Museo dell' Opera di Santa Croce
Tel. (055) 244619
Open Mon, Tues, Thurs – Sun: summer 9am – 12.30pm, 3 – 6.30pm, winter 9am – 12.30pm, 3 – 5pm
Closed Wed
🔳

This museum was severely damaged in the flood of 1966. Its most celebrated works are Cimabue's *Crucifixion*, now

heavily restored, and Donatello's majestic gilt bronze of *St Louis of Toulouse* ★ originally commissioned for ORSANMICHELE.

Santa Felicità
Piazzetta Santa Felicità
The first chapel on the right, the **Cappella Capponi** ★★ has decorations by Pontormo, assisted by Bronzino (1525 – 28). On the pendentives of the cupola are tondi of the four *Evangelists*; on the right wall, the *Annunciation*; on the altar, the *Deposition*, perhaps Pontormo's most moving work – the highly-wrought rhythms and unreal space, the weightless figures, with pallid, yearning faces, and the strange, heightened colours, convey an intense spirituality.

San Lorenzo ☆☆
Piazza San Lorenzo
🏛

This is an important Renaissance church, designed by Brunelleschi. Its greatest treasures are in the adjacent **Cappelle Medicee** (Medici Chapels), entered from Piazza Madonna degli Aldobrandini, but there are a number of outstanding works within the church itself.

In the second chapel on the right is the *Marriage of the Virgin* (1523) by Rosso Fiorentino. In the nave are two bronze **pulpits** ★ (c.1460) by Donatello and assistants. Donatello was more directly involved with the pulpit on the N side; the reliefs show the events after the Passion and are intensely personal and expressive – the resurrected Christ is no triumphant Saviour, but is shown horrifically clad in a tattered shroud, dragging himself painfully from his tomb. At the end of the right aisle is Desiderio da Settignano's finely-wrought **tabernacle** ★ In the left transept is Filippo Lippi's *Annunciation* (c.1440). To the left of the high altar is a fresco of the *Martyrdom of St Lawrence* (1565 – 69) by Bronzino.

The **Old Sacristy** (1421 – 28) by Brunelleschi perfectly expresses the Renaissance ideals of clarity and graceful proportion. The decorations by Donatello include four medallions, in the spandrels, of scenes from the *Life of St John the Evangelist* – free experiments in perspective; four roundels of the *Evangelists* in the lunettes; and two sets of bronze doors, the **Doors of the Apostles** and the **Doors of the Martyrs**, decorated with pairs of figures modelled against a flat background. The liveliness and dramatic quality of the figures on the doors – some gesticulating, involved in argument and discussion, others sunk in thought, reading and writing – break with the classical lucidity of Brunelleschi's design. To the left of the entrance is the majestic bronze and porphyry **monument to Piero and Giovanni de' Medici** (1472) by Verrocchio.

Cappelle Medicee *(Medici Chapels)* ★★
Piazza Madonna degli Aldobrandini
Open Tues – Sat 9am – 7pm,
*   Sun 9am – 1pm*
Closed Mon
🎫 🏛 ♿

The main chapel, the **Cappella dei Principi**, was the mausoleum of the Medici princes and is an ostentatious example of early 17thC taste. Infinitely more interesting is Michelangelo's **New Sacristy** (1520–34), the chapel that contains his celebrated **Medici tombs** ★★ The capricious architecture of the New Sacristy contrasts strongly with the lucid proportions of the Old Sacristy.

On the left is the **tomb of Lorenzo, Duke of Urbino**; on the right, the **tomb of Giuliano, Duke of Nemours**. The heroic effigies, in richly ornamented antique armour, are idealized portraits of the princes; the contrast in pose and mood suggests that they represent the active and contemplative life. They are, surprisingly, insignificant members of the declining family, although Machiavelli dedicated *The Prince* to them. Beneath, uneasily poised on the curving lids of the sarcophagi, are two pairs of allegorical figures, *Dawn* and *Dusk* and *Night* and *Day*. They symbolize the passing of time that leads to death; anguished, brooding and oppressed, they convey a profoundly tragic vision of life.

Opposite the altar is the simple tomb of the more renowned 15thC Medici princes, Lorenzo the Magnificent and his brother Giuliano. On this tomb is Michelangelo's ***Madonna and Child***★★ (1521), his last treatment of this theme. The elegant, mannered pose and grave, thoughtful beauty of the Madonna, in poignant contrast to the spontaneity of the Child, are in keeping with the disturbing melancholy of the chapel.

In a room below, fresco drawings on the wall by Michelangelo and his pupils were uncovered in 1975; sketches for many different works – some quite highly finished, others rapid jottings – seem to bring us closer to the artist.

San Marco See MUSEO DELL' ANGELICO.

Santa Maria del Carmine ☆
Piazza del Carmine
🏛 ♿
This Romanesque-Gothic church was largely rebuilt after a fire in 1771, which

left untouched the celebrated cycle of frescoes in the **Cappella Brancacci** ★★ (to the right of the crossing). The frescoes illustrate scenes from the *Life of St Peter*, the *Temptation* and the *Expulsion from Paradise*. They were begun by Masolino (1425–27), continued by Masaccio (1426–28) and, 50yrs later, completed by Filippino Lippi (1484–85).

The profound humanity of Masaccio's frescoes marks a turning point in Western art; his masterpiece is the *Tribute Money* (left wall, upper section), where the Apostles, noble and dignified figures, modelled in light and shade, are placed in a vast landscape that uses perspective to create the illusion of depth. The fresco looks back to Giotto, and forward to the grandeur of Raphael. The *Expulsion* (on the pier left of the entrance) is a deeply moving, tragic image.

The perspective space of Masolino's frescoes, the *Raising of Tabitha* and the *Healing of the Lame Man* (right wall), reflect the influence of Masaccio, yet the delicate, elegant figures show his continuing love of the characteristics of International Gothic. The frescoes by Filippino Lippi are on the lower section of the right wall.

In the left transept of the church, the Baroque **Cappella di Sant' Andrea Corsini** was designed by Silvani (1675–83); it has three high-relief sculptures by Foggini and, in the cupola, a glittering, richly composed fresco of the *Apotheosis of St Andrew Corsini* (1682) by Luca Giordano.

Santa Maria Maddalena dei Pazzi
Borgo Pinti 58
Convent open Tues – Sun 9am – noon,
*   5 – 7pm*
Convent closed Mon
In the chapter house of the attached convent is Perugino's fresco of the *Crucifixion* ★ (1493–96). The figures are shown, through an illusionistic Renaissance arch, poised against a serene, luminous landscape.

Santa Maria Novella ☆
Piazza Santa Maria Novella
🏛
This Dominican church was begun in 1246 and completed in 1360; the upper part of the facade was designed by the Renaissance architect Alberti in the 15thC and its pure geometry harmonizes brilliantly with the lower, Romanesque-Gothic portion.

In the second bay of the right aisle is the **tomb of Beata Villana** (1451) by Bernardo Rossellino. The marble pulpit in the left aisle was designed by Brunelleschi. Close by is Masaccio's celebrated fresco of the *Holy Trinity with the Virgin, St John the Evangelist and Donors* ★★ In it, the walls of the aisle seem to open into a Renaissance chapel inspired by Brunelleschi; the painting is revolutionary in its mastery over the new science of perspective and in the solid dignity of the figures.

In the left transept, the **Cappella Strozzi** has frescoes (c.1351–57) by Nardo di Cione, showing scenes from the *Last Judgment*, *Paradise* and *Hell*, and an altarpiece by Orcagna, Nardo's brother, of *Christ with Sts Peter and Thomas* (1354–57); the austere majesty of this altarpiece, with its solemn, hieratic figures, blaze of gold, and elaborate Gothic frame, ignores the warmth and animation of Giotto and looks back to Byzantine art.

In the sacristy there is a **crucifix** by Giotto; in the **Cappella Gondi** (by Giovanni da Sangallo), a **crucifix** ★ by Brunelleschi (c.1410–15).

The **Cappella Maggiore**, behind the high altar, has a cycle of **frescoes** ★ by Domenico Ghirlandaio depicting the *Life of the Virgin* and the *Life of St John the Baptist*. The scenes are shown as part of the everyday life of 15thC Florence and charmingly capture the feeling of a whole social era. The *Birth of the Virgin* depicts a rich house fashionably decorated with Renaissance ornament where St Anne sits up in bed to receive a group of dignified Florentine women.

In the right transept, the **Cappella Filippo Strozzi** has **frescoes** ★ (c.1487–1502) by Filippino Lippi of scenes from the *Life of St Philip the Apostle* and the *Life of St John the Divine* – strange, restless paintings, full of nervous twisting drapery and bizarre classical ornament. Behind the altar, the **tomb of Filippo Strozzi** (1491–93) is by Benedetto da Maiano. The **Cappella Rucellai** contains Nino Pisano's **Madonna** (after 1348) and, in the pavement, Ghiberti's bronze **tomb of Leonardo Dati** ★ (1425).

Chiostri *(Cloisters)*
Open Mon – Thurs, Sat 9am – 2pm, Sun 8am – 1pm
Closed Fri
📷 ♿

The **Chiostro Verde**, or Green Cloister, is named after the green *terra verde* hue that predominates in Uccello's scenes from the *Creation*, the *Deluge*, the *Sacrifice of Noah* and the *Drunkenness of Noah* – badly damaged works, now detached and shown in the entrance to the refectory. The *Deluge* ★★ (c.1445) is Uccello's great masterpiece; it shows, on the left, the terror of those outside the ark, abandoned to the rising water, and,

on the right, Noah welcoming the returning dove. The painting is remarkable for its extraordinary plastic strength and complex foreshortenings; Vasari commented in particular on the foreshortening of the strange Florentine headgear.

The **Cappellone degli Spagnoli**, or Spanish Chapel, has frescoes by Andrea da Firenze (1355). Over the doorway of the **Loggia di San Paolo** is a late 15thC terra-cotta lunette by Andrea della Robbia.

San Miniato al Monte ☆
Monte alle Croci
🏛

A superb example of the Florentine Romanesque, San Miniato has an elegant, geometric marble facade, its delicate patterns suggesting an unusually sensitive response to the spirit of classical art.

The Romanesque nave, decorated with green and white marble, and in part paved with 13thC marble inlay, contains Michelozzo's **Cappella del Crocifisso** ★ or Chapel of the Crucifix (1448); this is in perfect harmony with the delicate detail of its surroundings; the glazed terra-cotta vault is by Luca della Robbia. A magnificent marble **screen** ★ (1207) encloses the presbytery, which has a fine marble **pulpit** ★ (1209).

In the left aisle is the **Cappella del Cardinale di Portogallo** ★★ or Cardinal of Portugal's Chapel, an ornate 15thC funerary chapel, where architecture, sculpture and painting together create an almost Baroque impression of movement, colour and varied textures. To the right of the altar is Antonio Rossellino's **monument to the Cardinal of Portugal** (1461); marble curtains are drawn back to reveal a vivid tableau; the Virgin smiles down sweetly at the sleeping Cardinal; fluttering angels alight momentarily on the tomb.

On the left wall of the chapel, above the bishop's throne by Rossellino, is an *Annunciation* (1466–67) by Baldovinetti; facing the entrance, two angels by Antonio Pollaiuolo. The ceiling of glazed terra cotta is by Luca della Robbia.

Santo Spirito
Piazza Santo Spirito
🏛

One of the most perfect and serene of all Brunelleschi's achievements, the 15thC church of Santo Spirito contains many fine works of art. These include, in the right transept, Filippino Lippi's **Nerli altarpiece** ★ (c.1490) and, in the left transept, the **Cappella Corbinelli**

(1492), with architecture and sculpture by Andrea Sansovino.

The **refectory** has frescoes once attributed to Orcagna, and a small collection of Romanesque, Gothic and Renaissance sculpture.

Santa Trinità ☆
Piazza Santa Trinità

This is a Gothic church, with a 16thC facade by Buontalenti. In the fourth chapel of the right aisle are damaged frescoes (c.1420–25) and a gorgeously decorative altarpiece of the **Annunciation** ★ by Lorenzo Monaco; the predella panels of the altarpiece show a sensitive observation of nature close to that of Gentile da Fabriano.

In the right transept, the **Cappella Sassetti** ★ is decorated with frescoes of the *Life of St Francis* (1482–86) and an altarpiece of the *Adoration of the Shepherds* (1485) by Ghirlandaio. The frescoes are among Ghirlandaio's finest works, with a dignity and gravity that raise them above the pretty illustrations with which his name is often associated. They depict scenes from the Franciscan story, set in the world of contemporary Florence, with Florentine princes and nobles – Poliziano, the Medici, the Sassetti – and identifiable places – the Piazza della Signoria, the old bridge over the Arno, the Romanesque facade of Santa Trinità. On either side of the altarpiece – their simplicity contrasting with its rich pageantry – are portraits of the donors; they are buried in the austere tombs by Giuliano da Sangallo on the side walls.

In the left transept, second chapel on the left, is Luca della Robbia's **tomb of Bishop Benozzo Federighi** (1455–56), remarkable for its portrait of the ascetic bishop and for the contrast between the severe architecture and the delicate border of flowers in coloured terra cotta.

The left aisle has Desiderio da Settignano's gaunt wooden statue of *St Mary Magdalen* (c.1464), an unusually expressive work by this master of the sweet style of the 1460s and 1470s.

Spedale degli Innocenti ☆
Piazza Santissima Annunziata
Tel. (055) 284768
Open Tues–Sat, summer 9am–7pm, winter 9am–1pm; Sun 9am–1pm
Closed Mon
🕿 ▥ 血 ☑

Piazza Santissima Annunziata, enclosed by light, graceful Renaissance colonnades, is one of the most beautiful squares in Florence. At its center is Giambologna's rather dull equestrian statue of *Ferdinand I*, finished by Tacca

(1608), who also designed the two elegant yet bizarre **fountains** (1629). On the right is the Spedale degli Innocenti, the first foundling hospital in the world, and one of the seminal works of 15thC architecture.

Brunelleschi's facade is decorated with terra-cotta **medallions** ★ of babies (c.1487) by Andrea della Robbia. On the first floor, in the corridor overlooking the lovely cloister, is a series of detached frescoes and *sinopie*, including works by Alessandro Allori, strongly influenced by Michelangelo. On the second floor, the highlights are a *Madonna and Saints* by Piero di Cosimo; a late, exquisitely delicate *Madonna* ★ by Filippo Lippi; and a brilliantly colourful, festive *Adoration of the Magi* ★ (1488) by Ghirlandaio.

Uffizi See GALLERIA DEGLI UFFIZI.

FOLIGNO
Perugia, Umbria Map E4

Foligno is a modern town, sprawling around the edges, yet in the center the clarity of the street plan survives from Roman times and there is an unexpectedly grand main square.

Duomo
Piazza della Repubblica

The main structure of this church dates from 1133 but has been refashioned many times. The most interesting feature, dated 1201, is the facade of the transept facing on to Piazza della Repubblica. This work, which includes a **portal** with rich, classicizing sculpture, is by Rudolphus and Binellus, who also left signed work at nearby Bevagna.

Pinacoteca
Palazzo Trinci, Piazza della Repubblica
Tel. (0742) 53443
Open May–Oct Mon–Sat 9am–1pm, 2–7.30pm, Sun 8.30am–12.30pm; Nov–Apr Mon–Sat 9am–1pm, 2–4pm
Closed Nov–Apr: Sun
▥ ✗ 血 ▱

The gallery is housed in the 14thC Palazzo Trinci, where rooms decorated by Umbrian artists give a good idea of the culture of a provincial courtly society. There is a **chapel** decorated by Ottaviano Nelli, the chief and somewhat dull representative of late Gothic in Umbria. The **Sala delle Arti** or Room of the Liberal Arts is charmingly decorated by a 15thC Fabrianese master, with elegant female personifications beneath fantastic Gothic tabernacles; the **Sala dei Giganti** or Room of the Giants, by the school of

Nelli. Foligno was a significant artistic center in the Renaissance, influenced by Gozzoli at nearby **MONTEFALCO**, and there are good works by local artists, including Alunno, Pierantonio Mezzastris and Bernardino di Mariotto.

GALLUZZO
Firenze, Toscana Map C2

Galluzzo is a suburban area of Florence, celebrated for the monastery that was founded here in 1342.

Certosa del Galluzzo ☆
Tel. (055) 2049226
Open summer 9am – noon, 4 – 7pm, winter 9am – noon, 2.30 – 5pm
📷 *but gratuity appreciated* ▓ 🏛

The Pinacoteca is housed in the Gothic Palazzo degli Studi; the outstanding works are Pontormo's damaged frescoes on the theme of the *Passion* ★ (1522 – 24), detached from the lunettes of the Chiostro Grande (where they are replaced by copies by Jacopo da Empoli). The cycle is clearly influenced by Dürer's prints, but is also remarkable for its strange, distorted forms, taut, irrational space, and disturbing intensity.

From here one reaches the church of **San Lorenzo**; in the subterranean chapels, the Gothic **monument to Niccolò Acciaiuoli** (d. 1365) and the 16thC **tomb slab of Cardinal Agnolo II Acciaiuoli** are particularly interesting.

GROSSETO
Toscana Map B4

Grosseto retains an ancient center, encircled by a fine hexagonal rampart, yet it is a predominantly modern and rather characterless industrial city. It lies in the Tuscan Maremma, the coastal strip where Roselle, one of the most powerful of Etruscan cities, once flourished.

Duomo
Via Garibaldi 8
This is a 14thC building, heavily restored; the facade was added in 1845. In the left transept is a 15thC *Assumption* by Matteo di Giovanni.

Museo Archeologico e d'Arte della Maremma
Piazza Baccarini 3
Tel. (0564) 27290
Open Mon, Tues, Thurs – Sat 9.30am – 12.30pm, 4.30 – 7pm; Sun 9.30am – 12.30pm
Closed Wed
📷

This is a particularly well displayed and lavishly documented collection of archaeological finds taken from a wide area that embraces Roselle, Vetulonia, Populonia and Vulci. A large section consists of material from Roselle, some 10km (6 miles) N of Grosseto, tracing its artistic development from the Villanovan period, through the oriental phase, to late Hellenistic works. There are also sculptures from Vulci and Villanovan ceramics from Vetulonia.

On the second floor are some good Sienese paintings, including a *Madonna* by Girolamo di Benvenuto and Sassetta's charming *Madonna of the Cherries*.

San Francesco
Piazza dell' Indipendenza
The 13thC Gothic church has a lovely *Crucifixion* ★ over the high altar that is attributed to Duccio as an early work (c. 1290).

GUBBIO
Perugia, Umbria Map E3

An ancient center with Roman remains, Gubbio flourished as a powerful free commune in the Middle Ages; during the Renaissance it was governed by the Montefeltro family. It stands alone in the hills N of Perugia, an almost perfectly preserved 14thC town. Impressive medieval buildings rise, tier upon tier, against the steep slopes of Monte Ingino; two austere 14thC palaces, the Palazzo dei Consoli and Palazzo Pretorio, tower above the rooftops half way up the hill; higher still may be glimpsed the gentler lines of the Renaissance Palazzo Ducale and, over all, the campanile of the cathedral.

Museo del Duomo
Piazza del Duomo
Ring bell for custodian
📷 *but gratuity appreciated*
This tiny museum is attached to the 13thC cathedral and contains a haphazard assortment of objects. These include some 14thC detached **frescoes**; a 15thC ivory **crucifix**; and a delicately embroidered 15thC Flemish **cope** showing violent scenes from the *Passion*.

Museo e Pinacoteca Comunale
Palazzo dei Consoli, Piazza della Signoria
Tel. (075) 922341
Open Apr – Sept 9am – 12.30pm, 3.30 – 6pm; Oct – Mar 9am – 1pm, 3 – 5pm
▓ 𝑋 ♡ 🏛 🔲

First pause to enjoy the beauty of the palaces and the square between; planned as an architectural whole, they stamp an almost Renaissance lucidity on the haphazard growth of the medieval city round about.

The museum has a small collection of local archaeological finds and the famous **Eugubian tablets ★** These seven bronze tablets have inscriptions in Etruscan, and in Latin adapted to the ancient Umbrian language; they are an important historical document relating to the 3rdC–1stC BC.

The Pinacoteca is housed in dusty rooms on the second floor. It contains a few rather dull works by painters from Gubbio and some 17thC pictures (including a sketch by Sacchi) but it is worth visiting for the sweeping view from its arcaded loggia, over the medieval rooftops and Roman theater below.

San Francesco
Piazza Quaranta Martiri
In the chapel on the left of the chancel of this spacious Gothic church are frescoes of the *Life of the Virgin* (c. 1400) by Ottaviano Nelli, the leading painter from Gubbio; the frescoes are executed in a tired, late Gothic style that is generally typical of this artist.

Santa Maria Nuova
Via O. Nelli
🏛
This 13thC church has a simple yet exceptionally elegant facade. Inside, on the right wall, is the *Madonna del Belvedere* ★ (1413) by Ottaviano Nelli – perhaps his freshest, most appealing work, glowing with the lovely decorative details of International Gothic.

IESI
Ancona, Marche Map F3
The walls surrounding the medieval quarter are a good example of 14thC defences and enclose tortuous narrow streets, but the town has expanded considerably since those days. Birthplace of the composer Giambattista Pergolesi, Iesi was also host to Lorenzo Lotto, several of whose paintings are in the Pinacoteca.

Pinacoteca Comunale
Palazzo Pianetti-Tesei, Via XV Settembre
Tel. (0731) 58659
Open Tues – Sat 9.30am – 12.30pm,
*   4 – 7pm, Sun 10am – 1pm*
Closed Mon
📷 ➡ 𝗬 ♿
Housed in an 18thC palace, with a lovely Rococo gallery, this collection has an outstanding group of pictures by Lorenzo Lotto – a moving testimony to the

tribulations and uncertainties of the painter's life. The *Entombment* (1512), painted on his return from Rome, shows his attempt to imitate Raphael – not with outstanding success, for he is more at ease when not painting in a grand style. The large *St Lucy* ★ altarpiece (1532) is a strikingly original, expressive work, rich in unexpected effects of light; the predella panels – especially the scene of the *Charity of St Lucy* – show his feeling for popular imagery and for the poor and humble. Note, too, the *Madonna and Saints* and the *Visitation* (1532 – 34).

IMPRUNETA
Firenze, Toscana Map C2
A pretty village set in the hills near Florence, Impruneta is Etruscan in origin but prospered mainly in the Middle Ages.

Santa Maria dell'Impruneta
Piazza Buondelmonti
🏛
This church was consecrated in 1060 and has been altered many times. It was badly bombed in World War II but has been meticulously reconstructed. To the left and right of the presbytery are two lovely **tabernacles ★** which are sometimes attributed to Michelozzo; both have outstanding **terra-cotta decorations** by Luca della Robbia. The tabernacle on the left has an enamelled terra-cotta **frieze** of fruits and flowers of great beauty; that on the right has an inner **tabernacle** with a relief of the *Crucifixion* ★ a classical, direct and yet passionate and deeply moving work, one of Luca's greatest achievements.

LA VERNA
Arezzo, Toscana Map D2
La Verna is a Franciscan shrine, high in the wild solitude of the mountains of Casentino, where St Francis received the stigmata in 1224.

Convento della Verna ✩
Tel. (0575) 599016
Open 8am–1pm, 2–5pm
📷 ➡ 𝗬 🛏 ♿
The principal church, and the smaller chapels of the monastery, are decorated with a series of glazed **terra-cotta altars ★★** (1480s), possibly the most beautiful and influential works ever created by Andrea della Robbia. Andrea was the nephew of Luca, and developed his uncle's technique, brightening his colours and sweetening his style; the loveliest works here – the *Annunciation*

and the *Adoration* (in the **Chiesa Maggiore**) – suggest the influence of contemporary painting.

LIVORNO
Toscana Map A2

Livorno was created by the Medici and, in the 18thC, became a glamorous, cosmopolitan resort. It was badly bombed in World War II and is now a large, dull and mainly modern city, with an extremely busy port.

Monumento dei Quattro Mori
Piazza Micheli

The monument was erected in honour of Grand Duke Ferdinand I. It was designed by Giovanni Bandini in 1595; the four moors were added by Pietro Tacca, chief pupil of Giambologna, in 1626.

Museo d'Arte Contemporanea
Via Redi 22
Tel. (0586) 39463
Open Tues, Wed, Fri, Sun 10am–1pm;
*   Thurs, Sat: summer 10am–1pm,*
*   5–8pm, winter 10am–1pm, 4–7pm*
Closed Mon

This museum, although small, is lively and right up to the minute. It has a smattering of works by well-known 20thC masters – Renato Guttoso and Carrà among them – followed by examples of optical art and of experiments with light. The decorative textures, and electric colours, of Post-Modernist art are well represented in works by Enrico Baj and Ugo Nespolo from the 1970s. The gallery has some good temporary exhibitions.

Museo Civico G. Fattori
Villa Fabbricotti, Piazza Matteotti 19
Tel. (0586) 808001
Open Tues, Wed, Fri, Sun 10am–1pm;
*   Thurs, Sat: summer 10am–1pm,*
*   5–8pm, winter 10am–1pm, 4–7pm*
Closed Mon

Housed in a pretty 18thC palace, this is a small collection of works by the Macchiaioli, with the main emphasis on the Livornese painter, Giovanni Fattori. He is represented by battle scenes; seascapes; and a small, *plein-air* portrait of **Signora Martelli**, in which the soft light filtering through the leaves is almost Impressionist – Diego Martelli, the husband of the sitter, was the first Italian champion of Impressionism. Besides the modern collection, there is a handful of old masters and some 18thC Greek and Russian icons.

LORETO
Ancona, Marche Map F3

Surrounded by 16thC walls and battlements on a hill overlooking the sea, the little town of Loreto is dominated by the Santuario della Santa Casa, one of Italy's most celebrated monuments.

Pinacoteca
Palazzo Apostolico, Piazza del Santuario
Tel. (071) 970291
Open Thurs–Tues 9am–1pm, 3–6pm
Closed Wed

The Palazzo Apostolico was designed by Bramante in 1510. The Pinacoteca is most famous for eight pictures by Lotto, who spent several years in the Marches and ended his days as an oblate of the Santa Casa in Loreto. Many of the works he executed in Loreto show signs of decline, yet one stands out: the **Presentation in the Temple** ★ perhaps his last work. The painting's vivid, sketchy quality – not entirely due to its being unfinished – and the feeling for humanity and for the inner experience suggested by age, seem in a startling way to look forward to Rembrandt.

Santuario della Santa Casa ★★
Piazza del Santuario
Tel. (071) 970108
Open 6am–8pm

Legend relates that the Virgin's house was miraculously transported by angels from Nazareth, first in 1291 to Dalmatia and then in 1294 to the laurel woods near **RECANATI**, where the house became a major shrine for pilgrims.

The great basilica was begun in 1468 and, one by one, Italy's principal architects were called in to continue and complete the building – among them, Giuliano da Sangallo, Bramante, Andrea Sansovino and Antonio da Sangallo the Younger. The magnificent **bronze doors** ★ with reliefs illustrating scenes from the Old and New Testaments are the work of various artists including Girolamo Lombardo.

In the Gothic interior, under the main dome, is the **Santa Casa** itself, a small Romanesque construction with rough walls; it stands behind a marble **screen** designed by Bramante and decorated with statues and low reliefs of the *Life of the Virgin* by Sansovino.

The dome of the **Sagrestia di San Marco** at the end of the right aisle is decorated with **frescoes** ★ by Melozzo da Forlì (c.1480). The angels fluttering above the heads of the seated saints seem about to descend from their lofty perch and are good examples of Melozzo's mastery of remarkable illusionistic effects.

The **Sagrestia di San Giovanni** in the right transept has **frescoes ★** by Luca Signorelli. Painted between 1476 and 1479 they are notable for their dramatic lighting. Both Melozzo and Signorelli were perhaps pupils of Piero della Francesca who, according to Vasari, also worked at Loreto, although nothing here survives of his work.

LUCCA
Toscana   Map B2

Lucca, a Roman colony from 180BC, flourished in the Middle Ages as a rich independent city state; later it suffered from short periods of foreign domination, yet basically survived as a republic, independent of Florence, until the 19thC. The Roman city is still evident in the grid-like regularity of the streets, and especially in the Piazza Anfiteatro, where red-tiled medieval houses cluster around the oval site of a Roman amphitheater. Yet it is above all the wealthy Middle Ages, from the 11thC–13thC, that have left their mark upon the city; from the straight, narrow streets rise medieval palaces and towers – the Torre Guinigi bizarrely crowned with trees; small squares are dominated by the richly tiered facades of Romanesque churches. The loveliest views of the city are from the 16thC ramparts with, on one side, the distant Tuscan hills and, on the other, Romanesque belltowers and squares.

Duomo ☆
Piazza San Martino
🏛

The Romanesque facade, with three tiers of colonnaded arcading, emulates the Duomo at PISA; the upper part, by Guido da Como (1204) is richly and fantastically decorated, the spandrels inlaid with black and white marble. The three portals are decorated with **relief carvings** that are sometimes attributed to Nicola Pisano.

Inside, on the right of the central door, is a celebrated 14thC group of *St Martin and the Beggar*, once on the facade. In the right transept are works by Matteo Civitali, a renowned local 15thC sculptor; these include two *Angels* (1477), the **tomb of Pietro da Noceto** (c.1467) and the **altar of St Regulus**.

In the second chapel of the left transept is the *Madonna with Sts Stephen and John the Baptist* by Fra Bartolommeo. In the center of the chapel

is Jacopo della Quercia's **tomb of Ilaria del Carretto ★★** (c. 1406) – the light is very poor, so take plenty of coins. The base of this celebrated monument is modelled on a pagan sarcophagus; above, the young woman, touchingly beautiful in her marriage headdress and accompanied by a lively little dog – symbol of fidelity – movingly suggests a serene acceptance of death.

In the left nave is a **tempietto** (1484) designed by Matteo Civitali to house a sacred Byzantine Cross.

Museo Nazionale di Villa Guinigi
Via della Quarquonia
Tel. (0583) 46033
Open Tues – Sat 9am – 5pm, Sun
   9am – 1pm
Closed Mon
🚇 🏛 🌾

On the ground floor of the 14thC villa is a collection of Lucchese sculptures, dating from the Romanesque era to the Renaissance. In Room V is an interesting group of works by Matteo Civitali, a local sculptor who kept alive the style of the Florentine Renaissance in the late 15thC; note especially his *Ecce Homo*, an *Annunciation* and an *Annunciate Virgin*.

In the vast, rambling rooms of the first floor, the most interesting works are 12thC and 13thC **crucifixes**, including one signed by Berlinghieri and one by Deodato Orlandi; also, two large pictures by Fra Bartolommeo: *God the Father with Two Saints* (1509) – deeply influenced by the new High Renaissance ideals of Raphael and Leonardo – and the *Madonna della Misericordia* (1515) – a late work, unattractively grandiloquent.

Pinacoteca Nazionale
Palazzo Mansi, Via Galli Tassi 43
Tel. (0583) 55570
Open Tues – Sat 9am – 2pm, Sun
   9am – 1pm
Closed Mon
🚇 🏛

The Palazzo Mansi is a 17thC palace with, in one wing, a sequence of sumptuous Rococo rooms, some hung with splendid 17thC Flemish tapestries; notice especially the **Camera degli Sposi**, decorated with lovely Rococo ornament carved in gilded wood. The Pinacoteca is located in the small, drab rooms of the other wing, and is distinguished by a fine group of Mannerist portraits.

Room I has some interesting 17thC pictures, including a lyrical Vignali of *Tobias and the Angel*, and a mythological painting by Pietro Testa, who was a native of Lucca. Room II has Pontormo's tense portrait of *Giuliano de'*

Medici ★ also Bronzino's portrait of *Don Garzia de' Medici* as a small boy, and Barocci's portrait of *Federico Ubaldo della Rovere* – unexpectedly like a Velazquez. Room III has a handful of Venetian paintings; Room IV, paintings by Flemish artists including Bril.

San Frediano
Piazza San Frediano
🏛

The austere facade of the 12thC church is decorated by a large, much-restored mosaic of the *Ascension* in the Italo-Byzantine style of the Berlinghieri.

In the right aisle is an important 12thC **font**, reassembled in the 1950s; also, works by Matteo Civitali. In the left aisle, the **Cappella Trenta** has works by Jacopo della Quercia, including a marble **triptych** – note the violent realism of the predella panel, the *Martyrdom of St Lawrence* – and two **tomb slabs**.

MACERATA
Marche Map F3

Built on the ruins of the Roman city of Helvia Ricina, Macerata is well situated on a hill overlooking the Adriatic. Its university, one of the oldest in Italy, dates back to 1290, and although today Macerata looks more modern than medieval there is a picturesque old quarter with some fine Renaissance palaces.

Pinacoteca Civica
Piazza Vittorio Veneto
Tel. (0733) 49942
Open Tues – Sun 9am – noon
Closed Mon
📷 🚹 🔲

Paintings to note include a *Madonna* (1470) by Carlo Crivelli, a 15thC panel of the *Madonna with Angels and Saints* by Pietro da Montepulciano, a huge, late 16thC altarpiece of the *Madonna* by Andrea Boscoli and a late 17thC *Self-portrait* by Carlo Maratta.

San Giovanni
Piazza Vittorio Veneto
Built in the first half of the 17thC, this church has an elegant dome, rich stucco decorations and, in the third chapel on the left, a *Death of the Virgin* by Lanfranco.

MASSA MARITTIMA
Grosseto, Toscana Map B4

Massa Marittima, an ancient mining town, yielded its independence to the Sienese in 1337. It is divided into two parts; the old, walled, and mainly Romanesque lower town, and the Gothic upper town, which the Sienese defended with a formidable fortress. The splendid medieval center of the old town, the Piazza Garibaldi, is flanked by austere 13thC palaces and by the lovely facade of the cathedral.

Duomo
Piazza Garibaldi
🏛

The cathedral was built between 1287–1304 in the Pisan Romanesque-Gothic style. Over the portal, there is a 14thC low relief showing scenes from the *Life of St Cerbone*, featuring the saint to whom the cathedral is dedicated, charmingly aided by bears, deer and geese.

At the top of the right aisle is a **font** with reliefs by Giroldo da Como (1267) and, over it, a 15thC tabernacle. In the chapel to the left of the high altar is the *Madonna delle Grazie*, inspired by Duccio's *Maestà* in the Museo dell' Opera del Duomo in SIENA. The chapel to the right of the high altar has a 13thC painted wooden **cross** by Segna di Bonaventura.

In the subterranean chapel is the **tomb of St Cerbone** ★ with reliefs showing episodes from the life of the saint by the Sienese sculptor Goro di Gregorio (1324); the soft, flowing style of these reliefs looks back to Giovanni Pisano.

Pinacoteca Comunale
Palazzo Comunale, Piazza Garibaldi
Tel. (0566) 92051
Open summer Tues – Sun
10.30am – 12.30pm, 4 – 7pm
Closed summer: Mon; winter
📷 🏛

The highlight of this small collection of archaeological fragments and Sienese pictures is a large, early 14thC *Maestà* ★ by Ambrogio Lorenzetti, whose presence in Massa is mentioned by both Vasari and Ghiberti.

This is one of Lorenzetti's finest works, a brilliantly decorative and original interpretation of the theme made famous by Duccio and Simone Martini. Angels' wings cross to form the back of the Virgin's throne; the angels plump up the bolster over the seat; on the steps, their colours symbolic, sit personifications of the Theological Virtues: Faith, Hope and Charity. There is throughout an emphasis on surface – on the haloes that are like waves of gold, on the bright bands of colour that form the steps, on the sparkling dresses of the musician angels.

Painting in Umbria

Umbria, a fresh and lovely countryside of wooded valleys and plains, and of hills topped by formidable little fortress towns, developed its own school of painting in the 15thC. The dominant artistic centers to spread an awareness of new developments in Siena and Florence were Assisi and Orvieto; yet local schools of some charm arose at Gubbio, Foligno and Perugia. This tour concentrates on lesser Renaissance works in the medieval churches and palaces of tiny hill towns, where one may still turn from the fading landscape in a fresco, and see around one the hills and valleys that inspired it.

From PERUGIA, perhaps beginning with a visit to the **Galleria Nazionale dell' Umbria** to put one in the mood and give a good historical perspective, take the road S to SPELLO, a small but impressively walled town. A steep road winds up the hill through a crumbling Roman gate to the church of **Santa Maria Maggiore** where the **Cappella Baglioni** is beautifully decorated by Pintoricchio (1501); Pintoricchio's style was generally richer and more worldly than Perugino's, but these works, in the center of mystic Umbria, capture something of the older artist's spacious symmetry and peace.

Not far off is modern FOLIGNO, where one should visit the **Palazzo Trinci** (now the home of the **Pinacoteca**), with somewhat naïve, awkward decoration by local Umbrian artists, and the church of **San Niccolò**, with a *Coronation of the Virgin* by Niccolò Alunno, the leading local painter of the 15thC; Alunno's intense, expressive style was influenced by Crivelli; here, his harsh, angular figures are poised before a melancholy Umbrian landscape. A little further down the road is a spectacular view of TREVI, with its medieval rooftops patterning the whole side of the hill. Just outside Trevi, in the peaceful sanctuary of the **Madonna delle Lacrime**, is a fresco of the *Adoration of the Magi* (1521) by Perugino, a late variant of one of his favourite compositions.

From Trevi, the road leads through the valley to SPOLETO – past the source of the river Clitunno (Clitumnus), a deep pool evocatively fringed by

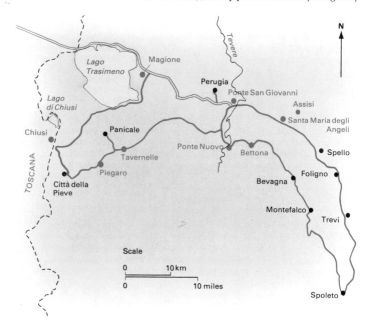

Views such as this gently rolling, wide-open landscape near Perugia have changed little since they were painted by Umbrian artists in the 15thC.

poplars and weeping willows and celebrated by Virgil and Propertius. Spoleto is a fine Roman and medieval town, and the apse of the **Duomo** has the last works of the Florentine Filippo Lippi, who died here in 1469. Only the dazzling, colourful *Coronation of the Virgin* can definitely be attributed to Lippi. The frescoes beneath are mainly by his assistant Fra Diamante, yet these too are lovely works; the dark, mysterious Gothic landscape of the *Nativity* contrasts with the elegant figures and dreamy, hazy Umbrian vista of Pintoricchio's *Madonna and Saints* in the **Cappella Eroli**.

Next, take the country road NW to MONTEFALCO, perched high on a hill, quiet and medieval. Here, the church of **San Francesco** (now the **Pinacoteca Comunale**) has paintings by Gozzoli and Perugino. Gozzoli's frescoes are sharper and more detailed than the soft, atmospheric distances of Perugino's *Nativity* in the left aisle. A sense of place is particularly strong in Gozzoli; in the **Cappella di San Girolamo** in the right aisle, St Jerome leaves the splendours of Rome – symbolized by the Castel Sant' Angelo – for the arid desert; in the *Life of St Francis* (1452) in the apse, the scenes on either side of the window reveal glimpses of the hills and neat fields of Umbria; St Francis preached to the birds at Bevagna and, beyond Montefalco, Gozzoli shows Bevagna on the plain and distant Assisi; one gets much the same view today from the tower of the town hall.

You may now continue across the valley to **Bevagna** itself, which has one of the most charming medieval squares in Italy, a smaller version of the grander square in Perugia. From here, carry on N to Perugia, diverting W and S (if time permits) to take in Panicale and Città della Pieve, both with important works by Perugino; alternatively, these two towns could be visited on another day. **Panicale** is set high above the southern shore of lake Trasimeno, which so frequently glitters in the distance in Perugino's paintings; in the church of **San Sebastiano** is his *Martyrdom of St Sebastian*, with lovely perspective architecture and landscape, yet clumsy figures. In CITTÀ DELLA PIEVE, Perugino's birthplace, **Santa Maria dei Bianchi** contains a large *Adoration of the Magi* – again, with a view of the lake – related to the compositions at Trevi and Montefalco but the most elaborate of the three.

A quick and pleasant way to return to Perugia is along the shore of the lake and then onto the *autostrada*.

MONTALCINO
Siena, Toscana Map C4

Montalcino is a medieval town, dominated by its massive fortress. Long stretches of 13thC walls offer lovely views over the surrounding Tuscan hills, silvery grey with olives.

Museo Civico e Diocesano
Via di Ricasoli 29
Tel. (0577) 848235
Open summer 9am–1pm, 3–7pm; winter
    Tues–Sun 10am–noon, 3–5pm
Closed winter: Mon
🎦 🎨 📖

This small museum is worth a visit. It has **Sienese pictures** from the 14thC–15thC, including works by Bartolo di Fredi and Girolamo di Benvenuto; a 12thC **crucifix** from the abbey of Sant' Antimo; a 16thC silk banner of the **Crucifixion** by Sodoma; a 12thC **illuminated Bible**; and a group of charming 15thC polychrome **wooden statues**.

MONTEFALCO
Perugia, Umbria Map E4

Montefalco is reached by a quiet road that twists W through gentle fields and hills from Spoleto; the road gradually climbs to this tiny medieval town, "the balcony of Umbria", jutting out over the plain. The little squares and streets of Montefalco are almost uncannily quiet, apparently untouched by the 20thC, yet in the Middle Ages this town was the scene of fierce rivalry between its powerful neighbours and an important artistic center.

Pinacoteca Comunale ☆
Via della Ringhiera Umbra
Tel. (0742) 79146
Open Mon–Sat 9am–12.30pm,
    3.30–6.30pm; Sun 9am–noon
🎦 *but gratuity appreciated* 🎨 📖

The old church of San Francesco, now a museum, has surprisingly important frescoes by Tuscan and Umbrian artists from the 13thC–16thC, and a few paintings randomly scattered about the rather bare interior, including works by Niccolò Alunno and Lo Spagna.

In the right aisle is a chapel frescoed by Benozzo Gozzoli. In the apse, the colourful fresco cycle of the *Life of St Francis* ★ is also by Gozzoli. Although the choice of episodes recalls Giotto's frescoes at nearby ASSISI, Gozzoli's touch is lighter and lacks Giotto's dignity and dramatic power. Yet they are charming

works, which movingly portray the saint at work in his much loved Umbrian countryside.

Note, in **St Francis Preaching to the Birds**, a view of Montefalco, little changed, with Assisi in the distance; and, in the **Expulsion of the Devils from Arezzo**, the fresh, springtime beauty of Umbrian hills and fields, with the sun catching little buildings and walled towns.

In the left aisle are Perugino's **Annunciation** and **Nativity** ★ The latter is a late work, which exists in many versions, and its authenticity has been questioned; yet the gentle gravity of the figures and the lyrical tranquillity of the landscape seem to rise above the many tired repetitions of this theme.

MONTE OLIVETO
Siena, Toscana Map C3

The vast, red-brick monastery of Monte Oliveto, circled by a dark band of cypresses, stands dramatically isolated in the clay hills – riven by deep gulleys and ravines – S of Siena.

Monastero di Monte Oliveto Maggiore
Open 9am–12.45pm, 3–7pm
🎦 *but donation appreciated* 🍴 📖 🍷 🏛 📷

The monastery was founded by Bernardo Tolomei in 1313 and the buildings heavily restored in the 19thC. The **Chiostro Grande** is decorated with an important fresco cycle, albeit in poor condition, of scenes from the *Life of St Benedict*, begun by Luca Signorelli (1497–98) and finished by Sodoma (from 1505).

The frescoes include an extraordinary *Self-portrait* by Sodoma, exotically robed, his black hair falling around his shoulders and, at his feet, his pet raven and badger. Sodoma was famous not only for sodomy but also for his dress and private zoo; Vasari describes him as "a merry and licentious man who kept others diverted and amused by leading a life of scant chastity . . . he delighted in having in his house many kinds of extraordinary animals: badgers, squirrels, monkeys, marmosets . . . above all he had a raven who had learned to talk so well that he could imitate the voice of Gianantonio . . ."

In the church, the intarsiaed **choir stalls** ★ (1503–5) by Giovanni da Verona are subtle and delicate perspective studies of little birds, musical instruments and ideal towns. The 17thC refectory has remnants of 15thC frescoes, while the library has illuminated hymn-books.

MONTEPULCIANO
Siena, Toscana Map C4

Montepulciano zig-zags along the crest of a steep hill, a small yet magnificent Renaissance city; the Via di Gracciano, which winds up to the center, is lined with splendid Renaissance palaces and churches by celebrated Italian architects – notably Vignola, Antonio da Sangallo and Michelozzo.

Duomo
Piazza Grande
The cathedral is an austere 17thC building. Inside are displayed fragments of Michelozzo's **tomb of Bartolommeo Aragazzi** (c.1427–37), which was dismembered in the 17thC. Notice especially the recumbent effigy of *Aragazzi* to the left of the entrance and the reliefs against the first two pillars of the nave. This was the first humanist tomb; the relief of *Aragazzi Taking Leave of his Family* ★ unites Christian belief with the noble elegaic quality of classical funerary stelae; the clamouring children were perhaps inspired by the Cantorie of Donatello and Luca della Robbia in **FLORENCE** (Museo dell'Opera del Duomo). On the right of the presbytery is Michelozzo's *St Bartholomew*; on the high altar, a **triptych** by Taddeo di Bartolo (1401).

Museo Civico
Via Ricci 11
Open Tues – Sun 9am – 1pm, 5 – 6pm
Closed Mon
This is a small collection of 13thC – 17thC painting and sculpture. It includes two pretty terra-cotta altarpieces by Andrea della Robbia; a *Nativity* by Girolamo di Benvenuto; and a portrait by Ribera.

MONTERCHI
Arezzo, Toscana Map D3

A visit to Monterchi is one of the most enchanting of all pilgrimages for the art lover. Monterchi itself is a small walled town; on a gentle hill outside the town, amongst fields and cypresses, is a tiny cemetery chapel, which contains one of the greatest of all Piero della Francesca's paintings.

Cappella del Cimitero ☆☆
Open during daylight hours

Piero's famous painting, the *Madonna del Parto* ★★ or Madonna of Childbirth, is guarded night and day. It shows two angels drawing back the brocaded curtains of a canopy, to reveal the grave, hieratic figure of the pregnant Madonna, pointing to her swollen belly. The extraordinary subject is not otherwise known in Italian art.

MONTE SAN GIUSTO
Macerata, Marche Map F3

Monte San Giusto is a small inland center, close to Corridonia.

Santa Maria in Telusiano
This church is famous for Lorenzo Lotto's **Crucifixion** ★ (1531), the most dramatic and powerful of all his large-scale works.

NARNI
Terni, Umbria Map D5

A medieval walled city, with Roman remains, Narni is pleasantly situated on the crest of a hill, overlooking olive groves.

Museo di San Domenico
Piazza XIII Giugno
To gain entry, inquire at Palazzo del Podestà, below

The 12thC church has been adapted into a museum, displaying frescoes, both *in situ* and detached from other churches, and a few interesting sculptures and paintings. The best of the paintings is an **Annunciation** by Benozzo Gozzoli (before 1450), a slightly stilted yet naïvely charming adaptation of Fra Angelico's great work at **CORTONA**.
There is also a strongly characterized 15thC portrait bust of *St Bernardine of Siena*, attributed to Vecchietta, a Sienese sculptor; a pretty 15thC Renaissance **tabernacle** – a provincial interpretation of Agostino di Duccio's style; and a late 17thC **reliquary urn**.

Palazzo del Podestà
Piazza dei Priori
Tel. (0744) 715171
Visits by request

The palace faces the 13thC Loggia dei Priori across a long, narrow piazza, with an elegant fountain (1301) on its left. It is made up of three medieval buildings and the facade, although altered in the 14thC, still incorporates interesting 13thC reliefs; there are further fragments of sculpture in the courtyard.
Inside, the Sala del Consiglio has Domenico Ghirlandaio's glittering

Coronation of the Virgin with Saints (1486), the best picture in Narni. It was executed with the aid of assistants, the most gifted of whom painted the three scenes on the predella.

NOCERA UMBRA
Perugia, Umbria Map E4

Nocera Umbra is an ancient hill-top city, surrounded by wooded hills.

Pinacoteca Comunale
Piazza Caprera
Tel. (0742) 81246
To gain entry, inquire at local police station
☒

This is a small collection with a few good works by minor Tuscan and Umbrian artists. The highlight is a well preserved **polyptych**, in a magnificent gilt frame, by Niccolò Alunno, a leading Umbrian painter of the 15thC. The painting dates from after Niccolò's visit to the Marches in 1466, when he met Crivelli; the bright colouring and precise technique show Crivelli's influence.

ORVIETO
Terni, Umbria Map D4

A distant view of Orvieto is one of the most spectacular sights in Italy; it rises dramatically from the sheer side of an isolated tufa plateau, dominated by the glittering facade of the cathedral. Orvieto is an ancient city and was very important in the Etruscan era; the most impressive monuments date from the 12thC to the 15thC, when the city, despite a stormy history, was wealthy and powerful. The splendour of its cathedral attracted artists from all over Italy.

Duomo ☆☆
Piazza del Duomo
▥

The cathedral was begun in 1290, perhaps by Arnolfo di Cambio, and finished in the 16thC. The colourful 14thC facade, richly decorated with sculpture and mosaics (much restored), was designed by Lorenzo Maitani and continued to his plans by Andrea Pisano and Orcagna.

The **Madonna** in the lunette of the central portal is attributed to Andrea Pisano, the six bronze **Angels** are by Lorenzo Maitani and the **bronze door** was designed by Emilio Greco (1964–70).

The **reliefs ★★** that cover the four piers are generally attributed to Maitani and his workshop (1310–30). Those to the left of the central portal show scenes from the Old Testament, those to the right, scenes from the New Testament and Apocalypse. The story of the **Creation and Fall** on the far left pier is told with a tender, lyrical grace and delicate beauty of line that yield to the crowded, violent drama of the **Last Judgment** on the far right pier.

Above the piers stand bronze emblems of the **Four Evangelists**, also by Maitani. The rose window was designed by Orcagna; the statues of **Prophets** and **Apostles** around it are by Raffaello da Montelupo (c. 1560).

Inside, in the left aisle, there is a frescoed **Madonna** (1425) by Gentile da Fabriano. The **Cappella del Corporale**, in the left transept, contains a celebrated 14thC silver and enamel **reliquary ★★** by Ugolino di Vieri, reputed to preserve the Holy Corporal of the miracle at Bolsena (1263); it is exhibited only on Corpus Christi and Easter Day; on the right wall of the chapel is a **Madonna** (1320) by Lippo Memmi.

The Cappella Nuova, in the right transept, has decorations begun by Fra Angelico and assistants in 1447; they painted two panels of the vault above the altar with **Christ in Glory** and **Prophets**. The work was continued in a sharply contrasting style from 1499–1505 by Luca Signorelli, whose fresco cycle of the **Last Judgment ★★** is his supreme achievement; his superb mastery over powerfully muscled nudes, and, in the **Damned**, his haunting images of suffering and despair, led onto the *terribilità* of Michelangelo.

In the niche to the right of the entrance is a **Pietà** by Signorelli. See also MUSEO DELL'OPERA DEL DUOMO.

Museo Claudio Faina
Palazzo Faina, Piazza del Duomo 29
Tel. (0763) 35216
Open Tues–Sun: Apr–Sept 9am–1pm,
3.30–6pm, Oct–Mar 9am–1pm,
2.30–5.30pm
Closed Mon
☒ ▥

This is an important private collection of Etruscan and Greek artifacts. It includes works in metal and ivory, a fine group of **Greek vases** – note especially the 5thC red figures vases – and two large Hellenistic **sarcophagi** with relief decorations. The celebrated marble **Venus ★** found in the nearby necropolis of Cannicella is also on display, with archaeological finds from continuing excavations in the area.

Museo dell' Opera del Duomo
Palazzo dei Papi, Piazza del Duomo
Tel. (0763) 35477

Open Tues – Sun 9. 30am – 12. 30pm,
  2. 30 – 4. 30pm
Closed Mon
🔄 💿

Housed in the gloomy 13thC palace of
the popes, this museum displays art
associated with the cathedral; it is richest
in works of the 14thC. The highlights are
Madonnas by Simone Martini, Lippo
Vanni (another Sienese painter) and
Andrea Pisano; also, a fragment of a
16thC fresco with a self-portrait by Luca
Signorelli.

San Domenico
Via Arnolfo di Cambio
This is a 13thC church, much altered. In
the S transept is the **monument to
Cardinal de Braye** ★ (d.1282), richly
decorated with coloured marble and
mosaics by Arnolfo di Cambio; it
established the pattern for wall tombs
throughout the next century.

PERUGIA
Umbria Map D4

Perugia was an important Etruscan center
until conquered by Octavian in 40BC; in
the early Middle Ages it became a
powerful free commune, dominating the
other Umbrian cities; its history was
particularly stormy, and in the 15thC it
witnessed bloody and tragic feuds
between the Oddi and Baglioni families.
Perugia remains a grim town, set high
above the Tiber valley; a road twists
sharply up through olive and cypress
plantations to forbidding Etruscan
gateways and cyclopean walls; outside the
city, lost among motorways, is the Ipogeo
dei Volumni, one of the grandest
Etruscan tombs. From the facade of the
grandly battlemented Palazzo dei Priori,
the bronze Perugian griffin and lion loom
defiantly over the irregular Piazza IV
Novembre, facing the dour, unfinished
cathedral. Dark streets and staircase
lanes, criss-crossed by arches and bridges,
and dotted with defensive towers, wind
down the hill; the main street, the Corso
Vanucci, opens into a sudden,
spectacular view of distant hills and
valleys.

Cattedrale
Piazza IV Novembre
In front of the cathedral is a bronze statue
of **Julius II**, by Vincenzo Danti, a 16thC
Umbrian sculptor. The rather
unattractive Gothic interior has, in the
right nave, the **Cappella di San
Bernardino**; this contains Barocci's
sombre **Deposition** ★ (1569), in which
the passionate gesture, stormy light and

swirling draperies look forward to the
Baroque. See also MUSEO DELLA
CATTEDRALE.

Collegio del Cambio *(Chamber of
Commerce)* ★
Palazzo dei Priori, Corso Vanucci
Tel. (075) 61379
Open Tues – Sat: summer 9am – 12. 30pm,
  2. 30 – 6pm, winter 9am – 12. 30pm,
  2. 30 – 5pm; Sun 9am – 12. 30pm
Closed Mon
🔄 🏛

The decoration of the **Sala dell'
Udienza** ★ or Audience Hall is Perugino's
most important work (1496 – 1500). The
end wall is frescoed with the **Nativity** and
the **Transfiguration**. On the left wall,
female figures personifing **Virtues** sit
solidly in the sky above the **Heroes and
Sages of Antiquity** whom they had
upheld on Earth.

Such abstract concepts were to be
given brilliant visual expression in
Raphael's Stanza della Segnatura (see
Musei Vaticani, Rome, **SOUTH CENTRAL
ITALY**). But here, despite the beauty of
the ceiling – an early use of delicate
grotesques – the wall frescoes dwindle
into somewhat dull rows of stiff,
mannered figures, suggesting Perugino's
lack of both intellectual power and ease
with large compositions. The highlight is
the more richly grouped frieze of
Prophets and Sibyls on the right wall;
some critics have seen traces of the young
Raphael's intervention in this fresco, and
in the figure of **Fortitude**. Perugino's own
pride in his achievement is revealed by
his inclusion of a blunt, lively **Self-
portrait** which, accompanied by a Latin
eulogy, hangs in a feigned frame against
one of the pilasters.

Fontana Maggiore
Piazza IV Novembre
The most celebrated fountain in Umbria
was designed between 1275 – 78 by Fra
Bevignate and decorated by Giovanni
and Nicola Pisano. It consists of two vast
polygonal bowls, one above the other,
decorated with reliefs representing the
Months of the Year, illustrated by
appropriate labours, signs of the zodiac,
biblical stories and other subjects.

Galleria Nazionale dell' Umbria ★★
Palazzo dei Priori, Corso Vanucci
Tel. (075) 20316
Open Tues – Sat 9am – 2pm, Sun
  9am – 1pm
Closed Mon
🔄 🏛 ☑

The gallery is housed in the spacious
rooms of the 13thC Palazzo dei Priori,
one of the most splendid medieval civic

palaces in Italy. The collection represents the major Italian regional schools but is naturally strongest on Umbrian art, charting the history of Umbrian painting from the 14thC to the 18thC.

In the 15thC, contacts with the art of the Florentine Renaissance increased – Domenico Veneziano worked in the Palazzo Baglione (since destroyed); the sculptor and architect, Agostino di Duccio, created in Perugia some of the most individual and exquisitely refined works of Tuscan architecture and sculpture; Fra Angelico was commissioned to paint an altarpiece for the church of San Domenico. A modest local school of painting began with Bonfigli's frescoes in the chapel of the Palazzo dei Priori, and reached a high point with the sweet tranquillity and poetic sense of space in works by Perugino and Pintoricchio.

This collection opens with 14thC and 15thC paintings of the Sienese, Tuscan and Umbrian schools, with useful notes that highlight the various cross-currents; the most interesting works are a *Madonna and Angels* (1308) by Duccio (**Room I**) and a *Madonna* (1408) by Gentile da Fabriano (**Room VI**). Also in Room VI is a 14thC polychrome wooden statue of *St Catherine of Alexandria*, in contemporary dress, with a curiously touching, fragile air.

Room VII is the showpiece of the museum, with works by celebrated Tuscan painters, albeit more interesting than beautiful. The polyptych by Fra Angelico, of the *Madonna with Angels and Saints*, was painted after 1437 for the church of San Domenico; it is a damaged, uneven work, yet the central panel and the tenderly meditative saints on the left hand side are of high quality; the gold ground of Gothic painting begins to yield to a more lucid space.

The Angelico polyptych hangs opposite an oddly assembled and puzzling altarpiece of the *Madonna and Four Saints* (c.1470) by Piero della Francesca and assistants. The disparity between the ornate Gothic frame of the lower half of this altarpiece and the perspective of the upper half is striking; Vasari commented on the beauty of the diminishing columns in the scene of the *Annunciation* above, and yet the space is not entirely clear. The finest passages occur in the predella panels – note especially those featuring the miracles of *St Elizabeth of Hungary* and *St Francis*.

This room also has a bronze plaque of the *Flagellation* (1481) by Francesco di Giorgio Martini.

Further on, in **Room IX**, Bonfigli's *Annunciation* is a response to the new

perspective of Florentine art; in **Room X**, there is a lovely *Madonna with Angels* by Girolamo da Cremona.

Rooms XIII and **XIV** have pictures by Perugino and his followers, including Perugino's crowded, elegantly detailed *Adoration of the Magi* (1475), unusually close to Florentine painting. A series of eight paintings by Perugino and Pintoricchio recording, with characteristic Umbrian delicacy, the *Life of St Bernardine of Siena* come from a chest in the oratory of SAN BERNARDINO. Perugino's panel of *St Bernardine Healing Polissena* ★ (1473) dominates the series with the bulky grandeur of its figures and new sense of space. Pintoricchio's panels are daintier and lighter; pretty, tightly-hosed youths pose gracefully before gentle valleys and idealized Renaissance buildings.

In **Room XV** a group of rather shadowy works by Perugino pales before the splendour of a richly decorative Pintoricchio altarpiece ★ still in its original frame. In **Room XVI** is a *Pietà* by Piero di Cosimo. **Rooms XVIII – XXI** have works by followers of Perugino; in pictures by Eusebio di San Giorgio and Lo Spagna, Perugino's already gentle art dwindles into a series of repetitively pious saints and soft vistas – not without a certain watery charm.

Room XXII, the Corridoio del Tesoro, has a collection of goldsmiths' work, ivory and bronzes; note especially the **reliquary of St Giuliana**, a work by an unknown Umbrian goldsmith of the 14thC.

Room XXIII, once the chapel of the Palazzo dei Priori, has late 15thC frescoes ★ *in situ* by Bonfigli of scenes from the *Life of St Louis of Toulouse* and the *Life of St Herculanus*; these, the artist's most important works, marked the beginning of an Umbrian school, influenced by Gozzoli and Fra Angelico, but with a darker range of reds and browns. **Room XXIV** has sculptures by Agostino di Duccio, who worked in Perugia from 1457–61, and again in 1473: there is an unusual terra-cotta *Madonna* ★ also fragments of a late work – in which there are signs of declining powers – from the facade of the Oratorio della Maestà delle Volte.

Room XXVI is a vast hall, with some good Baroque pictures dotted about. These include an unusually intimate Pietro da Cortona *Madonna and Saints* ★ a landscape by Agostino Tassi, who taught Claude; and two dark works by the French Caravaggesque painter, Valentin.

On the second floor, there are 18thC pictures and a collection of 19thC topographical paintings.

Ipogeo dei Volumni ★
6km (4 miles) SE of Perugia, near Ponte San Giovanni
Tel. (075) 393329
Open Tues – Sat: summer 9am – 6pm, winter 9am – 5pm; Sun 9am – 1pm
Closed Mon
🍴

This is a large Etruscan hypogeum or underground tomb, built as an almost full-scale imitation of an Etruscan house. In the main chamber are grouped seven sarcophagi belonging to the Volumnii family, where vivid effigies, forever partaking of a festive banquet, recline on couches.

The most elaborate and finely detailed sarcophagus belonged to the head of the family, the handsome, pensive Aruns Volumnius, a magistrate; his couch is richly draped and cushioned, its legs decorated with swans' head finials; the sarcophagus is supported at the base by large sculptures of *Winged Furies*, who sternly guard a painted doorway through which there is a glimpse of painted ghosts – perhaps welcoming, perhaps escaping. To the left, the sole woman, Veilia, sits grandly on a throne.

Museo Archeologico ★★
Piazza G. Bruno
Tel. (075) 27141
Open Tues – Sat 9am – 2pm, Sun 9am – 1pm
Closed Mon
🍴✓

This is one of the most important archaeological museums in Europe, with a particularly strong prehistoric section, displaying finds from Umbria, Tuscany and the Abruzzi. The Etruscan and Roman section are of greater artistic interest. The highlights are a series of **cinerary urns** ★ grouped according to provenance – the most elaborate bears on its lid a vivid portrayal of a married couple, tender, informal and richly dressed, and, on the sides, a deeply cut relief of a mythological scene; **bronzes** from Castel San Mariano; **Greek vases** and **bucchero ware**; and **coins** and **goldsmiths'** work. A famous stela, the **Cippus Perusinus**, carries an unusually long Etruscan inscription.

Museo della Cattedrale
Cattedrale, Piazza IV Novembre
Tel. (075) 23832
Open Wed, Thurs, Fri 9am – noon; Sat 9am – noon, 3.30 – 5.30pm; Sun 3.30 – 5.30pm
Closed Mon, Tues
🍴

The museum has paintings, detached frescoes, manuscripts, goldsmiths' work, vestments and chalices of various periods. There is a 15thC *Pietà* by the Umbrian painter Caporali, but the outstanding work is Luca Signorelli's great early altarpiece, the **Madonna with Sts John the Baptist, Onophrius and Lawrence, and a Bishop** ★ (1484) which shows the artist's interest in expressive poses and powerful outline.

San Bernardino ★★
Piazza San Francesco
🏛

The little oratory of San Bernardino, one of the most exquisite works of the early Renaissance, looks over the scruffy square of San Francesco. The polychrome facade was designed by the Florentine sculptor and architect Agostino di Duccio (1457–61) and is his most important architectural achievement.

The design suggests the influence of Alberti, with whom Agostino had worked at Rimini; and yet Alberti's powerful plasticity is transformed by the abundance of relief carvings that cover the entire facade, culminating, in the large arch, in the *Apotheosis of St Bernard*. Agostino's style is subtle, very linear and mannered; delicate draperies twist and flutter in intricate rhythms.

San Pietro
Borgo XX Giugno
🏛

The 10thC basilica preserves the beauty of its original structure despite the ornate decoration of later centuries; it has a rich gilt ceiling, finely intarsiaed **choir stalls** and an apse with elegant 16thC piers. In the sacristy are four small paintings by Perugino.

At the far end of the left nave is a *Pietà* attributed to Bonfigli; in the third chapel on the left, a **tabernacle** attributed to Mino da Fiesole; further down towards the entrance, a *Pietà* by Perugino. Other works are by Guercino, Sassoferrato and Guido Reni.

San Severo
Via Raffaello

This 11thC church was built over the site of a pagan temple, and restored in the 18thC. In the oratory adjoining the church, there is a damaged fresco by Raphael of the *Trinity and Saints* (1505), of great historical interest because it is Raphael's first fresco and the sweeping, semi-circular composition already looks forward to the celebrated *Disputà* in the Vatican Stanze (see Musei Vaticani, Rome, *SOUTH CENTRAL ITALY*). The row of six saints beneath was added by Perugino in 1521.

Sculpture in Tuscany

From the time of Nicola Pisano in the 13thC to Michelangelo in the 16thC, the greatest Italian sculptors were Tuscan; Tuscany is indeed the home of Italian sculpture, with Florence at its center. Yet the brilliance of Florence was heralded by Pisa and echoed by other, smaller sculptural centers. This tour starts at Pisa, where Nicola Pisano's pulpit marks one of the turning points in Italian art; it then takes in the historic towns of Lucca, Pistoia and Prato, where examples of Pisan Romanesque and Gothic may be seen side by side with works by Florentine and Sienese Renaissance sculptors.

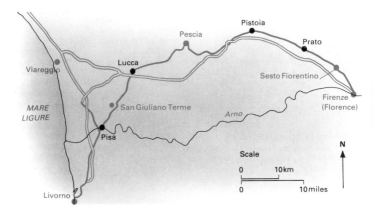

If you are starting from Florence, take the *autostrada* W to PISA. Once there, make for the green and tranquil setting of the cathedral complex. On the N side is the **Camposanto** where, encircled by lacy porticoes, one can still absorb something of the atmosphere that stimulated the Pisan rediscovery of antiquity. Against the shadowy background of the damaged frescoes – once so admired by the Pre-Raphaelites – stand many ancient Roman sarcophagi, appropriated for Christian burials in the 13thC. The ***Phaedra and Hippolytus*** sarcophagus was of outstanding importance to Nicola and Giovanni Pisano. Note especially the *contrapposto* pose of the man standing near the left end, and the man seated beside him.

Across the vivid expanse of grass, in the baptistry (**Battistero**), two figures on Nicola's famous **pulpit** were inspired by these models: the nude male symbolizing ***Fortitude***, and the Virgin in the ***Adoration*** panel. Nicola was the first Italian artist to understand and use the forms of classical art and his dignified realism is akin to that of Giotto. The five reliefs of his pulpit are saturated throughout with a feeling for antique sculpture; the draperies define the forms of the bodies; the grave figures are realistic and there are vivid, freshly observed details. In the **Duomo** is an even more intricately carved **pulpit** by Nicola's son, Giovanni. Particularly interesting is the figure of ***Prudence*** against one of the supports; she is clearly based on an antique ***Venus***. At least a day needs to be spent seeing Pisa; you can find some relaxation from the crowds, and a quiet hotel, in the university quarter.

Next day, take the slow but pretty road to LUCCA. Here, the arcaded facade of the **Duomo** is one of the most lavish works of Pisan Romanesque; yet within, Florentine and Sienese works dominate. In the left transept is the beautiful **tomb of Ilaria del Carretto** by Jacopo della Quercia; this is a transitional work, where the flowing grace of the Gothic effigy contrasts with the classical decorative motifs on the sarcophagus, perhaps derived from a

*The **Nativity** panel from Giovanni Pisano's pulpit in Sant' Andrea, Pistoia.*

Roman sarcophagus in Pisa. Matteo Civitali, a local sculptor, represents a later, purer Renaissance style; he was trained in Florence and his works, of outstanding technical skill, show his sensitivity to the lyrical beauty of Florentine decorative carving. Note especially, in the right transept, his **tomb of Pietro da Noceto**, inspired by the Bruni and Marsuppini monuments in Santa Croce in FLORENCE, and, in the left nave, his exquisite **tempietto**.

In the N of the old town is the church of **San Frediano**, with an outstanding marble **triptych** by Jacopo della Quercia (completed 1422); the Gothic form and elongated figures of the earlier, upper section – marked by Jacopo's highly individual style of falling draperies – contrast with the newer, more dramatic treatment of the predella panels; in the *Martyrdom of St Lawrence* the powerful nudes have a grandeur and vigour close to Donatello.

From Lucca, a winding road twists through hilly country to Pescia and PISTOIA. Here, Giovanni Pisano's **pulpit** in Sant' Andrea is the outstanding achievement of the greatest Italian Gothic sculptor. Its effect is overwhelmingly rich; Giovanni moves away from Nicola's classicism towards a dramatic style influenced by French Gothic. The panel of the *Nativity* makes an interesting contrast with Nicola's treatment of the same subject at Pisa; both artists crowd several stories into one panel but Giovanni breathes new life and expression into Nicola's heavy, impassive figures.

Also in contrast to Giovanni's vigour and drama are the clear grace and restraint of Luca della Robbia's *Visitation* in **San Giovanni Fuorcivitas**; this lovely Renaissance work, in white terra cotta, stands out startlingly in the dark, barn-like church; the young Virgin and ageing St Anne are poignantly suggested. Another Renaissance work, of far greater fame, is the elaborate silver **altar of St James** in the **Duomo**; Brunelleschi was among the many artists who contributed to its composition.

PRATO, a little further down the road towards Florence, is celebrated for its unusual covered **pulpit** by Donatello and Michelozzo; this stands outside the **Duomo**, to the right of the dazzling, green and white striped, marble facade; the originals of Donatello's lively relief panels may be seen in the **Museo dell' Opera del Duomo** nearby.

PESARO
Marche Map E2

Pesaro was ruled by the Sforza in the second half of the 15thC and, in the 16thC, by the delle Rovere who in 1508 succeeded to the duchy of Urbino and made Pesaro their capital. During this period, Pesaro became a splendid Renaissance city, enriched with fine buildings and walls. It is now a pleasant mixture of industrial city and seaside resort, a lively university town with plenty of bookshops; in the center, where the old Roman roads cross, is a fine Renaissance square dominated by the harmonious facade of the Palazzo Ducale (1450–65). Pesaro was particularly important for ceramics.

Pinacoteca e Museo delle Ceramiche ☆
Via T. Mosca 29
Tel. (0721) 31213
Open Tues–Sat: Apr–Sept
9.30am–12.30pm, 4–7pm, Oct–Mar
8.30am–1.30pm; Sun
9.30am–12.30pm
Closed Mon
🕿 *but* 🕿 *Sun*

The art gallery is small but has works of outstanding quality. The highlight is Giovanni Bellini's **Coronation of the Virgin** ★★ (c.1475), painted for the high altar of the church of San Francesco. Christ crowns the Virgin, not amid celestial golds and choirs of angels, but in the mellow beauty of the countryside around Pesaro – a view of the fortress of Gadara is glimpsed through a window in the back of the throne. The painting retains a splendid Renaissance frame.

Note also a harsh **Pietà** and macabre **Head of the Baptist** by the late 15thC painter, Marco Zoppo; 17thC pictures, including Cantarini's **Magdalen**, an elegaic painting in a lovely harmony of silvery greys and browns; and a terra-cotta model by Algardi for his relief of **St Leo Turning Attila away from Rome** (see San Pietro in Vaticano, Rome, *SOUTH CENTRAL ITALY*).

The collection of **ceramics** ★★ is one of the most beautiful and important in Italy. Note, especially, works by Maestro Giorgio Andreoli (145, 147) and Niccolò Pellipario (212–215).

PIENZA
Siena, Toscana Map C4

Pienza is a remote and tiny town, running along the crest of a hill and looking out over the plains of southern Tuscany. It was the birthplace of Aeneas Silvius Piccolomini who, as Pope Pius II (1458–64), rebuilt the medieval village of Corsignano, renaming it in his own honour. Bernardo Rossellino planned the new town; the buildings rose astonishingly quickly; within three short years the picturesque jumble of the medieval village had been replaced by buildings created in a single harmonious style, lucid and classical, and beautifully related to each other. Pienza is the earliest example of Renaissance town planning; it lacks both the deserted melancholy of Sabbioneta (see *NORTH & NORTH WEST ITALY*) and the vigour of *URBINO*; it has, rather, a frozen, unreal perfection – Pius stipulated that nothing should ever be altered; the stillness of the main square recalls those perspective studies of the ideal town, silent and empty, that lived in the imagination of the Renaissance artist.

Cattedrale
Piazza Pio II
🏛

Pius chose a Renaissance facade for his cathedral, crowning it with a tympanum proudly bearing the Piccolomini coat-of-arms, but the interior is Gothic and was inspired by the German hall churches he had seen and admired on his travels in northern Europe.

The most interesting paintings are, in the right transept, a **Madonna and Saints** by Matteo di Giovanni; in the chapel to the left of the high altar, an **Assumption** by Vecchietta; and, in the left transept, a **Madonna and Saints** by Sano di Pietro. The choir stalls (1462) are Gothic; in the crypt, there is a **font** by Bernardo Rossellino.

Museo della Cattedrale
Via Castello 1
Tel. (0578) 74644
Open Mar–Oct 10am–1pm, 3–6pm;
Nov–Feb 10am–1pm, 2–4pm
🕿

This small museum has works from the cathedral and nearby churches, including a **Madonna and Saints** by Vecchietta; a large **Madonna della Misericordia** by Bartolo di Fredi; 15thC and 16thC **Flemish tapestries**; and a famous **cope of Pius II**.

PISA
Toscana Map A2

Pisa was perhaps founded as a Greek colony in the 7thC or 6thC BC. But its most brilliant period was during the Middle Ages when, as a powerful maritime republic, it wielded great political power. In the 13thC Pisa was particularly famous for painted crosses, inspired by Byzantine models. The city saw the development of a brilliantly original form of Romanesque architecture, characterized by a rich blend of motifs from Roman, Italian and Oriental art. The buildings of its cathedral complex – the Duomo, baptistry and leaning tower, their white marble glittering against the vivid expanse of green, and their solid forms enriched by the fragile grace of delicate blind arcades and lacy Gothic pinnacles – form one of the most famous and celebrated architectural groups in the world. The atmosphere around the Piazza del Duomo is pleasantly bustling and festive – elsewhere Pisa is a quiet, rather sleepy city, with stately rows of medieval houses lining the banks of the Arno.

Battistero ☆☆
Piazza del Duomo
Tel. (050) 22531
Open Mon – Fri 9am – 1pm, 3pm – sunset
Closed Sat, Sun
🏛

The circular baptistry was begun in the 12thC, elaborated by Nicola and Giovanni Pisano (1260 – 90) and crowned by a Gothic dome and decorations in the 14thC. Figures by Nicola and Giovanni Pisano decorate the cusps of the loggia at the second level (many are now replaced by copies).

Inside, the **font** is by Guido da Como (1246). Around the walls are statues by Nicola and Giovanni Pisano from the exterior. Nicola's famous hexagonal **pulpit ★★** supported by columns, signed and dated 1260, is his earliest known work. Its architectural grandeur, and the grave realism of the five reliefs, broke dramatically with the more decorative style of earlier pulpits, and opened a new era in Italian sculpture. Nicola's realism was influenced by a study of classical art, and the pulpit incorporates direct quotations from the Roman sarcophagi then displayed in the CAMPOSANTO.

Camposanto ☆
Piazza del Duomo
Tel. (050) 22531
Open 9am – sunset
The cemetery or, literally, "holy field" of Pisa is reputed to have been overlaid with earth imported from the Holy Land in the 13thC. Around the oblong burial ground run porticoed galleries that once displayed a vast collection of Roman sarcophagi; celebrated artists from Tuscany, Umbria and the North were called in to fresco the walls. The building

was badly damaged by bombs in 1944 and what can now be seen is a monument to the restorer's art, but only a vestige of the Camposanto's past grandeur.

Note, especially, in the S gallery, the remnants of a series of 23 scenes frescoed by Benozzo Gozzoli. In the N gallery are Gozzoli's **Grape Harvest** and **Drunkenness of Noah**; in the center, amongst good Roman sarcophagi, the **Phaedra and Hippolytus** sarcophagus (2ndC AD), which inspired Nicola Pisano.

Off the portico is the **Salone degli Affreschi**, which displays the most important of the detached frescoes. The celebrated and macabre **Triumph of Death ★** long attributed to Francesco Traini, the leading Pisan artist of the 14thC, is now claimed for that mysterious painter, Buffalmacco. The terrible image of the three elegantly clad nobles who stumble across three rotting corpses has also been associated with an experience of the Black Death. This room also contains sculptures by Giovanni Pisano and Tino da Camaino.

Duomo ☆☆
Piazza del Duomo
Tel. (050) 22531
Open 7.45am – 1pm, 3pm – sunset
🏛
Begun by Buscheto in 1063, and continued by Rainaldo in the 12thC, the cathedral introduced a new, highly original style of Romanesque architecture which Lucca, Pistoia and other Tuscan cities were to emulate. From the 11thC to the 14thC, Pisa was an important maritime republic and trading center, in touch with the cities of the East; the outstanding feature of the cathedral is its decorative arcading and the distinctive blend of Western and Oriental motifs.

The three bronze doors on the W front are by followers of Giovanni Bologna. Entrance is usually by the Porta di San Ranieri in the S transept: the **bronze doors ★** (1180) by Bonanno show scenes from the *Life of Christ* with charming, ingenuous vigour.

On the left side of the nave, Giovanni Pisano's elaborate **pulpit ★★** (1302 – 10) is supported by an ambitious array of allegorical figure-sculptures, and decorated with dramatic relief panels illustrating the *Life of Christ* and the *Last Judgment*. The architectural detail of the pulpit is more correctly classical than in Giovanni's slightly earlier work at PISTOIA – note especially the capitals of the columns – but the relief style has lost something of the brilliant, fiery intensity that characterizes that work. The figures that stand at the base of the columns are the most interesting and revolutionary part of this pulpit; they are clearly influenced by classical art.

In the right transept is Tino di Camaino's **tomb of the Emperor Henry VII**. The entrance to the chancel is flanked by two bronze **candelabra** bearing angels by Giambologna. On the right is Andrea del Sarto's **St Agnes**; on the high altar, a bronze **crucifix** by Giambologna. The central apse is decorated with 13thC mosaics, finished by Cimabue, and pictures by Beccafumi and Sodoma. In the left transept, the Cappella del Sacramento has Baroque decorations by Foggini, Vanni and Paggi.

Museo Nazionale di San Matteo ✩✩
Lungarno Mediceo
Tel. (050) 23750
Open Tues – Sat 9am – 2pm, Sun
  9am – 1pm
Closed Mon
☎ 🏛 ☑ ♨ ▦

The museum houses an outstanding collection of Pisan Romanesque sculpture and Tuscan and Sienese painting, but only the ground floor section is now open. The second floor is being reorganized, and it is possible that the 17thC collection – which includes good works by Reni, Francesco del Cairo and Giambattista Crespi – will be rehoused in a separate building.

The atmosphere of this museum is particularly appealing; the history of Pisan sculpture, from the classical and early Christian period to the dramatic innovations of Nicola and Giovanni Pisano, unfolds in a series of small vaulted rooms that run around a lovely 14thC cloister, picturesquely strewn with classical and medieval capitals.

Note, especially, among the busts and figures that once decorated the baptistry, Giovanni Pisano's windswept figure of a **Dancer** and his **Saint with a Reliquary**; also, a pulpit from San Michele in Borgo, by a follower of Giovanni; and the grave **Madonna del Latte** or Madonna of the Milk (1365 – 68) by either Andrea or Nino Pisano.

Polychrome wooden sculptures by Nino Pisano's successors are softer, influenced by the gentler rhythms and swinging curves of Sienese painting; they include an outstanding group of **Annunciations**.

Among the paintings are a signed **polyptych** by Francesco Traini; works by Gozzoli and Gentile da Fabriano; and Masaccio's **St Paul**. The finest work is Simone Martini's polyptych of the **Madonna and Saints** ★ (1319), in which the main figures are exquisitely poised against a blaze of gold; the predella

figures, delicately coloured, subtly vary the central theme.

Museo delle Sinopie ✩
Piazza del Duomo
Tel. (050) 22531
Open 9am – 1pm, 3 – 5pm
☎ ☑

The museum exhibits a beautiful and very well documented display of *sinopie* – preparatory drawings for frescoes – salvaged from the destruction of the CAMPOSANTO frescoes during World War II.

The decoration of the Camposanto galleries was a great enterprise that involved some of the most famous 13thC – 15thC painters. The *sinopie* reveal fascinatingly different techniques: some of the drawings are unexpectedly sketchy (for example, those of Spinello Aretino and Taddeo Gaddi, both important 14thC Florentine artists); others (such as those attributed to Buffalmacco) are much more highly finished.

The great **Triumph of Death** is now claimed for Buffalmacco; this fascinating 14thC painter was well-known in his own day, and is mentioned by both Boccaccio and Vasari, yet no works can be definitely traced to him.

Palazzo dei Cavalieri
Piazza dei Cavalieri
🏛

The 13thC Palazzo degli Anziani was transformed into the Palazzo dei Cavalieri by Vasari, who decorated the facade with ornate grotesques. The busts of six Medici grand dukes, by Luni, glower pugnaciously from roundels across the facade; in front of the palace is a statue of **Cosimo I** (1596) by Pietro Francavilla.

PISTOIA
Toscana Map B2

Of Roman origin, Pistoia became a free commune in 1115; during the Middle Ages it was torn by bitter internal feuds and by wars with Lucca and Florence; in 1530 it fell to Florence. It is now a pleasant market town, with a wealth of Romanesque architecture – dependent on Pisan examples, but more finely patterned and colourful. In the center, the grand, spacious Piazza del Duomo is enclosed by a beautiful array of ancient buildings: the Romanesque cathedral with its heavy campanile; the elegant, octagonal Gothic baptistry, faced with green and white marble; and the austere 14thC Palazzo del Comune with, on the ground floor, the Centro Marino Marini and, on the first and second floors, the newly-opened Museo Civico.

Centro Marino Marini
Palazzo del Comune
Tel. (0573) 368182
Open Tues – Sat 9am – 1pm, 3 – 7pm, Sun
9am – 12.30pm
Closed Mon

Paintings, etchings, drawings and sculptures by Marino Marini, who was born in Pistoia, are displayed in three rooms off the courtyard of the Palazzo del Comune. There are very early drawings from the 1920s; a group of linear nude studies from the 1940s; many treatments, in different media, of his favourite horse and rider theme; and a series of illustrations to Shakespeare from the 1970s. His somehow ludicrous *Rider Miracle* (1953) stands in the courtyard of the palace.

Duomo
Piazza del Duomo

The cathedral was founded in the 5thC and rebuilt many times; its arcaded facade is Pisan Romanesque. The 14thC marble porch is decorated with terra cottas by Andrea della Robbia.

At the end of the right aisle is the 14thC **tomb of Cino da Pistoia**. Off the same aisle is the **Cappella di San Jacopo** (ask the sacristan to let you in) containing the celebrated silver **altar of St James ★★** (1287–1456). In the center of the altar is *St James* with, above, *Christ in a Mandorla*; on either side are scenes from the *Life of Christ* and *Life of St James*. Many artists contributed to this work; the oldest figures are the stiff, hieratic *Apostles* beside *St James*; the latest, the two vivid figures ★ by Brunelleschi on the left side.

The chapel to the left of the high altar has a *Madonna Enthroned with Saints*, begun by Verrocchio and completed by Lorenzo di Credi (1485).

Museo Civico
Palazzo del Comune
Tel. (0573) 367871
Open Tues – Sun: May – Sept
9am – 12.30pm, 3 – 7pm; Oct – Apr
9am – 12.30pm
Closed Mon

This is a new museum, beautifully displayed and documented, housed in the first and second-floor rooms of the 14thC Palazzo del Comune, many of which retain splendid wooden ceilings. The collection is of predominantly Pistoian

painting and ranges from the 13thC to the 19thC.

A rare painting of *St Francis with Scenes from his Life* ★ dates from the 13thC and is in the tradition of the Berlinghieri family. A series of 15thC and 16thC altarpieces from churches in Pistoia includes a late work by Lorenzo di Credi and an important early work by Gerino Gerini who introduced the style of Perugino to Pistoia. Among the sculptures, notice especially a charming wooden polychrome *Angel* attributed to the Sienese artist Francesco di Valdambrino.

Pictures by 17thC Pistoian and Florentine artists include two works by the rare painter Cecco Bravo, with the weird misty light and flickering brushwork that characterize his exotic style. Paintings from the once-celebrated **Puccini collection** include Cigoli's Correggiesque *Mystic Marriage of St Catherine*. Other works are by Coccapani and Matteo Roselli.

Ospedale del Ceppo
Piazza Giovanni XII

The hospital was founded in the 14thC. The portico is in the style of Brunelleschi and was added in 1514; around the top is an extraordinary polychrome **frieze ★** by Giovanni della Robbia and assistants, showing the *Seven Acts of Mercy*, with a wealth of fascinating realistic detail.

Sant' Andrea
Via Sant' Andrea

The church is 12thC and has a lovely arcaded facade; the fine reliefs above the central portal are by Gruamonte and Adeodatus (1166).

Inside, Giovanni Pisano's **pulpit ★★** (1298–1301) is the most celebrated work of art in Pistoia. The form of the pulpit is based on Nicola Pisano's earlier pulpit at PISA; five panels illustrate the *Life of Christ* and the *Last Judgment*. Yet these deeply undercut reliefs, crowded with twisting, sharply linear figures, reflect the intense emotion and dramatic movement that distinguish his art from his father's. The wooden **crucifix** in the right nave is also by Giovanni.

San Bartolommeo in Pantano
Piazza San Bartolommeo
This 12thC church, with a sculptured portal attributed to Gruamonte, is almost always closed; it has a **pulpit** (1250) by Guido di Como, a good example of the traditional kind of composition that was transformed by Nicola and Giovanni Pisano.

San Giovanni Fuorcivitas
Via Francesco Crispi
🏛

Built between the 12thC and the 14thC,
this church has an unfinished facade but
its arcaded lateral walls are vividly
decorated with bands of green and white
marble and geometric designs. The portal
has a decorated architrave by Gruamonte
(1162).

The interior has a single aisle and is
very dark. To the left of the entrance is a
passionate **Visitation** ★ of glazed terra
cotta by Luca della Robbia. To the left of
the altar is a **polyptych** by Taddeo Gaddi;
against the right wall, a **pulpit** by Fra
Guglielmo (1270); in the center of the
church, a **holy-water stoup** ★ by
Giovanni Pisano.

POGGIO A CAIANO
Firenze, Toscana Map B2

Poggio a Caiano is a suburban area W of
Florence, best known for its Renaissance
villa.

Villa Medicea di Poggia a Caiano ☆
Tel. (055) 877012
Gardens only open Tues–Sun: May–Aug
9am–6pm, Sept–Apr 9am–5pm
House closed for restoration; gardens closed
Mon
📷 🏛 ♥

This country seat was acquired by
Lorenzo the Magnificent in 1479. During
the next 5yrs it was remodelled and
turned into a princely Renaissance retreat
by the architect Giuliano da Sangallo,
who created a design inspired by the villas
of ancient Rome.

The symmetry of the plan, and the
pedimented temple front, influenced
later Medici villas and anticipate the
villas of Palladio; the startlingly
Neoclassical terra-cotta frieze, attributed
to Andrea Sansovino, was perhaps added
under the Medici pope, Leo X.

Leo X also commissioned a series of
frescoes for the vast entrance hall of the
villa (unfortunately now closed for
restoration) as a tribute to his father,
Lorenzo the Magnificent. Andrea del
Sarto, Pontormo, Franciabigio and Allori
all worked on the series. The outstanding
scenes are perhaps Andrea del Sarto's
Tribute Money (1521) where the main
action receives little attention, but the
genre-like scenes in the foreground are
brilliantly vivid; and, in the lunette of
the right wall, Pontormo's **Vertumnus
and Pomona** (1521) – a strange blend of
unconventional pose and pattern with
sharp observation, which perfectly
conveys the wonderful serenity of

country life celebrated in Lorenzo's
Arcadian poetry.

PRATO
Firenze, Toscana Map B2

Prato is a busy industrial city, where fine
Romanesque and Renaissance
monuments are surrounded by shabby,
traffic-polluted squares. Large 20thC
sculptures in streets and gardens – by
Henry Moore and Gio Pomodoro –
determinedly suggest its continuing
vitality. Prato lacks the charm of nearby
Lucca and Pistoia, but the quality of its
works of art is outstanding.

Duomo ☆
Piazza del Duomo
🏛

On the right of the vivid green and white
striped late Gothic facade is Donatello's
and Michelozzo's Renaissance **Pulpit of
the Holy Girdle** ★ (1428–38).
(Donatello's friezes are casts; the originals
are in the MUSEO DELL'OPERA DEL DUOMO).

The nave has an elegant Renaissance
pulpit by Mino da Fiesole and Antonio
Rossellino. The first chapel on the left,
the **Cappella del Sacro Cingolo** or
Chapel of the Holy Girdle, has late
14thC frescoes by Agnolo Gaddi; above
the altar is a **Madonna** by Giovanni
Pisano.

In the apse are Filippo Lippi's frescoes
of scenes from the **Life of St John the
Baptist** ★ (right wall) and the **Life of St
Stephen** ★ (left wall). These are Lippi's
richest and most dramatic narratives; the
scenes are ennobled by magnificent
Renaissance settings. In the **Feast of
Herod**, Salome's piquant dance takes
place before foppish Renaissance
courtiers; many of the figures are
portraits, and their expressions and
gestures are vivid and subtle; yet the
scene has a tender, melancholy air and
the graceful beauty of the line and
varying light looks forward to Botticelli.

The chapel to the right of the apse has
15thC **frescoes** begun by Uccello and
finished by Andrea di Giusto. In the right
transept is a 15thC **tabernacle** by the
Maiano brothers, enclosing a statue of
the **Madonna**, and a panel of the **Death
of St Jerome** by Filippo Lippi.

Galleria Comunale
Palazzo Pretorio, Piazza del Comune
Tel. (0574) 29396
Open Tues–Sat 9am–7pm, Sun
9am–noon
Closed Mon
📷 🗺 🏛 ☑

The severe 13thC palace towers over a

small square decorated by Tacca's charming **Bacchus Fountain** (the *Bacchus* is a copy); within is a lively collection, mainly of Tuscan and Sienese pictures of the 14thC.

On the first floor is a damaged but graceful **tabernacle** by Filippino Lippi. On the second floor, a large room with a fine 13thC wooden ceiling exhibits several altarpieces, including a **polyptych** by Bernardo Daddi featuring the *Story of the Sacred Girdle*, a **tondo** attributed to Luca Signorelli – note the perspective skill of the twisting band of paper which unfolds in the foreground – two works by Filippo Lippi (a *Madonna and Saints* and a *Nativity*) and a *Madonna and Saints* by Filippino Lippi.

A series of smaller rooms shows very different works: a dark, intensely spiritual *Noli Me Tangere* by the Neapolitan Caravaggesque painter, Caracciolo; Neapolitan still-lifes; and 18thC landscapes by Vanvitelli. The third floor has 18thC plaster models by Bartolini.

Museo dell'Opera del Duomo ☆
Piazza del Duomo 49
Tel. (0574) 29339
Open Mon, Wed – Sat 9.30am – 12.30pm,
* 3 – 6.30pm, Sun 9.30am – 12.30pm*
Closed Tues
🔛 🏛 ☑

To the left of the DUOMO is the former bishop's palace, with, on the ground floor, the cathedral museum – a comfortable, luxurious and beautifully-lit display of miniatures, goldsmiths' work, Renaissance sculptures, and paintings. The paintings include a cloyingly sweet *Guardian Angel* by Carlo Dolci and a dramatic Baroque canvas by Livio Mehus.

On the N side of the pretty cloister, a small room contains the original **reliefs ★** by Donatello from the pulpit outside the Duomo. The seven panels are linked by the lively rhythms of the dancing putti – wittily derived from Bacchic scenes on Roman sarcophagi. These rhythms later culminated in the wild abandon of the Cantorie in FLORENCE (Museo dell' Opera del Duomo). The theme is echoed, with exquisite charm, in Maso di Bartolommeo's **Reliquary of the Holy Girdle** (1446) in the same room.

RECANATI
Macerata, Marche Map F3

Recanati occupies a fine hill-top position, with panoramic views over the surrounding countryside, largely unchanged since the days of the poet Leopardi, born here in 1798.

Museo Diocesano
Via Falleroni
Open 8am – noon, 4 – 8pm
🔛 *but donation appreciated*

Housed in the former bishops' palace, the museum contains archaeological fragments and 15thC and 16thC paintings, including a polyptych by Ludovico Urbani.

Pinacoteca Civica ☆
Palazzo Comunale, Piazza Leopardi
Tel. (071) 982772
Open Tues – Sat 10am – 1pm, 4 – 6pm, Sun
* 10am – 1pm*
Closed Mon
🔛 ⬅ ✗ 🖫 ⁛ 🥄

The gallery is most famous for a group of works by Lorenzo Lotto (Room V). These open with the great **polyptych ★** of 1506 – 8; in this, the seminal work of his early period, Lotto begins to move away from his earlier dependence on Bellini and Giorgione towards a more dramatic style and lighter, softer colours; the *Transfiguration* dates from c. 1512, after a visit to Rome, and suggests an uneasy response to the monumentality of Raphael; finally, the *Annunciation* (c. 1526) is a strange and strikingly original work – with a curiously Pre-Raphaelite quality; the Virgin, pallid and agitated, is brought dramatically close to the spectator, as though seeking protection, while shrinking back in terror from the angel; a little cat arches its back in fury; the still quiet of the interior is disrupted by the uneasy mystery of the divine.

There is also an early 15thC **polyptych** by the local artist, Pietro da Recanati.

San Domenico
Piazza Leopardi
This 14thC church has a marble portal (1481) attributed to Giuliano da Maiano and, within (second altar on right), a detached fresco of *St Vincent Ferrer in Glory* (1515) by Lotto.

SAN GIMIGNANO
Siena, Toscana Map B3

San Gimignano is one of the most charming and complete little medieval towns in Tuscany. Enclosed within walls, a cluster of medieval towers rises arrogantly high from the narrow, twisting streets, overlooking a countryside of olives and vines. It is hard to believe that the towers represent a very small proportion of the original defensive system, and that most medieval towns had a similarly startling appearance. The most important monuments are Romanesque. San Gimignano was a free commune in the 12thC, but in 1354 became part of the Florentine Republic. Benozzo Gozzoli was born here.

Collegiata ☆
Piazza del Duomo
☎ *Cappella di Santa Fina – ticket also gives entry to Palazzo del Popolo*
This dark, heavily restored Romanesque cathedral is richly decorated with frescoes by leading Sienese and Florentine painters.

On the interior facade is the **Last Judgment** (1393) by Taddeo di Bartolo. Below is Benozzo Gozzoli's **Martyrdom of St Sebastian** (1465); on either side are polychrome wooden statues of the **Annunciation** (1421) by Jacopo della Quercia.

The right aisle has 14thC **frescoes** by Barna da Siena, strongly influenced by Duccio and Simone Martini, but nevertheless powerful works, and much admired by Ghiberti.

The **Cappella di Santa Fina ★** (1468), off the right aisle, is one of the loveliest early Renaissance chapels designed by the Florentine architect Giuliano da Maiano; the altar is by Benedetto da Maiano. Frescoes by Domenico Ghirlandaio show the **Life of St Fina**, a much-loved local saint who, after five years of severe illness spent lying on a board, died at the age of 15. On the right wall, **St Gregory Appearing to the Dying St Fina** is a touchingly simple composition, graced by the beauty of the light falling on the bare walls, and the little country scene beyond the window. On the left wall, the **Funeral of St Fina** shows the towers of San Gimignano beyond the window.

On the high altar is a **ciborium** by Benedetto da Maiano. In the left aisle are **frescoes** by Bartolo di Fredi. In the loggia of the baptistry (off the left nave) is an **Annunciation** by Ghirlandaio.

Palazzo del Popolo
Piazza del Duomo
Open Tues – Sun: Apr – Oct
9.30am – 12.30pm, 3.30 – 6.30pm;
Nov – Mar 10am – 1pm, 2.30 – 5.30pm
Closed Mon
☎ *ticket also gives entry to Cappella di Santa Fina in Collegiata* 🏛
This is a 13thC palace, with a fine tower; from the pretty interior courtyard, an external staircase leads to the **Sala di Dante**, where Dante in 1300 put forward the case for joining the Tuscan alliance. It contains Lippo Memmi's vast frescoed **Maestà** (1317); Lippo Memmi was the brother-in-law of Simone Martini, and this picture was inspired by Simone's great **Maestà** at SIENA. The Pinacoteca has some attractive 13thC – 15thC Sienese pictures, including two tondi by Filippino Lippi.

Sant'Agostino
Piazza Sant' Agostino
The Romanesque-Gothic church was built in the 13thC. To the right of the central door, the **Cappella di San Bartolo** contains a marble altar by Benedetto da Maiano; beneath the sarcophagus are scenes from the **Life of St Bartolo**. On the high altar is an outstanding work by Piero Pollaiuolo, the **Coronation of the Virgin ★**

In the choir there are frescoes of the **Life of St Augustine ★** by Benozzo Gozzoli. Running in three bands, these are vivid scenes of contemporary Florentine life, set against elaborate architectural backgrounds, and full of realistic portraits and lively incident. In the first scene, a sturdy Augustine is packed off to school by his mother; to the right, he is soundly caned, while more industrious pupils continue their studies.

In the left nave there is a frescoed **St Sebastian** by Gozzoli, and a **Madonna** (1330) by Lippo Memmi.

SANSEPOLCRO
Arezzo, Toscana   Map D3
This small market town in the upper Tiber valley is famous as the birthplace of Piero della Francesca. Throughout his life, Piero remained closely associated with the town, which has changed very little; as a young man, he was elected a town councillor, and he received his earliest great commission from the cathedral. Piero retired to Sansepolcro for the last 15yrs of his life and his fame persisted here after his death, although elsewhere he was neglected until his great rediscovery in the 20thC.

Duomo
Via Matteotti
A Romanesque-Gothic church, the Duomo has paintings by Bartolommeo della Gatta (right aisle) and two panels from a **polyptych** by Matteo di Giovanni.

Pinacoteca ☆
Via Aggiunti 65
Tel. (0575) 76465
Open 9.30am – 1pm, 2.30 – 6pm
☎ ♿
A varied collection of reliquaries, church furnishings, detached frescoes, 14thC *sinopie*, and paintings, is dominated by the works of Piero della Francesca.

The polyptych of the **Madonna della**

Misericordia ★ was Piero's first great commission; it is a markedly old-fashioned work, damaged, and executed with the extensive aid of assistants – yet the calm, noble beauty of the Madonna looks forward to later works.

The fresco of the **Resurrection** ★★ is perhaps Piero's greatest single painting. An aura of solemn majesty is created by the stark frontality and austere geometry of the composition; Christ, the promise of Salvation, rises slowly from the tomb, as the bare wintry landscape is touched by the first signs of spring and by the thin cool light of early morning; the four Roman soldiers slumber heavily.

Other works include Pontormo's *St Quentin* and a painted standard by Signorelli.

SIENA
Toscana Map C3

Lying on three hills amid countryside thick with olive groves and vineyards, Siena is one of the loveliest and most perfectly preserved medieval towns in Tuscany. It is surrounded by walls and has kept its medieval plan; the narrow, twisting streets are lined mainly with buildings of the 14thC and 15thC. Siena's most brilliant artistic period was during the 14thC, when it enjoyed political freedom and great commercial prosperity; in 1555 it became part of the Grand Duchy of Tuscany. The good government of 14thC Siena is movingly recorded in Ambrogio Lorenzetti's frescoes in the Museo Civico of the Palazzo Pubblico. Siena is rich in works of art – the brilliantly coloured Duomo and Duccio's *Maestà* in the cathedral museum mark one of the great turning points in Italian art; the font in the baptistry is a remarkable collaborative work of the most famous Renaissance sculptors; the Pinacoteca offers a unique collection of Sienese painting. The Campo, Siena's historic center, and the site of many colourful ceremonies, is perhaps the loveliest square in all Italy.

Battistero ☆
Piazza San Giovanni
The interior of the baptistry is very dark, so take plenty of coins for the lights. In the center stands Jacopo della Quercia's marble **font** ★★ (1411–30), decorated with bronze reliefs which provide a fascinating opportunity to compare the styles of the three leading contemporary sculptors – Ghiberti, Donatello and Jacopo himself – at an exciting moment when Gothic was yielding to the new naturalism of the Renaissance.

Ghiberti's panel, the **Baptism of Christ** ★ (1424–27), faces the entrance; its grace and clarity, and mixture of high and low relief, contrast with Donatello's complex and intensely dramatic **Feast of Herod** ★ one of the earliest uses of the new science of linear perspective, and with the weightier figures and more confused space of Jacopo's **Annunciation to Zaccharias** ★ Bronze statues soften the sharp lines of the font; *Faith* and *Hope* are by Donatello.

Duomo ☆☆
Piazza del Duomo
🚻 *Libreria Piccolomini* 🏛
The cathedral was begun about 1150 and building continued for the next two centuries. The brightly coloured marble facade – striped white, green and red, and lavishly decorated with sculpture and architectural ornament – is its most attractive feature. Originally the lower part of the facade was decorated with a series of life-size marble statues of **Prophets and Philosophers**, the first independent work of Giovanni Pisano. These are now mainly in the MUSEO DELL' OPERA DEL DUOMO, but it is worth studying the reproductions. When in their intended place, the distortions that seem so awkward at eye level disappear; only then does the connection between the figures, involved in animated discussion, with sharply turned heads and pointing gestures, spring to life.

The interior is startlingly patterned with bands of black and green marble leading to the blue, star-spangled vault. The unique **marble pavement** ★ was designed between the 14thC and 16thC by celebrated Sienese artists, among them Beccafumi. Note especially the dramatic **Massacre of the Innocents** (1481) by Matteo di Giovanni in the left transept. In the fourth bay of the left nave is the **Piccolomini Altar** (1503) designed by Andrea Bregno, with four small statues by Michelangelo.

The **Libreria Piccolomini** ★ off the left nave was built by Cardinal Francesco Piccolomini in honour of his uncle, the humanist scholar and diplomat, Aeneas Silvius Piccolomini, later Pope Pius II. It is decorated with charming **frescoes** ★ by Pintoricchio; a sequence of illusionistic arches, richly decorated with Renaissance ornament, opens onto airy landscapes, where the Pope's life unfolds in scenes full of lively incident and fresh colour. In the center of the room is a celebrated antique statue of the *Three Graces* ★

In the left transept, the circular Renaissance **Cappella di San Giovanni Battista** has frescoes by Pintoricchio and, in the center, a harsh, powerful bronze statue of *St John the Baptist* ★ (1457) by Donatello. Also in the left transept, the **Cappella di Sant'Ansano** has a **monument to Cardinal Petroni** by Tino di Camaino and the **tomb slab of Bishop Giovanni Pecci** ★ by Donatello. Nicola Pisano's **pulpit** ★★ (1265) is a more elaborate work than his earlier pulpit at PISA; the narrative panels are more crowded, and movement and expression more dramatic.

The pillars on either side of the presbytery are decorated with eight beautiful *Angels* ★ by Beccafumi, leading the eye to the high altar, with its **ciborium** ★ by Vecchietta. On either side of the altar are more *Angels* ★ – the higher pair by Giovanni di Stefano (1488), the lower pair by Francesco di Giorgio Martini (1499).

The **Cappella Chigi** in the right transept was designed by Bernini (1661) for Fabio Chigi, later Pope Alexander VII. The statues of *St Jerome* ★ and *St Mary Magdalen* ★ symbols of penitence, are late, visionary works by Bernini.

Museo Civico ☆☆
Palazzo Pubblico, Piazza del Campo
Tel. (0577) 280530
Open Mon–Sat: Apr–Sept
  8.30am–7.30pm, Oct–Mar
  8.30am–5pm; Sun 8.30am–1pm
🎟 🏛 ✓ 🚻

The Palazzo Pubblico, symbol of the city's proud independence and prosperity throughout the strife of the late Middle Ages, was built between 1297 and 1342, and the graceful Gothic building was decorated by the most celebrated Sienese artists of the early 14thC. It remains the seat of government, but the monumental apartments on the first floor are open as a museum.

Sala del Risorgimento Frescoes by late 19thC Sienese artists show scenes from the *Life of Victor Emmanuel II*.

Sala di Balia Frescoes by the Florentine artist Spinello Aretino relate the *Life of Alexander III*, the Sienese pope.

Sala dei Cardinali The sculptures are by followers of Jacopo della Quercia.

Sala del Concistoro Frescoes by the Sienese Mannerist, Beccafumi, strongly influenced by Michelangelo, illustrate the *Civic Virtues* with scenes from Greek and Roman history.

Antechapel and chapel The frescoes are by Taddeo di Bartolo. The Gothic choir stalls of the chapel are beautifully inlaid with scenes illustrating the *Nicene Creed*; over the altar is Sodoma's *Holy Family with St Leonard*.

Sala del Mappamondo The city council met in this vast room, which is proudly decorated with frescoes commemorating Sienese victories and Sienese saints. The frescoes movingly suggest layer on layer of history; they are an odd collection of survivals from different decorative schemes, often sharply contrasting in style and scale.

The large frescoed *Maestà* ★★ (1315) is Simone Martini's first documented work. A radiant, gorgeous, celestial vision, it invites comparison with Duccio's *Maestà* in the MUSEO DELL' OPERA DEL DUOMO; Duccio's rigid, horizontal rows of figures have yielded to a softer depiction of depth; the lovely patterned canopy introduces an elegant, courtly grace; there is a delicate rhythm of complex linear patterns.

Opposite this fresco is the later equestrian portrait of *Guidoriccio da Fogliano* (1328) whose traditional attribution to Simone Martini has recently become the subject of considerable controversy. This is a dazzling, bold design; the details are realistic and yet the haunting power of the wide, empty landscape, the intensity of the blues and the boldness of the movement transform the fresco into a deeply poetic vision of medieval valour.

Below this equestrian portrait, another 14thC fresco, showing two men talking before a castle, has recently been uncovered and attributed by some authorities to Duccio. On either side, *Saints* by Sodoma project dramatically from painted architectural niches; other, more static *Saints* decorate the pilasters of the long wall; above them are monochrome frescoes showing famous Sienese victories.

Sala della Pace Ambrogio Lorenzetti's frescoed *Allegory of Good and Bad Government* ★★ (1338–40) reminded the Sienese councillors that good government serves justice and the common good. On the right, *Good Government* is represented by the personification of the commune, wearing the black and white of Siena, and accompanied by symbolic Virtues; Peace, in white drapery – its crisp, transparent folds suggesting the influence of classical sculpture – is a particularly famous figure.

On the entrance wall, the *Effects of Good Government* are shown in the astonishingly recognizable streets of medieval Siena, and against the fields and hills of Tuscany – one of the earliest realistic landscapes in Italian art. The paper-thin walls suggest the easy relationship between town and country. The towers and arcaded loggias of the city rise with delightful Gothic profusion; in the narrow streets, the peaceful citizens dance, buy *salami*, take the sheep to the fields; beyond the walls, peasants walk towards the town, their sturdy vigour brilliantly contrasted with the grace of the elegant falconers.

Loggia This contains the damaged remnants of Jacopo della Quercia's celebrated **Fonte Gaia** from the Campo; the site of the original fountain is now occupied by a copy.

Museo dell' Opera del Duomo ✭✭
Piazza del Duomo
Tel. (0577) 283049
Open 9am – 7pm
🎦 🏛 ☑ 🦽

The ground floor has carvings from the cathedral facade, including a series of ten life-size figures of **Prophets and Philosophers** ✭ (1284–90) by Giovanni Pisano; these intensely dramatic, deeply undercut figures brought a new scale and power to Gothic sculpture in Italy. The low relief of the **Madonna and Saints** is by Jacopo della Quercia.

On the first floor, the **Sala di Duccio** contains Duccio's **Maestà** ✭✭ (1308–11), painted for the high altar of the DUOMO. In this, his most brilliant achievement, Duccio opened an important new era in art. Contemporary sources describe the jubilant procession, prayers and festivities that accompanied the progress of the altarpiece from Duccio's workshop to the cathedral. "On that day . . . all the shops were shut . . . and all the bells were ringing."

The altarpiece was painted on both sides with, on the front, the **Madonna in Majesty with Angels and Saints** and, on the back, 26 scenes from the **Passion**; it was completed by a predella showing scenes from the **Life of Christ**. The two sides were separated in the 18thC and now face one another, with the predella on the side wall.

The **Madonna in Majesty** remains linked to Byzantium – its sequence of grave, graceful figures creating a vision of celestial beauty, enriched by subtle variation of pose and delicate gesture – but the vivid panels of the **Passion**, full of sharply observed, tender details, reveal Duccio as a great narrator, alive to the discoveries of contemporary Florentine artists; note especially his superb control over large crowd scenes, as in the **Betrayal of Christ** and the **Agony in the Garden**. Duccio retained the gold background of medieval art and, against this, his delicate, harmonious colours and subtle linear rhythms create a richly patterned effect. Perhaps the most beautiful panels are the vividly observed **Christ Washing the Feet** and the deeply expressive **Deposition**.

Pietro Lorenzetti's triptych of the

Nativity of the Virgin ✭ (1342) is on the right wall of this room – a direct and powerful narrative.

The second floor has paintings by Luca Giordano and Beccafumi, and the **Blessed Agostino Novello with Four of his Miracles** ✭ (c.1330) by Simone Martini.

Palazzo Chigi-Saraceni
Via di Città 89
Tel. (0577) 46152
Visits by request
🎦 🏛

The 14thC palace houses the Accademia Musicale Chigiana and a good collection of Tuscan paintings.

The late Gothic period is particularly well represented; there are four paintings by Sassetta; a small and charming triptych by the Maestro dell' Osservanza, once attributed to Sassetta; and many pictures by the prolific and somewhat uninspiring Sano di Pietro. The 16thC is richest in pictures by Domenico Beccafumi, the greatest and most original of the Sienese Mannerists; the large **altarpiece of Santo Spirito** ✭ is one of his most accomplished achievements; the composition derives from Fra Bartolommeo, yet the soft, smoky colours and strange, dreamy mood are intensely personal.

The Sienese Baroque is relatively undistinguished; Rutilio Manetti brought an awareness of Caravaggio to Siena, and this collection has two rather dull Caravaggesque **Concert Scenes** by him – one with effects of artificial light that are close to the Dutch Caravaggesque painter, Honthorst.

The outstanding 17thC work, a **Self-portrait of a Warrior** ✭ is by the Neapolitan, Salvator Rosa. To poets and writers of the Romantic era, Salvator Rosa was a legendary figure, the symbol of a violent revolt against the forces of reaction and artistic convention; it was widely but incorrectly believed that he had fought in Masaniello's revolt against Spanish autocracy in Naples (1647) and that he had spent years wandering in the desolate mountains of the Abruzzi, a captive of savage bandits.

This glamorous portrait, which shows the artist drawing his sword – brooding, melancholy, Byronically sinister – is astonishingly Romantic in sentiment, yet it probably dates from c.1640 when Rosa was attaining fashionable success as court painter to the Medici.

The collection also has some good sculptures, including a vigorous *bozzetto* by Bernini for the **St Jerome** in the DUOMO; charming medieval ivory caskets; and majolica.

Siena recorded in frescoes

An unexpectedly full and lively picture of medieval life in central Italy can be gained from a visit to Siena, since the town retains much of its medieval appearance, and frescoes by her greatest early 14thC painters, in and around the city, show in great detail the contemporary fashions and activities of her inhabitants.

The best starting place is the **Palazzo Pubblico**, around which Siena's wealthy citizens planned an entire new city center during the early 14thC. The palace was the seat of government and is now the home of the MUSEO CIVICO. Inside, in the Sala del Mappamondo, Simone Martini's ***Maestà*** shows the Virgin, the city's special patron, as an enthroned queen surrounded by courtiers; on the facing wall is another fresco traditionally attributed to Simone, the equestrian portrait of ***Guido Riccio da Fogliano***, commander of the Sienese military forces. The city council conducted its meetings beneath these twin images of divine and human protection.

Further on in the palace, the Sala della Pace contains Ambrogio Lorenzetti's frescoed ***Allegory of Good and Bad Government***. On the right, ***Good Government*** personifies some of the qualities that facilitated the city's prosperity. At the foot of the imposing figure representing the commune is the she-wolf suckling Romulus and Remus; Siena saw herself as descended from Remus, as a counterpart of the magnificent city of Rome founded by his twin brother, and this image is repeated throughout the city. In the accompanying fresco of the ***Effects of Good Government***, the townswomen dance in flowing dresses made from the rich materials newly imported from the East; above them, men work on new buildings, standing on wooden platforms anchored into holes in the stonework – these holes are still visible on many Sienese buildings.

The expanding Franciscan and Dominican orders contributed to the city's growth by building new churches, whose vast walls provided room for more painted decorations. Some 10 to 15mins' walk NE of the Campo is the church of SAN FRANCESCO, containing Ambrogio Lorenzetti's fresco of ***St Louis of Toulouse before Pope Boniface VIII***. St Louis gave up the crown of Naples to become a Franciscan monk and here he is shown kneeling before the Pope to take his vows, watched by his brother, Charles, who became king in his place. Crowded into the side-aisles are courtiers in fashionably elaborate head-dresses. A companion fresco, the ***Martyrdom of the Franciscans***, shows a group of monks who were martyred in Morocco; increasing trade with the East had brought large numbers of Mongol slaves into central Italy, and Ambrogio must have based his images on their features and costumes.

Ambrogio Lorenzetti's fresco of the **Effects of Good Government** *(1338–40) in the Palazzo Pubblico, Siena.*

Extending your tour beyond the city, you can drive SW to **San Galgano**. Here, quite isolated in the countryside, approached by a rough path through fields thick with waving sunflowers, is a beautiful little red-brick Romanesque church. In the attached Gothic oratory are more remarkable frescoes by Ambrogio Lorenzetti. During the 1860s, conservators removed the frescoed **Annunciation** from the walls, revealing underneath a marvellous *sinopia* sketch, brushed in with quick, bold strokes, showing the Virgin trembling with fear at the sudden appearance of the angel and clinging desperately to a slim column for support. This figure was transformed to a more conventional image in the finished fresco, where the Virgin calmly accepts the message, humbly bowing to the angel, her hands folded across her breast. Strange too is the **Maestà** above, with a kneeling saint carrying a peculiarly modern-looking straw basket, and a voluptuous Eve lying languidly at the Virgin's feet. Nearby are the overgrown ruins of a splendid Cistercian abbey; these two buildings provide ample material for a day's visit.

Another day can be devoted to SAN GIMIGNANO, a town of clustering medieval towers NW of Siena. Here, Barna da Siena's grim paintings in the COLLEGIATA seem to reflect the troubled times of the mid 14thC, when a series of financial disasters hit central Italy and was followed by outbreaks of plague that wiped out more than half the Sienese population. The Collegiata frescoes focus on the more turbulent New Testament stories. The bobbing, twisting helmets of soldiers crowd around Christ at his betrayal; their threatening spears shoot up at different angles as they cast glances at Judas delivering the fatal kiss. Nearby, the mournful Saviour carries the cross beside a dark, menacing soldier brandishing a claw-hammer and a bunch of enormous spikes. Such a complete contrast to the peace and splendour of the Palazzo Pubblico frescoes is a timely reminder that the period of prosperity ended soon after the mid 14thC and that Sienese painting never again reached quite such heights.

Palazzo Pubblico See MUSEO CIVICO.

Pinacoteca Nazionale ☆☆
Palazzo Buonsignori, Via San Pietro 29
Tel. (0577) 281161
Open Tues–Sun 8.30am–1.45pm
Closed Mon
🚾 🏛 ☑ 🔦

This rich collection of Sienese painting, dating from the 12thC to the 17thC, is housed in a fine Gothic palace. From the pretty courtyard, a vaulted staircase leads to the second floor and to the earliest and most important pictures.

Second floor

Room I This room shows pictures by Sienese primitives; the most interesting is a small panel, dated 1215 (and thus the first dated work of Sienese painting) and still linked to Romanesque art; it shows, in the center, *Christ with the Symbols of the Four Evangelists* and, at the sides, scenes from the *Life of St Helen* and from the *Story of the True Cross*.

Room II A little later than the panel in Room I are the works of Guido da Siena, who is the earliest of the Sienese painters to emerge as a distinct personality. His *Madonna* (1262) is perhaps his earliest surviving work and clearly shows his conformity to Byzantine conventions.

Rooms III and IV The rigid works of the preceding rooms are followed by softer, more fluid pictures by Duccio and his school. The outstanding work is Duccio's very damaged *Madonna of the Franciscans* ★ (c.1295) which takes its name from three tiny monks – their disparity in scale the legacy of a medieval tradition – who adore the Virgin. Duccio is recorded as having decorated manuscript bindings, and the exquisite detail of this work may have something in common with this kind of decorative work; the cloth behind the Virgin and her halo create a strong accent on purely ornamental surface.

Room V Bartolo di Fredi's festive *Procession of the Magi* is a late 14thC work by an artist who brought the International Gothic style to Siena; the procession, enlivened by touches of sharp realism, wends its way across a fairytale landscape to the Virgin and Child; the composition looks forward to Gentile da Fabriano's great painting, the *Adoration of the Magi* in FLORENCE (Galleria degli Uffizi).

Room VI Simone Martini's *Madonna* (1320–25) is a refined, intensely spiritual work.

Room VII This room is dedicated to works by Ambrogio and Pietro Lorenzetti, artists who combined a Sienese love of ornament with something of Giotto's interest in solid form and modelling.

Ambrogio's small *Maestà* ★ is delicately and brilliantly patterned yet lucidly constructed. The *Annunciation* ★ (1344) is his last signed and dated work; the solidity and grandeur of the figures, and the calm restraint of the composition, suggest his response to the new art of Giotto. His small, magical panels, a *City by the Sea* and a *Castle by the Shores of a Lake*, provide a welcome relief from Madonnas and saints; they are the earliest examples of pure landscape in European art.

This room also has Pietro Lorenzetti's great Carmelite altarpiece, the *Madonna and Saints* with *Stories of the Carmelite Order* ★ Lorenzetti's interest in space is evident both in the grave, statuesque figures of the central panel, and in the charming scenes on the predella panels; his narrative is vigorous and direct, and the loveliest scenes, the *Dream of Sobach* and the *Fountain of Elias*, are full of touching, fresh observations of everyday reality. In the first, note the oddly moving little detail of the towel hanging on the wall; in the second, the monks reading, counting their rosaries and drawing water from the well.

Room IX The highlight of this room is a graceful *Madonna* by Lorenzo Monaco, a Sienese painter who brought something of the elegance of 14thC Sienese art to Florence.

Room XIII The leading painters of the mid 15thC, Sassetta and Giovanni di Paolo, continued to work in a sweet Gothic style. Sassetta is represented here by fragments from a highly important altarpiece, an early work of 1423–26, including a *Last Supper* and *Temptation of St Antony Abbot*; Giovanni di Paolo by a *Madonna of Humility*, with a magical Gothic landscape.

Room XIV In the late 15thC, the strongest and most fascinating personalities were Francesco di Giorgio Martini and Neroccio de' Landi, who both trained under Vecchietta and shared a studio from 1469–75. Yet they are very different painters.

Francesco, who is better known as an architect, quickly responded to the new art of the Florentine Renaissance, and his paintings suggest an awareness of Botticelli, Filippino Lippi and Antonio Pollaiuolo; they move from the lyrical *Annunciation* (1472) with just a hint of Florentine perspective, to the *Madonna and Angels* (1474–75) with its particularly lovely blond angel, and finally to the *Nativity* (1475) where the plasticity of Florentine Renaissance painting is very evident.

Neroccio's art, on the contrary, looks back to the Sienese 14thC. Bernard Berenson claimed that "he was Simone come to life again. Simone's singing line, Simone's endlessly refined feeling for beauty, Simone's grace and charm . . ." Here, the *Madonna with Sts Jerome and Bartholomew* ★ (c.1475) is a haunting, fragile, exquisitely elegant image of the Virgin, which pushes to its furthest point the refinement exhibited by Simone in Room VI.

From here, the display rapidly declines with a series of dull, repetitive works by Sano di Pietro. The only panel of interest is the predella from an altarpiece by the Maestro dell' Osservanza, once attributed to Sassetta (**Room XVI**).

First floor

Room XXIV Interest reawakens with an unexpected Baroque altarpiece by Pietro da Cortona.

Room XXVI A series of works by Sienese Baroque artists includes dramatically lit and luridly coloured Caravaggesque paintings by Rutilio Manetti.

Room XXXIII This has works by Domenico Beccafumi, a highly original Mannerist artist and the last great Sienese painter. His *St Catherine Receiving the Stigmata* (c.1515) is a lovely picture with a clarity and tranquillity indebted to Perugino and Fra Bartolommeo; yet the soft beauty of the light on the distant landscape is intensely personal and poetic. In the later *Birth of the Virgin* (1543) Beccafumi explores the magical, evocative effects of candlelight.

Room XXXVII The two large and elaborate Mannerist compositions, both depicting the *Descent into Hell*, are by Sodoma (c.1525) and Beccafumi (c.1532).

Sant'Agostino
Via Sagata

The 13thC church was restored in the 18thC. In the nave is a **crucifix** by Perugino; in the **Cappella del Santissimo Sacramento**, an unusual *Maestà* by Ambrogio Lorenzetti, a *Massacre of the Innocents* by Matteo di Giovanni and an *Adoration of the Magi* by Sodoma.

Santa Caterina
Costa di Sant'Antonio

This is a complex of little chapels, on different levels, clustering around the house of St Catherine Benincasa, a celebrated Sienese mystic (1347–80). The **Oratorio Superiore** has a precious majolica floor and, on the walls, fervent scenes from the *Life of St Catherine Benincasa* by Sienese Mannerists. The church of **Santa Caterina in Fontebranda** (part of the same complex) has a wooden statue of the saint by Neroccio and frescoes by Sodoma.

San Domenico
Piazza San Domenico

The **Cappella di Santa Caterina** opens off the right nave of this austere Dominican church; in the center is a **ciborium** (1475) by Benedetto da Maiano; frescoes by Sodoma of scenes from the *Life of St Catherine* (1526) cover the side walls – the fresco on the left wall is strongly influenced by Raphael.

San Francesco
Piazza San Francesco

In the left transept of this bleak, many-times rebuilt church is a powerful frescoed *Crucifixion* (1331) by Pietro Lorenzetti and two frescoes by Ambrogio Lorenzetti, *St Louis of Toulouse before Pope Boniface VIII* and the *Martyrdom of the Franciscans.*

Santa Maria dei Servi
Piazza Alessandro Manzoni

This church dates from the 13thC–15thC and has a Renaissance interior attributed to Baldassare Peruzzi. In the second chapel to the right of the high altar is a fresco of the *Massacre of the Innocents* by Pietro Lorenzetti; in the left transept, a *Madonna* by Lippo Memmi.

SPELLO
Perugia, Umbria   Map E4

Tiny Spello is built on the southern slopes of Monte Subasio. Stretches of Roman wall and three imposing gates recall its past grandeur; from the southern Porta Consolare the road twists up the hill, widening to take in the ornate facade of Santa Maria Maggiore, and offering sudden views over the Umbrian plain. From 1425, Spello was ruled by the bloodthirsty Baglioni, lords of Perugia, who kept a garrison here. Today the neat, pretty town is waking up to its tourist potential, and the restaurants have a chic, fashionable air.

Santa Maria Maggiore☆
Piazza Santa Maria Maggiore

🏛

The church dates from the 13thC and has a richly decorated Romanesque portal. In the left aisle, the **Cappella Baglioni** is now shielded by glass to protect Pintoricchio's **frescoes** ★★ and the precious majolica floor. (The light is expensive and requires notes.)

These frescoes are perhaps the most Umbrian of Pintoricchio's works; his love of rich decoration remains, but it is controlled within clear, spacious compositions; in the *Nativity*, the elaborate background serves as a foil to the quiet group of shepherds, who are depicted with a lively realism reminiscent of Northern painting.

The *Annunciation* is one of the most poetic and delicate of all Renaissance treatments of this theme; at the side, expressing his pride in his achievement, Pintoricchio includes a prominent self-portrait with, below, a trophy of pen and pencils and, above, an inscription that stresses his desire to paint for the glory of God.

On the pilasters before the apse are dull frescoes by Perugino.

SPOLETO
Perugia, Umbria Map E4

Spoleto is built on the side of a hill overlooking the gentle fields and woods of the Ticino valley. An ancient Umbrian center, it became powerful under the Roman Empire and remained so through successive eras. The city movingly suggests layer upon layer of history; fine Roman remains mingle with monuments of early Christian architecture; the Middle Ages left their imprint in the cathedral, the market place (built over the old Roman forum) and above all in the spectacular Ponte delle Torri or Bridge of Towers (built over the Roman aqueduct); modern art finds expression in the huge Alexander Calder sculpture in Piazza della Stazione. Spoleto is a wonderful city to walk around; it is full of little nooks and crannies, of stairs and tunnels, and of narrow, twisting lanes crossed by arches and lined with dark medieval houses.

Duomo ☆
Piazza del Duomo
🏛

The cathedral is built on a terrace near the top of the hill; the charming Renaissance loggia (by Ambrogio da Milano and Pippo di Antonio Fiorentino) was added to the severe Romanesque facade in the 15thC. The interior is dull Baroque.

On the internal facade is a bust of *Urban VIII* by Bernini. The first chapel on the right, the **Cappella Eroli**, has a fresco of the *Madonna Enthroned*, set against a calm Umbrian landscape, by the 16thC painter Pintoricchio. The adjoining chapel is charmingly decorated with contemporary frescoes by an unknown artist.

The right transept has an **altarpiece** by

Annibale Carracci. On the left wall is the **tomb of Filippo Lippi**, who died in Spoleto in 1469; the design is by his son, Filippino.

In the apse are frescoes of the *Life of the Virgin*, the last works of Filippo Lippi. Assistants played a large part in their execution, but they are nevertheless beautiful works. Note especially Filippo's tender observation of the ageing of the frail Virgin.

Pinacoteca Comunale
Piazza del Comune
Tel. (0743) 32141
Open Mon, Wed – Sun: May – Sept
  9am – 1pm, 4 – 8pm; Oct – Apr
  9am – 1pm, 3 – 5pm
Closed Tues
🔅

The Pinacoteca is characteristic of public galleries in small Umbrian towns. Tucked away on the second floor of the Palazzo Comunale or town hall, it consists of a rather haphazard array of paintings, detached frescoes, wooden statues and goldsmiths' work, contained in three rather gloomy rooms.

The most interesting pieces are a painted wooden **crucifix** by the Maestro di Cesi (late 13thC or early 14thC); a 12thC **reliquary**; a **triptych** by Niccolò Alunno; and a painting of the *Madonna* (1494) by Antonello da Saliba. There are dullish 17thC pictures by Conca, Spranger and Guercino.

Santi Giovanni e Paolo
Via Santi Giovanni e Paolo
This severe 12thC church has 13thC frescoes by Alberto Sozio of the *Martyrdom of St Thomas à Becket*, *Herod's Banquet* and the *Martyrdoms of Sts John and Paul.*

San Pietro in Valle ☆
8km/5 miles E of Spoleto, towards Monteluco
🏛

A flight of steps leads up to the terrace, from where there is a spectacular view of the medieval Ponte delle Torri.

The facade has the loveliest and most important **Romanesque carvings ★** in Umbria. Around the central doorway, flowers and leaves, exquisitely carved, twine in a richly decorative border. The reliefs to either side – of a farmer working with oxen and dog, a hind attacking a snake while suckling her young, a peacock eating grapes – are the freshest and most beautiful; beyond them are strange, symbolic scenes of struggling animals and monsters. The uppermost reliefs are duller and of recognizably Christian subjects.

TERNI
Umbria Map E5

Terni is the largest industrial city in Umbria. There are Roman and medieval remains but the overall impression is of a bustling, modern, provincial capital.

Pinacoteca
Via Manassei 6
Tel. (0744) 400290
Open Tues–Sat 8am–2pm, Sun 9am–1pm
Closed Mon
A handful of Tuscan and Umbrian paintings includes works by Niccolò Alunno and Lo Spagna; a gay, festive **Marriage of St Catherine** by Benozzo Gozzoli; and a **Madonna** by Pintoricchio.

TODI
Perugia, Umbria Map D4

This high, walled town was a powerful city throughout the 12thC and 13thC. A road rises steeply to the Piazza del Popolo, which – perhaps better than any other Umbrian square – movingly conveys the pride and defiance of these once forebidding towns; it is flanked by Gothic battlements and towers.

Pinacoteca
Palazzo del Capitano, Piazza del Popolo
Tel. (075) 883541
Closed for restoration
The Pinacoteca is housed in a severe 13thC palace and has a small but good Etruscan and Roman section; also, goldsmiths' ware and ceramics; and Lo Spagna's **Coronation of the Virgin**, commissioned as a copy of Ghirlandaio's painting at nearby NARNI – Lo Spagna's painting is softer, more gently pious, set against a gentle Umbrian vista; the artist was an important follower of Perugino.

San Fortunato
Piazza della Repubblica
The church was founded in 1292 and completed in the second half of the 15thC. The incomplete facade is Gothic, with a particularly fine **portal**. Inside, in the fourth chapel on the right, is a frescoed **Madonna** by Masolino.

TOLENTINO
Macerata, Marche Map F3

Tolentino is a lively city in the valley of the river Chienti, encircled by hills.

San Nicola da Tolentino ☆
Via San Nicola
This famous pilgrimage church was built in the 13thC and 14thC but later extensively altered; the 18thC facade retains a richly decorated Gothic **portal** by Nanni di Bartolo (1432).
The Gothic **Cappellone di San Nicola** ★ is decorated with one of the most famous 14thC fresco cycles in the Marches. The walls are almost entirely covered with scenes from the life of the saint; their attribution is controversial – the names of Pietro and Giuliano da Rimini and Baronzio have been suggested. The frescoes are lively narratives, still linked to the traditions of late Gothic, but revealing a response to the innovations of Giotto; note, for instance, the lively poses of the figures carrying jugs in the **Marriage at Cana**.

TREVI
Perugia, Umbria Map E4

A distant view of Trevi, dramatically spread out against a steep conical hillside, is one of the loveliest sights in Umbria; in the town itself, alleyways with cobbled steps and the odd frescoed house twist up to the still, quiet center and to marvellous views over the thick olive groves ringing the hill.

Pinacoteca Comunale
Piazza Mazzini
Tel. (0742) 78246
Open Mon–Sat 8am–2pm
Closed Sun
This small museum, in two rooms of the 14thC town hall, has a few Umbrian pictures – a **Madonna** by Perugino, and a **Coronation of the Virgin** by Lo Spagna – plus a miscellany of archaeological fragments, medieval and Renaissance sculpture, and detached frescoes.

URBINO
Marche Map E2

Medieval Urbino, a small, hill-top town, was transformed by Federico da Montefeltro into one of the finest Renaissance cities and an important art center, visited by painters from all over Italy. Piero della Francesca was a leading light at Federico's court in the 1450s and 1460s, here developing his theories of mathematical perspective and painting some of his greatest works. Urbino is beautifully set among soft green hills dotted with cypresses and vines. The approaches to it are dominated by the elegantly turreted facade of the Palazzo Ducale, which rises defiantly from a sheer cliff face; from within the city, however, the palace appears graceful and welcoming.

Casa di Raffaello
Via Raffaello
Tel. (0722) 4735
Open Apr–Sept Tues–Sat 9am–1pm,
3–7pm, Sun 9am–1pm; Oct–Mar
Tues–Sun 9am–1pm
Closed Mon
▨ ☑

Raphael was born in this large 14thC house, which is now preserved as a shrine to his memory. His father, Giovanni Santi, was a painter at the court of Urbino and the house has paintings by Giovanni as well as copies of paintings by Raphael. A small fresco of the *Madonna* is attributed by some authorities to Raphael; others claim it for Giovanni, and suggest that the models were his wife and the infant Raphael.

Duomo
Piazza Duca Federico
The medieval church was almost entirely rebuilt in the Neoclassical style between 1789 and 1801.

On the second altar on the right is the *Martyrdom of St Sebastian* (1557) by Federico Barocci. The chapel to the right of the high altar, the **Cappella della Concezione**, has on the right wall an *Assumption* (c.1707) by Carlo Maratta and on the left wall the *Birth of the Virgin* (1708) by Carlo Cignani. In the chapel to the left of the high altar is a *Last Supper* by Barocci.

See also MUSEO ALBANI DEL DUOMO.

Galleria Nazionale delle Marche ☆☆
Palazzo Ducale
Tel. (0722) 2760
Open Tues–Sat 9am–2pm, Sun
9am–1pm
Closed Mon
▨ ⏛ ☑ ↯

Under the last Montefeltro leaders, the court of Urbino was renowned for its inspired patronage of learning and the arts. The palace itself is the monument of the great Federico, duke from 1444–82. Its building history is long and complex; in 1468 Luciano Laurana was appointed architect, but contributions were also made by Piero della Francesca and Francesco di Giorgio Martini. Many brilliant artists were involved in the decoration of the interior, including Melozzo da Forlì and Domenico Rosselli.

Around the grand courtyard, with its commemorative inscription, runs a series

of light, exquisitely decorated and gracefully proportioned rooms; they are perhaps the loveliest and most perfect expression of the clarity and reason of the early Renaissance.

Federico himself epitomized the ideal of the Renaissance prince; he was a brilliant general, a scholar fascinated by every aspect of humanist learning, and a shrewd ruler – kind, humane and unusually accessible to his subjects. His court was disciplined, even austere – Vespasiano, the librarian, compared it to a monastery – and a brilliant intellectual center. The Flemish painter, Justus of Ghent, was summoned here from the North; and Vasari wrote that Piero painted for Federico "many beautiful pictures of small figures, most of which have been ruined or lost because of wars that ravaged that state".

Federico's ideals lived on in his son, the scholarly Guidobaldo, whose court, "the light of Italy", is movingly described in Castiglione's *Book of the Courtier*. Castiglione defines, with some nostalgia, the qualities of the ideal courtier, through an imaginary dialogue between the men and women who lived at the court of Urbino in 1506.

In these harmonious rooms, despite their emptiness, one can still sense something of Castiglione's vision of a serene and supremely accomplished society – and one that stands out in such sharp contrast to the bloody records of so many small Italian Renaissance courts.

The gallery is presently being rearranged. From the entrance, Laurana's lovely staircase leads to the first floor, where **Room 1** (Salone del Trono) most perfectly suggests the purity of Laurana's conception. A door at the end of this room, to the right, leads into **Room 2**, which has a collection of Venetian pictures including a **polyptych** by Antonio Vivarini (dated 1476).

Rooms 3–7 (Appartamento della Duchessa) culminate in a small room with an elegant plaster ceiling by Federico Brandani. Return from here to Room 1 and thence to **Room 8**, where there is a magnificent **chimney** by Domenico Rosselli and **intarsiaed doors ★** by Francesco di Giorgio Martini or Botticelli. The pictures include a double-sided **processional banner** by Signorelli.

In **Room 9** there is a remarkable portrait of *Federico da Montefeltro and his Son, Guidobaldo* by an unknown artist (perhaps Justus of Ghent or Pedro Berruguete). The portrait, which once hung in the duke's study, conveys his prowess in war and learning; clad in full armour, he pores over a weighty volume; the Order of the Garter from England,

and the mitre, a gift from the Shah of Persia, symbolize the range of his diplomacy; at his side his heir, the pallid Guidobaldo, bears the emblems of power. The portrait also suggests Federico's humanity, in the truthful observation of his remarkable profile and awkward hands – he had lost his right eye and broken his nose, and is always shown in left profile.

Federico's portrait appears again in the same room, in Justus of Ghent's **Institution of the Eucharist** ★ (1472) – a work distinguished by a grandeur and dramatic power rare in Flemish art. Also in this room are Uccello's predella panels of the **Profanation of the Host** ★ Delicately patterned and vividly coloured, they illustrate a particularly repulsive medieval legend.

In **Room 10** are 14 half-length figures of classical and humanist **Philosophers and Scholars** ★ variously attributed to Justus of Ghent or Pedro Berruguete; they once hung in Federico's Studiolo or study. From Room 10, a spiral staircase leads to **Room 11**, the Duke's private chapel, adjoining the Tempietto delle Muse or Temple of the Muses.

Room 12, above, is Federico's **Studiolo** ★★ It is decorated with sophisticated and playful *trompe l'oeil* wooden inlay, perhaps designed by Botticelli; cupboard doors open to reveal books and musical instruments; the Duke's armour stands against the door; a pet squirrel nibbles a nut.

Federico was deeply interested in mathematical perspective (Piero della Francesca dedicated a treatise to him) and beyond, in **Room 13** (the Cappellina di Guidobaldo) hangs the outstanding work of his collection and one of the greatest masterpieces of the Renaissance: Piero della Francesca's **Flagellation** ★★ (c.1456–57). In this small picture, the beauty of the architectural setting and of the complex perspective, and the lovely subtlety of the play of light, create a still and haunting poetry. Beside it hang Piero's **Madonna of Senigallia** and a perspective study of an **Ideal City** ★ now attributed to Piero's circle; the lucidity and classical purity of the second epitomize the Renaissance culture that flourished at Federico's court. There are also two fine Titians, a **Last Supper** and a **Resurrection**.

After this, it is hard to concentrate on the next three rooms, which have paintings by artists from Urbino, including Raphael's father, Giovanni Santi. However, attention revives in **Room 17** with Raphael's **Portrait of a Lady** ★ which is behind glass and hard to see. This is one of the last works of

Raphael's Florentine period, in which the subtlety of expression is emphasized by the exquisite precision of the detail – note the delicacy with which Raphael catches the play of light on the woman's gold chain and its shadow against her collar bone.

The last rooms are less interesting, with some 15thC and 16thC sculptures in **Rooms 23** and **24**, but on the second floor one large room has eight splendid canvases by Federico Barocci, who came from Urbino and was one of the most original painters of the late 16thC; his unusual colour harmonies and flickering touch are well displayed in his **Madonna with Sts Simon and Judith**.

Further on are a few good 17thC pictures by Orazio Gentileschi and Cantarini and, among a changing display of drawings and engravings, Annibale Carracci's **cartoon**★ for the central portion of the Farnese ceiling in Rome – a rich and powerful composition that heralds the exuberance of Rubens and the Baroque (see Baroque ceilings in Rome, *SOUTH CENTRAL ITALY*).

Museo Albani del Duomo
Piazza Duca Federico
Tel. (0722) 2892
Open 9am–12.30pm, 3–7pm
This is a collection of works of art associated with the cathedral, including detached frescoes, ceramics, goldsmiths' ware, and 14thC–17thC pictures. The outstanding work is an English 13thC **bronze lectern** (Room 3).

Oratorio di San Giovanni Battista
Via Barocci
Open May–Sept 10am–12.30pm,
*   4–7pm; Oct–Apr 10am–12.30pm,*
*   3–5pm*
 ticket also gives entry to Oratorio di San Giuseppe
The frescoes of the **Crucifixion** and of the **Life of St John the Baptist** (1416) that cover the walls of this 14thC chapel are the most significant work of the brothers Lorenzo and Jacopo Salimbeni; they are a late and charmingly detailed example of the International Gothic style, influenced by Sienese and Lombard painting.

Oratorio di San Giuseppe
Via Barocci
For entry details, see Oratorio di San Giovanni Battista, above
The chapel has a graceful stucco **Nativity** by Federico Brandani (1522).

Palazzo Ducale See GALLERIA NAZIONALE DELLE MARCHE.

VOLTERRA
Pisa, Toscana   Map B3

Located high in the Tuscan hills, Volterra is a brooding town of grim, almost gaunt aspect but with a certain austere beauty. Etruscan Velathri was about three times the size of the present town, which is mostly medieval. Bitter struggles for independence marked the early years of the Middle Ages and in 1470 a brutal siege organized by Lorenzo de' Medici resulted in a long-held hatred of Florence. Lorenzo completed the old fortress, another stark reminder of Florentine power.

Duomo
Piazza del Duomo
The facade is 12thC–13thC, the interior mainly 16thC. In the right transept is a larger-than-life, polychrome wooden group of the *Deposition* (13thC). The **ciborium** above the high altar and the two *Angels* on twisted columns on either side are the work of Mino da Fiesole (1471). The chapel at the w end of the N aisle has a 15thC fresco of the *Magi* by Benozzo Gozzoli, with a lovely, wide-open landscape; it serves as a background to the terra-cotta group of the *Nativity* by Zacci Zaccaria; in the niche on the left side is another terra-cotta group by Zaccaria, of the *Epiphany*. The *Annunciation* on the second altar of the N aisle is by Mariotto Albertinelli (1497).

The baptistry opposite the cathedral has a **font** (1502) by Andrea Sansovino.

Galleria Pittorica
Palazzo dei Priori, Piazza dei Priori
Tel. (0588) 86025
Open Mon, Wed–Sat 10am–1pm; Sun 10am–1pm, 3–6pm
Closed Tues
🌂 🏛
The Palazzo dei Priori, a handsome 13thC building with a crenellated tower, is the oldest civic monument in Tuscany. The gallery inside has a large 17thC painting of the *Marriage at Cana* by Mascagni (in the Sala del Consiglio) and, on the second floor, a good little collection of Tuscan and Sienese pictures; these include an *Annunciation* (1491) by Signorelli, a *Christ in Glory with Saints* (late 15thC) by Domenico Ghirlandaio and a *Deposition* ★★ by Rosso Fiorentino – where strangely disturbing, angular figures play their part in a passionate drama, suspended in a weirdly lit and unreal space.

Museo Diocesano di Arte Sacra
Via Roma 1
Open Tues–Sat summer 9.30am–1pm, 2.30–6pm, winter 2.30–4.30pm; Sun 9am–1pm
Closed Mon
🌂
Among the sculpture and architectural fragments in this cathedral museum are a bust of *St Linus* by Andrea della Robbia, nephew and pupil of the more famous Luca; a silver bust of *St Octavian* by Antonio Pollaiuolo; and a gilded bronze **crucifix** by Giambologna.

Museo Etrusco Guarnacci ☆
Via Don Minzoni 15
Tel. (0588) 86347
Open Mon–Sat: Apr–Sept 9am–1pm, 3–6pm, Oct–Mar 9.30am–1pm, 2.30–4.30pm; Sun 9.30am–1pm
🌂 ☑
This is a large and important collection of Etruscan art. Most of the ground floor and all of the first floor are given over to more than 600 **cinerary urns** ★ Made of alabaster, tufa and terra cotta, and dating from the 6thC to the 1stC BC, they are arranged according to the subject of the friezes on the sides – the lids all show the recumbent figures of the dead, often in a harshly realistic style that recalls late Roman portraiture. One married couple gaze at each other with alarming expressiveness.

Among the small bronzes in **Room 24** is the tiny, elongated statue known as the **Ombra della Sera** or Shadow of the Evening. Etruscan Velathri also produced fine pottery, coins and jewellery and good examples of these arts are on display.

LANDMARKS *in* ITALIAN ART

The story of Italian art is unparalleled in length, richness and diversity. For much of its duration it has also been the story of Western art, a source of classical inspiration and ideals. The classical link is fundamental, and Italian art can only be properly appreciated against this wider background. Yet the story does not even begin with the painters and sculptors of Imperial Rome. These artists drew on still earlier traditions, continuing and transforming the achievements of the Greeks and Etruscans.

CLASSICAL BEGINNINGS

Greeks colonized Sicily and the coastal mainland from as early as the 8thC BC. The art of these colonies reached its zenith in the 6thC and 5thC BC, in the magnificent cities of Paestum, Syracuse and Agrigento. Here, the temples were embellished with reliefs and colossal figure sculptures and the villas adorned with free-standing marble statues and a wealth of figured vases. The best of this colonial art shows a refinement and elegance that rival the achievements of Greece itself.

From the 6thC to the 2ndC BC, central Italy was dominated by the Etruscans. Their art stems from the Greek, but their sculpture is more crudely vital, and the rhythms of their painting more spontaneous. Most surviving Etruscan art comes from, or is still in, tombs. In the early period, it shows a charming preoccupation with all the good things of life: sculptured effigies recline as banqueters, smiling contentedly in the afterlife; wall paintings depict the pleasures of dancing, feasting, fishing and hunting. Later, this gaiety yields to greater restraint and, finally, to melancholy and foreboding.

By the 3rdC BC Etruscan civilization was on the wane and Rome dominated central Italy. The Romans were enthusiastic collectors of Greek art, and their patronage of Greek sculptors kept alive the classical tradition. Yet the skill of the Greek artists often served Roman taste; the dignified yet brutally honest portrait bust and the clear, direct narrative of the historical relief are the most characteristically Roman contributions to sculpture. The houses of the ancient Romans were lavishly decorated with paintings and mosaics. These blended the Greek taste for mythology with a liking for still-life, light and graceful romantic landscapes and idyllic garden scenes – all possibly inspired by Etruscan examples.

The DARK and MIDDLE AGES

Constantine, the first Christian emperor, moved his capital from Rome to Byzantium in AD330. For a while, the classical tradition persisted in Italian art – outstanding examples survive of the earliest mosaics at Santa Maria Maggiore in Rome – but it soon yielded to the majestic, awe-inspiring images of Byzantium. At Ravenna, the glittering beauty of Byzantine glass and stone mosaics transports the worshipper into a heavenly realm where solemn, hieratic figures symbolize sacred truths. The tradition remained alive well into the 13thC: the Norman invaders of Sicily summoned artists from the East in the 12thC; San Marco in Venice (begun 1063) is one of the finest of all Byzantine achievements outside the Eastern Empire.

In the 11thC and 12thC Byzantine and Roman elements fused into the early Romanesque style. A new realism and clarity are evident in the sculpture of Wiligelmo at Modena and Benedetto Antelami at Parma. By the late 12thC both Pisa and Lucca were flourishing artistic centers. At Pisa, where many Roman antiquities survived, the great innovators were Nicola Pisano and his son Giovanni. Nicola, deeply influenced by the warm dignity of classical sculpture, created a more solid and powerful figure style.

A new feeling for volume is also evident in the paintings of the Roman, Pietro Cavallini, and the Florentine, Cimabue, but it was another Florentine, Giotto, who at the turn of the 13thC finally and triumphantly rejected the weightless symbols of Byzantine art. In his frescoes in the Cappella degli Scrovegni (Arena Chapel) at Padua, solid figures move in a clearly defined space; human emotion is conveyed with strength and feeling.

Giotto's art was new, and his sense of the nobility of man decisively influenced the history of Italian painting up to the High Renaissance. But his followers failed to build upon his great achievements, and the first half of the 14thC was otherwise dominated by Sienese artists. Duccio's graceful line and lyrical colour softened the prevailing Byzantine style, endowing it with a new tenderness and humanity. His flowing rhythms were developed by Simone Martini into elegant patterns of line and colour, influenced by French Gothic. In the works of Ambrogio and Pietro Lorenzetti, Sienese grace blends with the grandeur of Giotto.

Further consolidation of Giotto's achievements was delayed by the refined and courtly style known as International Gothic. This spread through Europe in the later part of the 14thC, and was characterized by richly decorative patterns and a wealth of delicate and tenderly observed detail. In Italy its greatest exponents were Gentile da Fabriano and Pisanello. The style lingered longest in Siena, where it blended easily with the local tradition and with established French Gothic influences.

The BIRTH of a NEW ERA

In Florence, in the early years of the 15thC, the rise of humanism and the spread of the new learning in every intellectual sphere stimulated the development of a new art that strove to restore the grandeur of ancient Greece and Rome. Artists were no longer interested in elegance; instead, they strove to create an illusion of reality. By the discovery of the laws of mathematical perspective, the careful observation of the fall of light, and the study of anatomy, they created a vigorously naturalistic art.

Sculptors were the first to be influenced by the survivals of classical art. Lorenzo Ghiberti and Filippo Brunelleschi drew on classical sources in the designs they entered for a competition in 1401 to decide on the sculptor of the N doors of the Florence Baptistry. Ghiberti won the competition, and went on to win the commission for the later, E doors, in which he made full use of the new discoveries in perspective. Meanwhile, Donatello's famous *David* revived the free-standing, life-size nude; many classical types – the portrait bust, the equestrian statue, the memorial tomb, the medal, the small bronze – were recreated. In painting, the grave, austere figures of Masaccio's frescoes restored to Florentine art the nobility of Giotto; their new solidity and narrative power were matched only by Donatello's innovations.

The discoveries of these artists were immediately accepted and extended – in the radiant colour and clear-cut space of Fra Angelico, in the obsessively mathematical works of Paolo Uccello, and in Andrea del Castagno's concern with dramatic gesture. Towards the middle of the century artists developed a new gaiety and ornamental richness, and many responded to the realism of Flemish art. The frescoes of Benozzo Gozzoli and Domenico Ghirlandaio are graceful narratives, full of charming details of everyday life. Botticelli's mythologies – complex neo-Platonic allegories – express the interests of

1 **Riace Bronze**, *Greek, 5thC BC, Museo Archeologico Nazionale, Reggio di Calabria*

2 *Sarcophagus of the* **Bride and Groom**, *Etruscan, 6thC BC, Museo Nazionale di Villa Giulia, Rome*

3 *Wall painting (detail) from the* **Tomb of the Bulls**, *Etruscan, c. 540BC, Necropoli, Tarquinia*

1 **Marcus Junius Brutus**, *1stC BC*,
Musei Capitolini, Rome

2 **Trajan's Column** (detail), *AD113*,
Rome

3 **Strolling Players** (detail), *c.1stC BC*,
Museo Archeologico Nazionale, Naples

1 **Abraham and Lot** (detail), 5thC, nave, Santa Maria Maggiore, Rome

2 **Murano Diptych**, late 5thC or early 6thC, Museo Nazionale, Ravenna

3 **The Empress Theodora and her Court**, before 547, apse, San Vitale, Ravenna

1 *Nicola Pisano,* **Nativity***, 1260, pulpit, Baptistry, Pisa*

2 *Pietro Cavallini,* **Last Judgment** *(detail), 1293, Santa Cecilia in Trastevere, Rome*

3 *Giotto di Bondone,* **Flagellation***, 1303–5, Cappella degli Scrovegni, Padua*

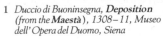

1 *Duccio di Buoninsegna,* **Deposition**
(*from the* **Maestà**), *1308–11, Museo
dell'Opera del Duomo, Siena*

2 *Simone Martini,* **St Louis of Toulouse
Crowning his Great-nephew, Robert
of Anjou, King of Naples**, *1317,
Museo e Gallerie Nazionali di
Capodimonte, Naples*

3 *Pisanello,* **St George and the Princess**
(*detail*), *c.1436, Sant'Anastasia,
Verona*

1 *Lorenzo Ghiberti,* **Joseph in Egypt**, *1424–52, east doors, Baptistry, Florence*

2 *Donatello,* **David**, *1430, Museo del Bargello, Florence*

3 *Masaccio,* **Tribute Money**, *1426–28, Cappella Brancacci, Santa Maria del Carmine, Florence*

4

4 *Fra Angelico,*
Annunciation, *1433,*
Museo Diocesano,
Cortona

5 *Andrea del Castagno,*
Last Supper, *1450,*
Cenacolo di Sant'
Apollonia, Florence

6 *Paolo Uccello,*
Monument to Sir John
Hawkwood, *1436,*
Duomo, Florence

5

6

1

1 *Benozzo Gozzoli,* **Journey of the Magi** *(detail), 1459–61, Palazzo Medici-Riccardi, Florence*

2 *Domenico Ghirlandaio,* **Birth of the Virgin**, *1485–90, Cappella Maggiore, Santa Maria Novella, Florence*

3 *Sandro Botticelli,* **Primavera** *(detail), c.1480, Galleria degli Uffizi, Florence*

2

3

4 *Andrea Mantegna,* **The Gonzaga Court** *(detail), 1465–74, Camera degli Sposi, Palazzo Ducale, Mantua*

5 *Piero della Francesca,* **Meeting of Solomon and the Queen of Sheba***, 1453–64, San Francesco, Arezzo*

6 *Giovanni Bellini,* **Pietà***, c.1470, Pinacoteca di Brera, Milan*

1 *Leonardo da Vinci,* **Portrait of a Musician**, *c. 1485, Pinacoteca Ambrosiana, Milan*

2 *Michelangelo Buonarroti,* **Ignudo**, *1508–12, ceiling, Sistine Chapel, Musei Vaticani, Rome*

3 *Raphael,* **Liberation of St Peter** *(detail), 1512–14, Stanza di Eliodoro, Raphael Stanze, Musei Vaticani, Rome*

4 *Giorgione,* **Tempesta**, *c.1505,
Accademia, Venice*

5 *Titian,* **Assumption**, *1516–19, Frari,
Venice*

6 *Lorenzo Lotto,* **Annunciation** *(detail),
c.1526, Pinacoteca Civica, Recanati*

7 *Paolo Veronese,* **Giustiniana Barbaro
with her Servant**, *1566–68, Villa
Barbaro, Maser*

1 *Agnolo Bronzino,* **Lucrezia Panciatichi**, *c. 1540, Galleria degli Uffizi, Florence*

2 *Jacopo Tintoretto,* **Flight into Egypt** *(detail), 1583–87, Scuola di San Rocco, Venice*

3 *Parmigianino,* **Madonna of the Long Neck**, *c. 1535, Galleria degli Uffizi, Florence*

1 *Annibale Carracci,* **Triumph of Bacchus and Ariadne** *(from* **The Loves of the Gods***), 1597–1600, Palazzo Farnese, Rome*

2 *Michelangelo Merisi da Caravaggio,* **Martyrdom of St Peter***, 1601–2, Santa Maria del Popolo, Rome*

3 *Gianlorenzo Bernini,* **Death of the Blessed Ludovica Albertoni***, 1674, San Francesco a Ripa, Rome*

1 *Antonio Canova,* **Hercules and Lichas***, 1795.–1802, Galleria Nazionale d' Arte Moderna, Rome*

2 *Giambattista Tiepolo,* **Meeting of Antony and Cleopatra***, c.1757, Palazzo Labia, Venice*

3 *Francesco Guardi,* **The Grand Canal***, c.1750, Pinacoteca di Brera, Milan*

1 *Giovanni Fattori,* **Signora Martelli at Castiglioncello,** *c. 1867, Museo Civico G. Fattori, Livorno*

2 *Carlo Carrà,* **Pine-tree by the Sea,** *1930, Galleria Nazionale d' Arte Moderna, Rome*

3 *Umberto Boccioni,* **Horse, Rider and Houses,** *1914, Galleria Nazionale d' Arte Moderna, Rome*

1 *Marino Marini*, **Horse and Rider**, *1946, Galleria Nazionale d'Arte Moderna, Rome*

2 *Alberto Burri*, **Sack**, *1952, Museo Burri, Città di Castello*

3 *Pino Pascali*, **Foreground Lip**, *1964, Galleria Nazionale d'Arte Moderna, Rome*

4 *Mario Ceroli*, **Last Supper**, *1965, Galleria Nazionale d'Arte Moderna, Rome*

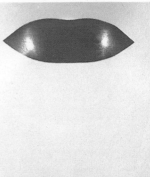

Lorenzo de' Medici and his humanist circle; his later style is more intense, and a similar disturbing restlessness runs through the works of Filippino Lippi.

The fame of Florentine discoveries spread through Italy. At Mantua, Andrea Mantegna's obsession with classical antiquity produced a precise, clear-cut style of painting and a revival of the techniques of illusionism. At Urbino and Arezzo, Piero della Francesca created a grave, silent poetry with his complex treatment of space and the beauty of the cool light that fills his works. At Perugia, Pietro Perugino developed a gentle, idealized art that often verges on the sentimental. Meanwhile, in Venice, growing interest in light and colour opposed the Florentine emphasis on line and form. Giovanni Bellini's use of pure oil paint enabled him to create a glowing, mellow atmosphere and to record with love the tiny details of plants and animals.

The ARTIST *as* GENIUS

Between 1480 and 1515 the fresh, bright colours of the Early Renaissance yielded to the delicate modelling and eerie poetry of Leonardo. In 1506 Julius II summoned Michelangelo to Rome and there followed a period of unparalleled creativity. A new ideal of beauty, harmony and the nobility of man found its most perfect expression in Leonardo's **Last Supper**, in Raphael's Vatican Stanze and in Michelangelo's mighty figures on the Sistine ceiling. The High Renaissance was dominated by great men, and by the artist's supreme confidence in the power of the divinely gifted imagination.

Rome was the main center of this unprecedented activity, yet in Venice Bellini's interest in light and colour was taken up and developed by Giorgione, whose small, idyllic paintings of pastoral subjects evoke a soft, dreamy and mysterious mood. Titian's early work was close to Giorgione's in its gentle lyricism but by 1518 he had evolved a new, heroic style, charged with dramatic movement and alive with brilliant colour. Although not in the same league as Titian, Lorenzo Lotto was another great Venetian colourist, whose best works are almost theatrical in their emphatic gesture and strong emotion. Meanwhile, in Parma, Correggio developed Mantegna's experiments with illusionism into dizzying airborne spectacles that prefigure the Baroque. In the second half of the 16thC Venice rather than Rome was the center of creativity, rejoicing in Titian's freely-handled, gloriously sensuous mythologies and in the decorative beauties of Paolo Veronese.

The last phase of the Renaissance, Mannerism, was both a refinement of and a reaction against the finest Renaissance achievements. A highly esoteric style, it was characterized by an irrational treatment of space, distortions of the human figure, and a sense of psychological unease. Its expression ranged from the horror of Michelangelo's **Last Judgment** and the agitated dramas of Rosso Fiorentino and Pontormo to the icy formality of Agnolo Bronzino's portraits; from the sophisticated elegance of Parmigianino to the nervous, flickering brushwork and weird spatial effects of Jacopo Tintoretto.

The AGE *of the* BAROQUE

The mood of 17thC papal Rome was one of triumph. Artists were called upon to exalt the renewed confidence of the church; they reacted against the artificiality of Mannerism and sought instead to create a religious imagery that could be easily understood, making intensely real the sufferings and martyrdoms, ecstasies and visions, of saints and mystics. Michelangelo Merisi da Caravaggio, scornful of all tradition, created a provocatively realistic art. His dark pictures are dramatically lit; scenes take place in squalid surroundings, and the protagonists are weather-beaten peasants. In sharp contrast, Annibale Carracci and his Bolognese followers sought to reform art by returning to the study of nature and to the grandeur of the High Renaissance: they brought back the joyful pagan subjects banned in the austere years of the Counter-Reformation.

By 1620 the warmth and humanity of the Early Baroque yielded to the increasingly overwhelming and theatrical imagery of the High Baroque. The surging rhythms and extended space of illusionistic ceiling paintings transported the spectator into heavenly spheres; the coloured marbles and painted and sculptured decoration of Roman churches created effects of unprecedented splendour. The High Baroque was dominated by Gianlorenzo Bernini, in whose most ambitious works sculpture, painting and architecture unite to express the most ecstatic emotion. Yet stylistic trends were complex, and throughout the period the Baroque was opposed by a classical movement. The severe style of Domenichino was developed by Nicolas Poussin, a French painter working in Rome, into an austere and profoundly moving classicism.

ROCOCO *and* NEOCLASSICISM

The transition from Baroque to Rococo occurred gradually. Luca Giordano in Naples and Sebastiano Ricci in Venice began to paint with a softer grace and charm; their brushwork is sketchy and light, their colours airy and luminous. The Venetian, Giambattista Tiepolo, was the last Italian artist to draw confidently on the grand subjects of mythology and history; his frescoes are filled with pale daylight and peopled by glamorous figures from an imagined Renaissance past. In total contrast are the unassuming genre pictures of Pietro Longhi and the cityscapes of Canaletto and Francesco Guardi.

The Rococo had little influence on Roman art; instead, the city became a center of Neoclassicism, a movement more European than Italian. Giambattista Piranesi's dramatic etchings of the most famous ruins created a lasting vision of the lost magnificence of Roman antiquity. The most celebrated Neoclassical sculptor, Antonio Canova, settled in Rome in 1781; his best works are frigidly erotic.

NINETEENTH *and* TWENTIETH CENTURIES

The 19thC was a dull period. Paris had supplanted Rome, and Italian artists were oppressed by the glamour of their own heritage. In Tuscany, Giovanni Fattori was the leading member of a group of painters known as the Macchiaioli, who experimented with *plein-air* techniques. More radical were the sculptures of Medardo Rosso, who took subjects from everyday life and caught transient effects of light and expression by dissolving solid form.

Futurism and Metaphysical painting both made significant Italian contributions to early 20thC art. The Futurists glorified the power of speed and the glamour of a machine-made society; their greatest exponent, Umberto Boccioni, used Cubist techniques to create the effects of vigour and movement. Metaphysical painting was associated with Surrealism and originated in Ferrara in the work of Giorgio de Chirico and Carlo Carrà; their deserted streets and squares are symbols of human loneliness.

Since the 1920s various kinds of abstract art have struggled for supremacy with figurative developments. A respect for the classical tradition is evident in the sculptures of Marino Marini and Giacomo Manzù. Important abstract artists include Lucio Fontana, whose stark, slit canvases are a form of conceptual art, and Alberto Burri, who uses damaged and wasted materials in a deeply expressive manner. Since the 1960s, many artists have participated in international movements such as Pop art; notable innovators include Pino Pascali and Mario Ceroli.

SOUTH CENTRAL ITALY

With its rich layers of history, archetypal grandeur and dazzling, world-famous collections, Rome dominates its surrounding region more forcefully than do most capital cities. Yet beyond this great metropolis, the south-central provinces offer wonderfully romantic landscapes and some fascinating art treasures.

LAZIO

North of Rome are many intriguing Etruscan sites, recalling a civilization even older than that of the ancient Romans. Tarquinia is famous for its wall paintings, Cerveteri for its architectural tombs; in the wild, craggy landscape between Viterbo and Tarquinia, rocky sepulchres are hewn out of the cliffsides of isolated valleys; the coast road leading from Tarquinia to the spectacular site at Vulci is studded with Etruscan remains.

From the 4thC BC, Rome dominated Lazio. There are important and evocative ruins at Palestrina, Ostia Antica and Tivoli; and at Sperlonga, on the dramatic, rocky coastline S of Rome, is the recently discovered Grotto of Tiberius, part of the summer palace where the Emperor entertained his guests, surrounded by magnificent sculpture and mosaics.

The Middle Ages were a period of flourishing artistic activity, producing the fine Romanesque churches at Anagni and Tuscania, and the picturesque Gothic monastic buildings at Subiaco. In the Renaissance, the influence of Rome was again dominant. Noble Roman families built splendid villas in the countryside around Rome – at Tivoli overlooking the wide plain of the Roman Campagna, at Frascati in the lush and gently rolling Colli Albani, and at Bagnaia and Caprarola in the rugged and densely wooded landscape of the Monti Cimini near Viterbo. Many of the villas are decorated with elaborate Mannerist frescoes and have spectacular gardens.

ABRUZZI and MOLISE

Although so close to Rome, the Abruzzi and Molise to the E feel remote; they form a wild and mountainous region, scattered with ancient and prehistoric remains; austere, isolated towns are linked by long, solitary roads that pass through rocky valleys and twist over precipitous crags to the coastal plains of the Adriatic.

Apart from a number of fine examples of Romanesque and Gothic architecture, showing strong Apulian influence, Molise has little to offer the art lover. The Abruzzi also produced important medieval churches – in a provincial but strong style, with severe rectangular facades and rose windows and often with elaborately carved pulpits – but they are notable for painting and sculpture as well.

The influence of the Tuscan and Venetian Renaissance reached the Abruzzi in the 15thC. It is evident in the charming frescoes of Andrea Delitio at Atri and Guardiagrele and, above all, in sculpture. The greatest sculptors were Silvestro dell'Aquila, who produced intensely realistic polychrome wooden statues, and the goldsmith Niccolò da Guardiagrele. Niccolò was the most celebrated of a flourishing school of goldsmiths, which had centers at Guardiagrele, Sulmona and Teramo.

ANAGNI
Frosinone, Lazio   Map B5

Anagni was an important papal city in the Middle Ages and retains many medieval buildings, including one of the finest Romanesque cathedrals in the region.

Cattedrale
Piazza Innocenzo III
🏛
The marble pavement dates from the 12thC but more interesting are the inlaid **Easter candlestick and bishop's throne** ★ by one of the Vassalletti family. This delicate style of inlay work, known as Cosmati, originated in Rome and the Vassalletti were among its greatest exponents.

In the crypt are 13thC **frescoes** ★ of biblical scenes, saints and scientific teachings – a rare example of wall painting from this period, and highly conservative in their formal and stilted style.

ATRI
Teramo, Abruzzi   Map D5

A small hill-top town with views towards the Adriatic, Atri was once the flourishing Imperial city of Hatria. In the Middle Ages, it was ruled by the dukes of Acquaviva.

Cattedrale
🏛
This is an important and sombre medieval monument with, in the apse, frescoes of the *Life of Mary and Christ* ★ by Andrea Delitio, the leading Abruzzi painter of the 15thC. These delicately patterned scenes are set in the fairytale landscapes of late Gothic art, with little arched rooms, many-towered castles, and precipitous rocks. Yet their lively realism and many charming genre details suggest a keen awareness of the new art of Florence.

Museo Capitolare
Via Roma
Tel. (085) 87241
Open mid-June to mid-Sept 10am – noon, 4 – 8pm; mid-Sept to mid-June, Sat 3 – 5pm, Sun 10am – noon, 3 – 5pm
Closed winter Mon – Fri
🔲 💟 ☑ ☙
The museum is attached to the cathedral and has a good collection of illuminated manuscripts, also goldsmiths' work of the 12thC and 13thC; note especially the crystal Byzantine **crucifix**.

BAGNAIA
Viterbo, Lazio   Map B2

Bagnaia is an attractive medieval town, best known for its spectacular late Renaissance villa.

Villa Lante della Rovere ☆
Via Jacopo Barozzi 71
Tel. (0761) 28008
Open Tues – Sun: Mar, Apr 9am – 5.30pm; May – Aug 9am – 7.30pm; Sept, Oct 9am – 5.30pm; Nov – Feb 9am – 4pm. Visits to palazzine by appointment only: tel. (06) 6791952
Closed Mon
🔲 🖪 *for palazzine* 🄿 *summer only* 🏛 ☙
The villa was completed in 1578 after a design attributed to Vignola. The **Renaissance garden** ★ is one of the most beautiful in Italy and is famous for its ornamental fountains.

The twin *palazzine* at the end are decorated with 16thC and early 17thC **frescoes**: the one on the right with mythological and hunting scenes by followers of the Zuccari and Antonio Tempesta; the one on the left with badly damaged works by Agostino Tassi, Cavalier d'Arpino and Orazio Gentileschi.

BASSANO ROMANO
Viterbo, Lazio   Map A3

This picturesque village is not far from Sutri and preserves a number of medieval buildings.

Palazzo Odescalchi
Piazza Umberto I
Visits by appointment only: tel. (06) 6789953 or write Amministrazione Odescalchi, Piazza Santi Apostoli 80, 00100 Roma
The medieval manor house was converted in the 16thC into an elegant *palazzo*. There are fine 16thC and 17thC decorations. Notice especially the dining room with mythological frescoes by Francesco Albani (1578 – 1660), a pupil of Annibale Carracci, and a smaller room frescoed with *Legends of Diana* ★ by Domenichino (1581 – 1641).

BOMARZO
Viterbo, Lazio   Map B3

On the slopes of a hill overlooking the Tiber valley, Bomarzo is dominated by the fine 16thC Palazzo Orsini, but is more famous for its terraced "Monster Park".

Parco dei Mostri (*Monster Park*) ☆
Tel. (0761) 42029
Open winter 8am – sunset, summer
7am – sunset
☒ ⌂ ⌺ ▣ ❧

This bizarre garden was created between 1552 and 1580 and features sculptures of imaginary and monstrous creatures, carved out of the rocky hillside. Its strange collection of conceits includes a small **temple**, dedicated to Giulia Farnese; the **mouth of Hades**, a monstrous mask of which the gaping mouth has been turned into a room; an **elephant** caparisoned for war; a giant **tortoise** carrying a goddess; and a **dragon** struggling with greyhounds.

The oddity of this assemblage contrasts strongly with the stately and ceremonial beauty of the nearby Renaissance gardens at BAGNAIA (Villa Lante) and CAPRAROLA (Palazzo Farnese). It was inspired by a Mannerist delight in fantastic and monstrous imagery and in witty contrasts between the natural and artificial.

BOMINACO
L'Aquila, Abruzzi   Map C5

A tiny mountain village on the slopes of Monte Buscito, Bominaco grew up around an ancient Benedictine foundation.

San Pellegrino
▥

This isolated church was built by the Benedictines from 1263. The walls and ceiling of the interior are almost completely covered with one of the richest cycles of medieval **frescoes** ★ in central Italy, in which three (unknown) hands have been discerned. Notice especially the huge, benign *St Christopher* near the entrance.

CAPRAROLA
Viterbo, Lazio   Map B3

Caprarola is a pleasant country town and tourist resort in the Monti Cimini, not far from Lake Vico.

Palazzo Farnese ☆
Via Antonio Sangallo 1
Tel. (0761) 646052
Open Tues – Sun: Apr – May 9am – 6pm,
June – Sept 9am – 8pm, Oct – Nov
9am – 5pm, Dec – Mar 9am – 4pm.
Visits to gardens by appointment only:
tel. (06) 6791952
Closed Mon
☒ ▥ ❧ *with permission*

The palace was begun by Antonio da Sangallo the Younger (1559) and completed by Vignola (1575). It is one of the most magnificent late 16thC buildings in Italy.

The **gardens** ★ are famous for their sculpture and monumental fountains; the **interior** ★ has one of the grandest decorative cycles of the late Renaissance. The beautiful spiral staircase by Vignola is frescoed by Antonio Tempesta; a suite of rooms decorated mainly by the brothers Taddeo and Federico Zuccaro celebrates the history of the Farnese family. The immensely erudite and complex iconography was planned by the humanist scholar Annibale Caro and in some of the rooms is made clear by inscriptions.

CERVETERI
Roma, Lazio   Map A3

From the 7thC to 5thC BC Cerveteri was a strong maritime power and a magnificent Etruscan city. It was conquered by the Romans in the 4thC and thereafter declined. Now a small modern town with a medieval center, it is best known for the Etruscan necropolises on the low hills surrounding it.

Museo Nazionale Cerite
Castello Ruspoli, Piazza Santa Maria
Tel. (06) 9950003
Open Tues – Sun: May – Sept 9am – 1pm,
4 – 7pm; Oct – Apr 9am – 4pm
Closed Mon
☒ ⌺ ▥

Housed in the 16thC Ruspoli castle, the collection traces the development of Cerveteri through archaeological remains found in the area.

Necropoli della Banditaccia ☆
2km (1¼ miles) N of Cerveteri
Tel. and opening times as Museo Nazionale
Cerite, above
☒ ⌂ ✗ *by arrangement*

The Banditaccia is the most splendid of the Etruscan necropolises outside Cerveteri. Its long, paved streets are lined with massive tumuli and rectangular tombs cut into the rock. Many of the burial chambers are built exactly like the interiors of houses – the great stone chairs eerily empty – and give a fascinating picture of Etruscan architecture.

The **Tomb of the Capitals** (6thC BC) is one of the earliest chamber tombs, with a roof that suggests the wooden beams of an Etruscan house and columns with Oriental capitals. Even more fascinating is the **Tomb of the Reliefs**, decorated with painted stucco reliefs of weapons and everyday household objects; at the back, a relief of **Typhon and Cerberus** is a grim reminder of the Etruscan Underworld – its gloomy mood contrasting strongly with the lyricism of the wall paintings at TARQUINIA (Necropoli).

CHIETI
Abruzzi Map D5

Chieti is a lively provincial capital not far from the Adriatic coast, with Roman and medieval remains.

Museo Archeologico Nazionale degli Abruzzi ☆
Via della Villa Comunale 3
Tel. (0871) 64175
Open Tues – Sun: June – Sept 9am – 1pm, 3 – 6pm; Oct – May 9am – 1pm
Closed Mon
📷 🎧 ✿

The museum has an important collection of archaeological material found in the surrounding region, including an elaborately decorated **bronze bed** (1stC AD). The enigmatic **Warrior ★** from Capestrano is the most celebrated of a group of rare and fascinating early Italian sculptures. Others include **Hercules** from Alba Fucens and a small bronze of the same subject from Sulmona.

CIVITA CASTELLANA
Viterbo, Lazio Map B3

Built on a tufa terrace, with an attractive medieval center, Città Castellana is not far from the ruins of Falerii Veteres, a town built by the Romans in the 3rdC BC.

Duomo
🏛

The magnificent Romanesque portico has exquisite early 13thC Cosmati work by the Roman marble workers, Jacopo di Lorenzo and his son Cosma. Inside are more Cosmatesque decorations, including the fine inlaid pavement and lecterns.

Museo Nazionale dell'Agro Falisco
Forte Sangallo
Tel. (0761) 53735
Open Tues – Sun 9am – 1pm
Closed Mon
📷 🏛 ✿

The museum is housed in a massive fortress, completed by Antonio da Sangallo at the end of the 15thC. It contains bronzes, ceramics and other findings from Falerii Veteres.

FRASCATI
Roma, Lazio Map A4

The town has been largely reconstructed after damage during World War II, but remains famous for the princely villas and gardens that surround it. The ancient Romans built villas at nearby Tusculum and the tradition was revived here in the 16thC by wealthy families. The series began in 1548 with the splendid **Villa Falconieri** (now closed to the public) and continued with the **Villa Torlonia** (1563), **Villa Aldobrandini** (1604) and many others. The Villa Torlonia was destroyed by bombing, but its gardens – now a public park – preserve a spectacular water theater by Maderno and splendid staircases linking the terraces.

Villa Aldobrandini ☆
Via Cardinale Massaia
Tel. (06) 9420331
House closed to public. For permission to visit gardens, inquire at Azienda di Soggiorno, Piazza G. Marconi 1
📷 🎧 🏛 ✿

The villa was begun by Giacomo della Porta and completed by Carlo Maderno and Giovanni Fontana but is mainly of interest for its splendid Renaissance **gardens ★** These are adorned with terraces, artificial grottoes, a water theater, fountains and statues. There are views of Rome from the terraces.

GAETA
Latina, Lazio Map A6

An ancient fortification, now a fishing town, Gaeta looks out over a sheltered bay. Near the cathedral there is a medieval quarter and castle.

Duomo
Piazza del Duomo

This has a celebrated late 13thC Easter **candlestick ★** with 48 low reliefs showing scenes from the **Life of Christ** and **Life of St Erasmus**. To the right of the high altar is the early 17thC **Martyrdom of St Erasmus** by Saraceni, a talented follower of Caravaggio.

Museo della Cattedrale
Piazza del Duomo
Tel. (0771) 461458
Closed for restoration

The museum has an early 16thC **Pietà** by Quentin Massys and an early 18thC **Madonna and Saints** by Sebastiano Conca; also, a fine 11thC Exultet parchment and beautiful fragments of an 11thC pulpit from the old cathedral.

Etruscan sites in Lazio

The great cities of southern Etruria developed earlier than the small inland centers and declined more rapidly; their abandoned sites were left untouched until their discovery in the desolate, marshy countryside by 18thC and 19thC travellers. Unlike the Tuscan center of Cortona and the Umbrian centers of Orvieto and Perugia, where medieval towns rose over the ancient Etruscan remains, these strange cities of the dead have been hardly touched by later civilization. The landscape is wild and rugged, cut by deep gulleys, waterfalls and cliffs, and studded with the grassy mounds of many tumuli. Rocky sepulchres lie almost hidden among fallen boulders and wild vegetation; or line the craggy sides of ravines hollowed out by rushing streams, their strange facades fashioned like house or temple fronts.

This tour may be made in two days from Rome, and easily extended into three. It takes in some of the more celebrated sites, victims of modern tourism, with tombs famous for their wall paintings and architectural features; also, some lesser known places, of merely archaeological interest but preserving more of the mysterious, uninhabited beauty that so moved the writers of the Romantic era.

Start at TARQUINIA, taking the *autostrada* from Rome and arriving early because the museum closes in the early afternoon. Tarquinia is famous both for its museum and for its necropolis, which has an unrivalled collection of wall paintings. These give a wonderfully vivid picture of the dancing, feasting and other activities that the Etruscans hoped to enjoy in the afterlife.

From Tarquinia, a road winds through the isolated valley of the river Marta to TUSCANIA, a small hilltop town. Tuscania has a slightly sad, dilapidated atmosphere, with crumbling towers and twisting medieval alleyways, in sharp contrast to the tourist smartness of Tarquinia. The necropolis is scattered around the town and a walk on nearby farmtracks will often reward you with a glimpse of an ancient tomb or stretch of Etruscan road. But the main tomb groups, from the 7thC to 4thC BC, are some 2.5km (1½ miles) from the town center and must be reached by car. These are clearly signposted. Most accessible are the Peschiera and Olivo groups (the latter with the labyrinthine Tomba della Regina or Tomb of the Queen).

Returning to the center of Tuscania, take the road E to VITERBO, pausing to look at the Etruscan and Roman remains at **Bagno delle Bussete**. Stretches of Etruscan wall bear witness to Viterbo's ancient origins and the local museum has an important collection of Etruscan finds, including decorative mirrors and vases. A road to the SW of the city leads to **Castel d'Asso**, one of the most beautiful and rewarding cliffside necropolises of ancient Etruria. A ruined medieval castle guards the wide valley and the cliffsides are thickly dotted with rocky sepulchres. The Tomba Grande and Tomba Orioli are the most interesting.

Returning to Viterbo, take the road S to Vetralla, then W to **Norchia**. The wild grandeur of its setting above twin river gorges makes Norchia extraordinarily spectacular. The temple tombs of the vast necropolis are, as at Castel d'Asso, built into the sides of the cliff; the two celebrated Tombe a Tempio or Temple Tombs have pediments with mythological figures, now sadly eroded.

Now return to Vetralla and make your way back to Tarquinia (perhaps for the night; there are good fish restaurants) and thence S, along the Via Aurelia towards CERVETERI. The coast road is lined with Etruscan and Roman sites – at **Civitavecchia** and **San Marinella**, and at **Pyrgi**, once the principal port of ancient Cerveteri, or Caere as it was then known. Pyrgi preserves the remains of an Etruscan sanctuary and polygonal walls of the 3rdC BC.

Cerveteri itself is now a small town, medieval in appearance, but it was once the most prosperous and splendid city of the Etruscan Empire. The town sits on a tufa spur, bounded by steep cliffs, and is surrounded by vast cemeteries. Most important of these is the necropolis of the Banditaccia. The great circular tumuli, and the rectangular tombs that line the regular streets and squares, are relatively untouched. In some places the tracks of cartwheels are still visible. Gently winding paths link the tombs, twisting among cypresses and crumbling hills; small steps lead down to burial chambers – sometimes built with windows and doors, in imitation of houses, yet forever uninhabited; stone seats and funeral couches remain eerily empty.

A tour of the Banditaccia could take anything from 2hrs to a day. You can then return to Rome on the Via Aurelia or the *autostrada*.

A detail of the stately frieze of the Tomb of the Baron at Tarquinia (c. 500BC).

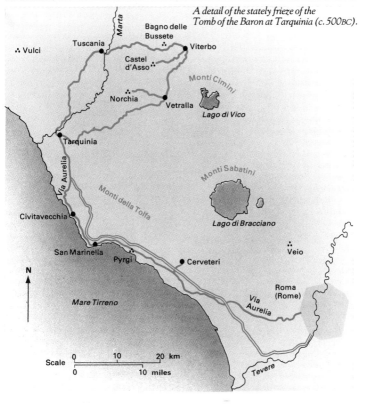

GROTTAFERRATA
Roma, Lazio Map A 4

Grottaferrata is an attractive town in the Colli Albani, famous for its scenic views and fortified abbey.

Abbazia e Museo di San Nilo
Corso del Popolo 128
Tel. (06) 945309
Open Tues – Sun 8. 30am – 12. 30pm,
4 – 6pm
Museo closed Mon
🔲 *but donations appreciated* ⓘ 🕮 🏛 ⚐

The abbey was founded in 1004 by St Nilus, for Basilian monks using the Greek liturgy. It was fortified by Giuliano da Sangallo at the end of the 16thC, and is surrounded by a moat and battlemented walls.

Inside, there is a **museum**, with ancient and Etruscan fragments and medieval sculpture; the **library** has rare Greek texts. The church of **Santa Maria** has a fine 13thC mosaic and some 12thC Byzantine frescoes. The **Cappella di San Nilo** ★ in the right aisle has good frescoes by Domenichino.

GUARDIAGRELE
Chieti, Abruzzi Map C6

This little hill-town was once an important center of goldsmiths' work. It is now a popular tourist resort.

Santa Maria Maggiore
The church has a late 15thC fresco of *St Christopher* by Andrea Delitio, better known for his work in the cathedral at ATRI. Niccolò da Guardiagrele's splendid early 15thC **silver cross**, once the pride of the treasury, was recently damaged during a theft and is being restored.

L'AQUILA
Abruzzi Map C4

L'Aquila is a dour, windy city, set high on a hillside and ringed by great mountains.

Museo Nazionale d'Abruzzo ☆
Castello Cinquecentesco
Tel. (0862) 64043
Open Tues – Sun 9am – 1. 30pm
Closed Mon
🖼 🚗 🏛 ☑ ⚐

The museum is housed in an imposing 16thC castle with great bastions. On the ground floor there is a small archaeological section. On the first floor, in a series of small rooms looking out over the mountains, is a richly varied and imaginative display of medieval art; outstanding polychrome wooden sculptures are exhibited with paintings, metalwork and ceramics.

Note especially two 12thC **carved wooden doors**, an early 15thC **polyptych** ★ by the Venetian artist, Jacobello del Fiore; a polychrome wooden statue of *St Sebastian* ★ by Silvestro dell'Aquila, which combines a startling surface realism with an almost Florentine nobility; a terra-cotta *Madonna*, also by Silvestro; and a superb **processional cross** ★ by Niccolò da Guardiagrele (1434).

On the second floor is a large group of 17thC pictures by secondary Flemish, Roman and Neapolitan artists; the Neapolitan section is the most interesting, with pictures by Bernardo Cavallino and Mattia Preti. There is also a section of dull contemporary pictures.

San Bernardino
Via di San Bernardino
🏛

The church has a fine Renaissance facade and a richly carved and gilded Baroque ceiling. In the third chapel to the right there is a late 15thC terra-cotta *Madonna* by the local sculptor, Silvestro dell'Aquila. The fifth chapel to the right has the **mausoleum of St Bernardine of Siena** (d. 1440), also by Silvestro; this is a less delicate work than his masterpiece, the **tomb of Maria Pereira** ★ (d. 1496), on the N wall of the choir.

Santa Maria di Collemaggio
Piazza di Collemaggio
🏛

This is an important Romanesque church, which was highly influential in the development of that style throughout the Abruzzi. In the chapel to the right of the high altar is the fine Renaissance **tomb of St Peter Celeste** ★ (1517) by Girolamo da Vicenza.

OSTIA ANTICA
Roma, Lazio Map A 4

The ruins of Ostia still vividly suggest the power and splendour of the seaport of ancient Rome; they yield a more immediate picture of daily urban life than do the scattered fragments in Rome itself.

Museo Archeologico Ostiense ☆
Scavi di Ostia Antica
Tel. (06) 5650022
Open Tues – Sun 9am – 1pm
Closed Mon
🖼 *Ticket to Scavi, below, gives entry to Museo* ☑ ⚐

This is a delightful small museum: cool, informative and beautifully arranged. The display traces the development of the sculptures found at Ostia; these date from the 2ndC BC and many are of very high quality.

Notice especially the almost Rococo grace of a group of sculptures deriving from Hellenistic art (Room VII); these include the **Cupid and Psyche ★** from the house of that name; the **Crouching Venus**, a lovely small marble work; and a fragment of a relief of **Arion on the Dolphin**. Portrait busts (Room VIII) include a group of the **Family of Marcus Aurelius ★** and **Sabina**, wife of Hadrian. Among a group of Roman paintings taken from tombs and buildings (Room XII) is a **Lion Attacking a Bull ★** notable for its lively detail.

Scavi di Ostia Antica ☆
Tel. as above
Open Tues – Sun 9am – 1hr before sunset
Closed Mon
🎫 *Ticket also gives entry to Museo, above*
🍴 X by appointment 🎧 🅿

The clarity of the excavated city's layout is evident as soon as you enter the long main street, with, on either side, the remains of the baths, theater and forum, *thermopolium* or bar (with marble counter and paintings of fruit and food) and four-storey apartment houses (a kind of middle-class dwelling very different from the low courtyard houses found at Pompeii).

The site, lined with cypresses and umbrella pines, is very beautiful; the fragments of ancient statues, the crumbling walls covered with mosaic, the shadowy paintings that linger on dark vaults, the mosaic floors that emerge from weeds and wasteland, create a moving sense of the past.

For works of art, the most important buildings are: the **Baths of Neptune**, with a lively **marine mosaic ★** characteristic of the rich, free compositions of the 2ndC AD; the **House of the Muses**, with both paintings and mosaics; and the **House of the Dioscuri**, with a fine mosaic of the **Birth of Venus ★**

PALESTRINA
Roma, Lazio Map A4

This attractive and largely medieval town is famous not only as the birthplace of the great 16thC composer of that name, but also for preserving the ruins of the vast Temple of Fortune (2ndC BC), which is dramatically sited on a series of monumental terraces.

Museo Nazionale Archeologico Prenestino ☆
Palazzo Colonna Barberini, Piazza della Cortina
Tel. (06) 9558100
Open Tues – Sat: May – Sept 9am – 6pm, Oct – Apr 9am – 1.30pm; Sun 9am – 12.30pm
Closed Mon
📷 🏛

The museum is housed in a stately 17thC palace that stands within the ruins of the Temple of Fortune. The outstanding work here is the **Mosaic of the Nile ★★** taken from the Sala Absidata or absidal hall of the temple. The fashion for these Nilotic scenes spread to Italy through Alexandrian mosaicists in the 1stC BC.

RIETI
Lazio Map B3

Once the capital of the Sabines, Rieti became a Roman municipality and, in medieval times, a residence of the popes. In the 14thC and 15thC it was a flourishing center of goldsmiths' work. It is a pretty town, dominated by the imposing Romanesque campanile of the Duomo.

Duomo
Piazza Cesare Battisti

In the first chapel of the left nave there is a 15thC fresco by Antoniazzo Romano; in the fourth chapel, **St Barbara** by Giovanni Mari, probably to a design by Bernini. In the second chapel of the right nave is Andrea Sacchi's **Guardian Angel**, another 17thC work. See also MUSEO DEL TESORO DEL DUOMO.

Museo Civico
Piazza Vittorio Emanuele II
Tel. (0746) 482231
Open Mon – Sat 8.30am – 1.30pm
Closed Sun
📷 🍴 X *by arrangement* 🎧

The museum has a small section devoted to Roman sculpture and coins, but the main collection centers on sculpture, painting and goldsmiths' work from the 13thC to 19thC. The sculpture includes a late 15thC terra-cotta **Madonna** by the school of Silvestro dell' Aquila.

Museo del Tesoro del Duomo
Duomo, Piazza Cesare Battisti
Tel. (0746) 41138
📷 🎧
Ask the cathedral sacristan for entry

The treasury is especially rich in medieval goldsmiths' work. Note the **processional cross ★** (1478) by Giacomo Gallina and a fine collection of 15thC chalices.

ROME (*ROMA*)
Lazio Map A4

Through more than two thousand years of cultural change and upheaval, Rome has acquired an overwhelmingly rich artistic heritage. As the center of a mighty military empire, the city in classical times collected the spoils of her victorious generals and became the greatest repository of Greek art in the world. Later, papal prestige and influence fostered a creative ferment that inspired, in the early 16thC, the classical purity and power of the High Renaissance and, in the 17thC, the virtuoso exuberance and drama of the Baroque. These two fundamental roles, as a place where art on a huge scale has been both collected and created, have combined to make Rome a center of pilgrimage for successive generations of artists and art lovers.

The vast papal palaces now known as the Vatican Museums (Musei Vaticani) are an essential starting point in any tour of Roman art. They house the finest collection of antiquities in the world, including the famous **Laocoön** group (venerated in antiquity, then lost until its sensational rediscovery in 1506), as well as two of the noblest achievements of High Renaissance art: Michelangelo's Sistine ceiling and Raphael's Stanze. More outstanding classical works are collected in the Capitoline Museums (Musei Capitolini), which occupy Michelangelo's spectacular Piazza del Campidoglio on the site of the ancient Capitol. The museums should ideally be visited late at night, when contrasts of darkness and light heighten the drama of the statuary within and of the giant figures of Castor and Pollux, the **Dioscuri**, outside.

Rome is also rich in 16thC and 17thC art collections, amassed by wealthy patrician families. The most famous of these is the Borghese Gallery (Galleria Borghese), now housed in the Villa Borghese, a *casino* or summer-house set in its own park in the northern heights of the city. Here the collection is dominated by that grand master of the Baroque, Bernini (1598–1680), and above all by his **Apollo and Daphne**, a tender, lyrical group that captures all the urgency and drama of the Baroque. In his later work, Bernini combined architecture, sculpture and painting in increasingly extravagant spectacles, culminating in the visionary splendours of the *baldacchino* (canopy) and throne in the great patriarchal basilica of St Peter's (San Pietro).

Rome is above all a city of churches – 280 of them within the old city walls alone and many with superb mosaics. These range in splendour from the exquisitely coloured and detailed 5thC panels in Santa Maria Maggiore, through the glowing and majestic 6thC Byzantine figures in Santi Cosma e Damiano, to Pietro Cavallini's lively 13thC narratives in Santa Maria in Trastevere. Other churches are worth visiting for their pulpits inlaid with brilliant marble (a medieval style known as Cosmati work), tomb reliefs and freestanding sculptures, and stupendous 17thC illusionistic ceiling paintings.

With so much to see, some organization of your time is prudent. The great masterpieces of the Vatican City may make your choice a little easier, perhaps suggesting a period or theme you would like to explore further. Popular sights become intolerably crowded in spring, particularly during Easter week, and if you have to visit them during this period it is wise to arrive early in the morning. August, with its enervating heat, is also best avoided. October is usually the ideal month, for the days are generally fine and warm and the main galleries only moderately crowded.

Ara Pacis Augustae (*Altar of Augustan Peace*) ☆
Via di Ripetta
Open June – Sept Tues – Sat 9am – 1pm, 3 – 6pm, Sun 9am – 1pm; Oct – May Tues – Sat 10am – 4pm, Sun 10am – 1pm
Closed Mon
📞 **𝓧** *tel. (06) 67101* 📷
The Ara Pacis was reconstructed in the 1930s and is now housed in its own pavilion near the mausoleum of Augustus. It was put up by Augustus between 13 and 9BC to mark his return to Rome after a long absence, and is in the form of an enclosure and altar on the Greek model. The whole structure is richly decorated with sculpture: scenes from legendary Roman history at each end, religious processions along the sides, and large areas of superbly carved acanthus scroll ornament.

Arco di Costantino (*Arch of Constantine*)
Piazza del Colosseo
The arch was erected between AD313 and 315 to commemorate Constantine's victory over Maxentius at the battle of Milvian Bridge. It incorporates a frieze from the time of Trajan, roundels from a monument to Hadrian, and panels from an arch in honour of Marcus Aurelius. In comparison with these earlier pieces, the narrow friezes showing episodes of Constantine's life are strikingly unclassical in feeling and technique.

Arco di Settimio Severo (*Arch of Septimius Severus*)
Foro Romano, Via dei Fori Imperiali
Tel. (06) 6792008
Forum open Wed – Mon: Oct – May 9am – 5pm, June – Sept 9am – 7pm
Forum closed Tues
📞 📷
The arch was erected in AD203 to commemorate Septimius Severus' Parthian victories. The most interesting parts of the sculpture are the four panels over the minor passages, which use a style adapted from that of the commemorative columns to illustrate episodes from the campaigns.

Arco di Tito (*Arch of Titus*)
Foro Romano, Via dei Fori Imperiali
For Forum entry information, see Arco di Settimio Severo, above
At the top of the Via Sacra, this was erected soon after Titus' death in AD81. The reliefs on the walls of the passage show the triumph of Titus and Vespasian after the capture of Jerusalem in AD70. The panel showing the booty from the temple being carried in procession under

a triumphal arch is remarkably illusionistic.

Borghese Gallery See GALLERIA BORGHESE.

Capitoline Museums See MUSEI CAPITOLINI.

Casino dell'Aurora
Via XXIV Maggio 43
Tel. (06) 4751224
Open first day of every month 10am – noon, 3 – 5pm
Closed at all other times
📷
The *casino* or summer-house is located in the garden of the Palazzo Pallavicini-Rospigliosi, which is closed to the public. It should be visited for Guido Reni's ***Aurora*** ★★ (1615), a ceiling fresco which throughout the 18thC and 19thC was one of the most celebrated of all paintings, and indeed one of the most lovely. The fresco glows with radiant light and colour; the graceful rhythms and ideal beauty of the figures were inspired by classical reliefs and by Raphael, and yet there is a sweet and tender poetry that is wholly of the 17thC. Reni resisted the illusionism of the nascent Baroque; the ***Aurora***, elegantly framed, is treated as if it were an easel picture to be hung on the wall. In the same room are contemporary frescoes by Bril and Tempesta.

Castel Sant'Angelo
Lungotevere Castello
Tel. (06) 655036
Open Tues – Sat 9am – 1pm, Sun 9am – noon
Closed Mon
📞 **𝓧** *by arrangement* 📷 🏛 ✓ ♨
The Castel Sant'Angelo was built as the tomb of the Emperor Hadrian; later it became a fortress and, during the Renaissance, a notorious prison; it now houses a museum. There is a large military collection; a series of rooms decorated with grotesques and elegant Mannerist friezes, many by Perin del Vaga; and some outstanding Renaissance pictures and furniture.
The finest rooms are the two **Rooms of Clement VII** on the second floor, with pictures by Crivelli and Signorelli. On the third floor are the **Papal Apartments**. These include the **Sala Paolina**, frescoed with the ***Deeds of Alexander the Great*** ★ by Perin del Vaga, and with works by Tibaldi; the **Camera del Perseo** and **Camera di Amore e Psiche**, also both frescoed by Perin del Vaga; and the **Room of the Mausoleum of Hadrian**, with fine pictures by Dossi and Lotto.

The fountains of Rome

Rome is rich in splendid fountains. Many were commissioned by the popes of the late 16thC and early 17thC, who were concerned to bring water to those areas of the city where it was badly needed. The most celebrated designer of the late Renaissance was Giacomo della Porta, whose architectural fountains were based on elegant contrasts of geometric forms. In the Baroque era, fountains became grander, more freely composed and more natural. Bernini delighted in the Baroque fusion of sculpture, architecture and nature, and created ever more spectacular ways of uniting mythological and allegorical figures – river gods, tritons and dolphins – with rushing water. This tour winds through the center of medieval and Renaissance Rome, taking in most of the city's best-known fountains and culminating in the most beautiful of all Baroque squares, Piazza Navona.

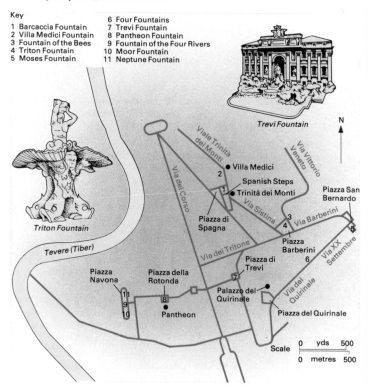

Key
1 Barcaccia Fountain
2 Villa Medici Fountain
3 Fountain of the Bees
4 Triton Fountain
5 Moses Fountain
6 Four Fountains
7 Trevi Fountain
8 Pantheon Fountain
9 Fountain of the Four Rivers
10 Moor Fountain
11 Neptune Fountain

Trevi Fountain

Triton Fountain

Tevere (Tiber)

Begin at Piazza di Spagna with Bernini's early **Barcaccia Fountain** (1627–29). This is shaped like a ship (an allegorical allusion to the Ship of the Church), with the Barberini arms emblazoned on the bows; the low siting is due to the low water pressure in this area. The fountain has a vivid, naïve charm and looks rather like the remnant of a Baroque naval spectacle, now incongruously surrounded by the flow of 20thC traffic; it is the focus of the traditionally Bohemian quarter of Rome.

From here, climb the graceful Spanish Steps to the imposing facade of the church of Trinità dei Monti, designed by Carlo Maderno. Turn left along Viale Trinità dei Monti; a little farther along, on the terrace to your left, is the peculiarly evocative **Villa Medici Fountain** (1587). Framed by ilexes and with water gently dripping from its wide, mossy bowl, the fountain forms the foreground to a splendid view over Rome towards the dome of St Peter's. This view was painted by Corot when he was at the French Academy in the Villa Medici and the area still retains something of the quiet, still charm that captivated the French Romantics.

From here, retrace your steps to the church, and thence down Via Sistina to Piazza Barberini. This is a busy, modern and rather unattractive square but it has two fountains by Bernini. The **Fountain of the Bees** (FONTANA DELLE API), at the corner of the Via Veneto, dates from 1644. It was not intended for this site and has been badly reconstructed; but the lovely double shell – a symbol of fertility – and the Barberini bees spouting water still suggest the poetry of Bernini's conceit. The **Triton Fountain** (1643), in the center of the piazza, is a magical, enchanting image. Four dolphins rise from the pool, their wide-open mouths drawing up water. The shell opens to free the triton, who blows a jet of water high into the air. Despite the 20thC buildings that tower over the relatively small group, its dynamic upward thrust still dominates the piazza.

From here, it is possible to go down Via del Tritone towards the Trevi Fountain, or to add an extra loop by going up Via Barberini to the **Moses Fountain** (1587) in Piazza San Bernardo. Also known as the Fountain of the Acqua Felice, this is an important post-Renaissance design by Domenico Fontana, in the form of a triumphal arch; the clumsy figure of Moses derives from Michelangelo. Now go down Via XX Settembre and Via del Quirinale, nasty roads enlivened at their junction by the grottoes of the **Four Fountains** or "Quattro Fontane" (1588–93). Go down the steps at the side of the Palazzo del Quirinale and on to the **Trevi Fountain** (FONTANA DI TREVI). Salvi's famous landmark, completed in 1762, almost fills the small and rather tatty piazza with its dynamic play of rushing water and natural rocks; the mighty figure of Neptune, standing on a huge shell drawn by sea horses, towers over the composition.

Next stop is Piazza della Rotonda, on the far side of the Corso. Here stands the **Pantheon Fountain** (1575) by Giacomo della Porta, who also designed the Tortoise Fountain (FONTANA DELLE TARTARUGHE) to the S of the medieval quarter and not therefore included in this tour. The Pantheon Fountain did not originally incorporate the Egyptian obelisk, which sits uneasily, somewhat dwarfed by its base. The ensemble cannot compete with the majesty of the Pantheon, but the piazza has the random charm – that sense of a haphazard mixture of ancient and Renaissance worlds – that is so often found in Rome.

A very different atmosphere, one of calculated theatrical splendour, characterizes nearby Piazza Navona. This famous Baroque showpiece is entirely dominated by the rushing water and vigorous, lively figures of Bernini's **Fountain of the Four Rivers** (FONTANA DEI FIUMI). The figures were executed by Bernini's assistants to his own designs and represent the rivers Danube, Nile, Ganges and Plate. The base of the fountain is a huge, craggy rock, surrounded by eddying water in which swim strange and delightful animals, attributes of the four rivers – notice especially the strange armadillo. The fountain was commissioned in 1648 by Innocent X, whose idea it was to incorporate the obelisk; this heavy, solid, mass rises from its startlingly insubstantial base as a symbol of the Triumph of the Church.

The fountains at either end of the piazza were designed by Giacomo della Porta; their bases were later altered by Borromini. The sculpture of the **Moor Fountain** (to the S) was executed by Gianantonio Mari in 1654 to a design by Bernini; that of the **Neptune Fountain** (to the N) dates from the 19thC.

Chiesa Nuova (*Santa Maria in Vallicella*)
Corso Vittorio Emanuele

The church was given to St Philip Neri by Gregory XIII in 1575. St Philip favoured an austere simplicity, but in the 1640s Pietro da Cortona began to transform the interior of the church with magnificent Baroque **frescoes** ★ Cortona's frescoes cover the dome (1647–51), the half-dome of the apse (1655–60) and the ceiling of the nave (1664–65); the last is less illusionistic, but elaborately framed, and enriched with gold and white stucco.

Over the high altar is a splendid *Madonna and Angels* ★ by Rubens; on the side walls of the choir, *Sts Domitilla, Nereus and Achilleus* ★ (right) and *Sts Gregory, Maurus and Papias* ★ (left), also by Rubens. All three pictures are painted on slate, to avoid reflection; they are one of the earliest Baroque attempts to link painted figures across real space.

In the left transept and fourth chapel of the left aisle are two late 16thC pictures by Barocci. The sacristy has a ceiling fresco by Cortona and, over the altar, Algardi's fine marble group of *St Philip Neri with an Angel* (1640).

Colonna di Marco Aurelio (*Column of Marcus Aurelius*)
Piazza Colonna

The column was erected between AD176 and 193 to commemorate the Emperor's victories in the German and Sarmatian campaigns, respectively shown in the lower and upper halves of the spiral relief. The column is fairly closely based on the COLONNA TRAIANA, but the carving is in deeper relief, more assertive, and easier to read from the ground. The statue of *St Paul* dates from 1589.

Colonna Traiana (*Trajan's Column*)
Foro Traiano, Via dei Fori Imperiali
Currently under restoration

Like the forum in which it stands, the column was put up as a piece of propaganda to commemorate Trajan's campaigns against the Dacians. It was dedicated in AD113 and just four years later the base was used as Trajan's own tomb.

The entire shaft of the column is covered by a spiral band of sculpture, which tells the story of the Dacian campaigns with extraordinary narrative clarity and precise attention to detail. The column was originally flanked by Trajan's Greek and Latin libraries and the reliefs could have been studied – as a monumental book – from the upper storeys of these buildings; much of the detail is too fine to distinguish from the ground.

Domus Aurea (*Nero's Golden House*)
Via Labicana
Tel. (06) 7316204
Closed for restoration

The dank and gloomy remains of the Domus Aurea give a poor idea of the magnificent palace that Nero built after the Fire of Rome in AD64. The Domus was celebrated by ancient writers for its lavish decorations and novel gadgetry (including a revolving banqueting table). Many of the surviving rooms are painted with extravagant architectural fantasies, in a style known as Fourth Pompeian; chief among the artists was Fabullus.

The ruins were excavated in the Renaissance, when they were visited by Giovanni da Udine, Raphael and Michelangelo. They were originally thought to be underground grottoes quite unrelated to Nero's palace, hence the term "grotesque" derived from their decorations.

Fontana delle Api (*Fountain of the Bees*)
Piazza Barberini

The fountain is by Bernini (1644), but has been badly reconstructed. It was commissioned to honour Urban VIII, the Barberini pope: hence the bees, the Barberini family emblem.

Fontana dei Fiumi (*Fountain of the Four Rivers*)
Piazza Navona

This is the most spectacular of Bernini's fountains (1648), richly textured, full of movement, and reigning over the long piazza. Four lively figures personifying the four great rivers – Danube, Nile, Ganges and Plate – sit at the corners of a craggy rock, encircled by rushing water; on the summit stands a massive Egyptian obelisk, crowned by a dove.

Fontana delle Tartarughe (*Tortoise Fountain*)
Piazza Mattei

This is one of the most sophisticated and graceful of all Mannerist fountains (1581–84). It was designed by Giacomo della Porta, with bronze figures by the Florentine sculptor Taddeo Landini. The tortoises were added later, in the 17thC.

Fontana di Trevi (*Trevi Fountain*)
Piazza di Trevi

The brilliantly imaginative design is by Niccolò Salvi; he used the side of the Palazzo Poli, enriched by a classical triumphal arch, as the backdrop for an exuberant display of allegorical and mythological figures, and for the rushing water that cascades over the rock formations. The fountain (completed 1762) almost fills the tiny square, and much of its startling effect depends on our sense of discovering so unexpectedly a monument of overwhelming Roman grandeur.

Galleria Borghese (*Borghese Gallery*) ☆☆
Via Pinciana
Tel. (06) 858577
Open Tues – Sat 9am – 2pm, Sun
    9am – 1pm
Closed Mon
🎫 𝘹 *by arrangement* 🎴 🅿 🏛 ☑ 🌱 🍴

The Villa Borghese on the Pincio was built in 1613 for Scipione Borghese, the wealthy nephew of Pope Paul V. The worldly, pleasure-loving Cardinal, famed for his magnificent banquets, was a zealous and often ruthless collector; his taste was wide and catholic, embracing ancient art, the great masters of the Renaissance, and contemporary artists of every school; he was an early admirer of Caravaggio, and his inspired patronage shaped the career of the young Bernini. The villa has been much altered, but the splendid collection (sculpture mainly on the ground floor, painting above) still suggests the powerful personality of the Cardinal – who is brought brilliantly to life in the fleshy features and jovial, penetrating expression of Bernini's **portrait bust** (Room XIV).

Ground floor
Salone This has five large fragments of 3rdC Roman mosaics; the vault was frescoed in 1782 by Mariano Rossi.
Room I This contains Antonio Canova's celebrated *Pauline Borghese* ★ in the attitude of Venus. Pauline was Napoleon's sister and married Prince Camillo Borghese in 1803.
Room II Bernini's *David* ★ (1623 – 24) is the climax of a brilliant group of early works commissioned from Bernini by Scipione Borghese. In this sculpture, Bernini attempted to destroy the boundaries between real and artistic space; the statue demands the presence of an unseen Goliath, and its dramatic movement seems to extend into the space of the spectator. The expression is strikingly realistic, and Bernini is said to have studied his own features in a mirror for inspiration.
Room III Bernini's *Apollo and Daphne* ★★ (1622 – 25) is an astonishing, exuberant display of technical virtuosity. The sculptor has created, in marble, richly pictorial effects – above all in the suggestion of a single, intensely dramatic moment, and in the contrasting textures of the hair, flesh and encircling bark, and

of the leafy branches that spring from the nymph's fingers. The group was planned for this room, but was intended to be set against the wall, and seen – as were the other sculptures of this series – from a single viewpoint.
Room IV In the center is Bernini's *Pluto and Persephone* ★ (1621 – 22). Again, the emphasis is on a transitory moment – Pluto with his victim strides past the threatening Cerberus, guardian of the Underworld – and on the soft, illusionistic carving of the marble.
Room VI Bernini's *Aeneas and Anchises Fleeing Troy* (1619) was his first work for the Cardinal. His later, unfinished *Truth Unveiled* was a personal allegory intended to answer attacks on the failure of his campanile for St Peter's.
Rooms VII and VIII have classical sculptures, including the *Dancing Faun* after Lysippus.
First floor
Room IX Besides Lorenzo di Credi's *Madonna and Child with St John the Baptist* and Pintoricchio's *Crucifixion with St Jerome*, there are two important works by Raphael – a quiet, lyrical *Portrait of a Woman with a Unicorn* ★ where the delicacy of his technique is indebted to Leonardo, and a dramatic *Deposition* ★★ (1507) in which he sought to emulate the powerful figures and elaborate composition of Michelangelo. This last was commissioned for the Baglioni chapel in San Francesco at Perugia, and stolen from there by Scipione Borghese.
Room X has Mannerist works by Bronzino, Cranach and Rosso Fiorentino.
Room XI has two works by Lotto; also Savoldo's *Tobias and the Angel*.
Room XII shows Sassoferrato and Domenichino.
Room XIV The vault frescoes by Lanfranco were inspired by Annibale Carracci's ceiling in the Palazzo Farnese (see BAROQUE CEILINGS IN ROME). The sculptures feature two busts of *Scipione Borghese* by Bernini; the first version, when nearly finished, revealed a crack in the marble and Bernini with dramatic speed made a copy. The pictures include Domenichino's *Hunt of Diana* (1618), a work of unexpectedly exquisite colouring and coy, erotic charm, and an outstanding group by Caravaggio. The *Sick Bacchus* ★ and *Boy with a Basket of Fruit* ★ are both early works, remarkable for the allure of the sitters and the fresh naturalism of the still-lifes. Their bright clarity contrasts with the dark stillness and brooding awareness of two later, more tragic works, the *Madonna of the*

Serpent and the *David with the Head of Goliath*. The head of Goliath is said to be a self-portrait.

Room XV The *Deposition* (1605) is an early work by Rubens. Three other pictures are attributed to Bernini.

Room XIX Correggio's *Danae* ★ is celebrated for its languid sensuality; Dosso Dossi's *Melissa* ★ shows the enchantress set against one of the most magical and glowing of all Dossi's landscapes.

Room XX An outstanding collection of Venetian pictures is dominated by Titian's *Sacred and Profane Love* ★★ usually interpreted as a Neo-Platonic allegory of different aspects of Venus. Other works include Antonello da Messina's *Portrait of a Man*, Giovanni Bellini's *Madonna and Child* ★ and Veronese's *St John the Baptist Preaching*.

Galleria Colonna
Palazzo Colonna, Piazza Santi Apostoli
Tel. (06) 6794362
Open Sat only, 9am–1pm
Closed Aug
Entrance in Via della Pilotta 17
🖼 🎭 🏛

The great attraction here is the immense gallery itself (opened in 1703 by Filippo Colonna), which provides a sumptuous setting for this princely collection. The gallery was decorated by Giovanni Coli and Filippo Gherardi, in a style deriving from Pietro da Cortona and from Venetian art. A Cortonesque framework surrounds the central panel – a dazzling, virtuoso performance, the *Battle of Lepanto* ★ (1675–78).

The collection has some good pictures by Bronzino and other Mannerists, also a fine portrait by Veronese and works by other Venetian masters, but its main strength lies in **17thC landscape** ★ with pictures by Mola, Testa, Rosa, and a series of light and lovely gouache scenes by Gaspard Dughet. Annibale Carracci's *Bean Eater* ★ is more realistic than anything painted by Caravaggio.

Galleria Doria Pamphili
Palazzo Doria Pamphili, Piazza del Collegio Romano 1A
Tel. (06) 6794365
Open Tues, Fri, Sat, Sun 10am–1pm
Closed Mon, Wed, Thurs
🖼 🏋 *for private apartments* 🎭

A visit to the Palazzo Doria Pamphili movingly suggests the rich past of a noble Roman family, most brilliant in the 17thC, when Giambattista Pamphili was elected Pope Innocent X (1644). The magnificent gilded galleries, enclosing a Renaissance courtyard, were built in

1731–34 to house the family collection and have changed very little; the pictures, gold frame to frame, are hung in rows often three deep, just as a 17thC connoisseur would have hung them. It is the most important collection left in private hands.

Gallery I This has a shadowy double portrait attributed to Raphael; a lyrical early Titian, *Salome* ★ two early and unexpectedly tender and detailed works by Caravaggio, the *Penitent Magdalen* and the *Rest on the Flight to Egypt* ★ also, pictures by Caravaggio's followers, notably Preti's *Tribute Money* and Saraceni's compassionate *St Roch Healed by an Angel* ★

Gallery II The main gallery is crowded with fine pictures by Bolognese Baroque painters. A series of small rooms opening from it shows Parmigianino's *Adoration of the Shepherds*, and many cabinet pictures by Flemish artists, highly prized by 17thC collectors. Works by Jan Brueghel and Paul Bril, and Pieter Bruegel's *Battle in the Gulf of Naples* ★ are outstanding.

Gallery III Also known as the Hall of Mirrors, this is one of the loveliest Rococo interiors in Italy. A small room at the end contains the finest work in the whole collection, Velazquez' portrait of *Innocent X* ★★ The harsh power of Velazquez' work contrasts with the polished virtuosity of Bernini's bust of the Pope nearby.

Gallery IV A rich collection of 17thC landscapes recalls the passion for this genre that was shared by the Pope's nephew, Camillo Pamphili. The most celebrated works are the six so-called Aldobrandini lunettes, by Annibale Carracci and his pupils, and five pictures by Claude. The clear structure and noble forms of Annibale's *Flight into Egypt* ★★ (c.1603) created the ideal landscape; its conventions were perfected in Claude's majestic *Sacrifice at Delphi* ★ (1648). Around these classical works hang lovely windswept landscapes by Dughet and Rosa; glowing, wooded vistas by the Dutch artist Herman van Swanevelt; and a rare group of pictures by Bartolommeo Torrigiani.

Salone Aldobrandini This has more grandiose landscapes, plus Guercino's luscious *Erminia and Tancred* ★

Private Apartments These may be visited on a guided tour only. A charming series of little Rococo drawing rooms contains many family portraits (two by Sebastiano del Piombo) and personal mementoes; other works of art include a 15thC **Burgundian tapestry** ★ a number of Gobelins tapestries, and an *Annunciation* by Filippo Lippi.

Galleria Nazionale d'Arte Antica – Palazzo Barberini ☆
Via delle Quattro Fontane 13
Tel. (06) 4754591
Open Tues – Sat 9am – 2pm, Sun
  9am – 1pm
Closed Mon
🎨 🏛 ♿

The Palazzo Barberini is a fine Baroque palace, which houses the greater part of the National Art Collection. (17thC pictures are mainly in the Palazzo Corsini – see following entry.)

First floor
The Baroque decorations are by Andrea Sacchi and Pietro da Cortona. The cool hues and restrained composition of Sacchi's *Allegory of Divine Providence* (Room VII) contrast strongly with the overpowering illusionism, rich Venetian colours, and surging movement of Pietro da Cortona's *Allegory of Divine Providence* in the Salone. Cortona also decorated the exquisite chapel that opens off Room VII.

Italian paintings from the 15thC include a triptych by Fra Angelico, Piero di Cosimo's *Mary Magdalen* ★ and Filippo Lippi's *Tarquinia Madonna* ★ and *Annunciation with Donors*. There is a strong 16thC Italian collection, with fine Mannerist portraits by Bronzino and Raphael (*La Fornarina* ★), also works by Barocci, Beccafumi, Fra Bartolommeo and Andrea del Sarto. Paintings from the 17thC range from the horrifying realism of Caravaggio's *Judith Beheading Holofernes* ★ to the warmth of Saraceni's *Holy Family*. Northern artists include Massys (a tender portrait of *Erasmus* ★) and a group of French 18thC painters.

Second floor
To your right is a suite of rooms decorated in a charming Rococo style; to your left, a large collection of 18thC Italian and some French pictures. The Italian pictures are arranged in regional schools: most interesting are sketches for Roman ceilings by Gaulli and Pozzo; the Neapolitan school, which includes some macabre, eerie works by Schönfeld; and the Venetian school, with works by Bazzani and Piazzetta. There are also some charming views of Rome by the Dutch-born Caspar van Wittel; and two outstanding works by Hubert Robert.

Galleria Nazionale d'Arte Antica – Palazzo Corsini
Via della Lungara 10
Tel. (06) 6542323
Open Tues, Thurs 9am – 6.30pm; Wed,
  Fri, Sat 9am – 2pm; Sun 9am – 1pm
Closed Mon
📷 *but* 🎨 *Sun ✗ Thurs, Sat, Sun* 🏛 ☑ ♿

The Palazzo Corsini houses mainly 17thC pictures from the National Art Collection. It is a fine old palace, rather out of the way and not much visited, but very pleasant to browse in.

The first two rooms display a charming group of small landscapes and still-lifes by 16thC Dutch and Flemish artists (among them, Jan Brueghel and Lucas van Uden); a *Holy Family* by van Dyck; and, close by, a *Flight into Egypt* by the Genoese artist Ansaldo, who was deeply influenced both by Rubens and by van Dyck.

Further on is Caravaggio's *Narcissus* ★ which brilliantly conveys the disturbing beauty of the youth, locked in a circle of self-love. Around it hang works by artists who responded in different ways to Caravaggio's revolutionary naturalism. Orazio Borgianni's *Holy Family* is a Renaissance design, disrupted by the startlingly naturalistic still-life of the cradle. The *Cake Vendor* by Pieter van Laer, the Dutch genre painter, introduces some of Caravaggio's realism to an ordinary Roman street scene.

There follow works by French and Flemish Caravaggisti, and small groups of paintings by 17thC Florentine, Genoese and Milanese painters. A room devoted to the Bolognese School has two outstanding works by Guercino: an *Adoration of the Shepherds* and the dusky *Et in Arcadia Ego* ★ the first painting of the theme that was to capture the Romantic imagination; two Arcadian shepherds are stopped by the sight of a human skull, which warns them that, even in Arcady, there is death.

Caravaggio's influence recurs in the Neapolitan pictures, in the dark and haunting intensity of Caracciolo's *St Onophrius* and in the repulsive violence of Rosa's *Prometheus* – yet the period also embraces the lyrical, elegant works of Cavallino, and Rosa's unexpectedly sweet *Poetry* and *Music*.

Galleria Nazionale d'Arte Moderna ☆
Viale delle Belle Arti 131
Tel. (06) 802751
Open Tues – Sat 9am – 2pm, Sun
  9am – 1pm
Closed Mon
🎨 ♿ 🍴 ☑ ⊞

The gallery was founded in 1883 when the ideals of the Risorgimento and the enthusiasm for the recent national unification were still very much alive. The idea was to show the development of the various regional schools towards what was considered the national art of the newly born country. The gallery is therefore strongest on 19thC and 20thC Italian art, although notable exceptions

include Klimt's ***Three Ages of Woman***
(1905) and a small, exquisite still-life by
Braque (both in Room XXXIX). The
enormous collection of contemporary
art, acquired since World War II, is due
to be rehoused in a new wing; the present
room arrangement must therefore be
considered temporary.

Canova's colossal group of **Hercules
Flinging Lichas into the Sea**
(1795–1802), just inside the entrance, is
a work of extraordinary sculptural
bravura. Most interesting among the
early sections of the gallery is Room IV
with works by the two founders of **Italian
Romantic painting**: Francesco Hayez and
Giovanni Carnovali (called Il Piccio).

The **school of Posillipo**, in Room VII,
flourished in and around Naples in the
late 19thC; Gioacchino Toma's *Luisa
Sanfelice in Jail* (1877) is a perfect
example of the warm colouring and
unheroic choice of subject that
characterized this group of painters. The
Tuscan Impressionists, in Room VIII,
were dubbed the **Macchiaioli** (literally,
"Blotters") by their contemporaries; most
of the works on display show the
limitations of a school that attached too
much importance to experimentation,
but some of Giovanni Fattori's paintings
rise above this purely technical level.

Of the Milanese **Scapigliati** or
"Bohemians," in Room XVI, the most
gifted painter was Tranquillo Cremona.
His idiosyncratic colour style is evident in
his ***Two Cousins*** and **Sick Girl**.

Room XVII is entirely dedicated to
the works of Medardo Rosso
(1858–1928). He was the first sculptor to
try to introduce Impressionist light
effects to sculpture. The next room,
Room XVIII, shows the **Divisionisti** or
"Divisionists", a group of artists who
painted fantastic subjects in a technique
similar to that of Seurat; outstanding
among this collection is Pellizza de
Volpedo's **Sun** (1904). In Room XXIII
the most monumental works of the
gallery are gathered together and
include ***Diana and the Slaves*** by
d'Annunzio's favourite painter, the
Symbolist Aristide Sartorio.

Outstanding among early 20thC
works are those by the Futurists Giacomo
Balla and Umberto Boccioni. The first is
best represented by one of his early
masterpieces, the **Villa Borghese
polyptych**, and the second by his portrait
of ***Ferruccio Busoni*** (1916). Notable
contemporary pieces include the puzzling
works of Lucio Fontana and the massive
bronze sculptures of the brothers
Pomodoro. Children will enjoy the
gallery's many amusing mechanical and
electronic exhibits.

Galleria Spada
Piazza Capo di Ferro 13
Tel. (06) 6561158
Closed for restoration

This collection was for the most part
formed by Cardinal Bernardino Spada, a
passionate 17thC connoisseur, and the
gallery vividly suggests the character of a
small private collection of the Baroque
era. There are pictures by celebrated
16thC artists – notably Andrea del Sarto,
Niccolò dell' Abbate and Titian (a ruined
Portrait of a Musician), but the 17thC
works are more interesting.

These open with two portraits of the
Cardinal, by Guercino and Guido Reni.
Works by the most important of the
Caravaggisti working in Rome include
Gentileschi's **David** and Borgianni's
Pietà. There is also a good collection of
genre – very popular with the 17thC
collector – featuring works by Jan
Brueghel, Pieter van Laer and
Michelangelo Cerquozzi. Cerquozzi's
Revolt of Masaniello ★ is perhaps his
masterpiece; it records, with remarkable
objectivity, the stirring revolt of the
fisherman, Masaniello, against Spanish
autocracy in Naples. Pietro Testa is
represented by a rare early work, the
Massacre of the Innocents, and by his
greatest and most confident painting, the
Sacrifice of Iphigenia ★ There are also
works by Gaulli and Furini.

Gesù ☆
Corso Vittorio Emanuele
🏛

This famous late 16thC church, with its
voluted facade by Giacomo della Porta
and aisleless, barrel-vaulted nave by
Vignola, has one of the most opulent
Baroque interiors in Rome. Gaulli's
brilliantly illusionistic frescoes
(1672–85) cover the vaults of the nave
and dome, pendentives and apse. The
Triumph of the Name of Jesus ★ on the
vault of the nave is a breathtaking blend
of painted figures, gilt stucco, stucco
figures, and stucco clouds that cast real
shadows. The vault of the church seems
open to a vision of the heavens; at the far
end, the damned tumble downwards to
the nave.

In the right transept is Maratta's
Death of St Francis (1674–79); in the
left transept, the **Cappella di
Sant'Ignazio**, with a sumptuous high
altar by Andrea Pozzo. In the first chapel
to the left of the nave are frescoes by Pier
Francesco Mola.

Museo Barracco
*Palazzo Piccola Farnesina, Corso Vittorio
    Emanuele*
Tel. (06) 6540848

Open Tues, Thurs 9am–2pm, 5–7pm;
   Wed, Fri, Sat 9am–2pm; Sun
   9am–12.30pm
Closed Mon
📷 ✗ *by arrangement* 🎧 🏛 ☑
A small but high quality collection of
classical, Egyptian, and Assyrian art
brought together by Baron Giovanni
Barracco in the late 19thC. It was
donated to the city in 1902, and is worth
visiting for its rare Egyptian and Greek
originals. The former include a relief of
the court official **Nofer★** (c. 2750 BC) –
possibly the oldest piece of Egyptian
sculpture in Italy; the latter, an elegantly
stylized **Head of a Youth ★** (late 6thC or
early 5thC BC).

Musei Capitolini (*Capitoline Museums*) ☆☆
Piazza del Campidoglio
Tel. (06) 6782862
Open Tues, Thurs 9am–2pm, 5–8pm;
   Wed, Fri 9am–2pm; Sat 9am–2pm,
   9–11.30pm; Sun 9am–1pm
Closed Mon
📷 🎧 🏛 ♿ ⛶

The **Palazzo Nuovo** and **Palazzo dei
Conservatori** stand on either side of
Michelangelo's Piazza del Campidoglio,
site of the historic Capitol. The first
palace houses the **Museo Capitolino**, the
second, the **Sale dei Conservatori**, the
Museo del Palazzo dei Conservatori and
the **Pinacoteca Capitolina**. Together,
the museums are known as the Musei
Capitolini and comprise the oldest public
art collection in the world, celebrated for
classical sculpture.
   The museums stay open late on
Saturday evenings, when the Piazza del
Campidoglio is perhaps at its most
spectacular. The famous bronze
equestrian statue of **Marcus Aurelius**,
dating from Imperial times, has been
temporarily removed for restoration, but
the giant, floodlit, marble statues of the
Dioscuri, Castor and Pollux, crowning
the monumental steps leading up to the
piazza, are still an impressive sight.
Museo Capitolino
Among the famous works of ancient art
are the **Capitoline Venus ★** a Roman
copy of a Greek original; the **Dying
Gaul ★** another Roman copy; and the
Mosaic of the Doves ★ a charming
Imperial work discovered in the Villa
Adriana at Tivoli. A large collection of
Roman portrait busts includes a moving
portrayal of the **Blind Homer** and a
1stC AD bust of a **Lady of the Flavian
Era ★** remarkable for its tender realism
and contrasting beauty of smooth-
textured skin and crisp ringlets.
Sale dei Conservatori
Outstanding classical works include the

Capitoline She-wolf ★ a 6thC BC
Etruscan bronze, and the **Spinario ★** a
1stC BC bronze of a boy removing a thorn
from his foot. There are also 17thC works
by Algardi and Bernini.
Museo del Palazzo dei Conservatori
Highlight of the collection is the graceful
Esquiline Venus ★ dating from the
1stC BC.
Pinacoteca Capitolina
This gloomy gallery houses a fine
collection of pictures dating from the
14thC to the 17thC, with the greatest
emphasis on 17thC Italian works.
16thC collection Important Venetian
pictures include a **Portrait of a Young Man**
by Giovanni Bellini; Titian's **Baptism of
Christ ★** (c. 1507), an early work close to
Giorgione in technique and in the lyrical
beauty of the landscape; also, Veronese's
splendidly rich and festive **Rape of
Europa ★**
17thC collection This includes a double
portrait by van Dyck; some small,
charming, Dutch landscapes;
Caravaggio's darkly sensual **St John the
Baptist ★** Pietro da Cortona's **Rape of the
Sabines ★** (1629); Guercino's vast
altarpiece, the **Burial and Reception into
Heaven of St Petronilla ★** a shadowy,
poetic **Erminia and the Shepherds** by
Lanfranco; and an array of late, silvery
pictures by Guido Reni – his half-length
figures of **Lucretia** and **Cleopatra** are
startlingly sketchy, pale evocations of his
earlier, more operatic treatments.

Museo Nazionale Romano ☆☆
Piazza dei Cinquecento 69
Tel. (06) 460530
Open Tues–Sat 9am–1.45pm, Sun
   9am–12.45pm
Closed Mon
📷 🎧 🅿 🏛 ☑ ♿

This museum has one of the most
celebrated and enjoyable collections of
antique sculpture in the world,
beautifully displayed in the halls and
cloistered gardens of the magnificent
ruins of the Baths of Diocletian – the
kind of setting in which many of the
Roman works would originally have been
seen.
   The museum is famous above all for
the **Ludovisi throne ★★** one of the most
beautiful Greek originals discovered in
Rome. The scene on the front is usually
described as the birth of Aphrodite from
the foam of the sea; the goddess,
radiantly joyful, stretches out her arms to
two attendants.
   Room III on the **ground floor** is the
main showpiece, with 15 statues of
superlative quality. Among them are two
fine copies of Myron's bronze
Discobolos; the **Daughter of Niobe ★** a

Greek original of the 5thC BC, showing the young girl fatally wounded by the arrows of Apollo and Artemis; the contrastingly slender and graceful **Venus of Cyrene** ★ probably a Roman copy of a Greek original, the goddess shown just risen from the sea; and the bronze **Boxer** ★★ signed by Apollonius son of Nestor, sculptor of the Belvedere torso (in the MUSEI VATICANI), a work of the 1stC BC that expresses extreme weariness and dejection through the heavy, abrupt rhythms of the powerfully muscled body and through the coarse, battered face.

Other rooms on the ground floor have fine sarcophagi, mosaics and portrait busts. On the **first floor** are paintings, stuccoes and frescoes from Roman buildings. Note particularly the stuccoes and frescoes from the VILLA FARNESINA, and the reconstruction of a room from the **House of Livia** at Prima Porta. The painting of the garden, glowing with fruit and alive with birds, was one of the most important Roman contributions to classical painting.

Museo Nazionale di Villa Giulia ☆
Viale delle Belle Arti
Tel. (06) 3601951
Open Tues, Thurs – Sat 9am – 2pm; Wed
9am – 6.30pm winter, 9am – 2pm,
3 – 7.30pm summer; Sun 9am – 1pm
Closed Mon
🎫 🎧 📽 🏛 ☑ ♨

The Villa Giulia is an elegant Mannerist building with a lovely nymphaeum. It houses a rich and beautifully displayed collection of Etruscan art.

The outstanding works are on the **ground floor**. In Room VII is a group of terra-cotta sculptures from the temple at Veio – perhaps by Vulca, who worked on the Capitol at Rome. The **Apollo of Veio** ★★ (late 6thC or early 5thC BC) was inspired by archaic Greek art but the powerful movement and crude vigour are wholly Etruscan; it formed part of a group showing Hercules' theft of the holy hind. In Room IX is the sarcophagus of the **Bride and Groom** ★★ from Cerveteri (late 6thC BC); this shows a man and his wife, relaxed and intimate, enjoying a banquet after death; the unswerving belief in the afterlife is touching, but it was the sense of equality between man and woman that shocked the Greeks.

On the **first floor** are many small bronzes, also decorative arts. Notice the beauty of the drawing on caskets and mirrors, often uncannily close to our own era and Picasso: the cylindrical **container from Palestrina** is a fine example. Room XXIX has important sculptures from the temples near Falerii Veteres, including elegant **terra-cotta pedimental figures**.

Museo di Palazzo Venezia
Via del Plebiscito 1
Tel. (06) 6798865
Open Tues – Sat 9am – 2pm, Sun
9am – 1pm
Closed Mon
🎫 ♨ *by appointment only* 🏛
The museum is currently undergoing
extensive reorganization and many rooms
are temporarily closed

The museum is mainly devoted to the decorative arts of medieval and Renaissance Rome. There is a good collection of small Renaissance bronzes; also medals, silver, ivories, tapestries, porcelain and majolica; medieval and Renaissance sculpture, including works by Nicola Pisano and Tino di Camaino; and terra-cotta models by Algardi and Bernini.

There is also a small collection of paintings. These include a **Portrait of a Young Man** by Giovanni Bellini; a **Vision of St Bernard** by Bachiacca (16thC); and two late works by Giambattista Crespi (c.1725) – **David and Abigail** and the **Finding of Moses** – the latter distinguished by the beauty of the dusky light and melancholy landscape.

Musei Vaticani (*Vatican Museums*) ☆☆
Viale Vaticano
Tel. (06) 6982
Open Mon – Sat and last Sun of month:
Oct – Mar 9am – 2pm, Apr – Sept
9am – 5pm. Entrance banned in last hr
before closing time
Closed Sun except last Sun of month
🍴 🎧 📽 🏛 ☑ ♨ ♿

The Vatican palaces are not only incomparably rich in antique sculpture; they also have Michelangelo's Sistine ceiling and Raphael's Stanze, perhaps the two noblest achievements in Western art. In summer the galleries become intolerably crowded and noisy and the authorities have now planned four alternative tours, each indicated by a colour code, to control the vast number of tourists. Yet it is fairly easy to ignore these routes, and perhaps the best way to approach this complex of museums is to decide if you most want to see the works of antiquity or of the Renaissance.

Many visitors are drawn to the Vatican by the fame of the Sistine ceiling; if this is your main interest, then make for it as rapidly as possible, otherwise you will arrive there, tired and sated, at the end of an already long tour. You may then go back into the Stanze, and on to the Pinacoteca. This freedom is easier to achieve in winter, when you may also linger to enjoy something of the beauty of the buildings – the long galleries lined with classical sculpture, the Pigna court, with its giant pine-cone fountain (1stC AD) and the lovely views over the Vatican gardens from the Gallery of the Maps.

Egyptian Museum This was founded by Gregory XVI in 1839. Note especially the huge granite statue of *Queen Tewe*, mother of Rameses II.

Chiaramonti Museum This was designed by the Neoclassical sculptor Antonio Canova. Pause at the top of the stairs to absorb the beauty of his intricate display: the entire length of the long gallery is lined with antique statues, portrait busts, urns and sarcophagi; in the lunettes are Neoclassical paintings. The **Lapidary Gallery** beyond is closed to the public.

Pio-Clementine Museum The museum was founded by Clement XIV and enriched by Pius VI. In **Room VIII**, the Octagonal Court, where Julius II began his great collection, are two of the most celebrated works of antique sculpture: the *Laocoön* ★★ and the *Apollo Belvedere* ★★

The *Laocoön* (2ndC BC) was rediscovered in 1506; Michelangelo and Giuliano da Sangallo rushed to the site, and immediately recognized the statue that Pliny himself had described as "a work to be preferred to all that the arts of painting and sculpture have produced". According to legend, Laocoön was a priest of Apollo who attempted to warn the Trojans against the wooden horse; Apollo as revenge sent serpents to destroy him and his two sons. Michelangelo was deeply impressed by the tragic grandeur and violently expressive movement of the writhing figures.

The grace of the *Apollo Belvedere* (a copy of a 4thC BC Greek original) was lavishly praised by Renaissance and Neoclassical artists and writers; in recent years critics have expressed a low opinion of this once most celebrated work. Its influence may be seen in Canova's vacuous *Perseus* nearby.

Room V (the Gallery of the Statues) has the *Apollo Sauroctonos* ★ a marble Roman copy of a 4thC BC bronze original by Praxiteles; and the *Sleeping Ariadne* ★ after a 2ndC BC Greek original. **Room VII** has the *Cnidian Venus* ★ a celebrated copy of the *Aphrodite* of Praxiteles. In **Room III** is the *Belvedere Torso* ★ a fine Hellenistic sculpture, signed by Apollonius son of Nestor; the power of the superbly muscled, twisting body deeply influenced later artists; echoes of it occur throughout the work of Michelangelo.

Room II has the *Jupiter of Otricoli* ★ a copy of a 4thC BC original, and the classic representation of Jupiter's grandeur and majesty. In **Room I** are two vast porphyry sarcophagi, the **sarcophagus of St Helena** and the **sarcophagus of Constantia** (both 4thC AD); the latter is decorated with putti gathering grapes and with peacocks and lambs.

Gregorian-Etruscan Museum This museum was founded in 1837 by Gregory XVI. It is most celebrated for the **Regolini Galassi tomb** ★ (7thC BC) discovered at Cerveteri in 1836 (**Room II**). The tomb held three burials. The inner chamber contained the remains of a woman named Larthia, and yielded an astonishing wealth of Etruscan jewellery; note especially the large gold breastplate and the lavish gold fibula ornamented with rows of tiny ducks and winged animals, which suggest the influence of Eastern art. In **Room III** is the *Mars of Todi* ★ (4thC BC), one of few surviving large Etruscan bronzes, whose strange, sprightly pose is derived from archaic Greek art. **Rooms XIV – XVIII** feature a collection of Greek and Etruscan vases.

Room of the Biga The **biga** is a splendid chariot, reconstructed from ancient fragments by Franzoni in the 18thC. From here, the visitor passes through the **Gallery of the Candelabra**, decorated with antique marble candelabra, the **Gallery of the Tapestries**, the **Gallery of the Maps** and some less interesting rooms, to the Raphael Stanze.

Raphael Stanze ★★ Julius II commissioned the young Raphael to decorate these rooms in 1508.

    Room 1: Stanza dell'Incendio (1514–17). This room is the first on the tour, but was painted mainly by Raphael's assistants. The scenes glorify the power of the pope; the *Fire in the Borgo* ★ shows Leo IV extinguishing, with the sign of the cross, the terrible fire of 847. The composition was entirely new and deeply influential: the main event is thrust into the background; the enlarged foreground figures attain the grandeur of classical tragedy, deepened by the inclusion of Aeneas and Anchises escaping from the legendary flames of Troy.

    Room II: Stanza della Segnatura (1508–11). The frescoes here celebrate the ideas of Truth, Beauty and Goodness, conveying a humanist faith in the unity of classical philosophy and Christian learning. On one wall, the *Disputà* is a vision of the Church Triumphant, with the faithful adoring the Host, and the Trinity encircled by saints and martyrs. Opposite, the *School of Athens* represents a different aspect of Truth, through the philosophers of antiquity. At the center stand Plato and Aristotle, their philosophies suggested, with brilliant simplicity, by their gestures;

Plato points to the sky, Aristotle to the earth. Above them rises a majestic coffered vault, a vision of the future grandeur of St Peter's.

The vividness of Raphael's treatment of so abstract a theme depends on the variety and aptness of expression and gesture, and on the immediacy of several portraits. Plato resembles Leonardo; to the far right is Raphael himself, with Sodoma. Heraclitus, in the foreground, his head on his hand, is a portrait of Michelangelo; the figure is apparently a late addition, painted in homage after the unveiling of the Sistine Chapel. These portraits drew a parallel between the glory of Athens and the Rome of Julius II. The grandeur of the two frescoes was entirely new; their spaciousness, and the beautiful relationship between the groups of figures, makes them one of the most perfect achievements of High Renaissance design.

Above the window, *Parnassus*, a celebration of Beauty, shows Apollo surrounded by the Muses and the poets of antiquity. In the lunette opposite is a graceful frieze of the three *Virtues*, representing the Good; below are two much damaged frescoes showing the *Institution of Law*.

Room III: Stanza di Eliodoro (1512–14). The theme of these four frescoes is divine intervention in aid of the Church; dramatic events from Christian history glorify the papacy of Julius II. The harmony of the Segnatura yields to a more expressive style in *Leo I Repulsing Attila* and the *Expulsion of Heliodorus*; the latter shows Heliodorus driven from the temple of Jerusalem by an angelic horseman – it is full of strong lighting effects, violent emotion, and powerful rhythms. In the *Mass of Bolsena*, the rich colour of the Swiss guards suggests the influence of Venetian painting. The visionary beauty of the *Liberation of St Peter* depends entirely on effects of light; in the center, the black grating of the prison emphasizes the heavenly light of the angel, brilliantly reflected in the soldier's armour.

Room IV: Sala di Costantino (1517–24). This room was finished by assistants after Raphael's death. Giulio Romano's *Battle of the Milvian Bridge* is deeply influenced by antique sarcophagi reliefs.

Loggia of Raphael The pilasters and arches of this long gallery were covered by Raphael and his pupils with stuccoes and grotesques – a kind of classical ornament, delicate and fanciful, that had recently been rediscovered in the DOMUS AUREA. In the vaults of the bays are paintings known as *Raphael's Bible*.

Chapel of Nicholas V ★ This was frescoed by Fra Angelico from 1447–49, with the assistance of Benozzo Gozzoli. In the three lunettes are six scenes from the *Life of St Stephen*; beneath are five scenes from the *Life of St Lawrence*. Fra Angelico's vivid, delicately-coloured narratives here attained a new weight and dignity.

Borgia Apartments In the **Room of the Saints ★** the lavish ornament and deep blues and golds of Pintoricchio's rich decorative style contrast with the purity of Fra Angelico's work in the Chapel of Nicholas V. Pintoricchio's style was more suited to the taste of the dissolute Borgia Pope, Alexander VI.

Collection of Modern Religious Art This includes work by American and European artists, notably Bacon, Chagall, de Chirico, Dix, Manzù, Moore, Sutherland, Ben Shahn and Severini. Yet the total effect is somehow depressing; the predominant style, determinedly avant-garde, is a watered down Expressionism.

Sistine Chapel ★★ The chapel was originally built by Sixtus IV (c. 1475) and the walls beautifully decorated throughout by 15thC Florentine and Umbrian artists including Perugino, Botticelli, Cosimo Rosselli and Domenico Ghirlandaio. The side walls still bear these original frescoes, illustrating, on the right, the *Life of Moses* and, on the left, the *Life of Christ*; clear parallels are drawn between the two texts. Most beautiful are Botticelli's *Trials of Moses*, a work stylistically close to his famous *Primavera* in Florence, and Perugino's *Christ Giving the Keys to St Peter*, where the even light and poetic mastery of perspective contrast sharply with the busy narratives of the Florentine frescoes.

Ceiling In 1508, Michelangelo overcame his initial reluctance and began to fresco the Sistine ceiling. In four years he had completed perhaps the noblest of all works of art. The physical effort alone was incredible; Michelangelo described himself as having "a goiter from this strain. . . I feel the back of my brain upon my neck. . . My brush above my face continually makes it a splendid floor by dripping down".

First, he enlivened the simple barrel vault and established a flowing rhythm by a painted architectural framework. In the center are nine scenes from Genesis. They are 1 the *Separation of Light and Darkness*, 2 the *Creation of the Sun*, 3 the *Separation of Land and Water*, 4 the *Creation of Adam*, 5 the *Creation of Eve*, 6 the *Fall and Expulsion from Paradise*, 7 the *Sacrifice of Noah*, 8 the

VATICAN MUSEUMS TOP TEN

The museums are too vast and their collections too important to be visited in a hurry, but this list narrows down your choice to some of the most celebrated and lovely of the Vatican treasures.

1 ***Laocoön*** (Pio-Clementine Museum)
2 ***Apollo Belvedere*** (Pio-Clementine Museum)
3 ***Belvedere Torso*** (Pio-Clementine Museum)
4 ***Regolini Galassi Tomb*** (Gregorian-Etruscan Museum)
5 Raphael: ***School of Athens*** (Raphael Stanze, Stanza della Segnatura)
6 Perugino: ***Christ Giving the Keys to St Peter*** (Sistine Chapel, N wall)
7 Michelangelo: ***Creation of Adam*** (Sistine Chapel, ceiling)
8 Michelangelo: ***Last Judgment*** (Sistine Chapel, W wall)
9 Melozzo da Forlì: ***Musician Angels*** (Pinacoteca)
10 Raphael: ***Madonna of Foligno*** (Pinacoteca)

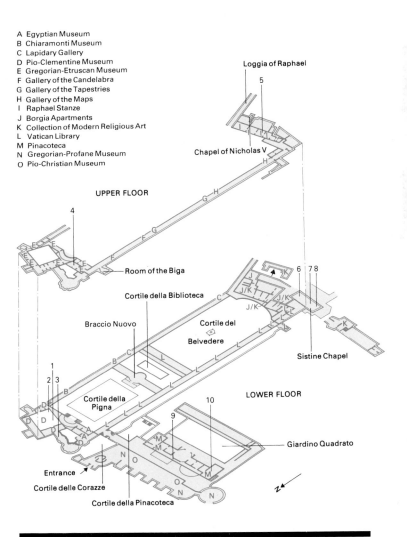

A Egyptian Museum
B Chiaramonti Museum
C Lapidary Gallery
D Pio-Clementine Museum
E Gregorian-Etruscan Museum
F Gallery of the Candelabra
G Gallery of the Tapestries
H Gallery of the Maps
I Raphael Stanze
J Borgia Apartments
K Collection of Modern Religious Art
L Vatican Library
M Pinacoteca
N Gregorian-Profane Museum
O Pio-Christian Museum

Loggia of Raphael

Chapel of Nicholas V

UPPER FLOOR

Room of the Biga

Cortile della Biblioteca

Braccio Nuovo

Cortile del
Belvedere

Sistine Chapel

LOWER FLOOR

Cortile della
Pigna

Giardino Quadrato

Entrance

Cortile delle Corazze

Cortile della Pinacoteca

Flood and **9** the ***Drunkenness of Noah***. The last pictures in the story were painted first; the cycle reveals a clear progression towards a broader and more monumental style. Compare, for example, the rich grouping and detail of the *Flood* – the detail hardly visible from the floor – with the simplicity of the later ***Fall and Expulsion***, where the soft, yielding pose of Eve contrasts forcefully with the tormented figures driven into a desolate world. Still later, and still more powerfully conceived, is the ***Creation of Adam*** where, at the touch of God's finger (perhaps the most moving and celebrated gesture in art), the inert beauty of Adam quickens with energy.

Large scenes alternate with small ones, and the latter are framed with beautiful male nudes, or *Ignudi*, whose immense variety of poses display Michelangelo's complete mastery of the nude. The *Ignudi* defy a precise interpretation and yet in a sense they are at the center of Michelangelo's art. As Kenneth Clark wrote, "Their physical beauty is an image of divine perfection; their alert and vigorous movements an expression of divine energy".

Below them are the mighty figures of the *Prophets* and *Sibyls* who foretold Christ's birth; their grandeur and latent energy contrast with the grieving figures of the *Ancestors of Christ* in the dark spandrels below. In the four corner spandrels are Old Testament scenes associated with the salvation of Israel, anticipating the distortions and irrational space of Mannerist art; the ***Death of Haman*** (in which the dramatically foreshortened body derives from the *Laocoön*) and the ***Brazen Serpent*** are full of violent movement.

Last Judgment This later masterpiece by Michelangelo was begun in 1533, and expresses the despair of the troubled years that followed the Sack of Rome in 1527. It occupies the entire end wall of the chapel.

At the center, the terrible figure of Christ the Judge condemns the damned; the Virgin turns from his anger; the huge, menacing figures of saints and martyrs clamour for vengeance. St Bartholomew holds a flayed skin with a desolate portrait of Michelangelo. Below, the dead awaken at the last trump; the damned are dragged to Hell and beaten by Charon in his boat. The dark pessimism of the fresco is unrelieved; the joy of the elect plays little part; the colours are murky; the figures massive and heavy; the expressions violently distorted.

Vatican Library In Room X is the **Odyssey landscape series ★** found on the Esquiline in 1848, the most complete

known cycle of Hellenistic landscapes; also the ***Aldobrandini Wedding ★*** the only Roman fresco known in the 17thC and 18thC, and deeply revered by classical artists of this period.

Braccio Nuovo This "new wing" of the Chiaramonti Museum was in fact opened in 1822. It is one of the most successful of the Neoclassical galleries and is famous for the ***Augustus of Porta Prima ★*** showing the Emperor, in military dress, as the symbol of Imperial power.

Pinacoteca The Vatican picture gallery houses an exceptionally fine collection, which tends to be overshadowed by the preceding works by Raphael and Michelangelo.

In Rooms II – VII the regional schools of early Renaissance painting are well represented. In **Room II**, the monumentality of Giotto's **Stefaneschi triptych ★** (c. 1330–35) contrasts with the sweet Sienese poetry of Giovanni di Paolo's night *Nativity*. In **Room III** the Renaissance grandeur of Filippo Lippi's *Coronation of the Virgin* may be compared with Fra Angelico's backward look at the fantasies of Gothic landscape in *St Nicholas of Bari ★* **Room IV** has Melozzo da Forlì's ***Musician Angels ★*** and his fresco of the ***Inauguration of the Vatican Library ★*** (1477), in which the beauty of the perspective emphasizes his link with Piero della Francesca.

Room VIII has three great altarpieces by Raphael. These move from the sweet, Peruginesque grace of the early ***Coronation of the Virgin ★*** (1505) to the drama and elaborate poses of his last work, the ***Transfiguration ★*** (1519–20). The ***Madonna of Foligno ★★*** (1511–12) is a lovely work of his full maturity. **Room IX** has Leonardo's unfinished *St Jerome* and a *Pietà* by Bellini; **Room X**, Titian's *Madonna of the Frari* and works by Veronese.

The Baroque altarpieces in **Room XII** show the rich complexity of stylistic trends in the early 17thC. The theatrical, frozen emotion of Caravaggio's *Deposition ★* contrasts with the clarity and warm humanity of Domenichino's ***Last Communion of St Jerome ★*** There is an unusually Caravaggesque Guido Reni, the ***Crucifixion of St Peter***, and an unusually Baroque Poussin, the ***Martyrdom of St Erasmus ★***; also, fine works by Guercino and Sacchi. Pictures by Pietro da Cortona in **Room XIII** include the soft, almost Rococo ***Madonna Appearing to St Francis ★***

Gregorian-Profane Museum This collection of pagan antiquities features Roman Imperial sculpture, urns and sarcophagi.

Pio-Christian Museum This is mainly a

collection of sarcophagi from the cemeteries of the Early Christians.

Palazzo del Quirinale
Piazza del Quirinale
Tel. (06) 4699
Visits by appointment only: write to Ufficio Intendenza, Palazzo del Quirinale, Rome 00137

The Quirinal Palace, now the residence of the President of the Republic and formerly of the kings of Italy (1870–1944), was originally used as a summer retreat by the popes. Many celebrated architects – notably Maderno, Bernini and Fuga – have been associated with various phases of the building, begun in 1573.

On the grand staircase is Melozzo da Forlì's magnificent late 15thC fresco, **Christ in Glory** ★ taken from the church of Santi Apostoli. The **Sala dei Corazzieri** is decorated with a Baroque frieze of illusionistic architecture by Agostino Tassi and with figures by Lanfranco, Saraceni and Gentileschi. The **Cappella Paolina** has superb contemporary stuccoes by Martino Ferabosco. The **Galleria** was decorated, under the direction of Pietro da Cortona, by the leading artists of the day – including Lauri, Dughet and Mola; the outstanding work is Mola's **Joseph Recognizing His Brothers** ★ (1657), a composition influenced by Raphael.

The **Cappella dell'Annunciata** has the most beautiful decorations in the palace, commissioned by Paul V from Guido Reni (1609–12). On the altar is the **Annunciation** ★ – its idealized grace contrasting with the naturalism of the pictures on the side walls. These depict the **Birth of the Virgin** ★ and the **Madonna Sewing** ★ in a tender poetry reminiscent of 15thC Florentine art. On the dome is the **Madonna in Glory** ★ – its composition and radiant golden light both indebted to Correggio.

Outside the palace, in the Piazza del Quirinale, is an ancient obelisk flanked by Imperial statues of the **Dioscuri**, Castor and Pollux.

Raphael Stanze See MUSEI VATICANI.

Sant'Agnese in Agone
Piazza Navona
🏛

The famous facade of Sant'Agnese is largely the work of Borromini. Inside are sumptuous Baroque decorations. The dome was frescoed by Ciro Ferri, the pendentives by Gaulli. The seven altars have splendid marble reliefs by sculptors including Caffa, Campi,

Ferrata and Raggi. Outstanding are Ferrata's **St Agnes on the Pyre** ★ (1660, second on right from central door), a compromise between the classicism of Algardi and the emotional intensity of Bernini; also, his **Stoning of St Emerenziana** (begun 1660, third on right); and Raggi's more Baroque **Death of St Cecilia** (1660–67, third on left). In the oratory beneath the church is Algardi's last work, the **Miracle of the Hair of St Agnes** (c.1653).

Sant'Agnese fuori le Mura
Via Nomentana
This much-restored early Christian church, some way out of the city center, is worth visiting for its fine 7thC Byzantine **apse mosaic** ★ With eloquent simplicity, this shows the hand of God reaching down to place a crown on the head of St Agnes, who stands, in Byzantine dress, with the sword of her execution at her feet.

Sant'Agostino
Piazza di Sant'Agostino
This early Renaissance church with remodelled 18thC interior contains (first chapel on left) Caravaggio's **Madonna of Loreto** ★★ (1603–5); the muddy feet and torn bonnets of the pilgrims scandalized contemporary taste; today we are more moved by the picture's compassionate and tender naturalism. On the third pillar, left of the nave, is Raphael's **Prophet Isaiah**, said by Vasari to have been repainted after the unveiling of the Sistine ceiling. Beneath it is Andrea Sansovino's **Madonna and Child with St Anne** ★ (1512); on the entrance wall, Jacopo Sansovino's **Madonna del Parto** ★ (1521); in the right transept, **Sts Augustine, John and Jerome** by Guercino.

Sant'Andrea delle Fratte
Via Capo le Case
🏛
The dome and campanile are among Borromini's most exuberant creations. To right and left of the high altar stand Bernini's **Angel with the Superscription** ★ and **Angel with the Crown of Thorns** ★ (both 1667–69); these were the two angels sculpted by Bernini for the Ponte Sant'Angelo: those now standing on the bridge were produced by his workshop.

Sant'Andrea della Valle
Corso Vittorio Emanuele
🏛
Here architecture, painting and sculpture unite to create a sumptuous Baroque interior. Many of the greatest artists of

the early 17thC are represented, and the conflict between the Baroque of Lanfranco and the elegant classicism of Domenichino suggests the rich complexity of stylistic trends during this period.

The vault of the apse is decorated with frescoes of the *Life of St Andrew* ★ by Domenichino, framed by graceful stuccoes; one of the most moving scenes is *St John the Baptist Revealing Christ to Sts Peter and Andrew*, in which the figures are beautifully related to a fine Venetian landscape. The walls of the apse were frescoed in 1650–51 by Mattia Preti.

The dome is frescoed with an *Assumption of the Virgin* ★ by Lanfranco (1625–27). This work, deeply influenced by Correggio, introduced the overwhelming illusionism of the High Baroque. The splendid **pendentives** ★ are by Domenichino; the powerful figures contrast with his more restrained style in the apse, and suggest Domenichino's response to the triumphant Baroque of Lanfranco.

In the right transept is Lanfranco's *Vision of St Andrew Avellino*; in the first chapel on the right, a relief and statues by Antonio Raggi (1671–75); in the first chapel on the left, *St Martha* by Francesco Mochi and *St John the Baptist* by Pietro Bernini.

Santa Bibiana
Via Giolitti
🏛

The two greatest artists of the Roman High Baroque collaborated here in the early development of that style. The facade was designed by Bernini; his statue of *St Bibiana* ★ (1624–26), above the high altar, established the type of the Baroque female saint, where emotion is expressed by the fluttering lines of the drapery and by the ecstatic tenderness of expression. In his frescoes of the *Life of St Bibiana* ★ (left wall of nave), Pietro da Cortona brought a new boldness to 17thC classicism: the dramatic events unfold against a background of grandiose Imperial architecture.

San Carlo ai Catinari
Piazza Cairoli

This church is rich in splendid Baroque works. The **pendentives** ★ are frescoed by Domenichino (c.1630); over the high altar is a powerful late altarpiece by Pietro da Cortona, the *Procession of St Charles Borromeo* (1667); Lanfranco's last work, a fresco of *St Charles Borromeo in Glory* (1647), decorates the apse. Other works are by Preti, Lanfranco, Andrea Sacchi and Guido Reni.

Santa Cecilia in Trastevere
Via di San Michele
🏛 ❧

This ancient church was founded before the 5thC and is now a charming blend of later styles, with a pretty garden, a 12thC portico and campanile, and a graceful Rococo facade by Fuga (1741).

A Gothic **canopy** ★ (1283) by Arnolfo di Cambio covers the high altar; beneath is Stefano Maderno's touching statue of the body of the martyred *St Cecilia* ★ (1600), showing the saint exactly as she was found in 1589. In the apse is a 9thC **mosaic** which sadly lacks the power and grandeur of other contemporary Roman examples.

In the first chapel to the right is an early 17thC altarpiece of the *Martyrdom of St Cecilia* by Guido Reni; also, contemporary landscapes by the Flemish artist Paul Bril.

The adjacent convent has Pietro Cavallini's *Last Judgment* ★ (1293), an important work in which the dignity of the figures heralds the innovations of Giotto.

San Clemente
Via di San Giovanni in Laterano
🏛

With an upper and lower church built over the remains of a Roman mithraeum, San Clemente is the best preserved medieval basilica in Rome; it was restored in the 18thC. The upper church has a richly symbolic 12thC **apse mosaic** ★ featuring an elaborately branching Tree of Life, the four Doctors of the Church and other figures, and exotic birds and animals.

The **Cappella di Santa Caterina** has important frescoes by Masolino (c.1428). On the left of the chapel is the *Life of St Catherine*; on the right, scenes from the *Life of St Ambrose of Milan*; above the altar, the *Crucifixion* ★ This large, sombre work, with its deep space, contrasts with the lighter, more graceful and anecdotal style of the other scenes; some critics have detected in it the hand of Masaccio.

In the lower church are some damaged but still interesting examples of Italian Romanesque painting, dating from the 9thC and 11thC.

Santi Cosma e Damiano
Via dei Fori Imperiali
🏛

This church was founded by Felix IV in 527 in the former library of the Emperor Vespasian's Forum of Peace. The 6thC **mosaics** ★★ of the apse and triumphal arch are among the most beautiful of all medieval works.

In the apse, the majestic gold-robed figure of the Risen Christ appears in splendour before the pink and orange clouds of a dawn sky. On either side are Sts Peter and Paul, who turn to present the martyrs, Cosmas and Damian, for whom the church is named. The noble, hieratic figures, with wide staring eyes, opened a new era in Byzantine art; the bearded Christ leads onto those severe Christ Pantocrators that look down from so many Byzantine domes. The composition was very influential, both on medieval and Renaissance art.

Santa Costanza
Via Nomentana
🏛

An unusual centrally-planned church, thought to have been built as a mausoleum for the Emperor Constantine's daughter, Constantia, whose vast porphyry sarcophagus is now in the MUSEI VATICANI.

The vaults of the ambulatory are decorated with charming **mosaics ★** of birds, flowers, putti and geometrical designs. These date from the 4thC, and in both imagery and style – which is reminiscent of a floor mosaic – they seem entirely pagan, although the symbols have been interpreted as an obscure Christian allegory.

Santa Croce in Gerusalemme
Piazza Santa Croce in Gerusalemme
🏛

Santa Croce was founded in the 4thC, rebuilt in the 12thC and embellished and restored in the 18thC; traditionally it is associated with a relic of the True Cross. The Baroque vault painting, *Apparition of the Cross*, is by the Neapolitan artist Corrado Giaquinto (c.1744). In the apse is a late 15thC fresco of the *Invention of the True Cross* by an unknown painter. The lovely late 15thC **mosaic ★** in the Cappella di Sant'Elena is attributed to Melozzo da Forlì.

San Francesco a Ripa
Piazza San Francesco d'Assisi
This 13thC church, rebuilt in the 17thC, has Bernini's *Death of the Blessed Ludovica Albertoni ★* (1674, fourth chapel on left), a deeply moving image of pain and mystical rapture. The dying saint lies on a great marble couch at the end of the dark chapel, appearing like a vision above the altar; the bright light falls from a concealed window on the left. The painting above is by Gaulli; other pictures are by Vouet (first chapel on left) and Salviati (second chapel on left).

San Giovanni in Laterano
Piazza San Giovanni in Laterano
🏛
The cathedral of Rome and first church of Christendom has been rebuilt many times since its foundation in the 4thC; the interior was completely remodelled by Borromini from 1646–50.

Some works from the earlier period remain: Jacopo Torriti's **apse mosaic** (1291) was reset in the 19thC; the papal altar is covered by a fine Gothic **canopy** (1367) with frescoes attributed to Barna di Siena (1368).

Yet the great beauty of the church is the splendidly rich and brilliantly imaginative decorative scheme by Borromini. The niches of the nave piers hold vast 18thC statues of the *Apostles* by Carlo Maratta; above are 17thC reliefs and oval paintings; the whole is embellished by fresh floral ornament and interlaced palm leaves. On the vault of the aisles are charming winged cherubs' heads. Against many of the piers are monuments designed to incorporate many of the old medieval and Renaissance tombs.

The **cloister ★** has superb Cosmati decorations by Jacopo and Pietro Vassalletto (1223–30).

San Gregorio Magno
Via di San Gregorio
The church is of ancient foundation but has been rebuilt many times; the severe 17thC facade is by Soria. The most interesting works of art are in the three chapels in the grounds of the church.

The **Cappella di Santa Silvia** has a lovely fresco by Guido Reni, *God the Father with Angels ★* (1608). In the **Cappella di Sant'Andrea**, Domenichino's austerely classical *Flagellation of St Andrew ★* challenges the greater richness and freedom of Reni's *St Andrew Led to Execution ★* (both 1608). In the **Cappella di Santa Barbara** are frescoes by Viviani (1602), and a contemporary statue of *St Gregory* by Nicolas Cordier.

Sant'Ignazio
Via di Sant'Ignazio
This Baroque church is celebrated for the spectacular illusionistic frescoes by Andrea Pozzo on the vaults of the nave, apse and right transept. Over the crossing, painted on canvas, is a cupola in feigned perspective, also by Pozzo. The fresco on the ceiling of the nave is an elaborate allegory of the missionary work of the Jesuits, the *Apotheosis of St Ignatius* (1691–94). The illusion only works from a single point in the nave, which is marked.

Baroque ceilings in Rome

Illusionism was used by Baroque artists to astonish and overwhelm the spectator and to enhance the emotional intensity of a work of art. Many of the most dazzling achievements of the Italian Baroque are found on ceilings; in many churches the nave or dome seems open to the sky, involving the spectator in the heavenly vision thus revealed and, by the sense of infinite space, creating a mood of spiritual exaltation. The ceiling tradition that developed in Rome was inspired above all by Correggio's famous domes in Parma (see *NORTH & NORTH WEST ITALY*). Most of the major Roman ceilings date from the last third of the 17thC and are located conveniently close to one another.

This tour begins with the CHIESA NUOVA on the Corso Vittorio Emanuele. This church has frescoes of different periods by Pietro da Cortona. The frescoes in the dome (the *Holy Trinity in Glory*) and in the half-dome of the apse (the *Assumption of the Virgin*) look back to Correggio. Yet the two compositions are united: the Virgin seems to ascend, across the real space of the church, towards the Holy Trinity; the linking of real and painted space is characteristically Baroque. These two works are far more illusionistic than the clearly framed picture on the nave ceiling (the *Vision of St Philip Neri*) painted in a later, more classicizing period of Cortona's career.

Unfortunately, it is no longer possible to visit the greatest of all early Baroque ceilings, Annibale Carracci's *Loves of the Gods* (1597–1600) in the gallery of the **Palazzo Farnese**, S of the Corso Vittorio. The palace is now the French Embassy and the gallery is closed to the general public. Instead, walk E along the Corso Vittorio, past the strangely curving facade of the Palazzo Massimo alle Colonne, to SANT' ANDREA DELLA VALLE. Lanfranco's dome (the *Assumption of the Virgin*) was directly inspired by Correggio; it opened up a new era in High Baroque painting. Bright shafts of light (from the windows at the top of the lantern) flicker across Lanfranco's fresco, enhancing the beauty of his vision of celestial glory; the inclusion of real light in a painted composition was a new and dramatic Baroque device. The conflict between Lanfranco and the more classical Domenichino is fascinatingly evident in the decorations. Domenichino's pendentives reveal his desire to rival the new, dynamic art of Lanfranco; their dramatic power contrasts with his much calmer paintings in the vault of the apse, painted exactly as if they were easel paintings, with no concession to their position.

Further along the Corso Vittorio is the GESÙ. The vault was frescoed by Gaulli, a Genoese artist who had studied Correggio's domes in Parma and later joined Bernini's studio in Rome. In his fresco (the *Adoration of the Name of Jesus*), the church seems to open to reveal a vision of the monogram *IHS* in an aureole of light and adored by the heavenly host. The painted figures spill over the coffered vault, and tormented souls hurtle into the darkness of the nave. The soft colour is Correggiesque, and the figures have

A detail of the vault of Sant' Ignazio, frescoed by Andrea Pozzo.

something of the ecstatic tenderness of late Bernini; the quality of lightness and grace heralds the late Baroque.

North of the Gesù, past Piazza del Collegio Romano, is SANT' IGNAZIO, facing a lilting Rococo square. The fresco on the vault of the nave is Andrea Pozzo's *Apotheosis of St Ignatius*. Pozzo's ceiling does not derive from Correggio; instead he extends the space of the church by a virtuoso display of feigned architecture; a second storey seems to open out above the nave. The illusionism only works from one spot; from elsewhere the columns tumble about us; Waterhouse has wondered whether "the Jesuits conceived this bizarre scheme of decoration as a lesson to those who were not altogether on the correct spot in their religious beliefs".

From this church, the swan song of the late Baroque, turn S to Piazza Venezia; beyond the Foro Traiano (Trajan's Forum), on the right of the Via Panisperna, is **Santi Domenico e Sisto**. The ceiling fresco, the *Apotheosis of St Dominic* (1674) is by Domenico Maria Canuti, and its light and lovely style was influenced by the Gesù; small, ethereal figures melt into infinite space. The center of the ceiling opens, yet here it is framed by a complex architectural framework – a tradition more Genoese than Roman.

If you still have time left, you can now walk N to the Palazzo Barberini (GALLERIA NAZIONALE D' ARTE ANTICA) where Pietro da Cortona's great fresco, the *Allegory of Divine Providence* (1633–39) is perhaps the finest illusionist masterpiece of the Italian late Baroque. Cortona created a painted architectural framework; figures appear above and before it, and seem to float in a vast open space just above the spectator's head.

San Lorenzo in Lucina
Piazza San Lorenzo in Lucina

The church dates from the 5thC, but has been much rebuilt. The **Cappella Fonseca** (fourth chapel on right) was designed by Bernini; his bust of *Gabriele Fonseca* (probably 1670s) is a late, intensely emotional work; the doctor gazes with fervent adoration at the mystery of the altar. In other chapels are paintings by the Caravaggesque artists, Saraceni and Vouet; Vouet's scenes from the *Life of St Francis* (fifth chapel on left) show a highly original interpretation of Caravaggio's chiaroscuro.

San Luigi dei Francesi
Piazza di San Luigi dei Francesi

The French national church of Rome dates from the 16thC; the interior was remodelled in the late 18thC and has fine stucco decorations by Antoine Derizet.

In the second chapel on the right are Domenichino's frescoes of scenes from the *Life of St Cecilia* ★ (1616–17). These are elegant and severely classical works, deeply influenced by Raphael, and looking forward to Poussin; their muted colours and refined, clear compositions contrast sharply with Caravaggio's canvases in the fifth chapel on the left (1599–1602).

These are *St Matthew and the Angel* ★ replacing an earlier version which the clergy had found indecorous, the *Calling of St Matthew* ★★ and the *Martyrdom of St Matthew* ★ The *Calling* introduced a new and vivid narrative realism into Roman painting; the setting is squalid, the figures taken from low life; only the famous cellar light suggests the profound significance of the drama.

Santa Maria d'Aracoeli
Piazza d'Aracoeli
🏛

An ancient church, built on the site of the Temple of Juno Moneta, Santa Maria d'Aracoeli was rebuilt in an austere Romanesque style by the Franciscans in the 13thC. The church movingly suggests those layers of history that are so characteristic of Rome; the interior has classical columns and fine Cosmati work in the monuments and pavement.

To the right of the central door is Andrea Bregno's **tomb of Cardinal d'Albret** (1485); nearby is Donatello's **tomb of Giovanni Crivelli** (1432). The first chapel on the right is decorated with frescoes of the *Life of St Bernardine* ★ (c.1485) by Pintoricchio. These are works of Pintoricchio's early maturity, and show him breaking away from his master Perugino to develop his own, richly decorative and festive style. In the

right transept, the **Cappella Savelli** has two late 13thC Cosmati tombs. In the left transept is the **monument to Cardinal Matteo d'Acquasparta** ★ perhaps the most gorgeous of all the Cosmatesque monuments in this church.

Santa Maria in Domnica
Via della Navicella
🏛

This early Christian church was altered in the reign of Pope Paschal 1 (817–24) and restored in the 16thC by Andrea Sansovino. There is a lovely 9thC **mosaic** ★ in the apse, featuring for the first time the *Virgin Enthroned in Glory*. The fine frescoed **frieze** ★ over the windows is by Perin del Vaga, based on drawings by Giulio Romano.

Santa Maria di Loreto
Piazza Venezia

Located in Trajan's Forum, this Renaissance church contains (left of altar) Duquesnoy's *St Susannah* ★ (c.1626–33). The classical purity of this work, highly celebrated in the 17thC, sharply challenged the drama of Bernini's *St Bibiana* (see SANTA BIBIANA).

Santa Maria Maggiore
Piazza di Santa Maria Maggiore
🏛

The fourth of the great patriarchal basilicas was built by Sixtus III soon after the Council of Ephesus in 431, and dedicated to the Virgin Mary, whom the Council had officially proclaimed the mother of God. The facade was designed by Fuga (1741), who also made substantial alterations to the interior of the medieval church. Despite this, the rich 5thC **mosaics** ★★ have survived virtually intact.

The **nave mosaics** are a series of 27 small scenes (originally 42) that are tantalizingly difficult to see. The figures are shown frontally, the colours are vivid, and the settings are full of lively naturalistic detail; the narrative unfolds with charming simplicity and directness. These traditional works contrast with the grandeur of the mosaics on the triumphal arch, which, although only a few years later, form a prelude to the early Byzantine style. The **arch mosaics** are the first gospel stories to be illustrated in art and show scenes from the *Infancy of Christ*. In the **Annunciation**, Mary is shown robed and jewelled as a Byzantine princess, suggesting the new grandeur bestowed upon her by the Council of Ephesus. Beside her, the enthroned Christ Child receives the gifts of three exotically clad kings. The 13thC **apse mosaic** is by Jacopo Torriti.

Across the nave, two splendid early Baroque chapels rival one another in their profusion of coloured marble, frescoes and sculpture. The third chapel on the right, the **Cappella Sistina**, contains the **Oratory of the Crib** ★ with 13thC reliefs by Arnolfo di Cambio. Third on the left, the **Cappella Paolina** has decorations in the pendentives by Cavalier d'Arpino; in the dome, by Cigoli; in the lunettes around the **tomb of Clement VIII**, by Guido Reni and Lanfranco. These chapels were highly influential in establishing a taste for splendid, highly-coloured and lavish decoration that lasted well into the 18thC. At the end of the right aisle is the fine Cosmatesque **tomb of Cardinal Rodriguez** (d. 1299).

Santa Maria sopra Minerva
Piazza della Minerva
The only Gothic church interior in Rome was brutally restored in the 19thC. On the left of the high altar, Michelangelo's **Risen Christ** is an unusually feeble work. The **Cappella Carafa** ★ (1488–92), in the right transept, is richly frescoed by the Florentine Filippino Lippi. Bernini's **tomb of Maria Raggi** (1643) is on the fifth pier of the nave.

Santa Maria della Pace
Vicolo della Pace
🏛
This is a delightful early Renaissance church, with a charming Baroque facade by Pietro da Cortona. The first chapel on the right was painted by Raphael for Agostino Chigi in 1514. His frescoed **Sibyls** ★ and **Prophets** were incomplete at his death and were finished by Sebastiano del Piombo. The fresco over the altar of the first chapel on the left is by Peruzzi (1516), who is most famous for his work in the VILLA FARNESINA.

Santa Maria del Popolo
Piazza del Popolo
🏛
This medieval church was rebuilt in the Renaissance and later enriched and restored under the direction of Bernini. It has fine works of art from many periods.

The first chapel on the right has frescoes by Pintoricchio (1485–89). The second chapel, lavishly decorated with marble, has a late 17thC altarpiece by Maratta, showing the influence of Raphael. The apse has splendid **frescoes** ★ by Pintoricchio in the vault, and two important **tombs** by the Florentine sculptor, Andrea Sansovino (c. 1505).

The first chapel on the left of the transept has the **Assumption of the Virgin** by Annibale Carracci and two side pictures by Caravaggio, the **Conversion of St Paul** ★ and the **Martyrdom of St Peter** ★ (both 1601–2). The harsh realism of the two Caravaggios introduced a new kind of religious imagery: steep foreshortening and grand gestures draw the spectator into the drama; the darkness behind St Peter creates a sense of horror.

The second chapel on the left of the nave is the **Cappella Chigi** ★★ built and decorated by Raphael as a mausoleum for the family of Agostino Chigi. The chapel is rich with sculpture, mosaic and painting, yet is restrained and harmonious, and altogether one of the most perfect achievements of the High Renaissance. The altarpiece of the **Birth of the Virgin** is by Sebastiano del Piombo. The dome mosaics and two obelisk tombs were designed by Raphael; the frescoes are by Salviati. Of the four statues of prophets, **Jonah** and **Elijah** are by Lorenzetto after Raphael; the **Daniel** and **Habakkuk** are by Bernini. The strong relationship between these figures, linked by dramatic gestures, transforms the space of the entire chapel.

Santa Maria in Trastevere
Piazza di Santa Maria in Trastevere
This early Christian church has been rebuilt many times, but is still famous for its mosaics. Those on the facade date from the 12thC or 13thC but are heavily restored. In the upper apse, the 12thC mosaic of the **Virgin and Christ Enthroned** ★ is an outstanding work of the Byzantine revival, charged with solemn majesty. Beneath it are Pietro Cavallini's mosaics of scenes from the **Life of the Virgin and Christ** ★ (1291). These are Cavallini's most famous early works; their lively narrative quality and greater concern with depth contrast with the renewal of early Christian simplicity in the upper mosaic.

The ceiling was designed by Domenichino, who painted the **Assumption** (1617) in the center. The fifth chapel on the left is the Baroque **Cappella Avila**, designed by Antonio Gherardi (c. 1680).

Santa Maria della Vittoria
Via XX Settembre
This fine Baroque church is mainly famous for the **Cappella Cornaro** (left transept), containing Bernini's **Ecstasy of St Teresa** ★★ (c. 1647–52). This is Bernini's most perfect attempt to render mystical experience credible. St Teresa described how the angel pierced her heart with "a long barb of gold. . . The exquisite joy caused by this incomparable

pain is so excessive that the soul cannot want it to cease". The white marble group, framed by darker columns, seems to float before us as if in a vision; golden light floods down from a concealed source; carved spectators, as in theater boxes, eagerly discuss the event.

San Martino ai Monti
Via Lanza
The church contains frescoed landscapes by Gaspard Dughet (1647–51), illustrating stories from the Carmelite legends; the series introduced into landscape painting a new sense of the immensity of the natural world.

St Peter's See SAN PIETRO IN VATICANO.

San Pietro in Montorio
Via Garibaldi
🏛
Outside this church stands Bramante's **Tempietto**, one of the most famous architectural statements of the High Renaissance. Inside, in the first chapel on the right, is Sebastiano del Piombo's **Flagellation** ★ (c.1520), based on drawings by Michelangelo of 1516. In the fourth chapel on the left is Dirck van Baburen's sombrely Caravaggesque **Deposition** (1617).

The second chapel on the left is the **Cappella Raimondi**, designed by Bernini (1638–48) and executed by pupils. The chapel is important for its early use of a concealed light source, and for the fusion of architecture and sculpture. The tombs show both living and dead images of the deceased, a theme that is more commonly found in French Gothic than Italian sculpture.

San Pietro in Vaticano (*St Peter's*) ☆☆
Piazza San Pietro
Tel. (06) 6984466
Open Oct–Mar 7am–6pm, Apr–Sept 7am–7pm
✗ ⛪ 🏛 ⚒
In the 17thC, Bernini's inventive genius wonderfully transformed both the interior of Michelangelo's great church and the approach leading up to it. The climax of the pilgrim's journey begins on the **Ponte Sant'Angelo**, where ecstatic angels bear the instruments of the cross; continues through the oval **piazza** – symbol of the all-embracing arms of the Church; and ends inside the basilica with the splendid finale of the **baldacchino** and **throne of St Peter**, which together celebrate the triumph of the Church.
Portico The central **bronze doors** ★ are by Filarete (mid 15thC); the left-hand doors by Giacomo Manzù (1964). Above the

central entrance, on the inside of the facade, is Giotto's damaged **Navicella**; facing it, over the central door, Bernini's relief, **Feed My Sheep**. At the entrance to the Scala Regia – on the right, behind glass doors – is Bernini's **Constantine** ★ (1670) a dramatic portrait of the first Christian Emperor at the moment of his conversion.
Crossing This is dominated by Bernini's **baldacchino** ★★ a gorgeous canopy with four twisted bronze columns, standing over the tomb of St Peter. In the niches of the four crossing piers are statues of saints associated with the four chief relics; Duquesnoy's **St Andrew** ★ (SE), Mochi's **St Veronica** (SW), Bolgi's **St Helena** (NW) and Bernini's **St Longinus** ★ (NE); in the galleries above, against coloured marbles, angels bear their respective relics. In the sunken *confessio* in front of the high altar is Canova's **Pius VI** ★ (1820); at the end of the nave, on the right, Arnolfo di Cambio's **St Peter** ★ (late 13thC).
Apse The magnificent conclusion of this progress, the **throne of St Peter** ★★ was designed by Bernini to enclose the wooden chair believed to have been used by the saint. Above, gilt angels and cherubs float in glory on stucco clouds; at the center, light pours through an oval window on which is outlined an image of the Holy Dove; beneath are bronze figures of the Greek and Latin Fathers of the Church.

The monument on the left is Guglielmo della Porta's **tomb of Paul III** (1551–75); that on the right, Bernini's **tomb of Urban VIII** (1642–47). Both were influenced by Michelangelo's Medici Chapel in Florence. Bernini's richer colour and texture and more dramatic interpretation became the prototype for later Baroque tombs.

It is important first of all to submit to Bernini's gifts as a decorator, but you can now return to the foot of the right aisle for a more detailed tour.
Right aisle In the first chapel is Michelangelo's **Pietà** ★★ The image of the Madonna, grieving over the body of the dead Christ, and holding him on her lap as though he were a child, is Northern; the high finish, and tender, Florentine beauty of the Madonna, are rare in Michelangelo's work.

In the passage behind the second pier are (on the right) Fuga's **tomb of Innocent XII** (d.1700) and (on the left) Bernini's **monument to Countess Matilda**. The third chapel is the **Cappella del Santissimo Sacramento** ★ with a **fresco** by Pietro da Cortona and **ciborium** by Bernini – one of his last great works (1674).

Left aisle The **Cappella della Colonna** (at the apse end) has Algardi's spirited relief of *St Leo Turning Attila away from Rome* ★ (1646–50). Over the door in the passage leading back to the left transept is Bernini's **tomb of Alexander VII** ★ (1672–78). In the passage behind the second pier (on your right, facing towards the high altar) is Pollaiuolo's **tomb of Innocent VIII** ★ (1498); against the first pier (also on the right) is Canova's **monument to the Last Stuarts** ★ (1817–19), a beautiful Neoclassical monument revered by Stendhal. In the first chapel, the late 17thC **font cover** was designed by Carlo Fontana.

Museo Storico
Tel. (06) 6984587
Open Oct–Mar 9am–2pm, Apr–Sept
*   9am–6.30pm*
🎫 ⌑ ☑
Access from left aisle, E of transept
Donatello's **Tabernacle of the Blessed Sacrament** ★ (1432–33), in the Cappella dei Beneficiati, is one of the most perfect Florentine works in Rome. Elsewhere, there are some good early Christian ivories; the **Cross of Justin II** ★ presented to St Peter's in 570 by the Byzantine Emperor Justin II and the Empress Sophia; a rich collection of 17thC and 18thC altar plate; and a full-size plaster model for one of the angels designed by Bernini for the Cappella del Santissimo Sacramento. Pollaiuolo's **tomb of Sixtus IV** ★★ is a work of astonishing technical brilliance, an eloquent tribute to the Christian humanism of Sixtus IV; around the startlingly realistic effigy of the Pope are the seven Virtues; lower down, the nine Muses, with the added personification of Perspective – central to 15thC aesthetics – render homage to their protector.

Grotte Vaticane (*Vatican Grottoes*)
Tel. (06) 6384587
Open Oct–Mar 7am–5pm, Apr–Sept
*   7am–6pm*
📷 𝕏 ⌑
Access from SE corner of crossing
The grottoes have some interesting papal tombs; also the **sarcophagus of Julius Bassus** (late 4thC), an important early Christian sarcophagus; and a mosaic roundel of an **Angel** ★ by Giotto, a fragment of the *Navicella*.

San Pietro in Vincoli ☆
Piazza San Pietro in Vincoli
Michelangelo's tomb for his great patron, Julius II, was originally planned as a vast, free-standing mausoleum for St Peter's; after 42yrs it was finally built here (in the right transept), in an uneasy blend of different styles.
    The celebrated *Moses* ★★ (c.1515)

was conceived as one of several corner figures; Vasari wrote that "Michelangelo expressed in marble the divinity that God first infused in Moses' most holy form". The sculptures to left and right, *Rachel* and *Leah*, are Michelangelo's last finished works; they symbolize active and contemplative life.
    The rest of the monument is by his pupils. In the upper tier, the statues of the *Virgin*, a *Prophet* and a *Sibyl*, are by Raffaello da Montelupo and were greatly scorned by Michelangelo; the ridiculous effigy of *Julius II* is by Boscoli after designs – influenced by Etruscan monuments – by Michelangelo.

Santa Prassede
Via Santa Prassede
Legend relates that Prassede sheltered persecuted Christians and saw 23 of them executed; she mopped up the blood with a sponge, and squeezed it into a well, the site of which is marked in the center of the nave with a porphyry slab.
    The church was originally built in the 9thC and is famous for its glorious medieval mosaics, on the triumphal arch and in the apse, and above all in the small **Cappella di San Zenone** ★ (third on right of nave). Here the walls and vault glow with gold mosaic. Among the rigid figures is Theodora, mother of Pope Paschal I; the chapel was built as her mausoleum and her square halo indicates that she was still alive at the time the chapel was decorated.
    In the right aisle, against the last pillar to the left, is Bernini's **tomb of Monsignor Giambattista Santoni** (d.1592), a very early work.

Santa Pudenziana
Via Urbana
This early Christian church, rebuilt over the centuries, retains a fine **apse mosaic** ★ (5thC) – one of the first surviving examples in Rome. Although restored in the 16thC (when the edges were cut down) and in the 19thC, the mosaic is still remarkable for the lively movements and solid modelling of the Apostles who surround the enthroned Christ. In the background are the four emblems of the Evangelists and a symbolic representation of Jerusalem.
    The first chapel on the left is the Baroque **Cappella Caetani**, with mosaics in the dome after designs by Federico Zuccaro.

Santi Quattro Coronati
Via dei Santi Quattro Coronati
The early 17thC **apse frescoes** in this church of mainly medieval appearance are by Giovanni da San Giovanni, the

only Florentine artist of the period to work mainly in fresco. The Romanesque wall paintings (1246) in the **Oratorio di San Silvestro** are well preserved and historically important but stylistically rather dull.

Sistine Chapel See MUSEI VATICANI.

Vatican Museums See MUSEI VATICANI.

Villa Farnesina
Via della Lungara
Tel. (06) 650831
Open Mon–Sat 8.30am–1.30pm
Closed Sun
📷 �;; 🏛 🐾
This fine Renaissance villa was built between 1508 and 1511 by Baldassare Peruzzi for the Sienese banker Agostino Chigi. The **gallery** or loggia on the ground floor was originally open to the garden, so that Giovanni da Udine's lovely painted arbour seemed to continue the leaves and flowers outside. The fresco cycle, **Cupid and Psyche** ★★ (1517), was designed by Raphael and executed mainly by assistants; it is a light-hearted, witty illustration of the gods of antiquity brought low by the power of love.

In the room next door is Raphael's richly composed **Galatea** ★★ (1511), a fresco celebrated for its varied and apparently effortless arrangement of radiantly beautiful and freely moving figures. In the same room and of the same date is Sebastiano del Piombo's colossal **Polyphemus**. Upstairs, the **Salone delle Prospettive** or Hall of Perspectives is decorated with *trompe l'oeil* pictures by Peruzzi. In the next room are frescoes by the Sienese painter Sodoma (1511–12).

SPERLONGA
Latina, Lazio Map A6

The old part of Sperlonga is a cluster of white-washed houses, glittering in the sun and perched on a steep, rocky slope at the edge of the sea; dark, narrow passages and staircase-lanes climb steeply from the harbour to the market place, linked by tunnels hewn out of the solid rock; arched doorways frame spectacular views of the sea beneath.

Grotta di Tiberio e Museo Nazionale Archeologico ✩
1km (½ mile) SE of Sperlonga
Tel. (0771) 54028
Open Tues–Sun 9am–4.30pm
Closed Mon
📷 🐾

In 1957 the large cave near Sperlonga, known as the Grotto of Tiberius, was explored for the first time. The result was one of the most romantic finds of the 20thC, linking the gloomy and tyrannical Emperor Tiberius with the sculptors of the celebrated *Laocoön* (see Musei Vaticani, ROME).

The deep and sheltered cave was once the Emperor's summer banqueting hall, richly decorated with glass wall-mosaics and large groups of sculpture.

Many statues were rediscovered and are now in the nearby museum; the most interesting are three groups illustrating scenes from Homer's *Odyssey*: the **Blinding of Polyphemus**, **Scylla Attacking the Ship of Odysseus** and the **Wreck of Odysseus' Last Ship**. On the ship of the second is an inscription bearing the names of Atanodorus, Polidorus and Agesandrus, whom Pliny named as the sculptors of the *Laocoön*. These works, like that famous Hellenistic statue, are intensely expressive and powerful.

SUBIACO
Roma, Lazio Map B4

A mountain village in lovely countryside, Subiaco is celebrated for the extraordinarily evocative Sacro Speco or monastery of San Benedetto. The village was originally the site of a villa built by Nero, of which interesting ruins remain. In the early 6thC, St Benedict founded his monastic order here, beginning his devotional life in the Sacro Speco or grotto from which the monastery takes its name.

Monastero di Santa Scolastica
Tel. (0774) 85525
Open 9am–12.30pm, 4–7pm
📷 🚌 🊿 🐾
The convent of Santa Scolastica was founded by St Benedict's twin sister in the 6thC. It has three **cloisters**, of which the third is the work of Luca and Jacopo Cosma, a celebrated family of Roman marble workers.

Sacro Speco (*Monastero di San Benedetto*) ✩
Tel. (0774) 85039
Open 9am–12.30pm, 3–6pm
📷 🏚 🐾
The Sacro Speco grew up haphazardly in the 13thC, around little hermitages hewn out of the rocky cliffside. It consists of an upper and lower church and several chapels. Three corridors, frescoed by 14thC and 15thC Umbrian and Sienese artists, lead into the irregular sequence of

frescoed rooms that comprise the **upper church**.

The most interesting works in the **lower church** are in the **Cappella di San Gregorio ★** Here, the different styles of two Roman artists are apparent in the 12thC and 13thC frescoes – one classical, the other livelier and more individual (notice especially the elegance of his *Pope Gregory IX Consecrating an Altar*); the chapel also has a famous portrait of *St Francis* (1223), painted before he was canonized.

Further on, the walls of the lower church are frescoed with scenes from the *Life of St Benedict* (c.1280), their lively expression and gesture and genre-like detail deriving from popular narrative art.

Stairs lead down to the oldest part of the monastery, the **Sacro Speco** itself, also known as the Grotto of Angels and preserving a 9thC fresco.

SULMONA
L'Aquila, Abruzzi Map C5

Once an important Roman town, birthplace of the poet Ovid, Sulmona was ruled by the dukes of Spoleto during the Middle Ages and retains a number of fine medieval monuments. A school of goldsmiths prospered here in the 14thC and 15thC. The town enjoys a spectacular location, surrounded by a great ring of mountains.

Duomo
The lovely porch is part of the original medieval building. In the crypt are a remarkable 12thC stone relief of the *Madonna and Child* and a 15thC silver gilt bust of *St Pamphilus*.

Museo Civico
Annunziata, Corso Ovidio
Tel. (0864) 53276 (local tourist office)
Open Tues – Sun 9am – noon, 4 – 6.30pm
Closed Mon
☎ ✗ *tel. (0864) 52333* ▯ ❤
The Annunziata (begun 1320) is an impressive civic building – an oddly pleasing blend of Gothic, Renaissance and Baroque styles. One part of it houses the museum, which is worth visiting for its fine collection of Abruzzi goldsmiths' work.

TARQUINIA
Viterbo, Lazio Map A2

Once among the grandest cities of Etruria, Tarquinia rose to power and prosperity in the 7thC BC. It fell to Rome

in the 3rdC BC, yet flourished under the Empire. In the Middle Ages the Etruscan city was destroyed and a new town, Corneto, was built nearby. In the 20thC, this picturesque medieval town, with winding streets, towers and turrets, took the name of Tarquinia. The famed Etruscan necropolis nearby has brought to Tarquinia the full weight of modern tourism and it is best avoided in the high season.

Museo Nazionale Tarquiniese ☆
Palazzo Vitelleschi, Piazza Cavour
Tel. (0766) 856036
Open Tues – Sun 9am – 2pm
Closed Mon
☎ ▯ 🏛
A rich collection of Etruscan art is displayed in an elegant Renaissance palace with lovely courtyard and loggia. On the ground floor, among many fine stone sarcophagi, note especially the **tomb of Laris Pulena**, with an expressive portrait and long Etruscan inscription, and the **tomb of Velthu the Magistrate ★** a powerfully realistic portrayal of a paunchy, middle-aged man mournfully sunk in reverie (mid 3rdC BC).

On the first floor are Greek and Etruscan vases, and the celebrated terracotta *Winged Horses ★* from a temple relief. On the second floor (currently under restoration) are detached tomb frescoes from, among others, the **Tomb of the Ship** (500BC), the **Tomb of the Olympiads** (600BC) and the **Tomb of the Triclinium ★** (500BC). The first is remarkable for the strange juxtaposition of ship and feasting men and women – perhaps a reference to the journey of death; the last, for the subtle and witty grace of the dancing figures.

Necropoli ☆
3km (2 miles) E of Tarquinia
☎ 🏃 *start from Museo, above*
The necropolis is famous for its unrivalled collection of Etruscan wall paintings. These depict, in scenes of hunting, fishing, dancing and, above all, feasting, the blissful happiness that was believed to wait beyond the Etruscan grave.

The frescoes develop from the vivid, exuberant detail of the early tombs to a greater elegance and restraint. One of the earliest tombs that may be visited is the **Tomb of the Bulls ★** (c.540BC), showing *Achilles Ambushing Troilus*. The slightly stiff composition, charming array of odd objects and vivid natural detail contrast with the stately frieze of horsemen and stylized trees against a neutral background of the later **Tomb of the Baron ★** (c.500BC).

TERAMO
Abruzzi Map D4

Teramo is now a mainly modern town,
but Roman remains and fragments of
medieval walls and palaces recall its past
importance. The greatest period of
prosperity was under the Angevins
(12thC to 14thC), when the town was an
important center of goldsmiths' work.

Cattedrale
Piazza Martiri di Libertà
🏛

The Gothic portal has mosaics and reliefs
by Deodato di Cosma (1332). The glory
of the interior is a magnificent **silver altar
frontal ★★** (1433–48) by Niccolò da
Guardiagrele. Niccolò was the greatest of
the Abruzzi goldsmiths; his early works
are late Gothic, but here the influence of
Ghiberti's Baptistry doors is evident in
the elegant compositions and delicate
modelling (see Florence, *NORTH
CENTRAL ITALY*). On the right wall of
the presbytery is a **polyptych** by Jacobello
del Fiore (1450).

TIVOLI
Roma, Lazio Map B4

An ancient city that continued to prosper
throughout the Middle Ages, Tivoli has
fine Roman remains and medieval
churches. It was painted and extolled by
many 17thC and 18thC artists and
writers, who came here for the poetic
charm of the cascades, the wild beauty of
the Campagna and the dramatic ruins of
the Temple of Vesta and Hadrian's so-
called Villa Adriana.

Duomo
Via del Duomo
In the fourth chapel on the right of the
nave is a 13thC wooden group of the
Deposition ★ Wooden sculptures are rare
in Lazio, and this is an exceptionally fine
work – restrained and deeply moving.

San Giovanni
Viale Trieste
The presbytery has a fine series of late
15thC frescoes that have been associated
with the name of Melozzo da Forlì – a
somewhat unlikely attribution.

San Silvestro
Piazza di Colonnato
The frescoes in the apse are related to the
12thC Roman school. In generally poor
condition, they show ***Christ Handing
down the Law to St Peter*** and scenes
from the ***Life of St Silvester***.

Villa d'Este ☆ ☆
Piazza Trento 1
Tel. (0774) 22070
Open Tues – Sun 9am – 1½hrs before sunset
Closed Mon
📷 🛏 🅿 🏛 ☑ ♨

The most extravagant and varied water
garden in the world was designed in the
1570s by Pirro Ligorio for Cardinal
Ippolito II d'Este. The interior of the villa
is frescoed by 16thC artists but the main
attraction remains the garden.

The magical effects of water range
from the great cascades of the **Organ
Fountain ★** (a monumental structure
encrusted with fantastic Mannerist
imagery) to the still, slow water of the
fishpond pools. A tour should also take in
the mossy **Terrace of the Hundred
Fountains ★** where many thin jets play in
the green shade; the **Ovato Fountain ★** by
Pirro Ligorio; the **Rometta Fountain**,
where models represent the monuments
of antiquity; and the **Dragon Fountain**,
again by Pirro Ligorio.

The pleasure of the 16thC
connoisseur would have been heightened
by the witty references to antiquity; he
would have suffered tedious dousings
from the *giochi d'acqua* or hidden sprays
that were so fashionable in the 16thC,
and been startled by acoustic effects (the
Organ Fountain originally played music).

TUSCANIA
Viterbo, Lazio Map A2

Tuscania is a largely medieval town,
famous for its Romanesque churches and
Etruscan remains. In 1971 it was badly
damaged in an earthquake.

Santa Maria Maggiore
Strada Santa Maria
🏛
This lovely Romanesque church with
richly decorated portals has a fine 13thC
font in the right aisle. In the apse is a
large 14thC fresco of the *Last Judgment*.

San Pietro
Via del Comune
🏛
The church dates from the 8thC and has
a 12thC facade of outstanding beauty.
The 12thC Byzantine **frescoes** in the apse
were damaged in the earthquake.

VEIO
Roma, Lazio Map A3

Veio once dominated a large and
powerful Etruscan territory. It fell to
Rome in 396BC after a long siege. The

city was an important artistic center, renowned for terra-cotta sculpture. The only Etruscan artist mentioned by name in literary sources is the Veientine master, Vulca, whose works are described by Pliny; the celebrated *Apollo of Veio*, now in the Museo Nazionale di Villa Giulia, ROME, came from the Temple of Portinaccio just outside the city.

Necropoli
1km (⅔ mile) N of Isola Farnese
Tel. (06) 3790116
Open Tues–Sun: summer 9am–1hr before
sunset, winter 10am–2pm
Closed Mon
🚻 🍴
Vast cemeteries lay outside the ancient city, and the ruins, in a splendid ravine, may be reached from the dramatic hill-top village of Isola Farnese. The most interesting of the many tombs is the **Tomba Campana**. This has faded frescoes featuring fabulous monsters and animals – the earliest significant example of Etruscan painting. The nearby **Ponte Sodo** is an extraordinary tunnel bored through the tufa cliffs.

VITERBO
Lazio Map B2

Viterbo was an important city in the 12thC and 13thC when many papal elections were held here. It suffered terrible bomb damage in World War II but still has an impressive but rather charmless area of medieval buildings.

Cattedrale
Piazza San Lorenzo
The cathedral has two paintings by the Baroque artist Giovanni Romanelli: a *Holy Family* in the right aisle and *St Lawrence in Glory* in the presbytery. The *Christ Redeemer with Four Saints* (1472) in the left aisle is by Girolamo da Cremona (1472).

Museo Civico ☆
Piazza Crispi
Tel. (0761) 30810
Open Mon–Sat: Apr–Sept
8.30am–1.30pm, 3.30–6pm,
Oct–Mar 9am–1.30pm; Sun
9am–1pm
Closed public holidays
🚻 🏚 🏛 ☑ 🌱
The museum is housed in the convent buildings adjoining SANTA MARIA DELLA VERITA. The ground floor rooms display a good collection of Etruscan finds.

The picture gallery on the first floor is at present closed for restoration. The outstanding work, and by far the finest

painting in the city, is Sebastiano del Piombo's *Pietà* ★★ based on a lost drawing by Michelangelo of 1512. The powerful, tragic figures are Michelangelesque, but the colouristic brilliance and the intense poetry of the nocturnal landscape reflect Sebastiano's Venetian origins. Another work, the *Flagellation*, is obviously related to Sebastiano's mural in San Pietro in Montorio, ROME, and is generally attributed to him.

The collection also includes a locally celebrated 14thC *Madonna* by Vitale da Bologna; and, from the 17thC, two paintings by Giovanni Romanelli and an early altarpiece by Salvator Rosa.

San Francesco
Piazza San Francesco
This 13thC church was extensively rebuilt in 1953. It has two important monuments: in the left transept, the **tomb of Clement IV** (d.1268), attributed to Pietro di Oderisio; in the right transept, the **tomb of Adrian V** ★ (d.1276), attributed to Arnolfo di Cambio.

Santa Maria della Verità
Via Lorenzo da Viterbo
The Cappella Mazzatosta, to the right of the nave, has a lovely fresco cycle of the *Life of the Virgin* ★ (1469) by Lorenzo da Viterbo. The frescoes were badly damaged by a bomb, but have been wonderfully restored.

VULCI
Viterbo, Lazio Map A2

Once a powerful Etruscan city, famous for its sculpture, Vulci was conquered by the Romans in 280BC. It is now a vast archaeological site in one of the most wild and desolate areas of central Italy.

Museo Nazionale di Vulci
Ponte Abbadia, 10km (6 miles) N of
Montalto di Castro
Tel. (0761) 437787
Open Tues–Sun: May–Sept 9am–2pm,
3–7pm; Oct–Apr 10am–4pm
Closed Mon
📷 🍴 🌱
This is a small and isolated museum of Etruscan artifacts, housed in a medieval fortified abbey known as the **Abbadia**. It is notable chiefly for its ceramics and jewellery, the latter taken from tombs. The view of the Abbadia, on the edge of a rocky abyss, across the **Ponte di Vulci** – a spectacular Etrusco-Roman bridge spanning the river Fiora – was dear to the writers and travellers of the Romantic era.

SOUTHERN ITALY

Southern Italy – the largely mountainous area extending S from Campania into the heel (Apulia), the instep (Basilicata) and the toe (Calabria) of Italy – is today still noticeably poorer and more backward than the North, although it has recently started to pick up economically. Apulia, with its ports of Bari, Brindisi and Taranto, and its flatter and more fertile terrain, has long been an exception to the rule, enjoying a relatively rich concentration of Romanesque architecture and sculpture. Generally, however, the art lover visiting the South will have to travel long distances between important monuments; the most outstanding works are often isolated treasures, imports or lucky finds retrieved from a cultural ambiance otherwise destroyed.

CAMPANIA, BASILICATA *and* CALABRIA

The South begins at Naples, capital of Campania and the one great city of the region. The Bay of Naples has been a coastal resort since Roman times, and

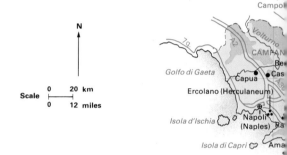

the eruption of Vesuvius that buried Pompeii and Herculaneum has made these excavated towns, and the archaeological museum at Naples that houses most of their treasures, a mecca for students of ancient art. To the N and E of Naples, Campania is a pleasant countryside of hills and valleys but past Salerno, to the S, the landscape becomes bleak and forbidding and remains so into Basilicata and Calabria. The astonishing survival of the Greek temples at Paestum, which stood undisturbed for centuries, indicates the slow cultural tick-over of these areas in the post-Classical period.

Cosenza, capital of northern Calabria, is probably the most attractive city of the interior: it has a fervent new town and a beautifully picturesque and sleepy medieval quarter. Apart from Altomonte, housing a fragment by Simone Martini, Calabria's charming small towns have little art, while a commercial and administrative capital such as Reggio, with its important archaeological museum housing the two superb, over-lifesize 5thC BC bronzes recently found near Riace, has little charm. Basilicata is dry and dusty and one of the poorest parts of Italy; with the exception of the spectacularly situated town of Matera, it has virtually nothing to offer the art lover.

PUGLIA (*Apulia*)

Apulia is less mountainous than the rest of southern Italy, but it is still rocky – providing good stone for its fine churches with their celebrated architectural sculpture. The coastline offers the classic Mediterranean ingredients and is in fact far superior to many other more famous rivieras, and much less crowded. Beside its peaceful harbours stand the great castles built by the Emperor Frederick II and pretty replicas and variations on the famous 11thC pilgrimage church of San Nicola at Bari; although relics of the brilliant court of the Emperor are few, these churches and their lively animal sculpture have survived, scarcely altered or damaged, up and down the E coast.

In later periods Apulia produced little native culture, importing largely from Venice during the Renaissance (there are outstanding pictures by the Vivarini at Bari) and from Naples during the Baroque era. Yet the small town of Lecce enjoyed a remarkable flowering of architecture and sculpture in the 17thC and 18thC, exploiting its extremely ductile local stone as if it were stucco. Last but not least, modern archaeology has unearthed treasures from what was a flourishing and sometimes very rich area in Greek and then Roman times; the museum at Taranto rivals that of Reggio.

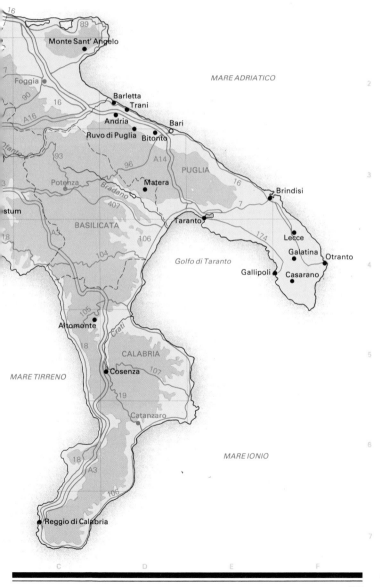

ALTOMONTE
Cosenza, Calabria Map C5

Set up in the remote and scenic hills circling Castrovillari and the Sibari plain, Altomonte is a pleasant village with a pretty 14thC church.

Museo Civico
Piazza Santa Maria della Consolazione
Tel. (0981) 948261
Open 9am–noon, 4.30–7.30pm
🔲 ✗ 💯

On the left wall of the second room, Simone Martini's *St Ladislas* ★ is assumed to be the last remaining fragment of a polyptych commissioned in 1326 by Filippo Sangineto, a local baron. St Ladislas has been given a moustache and a splendidly baronial expression. His forward-stepping body is established in space with just a few touches of masterly delicacy (notably around the left arm).

Santa Maria della Consolazione
Piazza Santa Maria della Consolazione
🏛

Founded in the 14thC by Filippo Sangineto, as part of a Dominican monastery, this fine Gothic church has been recently restored. It contains a good 14thC **recumbent effigy** on the left of the nave and, against the back wall of the choir, the grand mid-14thC **tomb of Filippo Sangineto**, the founder, by a southern Italian sculptor influenced by Tino di Camaino; the tomb is unusually well preserved, even down to the paint.

AMALFI
Salerno, Campania Map B3

Amalfi has long been a famous seaside beauty-spot: in the nature of such places, it can become either sad and tatty or exploitative and vulgar, depending on the season. It was once (9thC–11thC) a powerful medieval trading republic.

Duomo
Piazza del Duomo
Open 8.30am–7.30pm in summer,
otherwise usual church opening times
💯 🏛

The cathedral was founded in the 9thC, but the basis of its present appearance is early 13thC Romanesque, heavily restored in the 19thC. As such, it is rather charming, and the early 20thC mosaics and frescoes (in a diluted Symbolist, Puvis de Chavannes-like style) complement it well; contributing to the overall effect is the majolica facing, common throughout the peninsula.

The niello bronze doors were made in 1060 in Constantinople; their colours are faded and the design is hard to make out. The pretty 13thC "Moorish" cloister – with very steeply pointed, interlaced arches – is littered with odd remnants, including a Roman sarcophagus featuring the **Rape of Persephone**.

ANDRIA
Bari, Puglia Map D2

This is a busy town, predominantly modern in aspect; its medieval churches have been much altered.

Palazzo Vescovile
Via Corrado
🔲 *but gratuity appreciated*
Ask the sacristan of the adjacent Duomo to let you in

The archbishops' palace contains a 15thC **Madonna** by the Venetian painter, Antonio Vivarini.

San Domenico
Piazza Manfredi
🏛

This church is 18thC in appearance, although founded in the 14thC. In the sacristy, the bust of **Francesco II del Balzo** ★ (1472) by Francesco Laurana is worth seeking out; even in a male portrait Laurana manages to impart a kind of fragility to the marble.

BARI
Puglia Map D3

Bari is not only the capital of Apulia but also in many ways a model to which other towns of the region conform. It has an old and a new town – the old town on a promontory beside the harbour, the new town grid-like, busy and almost entirely separate. The old town has become poor, even a slum – despite its famous churches; the modern town is clean and slick.

Castello Svevo
Piazza Federico II di Svevia
Tel. (080) 214361
Open Tues–Sat 9am–1pm, 4–7pm, Sun 9am–1pm
Closed Mon
🔲 💬

The castle was built by the Emperor Frederick II to protect his lands from invasion, particularly by the pope, during the 1230s. It is well preserved and features the occasional finely carved capital. Through a door beneath the external staircase of the central courtyard is a sculpture gallery, containing casts of the finest 11thC–14thC church sculpture of the region.

Cattedrale ☆
Piazza del Duomo
🏛

This outstanding Romanesque building, dating from the late 12thC, no longer contains any notable works of art. It should, however, be visited for its superb external sculpture; notice especially the wonderfully inventive carvings of the E **window**.

Pinacoteca Provinciale
Via Spalato 19
Tel. (080) 334445
Open Tues–Sat 9am–1pm, 4–7pm, Sun 9am–1pm
Closed Mon
📷 🎧

The building is undergoing repairs that affect some of the rooms of the museum, the more important contents of which are displayed in other rooms. In these, despite the additions, the permanent scheme of exhibition remains unaltered. The arrangement is chronological with interpolations.

Room I displays sculpture and painting from the 11thC to the 13thC. Outstanding pieces are two panels from Santa Margherita in Bisceglie, a *St Margaret* and a *St Nicholas*, both local Byzantinizing works of the 13thC.

Room II contains an important **series of paintings** ★ by Antonio and Bartolommeo Vivarini, the 15thC Venetian painters who ran a flourishing export drive to this part of the world. First comes a *Madonna* by Bartolommeo, a very early work, in which he is still reproducing the closely worked and lavish late Gothic surface of his father, Antonio. After four nondescript half-length saints from a polyptych, there is an **altarpiece** by Antonio – a late work (1467, although the date and signature are false) in which he is now copying the sculptural, much gaunter figures of his son. The *Annunciation* that follows is by Bartolommeo, commissioned by the same Venetian canon who ordered the *Madonna and Saints* by Bartolommeo of SAN NICOLA, and of equally high quality, although not in such good condition. The last **polyptych**, again by Bartolommeo, is the most typical of his usual production.

In **Room III** is a large, fairly late and rather dull *St Peter Martyr* by Giovanni Bellini. A good-quality late Tintoretto, *St Roch and the Plague-stricken*, hangs next to a work by a local early 16thC practitioner of the Venetian idiom, Constantino da Monopoli, and to a

workshop Paolo Veronese. Best in the room is an altarpiece by Paris Bordone of the *Madonna and Saints* ★

Rooms IV and **V** are devoted to local artists. The first has a large *St Michael* after a design by Memlinc, clearly by a contemporary Italian; the second, a **polyptych** by the prolific but weak painter known only by his initials "Z. T.".

Returning to the entrance and proceeding in the opposite direction, one passes through **Room XV**, with a pleasant collection of **19thC paintings**, to **Room XIV**, with **Baroque and Rococo works**. The best of these are by Giaquinto – not the full-size *Nativity of the Baptist*, but the *Triumph of Joseph* ★ and the *Nativity*, both small-scale pictures, in which Giaquinto's Rococo effervescence remains undissipated by the demands of scale and grandeur. There are also two good works, an *Annunciation* and a *Visitation*, by Francesco de Mura, a local follower of Solimena.

San Nicola ☆
Piazza San Nicola
🎧 🏛

There are two magnificent Romanesque churches in Bari old town; but whereas the CATTEDRALE is interesting now only as a building and for its external sculpture, San Nicola also retains some splendid furnishings.

Its greatest treasure is the famous **bishop's throne** ★ set on a round dais behind the main altar. The carving, of the late 12thC, is not fundamentally different from the run of southern Italian sculpture; the motif of the Atlas figures who struggle to hold up the seat is quite common, too; but the object as a whole, in all its hand-made crookedness, is a joy to look upon. The figures of the capitals of the **baldacchino** of the altar, just in front, are also worth studying; slightly earlier, of the mid12thC, they are more delicate.

Around the main apse, the reliefs of the **monument to Bona Sforza** are late 16thC Neopolitan Michelangelizing work. On the altar of the **crypt** is an interesting 14thC icon of *St Nicholas*, of Hungarian manufacture. In the left transept is one of Bartolommeo Vivarini's best paintings, signed and dated 1476, showing the *Madonna and Saints* ★ in a walled garden.

Tesoro
Tel. (080) 211269
Open Mon, Tues, Thurs, Fri 10am–noon
Closed Wed, Sat, Sun
📷 *but gratuity appreciated*
The church treasury contains 13thC and 14thC reliquaries and precious objects.

BARLETTA
Bari, Puglia Map D2

Barletta is one of the pleasantest and
most important of the cluster of small
towns surrounding Bari, and it has rather
more to offer artistically than the rest.
The area in the immediate vicinity of the
Duomo is typically sleepy.

Museo Civico/Pinacoteca de Nittis
Via Cavour 8
Tel. (0883) 33005
Open Tues – Sun 9am – 1pm
Closed Mon
📷 ♿

The Museo Civico proper is a typical
minor-town collection, combining
Garibaldi trophies with Greek vases and
crude medieval and Renaissance statuary
rescued from local churches. Attached to
it, however, are the contents of the
studio of the native Giuseppe de Nittis
(1846 – 84), successful painter of 1870s
Paris and close friend of Degas.

In the entrance corridor of the
museum is, furthermore, one of the most
stupendous pieces of sculpture to have
survived from the Middle Ages. This is
what is reasonably assumed to be a
portrait of the *Emperor Frederick II* ★★ a
half-length, over-lifesize stone figure
retrieved from a nearby ruined castle in
the 19thC. The classicism of this figure is
extremely advanced: indeed, the only
feature that clearly separates it from the
kind of Roman consular bust it
reproduces is the more energetic twist of
the neck. The Roman haircut and the
garland with its trailing fillets are
striking; but the lips and nose are
unfortunately damaged, giving this
severe image a more conversational air
than was intended. Even so, it is a worthy
and rare monument to the reported
sophistication of Frederick's court.

The **de Nittis collection** (across the
courtyard) is arranged chronologically,
beginning in **Room I** with works of the
late 1860s. The *Passing Train* (1869)
anticipates the landscape realism and
search for striking viewpoints of the
Dutch Hague School.

In **Room II**, *Spring*★ (1871) is
perhaps the most interesting work in the
whole collection; the effect of white and
pink blossom is extremely close to
contemporary Impressionism. Later
pictures, notably those in **Room VIII**,
show the influence of Degas. In **Room IX**
there are some nice snow scenes; at the
end of **Room XI**, the *Garden Scenes*
painted in 1884 show de Nittis still a
weak Impressionist but a still-life painter
of rare talent.

Sant' Andrea
Via Sant' Andrea
🏛

This little 12thC church is at the top of a
steep flight of steps, and is entered by a
modern door on the right. The front
portal preserves an unusual *Christ
between the Madonna and St John the
Baptist and Two Angels* – clearly
Apulian in workmanship, but perhaps
imitating a Byzantine scheme. Ask the
sacristan to let you into the sacristy,
where there is an important *Madonna*★
(1483) by Alvise Vivarini.

San Sepolcro
Corso Vittorio Emanuele
🏛

The building is late 13thC, incorporating
Romanesque remains of an earlier
foundation, and is rather charmingly
dark and dank. It contains paintings of no
great interest. Outside, however, stands a
unique example of late antique
bronzework, the **Barletta Colossus** ★
This statue is thought to be 4thC, and
may represent the Emperor
Valentinianus I (364 – 75); in the 14thC
the legs and arms were removed by the
local Dominicans to make a bell, but were
restored in 1491. The armoured trunk is
original, as is the head, with sharp, rather
schematized features.

BENEVENTO
Campania Map B2

Benevento is an uninteresting town, still
serving essentially the same function now
as in Roman times: it lies on the route
between Naples and Apulia, marking the
way with its famous Arco di Traiano. In
the early Middle Ages, it was a power
center into which Campania and Apulia
threatened to be drawn, yet sadly little
survives from this illustrious period.

Arco di Traiano (*Arch of Trajan*) ☆
Via Traiano

Erected by Trajan in AD114, this is one of
the best preserved Roman triumphal
arches, and its unusually rich cladding of
relief sculpture is entirely complete
except for two figures at the top left of the
outer side of the arch (facing away from
the town, down the hill). That said, it
must also be pointed out that the arch is
dirty, and so weathered that the fine
detail is all gone.

What remains is the fluent
composition, the discipline and variety of
the grouping, and the sense of order and
commonweal that the arch was always
intended to convey. Much effort has
been spent on the elucidation of the

individual scenes, but they are too damaged to permit a definite identification, and the current detailed explanations bringing to bear virtually every known circumstance of Trajan's reign are patently imaginary. The scenes must remain generic – ceremonies of giving, welcoming, honouring, worshipping and providing that were part of the daily round of a Roman emperor.

Trajan's era represents an apogee in Roman art: one can compare these reliefs with those honouring Augustus on the Ara Pacis Augustae in Rome, which are much stiffer and more severe; or with those on the inside of the Arco di Tito in Rome, which are much like these but not so grand or confident. (See *SOUTH CENTRAL ITALY*.)

Museo del Sannio
Corso Garibaldi
Tel. (0824) 21818
Open Mon – Sat 9am – 1pm
Closed Sun
🔾 🏛 ✿

The museum occupies a modern building beside the cloister and in the grounds of the ancient church of Santa Sofia. Founded on its present shell-shaped plan in the 8thC, but rebuilt in the 12thC, this unusually subtle, centrally-planned church is some reflection of the cultural importance of Benevento in the 8thC.

The museum, entered through the gates at the right of the church, is primarily archaeological in content. The considerable collection of **statuary** includes Roman copies of Greek originals – notably, in **Room 10**, a *Doryphoros*, or spear-carrier, after Polykleitos (see **NAPLES**, Museo Archeologico Nazionale). There are also Roman copies of Egyptian originals (**Rooms 5 – 9**) coming from the 1stC AD Temple of Isis in Benevento. **Room 11** has vases; then, in **Rooms 12 – 16**, there is more Roman statuary, also some good sarcophagi.

From **Room 17**, exhibiting small-scale pieces, one enters the **12thC cloister**, which has figurated capitals and "Moorish" ornament recalling, for instance, Monreale in Sicily (see *SICILY & SARDINIA*). Across the cloister, one climbs the stairs to a small collection of medieval sculpture and the picture gallery.

There is virtually nothing before the 17thC, and the **Baroque pictures** are almost all in the nature of large religious altarpieces that achieve at best a ponderous monumentality. The small 19thC works in **Room 31** include a group of *Goats* by Jacob Philipp Hackert, a German artist who became court painter at Naples.

BITONTO
Bari, Puglia Map D3

The new town is wrapped around three sides of the old town; at the center is the cathedral, one of the richest examples of Apulian Romanesque.

Cattedrale
Piazza del Duomo
🏛

The church belongs to the second half of the 13thC, but adheres strictly to the model of San Nicola at **BARI**: there has been no evolution in style. **External sculpture** is plentiful – notably the carved capitals of the outside gallery, with their divers beasts. There are more creatures on the jambs of the portal, which has a tympanum featuring *Christ with the Resurrected*, and a lintel showing the *Annunciation* to the *Circumcision* in continuous narrative.

Inside is a well preserved early 13thC carved and intarsiaed marble **pulpit**, with odd half-figures on the aisle side. Over the steps descending to the crypt, note the **Atlas figures**: they are just like those of the bishop's throne in San Nicola.

BRINDISI
Puglia Map E3

Modern Brindisi has taken on a new industrial importance, although it has a sizeable old town with some interesting Romanesque churches. Of the Roman port, which has associations with Caesar, Mark Antony and Virgil (who died here), nothing evocative remains.

San Benedetto ☆
Piazza San Benedetto
🏛

The Norman cathedral of Brindisi has been rebuilt and is an ugly church, although a few patches of 12thC mosaic remain. The loss is made up for by the 11thC round Templar church of San Giovanni al Sepolcro and by the exceptionally charming little late 11thC church and cloister of San Benedetto.

San Benedetto is adorned with fine **Apulian Romanesque sculpture**, with particularly endearing escapees from the bestiary in the capitals of the cloister, on the first, right-hand capital of the nave and on the lintel and jambs of the portal.

Santa Maria del Casale
2km (1¼ miles) N of the city
🔳 🏛

The large, empty, echoing, wooden-roofed late 13thC church preserves several areas of **14thC frescoes**, in particular (covering the entire entrance wall) a *Last Judgment* by Rinaldo da Taranto. This consists of Byzantine forms and a Byzantine iconography translated rather grossly into a Romanesque idiom still ignorant of Gothic. By a different artist, of higher quality but very damaged, are the frescoes in the choir, notably the *Deposition* on the left, where the stylized lines take on some expressive force.

CAPUA
Caserta, Campania Map A2

Once an ancient walled city, lying on the left bank of the river Volturno, Capua is now a sleepy, rather dusty little town of diminished importance.

Museo Campano
Palazzo Antignano, Via Roma
Tel. (0823) 971402
Open Tues – Sat 9am – 2pm, Sun
* 9am – 1pm*
Closed Mon
🔲 🎴 🏛 ☑ ❦

One now usually enters this museum through a pretty garden of palm and lemon trees and up a staircase to the first floor. This means that the tour goes backwards chronologically, ending with the pre-Classical period.

In **Room XXVI**, the Sala Federiciana, is a series of **busts ★** which once decorated a triumphal arch built in the 1230s by Frederick II. These are austere, surprisingly classical works that look forward to the Renaissance. Among the Renaissance works in **Room XXVII** note especially the 16thC **tomb slab of Cristina Ferrero** – a deeply moving work. The small **Pinacoteca** in **Room XXVIII** has a handful of 15thC – 17thC pictures, including a harsh, linear *Deposition* by Bartolommeo Vivarini (15thC).

Rooms I – X contain a large collection of objects of mainly archaeological interest, including small terra-cotta figures and architectural fragments from the 9thC – 6thC BC (note especially in Room VI the pretty bust of a *Woman Holding a Pomegranate*).

From Room X stairs lead down to the ground floor where is displayed a series of statues of *Mothers* (6thC – 1stC BC) dedicated to the Mater Matuta, an ancient Italian divinity of dawn and birth, the remains of whose temple near Santa Maria Capua Vetere were discovered in the late 19thC. These seated women – grim, squat, hunched up, clutching as many as 12 babies – create a weird and moving impression.

CASARANO
Lecce, Puglia Map F4

The town itself is not for visiting, except that one has to go to the Municipio for the keys to the church of Casaranello, a village engulfed by its outskirts.

Santa Maria della Croce
Casaranello, at southern edge of Casarano
Municipio open Mon – Fri 10am – noon
🔲 🎇

The church is a solitary vestige of early Christian culture in southern Italy; although the building was given aisles in the 13thC (the date of the occasional coarse fresco surviving in them), the nave and the crossing cupola are 5thC. Also 5thC are the spare, purely decorative mosaics of the choir and an area of fresco surviving on the vault of the nave, showing the *Life of St Catherine* and the *Last Supper* in a catacomb-like style.

CASERTA
Campania Map A2

Caserta is a dull little town to the N of Naples, dominated by the vast mass of the Palazzo Reale and by the obtrusive presence of the military.

Palazzo Reale ☆☆
Parco Reale
Tel. (0823) 321127
Open 9am – 1.30pm
🆒 *but* 🔲 *Sun* 🎴 🅿 🏛 ❦

The palace of Caserta was begun by the Neapolitan architect Luigi Vanvitelli in 1752 for Charles III, the Bourbon king of Naples. Its sheer magnificence and vast scale – the formal gardens, where nature is ruthlessly controlled and ordered, extend for some 3km (2 miles) to the N – rival and were influenced by Versailles, but Vanvitelli's wonderful scenographic sense makes this an infinitely more exciting building than Versailles.

Through the main gate, a long open gallery sweeps dramatically onward until it merges with the distant greens of the gardens. From the octagonal rotunda in the center are views of the inner courts. From the right of the rotunda an overwhelmingly majestic **staircase ★** leads to the **Appartamenti Reali** or royal apartments, offering vistas that look like "a Piranesi or Bibiena phantasmagoria in solid stone" (Rudolf Wittkower).

The Appartamenti Reali are preceded by three large halls decorated in a rather frigid Neoclassical style. In the wing to the left – the **Appartamento Vecchio** – the first four rooms, dedicated to the Four Seasons, are frescoed with pretty Rococo garlands and figures and the walls are covered with silk. Note especially the charming musicians leaning over balustrades in the **Salone Primavera**, where there are also some good pictures by Francesco de Mura. Further on, in the small rooms beyond the library, there is a spectacular 18thC **crib** and one or two reasonable 18thC pictures including works by Solimena. The wing to the right of the stairs – the **Appartamento Nuovo** – was decorated in the early 19thC in an ornate but dull classical style.

Gardens The gardens are immense and, on a hot day, very exposed. There is, however, a bus that runs quite often up to the **Grande Cascata**, where one may also buy postcards and a drink.

A sequence of terraced pools and fountains culminates in the celebrated group of *Diana and Actaeon* ★ at the bottom of the Grande Cascata. The over-lifesize marble figures, executed by various sculptors under Vanvitelli's direction, are divided into two groups. On one side of the cascade are Diana and her startled nymphs, who have been stumbled upon by Actaeon while he is out hunting; on the other side Actaeon is transformed into a stag and killed by his own dogs – the rather harsh punishment meted out by Diana for his accidental glimpse of her divine nudity. The figures blend with their rocky surroundings, and the freedom of design and union of art and nature are the climax of a tradition that had opened with Bernini's Fontana dei Fiumi in the Piazza Navona in Rome (see *SOUTH CENTRAL ITALY*).

COSENZA
Calabria Map D5

Cosenza is a town in two parts – the streamlined, modern capital of northern Calabria, with its tidy grid-plan, and, across the river, the winding, hilly old town. Cosenza old town is particularly charming; every single one of its shopfronts is in wood or iron, and lit by the gentle light of bracket lamps.

Duomo
Piazza del Duomo
🏛
The 13thC church (consecrated in 1222 in the presence of the Emperor Frederick II) and its beautiful Gothic facade are the town's main reminder of its importance during the Middle Ages. Inside, in the right aisle, there is a good-quality 4thC **sarcophagus** featuring the *Hunt of*

Meleager and, in the left transept, the **tomb of Isabella of Aragon** ★ wife of Philip III of France, who died here in 1271; the workmanship is French.

Museo Diocesano
📷 *but gratuity appreciated*
Ask the sacristan to let you in
The prize exhibit of the museum is a 12thC **enamelled crucifix** ★ given by Frederick II in 1222. Its second most important holding, the 13thC *Madonna del Pilerio*, totem of the city, by a local Byzantinizing artist of distinctive style, is at present housed in the convent of SAN FRANCESCO D'ASSISI.

San Francesco d'Assisi
Via San Francesco
For appointment to visit Soprintendenza dei Beni della Calabria, tel. (0984) 26459
Set above steep twisting alleys or steeper steps, at the bottom of a lane leading to the historic castle, San Francesco dates from the 13thC but has been much rebuilt. The church itself contains only one item of interest, a strangely stylized over-lifesize wooden **crucifix** (15thC?) in the right transept. However, the conventual buildings are the seat of the Soprintendenza dei Beni della Calabria and contain many unreturned exhibits of a past show of Calabrian art.

At present the collection includes: two altarpieces by Bernardo Daddi; a large and quite good-quality polyptych by Bartolommeo Vivarini; several works by Mattia Preti; a large *Madonna and Saints* by Caracciolo; and the *Madonna del Pilerio* (see DUOMO).

ERCOLANO (*HERCULANEUM*)
Ercolano, Campania Map A3

Like its larger and more famous neighbour POMPEI, Ercolano or Herculaneum was completely buried in the eruption of Vesuvius in AD79. The first ruins were discovered during the sinking of a well-shaft in 1709.

Scavi di Ercolano
Corso Vesina
Tel. (081) 7390963
Open Tues–Sun 9am–3pm (Jan 1), 9am–6.20pm (July 1); for closing times of dates in between, Jan–June add 20mins every fortnight, July–Dec subtract 20mins every fortnight
Closed Mon
🔀

At Pompeii, the eruption of Vesuvius seems to have taken most people by surprise; but at Herculaneum the inhabitants had time to escape, there was almost no loss of life, and the city was slowly engulfed by the lava flow rather than buried under a rain of ash. The ruins here therefore have a rather different character, offering greater traces of a second storey than at Pompeii. The present site is surrounded by cliff-walls as if it were a quarry. It is much smaller than the excavated area of Pompeii; Herculaneum was anyway a smaller city, although its houses were often distinctly richer and smarter.

Today, the ruins of Herculaneum are almost astonishingly uninteresting. Even those professionally involved exude a lack of enthusiasm. A museum built at the seaward end of the site will remain unopened indefinitely. In the center of the ruins, the abandoned tourist office reeks gently in the sun; the posters that hang from it are rather more evocative than anything else among the ruins, for almost all of Herculaneum's treasures have been transferred to the Museo Archeologico Nazionale in NAPLES.

The most interesting houses are the **Casa Sannitica** (Samnite House), distinctive in the center of the site for its first-floor loggia; the **Casa del Tramezzo di Legno** (House of the Wooden Beam) on the opposite side of the crossroads from it, with a complete first floor; and the **Casa di Nettuno** (House of Neptune), NE of the same crossroads: this is most interesting for its well-preserved shop and shop-front.

GALATINA
Lecce, Puglia Map F4

Galatina is a flourishing agricultural center that has never been of any great importance, but it possesses in Santa Caterina a large, late 14thC Franciscan church with some of the best Gothic frescoes in Apulia. On the way to Santa Caterina, adjacent to the central Piazza Dante, is the splendid late 17thC Baroque facade of Santi Pietro e Paolo.

Santa Caterina d'Alessandria ☆
Via Umberto I
🏛

The church has the unusual design of a nave separated from its aisles by two smaller, vaulted corridors – hence the triple-gabled facade, adorned with fine carving in the rose-window and portals.

The most important **frescoes** are those in the nave and choir, all early 15thC and International Gothic in style. The first bay is the work of one artist; the next two bays are by another hand; and the choir frescoes are by yet another artist.

The frescoes in the first bay represent the **Apocalypse** as a kind of chivalric

ordeal, and reveal occasional flashes of inspiration; notice, for instance, the face of haunting anxiety in the left spandrel of the right arch.

The artist in the next two bays delineates his figures less clumsily, and achieves more effective naturalistic details; admittedly his subject matter – the **Seven Sacraments**, the **Allegory of the Priesthood** and **Heaven** (vault) and **Genesis** and the **Passion** (walls) – gives him more opportunity. The **Tasting of the Fruit of the Tree of Good and Evil**, for instance, is a gourmet affair, even though Adam holding his throat in the second scene shows clearly that he is not enjoying the experience.

The naturalism has a distinctly clerical perspective: **Christ in the Temple** seems to be hammering the sides of the pulpit, and is tempted by a devil convincingly dressed as a friar but given away by his taloned feet. It is a fascinating reflection on the late Gothic outlook that the angels in Heaven wear Roman armour while the soldiers who enforce the judgment of Pilate are contemporary knights.

In the choir, the same kind of naturalism characterizes the **Story of St Catherine** (walls) and the **Evangelists** and **Doctors of the Church** (vault): the angels bring axes to chop up St Catherine's wheel, and one of her executioners makes off holding his hand and grimacing in pain.

Also to be seen in the church is the charming **tomb of Raimondello Orsini** in the choir, combining the most superbly carved friezes and capitals with crudely worked figures; and the much more impressive and important **tomb of Giovanni Antonio Orsini**, which occupies the back wall of an octagon built on to the choir; both are late 14thC.

GALLIPOLI
Lecce, Puglia Map F4

Gallipoli (Greek *"Kale polis"* – beautiful city) is one of the most attractive of all Apulian sea-ports. The old town, occupying its own little island joined to the new town by a bridge, varies whitewash with the austere stone of its Norman churches; the sea laps the splayed bulk of Frederick II's castle; and the rebuilt cathedral is a kind of picture gallery of local Baroque.

Cattedrale
Via Antonietta de Pace
🏛

The early 17thC cathedral has abundant paintings and the general effect is most impressive. The pictures by the Gallipolitan Giovanni Andrea Coppola, in the chapels flanking the nave, show a clear classicism of design – in bright colours, in which white and blue predominate.

The canvases in the nave, choir and transepts are by the Neapolitan Nicola Malinconico or by his less well documented relative Carlo, whose works are muddier and less orderly.

The altarpiece in the first chapel on the left may be by Giovanni Andrea Coppola: the style is markedly different from the rest, and whoever painted it must have been studying van Dyck. The fourth **altar** on the right is a remarkable, twisted-column Baroque confection, similar to those found in LECCE, incorporating hobgoblin putti.

LECCE
Puglia Map F4

Lecce is the pretty and vivacious capital of the province of Salento, and is famous above all for its remarkable local 17thC–18thC school of Baroque stone-carvers, by whom the heart of the city was transfigured. They exploited the superb quality of the local golden sandstone to achieve effects the equal of stucco. The stone is easily worked when it is quarried, but hardens with time.

Chiesa del Rosario
Via Libertini
🏛

The Rosario is by Giuseppe Zimbalo called Lo Zingarello, the outstanding Leccese Baroque architect, and its facade is equalled in the city only by that of SANTA CROCE. It is indeed difficult to describe these columns with their reversing spirals and garter-coronets, these plinths more ornate than the statues they carry, these vases spilling geometric growths, with putti revelling and birds tweeting.

Duomo
Piazza del Duomo
🏛

The cathedral is entered through a side door at the W end in the Piazza del Duomo; the piazza itself can be entered only from the Via Libertini/Via Vittorio Emanuele, and the fact that it is closed off certainly enhances its dramatic effect. The adjoining Palazzo Vescovile and Seminario merely contribute to the *mise-en-scène*; the flowering **portal** of the cathedral and its stupendous **campanile**, both by Lo Zingarello, steal the show.

In both of these, the main principles of Lecce Baroque are clear. It is essentially a style of surface decoration. The underlying forms may be clear and classical, but the standard classical ornament breaks out and sprouts unexpected form in unexpected places – hence the wonderful doorheads, hanging pomegranates, jutting vignettes, and plinths bearing fantastic vases.

Inside, the splendid overall effect is also due to Lo Zingarello. The intarsiaed, curvilinear, marble **balustrade** is of Neapolitan type, but the **altars**, with their gilt spiral columns into which foliage, animals and birds interlace, are typically Leccese. It needs repeating that these altars are not stucco, but stone. The big, heavenly, Giordanesque canvases in the choir are by the local 18thC painter Oronzo Tiso.

Museo Provinciale Sigismondo Castromediano
Palazzo Argento, Via Gallipoli
Tel. (0832) 47025
Open Mon – Fri 9am – 1.30pm,
* 3.30 – 7.30pm, Sun 9.30am – 1pm*
Closed Sat
🔁 📖 ☑

This is a modern museum, installed in the newly converted and extended Palazzo Argento. It consists of an archaeological collection (ground and first floor) and a picture gallery (third floor), which also has sculpture and minor arts.

The **archaeological collection** is divided into a chronological section, in which its more important vases, terra cottas and bronzes are displayed, and a topographical section. The chronological section is entered first, up a ramp to the first floor. One descends another ramp to the topographical part; this includes marble statuary from the amphitheater that lies off Piazza Sant' Oronzo, the main square of the town.

The **picture gallery** is reached from the ground floor by stairs to the right of the ramp. At the top of the stairs is an ugly, mask-like bust of **Giuseppe Palmieri**, inscribed as by Canova – the first of many optimistic attributions in the museum.

In **Room I**, to the right, is a late 14thC/early 15thC **polyptych** by Jacobello di Bonimo; at right angles to it, a *Madonna of Humility* attributed to a more important Jacobello, the early 15thC Venetian painter, Jacobello del Fiore: the coarse drawing of the face makes the attribution hard to accept. There follows, among other weak paintings, a **polyptych** in which the types are clearly those of Antonio Vivarini but the handling is so bad that it cannot even be from his workshop: it must be a local copy after a lost original.

More worthwhile are a ***Prophet Writing*** by the local sculptor and architect Gabriele Riccardi, a 16thC precursor of Lecce Baroque stone-carving, and some 16thC–18thC Byzantinizing icons, notably a *St Demetrios*.

Room II, to the left, contains canvases by the local Baroque artist Oronzo Tiso (see DUOMO), an ***Ecce Homo*** by the Neapolitan Andrea Vaccaro and three ***bozzetti*** ★ for lunettes by Giaquinto – his firm, clear, space-creating colours are a welcome refreshment.

Santa Croce
Via Umberto I
🏛

This spacious church was designed in the late 16thC by Gabriele Riccardi, but its 17thC facade is by Lo Zingarello. The ornament is typically effervescent, but the explosion of motifs does not obscure the lines of the architecture; indeed, this is the most monumental of the Lecce facades, since the horizontals and verticals are strong and the decoration swells around and clings to the facade elements rather than sallying off them.

Inside, Riccardi created a novel effect by loading the arches and spandrels (copied from Brunelleschi's Santo Spirito in Florence – see NORTH CENTRAL ITALY) with festoons and acanthus decoration. The side-chapels are fitted with typical Leccese **carved altars**, some attributed to Riccardi; the altar of the chapel to the left of the choir, by Francesco Antonio Zimbalo, is unusual in having figured reliefs of the ***Life of St Francis*** (1614–15).

Other churches in Lecce with interesting facades and altars include the **Gesù**, Via Rubichi; **Sant' Irene**, Via Vittorio Emanuele; **Santa Chiara**, Piazza Vittorio Emanuele; **San Matteo**, Via d'Aragona; and **Santa Maria delle Grazie**, Piazza Sant' Oronzo. They are all within easy walking distance of each other.

MATERA
Basilicata Map D3

Spectacularly situated above a deep ravine, Matera is one of the most prosperous towns in Basilicata and is noted for the manufacture of terra cotta and ceramics. The lower, older part of the town is remarkable for its caves: along the slopes of the ravine, houses and chapels (some with frescoes) are excavated into the rock.

Duomo
Piazza del Duomo
🏛

The Romanesque cathedral dates from 1268–70 and has a handsome campanile. Otherwise the most striking feature of the exterior is a fine rose window supported by carved angels.

Inside, the most spectacular piece is a huge **crib** (1534) by the local sculptors Altobello Persio and Sannazaro d'Alessandro, whose work figures prominently elsewhere in the building.

Pinacoteca d' Errico
Palazzo Duni, Piazza Pascoli
Open Mon–Sat 9am–1pm, Sun 9am–noon

The Pinacoteca is housed in a former seminary. It contains an interesting collection of 17thC and 18thC paintings, predominantly of the Neapolitan school, but there are no outstanding works.

San Francesco d' Assisi
Piazza San Francesco

The church was founded in the early 13thC, but rebuilt in the late 17thC. It contains various minor works and one outstanding item – a set of eight panels from a **polyptych** by the 15thC Venetian, Bartolommeo Vivarini; these are set into the organ case behind the main altar.

MONTE SANT' ANGELO
Foggia, Puglia Map C2

This is a hill-town with magnificent panoramic views and crowded streets leading to the venerable sanctuary of San Michele Archangelo.

Basilica di San Michele Archangelo
Piazzale della Basilica

In the mostly 19thC facade, the portal frames magnificent **bronze doors** ★ with coloured niello inlay, made in Constantinople in 1076: they are better preserved than those at AMALFI.

Inside, at the rear of the shrine, the **bishop's throne** shows good Romanesque lions beneath, with a more Oriental design in the upper part; it is somewhat similar to the bishop's throne in San Nicola, BARI. On the right is a Renaissance marble statue of *St Michael* attributed to Andrea Sansovino.

Museo
📷 *but gratuity appreciated*
Ask the sacristan to let you in

The museum contains most notably a 7thC icon of *St Michael* and a **crucifix** donated by Frederick II, both of high quality.

NAPLES (*NAPOLI*)
Campania Map A3

The legendary beauty of Naples – a city curving around the shore of a spectacularly beautiful bay and looking towards the romantic islands of Ischia and Capri – has today sunk beneath the vast and ugly sprawl of modern developments. Naples has little of the enchantment of Rome or Florence, and many tourists, frightened by its reputation for violence and theft, linger only to see the nearby sites of Pompeii and Herculaneum. Yet the historic center – despite a long history of fire, bombs and earthquakes – remains vital, intensely picturesque and slightly sinister, with much that absorbs and fascinates.

Naples was founded by the Greeks around the 7thC BC and the ancient city plan has survived with astonishing completeness; three long parallel roads sweep dramatically through the center; between them lies a grid of dark, narrow streets and alleyways, overshadowed by high buildings. Life takes place in these crowded warrens, deep in litter, festooned with lines of washing and made brilliantly colourful by the stalls of fruit and fish, displayed with all the exuberance of a Baroque still-life.

The squalor of the houses of the poor contrasts with the grandeur of the churches that line every street. These are predominantly Baroque and Rococo, but there are some interesting medieval survivals which contain reminders of how Naples could always attract the best artists. Giotto's sojourn in Naples (1329–33) has left no trace, but Santa Maria Donnaregina Vecchia has frescoes convincingly attributed to his great Roman contemporary Pietro Cavallini, as well as one of the finest works of Tino di Camaino, the leading sculptor of the early 14thC.

There are splendid Renaissance monuments, too, most notably the Castel Nuovo's huge triumphal arch, but the greatest period of Neapolitan art was undoubtedly the 17thC. By this time Naples was the largest city in southern Europe, and the churches especially seem to have had an insatiable demand for art of all kinds. Caravaggio was the impetus behind the development of a strong local school of painting, distinguished by its often violent realism. The richness of Neapolitan Baroque is expressed also in the marvellous decorative sculpture and inlaywork found in so many churches. Cosimo Fanzago – brilliant, versatile, long-lived and energetic – was the supreme figure in this field, but his tradition was carried on into the 18thC by virtuoso sculptors such as Giuseppe Sammartino. Painting also flourished well into the 18thC, and the light, decorative works of Giordano and Solimena were seminal in the development of the new Rococo style.

Apart from the churches, there are exceptionally fine museums, in particular the Museo Archeologico Nazionale and the Museo e Gallerie Nazionali di Capodimonte. The archaeological museum, with its incomparable treasures from Pompeii and Herculaneum, is one of the greatest in the world, and Capodimonte boasts one of the choicest collections of paintings in all Italy.

The city itself is both exciting and dramatic, but can easily seem unbearably hot and claustrophobic. It is undeniably tiring, and the awkward opening hours of the churches can be maddeningly frustrating; some churches close immediately after early morning mass, and many are shut in the evening. In addition, several churches and museums are at present closed due to the damage wrought by the earthquake of 1980. Some of their pictures are now displayed in Capodimonte and restoration could take some years.

Cappella Sansevero
Via de Sanctis 19
🏛

This little chapel is one of the most bizarre and elaborate late Baroque works in Naples. Founded in 1590 as the burial chapel of the del Sangro family, it once stood in the garden of the Palazzo Sansevero (now destroyed).

The allegorical statues that dominate the chapel were commissioned by Raimondo del Sangro between 1749–66. They are remarkable above all else for their technical bravura, so much so that it is easy to forget the function of the building and see it as a shrine to virtuoso stonecarving rather than as a memorial to the departed members of the del Sangro family.

The most interesting sculptures are at the end of the right and left naves. On the right is a group of **Deception Unmasked** ★ by the Genoese sculptor Francesco Queirolo. This shows a nude man struggling to free himself from the meshes of a net – the snares of deceit – helped by a winged angel, symbol of the human mind; in a complementary scene on the base, Christ is shown opening the eyes of the blind. The net – carved in marble – is an astonishing *tour de force*.

At the end of the left nave is Antonio Corradini's **Chastity Veiled**; here the thin swathes of drapery subtly – and sexily, despite its title – suggest the forms of the nude body beneath. In the center of the chapel is Giuseppe Sammartino's **Christ Lying under the Shroud**. Again the body is revealed by thin drapery; yet, despite its virtuosity, this is a moving blend of realism and poetic feeling.

Castel Nuovo ★
Piazza del Municipio
Courtyard open 9am–6pm
📷 ✿

The Castel Nuovo was originally built in 1279–82 for Charles I of Anjou but has been much altered through the centuries. Externally, it is largely 15thC in aspect. Its vast and impressive bulk is now stranded in a squalid, run-down part of the city. But a visit to the Castel Nuovo is an essential part of any stay in Naples, for between the two towers on either side of the entrance is the **triumphal arch of Alfonso I** ★ the most significant Renaissance monument in the city.

The arch celebrates the triumphal entry of Alfonso I of Aragon into Naples in 1443, but it was not built until 1453–67. Its history is complex and the artist responsible for the overall design is unknown, although the tendency is to attribute it to Francesco Laurana. Domenico Gaggini was also involved.

Cattedrale di San Gennaro ★
Via del Duomo
🏛

The cathedral was begun in 1272 by Charles I of Anjou on the site of an early Christian basilica and completed by Robert of Anjou c.1314. It was seriously damaged in an earthquake in 1456, rebuilt, and many times altered and restored in the 17thC and 18thC. The facade is mainly 19thC Neo-Gothic, yet in keeping with the elaborate **Gothic portals** (1407) by Antonio Baboccio.

The **interior** is dominated by a splendid **coffered wooden ceiling**, commissioned in 1621; the paintings in the coffers are by minor artists including Fabrizio Santafede. The **frescoes** high on the walls of the nave and transept are by Luca Giordano and pupils. Beneath the second arch is a **font** (1613–26) by Decio Carafa. It is of green basalt and decorated with Bacchic motifs.

The third chapel of the right aisle is the **Cappella del Tesoro di San Gennaro**★ built in 1608–37 to house the celebrated relics of St Januarius, who was martyred in 305. A **silver gilt bust** (1305) behind the altar preserves his skull and two vessels contain his blood, said to liquify miraculously three times a year.

The decoration of the chapel constitutes one of the most splendid High Baroque ensembles in Naples. The magnificent **bronze gates** are by Fanzago. Four of the small altarpieces on copper are by Domenichino, who in 1630 was commissioned to decorate the **pendentives** and dome. The pendentives have an oddly clumsy look, and are much less successful than his pendentives in Sant' Andrea della Valle in Rome.

After Domenichino's death the **dome** ★ was frescoed by Lanfranco, who created here one of the outstanding works of High Baroque illusionism. The altarpiece on the right, the **Martyrdom of St Januarius**, is by Ribera. To the left and right of the entrance are two marble statues by Giuliano Finelli (a former assistant of Bernini), who also designed the bronze statues around the high altar. The 49 silver busts date from the early 17thC.

Beneath the main altar is the **crypt** ★ (also called the Cappella Carafa), one of the loveliest Renaissance works in Naples. It dates from 1497–1506 and was designed by Tommaso Malvita, a sculptor from Como, who also created the kneeling statue of **Cardinal Carafa**.

In the middle of the left aisle a door leads into the church of **Santa Restituta**, the oldest church in Naples. At the end of the left aisle of this church, the **Cappella di Santa Maria del Principio** has a mosaic of the *Virgin with Sts Januarius and Restituta* (1322) by Lello da Orvieto, which shows the influence of Sienese art and of Cavallini. The ceiling painting is by Luca Giordano.

At the far end of the right aisle of Santa Restituta, one reaches the **Battistero di San Giovanni in Fonte**, a small, early Christian baptistry with the remains of fine 5thC mosaics.

Certosa di San Martino ☆☆

Via Angelini, Vómero
Tel. (081) 377005
Open Tues–Sat 9am–2pm, Sun
9am–1pm
Closed Mon
🕿 🏛 ♨

Very many churches and religious institutions arose amid the miserable poverty of 17thC Naples, and the Certosa di San Martino – a Carthusian monastery – was the wealthiest and most sumptuously decorated of them all; its church is the greatest monument of the early Baroque style in Naples. The monastery rises on a high spur, below the Castel San Elmo and overlooking the sprawling modern city.

The church itself is richly decorated. The frescoes on the vault of the nave are by Lanfranco, who subtly transformed the compartments of the Gothic vault with his illusionistic skill. Over the door of the entrance wall is a *Lamentation over the Dead Christ* ★ (1638) by Massimo Stanzione, an eloquent and moving work in spite of its rather poor condition. Also on the entrance wall, the *Moses* and *Elijah* (1638) are by Ribera, as is the series of 12 over-lifesize *Prophets* ★ (1638–43) in the spandrels along the nave.

In the left aisle, the first chapel has very dark pictures by Caracciolo, perhaps the greatest of Caravaggio's followers. Caracciolo was an accomplished fresco painter, and the third chapel has, on the vault, the finest of his works in this medium. The much lighter *Visitation*, *Annunciation* and *Assumption* are by the 18thC painter Francesco de Mura.

The choir is dominated by two huge paintings: in the lunette, Lanfranco's fresco of the *Crucifixion* ★ and, beneath it, behind the altar, a very late work by Guido Reni, the *Nativity* ★ The left wall of the choir has two more large, impressive paintings: the still, intense *Washing of the Feet* ★ (1622), Caracciolo's finest work; and Ribera's last great masterpiece, the *Communion of the Apostles* ★ (1651).

To the right of the choir is the **Sala Capitolare**, with vault frescoes by the Mannerist painter Belisario Corenzio and

a series of ten lunettes portraying the *Founders of the Religious Orders* by Paolo Finoglia. Finoglia's sharp light is influenced by Caracciolo, but the powerful realism of these striking portraits suggests Ribera, especially in such details as the rendering of wrinkled brows and veined hands – and yet these were painted before Ribera's *Prophets* in the nave. The room also has pictures by Caracciolo, and Simon Vouet's *St Bruno Receiving the Rule of the Carthusian Order*, painted in the 1620s.

A small door to the right of the high altar leads to the **Coro dei Conversi**, with fine 15thC **choir stalls** with intarsia decoration. On the walls are frescoes by Micco Spadaro, painted as feigned tapestries; they are predominantly landscapes with small biblical stories and Carthusian legends. These romantic woodland and mountain scenes derive from the tradition of decorative landscape established in Rome and Naples by the Flemish painter Paul Bril.

From the left-hand side of the choir a further sequence of rooms opens out. First is the **sacristy**; on the arch is an *Ecce Homo* by Stanzione and, beyond, two brilliantly free canvases by Luca Giordano. The last room is the **Cappella del Tesoro**, with a ceiling by Luca Giordano (his last work) and, on the lavishly decorated high altar, a *Pietà* ★ (1637) by Ribera. At this time, Ribera was moving away from his earlier, aggressive naturalism towards a more graceful and painterly style that draws close to van Dyck; yet, despite its Baroque drama, this is a grave and tender work. Giordano's small dome, decorated with *Stories of Judith and Other Heroines* ★ is a sparkling, luminous work that looks forward to Tiepolo and even Fragonard.

Museo e Pinacoteca di San Martino
Open Tues–Sat 9am–2pm, Sun
9am–1pm
Closed Mon
🕿

The museum consists mainly of historical, naval, and topographical collections. Artistically, its most interesting feature is the collection of **Neapolitan cribs**. These were a speciality of Neapolitan Rococo art, exotically detailed and combining a sweet grace close to contemporary porcelain with the fairy-tale fantasy of the theater. The large **Cucimiello crib** ★ is one of the most spectacular to have survived.

The Pinacoteca is mainly closed, but the 19thC Neapolitan collection is open. **Rooms 67–69** show paintings by the **school of Posillipo**, whose members worked in and around Naples in the late

19thC. They were predominantly landscape painters, who gradually moved away from tired 18thC formulae to a fresher, more direct observation inspired by Corot.

Room 70 has paintings by artists of the **school of Resina**, a group committed to landscape and to the observation of reality. The most attractive pictures are Giuseppe de Nittis' *Little Courtyard Open to the Sun* (1867) and Alceste Campriani's painting of the corner of a sunlit square. **Rooms 71–76** display the **Rotondo Collection**, recently transferred from the MUSEO E GALLERIE NAZIONALI DI CAPODIMONTE. There are some touchingly fragile busts by Vincenzo Gomito and street scenes of Neapolitan squalor by Vincenzo Migliano.

Gesù Nuovo
Piazza del Gesù
🏛

The Gesù Nuovo was designed by the Jesuit architect Giuseppe Valeriano and built between 1584–1601. It is based on the highly influential Gesù in Rome, but the interior is more successful than its model in its lucid spaciousness.

Over the entrance door is Solimena's fresco of the *Expulsion of Heliodorus from the Temple* ★ (1725). Solimena was heir to Luca Giordano, and the last great painter of the Neapolitan Baroque – yet this fresco is more measured and classical than Giordano's explosively Baroque *Christ Driving the Money-lenders from the Temple* in the GIROLAMINI, with which it invites comparison. The splendid *Evangelists* (1634–36) in the pendentives of the dome are by Lanfranco; the cupola was also painted by Lanfranco, but it was destroyed in 1688. The present dome dates from 1744.

The vault of the choir is frescoed by Massimo Stanzione (1639–40); the vault of the sacristy by Aniello Falcone, Salvator Rosa's master. The second chapel of the left aisle, the **Cappella Fornaro** (1600–2), is one of the most ambitious and lavish decorative schemes of its period. The **marbling** is by Mario Marasi and assistants; and the **statues** on either side of the altar by Michelangelo Naccherino and Pietro Bernini, the great Gianlorenzo's father.

Girolamini
Piazza dei Girolamini
🏛

This is one of the grandest late 16thC churches in Naples. It was built for the Oratorians between 1592–1619 by the Florentine architect Dionisio Nencioni and is strongly Florentine in feeling, although its clarity of form has been

modified by later lavish decoration.

The most famous painting in the church is Luca Giordano's fresco of *Christ Driving the Money-lenders from the Temple* ★ on the entrance wall (1684). This is a powerful and dramatic work which seems to explode in waves of violent movement from the central dominating figure of Christ.

On the altar in the sacristy is Guido Reni's *Meeting of Christ with St John the Baptist* ★ (c.1628), a work distinguished by its grace of line, delicate colouring and gentle poetic mood.

Museo Archeologico Nazionale ★★
Piazza Museo
Tel. (081) 294502
Open Tues–Sat 9am–2pm, Sun 9am–1pm
Closed Mon
🚋 ✿

A 16thC palace houses one of the most celebrated and varied collections of antiquities in the world. The palace was built as a barracks but occupied by the university throughout most of the 16thC and 17thC. In the late 18thC it was converted into a museum to house the two groups of antique art that still form its nucleus – the spectacular finds from POMPEI and ERCOLANO and the collection inherited by the Bourbon dynasty from the Farnese family, who had numbered some of the greatest patrons and collectors of the 16thC. The Farnese paintings were also housed here, but in 1957 they were transferred to the MUSEO E GALLERIE NAZIONALI DI CAPODIMONTE.

The museum is at present undergoing extensive reorganization; large and important sections are now closed and their future arrangement is uncertain. This guide therefore mentions such sections only briefly.

Ground floor   To the right of the large entrance hall, displaying impressive **Roman sarcophagi**, the **Galleria dei Tirannicidi** is followed by the **Galleria dei Grandi Maestri** (Rooms II–VI). In **Room II** is an *Aphrodite* from Herculaneum and a lovely relief of *Orpheus, Eurydice and Hermes*, a high-quality copy of a work by Phidias, the most celebrated of all Greek sculptors. The most important work in **Room III** is a Roman copy of one of the most famous and influential works of antiquity, Polykleitos' statue of a youth carrying a spear, known as the *Doryphoros* ★ (the original of c.450BC is lost and this is the best of numerous copies).

To the right of **Room VIII** is the **Galleria del Toro Farnese**, a series of small rooms dominated at opposite ends by the gigantic figure of the *Farnese*

Hercules ★ and the vast sculptural group of the *Farnese Bull* ★ These two works are the most celebrated in the museum, but by no means the most beautiful.

The *Farnese Hercules*, showing the hero resting on his club after his labours, was discovered in 1540 in the Baths of Caracalla in Rome – where it would have looked much more at home. Signed by the Athenian sculptor Glycon, it is a version of an original of the late 4thC BC by Lysippos. It was deeply admired by artists of the Baroque, and the power of the muscles and the realism of the surface still command respect.

The *Farnese Bull* is probably a Roman copy of a Greek original dating from c.150BC; the subject is from Theban legend and shows Dirce tied to the horns of a bull and being trampled to death. The work is an unforgettable virtuoso performance, but it is not easy to like.

The two Farnese sculptures are so over-powering that it is easy to miss some excellent pieces in the small rooms forming the gallery between them. Among these are an *Aphrodite* ★ attributed to Praxiteles (**Room XII**); a relief showing the *Meeting of Paris with Helen and Aphrodite* and a large vase signed by the Athenian Salpion (1stC BC), depicting the *Birth of Bacchus* (both **Room XIII**); and, in **Room XV**, a much copied *Pan and Olympus* and a lively, almost Rococo *Satyr with the Infant Bacchus* (3rd–2ndC BC).

Mezzanine floor This displays in **Rooms LVII–LXIV** an outstanding collection of **mosaics from Pompeii.** Many of the floors of Pompeian houses were decorated with all-over mosaic patterns, but there are also some beautiful examples of mosaics that were set into the floor like pictures. The most spectacular example, based on a Greek painting of the 4thC BC, shows *Alexander's Victory over Darius at Issus* ★★ It is an exciting work, full of dramatic foreshortenings and effects of light and shade – note the startling modelling of the horse's rump in the center – and gives a vivid sense of what ancient Greek painting would have been like.

Another Roman fashion – showing the influence of Alexandria – was for **Egyptian scenes** ★ There is a particularly charming example in **Room LX**, with a hippopotamus and crocodile cheerfully baring their teeth.

In **Room LIX** two small **mosaics** ★ are signed by Dioskourides. They may be copied from Greek originals, but the lively realism of the *Strolling Players*, with its squat, vivid figures and sad child, is more Roman than Greek. Such scenes stood on shelves or in niches – unlike the sweeping floor mosaic of an *Underwater Scene* ★ with an octopus, eyes popping and tentacles swirling, engulfing a lobster. The sensitively modelled *Portrait of a Woman* ★ was also, surprisingly, intended as a floor mosaic.

First floor In the center of the vast **Salone della Meridiana** stands the *Farnese Atlas* ★ a celebrated Hellenistic sculpture. To the right of the stairs, a sequence of rooms displays works discovered at the **Villa of the Papyri**, on the slopes of Vesuvius, including the most spectacular group of ancient bronzes ever unearthed.

Another startling find was a large number of **papyri**, some of which, together with a landscape frieze, are exhibited in a small room to the right. Beyond, large and magnificent rooms display the **bronzes**. The most celebrated work in **Room CXVI** is the seated *Hermes* ★★ based on an original by Lysippos (4thC BC), but also outstanding are two graceful *Fauns* and a series of *Dancers* ★ In **Room CXVII** note especially the taut, intensely expressive **portrait bust** ★ – it is usually called *Seneca* but probably represents a tragic actor.

To the left of the stairs, a series of rooms (**LXVI–LXXVII**) displays the richest collection of **Roman painting** in the world. Recovered from the walls of houses at Pompeii, Herculaneum and Stabiae, the collection shows the fascinatingly wide variety of styles and subjects in Roman painting. Many scenes represent Greek myths, and derive from Greek painting, but a more distinctively Roman contribution lies in the field of landscape art: Roman artists excel both in idyllic pastoral scenes, studded with little classical ruins and goatherds tending their herds, and in tranquil garden scenes, with detailed plants and birds.

In **Room LXXI** the outstanding painting is *Hercules and Telephus* ★★ from Herculaneum. This is a vigorous, powerfully modelled work, full of bold detail; note the vivid grace of the hind and child, and the dark, mischievous vitality of the faun playing his pipes.

In the next room (**LXXII**) there is the dramatic *Sacrifice of Iphigenia* ★ adapted from a theatrical presentation, and *Perseus Freeing Andromeda* ★ a grave, yet softer and more melancholy treatment of antique myth. There are also two unusual paintings on marble, one showing *Niobe's Daughters Playing with Knucklebones* ★

The next room (**LXXIII**) has a group of landscape paintings in a different style, with figures very small in relation to their surroundings. In **Room LXXIV** there are **pictures from Stabiae**, a town just S of

Pompeii that was likewise buried in the eruptions of Vesuvius in AD79. A distinct decorative style flourished at Stabiae, and this room has characteristically light-hearted and witty friezes of putti playing. In the center are four paintings of the seasons; *Spring*★★ (represented by a maiden gathering flowers) is one of the loveliest images to have survived from the ancient world. Its linear grace and sense of freshness are exquisite.

Room LXXVII has some outstanding and sensitive examples of **Roman portraiture**★ Beyond, in **Rooms LXXIX – LXXXIII**, are collections of armour, glass, gold and silver. In **Room XCVI** are some exceptional examples of **Roman still-life painting**★

Museo e Gallerie Nazionali di Capodimonte ☆☆
Parco di Capodimonte
Tel. (081) 7410881
Open Tues – Sat 9am – 2pm, Sun
  9am – 1pm
Closed Mon
🎦 📽 🏛 🛥 🍴

Occupying a fine Neoclassical palace set in a scruffy park on a hill overlooking the city, the Museo e Gallerie Nazionali di Capodimonte combine three museums in one. They were established in 1957 to house the Galleria Nazionale; a collection of 19thC Italian art from the Accademia di Belle Arti; and the former royal collections, consisting primarily of porcelain, bronzes and armour.

On the first floor are the state apartments with the royal collections, and the 19thC collection. Capodimonte is, of course, the name of one of the most famous types of porcelain: the factory was founded in 1743 in the grounds of the palace and the collection here is not surprisingly the best in the world. It includes a remarkable porcelain room, the **Salottino di Porcellano**★ (1757–59) designed by the German artist Johann Sigismund Fischer for the Villa Reale at Portici. Everything except the mirrors and the stucco ceiling is of porcelain.

The 19thC collection is presently closed after damage in the 1980 earthquake; part of it (the Rotondo Collection) has been transferred to the Pinacoteca in the CERTOSA DI SAN MARTINO. The Galleria Nazionale, on the second floor, has paradoxically been enriched by the earthquake: several important paintings have been moved here temporarily from elsewhere.
Galleria Nazionale   This is one of the most enjoyable and comprehensive of the great Italian collections. Its most outstanding features are the unrivalled display of 17thC Neapolitan paintings

and a magnificent group of Titians.

The display opens with a splendid series of 16thC **Flemish tapestries**. Beyond, a sequence of small rooms shows **14thC and 15thC Sienese and Florentine works**. The outstanding Sienese painting is Simone Martini's *St Louis of Toulouse Crowning his Great-nephew, Robert of Anjou, King of Naples*★ and there are some good pictures by Bernardo Daddi and Masolino.

This group is, however, dominated by Masaccio's *Crucifixion*★★ which was once the topmost part of a polyptych painted in 1426 for the Chiesa del Carmine in Pisa. Although a fairly small painting, it has astonishing grandeur; the startling image of Mary Magdalen – her arms flung wide in grief, her golden hair spilling over the vivid red of her robe – is intensely dramatic. Masaccio was a master of perspective, and the cross and Christ's body are shown as if the spectator were looking up at them, to accord with the low viewpoint from which they would have been seen when they were at the top of the polyptych.

Beyond this room, there is a small but high-quality group of **Renaissance pictures from Florence and Umbria**; the loveliest painting is Botticelli's *Madonna and Angels*★ (c.1470), an early work, still linked to the delicate style of Filippo Lippi, yet already hinting at the subtler rhythms of Botticelli's mature style.

Room VIII has **northern Italian Renaissance pictures**. There is a strikingly realistic portrait of *Cardinal Bernardo de' Rossi*★ (1505) by Lorenzo Lotto; a small, profile portrait of *Francesco Gonzaga as a Boy*★ (c.1460) by Mantegna; and Giovanni Bellini's overwhelmingly beautiful *Transfiguration*★★ (1480s). The poetry of this work depends on the tension between the rigid, almost Byzantine grouping of the figures and the fresh, naturalistic detail of the landscape setting: little hills and paths lead into the distance; the bare branches of a tree are poignantly silhouetted against the soft clouds; men herd sheep and goats; the flowers and rocks in the foreground are painted with loving precision.

Through **Rooms X and XI**, with **15thC Neapolitan and Flemish pictures**, **Room XII** has some fine **High Renaissance works**, with cartoons by Michelangelo and Raphael, and an impressive group of pictures by Sebastiano del Piombo. Of these the finest is a *Portrait of Clement VII*★ (1526); the grandeur of the forms suggests Sebastiano's allegiance to Michelangelo, yet the brilliance of the colour and the intensely romantic lighting show his Venetian origins.

Rooms XIII–XVIII contain a particularly good collection of **Mannerist pictures**. **Room XVII** has the outstanding works, with masterpieces by Parmigianino, the most refined and elegant of Mannerist artists. They include *Lucrezia*, an early work; and the *Holy Family with St John* (1527), distinguished by its lovely rhythms and windswept landscape; but these take second place to his superb portraits of *Galeazzo Sanvitale★* (1524) and of a young woman known as *Antea★* The latter is a late work, assured and confident in its monumental breadth of design. The tiny head attains an almost abstract beauty – and yet it is a psychologically complex picture, the mood slightly melancholy and inward-turned. The ferret, its teeth bared and a ring in its nose, adds a disturbing note.

The same room has two intimate, charming works by Correggio: the *"Zingarella" Madonna★* (named after the Madonna's gypsy headdress) and the *Mystic Marriage of St Catherine★* There are also some strange, disturbing fantasies by Lelio Orsi; and a cool, slightly watchful *Self-portrait* by Sofonisba Anguissola, oddly reminiscent of Degas.

Room XVIII has two outstanding works; an unusually vivid and spontaneous picture by El Greco of a *Young Boy Blowing on Charcoal★* (one of several versions by El Greco or his studio) and Titian's *Annunciation★*

The Titians in the room beyond, **Room XIX**, are one of the great glories of Capodimonte. The range of Titian's powers is suggested in two paintings produced during his stay in Rome from 1545–46: the marvellously erotic *Danae★★* (the first of several versions of the subject by Titian); and the brilliantly characterized portrait of *Pope Paul III with his Nephews Alessandro and Ottavio Farnese★★* It may be unhistorical to read into the picture our knowledge of Farnese family intrigue, but the atmosphere of cunning and deceit is intensely gripping.

The individual portrait of *Paul III★* dates not from the time of Titian's visit to Rome, but from 1543, when the Pope visited Bologna and requested the artist to go there to paint him. Here also the shrewd old face is superbly captured, but what perhaps lies in the memory longest is Titian's handling of the velvet cape – an electrifying piece of painting.

In **Room XX** there is a change of feeling with a group of **Flemish and Dutch pictures** that includes two works by the greatest 16thC Flemish painter, Pieter Bruegel – the *Misanthrope★* and

the *Parable of the Blind Men★★* Both were painted in 1568, the year before his death, and both reveal a basic view of man. The gloomy misanthrope is being robbed by a figure symbolizing the wicked world from which he tries to escape. The *Parable of the Blind Men* illustrates the passage from St Matthew's Gospel: "If the blind lead the blind, both shall fall into the ditch." Physical blindness, pitilessly observed by Bruegel, is a metaphor for spiritual blindness.

The 17thC opens in **Room XXVI** with an outstanding group of works by the Bolognese painter Annibale Carracci. These range from one of his prettiest, and most Correggiesque early pictures, the *Mystic Marriage of St Catherine* (1586–87), and a small, poetic Venetian landscape, the *Vision of St Eustace* (1585–86), to the noble forms and tragic grandeur of the *Pietà* (c.1600). Another Bolognese painter, Guido Reni, is the highlight of **Room XXVII** with his *Atalanta and Hippomenes*, a work of extraordinary, unreal elegance. **Room XXVIII** has some fascinating, slightly disturbing works by the Parmese painter Bartolommeo Schedoni.

The collection of **17thC landscape paintings** in **Room XXIX** is dominated by Claude's *Landscape with the Nymph Egeria★* (1669). The silvery greys and greens, the strangely elongated figures, and the muted, melancholy poetry are characteristic of his late style. Apart from the Claude, the most poetic evocation of the Roman Campagna in this room comes rather surprisingly from Lanfranco – an artist better known for his Baroque frescoes – in his highly original *St Mary Magdalen Transported to Heaven★* A group of landscapes by the Roman Caravaggesque painter Carlo Saraceni suggests his response to the intimate mood and intense light of landscapes by the German artist Adam Elsheimer.

Room XXIX also heralds the Neapolitan Seicento, with two great altarpieces by Caravaggio, whose visits to Naples induced the birth of a vigorous native school of painting. The first is the huge *Seven Acts of Mercy★* which is at Capodimonte after earthquake damage to the church of the Monte della Misericordia, for which it was commissioned (for the high altar) in 1607. The subject is from St Matthew's Gospel: "For I was an hungered, and ye gave me meat; I was thirsty, and ye gave me drink . . ." The painting draws the Seven Acts together into one scene; the other altarpieces from the church are more traditional in showing individual Acts. Apart from its novel iconography, Caravaggio's picture is distinguished by its astonishing compositional freedom and compassionate naturalism; it is crowded with scenes from everyday life, and suggests all the dark squalor of a Neapolitan street scene.

The *Flagellation*★ probably also dates from 1607. This, however, is a brutal and tragic painting, and echoes of its violent mood run throughout Neapolitan painting of the period. The taste for horrifying, bloody subjects is seen at its most sensational in Artemisia Gentileschi's *Judith and Holofernes*★

Caravaggio's aggressive naturalism also influenced the Spanish painter Ribera; his *Drunken Silenus*★ (1626) is a coarse, vital picture of startling originality. The vigorous, scratchy brushwork suggests, with virtuoso skill, the grotesque bulk of Silenus' body and the stubble on his unshaven face. Two other moving works by Ribera are the *Head of St John the Baptist*★ (1646) and *St Mary of Egypt*★ (1651).

Room XXX suddenly leaps into the 20thC with a large, dull work by the abstract artist Alberto Burri. Beyond, the Neapolitan 17thC continues with works by the mysterious Master of the Annunciation to the Shepherds. This artist painted the world of the poor and suffering without violence, but with true compassion and dignity; his *Return of the Prodigal Son* shows a popular 17thC Neapolitan theme treated in a deeply human, tender way.

Aniello Falcone's *Charity of St Lucy* (c. 1630) has a similar grave realism; Falcone is better known as the inventor of a new kind of subject, "the battle scene without a hero" (Fritz Saxl), of which there are good examples here. The early 17thC in Naples also saw the growth of a new kind of fresh and spontaneous landscape. Micco Spadaro and Salvator Rosa made sketching tours together in the countryside around Naples; although there are here only dull figure paintings by Rosa, the most glamorous of all Neapolitan painters, Spadaro, is represented by an attractively sketchy *Coastal Scene* and two elaborate *Landscapes with Hermit Saints*.

Room XXXVIII features the work of Bernardo Cavallino, the most graceful and lyrical painter of the Neapolitan Seicento. His *Judith and Holofernes* is altogether less gory than Artemisia Gentileschi's and his *Singer* has an almost fragile delicacy – the expressive, half-open mouth is a Cavallino trademark.

One of the artists closest in style to Cavallino was Francesco Guarino, represented here by his superb *St Agatha*★ This shocking combination of eroticism and violence was formerly attributed to Stanzione and for a long time was one of the most famous of all Neapolitan paintings.

Room XXXIX has a pretty, almost Rococo *Erminia and the Shepherds* by Cavallino and a further array of 17thC pictures. **Rooms XL** and **XLI** are devoted to Mattia Preti and Luca Giordano. Preti arrived in Naples after the terrible plague of 1656; he was given the commission for a series of huge frescoes, commemorating the plague, for the city gate. These no longer survive, but sombre *bozzetti* for two of them are displayed here.

Room XLII has a marvellously lush and beautiful display of **17thC Neapolitan still-life paintings**. These range from the naturalistic, descriptive compositions of food and kitchen utensils, influenced by Caravaggesque realism – a *Still-life with Goat's Head* attributed to Giambattista Recco is a good example – through more elaborate Baroque designs of flowers and fruits by Paolo Porpora, to the subtler poetry and Rococo grace of Andrea Belvedere's *Convolvulus and Guelder Rose*★

Room XLIIA has the collection of the Banco di Napoli with works by Artemisia Gentileschi and by the 18thC painters Francesco de Mura and Gaspare Traversi. Traversi is not well known, but he was one of the most interesting genre painters of his time; the *Concert* and the *Letter* are strange, ambiguous works, with an odd mixture of the shadowy and the concrete.

Room XLIII has a large collection of **Flemish genre** and, with **Room XLIV**, introduces the lighter, gayer style of the **Rococo**; the finest work here is Corrado Giaquinto's *Aeneas and the Sibyl*.

Museo Nazionale della Ceramica Duca di Martina

Villa Floridiana, Vômero
Tel. (081) 377315
Open Tues–Sat 9am–2pm, Sun 9am–1pm
Closed Mon
▨ ☑ ❧

The elegant, Neoclassical Villa Floridiana stands on a spur overlooking the Bay of Naples; the view is spectacular – one of the few that actually lives up to its reputation. The museum has a fine collection of European, Chinese and Japanese porcelain and majolica; ivories and enamels; and some good 18thC oil sketches, mainly by Neapolitan artists.

In **Room III** are two melancholy, misty *Bacchanals* by Giacomo del Po. **Room V**, the ballroom, has 18thC stucco decorations and chiaroscuro sketches by Francesco de Mura. In **Room VI** there is a particularly fine oil sketch by Corrado Giaquinto – *St Nicholas Blessing a Warrior*; in **Room VIII**, a *Nativity* by Filippo Falciatore and five playful, decorative, coyly erotic *Mythological Scenes*★ by the same artist, perhaps painted for the doors of a carriage. **Room IX** has a vast sketch by Solimena, the *Massacre of the Giustiniani at Scio*.

Museo di Palazzo Reale
Piazza del Plebiscito
Tel. (081) 417010
Open Tues – Sat 9am – 2pm, Sun
    9am – 1pm
Closed Mon
📷 🏛

The vast block of the Palazzo Reale was built by Domenico Fontano from 1600–2 and extended and refurbished in the 18thC. From the left of the courtyard, a spectacular marble staircase leads to a suite of rooms on the *piano nobile*; at the foot of the staircase stands a set of **bronze doors** (1462–68) from the CASTEL NUOVO, with six reliefs showing Ferdinand of Aragon's campaign against the barons. Before coming to the suite of rooms one enters a lovely Rococo **theater** (1768) attributed to Ferdinando Fuga. Around the walls are late 17thC statues of the *Muses* and some pretty (much restored) 18thC fantasies of ruins and landscapes.

Room I, the **Sala Diplomatica**, has some Gobelins tapestries and a ceiling painting by Francesco de Mura, in a heavy *quadratura* framework. **Rooms II** and **III** show some rather vapid, classicizing works by Massimo Stanzione and Paceco de Rosa, strongly influenced by Guido Reni. The next few rooms are of little interest – although there is a good view from the terrace of the Bay of Naples – but **Room XI** has a spectacular Baroque picture by Luca Giordano, the *Patron Saints of Naples Adoring the Cross*, and a powerful *Annunciation* by Artemisia Gentileschi.

A series of light, decorative landscapes in **Room XII** follows these dramatic works. Most interesting is a *Landscape with Figures* by Micco Spadaro and Viviano Codazzi; Codazzi specialized in producing scenes into which others painted the figures. **Room XIII** has an impressive group of pictures by Luca Giordano, and a *Martyrdom of St Sebastian* by Micco Spadaro. There are also good Caravaggesque works: an *Adoration of the Shepherds* by Matthias Stomer; a *Judith with the Head of Holofernes* by Pietro Novelli; and a *Return of the Prodigal Son*★ by Mattia Preti, perhaps the finest work here.

Sant' Anna dei Lombardi ☆
Via Monteoliveto

This church, begun in 1411, was completely altered in the 17thC. It has an outstanding array of Florentine sculpture that seems strange in Naples.
Right aisle   The first chapel has a pretty majolica floor and, over the altar, an *Annunciation*★ by Benedetto da Maiano. From the fifth chapel, one reaches the **Cappella di Santo Sepolcro**, with a terra-cotta *Pietà* (1492) by Guido Mazzoni (the figures are rearranged).
Left aisle   The sixth chapel is a graceful Renaissance design by Giuliano da Maiano, indebted to Brunelleschi's Cappella Pazzi at Santa Croce in Florence (see *NORTH CENTRAL ITALY*). It is decorated with 16thC frescoes (heavily restored). In the fifth chapel there is a *St John the Baptist* by Giovanni Nola and a *Pietà* by Santacroce. From the first chapel, one enters the **Cappella Piccolomini**. Over the altar, the sculptured relief of the *Adoration of the Shepherds*★ with two small statues of saints is a lovely work by Antonio Rossellino (c.1475). The **monument to Maria of Aragon** (d. 1470) was begun by Rossellino and finished by Benedetto da Maiano; it is almost a copy of Rossellino's monument to the Cardinal of Portugal in San Miniato al Monte in Florence.

Santi Apostoli
Largo Santi Apostoli 8
🏛

The church was designed by Fabrizio Grimaldi in 1609–10, and built after his death, from 1626–32. The **vault of the nave**, which has lavish stucco decoration, was frescoed by Lanfranco from 1634–46, the **cupola** by Giambattista Beinaschi in 1680. Beinaschi was heavily influenced by Lanfranco, and his work forms a link between Lanfranco and Giordano, by whom there are four canvases on the walls of the crossing.

Santa Chiara
Via Benedetto Croce
🏛

This early 14thC church is one of the finest Angevin monuments in Naples. In the 18thC it was given a lavish Rococo interior, but after heavy damage by air raids in 1943 the church was restored in its original Gothic style. It is famous for its Gothic sepulchral monuments: on the right wall of the choir, the **tomb of Marie de Valois** (d.1331) by Tino di Camaino and assistants; and, behind the main altar, the remnants of the **tomb of Robert I of Anjou** (d.1343) by Giovanni and Pacio Bertini da Firenze.

Chiostro delle Clarisse

Open Apr – Sept 8.30am – 12.30pm,
4 – 7pm; Oct – Mar 8.30am – 12.30pm,
4 – 6pm

🖭 🏛 ☑ ⚲

This cloister, attached to Santa Chiara, is
an oasis of green enchantment in the very
heart of the most crowded and noisy part
of old Naples. It was designed from
1739 – 42 by the Rococo architect
Domenico Vaccaro, who created a light
and fanciful blend of art and nature.
Avenues of octagonal majolica piers,
linked by majolica benches, support
trellises covered with climbing plants; the
real foliage mingles with the majolica
garlands of flowers encircling the piers.
The benches have little Arcadian scenes
and seascapes, all in majolica.

San Giovanni a Carbonara

Via Carbonara 5

This church was built in the 14thC, but it
was later enlarged and altered, and then
badly damaged in World War II.

Behind the high altar is the **tomb of
King Ladislas** (d. 1414), an elaborate
Gothic work by Marco and Andrea da
Firenze. Behind this is the circular
Cappella Caracciolo del Sole (1427),
with a fine majolica floor and 15thC
frescoes by Leonardo da Besozzo (upper
part) and Perrinetto da Benevento (lower
part), as well as the **tomb of Ser Gianni
Caracciolo** (c. 1433) attributed to
Andrea da Firenze.

To the left of the chancel is the
strikingly original **Cappella Caracciolo di
Vico★** (begun 1516). The architect of
this impressive circular building is
unknown. It was perhaps inspired by
Bramante's Tempietto at San Pietro in
Montorio in Rome (see *SOUTH CENTRAL
ITALY*), but is grander and more vigorous,
and lavishly ornamented with sculpture.

San Gregorio Armeno

Via San Gregorio Armeno 44

This church lies in one of the most
picturesque streets in the center of old
Naples. It is a 16thC building (begun
1574) with sumptuous Baroque and
Rococo decoration.

The third chapel on the right has the
most interesting paintings in the church,
two large canvases showing scenes from
the *Life of St Gregory of Armenia*
(1635) by Francesco Fracanzano, the
brother-in-law of Salvator Rosa. In the
first, King Tiridates, opposed to
Christianity, has St Gregory, the first
patriarch of Armenia, thrown into a pit
of wild beasts; in the second, the King has
been transformed into a wild boar and
begs Gregory to help him regain human
form. Fracanzano trained with Ribera

and his impressive naturalism reflects the
influence of his master.

San Lorenzo Maggiore

Piazza San Gaetano

This Gothic church, with a fine 13thC
French-style apse, is best known for its
medieval monuments. In the ambulatory
behind the high altar is the **tomb of
Catherine of Austria ★** (d. 1323). This is
the first Neapolitan work attributed to
Tino di Camaino, who worked for the
court of the Angevins from 1323; the
delicate, tranquil effigy, the four
attendants at the head and foot, and the
fine sculptural supports are generally
accepted as being from his hand.

The church also has two typically
sumptuous chapels (1643 – 55) by Cosimo
Fanzago: the **Cappella Cacace** (third on
the right) and **Cappella di Sant' Antonio**
(in the left transept).

Santa Maria Donnaregina Nuova

Largo Donnaregina 81a

The new church of Santa Maria
Donnaregina is a splendid Baroque
building (1620 – 49) by Giovanni
Guarini, with early frescoes by Solimena
in the chancel. More interesting,
however, is the adjacent old church,
SANTA MARIA DONNAREGINA VECCHIA.

Santa Maria Donnaregina Vecchia

Vico Donnaregina

The church was begun in the early
14thC, and is visited mainly for the
contemporary cycle of **frescoes ★** in the
nun's choir (a gallery over the W end of
the church). They represent the *Last
Judgment*, scenes from the *Passion* and
legends of *St Agnes*, *St Catherine* and *St
Elizabeth of Hungary* (the church was
built by Queen Mary of Hungary, wife of
Charles II of Anjou). Pietro Cavallini,
the Roman painter and mosaic designer,
is known to have been in Naples in 1308,
and it is highly likely that he was
responsible for the design and some of the
execution of these frescoes.

Also of interest here, on the left wall
of the chancel, is the **tomb of Queen
Mary of Hungary ★** by the Sienese
sculptor Tino di Camaino.

San Paolo Maggiore

Piazza San Gaetano

This late 16thC/early 17thC church,
approached by a splendid double
staircase, is by the Neapolitan architect
Francesco Grimaldi. It is built on the
ruins of a 9thC church, which was in turn
built over the site of a Roman temple; it
lies at the very heart of ancient Naples.

The sumptuous Baroque interior
contains some of the loveliest **inlaid**

marble work in Naples. The vault of the nave is decorated with badly damaged **frescoes** (1644) by Massimo Stanzione. In the sacristy, there are brilliant **frescoes** (1689–90) by Francesco Solimena, whose light, enchanting colours and vivacious, multi-figured compositions are indebted to Luca Giordano.

San Pietro a Maiella
Piazza Luigi Miraglia
🏛
This church is a particularly lucid and beautiful example of Angevin Gothic; its plain arches and bare surfaces create a startling – and yet utterly successful – contrast with the rich **Baroque ceiling ★** This was designed by Mattia Preti, who worked in Naples from 1656–60; in form – heavy compartments with inset canvases – it is Venetian, and the influence of Veronese is clear in the sweeping grandeur and brilliant colours.

Santa Restituta See CATTEDRALE DI SAN GENNARO.

OTRANTO
Lecce, Puglia Map F4

The hilly, picturesque ferry-port of Otranto is notable chiefly for the Romanesque mosaic floor of its cathedral, the only one of its kind surviving in Apulia.

Duomo
Piazza Basilica
The Baroque facade gives entrance to a spacious 12thC church, restored after the sack of the city by the Turks in 1480. The floor of the nave is a faded and in places much restored mosaic tree, from the branches of which spring a diverse collection of scenes. These include *Arion on a Dolphin*, figures from chivalric romance, *Adam and Eve* and other biblical persons. Quite apart from the style, the large size of the tesserae, and the appearance of mortar between them, mark the work as Romanesque rather than Byzantine.

PAESTUM
Salerno, Campania Map B3

The Greek city was founded in the 6thC BC. After various vicissitudes, it flourished under Roman rule, proving itself loyal during the Carthaginian invasion led by Hannibal (3rdC BC) and being duly rewarded. The failure of the port and outbreaks of malaria brought about a rapid decline in the early Middle Ages and Paestum was almost forgotten for centuries. The city's mighty temples remained unknown until the late 18thC.

Città Antica
Tel. (0828) 811016 (local tourist office)
Site open Tues – Sun 9am – 1hr before sunset
Closed Mon
📷 𝄞 ⛩ 🚻 🏛
The complete town, with its walls, survives; but the only buildings to rise to any height are its temples. Of these the **Basilica** (Temple of Hera) and **Temple of Neptune** (in fact, another Temple of Hera) are justly famous. Both conserve all their columns.

The Basilica is 6thC BC, and Archaic: it has a single row of columns down the *cella*, and nine columns on its short ends instead of the six or eight canonical in the Classical era.

The Temple of Neptune (c. 460 BC) is slightly earlier than the Parthenon in Athens. It is heavier looking than the Parthenon, but shares with it some of the optical refinements (for example, the curvature of the column shafts) that give a sense of energy and lite.

Museo di Paestum ☆
Tel. as Città Antica, above
Open Tues – Sat 9am – 2pm, Sun 9am – 1pm
Closed Mon
📷 𝄞 ⛩ 🚻 🏛
On the opposite side of the road from the temples, the museum houses metopes retrieved from the sanctuary of Hera near the port and finds made in and around Paestum – in particular rare examples of Archaic wall-painting from its tombs.

The temple-like main chamber of the museum contains the **metopes**, all Archaic. Notable is a *Warrior* brandishing a spear (early 5thC BC) on the ground floor, but one mounts a stair to the gallery to see the frieze that comes from the main building of the sanctuary of Hera. Only three of its original 36 metopes are missing, and these late 6thC BC reliefs almost constitute an encyclopaedia of Greek mythology.

In the following rooms, amidst the vases and terra cottas, some of them preserving their paint, there are articles of bronzework, notably three bronze *hydriae* (water jugs) with fine relief decoration. In **Room VIII** are the examples of **wall-painting**: the figure from the **Tomb of the Diver ★** (early 5thC BC) plunging through his blank landscape is somehow cheery. It is important as a very rare survival of full-scale rather than vase-scale painting of the period, although it shows exactly the same conventions.

Apulian church sculpture

The old Roman province of Apulia played an important role in the general resurgence of late 11thC Europe – first as part of the territory that the Norman Robert Guiscard acquired and rapidly developed into a flourishing kingdom; and secondly as a main point of embarkation for the Crusades. Symbol of this upturn is the church of San Nicola at Bari, founded in 1087 when the relics of the saint were brought from Asia Minor. It became the model for a series of churches around the region, and the start of a school of stone sculpture which thrived right up until the 14thC.

The Apulian style of stone-carving is characterized by smooth surface and powerful animal imagery. Its distinctive repertoire of motifs features griffins, creatures bearing columns on their backs, and Atlas figures. Often these appear at the same points of the church: lions may support the columns of the porch (a motif common all over Tuscany and in northern Italy, but believed to have originated at Bari); and elephants are often used to bear the columns that flank the central arched window of the E end. In the Romanesque period, the region had strong links with Sicily, another Norman conquest, but Apulian sculpture was otherwise extraordinarily isolated, continuing its traditions, untouched by Gothic innovations, until the late 13thC. In the 14thC, Gothic influences were finally absorbed, but the richness and invention of the Apulian style remained undiminished.

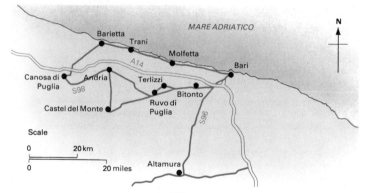

A tour must of course begin with San Nicola in BARI, with its bishop's throne – the acknowledged masterpiece of Apulian sculpture – and fine external sculpture including the Porta dei Leoni or Portal of the Lions, on the N side. The nearby cathedral, built nearly a century later, exhibits the same fundamental plan and has particularly fine carved creatures along the roof galleries and on the E end. San Gregorio, rebuilt in the 12thC just opposite San Nicola, is another beautiful, much smaller church, with fine capitals. Smaller variations of San Nicola are found in the ports N of Bari – Molfetta, Trani and Barletta – and in various towns in the hinterland.

All the places mentioned here can easily be reached along direct main roads if you have a car. Saving Altamura for another occasion, the other towns make an enjoyable round trip in a day. Avoiding the *autostrada*, take the coast road W as far as Barletta, then drive inland to Canosa di Puglia and return to Bari along the S98, diverting only to take in Terlizzi (and possibly a 13thC castle S of Andria). If you are without a car, trains run from Bari up the coast; there is also an independent railway, leaving from a separate station to the right of the main one in Bari, which serves Bitonto, Terlizzi, Ruvo di Puglia, Andria and Barletta. (*Trains on both lines are reasonably frequent –*

The Atlas figures of the 12thC bishop's throne in San Nicola, Bari.

about one every hour.) Altamura and Canosa di Puglia can be reached only by car or bus. (*Enquire at the Ente Provinciale di Turismo, to the left of the main station in Bari, or at the bus company office opposite.*)

The Duomo Vecchia at **Molfetta** is located down by the waterfront: domed, dark, shut in by abutting buildings, it makes a distinctly medieval impression, but in no way prepares one for the splendours of TRANI. Here, the enormous, extremely impressive Duomo, newly restored (1981) to an almost shining beauty, is also set on the waterfront – but in superb isolation, its mellowed white stone singing out against blue sky and sea. The Duomo at BARLETTA is less romantically situated, but has particularly good sculpture – lions jutting out from the ends of the facade, odd reliefs set into the walls all around, a nice array of corbel-faces on the flanks; close by is the little church of Sant' Andrea, also with 12thC external sculpture.

Inland, at **Canosa di Puglia**, the 11thC cathedral has undergone later modification but retains a finely sculpted bishop's throne. Sant' Agostino at ANDRIA has also been drastically remodelled, although it still has a richly carved 14thC Gothic porch. Now, if you have time, you should turn off the main road to **Castel del Monte**, where there is an amazingly well preserved 13thC castle, perfectly intact in its symmetry.

Returning to the sculpture tour, the next stop is RUVO DI PUGLIA – an attractive town with one of the loveliest of all Apulian cathedrals, with a steeply gabled facade and a profusion of sculptural decoration. At **Terlizzi**, the church of San Rosario, although modified, still has an interesting 12thC portal with reliefs signed by Anseramo da Trani. Farther on, the cathedral at BITONTO is one of the finest examples of Apulian Romanesque, with a wealth of external ornament. But the most elaborate sculpture of all, still farther inland, is around the 14thC portal of the Duomo at **Altamura**; these numerous cramped little scenes of the *Life of Christ* show, in the drapery at least, and perhaps for the first time in Apulia, the influence of Gothic.

POMPEI (*POMPEII*)
Napoli, Campania Map B3

Pompeii was a busy port and a prosperous resort (with a population of about 20,000) when it was buried by the eruption of Vesuvius in AD79. The site was discovered in the 1590s but excavations only began in 1748. The unearthing of the town has made Pompeii the most famous name in archaeology.

Pompei Scavi ✩✩
Tel. (081) 8610744
Open Tues – Sun 9am – 3pm (Jan 1),
9am – 6.20pm (July 1); for closing times
of dates in between, Jan – June add 20
mins every fortnight, July – Dec subtract
20 mins every fortnight
Closed Mon
▨ ⅋ ▥ ▣

The first-time visitor to Pompeii should be alert to the two following facts. First, this enormous site is not a museum but an unearthed town no longer provided with elementary comforts such as bars, lavatories, shade or even somewhere to sit down. As one can very well see, the Romans had all these things, but today they are provided only outside the site (with the exception of the rather unsatisfactory café in the Forum).

Secondly, the best things discovered in Pompeii are no longer here but in the Museo Archeologico Nazionale in NAPLES, or in the Metropolitan Museum in New York, or in museums great and small elsewhere. The only exception is the Villa dei Misteri (Villa of Mysteries), which has its frescoes intact *in situ*: these frescoes are the most important single series of the whole site, but they are some way outside the main area.

If you do not mind being shepherded, it is really best to use a guide. This will also guarantee entry to some of the houses for which you would otherwise have to find one of the warders posted in the site, and may result in your being shown some of Pompeii's erotica – sexual images of pornographic or quite other kind.

The main point of going to Pompeii is of course to marvel at the complete organism of a Roman town suspended in time on August 24, AD79. Unlike the inhabitants of ERCOLANO, those of Pompeii had little warning: for anyone who did not immediately abandon everything, it was too late. The ash, pumice and sulphur engulfed the town to the level of the first floor; Pompeii is not perfectly preserved, but in contrast to virtually every other excavated Roman site one may visit ground-floor rooms rather than a ground-floor plan.

Entering the site from the W, by the **Porta Marina**, served by a main road and by the two railway stations of Pompei Scavi (state railway) and Pompei Villa dei Misteri (Circumvesuviana), one soon reaches the **Forum**, the administrative and business heart of the city. Close to the entrance gate is the **Antiquarium**, a museum opened in 1948. **Rooms I** and **II** are devoted to the occasional remains of earlier settlement at Pompeii. Roman Pompeii proper begins in **Room IIA**, with 1stC AD statues and heads of the Imperial family: outstanding is the statue of *Livia* from the Villa dei Misteri. **Room III** has utensils of all kinds, often of superior workmanship. **Room IIIA** provides the thrill obligatory for any visit to Pompeii: casts formed by the hollow left in the set tufa by decayed corpses, vividly expressive of their desperation.

A typical house is the so-called **Casa del Poeta Tragico** (House of the Tragic Poet – the name, like most of the house names, is quite arbitrary). You reach it after crossing the length of the Forum, passing one arch, and turning left before the Arch of Caligula down the Via delle Terme. On the doorstep is one of the most famous images of Pompeii, a mosaic showing a dog with the inscription *Cave Canem* (Beware of the Dog).

At some point, mention of the "Four Pompeian Styles" of painting (and relief stuccowork) will arise. The first style is hardly painting at all, but a fictive marble wallcovering or even just coloured squares. The second style is more or less straightforward illusionistic figure-painting. The third style is the typically Pompeian one, enjoying a fashion during the first half of the 1stC AD, consisting of perspective puzzles hung with little tablets offering mythological and landscape scenes. The fourth style is a variation on this, with a tendency towards a greater impressionism and is typical of the redecoration given to many houses after the earthquake of AD63.

The fourth style can best be seen in its singular charm in the **House of the Vettii ★** in the Vicolo di Mercurio, the street behind the Via delle Terme, towards the Porta di Vesuvio in the N. Close by are other interesting houses, such as the **Casa del Fauno** (House of the Faun) or **Casa degli Amorini Dorati** (House of the Golden Cherubs).

Downtown Pompeii is at the opposite, S end, by the Porta di Stabia. Here, there is a second center with more temples, more fora, and **two theaters**. To reach the Palaestra and the **Amphitheater** one goes E from here to the area of the Nuovi Scavi or New Excavations (in fact begun

in 1911), where the **House of Menander**
and the **House of the Cryptoporticus** are
the most interesting buildings.

There remains the **Villa dei Misteri**,
at the NW end of the town – past the
once-luxurious **Villa di Diomede**, which
is now stripped of its decoration. The
whole complex of the Villa dei Misteri is
interesting, but the outstanding feature is
the **Sala del Grande Dipinto**, which is on
your right straight after entering.

If the rest of Pompeii has revealed the
everyday life of 1stC AD Romans, the
Villa dei Misteri paintings ★★ give an
insight into their spiritual life.
Represented here are preparations for the
great revelation (wall on left of
entrance), the moment just before it (end
wall) and, probably, the rites after it
(right wall). The cult is that of Dionysus
(Bacchus), which enjoyed a considerable
vogue in the Imperial age (judging not
only by this painting but by large numbers
of surviving sarcophagi that allude to the
same rituals), despite being banned by
the Senate.

The various objects handled by the
servants of Dionysus on the end wall are
the props and emblems of his
intoxication; the most important of all,
the sacred phallus, cannot be shown, but
is about to be revealed on the right, where
a woman reaches her hand under a
curtain and an avenging angel raises a
whip to indicate the consequences. But
the quiet scenes on the opposite wall
surely illustrate the ultimate aim of this
journey into pleasure and pain –
catharsis, purification, the peace of urges
and guilts sated and expiated.

RAVELLO
Salerno, Campania Map B3

Ravello is a small medieval town located
in a picturesque position above Amalfi. It
has become – like Taormina or Erice in
Sicily – a tourist village, and concerts are
held in the gardens of the Villa Rufolo.

Duomo
Piazza del Duomo
🏛

Founded in 1086, the church was rebuilt
in the 12thC and remodelled in the
18thC, but its Baroque redecoration has
recently been removed. The fine **bronze
doors** (1179) are by Barisano da Trani,
who also made the doors of the Duomo at
TRANI. Inside, there is a beautiful 13thC
pulpit ★ borne on magnificent lions and
with a rich cladding of carved friezes and
mosaic. The **ambo** opposite is early
12thC, with two charming, though
primitive, mosaics.

REGGIO DI CALABRIA
Calabria Map C7

Like Messina, and due to the same
earthquake of 1908, Reggio di Calabria is
a featureless modern city, although its
sloping site gives it hilly streets like those
of San Francisco or Brighton. The
collections of its archaeological museum
are, however, outstanding.

Museo Archeologico Nazionale ★★
Piazza de Nava
Tel. (0965) 22005
*Open Tues – Sat 9am – 1.30pm, 4 – 7pm,
   Sun 9am – 12.30pm*
Closed Mon
📷 ☑

This is a large museum, with a modern
layout, displaying the archaeological
treasures of all southern Calabria. The
top floor is given over to post-classical
exhibits; the lower ground floor to
submarine archaeology and so to one of
the most important classical finds of this
century, the Riace bronzes – two superb
5thC BC statues of warriors found in the
sea near Riace in 1972.

Even before reaching the reception
desk on the **ground floor**, immediately
upon entering the main door, one should
not miss the **Montescaglioso telamon**, a
splendid baboon-chested Hellenistic
Atlas figure. Circulating around to the
right, past the prehistoric collection, one
passes through bright, orderly rooms
arranged topographically. In **Room XI**,
look out for a fine, almost life-size terra-
cotta *Youth on a Horse* (5thC BC),
thought to have been the roof finial of a
temple. In **Room XII** are more youths
with horses – the *Dioscuri* (late 5thC BC)
from Marasa: these are very similar to the
Dioscuri outside the Musei Capitolini in
Rome (see *SOUTH CENTRAL ITALY*).

On the **first floor** are further rooms
arranged topographically. In **Room
XXIII** are some interesting pieces of
armour, especially two bronze **belts** with
good-quality relief figures and a figurated
cuirass. In **Room XXIV** is a fine **mosaic**
from Hellenistic Kaulonia; in **Room
XXVI**, interesting metalwork from the
Temple of Apollo at Krimisa (mid 5thC
BC). Throughout this section are cases
containing fine terra cottas and vases.

On the **second floor**, passing a few
finely carved medieval marbles, one
enters **Room XXVI**, where there are two
small oil-paintings attributed to
Antonello da Messina: *St Jerome ★* and
Three Angels. Both paintings have been
cut down from larger works.

On the **lower ground floor**, the hall of
the Riace bronzes is preceded by a room

discussing the bronzes and exhibiting fragments of another bronze statue, found in the sea near Ponticello; the head of this statue, called the **Head of a Philosopher** ★★ is next door with the Riace finds. Because it is incomplete, the statue has had much less publicity, but it was evidently every bit as fine, and the **Head** is even better than those of the Riace warriors. The forehead curves slightly inward at the center; the nose projects strongly, hooked in profile but flattened from the front; above all, the bright, far-seeing quality of the eyes makes this a fascinating face, although the idealized features make it unlikely to be a portrait. Like the Riace bronzes, it dates from the mid or late 5thC BC.

The most attractive idea advanced for the **Riace bronzes** ★★ is that they originally formed part of a monument erected at Delphi by the Athenians to celebrate their victories over the Persians in 480 and 479BC; the monument is known to have included warriors, but its date, c.470, ill accords with the preponderance of scholarly opinion on the Riace pieces, which places them towards 450 or even 420BC. Statues A and B are markedly different: B is more at rest, although the *contrapposto* is emphatic; in A, the spiral along which the man bears his weight is much more taut. Both are wonderfully well preserved (and well restored) – even down to the colouring of their eyes; the lips and nipples are of copper; the ringlets of the hair are a joy – almost identical with those of the **Head of a Philosopher**. Their importance derives not only from their quality but from their rarity: very few Greek bronze statues survive.

RUVO DI PUGLIA
Bari, Puglia Map D3

Ruvo is a pleasant, mainly modern town. In its medieval quarter are whitewashed streets and one of the most appealing Romanesque cathedrals in Apulia.

Museo Jatta
Piazza Bovio
Tel. (080) 811042
Open Mon–Sat 9am–noon
Closed Sun
▨

The collection consists almost entirely of **classical vases** and has been formed around a nucleus assembled by two Giovanni Jattas, father and son, in the 19thC. The majority of the vases are of local workmanship; the prize piece is an Attic krater of the late 5thC BC, figuring the **Death of Talos**.

SALERNO
Campania Map B3

Salerno became the dominant city of the gulf that bears its name after the eclipse of Paestum in the early Middle Ages. In the 11thC it was famous throughout Europe for its medical school. While the city's sloping site and surviving medieval buildings give it character, it is mainly modern in aspect.

Duomo
Piazza del Duomo
🏛

The cathedral dates from the time of the town's zenith, in the late 11thC. Completely redecorated in the 18thC, it has since been gradually returned to its original condition, and the earthquake of 1981 has revealed the Norman columns inside the Baroque piers. Repairs at present occupying the right side of the nave will be completed by 1985, the ninth centenary of the death of Pope Gregory VII, who is buried here.

To the left and right of the nave are two glistening marble and mosaic **ambos** ★ (late 12thC and early 13thC). They are very fine, even by Apulian standards. There is also, on the right, an early 13thC **Easter candlestick**, showing the same vigorous animal sculpture as its companion ambo. Beyond are remains of the 12thC **screen** and **floor mosaic**.

In the right and left transepts, and in the atrium fronting the Duomo, are numerous **sarcophagi**, mostly of high quality. But much the finest of the many monuments in the church is the **tomb of Margherita di Durazzo** ★ (d.1412) in the last chapel before the left transept.

Museo del Duomo
Via Monterisi 2
Closed for restoration
The museum has been closed since the 1981 earthquake, but should be open by 1985 (see DUOMO).

Its possessions include several quite good Baroque paintings, notably *Sts Archelaide, Thecla and Susanna* by Solimena and a *St Jerome* by Ribera, and some 15thC and 16thC altarpieces by local masters. There are also a number of medieval ivories.

TARANTO
Puglia Map E3

The old town has fallen, like that of Bari, into the condition of a slum, but is being restored in parts; meanwhile it still offers that unbeatable Apulian combination of sea, sky, 13thC castle and Norman churches – with the addition here of a few columns from a Greek temple. The new town is again like that of Bari, but quieter.

Duomo
Piazza del Duomo
🏛

Built, or rebuilt, in the second half of the 11thC, the Norman Duomo of Taranto is a particularly interesting church, not least for the original cupola over the crossing. Inside, this now has a Baroque covering, and the facade is a magnificent early 18thC addition.

The capitals of the columns are lively and it is interesting to compare the evident Norman copy, second left, with Roman and Byzantine originals.

Museo Archeologico Nazionale ☆
Piazza Archita
Tel. (099) 22112
Open Mon – Sat 9am – 2pm, Sun 9am – 1pm
🔳 ☑

This large, modern museum houses the relics not only of the exceedingly rich Greek and Roman town but also of the province.

Room I contains fragments of early **Greek stone sculpture**, all of which are worth examining. Outstanding, however, is the **female head ★** (late 5thC or early 4thC BC) on the reverse of the display-partition on your right as you enter. The great quality of this work is its purity; the Archaic type of the chin is still clear, even at this date. The use of the chisel is unknown or unwanted: it has been worked all over with a point, hence the bloom of the surface.

Among the items of Hellenistic stone sculpture and the mosaics in **Room II**, one should not miss, first on the left, the expressive **head**, perhaps of a fighter and of uncertain date. The Roman sculpture in **Room III** is also of a consistently high standard, particularly the *Bust of a Youth* (1stC BC) immediately on the left. The best of the hunting-scene **mosaics** is the one on the right beside the window.

Room IV has finds from a Tarentine necropolis, including some outstanding small **reliefs** of local stone (on the shelves on the left). Roman Tarentum could afford quality and a fragmentary *Peleus and Thetis* is particularly good.

The next rooms contain **vases ★** arranged chronologically or by origin. Taranto was an early Spartan colony, and the collection of pottery is more varied than most others in Italy. Attic vases predominate, but of even greater interest are the Corinthian vases in

Room V. These are much smaller than Attic vases, and the impulse towards decoration is stronger and bolder. Spartan pottery is in **Room VI**, with a distinct repertoire of animal designs and colours.

Rooms VII, VIII, IX and **X** comprise the Attic collection, trailing off towards the end with later (4thC – 3rdC BC) local ware. The examples shown here are numerous and include best-quality pieces; besides the common motifs and scenes you will find a rich harvest of mythological and everyday episodes, for example *Hermes Stealing Cattle*.

Room XI, with a large collection of jewellery, is also important. A fragmentary terra-cotta head, on the right, bears the jewellery with which it was found. Here also is displayed a late 6thC Archaic bronze of *Poseidon ★* about half life-size. In a corridor running all the way around the cloister (**Rooms XII–XV**) are terra cottas, including a set of **masks** with grotesque, long, sideways-squashed noses.

TRANI
Bari, Puglia Map D2

Trani is a peaceful, easy-going town. It would be of little interest without its cathedral which, taken with its setting, is one of the most beautiful in the world.

Duomo ☆
Piazza del Duomo
🏛

This tall, elegant, building dates from the late 11thC to the mid13thC. Instead of a crypt, it has an entire lower church. A majestic double staircase leads up to the main entrance; to the right, the campanile is set above a fine Gothic arch.

Adorning the architecture are the usual heraldic beasts of Apulian sculpture, but worth particular attention – high up on the exterior of the transept – is the *Spinario* (a youth removing a thorn from his foot), a Hellenistic motif known in the Middle Ages from the bronze now in the Musei Capitolini in Rome (see *SOUTH CENTRAL ITALY*). Also noteworthy is the way the **Atlas figures** of the main portal do not merely support the bases of the columns but attempt to climb up over them.

The portal frames **bronze doors ★** made in the 1180s by Barisano da Trani, who also made doors for the cathedrals at RAVELLO and at Monreale in Sicily (see *SICILY & SARDINIA*). These are the finest. The ornament is classical, presumably learnt from Byzantine sources, but translated into Romanesque form.

SICILY & SARDINIA

Sicily and Sardinia are the two largest islands in the Mediterranean. They have equally ancient but very different artistic traditions, reflecting the islands' colourful and often bloody histories, in which conquests by foreign powers have played a large part.

SICILIA (*Sicily*)

With its wonderful climate, agricultural riches and central trading position between the Atlantic and the East, Africa and Europe, Sicily has been the Mediterranean's richest prize throughout most of its history. It was colonized or conquered successively by the Greeks, Phoenicians, Romans, Goths, Byzantines, Saracens, Normans, Swabians and Angevins. Later the island was ruled by Spain, then by the Bourbons of Naples. In 1815 Sicily was united with Naples, and in 1861 it became part of the new Kingdom of Italy.

The cosmopolitan nature of Sicily's history and art is eloquently witnessed in the inscription outside the Cappella Palatina in the Palazzo dei Normanni in Palermo, written in Greek, Latin and Arabic. Of all foreign artists to work on the island, Caravaggio was the most celebrated; he visited Messina and Palermo in 1608 and his style had lasting influence on local painters. But the island has also produced outstanding native artists, notably Antonello da Messina in the 15thC and Giacomo Serpotta in the 18thC.

In landscape, Sicily continues the mountain chain of southern Italy, although in the W it levels out into undulating hills and broader valleys. Fields of waving corn spread along the fertile central plains; citrus groves and vineyards wind along the coast; in spring the entire island is brightly carpeted with wild flowers. The major cities are still, as they always have been, on the coast, and there will only exceptionally be occasion for the art-lover to visit the remote interior. The capital and most important city is Palermo; Syracuse is perhaps the most attractive; Messina is pleasant, but has suffered terribly from earthquakes, to which indeed the whole island is prone.

SARDEGNA (*Sardinia*)

Sardinia is much less fertile than Sicily and makes an unforgettable impression on the traveller through its enormous expanses of bare, rugged landscape. Spectacular mountains, capped by swirling mists, hug the center of the island; along the coast, jagged rocks pitted with grottoes drop down to turquoise and emerald seas.

No other part of Europe is still so affected by its prehistoric past. The greatest era in Sardinian history was the Nuragic period (c. 1300–250BC), and the most dominant landmarks of the interior are the tower-like stone structures known as *nuraghi*. The bronzes fashioned by the Nuragic people are by far the most interesting works of art in Sardinia's two main museums.

The Romans ousted the Carthaginians in 238BC and controlled the island until the 5thC AD. Sardinia never fully regained its former autonomy, and its art and architecture came to be a pale provincial reflection of work in other countries. Brutally devastated in the Dark Ages by the Saracens and others, Sardinia was then fought over by the Genoese and Pisans until conquered by the Aragonese in the early 14thC. In the 18thC it passed to the Austrian Hapsburgs and then to the dukes of Savoy.

By 1861, when Vittorio Emanuele II of Sicily became king of a united Italy, Sardinia was a desperately backward place, and indeed remained so until comparatively recent times. The Costa Smeralda in the NE is now a smart tourist area, and there are a number of busy ports around the island, but the mountainous interior remains isolated and inhospitable.

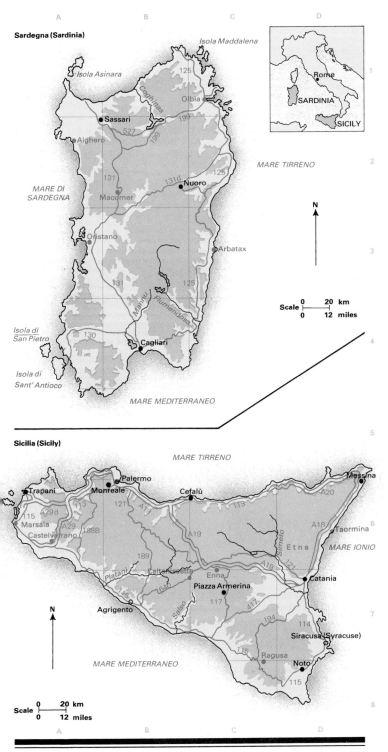

Sardegna (Sardinia)

Isola Maddalena

Isola Asinara

MARE TIRRENO

125

Coghinas

Olbia

199

● Sassari

527

Alghero

199

131

131d ●Nuoro

125

Macomer

MARE DI SARDEGNA

N

Oristano

●Arbatax

131

Mannu

Flumendosa

125

Isola di San Pietro

130

● Cagliari

Isola di Sant' Antioco

Scale 0 — 20 km
0 — 12 miles

MARE MEDITERRANEO

SARDINIA

Rome

SICILY

Sicilia (Sicily)

MARE TIRRENO

● Palermo

Messina ●

Trapani ●

Monreale ●

Cefalù ●

A20

115

A29d

113

121

A19

113

A18

Taormina

Marsala

A29

188B

Etna

MARE IONIO

Castelvetrano

189

A19

Simeto

121

Platani

Caltanissetta ●

A19

Saleso

Enna ●

Piazza Armerina

● Catania

N

640

117

417

Agrigento ○

194

114

Siracusa (Syracuse)

115

Ragusa ●

● Noto

115

MARE MEDITERRANEO

Scale 0 — 20 km
0 — 12 miles

SICILIA (*SICILY*)

AGRIGENTO
Sicilia Map B7

Agrigento was a wealthy Greek colony during the 6thC and 5thC BC and has an evocative history. Here the tyrant Phalaris roasted his enemies in a horrible bronze bull; here Empedocles philosophized; and here one of the best preserved Greek temples survives, amidst a large complex of ruins. The modern city is set high on a hill above the Zona Archeologica or ancient city – so high that from below its buildings look like skyscrapers. The view is memorable.

Museo Archeologico Nazionale e Zona Archeologica
Via Passeggiata Archeologica
Tel. (0922) 29008
Museo open Tues–Sat 9am–2pm, Sun
*   9am–1pm. Zona Archeologica open*
*   9am–1hr before sunset*
Museo closed Mon
🖂 ⟲ 🏛 ⬛ ✓

The museum is built around the 13thC Cistercian church of San Nicola, but has a modern layout. Before entering the museum, the well-preserved 2ndC AD Roman **sarcophagus** in the second chapel on the right of the church is worth a look.

After the prehistoric exhibits, **Room III** offers an important collection of **Greek vases** – their quality is a reflection of the wealth of classical Agrigento. Among many items of browsing interest, note a white-ground krater depicting *Perseus and Andromeda* (5thC BC) – Perseus contemplating the unfortunate Andromeda hung out on a scaffold.

At the far end of the room, on the left, a sole **marble torso**, displayed with a drawn reconstruction, is the only remaining fragment of the 5thC BC sculpture of the Temple of Zeus Olympios, except for the famous colossal **telamons** (Atlas figures used as columns). The only intact telamon is exhibited in all its grandeur in **Room VI**: here also are heads of other telamons, and models showing how these figures may have been set between the columns of the vast temple. (Another telamon, a composite of several, can be found amidst the ruins of the temple itself.)

Leaving the room at the upper level, into **Room X**, you find three important pieces of marble sculpture – an Archaic torso of an *Ephebe* or youth (early 5thC BC); a small Hellenistic *Aphrodite Bathing* and a Hellenistic **male torso** ★ (both c. 3rdC BC).

Across the road a small section of the ancient city has been unearthed: the best entrance to the great temples is down the hill to the right.

Santo Spirito
Via Santo Spirito
🛈 🏛 ⬇

The most important things in Agrigento are classical, but a visit to Santo Spirito gives a taste of the winding, climbing streets of medieval and modern Agrigento, and also offers a charming ruined cloister with quantities of crumbling late 13thC stonework. Inside the church is much statuary and a Berninesque **sunburst** over the main altar by the celebrated Rococo stuccoist Giacomo Serpotta.

CATANIA
Sicilia Map D6

Catania has become more important in recent times than either Messina to the N or Syracuse to the S, but much of it is less attractive – with the exception of the Via Crociferi and the gardens of the Villa Bellini above. It preserves a Roman theater and a 13thC castle but otherwise the buildings are mainly 18thC (after the earthquake of 1693) or later (the city suffered considerably in World War II).

Museo Civico
Castello Ursino, Piazza Federico di Svevia
Tel. (095) 583035
Open Tues–Sun 9am–1.20pm
Closed Mon
🖂 🏛

The castle, built in the mid 13thC by the Emperor Frederick II and fairly well preserved, is typical of his fortifications in Sicily and Apulia. The museum is a rambling collection of objects of sometimes dubious value. The best things are probably the **Greek and Roman sculptures** in **Rooms III** and **IV**: a 6thC BC Archaic head from Lentini in Room IV; and Roman torsos and heads in both rooms, including a version of Polykleitos' *Doryphoros* (see NAPLES, Museo Archeologico Nazionale). The medieval and Renaissance sculpture in **Rooms X** and **XI** includes a fine recumbent **effigy** of a knight (Room XI).

Room XV on the first floor features Baroque paintings by local and mainland artists; the latter include *Tobias Healing his Blind Father* by Mattias Stomer (early 17thC), which is notable for its grotesque but striking realism. On the second floor, in **Room XIX**, are medieval and early Renaissance works; note especially a *Madonna* and other pictures by Antonello de Saliba, the nephew and imitator of Antonello da Messina. The **small bronzes** in **Room XXII** are quite interesting, although the attributions to Riccio or Giambologna are highly optimistic. The **18thC works** of all kinds in **Room XXV** instance the upturn in energy of Sicilian late Baroque.

CEFALU
Palermo, Sicilia Map B6

Without a visit to Cefalù a tour of Sicily would be incomplete. The winding little town with its fine beach and world-famous cathedral also boasts an important portrait by Antonello da Messina. The only drawback to visiting Cefalù is the sometimes frustrating attitude of the authorities, who seem intent on imposing unnecessary difficulties on sightseeing.

Cattedrale
Piazza del Duomo
🏛 🏛

The church was begun by Roger II in 1132, but not completed for more than a century: the facade dates from 1240. In the mosaic decoration of the capitals and in the awkward mounting of two classical columns one above another at the jambs of the crossing, the cathedral closely resembles Norman churches in **PALERMO**.

Access is forbidden to the choir, which hinders enjoyment of the **mosaics** there; these are by Byzantine workmen imported soon after the church was begun. The *Christ Pantocrator* in the apse is more finely characterized, indeed a more suffering and concerned figure, than that in the cathedral at **MONREALE**. The warrior saints beside the lower window of the right side-wall are particularly splendid.

Museo della Fondazione Mandralisca
Via Mandralisca
Tel. (0921) 21547
Open 9am–12.30pm, 3.30–7pm
📷 🏛

This is a rather typical municipal collection, consisting mostly of furniture, coins and terra cottas.

The museum's one outstanding possession, Antonello da Messina's *Portrait of an Unknown Man* (c.1465–70) has a separate chamber where, in the worst display in all Italy, it is roped off and shown at an angle of some 30° to the spectator (to reinforce the effect of the eyes turning to meet your gaze from the head set at an angle to the picture plane!). If you ask to see it properly you will be offered a same-size photograph.

MESSINA
Sicilia Map D5

The various earthquakes that have ruined Messina during the course of its history have left it a featureless city, although the center around Piazza Cairoli is bustling and full of life. Nothing remains of the Greek colony and Roman city, and the pretty 12thC church of Santa Maria Annunziata dei Catalani is virtually the only survivor of the Norman city.

Museo Nazionale
Viale della Libertà
Tel. (090) 41110
Closed for restoration

The rich collections of the museum range from Greek and Roman sculpture to 17thC and 18thC painting, sculpture and minor arts. There are several Byzantine or Byzantinizing paintings from the 13thC to the 15thC, and a fine 14thC marble *Madonna* of Sienese workmanship.

The early Renaissance works are important. There is a beautiful *Madonna* ★ (1469) by Francesco Laurana, together with a *St Antony* and a *St Catherine* by Antonello Gagini and an anonymous wooden **crucifix** (thought to be Catalan in derivation) of considerable power. Although badly damaged in the 1908 earthquake, Antonello da Messina's **St Gregory polyptych** ★ (signed and dated 1473) is still a striking work; the head of the Madonna, solid and palpable, has remained intact. Several contemporary or slightly later Netherlandish works, three or four of high quality, attest to the abundance of such art in Sicily for Antonello to study.

From the 16thC there is a fragmentary picture by the rare artist, Polidoro da Caravaggio, who died in Messina in 1543, and a *Madonna* by Bronzino.

Next come two famous pictures by Caravaggio: the **Resurrection of Lazarus** ★ (1609) for the Chiesa dei Crociferi and the **Adoration of the Shepherds** ★ (also 1609) for the Chiesa dei Cappuccini. The grandeur of conception of the **Lazarus** and the bold void of the entire upper part of the canvas survive, but the painting has long been in bad condition and seems to have reached the limits of restoration. The **Adoration** was another of Caravaggio's "proletarian" pictures: it shows the Virgin hugging the Child like a beggar-woman in the street.

Classical sites in Sicily

Sicily is extremely rich in classical, particularly Greek, remains – hardly less rich than Greece itself. There are about 40 classical sites where there is something considerable to see, and many of these are set in the most romantic Mediterranean scenery, which even the most blinkered specialist would find difficult to ignore. Some of the more remote sites are difficult to reach, but others are major tourist attractions. Coaches to all sites mentioned here are run by Suntours of Palermo (*Via Emerico Amari 34, tel. (091) 587144*).

The heyday of classical Sicily was during the 6thC and 5thC BC: this was the period when its remarkable surviving temples were built – although other parts of the sites tend to belong to later, less heroic periods. Undoubtedly the richest site on the island is the archaeological zone of AGRIGENTO (*open 9am to 1hr before sunset*), offering the **Temple of Concord**, the best preserved temple in Sicily (it was adapted as a church, and the *cella* or central part survives intact); the **Temple of Hera** and **Temple of Castor and Pollux**, which look superb against the skyline; and the extremely impressive ruins of the vast **Temple of Zeus** (important sculptural fragments from this are on display in the local museum). All these temples were begun in the 5thC BC; the Temple of Zeus was never completed.

The modern city of Agrigento rises on a separate hill, but many towns still occupy their ancient sites, their more fragmentary classical remains poking up in bare, deserted enclosures between noisy, traffic-filled streets. SIRACUSA is an example (and its cathedral, converted from a Greek temple in the 7thC, is an essential part of any classical tour), although it also has an archaeological zone outside the modern city (*open Tues – Sun 9am – 6pm or 1hr before sunset if earlier*). A disappointment after Agrigento, this site is still interesting for its quarries; here the Athenians were imprisoned after their disastrous expedition of 416 – 413BC; no one who has read Thucydides' vivid account of this episode can see these pits without being moved.

However splendid these archaeological zones may be, they cannot compare with ancient cities exposed on hill tops or sea shores far away from any modern settlement. **Segesta**, in western Sicily, is the finest example of a hill-top site, offering not only a charming small theater and magnificent temple, but also panoramic views over beautiful, saucer-shaped valleys. As one approaches the temple at Segesta (late 5thC BC), it emerges unforgettably from behind a hill, tawny as a great, placid lion. (*Segesta is an exit from the Palermo-Trapani autostrada and has a railway station. The site is open 9am to 1hr before sunset.*)

Selinunte, again in western Sicily, offers by contrast an enchanting strip of deserted beach, as well as much more of a town on its acropolis; the temples include the well-preserved **Temple E** and the gigantic sprawl of **Temple G** – only slightly smaller than the Temple of Zeus at Agrigento, and with much more of its stone remaining. Both again are 5thC BC. (*Selinunte is served by a branch-line and road from Castelvetrano. It is open 9am to 1hr before sunset.*)

Selinunte marks the westward end of Greek colonization and **Mozia** near Marsala was, by contrast, a Phoenician settlement. Lying on a romantically deserted island, this has the most beautiful setting of all the classical sites, although little remains of the buildings above foundation level. (*A boat makes the crossing Tues – Sun 8.30am – 1pm from Ettore Infersa on the facing shore, on the Trapani-Marsala road.*)

Other important sites, such as **Tindari** on the northern coast or **Taormina** on the eastern coast, are more easily accessible and have virtually become tourist villages. Tindari has extensive and important ruins, including a Greek theater. Taormina, a charming hill town, offers a Roman theater with comparatively well preserved stage architecture. **Erice**, above Trapani, is an even prettier medieval town, enjoying vertiginous views along the western coast; it was once the site of a world-famous sanctuary of Venus, although her temple is now entirely buried beneath the castle.

The imposing Greek ruins of Selinunte, on the SW coast of Sicily.

MONREALE
Palermo, Sicilia Map B5

The town of Monreale, picturesquely set near the foot of Monte Caputo, grew up in the 12thC around William II's celebrated cathedral. It is now a busy market center for the olive and fruit trade of the Conca d'Oro or Golden Valley.

Cattedrale ☆
Piazza Vittorio Emanuele
📖 🏛 ♨

The cathedral is set high on a hill overlooking Palermo, much as Fiesole overlooks Florence; the view is perhaps not quite so good, but the cathedral, one of the greatest Romanesque buildings in Italy, is incomparable. The outstanding architectural features externally are the interlacing arcades of the apses and the magnificent cloister, with its exotically rich and ingenious decoration.

William II founded the cathedral in 1174, and thus the superb **mosaics** ★★ covering the nave, aisles, apse and transepts are rather later than those commissioned by Roger II from Greek artists (see Palazzo dei Normanni, **PALERMO**) and are the work of Sicilian and Venetian masters.

Easiest to see, and perhaps best of all, are the mosaics of the **nave**. These tell the story of *Genesis*, starting top right and continuing all the way round, then dropping to the layer beneath the windows. In the **aisles** are scenes from the *Life of Christ*. Although the emotional range is limited, the charm with which details of the story are depicted is constantly rewarding, and some of the figures are striking – the golden-haired athlete sawing planks for Noah's ark, for instance, or the warrior figure of Esau.

In the **apse**, *Christ Pantocrator* reaches out an embracing arm of awesome majesty. In the **transepts** is the continuation of the *Life of Christ* from the aisles; also, scenes from the *Lives of Sts Peter and Paul*, whose monumental figures as usual occupy the side apses. One of the finest images of all is the *Madonna* in the lunette inside the W portal – but more important than any individual scene is the coherence and grandeur of the whole, which it is possible to appreciate because the building is so well lit.

The cathedral also has two sets of **bronze doors** ★ Those on the main facade (1186) are by Bonanno, who also made bronze doors for the Duomo at Pisa (see *NORTH CENTRAL ITALY*); those on the N side are probably of the same date and are by Barisano da Trani: they show the same repertoire of motifs as his doors for the cathedral of his native Trani (see *SOUTHERN ITALY*). Bonanno's doors display a lively narrative unknown to Barisano, whose approach is more Byzantine than Romanesque.

NOTO
Siracusa, Sicilia Map D7

Noto, an easy day-trip from Syracuse, is one of the most charming hill-towns in Sicily, and also possesses the only signed Francesco Laurana sculpture on the island. The town was rebuilt after the earthquake of 1693, and is characterized by the ornate facades of its late Baroque palaces and churches.

Santissimo Crocifisso
Piazza Mazzini
🏛

The facade of this Baroque church is incomplete. Inside, in the right transept, only the *Madonna of the Snow* (1471) by Francesco Laurana is of interest; it is a very beautiful work – simple in conception and with the most exquisite handling of the surface.

PALERMO
Sicilia Map B5

The capital and most important city of Sicily, Palermo has a distinguished past and the richest collection of medieval monuments in the island. Palermo became the capital of Sicily when conquered from the Arabs by the Norman adventurer-baron Robert Guiscard, and its splendid Norman heritage reflects the rapid elevation of its Norman kings to third place in 12thC Europe after the Holy Roman Emperor and the Pope. The courts of Roger I, Roger II, William I and William II (d.1189) were brilliant and cosmopolitan. Most of modern Palermo is pleasant enough, but around the port, particularly in the historic center of the city – the Kalsa – the dirt and dereliction are even worse than in Naples. This area was devastated by bombs in World War II and is still ruined. Palermo has a bad reputation for crime, and its picturesque street markets have been the scene of sinister events. Palermitans themselves advise tourists to take elementary precautions, but the situation has been exaggerated by rumour and is not as bad as in Naples.

Cattedrale di Monreale See
MONREALE.

Chiesa della Martorana ☆
Piazza Bellini
🏛

The Martorana is masked by an inappropriate Baroque portal, but has a particularly fine Norman campanile and, inside, 12thC **mosaics ★** in a pure Byzantine style, among the most important in Palermo. There is also the adjacent, triple-domed Cappella di San Cataldo (c.1160). The church was built and decorated from 1143 by Roger II's admiral, George of Antioch: both appear in donor portraits.

The mosaics are by imported Eastern artisans and are arranged according to Byzantine conventions: in the dome, **Christ Pantocrator**; below, **Seraphim** – particularly interesting figures, showing the established patterns elongated for the sake of elegance and distorted to show movement; then **Prophets, Evangelists** and **Apostles**. In the areas flanking the dome are scenes from the **Life of the Virgin** (note the **Nativity** on the right of the vault preceding the dome, with the midwives bathing the Child) and, on the walls, **Patron Saints**. Also worth noting is the magnificent **mosaic pavement**.

Duomo
Corso Vittorio Emanuele
🏛

The Romanesque E end and the Gothic facade are outstanding architecturally, but the interior, refurbished in the late 18thC, is cold and dull. It does, however, contain the impressive 13thC **tombs ★** of several Norman rulers (in a side-chapel immediately to the right of the W entrance); each is a vast, curved, utterly plain sarcophagus, all of porphyry, of terrifying, absolutist dignity.

Galleria Nazionale della Sicilia ☆
Palazzo Abatellis, Via Alloro 4
Tel. (091) 233317
Open Wed, Fri, Sat, 9am–1.30pm, Tues, Thurs 9am–1.30pm, 3–5.30pm, Sun 9am–1pm
Closed Mon
🎨 ♿ 🏛 ☑

The building is a palace of the 1490s, combining Aragonese-Gothic forms with a few hints of the Renaissance. It contains masterpieces by the leading lights of the southern Renaissance – Francesco Laurana and Antonello da Messina – and by a slightly later Netherlandish artist, Jan Gossaert.

In **Room II**, the old palace chapel, is a detached fresco of the **Triumph of Death ★** by an unknown artist. It dates from around the middle of the 15thC, and is commonly but unconvincingly associated with Pisanello. Around the

ramping skeleton horse ridden by Death, pious and profane collapse alike; friends are shown succouring the stricken; on the right (lower corner) a doctor intercedes uselessly. Just above, three women with intertwining hands unexpectedly turn out to be the Three Graces, dancing to a lutenist.

Laurana's late 15thC **bust ★** (said to be of Eleonora of Aragon but the identification is not secure) is in **Room IV**. Like many other Laurana busts, it may have been executed after the sitter's death; the peculiarly ethereal, idealized quality makes one think so. The sculptor seems to deny all volume to the markedly simplified form of the head; it is worth recalling contemporary painted portraits, often seen in flattened profile, because this bust also demands to be seen in profile, and hardly offers even a frontal view, let alone a three-quarters one.

Room V contains sculpture by Antonello Gagini, son of Domenico, and well represents the all-pervasive Gaginesque current; the **Madonnas** in particular show the evident links with Laurana. Up the stairs, **Room VII** reveals the rich mix of influences on 14thC and 15thC Sicilian painting. All on a small scale, these imports come from Tuscany (particularly Siena); Venice and Padua (the **Madonna** by Antonio Veneziano is of high quality); the Marches; and also Catalonia. **Rooms VIII** and **IX** are given to local artists, in which these various influences can be traced – but most of the works in Room IX post-date the arrival of Antonello da Messina.

Antonello's **Madonna Annunciate ★★** (once presumably but not necessarily accompanied by an angel) is in **Room X** with three works from a dismembered polyptych, showing **St Jerome, St Gregory** and **St Augustine**. The three saints are beautiful and have a kind of special glow but the Madonna is, quite simply, spellbinding. Much of the blue of her mantle is lost, but still evident is the extremely sharp distinction between light on one side and shade on the other, creating a forward and backward plane between which the face takes sculptural form. Throughout the picture Antonello does not model in gradations of shade but contrasts block against block, with greatest virtuosity in the Madonna's raised, foreshortened hand.

This kind of sophistication was beyond the capabilities of Antonello's followers in **Rooms XI** and **XII**. In **Room XIII** is the **Malvagna triptych ★** of Jan Gossaert, a tiny work of the most fastidious detail, especially in the rich Gothic tracery of the thrones, but moving and devout as well.

Museo Archeologico Nazionale ☆
Piazza Olivella 4
Tel. (091) 587825
Open Tues–Sat 9am–1.30pm, Sun
9am–12.30pm
Closed Mon
📷 💷

Founded at the beginning of the 19thC, this is the most important archaeological museum in Sicily, although those of Agrigento and Syracuse are close rivals. Housed in 17thC monastic buildings, it is devoted mainly to cultural artifacts and the classical history of western Sicily; the pride of the museum is the sculpture found at Selinunte.

Across the first, smaller cloister, the room on the left has Egyptian sculpture; the room on the right, two interesting **sarcophagi** of Carthaginian manufacture (6thC/5thC BC), resembling Etruscan examples in general scheme but quite different from these and from Greek art in style.

Across the second, larger cloister, through the door at the end on the right, it is impossible to miss the vast *Gorgon* that once occupied the center of the pediment of Temple C at Selinunte (late 6thC BC). To the right, through a room with a collection of lionhead-gutters (early 5thC BC) from Himera, one reaches the bronze *Ephebe of Selinunte* ★ and the surviving **metopes** ★ of Temples C, E and F of Selinunte.

The *Ephebe* (early 5th BC), although not much bigger than a statuette, has aroused local attention because, despite its evident dependence on Greek art, the proportions are subtly different; it is thought to be of native workmanship.

On the left wall are three quite well preserved metopes from the same temple as the *Gorgon*, Temple C, showing *Perseus Killing the Gorgon*, *Hercules Punishing Robbers* and the *Chariot of the Sun*. For all their beauty, these are in a fairly undeveloped Archaic style, with little progress towards movement, truly rounded form or distinction of types.

Clearly later (of the late 5thC BC) are four metopes from Temple E on the back wall. Their greater sophistication is evident in the much more fluent movements of *Hercules Fighting the Amazons*, *Actaeon Transformed into a Stag*, *Athena Overcoming the Giant Enceladus* and the *Marriage of Zeus and Hera*.

To the right of the Temple C metopes, on the same wall, are other, more fragmentary metopes from Temple E, intermediate in date (early 5thC BC). The *Head of a Giant* ★ is a striking mask of pain, and comparable with similar things from the Temple of Zeus at Olympia. Further metopes on the right wall, found re-used in fortifications, are also of high quality. Through this room is an Etruscan collection.

Up the stairs from the first, smaller cloister are numerous cases of terra cottas, also a large bronze *Ram*, and a virtuoso Hellenistic piece of an *Athlete and Stag* presented to the museum after its discovery in Pompeii. Further on are two rooms of Greek and Roman marble sculpture of fair quality, but this is a 19thC collection without provenance and so of limited interest.

The second floor has a few mosaics and an enormous collection of **vases**.

Museo Diocesano
Palazzo Arcivescovale, Via Bonello
Closed for restoration
This is a good collection, with several pictures by or from the workshops of well-known artists, such as Vasari or Luca Giordano. Most interesting are 14thC and 15thC works, revealing the wide range of artistic currents present then in Sicily. Among them is a picture painted for the confraternity of San Niccolò Reale by the Paduan artist, Antonio Veneziano (1388); also, works by Tuscan, Flemish, Catalan and native masters.

Oratorio del Rosario di San Domenico
Via Bombinai 16
The **stucco decorations** (1714–17) are by Serpotta and the life-size statue of *Fortitude* ★ is perhaps the finest single figure he ever produced. Fortitude is usually represented as a rather severe woman, but here she is a delicious coquette. She retains the traditional emblems of a column and a lion's skin (allusions to Samson and Hercules), but instead of armour and a helmet she wears a tight bodice and a jaunty headdress of ostrich feathers.

Over the main altar is the enormous *Virgin of the Rosary* ★ (1624–28) by van Dyck. It is rather dirty, but still stupendous: the Madonna bursts through an arch, causing wonder amidst the saints, while a putto scampers through their legs to point to a skull beside a bouquet of flowers.

Oratorio di San Lorenzo
Via Immacolatella 5
Closed for restoration
The early 18thC **stucco decorations** are by Giacomo Serpotta and are similar to those of the ORATORIO DEL ROSARIO DI SAN DOMENICO. The church's greatest treasure, Caravaggio's altarpiece of the *Nativity* (1609), was stolen in 1969 and has not yet been recovered.

Oratorio di Santa Zita
Via Squarcialupo
The oratory has more splendid **stucco decorations** (1688–1718) by Serpotta, again featuring allegorical figures.

Palazzo dei Normanni ☆
Piazza del Parlamento
Tel. (091) 484700, 788449
Palazzo open Mon, Fri, Sat 9am–12.30pm;
  Cappella Palatina open Mon, Tues,
  Thurs–Sat 9am–1pm, 3–5.30pm,
  Wed 9am–1pm, Sun 9–10.20am,
  12.15–1pm
Palazzo closed Tues–Thurs, Sun
🔲 *but gratuity appreciated for guided tour*
🚹 *Palazzo* 📱 🏛
The great palace of the Norman kings was only partly rebuilt in the 16thC and 17thC, and still preserves in all its glory (vitiated only by occasional restoration or replacement) the **Cappella Palatina ★★** of Roger II.

Entry to the chapel is across the courtyard, and left at the top of the stairs. The **painted wooden roof ★** is almost pure Moorish work, unique in Europe and the equal of most such things in Tunisia – endless interrelating wooden stalactites to bamboozle and create wonder. The **mosaics ★** with which every remaining inch of the quite large, aisled chapel is filled range from those of Roger's time (1140s) in the dome and choir to the slightly later ones of the walls beneath the nave windows (1150s–60s) to the 13thC ones of the aisles. The chapel is completed by a magnificent **mosaic floor**, marble facings on the lower walls, a fine **pulpit** and a **candlestick ★** with lively marble sculpture.

The mosaic scheme of the dome and choir is the work of Greek artists and follows Byzantine patterns, with *Angels* beneath the *Christ Pantocrator*, then *Prophets*, *Evangelists* and *Apostles*, the *Life of Christ* and *Life of the Virgin*, and *Patron Saints*. (The obvious replacements are 17thC and 18thC.) Notable is the awesome *St Paul* in the right apse; the awe is created by the larger scale of this bust-figure, but also by the lean, uncompromising energy of the colossal face. The faces of the wall saints also have marked character, a sign of the unusual quality of the workmanship.

The narrative scenes here are much more impressive than those of the aisles, which retain a full classical grandeur (for instance, *Sts Peter and Paul before Nero*, last but one before the choir in the left aisle) but seem peculiarly lifeless, as if they were the work of an extremely good copyist – indeed they are considered native workmanship. Also by Sicilian artisans are the smaller and more zestful narrative scenes of the nave.

Despite its restricted viewing times, and the unwanted tour of neighbouring 19thC rooms, the **Sala di Re Ruggero ★** (second floor) is not to be missed. Here the mosaics are secular. Oddly enough, they are more stylized than the religious ones in the Cappella beneath, and the symmetrical pattern by which the isolated animals and hunters are imprisoned is even more insistent. The stylization is not of the usual Romanesque kind but is influenced by Moslem art, and these mute, strange beasts have an arcane simplicity that is unforgettable.

Down the road to the left of the Palazzo dei Normanni, in the Via dei Benedettini, is the empty but evocative church and flowering cloister of **San Giovanni degli Eremiti**, a domed chapel built in the 1130s by Roger II.

Sant' Agostino
Via Favaro
🏛
The particularly beautiful Gothic portal is 15thC. Inside, the entire interior is a playground for the **stucco decorations ★** (1711–29) of Giacomo Serpotta, the one genius in 18thC Sicilian art. It is likely that Serpotta trained in Rome, and his icing-sugar-white figures show an affinity with Bernini in their energy and vivacity; yet they are more elongated and elegant than Bernini's figures, with an enchanting air of festive well-being that places them among the most delightful expressions of the Rococo in Italian art.

San Domenico
Via Roma
The Baroque church is of little interest but is on the way to the ORATORIO DEL ROSARIO DI SAN DOMENICO. Its abundant **Neoclassical tombs** are not individually outstanding but they do represent Risorgimento Palermo.

San Francesco d'Assisi
Piazza San Francesco
📱 🏛
This attractive 13thC church (restored to a pristine state after war damage) has several interesting Renaissance monuments. Most important of these is the **arch ★** that now leads to the fourth chapel on the left, by Francesco Laurana assisted by Pietro de Bontade (1468): the jambs are lined with low relief panels of *Evangelists* and *Doctors of the Church*. In the fifth chapel on the left is the *Madonna* to which the arch once gave entrance; this is presumably by Pietro de Bontade, since it is heavy and dull compared to *Madonnas* by Laurana (such as his *Madonna of the Snow* in the

Santissimo Crocifisso at **NOTO**). Of finer quality is the **Madonna** on the right in the first chapel on the left; this is the work of Domenico Gagini and went with his arch of 1465 that is now on the entrance wall on the immediate right of the door; it has something of Laurana's striking serenity, achieved by simplicity of form and enhanced rather than marred by refined decoration.

Domenico Gagini was the father of a clan of marble sculptors who dominated Renaissance Sicily even more than the Lombardo family dominated Renaissance Venice: the **Madonna** on the left in the same chapel is typical of the style of his followers in its greater roundness of form and lavish gilding.

Also to be seen are eight **Virtues** (1723) by Serpotta against the entrance wall; and several other arches and **Madonnas** of Gaginesque type and good quality. Worth special mention is the **recumbent effigy** of a fragmentary tomb now against the outside wall of the fifth chapel on the right – a charming and tragic memorial to a young knight.

San Giovanni degli Eremitti See
PALAZZO DEI NORMANNI.

PIAZZA ARMERINA
Enna, Sicilia Map C7

A pleasant town with some interesting buildings, Piazza Armerina has become part of the tourist route (acquiring hotels and restaurants) solely thanks to the remarkable Roman mosaics found at nearby Casale. The main square, Piazza Cascino, has a bizarre war memorial, inscribed "It is blood that gives movement to the sounding wheel of history".

Duomo
Piazza del Duomo
The rather grand, Baroque Duomo preserves, in a small chapel to the left of the main altar, an interesting painted **crucifix**, dated 1485, of good quality but by an unknown artist. The solidity of the lighting of the forms strongly suggests Provençal painting.

Villa Filosofiana ☆☆
Casale
Tel. (0935) 81037
Open 9am–2hrs before sunset
🗺 🚗 ⛽ 🅿 ⏞ 🏛 ☑
Casale lies 6km (4 miles) SW of Piazza Armerina
The splendour and extent of this early 4thC AD villa are very striking, and a tour of its magnificent **mosaics ★★** takes quite

a long time. At the center is a largish garden, surrounded by an elegant colonnade with a lovely mosaic pavement – a design of isolated medallions containing mostly animal heads. Around this, in an asymmetrical plan, open the rooms of the house, each furnished with a mosaic floor of similar quality; in addition there is a bath-house (which you come to on first entering the complex) and a *triclinium* (to be translated here as "banqueting-house" rather than "dining-room").

Among the most outstanding mosaics of the villa are: the enormous composition running the length of the raised corridor at the far end of the garden, with its scores of animals and hunters; the set-pieces showing a god in the midst of a sea inhabited by mythological creatures, Ulysses and the Cyclops, girls in bikinis playing ball or even weightlifting and – the *pièce de résistance* – the **Destruction of the Giants ★** in the *triclinium*.

The workmanship is African, for the entire villa is a reflection of the close links between Roman Sicily and the neighbouring province of North Africa. The style must be related to the "impressionistic" mode of Roman painting, in particular to its "broken" brushwork: hence the sloppy delineation, the use of strips of varied colour instead of a regulated modelling. In compensation, what elegances of pose are achieved in the figures! This sophisticated art is perhaps most successful in the furthermost lobe of the *triclinium*, where passionate giants writhe in muscular frenzy beneath an onslaught of arrows; the scene is all the more moving because the arrows seem to have been issued from mere supernatural whim: the iconography is obscure.

SIRACUSA (SYRACUSE)
Sicilia Map D7

Syracuse is a sizable city in the typical southern Italian pattern of old town on a promontory, modern and commercial city behind it and around the bay. It is prosperous but not heavily industrialized, and one of the pleasantest and most cultivated cities in Sicily.

Duomo
Piazza del Duomo
🏛
Entering the cathedral of Syracuse is a unique and fascinating experience. Although the building has been refurbished in some important ways, this is still essentially the early 5thC BC

Temple of Athena, which was converted to a Christian church in AD640. Even if the spaces between the columns have been walled up, and the wall of the *cella* has been opened up by arches, an ancient Greek *cella* must have been dark and was roofed, so the experience is as genuine as entering a comparable derelict temple.

Works of art in the church are not so impressive, and the most interesting – three late 15thC paintings in the style of Antonello da Messina (*St Zosimus*, *St Jerome* and *St Marcian*) – are now kept in the sacristy (ask a priest to let you in).

Museo Archeologico
Piazza del Duomo
Tel. (0931) 69291, 68791
Open Tues – Sat 9am – 2pm, Sun
  9am – 1pm
Closed Mon
🖭

Somewhat confusingly, the tour of the ground floor usually begins in Room XIV (first on the right), since access to Rooms I–IV (containing only inscriptions and architectural fragments) is closed, and Rooms V–XIII must be visited in inverse order. Indeed the entire museum is suspended in a temporary state, pending the decision to close it and move the collection to a new building.

Dominating **Room XIV** is a large 4thC AD **sarcophagus** in good condition, showing Christian scenes in considerable profusion. Next, in **Room XII (Room XIII** is a small chamber off it at the opposite end, containing rows of busts), is a crowded collection of **Hellenistic and Roman marble sculpture**, many pieces being of good quality. **Room XI** has earlier Greek sculpture or copies after it, but not of such a high standard. **Room X** has Archaic Greek works, including a noteworthy puffed-out *Demeter* sheltering two children in her mantle (late 6thC BC).

One then enters the large central **Room VII**, mainly given over to **architectural sculpture**, unusually interesting because on many pieces the original colours have been preserved, even if they have faded. There is also a small running *Gorgon* (early 5thC BC) with many of its original colours.

The pride of the museum is housed across in **Room IX**: the white marble statue of *Venus*★ in the act of covering her nudity, of Roman date but after a Hellenistic conception originating in the 2ndC BC. It is close to the *Medici Venus* in the Uffizi in Florence (see *NORTH CENTRAL ITALY*). The marble is finely finished to achieve a distinctly fatty quality in the flesh. In the same room is a Hellenistic statuette of *Hercules*★ of

elongated, Lysippan proportions, and perhaps close in date to Lysippos' career (ending in the 4thC BC); also, another Lysippan work, an expressive **torso**★

Museo Regionale di Palazzo Bellomo
Via Capodicci
Tel. (0931) 65343
Open Tues – Sat 9am – 2pm, Sun
  9am – 1pm
Closed Mon
🖭 🕮 🏛 ☑

This charming 13thC palace, reworked in the 15thC, houses a well-presented collection of local provenance.

Room III, first on the left after passing into the courtyard, contains several good Renaissance marble sculptures: besides the **tomb of Eleonora Branciforte d'Aragona** (1525) by Giambattista Mazzolo on the far wall, there is an endearing 15thC *Madonna* by Domenico Gagini and a fine early 16thC **tomb figure** by Antonello Gagini.

The **picture gallery** is on the first floor. **Room V** has Creto-Byzantine icons datable up to the 17thC, and a late 16thC Russian (Stroganov school) icon of the *Assumption*.

Room VI contains the pride of the museum, a large panel *Annunciation*★ by Antonello da Messina, documented 1474, unfortunately much damaged and restored. The room also contains some charming early 15thC polyptychs by local masters. By the door to Room VII are the separated parts of a polyptych reasonably attributed to the 15thC Venetian painter Lazzaro Bastiani.

Room VII has altarpieces of the turn of the 15thC, and a copy after Antonello's lost *St Thomas Aquinas*. In **Room VIII** are dull 16thC paintings; in **Room IX**, Baroque works, similarly undistinguished.

Santa Lucia
Piazza Santa Lucia
The church, some distance from the old town, has a Byzantine foundation and catacombs, but the present building is entirely 18thC in aspect. St Lucy was a Syracusan virgin martyr, killed in about 304, and this is her cult church. Its greatest glory, hanging over the main altar, is the *Burial of St Lucy*★ by Caravaggio. In bad condition, it is still immensely impressive. Probably painted in late 1608, just before the MESSINA Museo Nazionale pictures, it is indebted to the artist's own *Death of the Virgin*, now in the Louvre, for mood and basic composition, although the enormous void above the figures is perhaps the most effective of its kind in Caravaggio's work.

TRAPANI
Sicilia Map A6

Trapani is a charming sea-port, typical in having its old town set out on a narrow promontory – although its old streets are straight and grid-like. Trapani is all the more delightful for no longer being on the route to anywhere. Above it rises the vertiginous mountain of Erice, with its medieval walled settlement, now a modern tourist village.

Museo Pepoli
Via Conte Agostino Pepoli
Tel. (0923) 35444
Open summer Tues, Thurs, Sat
  9am – 1.30pm, Wed, Fri 9am – 1.30pm,
  3 – 6pm, Sun 9am – 12.30pm; winter
  Tues, Thurs, Sat 9am – 1.30pm, Wed,
  Fri 9am – 1.30pm, 3 – 5.30pm, Sun
  9am – 12.30pm
Closed Mon
🕿 🏛 ☑

Formed from 19thC bequests and from that of Conte Agostino Pepoli in 1906, the museum was nationalized in 1925 and is housed in the ex-conventual buildings of the neighbouring Annunziata.

The ground floor has a number of Arabic funerary inscriptions (**Room I**) and **sculpture** by the Gagini family (**Room II**). The first floor begins with the **picture gallery**. **Room III** contains interesting 14thC and 15thC local masters; **Room IV**, 15thC and 16thC imports or copies, including a copy of a van Eyck *Madonna and Angels* that is otherwise unknown.

Passing through **Room VI**, with Baroque paintings that include a *St Antony* by the local 17thC master Andrea Carreca, you reach the pride of the museum, *St Francis Receiving the Stigmata* ★ Although attributed to Titian, this painting is in fact by his workshop or his brother.

Santuario dell' Annunziata
Via Conte Agostino Pepoli
The 14thC church has, attached to its N flank, a 15thC chapel ornamented in a distinct local Gothic style: just beyond this is the present entrance to the church, from Via Pepoli. Turning left into the Cappella della Madonna you find the marble *Madonna of Trapani*, attributed to the workshop of the late 14thC Tuscan sculptor Nino Pisano.

SARDEGNA (*SARDINIA*)

CAGLIARI
Sardegna Map B5

Cagliari, the capital of Sardinia, is beautifully situated on a hill that slopes steeply down to the sea. Unfortunately, half the town was destroyed in World War II, and since then its population has more than doubled, accompanied by much ugly industrial and residential development. There remains, however, an attractive if rather neglected old quarter, with many charming 15thC to 17thC Spanish buildings, as well as earlier monuments built when the town was under Pisan domination. This quarter extends from just behind the port up through a series of alleyways and steps into the Pisan-built citadel.

Cattedrale
Piazza Palazzo
Founded in the 13thC, the cathedral was largely rebuilt in a heavy Baroque style in the 17thC; the hideous facade in a 12thC Pisan style dates from 1933. Inside, the outstanding attractions are near the main entrance: two superlative **marble pulpits ★** (1159–62) by the Pisan artist Maestro Guglielmo. They were originally made for the Duomo at Pisa, but were given to Cagliari in 1312 after Giovanni

Pisano had made his celebrated pulpit (see Pisa, *NORTH CENTRAL ITALY*).

Museo Nazionale Archeologico e Pinacoteca
Piazza Indipendenza
Open Tues – Sat 9am – 2pm, Sun
  9am – 1pm
Closed Mon
🕿 ♥ ⸬

A Neoclassical building on the edge of the citadel houses two separate institutions – an archaeological museum on the ground floor and a picture gallery on the first floor. The Museo Nazionale Archeologico developed out of a private collection of ancient art left to the town's university in 1806 by Duke Carlo Felice of Savoy, later King of Sardinia. The interior is rather seedy, and the style of display old-fashioned, but the collections are the finest in Sardinia.

Although there are numerous Roman, Punic and Early Christian finds, the highpoint of the collections is undoubtedly the **Nuragic bronzes ★** These are small objects featuring strikingly naturalistic and sometimes humorous representations of animals (including bears and monkeys), boats, and human figures engaged in such varied activities as fighting, riding a donkey, playing a traditional Sardinian game called Launedda, and even making love.

The Pinacoteca has mainly **Sardinian religious paintings** from the 14thC to 17thC, many of which were originally in the Cagliari church of San Francesco da Stampace, destroyed by fire in 1872. These paintings are more interesting than attractive, reflecting the very eclectic and parochial nature of Sardinian art. The polyptych of *St Francis and St Nicholas of Mira* (1338–44) by an unknown artist is the finest of the earlier works, and is painted in a contemporary Tuscan style.

Later Sardinian artists blindly followed Spanish example, which in turn was strongly influenced in the 15thC by Flemish art, and in the 16thC by the art of Raphael and his Italian followers. The two finest works in the Pinacoteca are by artists working in a Hispano-Flemish style. These are the *Visitation* by Giovanni Barcelo, whose works echo Spanish interpretations of the art of Rogier van der Weyden, and the various fragments from the **Polyptych of the Porziuncola** by the so-called Master of Castelsardo, who appears to have been trained in the Spanish town of Valencia.

NUORO
Sardegna Map B2

Remotely situated in the central mountains of Sardinia, Nuoro is the most intensely and traditionally Sard of the major towns of the island. On arriving in Nuoro, D.H. Lawrence expressed his pleasure that there was nothing to see – in other words, it was the place itself that mattered, not the buildings or monuments it contained. The folk culture of Nuoro, perhaps best expressed in the traditional costume of the area, has recently had a remarkable efflorescence in painted form. Many of the town's buildings are covered with political (pro-Communist, anti-Fascist) murals. These are somewhat amateurish, but often remarkably lively. Similar murals can be seen in the nearby town of Orgosolò. Just outside Nuoro is Monte Ortobene, at the top of which is a colossal statue of the *Redeemer* (1901) by Vincenzo Ierace.

Duomo
Piazza Santa Maria della Neve
The cathedral is situated on a hill in the old part of the town, but it is an entirely 19thC building, in a sober classical style. To the right of the main altar is a picture of the *Dead Christ* attributed to the 17thC Bolognese painter Alessandro Tiarini.

SASSARI
Sardegna Map A1

The second largest town in Sardinia, Sassari is also the most beautiful. In contrast to the old buildings in Cagliari, those here are in good condition and blend well with the modern ones. Sassari also has a richer artistic history than Cagliari. In the 15thC it was the center of a thriving school of painters headed by one of Sardinia's leading artists, Giovanni Barcelo. Although there was little in the way of painting activity in Sassari in the 16thC and 17thC, this period saw the importation of a large number of works of art from the Italian mainland, particularly from Liguria and Tuscany. At the same time there developed a high level of local craftsmanship, especially in wood and marble intarsia work. The numerous inlaid altarpieces in the town's churches bear eloquent testimony to this.

Museo Nazionale G.A. Sanna
Via Roma
Tel. (070) 272203
Open Tues–Sat 9am–2pm, Sun
*   9am–1pm*
Closed Mon
🏛 ☑ ♨
Named after a mining engineer whose collection was given by his family to the state, the Museo Nazionale G.A. Sanna is in a garden off the town's liveliest street. The building dates from the 19thC, but has a well-modernized interior.

The **archaeological collections** are adventurously and clearly displayed, with extremely helpful information panels. However, these collections are not as rich as those in Cagliari, containing much unexciting Roman work (including a large collection of coins and medals) and relatively few Nuragic bronzes.

The **painting collection** also is weak in Sardinian art, but makes up for this by having a large number of interesting works by artists from mainland Italy and elsewhere. Most notable of the earlier paintings are the *Madonna of the Grape* by Jan Gossaert, a *Madonna* (signed and dated 1473) by Bartolommeo Vivarini and a *Portrait of a Woman* by Piero di Cosimo; there are also numerous works by 17thC and 18thC painters, including Domenichino, Guercino, Lanfranco, Rosa, Solimena and Strozzi.

A smaller building in the garden houses the museum's ethnographic collection, which has some wonderful Sardinian costumes and other examples of local folk art.

BIOGRAPHIES

A selective list of Italian artists, also featuring a number of European artists whose work has been influential in Italy or who have themselves been deeply influenced by Italian art.

Abate, Niccolò dell' c. 1512–71
Painter from Modena, active also in Bologna and France. He is most important for his landscapes with mythological figures, which look forward to Claude and Poussin.
Agostino di Duccio 1418–81
Florentine sculptor and architect, active in various parts of northern Italy. His lively, graceful style shows the influence of antique relief sculpture.
Albani, Francesco 1578–1660
Bolognese painter. He is best known for his mythological and allegorical scenes in landscape settings, which were popular collectors' pieces in the 18thC.
Algardi, Alessandro 1598–1654
Bolognese sculptor, active mainly in Rome. Apart from Bernini, he was the most important Italian sculptor of the 17thC. His style was much more sober and classical than that of his rival.
Allori, Alessandro 1535–1607
Florentine painter and tapestry designer, active also in Rome. He worked in a graceful Mannerist style. His son **Cristofano** (1577–1621) was one of the most attractive Florentine painters of the 17thC and was particularly skilled at depicting rich materials.
Altichiero da Zevio a. late 14thC
Painter, born in Verona and active in Padua, where he was the most distinguished of Giotto's followers. In the Oratorio di San Giorgio he collaborated with an otherwise unknown artist called Avanzo.
Amigoni, Jacopo 1682–1752
Decorative painter, born in Naples and working in Bavaria, England, Flanders and Spain as well as various Italian centers. His style is light and colourful.
Ammanati, Bartolommeo 1511–92
Florentine Mannerist sculptor and architect. As a sculptor he is best known for the Neptune Fountain in Piazza della Signoria.
Andrea del Castagno c. 1421–57
Florentine painter, one of the outstanding artists of the generation following Masaccio. His powerful, sinewy style found a convincing pictorial equivalent for Donatello's sculpture.
Andrea del Sarto 1486–1530
Florentine painter. With Fra Bartolommeo he was the leading painter in Florence in the second decade of the 16thC. His works are noted for their fluent grace of draughtsmanship and composition and for their beautiful colouring.

Angelico, Fra (Guido di Pietro) d. 1455
Florentine painter. A Dominican monk, he is celebrated mainly for the fresco decoration of his monastery of San Marco, in a style of radiant simplicity and great emotional directness. In the 19thC he was considered an "inspired saint", but he was, in fact, one of the most progressive artists of his generation.
Anselmi, Michelangelo c. 1492–1556
Painter active mainly in Parma. His elegant Mannerist style was influenced by Parmigianino.
Antelami, Benedetto a. late 12thC
Romanesque sculptor, active in Parma. He was the most notable Italian sculptor before Nicola Pisano and had wide influence.
Antonello da Messina c. 1430–79
Painter from Sicily, a pioneer of the oil-painting technique in Italy. He visited Venice in 1475–76 and was an important influence on Giovanni Bellini.
Arnolfo di Cambio c. 1245–1302?
Pisan architect and sculptor, active in Florence, Rome and Siena. He was the original designer of the Duomo in Florence (the nave is largely his work) and as both architect and sculptor ranks as one of the most important Italian Gothic artists. His sculpture continued the heroic style of Nicola Pisano.
Arpino, Il Cavaliere d' (Giuseppe Cesari) 1568–1640
Mannerist painter, active in Rome. In the earlier part of his career he was highly favoured with decorative commissions by successive popes, but his style was long outmoded by the time of his death. Caravaggio was briefly his assistant.
Aspertini, Amico c. 1475–1552
Bolognese painter. His output included frescoes, facade decorations and altarpieces painted in a complex Mannerist style. He also made drawings of classical remains in Rome.
Avanzo See ALTICHIERO DA ZEVIO.

Balla, Giacomo 1871–1958
Painter and sculptor, one of the leading Futurist artists. His paintings fulfilled the Futurist demand for art that probed the essence of speed and light and of human reactions to them.
Barna da Siena a. third quarter of 14thC
Sienese painter, probably the most important of his time, although his career is obscure. The works attributed to him are influenced by Duccio and Simone Martini.

Barocci, Federico c.1535–1612
Painter from Urbino, where he spent
almost all his career. The vigour and
freshness of his design and handling place
him apart from the main currents of
Mannerism, making him a forerunner of
the Baroque.

Bartolo di Fredi a.1353–97
The foremost Sienese painter of the
second half of the 14thC apart from
Barna. He was influenced by Barna and
by the Lorenzetti.

Bartolommeo, Fra (Baccio della Porta)
1472/75–1517
Florentine painter, one of the leading
artists of the High Renaissance. He was a
Dominican monk in the convent of San
Marco, where Fra Angelico had worked.
His graceful, idealized style was highly
influential, notably on Andrea del Sarto.

Bassano, Jacopo (Jacopo da Ponte)
c.1510–92
The most important member of a family
of painters from Bassano, the town from
which he takes his name. His style was
robust and bucolic and he helped to
popularize the taste for paintings in
which the genre content takes over from
the ostensibly religious subject. He had
four painter sons, **Francesco** (1549–92),
Gerolamo (1566–1621), **Giambattista**
(1553–1613) and **Leandro**
(1557–1622).

Beaumont, Claudio Francesco
1694–1766
The leading 18thC decorative painter in
Piedmont. He worked mainly in his
native Turin for the Piedmontese royal
family.

Beccafumi, Domenico c.1486–1551
The outstanding Sienese Mannerist
painter. He is particularly noted for his
complex light effects.

Bellini, Giovanni c.1430–1516
The greatest Venetian artist of his day,
largely responsible for making Venice an
artistic center to rival Florence. Two of
his great achievements were the
development of the oil technique to new
heights of subtlety and expressiveness
and the integration of figures and
landscape in perfect harmony. Giorgione
and Titian were among his pupils. His
brother, **Gentile** (c.1429/30?–1507),
was also very talented and is best known
for his large views of religious events in
Venice, full of rich anecdotal detail.
Their father, **Jacopo** (c.1400–70/71),
ran a flourishing workshop but few
paintings by him survive.

Bellotto, Bernardo 1720–80
Venetian view-painter, active mainly
outside Italy. His meticulously detailed
works are sometimes indistinguishable
from those of his master and uncle,
Canaletto.

Benedetto da Maiano 1442–97
Florentine sculptor and architect, who
frequently worked with the assistance of
his brother, **Giuliano** (1432–90). His
work, especially his portraiture, is noted
for its careful naturalism.

Berlinghieri family
Family of painters living in Lucca in the
13thC, among the earliest Italian
painters to be identified by name.
Berlinghiero Berlinghieri was the
founder of the family and he had three
painter sons – **Bonaventura** (the most
talented of the three), **Barone** and
Marco.

Bernini, Gianlorenzo 1598–1680
Sculptor, architect, painter, playwright
and theater designer, the dominant figure
in Italian Baroque art. The son of a highly
accomplished Mannerist sculptor, **Pietro**
(1562–1629), he was remarkably
precocious and astonishingly energetic,
and by his mid-twenties was virtually
artistic dictator of Rome. With his
buildings, fountains and other statuary,
Bernini left a deeper impression on the
face of Rome (almost all his work is
there) than any artist has on any other
city.

Bernini: *Self-portrait, c.1625, Rome,
Galleria Borghese*

Boccioni, Umberto 1882–1916
Painter and sculptor, one of the leading
Futurist artists. He was innovatory in
both mediums, and his semi-abstract
work powerfully expresses the dynamism
of his times. He was killed in World
War I.

Boldini, Giovanni 1842–1931
Painter active mainly in Paris. He had an
international reputation for his
fashionable portraits and also painted
fine street scenes.

Boltraffio, Giovanni Antonio
c. 1466–1516
Milanese painter. He was a pupil of
Leonardo da Vinci and one of his closest
followers.

Bordone, Paris 1500–71
Painter active mainly in Venice, where
he was a pupil of Titian. He is best known
for his Giorgionesque pastoral scenes.

Botticelli, Sandro c. 1445–1510
Florentine painter, one of the most
popular of Renaissance artists. His linear
style owes something to his master Filippo
Lippi, but Botticelli's expressive
gracefulness is highly personal and
distinctive. Paintings such as the
Primavera and *Birth of Venus* are among
the most enduring images in world art.

Bramante, Donato 1444–1514
Architect and painter, born near Urbino.
The foremost architect of the High
Renaissance, he seems to have spent most
of his early career as a painter. His style
was influenced by Piero della Francesca,
who may have taught him.

Bril, Paul 1554–1626
Flemish painter working mainly in Rome,
where he was one of the pioneers of ideal
landscape. His brother, **Matthew**
(1550–83), likewise a landscape painter,
also worked in Rome.

Bronzino, Agnolo 1503–72
Florentine Mannerist painter, the pupil
and adopted son of Pontormo. He is best
known for his elegant and highly polished
court portraits, but he also painted
religious and mythological works.

Bruegel, Pieter c. 1525–69
The greatest Netherlandish painter of the
16thC. In the early 1550s he travelled to
Italy and his experience of the Alps seems
to have inspired his preference for the
high viewpoint and majestic breadth of
vision that characterize many of his
paintings. His sons **Pieter Brueghel the
Younger** (1564–1638) and **Jan "Velvet"
Brueghel** (1568–1625) were also
painters. Pieter imitated his father's
peasant scenes; Jan, a friend of Rubens,
was a celebrated flower painter and noted
for his ability to depict rich textures,
which earned him his nickname.

Brunelleschi, Filippo 1377–1446
Florentine architect and sculptor, one of
the creators of the Renaissance style.
Famous above all as the designer of the
superb dome of the Duomo in Florence,
he was also, early in his career, an
accomplished sculptor (he trained as a
goldsmith). He was not a painter as such,
but he made important contributions to
the development of perspective,
influencing his friend Masaccio.

Buffalmacco (Buonamico Cristofani)
a. first half of 14thC
Painter with a wide contemporary

reputation, but so little is known about
him that he is considered by some to be a
figure of legend rather than history.

Burri, Alberto b. 1915
Artist best known for his disturbing
collages, composed of such diverse
materials as cloth, paint, metal and
charred wood.

Cambiaso, Luca 1527–85
Mannerist painter working chiefly in
Genoa, where he was the outstanding
painter of the 16thC.

Canaletto (Giovanni Antonio Canal)
1697–1768
Venetian painter, active mainly in his
native city apart from a period in England
(1746–56). The most famous view-
painter of the 18thC, he had a virtual
monopoly over the tourist trade in
Venice and his paintings have helped to
form the popular image of the city.

Canova, Antonio 1757–1822
The most celebrated sculptor of the
Neoclassical movement. His fame and
prestige were enormous; he worked for
Napoleon, the papacy and various
members of Europe's royalty and
aristocracy. He was noted for his
generous nature and his influence on
younger sculptors was immense.

Caracciolo, Giambattista 1578–1635
Neapolitan painter, one of the greatest of
Caravaggio's disciples. Whereas most of
Caravaggio's Italian followers imitated
the superficial characteristics of his style,
Caracciolo understood the tragic
grandeur of his art. He had great
influence in Naples.

Caravaggio, Michelangelo Merisi da
1571–1610
The greatest Italian painter of the 17thC,
active mainly in Rome and then in
Naples, Sicily and Malta. His
revolutionary style – characterized by
bold, strongly lit, realistically painted
figures emerging dramatically from dark
shadows – was immensely influential, in
Spain and northern Europe as well as
Italy. Caravaggio's life was as stormy and
intense as his art and in some ways he is
the prototype of the Romantic concept of
the artist as a rebel against society.

Carlevaris, Luca 1665–1730
View-painter, based in Venice. He was
one of the first artists to specialize in this
genre and was a major influence on
Canaletto.

Carlone family
18thC family of frescoists and stuccoists
from Lombardy. The most talented
member was **Carlo Innocenzo**
(1686–1775).

Carpaccio, Vittore c. 1460/65–1525/26
Venetian painter. He painted mainly

religious subjects, but they are set amid the pageantry of 16thC Venice and crowded with charming details.

Carrà, Carlo 1881–1966
One of the leading Futurist painters and later, with de Chirico, the founder of Metaphysical painting.

Carracci, Annibale 1560–1609
Important Bolognese painter, one of the founders of Baroque history painting and the father of ideal landscape. With his brother, **Agostino** (1557–1602), and cousin, **Ludovico** (1555–1619), he played a leading role in the revival of Italian painting from the prevailing rather sterile Mannerism. The Carracci based their work on drawing from nature, encouraging a realistically solid sense of form.

Carriera, Rosalba 1675–1757
Venetian pastel portraitist, the sister-in-law of Pellegrini. She had a remarkable international reputation and received commissions from many of the most eminent patrons of Europe. She became blind in 1743 and died insane.

Carriera: *Self-portrait, 1709, Florence, Galleria degli Uffizi*

Castiglione, Giovanni Benedetto (Il Grechetto) c.1610–65
Versatile and prolific Genoese painter, engraver and draughtsman, active also in Mantua. His works often contain a bizarre or fantastic element and, unusually for an Italian, he was open to foreign influences.

Catena, Vincenzo c.1495–1531
Venetian painter. His derivative but often charming work shows the influence of Giovanni Bellini, Titian and Giorgione.

Cavallini, Pietro a. 1273–1308
Fresco-painter and mosaic designer working in Rome and also Naples. He is often considered a Roman equivalent to

Cimabue, for although his iconography is essentially Byzantine, his figures have a solidity deriving from the antique that looks forward to Giotto.

Cavallino, Bernardo 1616–56?
Neapolitan painter, chiefly of religious works. He developed a sweet and graceful style that was without parallel in contemporary Italian painting.

Cellini, Benvenuto 1500–71
Florentine sculptor and goldsmith, active also in Rome and France. He was one of the most accomplished Mannerist sculptors, but his fame depends largely on his *Autobiography*, one of the most colourful ever written.

Ceroli, Mario b. 1938
Sculptor whose recurrent theme – the individual reduced to a type – is manifested in series of identical, flat, faceless figures.

Cerquozzi, Michelangelo 1602–60
Painter, best known for his battle scenes. He also painted small scenes of street life, peasants and other picturesque subjects in the manner of Pieter van Laer.

Chirico, Giorgio de 1888–1978
Painter, a forerunner of Surrealism, whose works are characterized by an enigmatic, dreamlike quality. With Carrà, he founded Metaphysical painting.

Cigoli, Il (Ludovico Cardi) 1559–1613
Florentine painter and architect, working in Rome as well as his native city. His art lacked consistent direction, but he was the most powerful and original Florentine painter of his time.

Cimabue (Cenni di Pepi) a. c.1272–1302
Florentine painter. There is little secure knowledge concerning him, but he was said to be Giotto's teacher and therefore stands at the beginning of the line of great Italian painters.

Cima da Conegliano, Giovanni Battista c.1459–c.1518
Painter, active mainly in Venice. An accomplished painter of altarpieces, his work resembles that of the mature Giovanni Bellini.

Claude Gellée called **Claude Lorraine** 1600–82
French painter, active in Rome for almost all his life. He was the most famous exponent of ideal landscape painting and was enormously influential. His works, which show extraordinary sensitivity to effects of light, are much more gentle and elegiac than those of his friendly rival Poussin.

Conca, Sebastiano 1679–1764
Painter of religious and historical scenes, active mainly in Naples and Rome. His work successfully fused influences from Giordano and Maratta.

Correggio (Antonio Allegri) d. 1534
Painter, named after his birthplace in
Emilia, but active mainly in Parma. He
was one of the most inventive and
influential artists of the High
Renaissance. His dome paintings form a
link between the illusionism of Mantegna
and that of the great Baroque ceiling
decorators, and his brilliant handling of
erotic subjects was an inspiration for
Rococo painters.

Cortona, Pietro da (Pietro Berrettini)
1596–1669
Painter and architect. Next to Bernini,
the most versatile genius of the Italian
Baroque. As a painter he was at his best
with large-scale decoration and his use of
rich stucco to embellish his frescoes was
highly influential.

Cosmati family
Family of 12thC Roman marble-workers
after whom a type of decorative inlay
work using coloured stones and glass is
named.

Cossa, Francesco del c. 1435–c. 1477
With Tura and Roberti, the principal
painter of the 15thC Ferrarese school.
His style is less wiry than Tura's, but just
as sharply focused.

Costa, Lorenzo c. 1460–1535
Painter, born in Ferrara and active in
Bologna and then in Mantua, where he
succeeded Mantegna as court painter to
the Gonzaga. His style was influenced by
Tura and Roberti as well as Mantegna,
and he mainly painted mythological and
allegorical scenes.

Credi, Lorenzo di c. 1458–1537
Florentine painter, a pupil of Verrocchio
at the same time as Leonardo. He was a
superb craftsman but rather uninventive.

Cremona, Tranquillo 1837–78
Painter, specializing in portraits and
genre scenes. His rapid, fluid
brushstrokes influenced the Divisionisti.

Crespi, Daniele c. 1598–1630
Milanese painter of austere religious
works reflecting the spirit of the Counter-
Reformation. His prolific career was cut
short by the plague.

Crespi, Giambattista (Il Cerano)
c. 1575–1632
Painter, sculptor, architect, engraver and
writer, active mainly in Milan, where he
was one of the most important artists of
the early 17thC. His paintings are often
reminiscent of Barocci, but have a
distinctive feeling of morbid mysticism.

Crivelli, Carlo 1435/40–1495/1500
Painter, born in Venice and active
mainly in the Marches. His paintings are
extraordinarily richly detailed and the
effect of density is often increased by the
use of raised gesso detailing. **Vittorio** (a.
1481–1501/2), probably his brother, was
a faithful but pedestrian follower.

Daddi, Bernardo a. c. 1290–1349
The leading Florentine painter of the
generation after Giotto. He had a large
workshop specializing in the production
of small devotional panels.

Danti, Vincenzo 1530–76
Sculptor from Perugia, active mainly in
Florence. His style was inspired by
Michelangelo's, but had more grace and
much less power.

Desiderio da Settignano c. 1430–64
Florentine sculptor. He is noted for the
subtle delicacy of his marble technique
and his sensitivity to individual
expression.

Dolci, Carlo 1616–86
Florentine painter. His sweet, enamel-
smooth religious paintings won him an
international reputation, but today
appear rather sickly. His portraits are now
considered his finest works.

Domenichino (Domenico Zampieri)
1581–1641
Bolognese painter, Annibale Carracci's
favourite pupil. Working chiefly in Rome
and then in Naples, he produced some of
the finest fresco decoration of his time.
He was also one of the pioneers of ideal
landscape painting, an incisive portraitist
and a superb draughtsman.

Domenico Veneziano d. 1461
Painter of Venetian origin, working
chiefly in Florence. He is noted for his
soft atmospheric colour and subtle light
effects, which influenced his one-time
assistant, Piero della Francesca.

Donatello (Donato di Niccolò)
1386–1466
Florentine sculptor, active in Padua as
well as his native city. He was not only
the greatest Italian sculptor before
Michelangelo but also probably the single
most influential artist of the 15thC.
With Brunelleschi and Masaccio, he was
one of the creators of the Renaissance,
and a pioneer of perspective and the
understanding of antique art.

Dossi, Dosso (Giovanni Luteri)
c. 1490–1542
Painter, working at the court of Ferrara
for most of his career. He is noted for his
opulent textures and colours, often
accompanied by a striking sense of the
exotic. His brother, **Battista**
(c. 1497–1548), worked in a similar
manner.

Duccio di Buoninsegna a. 1278–1318
The greatest painter of the Sienese
school. He is comparable to Giotto in the
way he broke away from Byzantine
conventions, although his figures are less
solid. Unlike Giotto, he did not work in
fresco. His panels are marked by
wonderful colouring and superb
craftsmanship, and he renders human
relationships with exquisite sensitivity.

Dughet, Gaspard (also called Gaspard Poussin) 1615–75
French landscape painter active in Rome, the pupil and brother-in-law of Poussin. His style contains elements of Poussin and Claude, and his work was very popular and influential in the 18thC.

Duquesnoy, François (Il Fiammingo) 1594–1643
Flemish sculptor active in Rome, where he and Algardi were the leading sculptors apart from Bernini. His style is more classical and restrained than Bernini's, showing the influence of his friend Poussin.

Dürer, Albrecht 1471–1528
German painter, printmaker and writer on art, the greatest artist of the northern Renaissance. He twice visited Italy and was particularly influenced by Giovanni Bellini. His work reconciles German intensity of vision with Italian idealism of form, and was enormously influential in Italy as well as northern Europe.

Dyck, Sir Anthony van 1599–1641
The most important Flemish painter of the 17thC apart from Rubens. He was in Italy 1621–28, working chiefly in Genoa, where he developed his aristocratic portrait style, distinctive for its dazzling brushwork and exquisite sensitivity of characterization.

Elsheimer, Adam 1578–1610
German landscape painter working mainly in Italy. Despite his short career and small output, he was a major influence on the development of landscape painting as an independent genre. Rembrandt and Rubens (a friend of Elsheimer) were both inspired by his poetic sense and exquisite lighting effects.

Fanzago, Cosimo 1591–1678
Architect and sculptor, active in Naples from 1608. He was more interested in the decorative aspects of architecture than in structure, and his church interiors are exuberant and colourful.

Fattori, Giovanni 1825–1908
The leading painter of the Macchiaioli group. Best-known for his portraits, he was a masterly handler of brilliant light effects.

Ferrari, Gaudenzio c. 1475–1546
Painter active in Piedmont and Lombardy. His elaborate work is highly individualistic, drawing on a number of sources, including German art.

Feti (Fetti), **Domenico** 1588/9–1623
Painter, working principally in Mantua and Venice. He is best known for his highly original paintings of subjects drawn from the Parables – a kind of Venetian version of Dutch genre.

Filarete (Antonio di Pietro Averlino) c. 1400–69?
Florentine sculptor, architect and theorist, active mainly in Milan, where he settled after being accused of stealing a relic in Rome. He was an idiosyncratic artist, and his work is a fascinating mixture of old and new, of medieval and Renaissance ideas.

Filarete: *Self-portrait medal, c. 1466, London, Victoria & Albert Museum*

Foggini, Giambattista 1652–1737
The leading Florentine sculptor of his generation, active also in Pisa and Pistoia. His style shows some influence from Bernini but is rather dry.

Fontana, Lucio 1899–1968
Abstract painter and sculptor. He is best known for introducing the concept of Spatialism, in which artists and scientists would cooperate to express new ideas in a total art form synthesizing colour, sound, movement, space and time.

Foppa, Vincenzo c. 1428–c. 1515
Painter, born in Brescia, and active also in Genoa, Milan and Pavia. He was the leading painter in Lombardy before the arrival of Leonardo da Vinci in Milan in 1481/2.

Francesco di Giorgio Martini 1439–1501/2
Sienese painter, sculptor, architect and military engineer, active also in Milan, Naples and Urbino. He is best known for his influential architectural treatise. His paintings and sculpture continued Sienese traditions.

Franciabigio (Francesco di Cristofano) c. 1482/3–1525
Florentine painter, a pupil of Piero di Cosimo and collaborator of Andrea del Sarto and Fra Bartolommeo. His portraits are his best works, but his spacious architectural settings are also impressive.

Furini, Francesco c.1600–46
One of the most distinctive Florentine painters of the 17thC, best known for his paintings of morbidly erotic female nudes emerging mysteriously from dark backgrounds.

Gaddi, Taddeo c.1300–c.1366
Florentine painter, the closest follower of Giotto, for whom he is said to have worked for 24yrs. His father, **Gaddo** (c.1250–1327/30?), was a painter and mosaicist and his pupil and son, **Agnolo** (d.1396), perpetuated a direct line of descent from Giotto to the end of the 14thC.

Gagini, Domenico d.1492
Sculptor, born at Bissone and active in Genoa, Naples and finally Sicily. His style is often close to Francesco Laurana's and the two may have worked in partnership. Domenico's son, **Antonello** (1478–1536), was the foremost Sicilian sculptor of the Renaissance. His output was prodigious.

Gaulli, Giambattista (Il Baciccio) 1639–1709
Genoese painter, active mainly in Rome, where he was a protégé of Bernini. He was a master of Baroque illusionism and is remembered chiefly for his fresco decorations in Roman churches, but he was also a distinguished painter of altarpieces and portraits.

Gentile da Fabriano c.1370–1427
Painter, presumably from Fabriano in the Marches, active in Venice, Florence, Siena, Orvieto and Rome. He was the outstanding International Gothic painter in Italy and his work – colourful, courtly, graceful and exquisitely detailed – was widely influential.

Gentileschi, Orazio 1563–1639
Caravaggesque painter, born in Pisa and active mainly in Rome but also in Genoa, France and England, where he settled in 1626. One of the most distinctive of Caravaggio's followers (and one of the few to know the master personally), he is noted for his graceful draughtsmanship and poetic feeling. His daughter, **Artemisia** (1593–c.1652), was also a Caravaggesque painter. She worked in Rome and Florence, then in 1630 settled in Naples, where she was based for the rest of her life. Her powerful, sombre works mark her out as one of Caravaggio's outstanding followers and as perhaps the greatest of all women painters.

Ghiberti, Lorenzo 1378–1455
Florentine sculptor, goldsmith, stained-glass designer, architect and writer, a major figure in the transition between Gothic and Renaissance. His flourishing workshop provided the training ground for Donatello, Uccello and other important artists. His *Commentaries* are the first autobiography of an artist.

Ghirlandaio, Domenico 1449–94
Florentine painter. He had a large workshop and his frescoes in Florentine churches provide a vivid record of contemporary life. His son, **Ridolfo** (1483–1561), was an accomplished portraitist and a friend of Raphael.

Giambologna (Giovanni Bologna) 1529–1608
Italian sculptor of Flemish origin, the most important sculptor in Italy between Michelangelo and Bernini. He worked mainly in Florence and was one of the leading figures of Mannerism.

Giambologna: *Drawing by Goltzius, 1591, Haarlem, Teylers Museum*

Giaquinto, Corrado 1702–65
Neapolitan Rococo painter, active also in Rome, Turin and Madrid, where he became court painter to Ferdinand VI. His work is light-hearted and colourful.

Giordano, Luca 1634–1705
The most important Neapolitan painter of the later 17thC, known as "Luca fa presto" (Luke go quickly) for the speed at which he produced his enormous output in oil and fresco. He travelled widely in Italy and also spent ten years in Spain.

Giorgione da Castelfranco 1476/78–1510
Venetian painter. Giorgione is an enigmatic figure and very few paintings are certainly known to be by him, but his importance is great. He was one of the first artists to paint small pictures for private collectors and the mood of his works, usually one of poetic reverie, is often more important than the subject. Many Venetian painters, including Titian, imitated the Giorgionesque mood in pastoral paintings and portraits.

Giotto di Bondone c. 1267–1337
Florentine painter and architect, the
founder of the main tradition of Western
painting because of the way he broke
away from the flat Byzantine style and
introduced concern with an illusionistic
pictorial space. He worked all over Italy
and had immense prestige and influence.
Little of his work survives intact, but his
frescoes in the Cappella degli Scrovegni
in Padua are unsurpassed in their
grandeur and intensity of feeling and
place him among the giants of European
art.

Giovanni da Milano a. 1360s
Painter, Milanese by birth, but active in
Florence. His career is obscure, but he
was one of the outstanding artists of the
mid 14thC.

Giovanni da San Giovanni (Giovanni
Mannozzi) 1592–1636
Florentine painter. An isolated figure, he
was the only 17thC Florentine painter to
work mainly in fresco.

Giovanni di Paolo a. late 1420s–1460s
Sienese painter of small-scale religious
works. His elegant style continued the
tradition of Duccio and Simone Martini,
but he added a delightful wistfulness of
his own.

Giovanni di Pietro See SPAGNA, LO.

Giuliano da Maiano See BENEDETTO DA
MAIANO.

Giulio Romano 1499?–1546
Painter and architect, Raphael's chief
pupil and assistant and one of the most
important Mannerist artists. His finest
work is in Mantua, where he designed the
Palazzo del Tè and decorated it with
virtuoso illusionistic frescoes.

Goes, Hugo van der d. 1482
The greatest Netherlandish painter of the
later 15thC. His masterpiece, the
Portinari altarpiece, was shipped to
Florence in the mid 1470s and its brilliant
oil technique had a lasting effect on
Italian artists.

Gozzoli, Benozzo c. 1421–97
Florentine painter, remembered
primarily for his frescoed decoration of
the chapel in the Palazzo Medici-Riccardi
in Florence. His other works rarely
approach the captivating brilliance he
showed there.

Greco, El (Domenikos Theotokopoulos)
1541–1614
Cretan-born Spanish painter, one of the
most individual artists of his time. He
lived in Italy in the 1560s and 1570s and
is said to have been one of Titian's last
pupils. Tintoretto, however, is a much
more obvious influence on his intensely
emotional style.

Guardi, Francesco 1712–93
Venetian painter, best known for his
view-paintings, which are remarkably
freely painted and much more
atmospheric than Canaletto's. His output
was enormous, but he died in poverty. He
came from a family of artists, and his
brother, **Gianantonio** (1699–1760), also
painted in a vibrant, sketchy style. It is
sometimes not possible to distinguish one
brother's work from the other's.

Guariento di Arpo a. 1338–70
Paduan painter, a follower of Giotto,
active also in Venice. Much of his most
important work has unfortunately been
destroyed.

Guercino, Il (Gianfrancesco Barbieri)
1591–1666
Painter from Cento, near Ferrara, active
mainly in Rome and Bologna, where he
became the city's leading painter after
Reni's death. He was one of the most
individual of Italian Baroque painters,
although the originality of his youth
gradually faded. His nickname means
"squint-eyed".

Guglielmo della Porta d. 1577
Sculptor, active mainly in Rome. He was
a prolific artist and there are many tomb
sculptures by him in Roman churches. He
also made several papal busts.

Hayez, Francesco 1791–1882
Painter of religious, historical and
mythological works and portraits, active
mainly in Milan. He was an important
figure in the transition from
Neoclassicism to Romanticism and
exerted great influence as a teacher.

Jacobello del Fiore a. 1401–39
The most important Venetian painter of
his time. He worked in a somewhat stiff,
formal International Gothic style and
had many state commissions.

Laer, Pieter van 1592–1642
Dutch genre painter, known as
Bamboccio ("clumsy baby") because of
his deformed body. In 1625 he went to
Italy, where he specialized in Roman
street scenes. These popular works
inspired a host of followers known as
Bamboccianti – mainly other northern
artists working in Rome.

Lanfranco, Giovanni 1582–1647
Painter from Parma, active mainly in
Rome and Naples. An outstanding fresco
decorator, he was one of the founders of
the mature Baroque style in painting and
had wide influence.

Laurana, Francesco c. 1430–1502?
Sculptor of Dalmatian birth, working in
France as well as various parts of Italy. His
finest and most original works are his
female portrait busts.

Leonardo da Vinci 1452–1519
Florentine artist, scientist and writer, one
of the greatest of Renaissance painters
and perhaps the most versatile genius
who has ever lived. He was the creator of
the High Renaissance style, and his
modelling through light and shade was
one of the foundations of later European
painting. Leonardo's immense prestige
and fame helped to raise the status of the
visual arts: the idea of the artist as a
creative thinker rather than an artisan
stems chiefly from him.

*Leonardo da Vinci: Self-portrait
drawing, c.1512, Turin, Palazzo Reale*

Liberale da Verona c.1455–c.1529
Painter and manuscript illuminator,
working mainly in his native Verona but
also in Siena and Venice. He painted
frescoes but was happiest with exquisite
small-scale illuminations.
Lippi, Filippino c.1457–1504
Florentine painter, the son of Filippo
Lippi. His best works are his frescoes,
which anticipate something of the
monumental grandeur of the High
Renaissance.
Lippi, Fra Filippo c.1406–69
Florentine painter, a Carmelite monk
who caused a scandal because of his love
affair with a nun. He was one of the finest
painters of the generation following
Masaccio, evolving a much more delicate
and linear style. He taught Botticelli.
Liss (Lys), **Johann** c.1597–1631
German painter working mainly in Italy,
particularly Venice. The looseness and
freedom of his brushwork and his high-
keyed colour influenced the great
Venetian painters of the 18thC.
Lomazzo, Giovanni Paolo 1538–1600
Milanese painter. He became blind in
1571 and turned to writing, producing his

influential *Treatise on the Arts of Painting,
Sculpture and Architecture* in 1584. It has
been described as a Mannerist bible.
Lombardo family
Family of Venetian sculptors consisting
of **Pietro** (c.1435–1515) and his sons,
Tullio (c.1455–1532) and **Antonio**
(d.1516). Their successful workshop
produced monuments and chapel
decorations in Venice, Padua and
Treviso. Tullio, the most individual
member of the family, developed a fluent
and original classical style.
Longhi, Pietro 1702–85
Venetian genre painter. His charming,
small-scale paintings provide a record of
fashionable life in 18thC Venice. His
son, **Alessandro** (1733–1813), was the
foremost Venetian portraitist of his day.
Lorenzetti, Ambrogio a. c.1319–c.1348
Sienese painter. Ambrogio was one of the
leading painters to develop the
innovations of Giotto and Duccio and, in
particular, was among the first artists to
paint realistic landscape. His brother,
Pietro (a. c.1319–c.1348), was also one
of the outstanding painters of his time,
with a keen awareness of Florentine art.
Both brothers probably died in the Black
Death of 1348.
Lorenzo Monaco c.1370–c.1425
Sienese painter, a monk, working mainly
in Florence. His brightly coloured,
elegant style was rooted in Sienese
tradition, but also showed the influence
of International Gothic. His work was
rather outmoded by the time of his death.
Lotto, Lorenzo c.1480–1556/57
Venetian painter. He was something of a
stylistic maverick and his work is uneven,
but at his best he was an artist of great
distinction. His finest works are his
portraits, usually bold in design and
moody in atmosphere.
Luini, Bernardino a.1512–32
Prolific Milanese painter, one of the most
prominent of Leonardo's followers. He
vulgarized Leonardo's style, but was
highly successful.

Maderno, Stefano 1576–1636
Sculptor from Bissone, active in Rome.
He was one of the leading sculptors in
Rome until eclipsed by the young
Bernini.
Maffei, Francesco c.1600–60
Baroque painter from Vicenza, active in
various parts of northern Italy. His style
was refreshingly unorthodox,
characterized by nervous brushwork and
strangely elongated figures.
Magnasco, Alessandro 1667–1749
Genoese painter of religious scenes and
fantastic, eerie landscapes, active mainly
in Milan. The drama of his style and the

freedom of his technique owe much to Rosa and he was particularly appreciated in the Romantic era.

Maitani, Lorenzo d. 1330
Sienese sculptor and architect. From 1310 he was architect to the Duomo at Orvieto, and much of the rich sculptural decoration of the facade is credited to him.

Manfredi, Bartolommeo c. 1587–1620/1
Painter, active mainly in Rome, where he played an important role in the dissemination of Caravaggio's style. His genre scenes of taverns and other low-life subjects were particularly popular.

Mantegna, Andrea c. 1430–1506
Paduan painter and engraver, one of the most renowned artists of the 15thC. He worked mainly for the Gonzaga court at Mantua, where he created brilliant illusionistic decorations in the Palazzo Ducale. His paintings reveal his devotion to classical antiquity, but although his style is precise it is never dry – indeed he was one of the wittiest of great painters. Giovanni Bellini, his brother-in-law, was one of many artists influenced by him.

Manzù, Giacomo b. 1908
One of the most individual of contemporary sculptors. Much of his work is religious, and demonstrates the possibility of producing figurative sculpture relevant to 20thC concerns.

Maratta or **Maratti, Carlo** 1625–1713
The leading painter in Rome in the second half of the 17thC. He is best known for his calm and dignified religious works, but he was also a fine portraitist. He had many pupils and imitators and his reputation has suffered because their inferior works have often been attributed to him.

Marini, Marino 1901–80
Sculptor, painter and graphic artist. He is best known for his bronze sculptures, in which he brilliantly exploits the varied surface qualities of the medium.

Masaccio (Tommaso di Ser Giovanni di Mone) 1401–28?
Florentine painter, one of the great innovators of the early Renaissance. His mastery of perspective and understanding of light provided the first great advance in naturalism in painting since Giotto. Among contemporary artists only his friend Donatello matched the grandeur and emotional intensity of his work. He died tragically young.

Masegne brothers
Venetian late Gothic sculptors, **Jacobello dalle Masegne** (d. c. 1409) and his brother, **Pierpaolo** (d. 1403?). They worked also in Bologna, Pavia and Milan, and were the dominant sculptors in northern Italy between about 1380 and 1400.

Masolino da Panicale 1383/4–1447
Florentine painter, active in Hungary as well as in various Italian centers. He briefly worked with Masaccio and was for a time strongly influenced by him before returning to the more decorative style of his youth.

Mazzoni, Guido a. 1473–1518
Sculptor, painter and miniaturist from Modena, active there and in Naples and France, where he worked for Charles VIII. He is best known for his life-size terra-cotta groups.

Mazzoni, Sebastiano c. 1611–78
Baroque painter of bizarre originality, also a poet and architect, born in Florence and active mainly in Venice. He was highly imaginative in his choice and treatment of subject matter, and his brilliantly free brushwork looks forward to the great 18thC Venetian painters.

Melozzo da Forlì 1438–94
Painter from Forlì in the Romagna, active chiefly in Loreto, Urbino and Rome. He was one of the most appealing and idiosyncratic painters of his time, but little of his work survives and he has been somewhat neglected until recently. His virtuoso skill at foreshortening is comparable with Mantegna's.

Memmi, Lippo a. 1317–57
Sienese painter, remembered chiefly as the brother-in-law and collaborator of Simone Martini. His independent work consists mainly of small panel paintings.

Michelangelo Buonarroti 1475–1564
Florentine painter, sculptor, draughtsman, architect and poet, one of the supreme giants of world art. In his early career he expressed the most sublime concepts through ideally beautiful figures, and in his later years created religious works of an awesomely intense piety. His effect on European art has been incalculable: for three centuries after his death, hardly any artist who expressed himself through the medium of the human body remained untouched by his influence.

Mochi, Francesco 1580–1654
The most original Italian sculptor of the early 17thC until overtaken by Bernini. He worked mainly in Rome and his best works are among the first pieces of Baroque sculpture.

Mola, Pier Francesco 1612–66
Painter, active mainly in Rome. He was one of the chief representatives of the Romantic strain in Roman painting that ran alongside Cortona's Baroque and Sacchi's classicism.

Morandi, Giorgio 1890–1964
Painter who was deeply influenced by Surrealism and the Metaphysical movement. He is best known for his still-lifes.

Moretto (Alessandro Bonvicino)
c. 1498–1554
Painter, active mainly in his native
Brescia and in Bergamo. He is best known
for his strong and direct portraits and
seems to have introduced the
independent full-length portrait to Italy.

Morlaiter, Gianmaria 1699–1781
German-born Italian sculptor, active in
Venice, where at the peak of his career he
received virtually all the major sculptural
commissions.

Moroni, Giambattista c. 1525–78
Painter, a pupil of Moretto and, like him,
active mainly in Bergamo and Brescia.
He continued his master's sober style of
portraiture, adding to it his own
distinctive, delicate, silvery tonality.

Mura, Francesco de 1696–1784
Neapolitan painter, active also in Turin.
He was the leading pupil of Solimena,
whose style he continued.

Niccolò dell'Arca (or d'Apulia)
c. 1435–94
South Italian sculptor active mainly in
Bologna. His style is realistic and highly-
charged emotionally.

Niccolò da Guardiagrele 1395?–before
1462
Goldsmith and painter from
Guardiagrele in the Abruzzi. He is best
known for his richly decorated silver
processional crosses.

Nittis, Giuseppe de 1846–84
Painter from Barletta, specializing in
landscape, bourgeois interiors and scenes
of contemporary city life. In 1867 he
moved to Paris, where he exhibited with
the Impressionists.

Orcagna (Andrea di Cione) a. 1343–68
Painter, sculptor and architect, the most
important Florentine artist of the third
quarter of the 14thC. His two brothers,
Nardo di Cione (a. 1343/6–65/6) and
Jacopo (a. 1365–98), were also leading
painters in Florence. Their style was
somewhat softer than Andrea's, which
was impressively severe.

Palma, Jacopo (called Palma Giovane)
1548–1628
Venetian painter, the great-nephew of
Palma Vecchio. He trained with Titian
and after the death of Tintoretto was the
leading painter in Venice.

Palma Vecchio (Jacopo Negreti)
c. 1480–1528
Painter active mainly in Venice. His
richly sensuous paintings are similar in
style to early Titian. He is particularly
noted for his superbly voluptuous blond-
haired women, who are found not only as
portraits or allegories but also as saints.

Paolo Veneziano a. 1321–62
The most important Venetian painter of
the 14thC. His characteristic products
were large, sumptuous polyptychs, many
of which were exported to the Venetian
colonies of the Adriatic coast.

Parmigianino (Girolamo Francesco
Maria Mazzola) 1503–40
Mannerist painter and engraver from
Parma, active there and in Rome and
Bologna. His extraordinarily graceful and
sophisticated style had wide influence,
spread partly by his etchings.

Pascali, Pino 1935–67
Painter and sculptor, one of the major
innovators in Pop art in the 1960s.

Pellegrini, Gianantonio 1675–1741
Venetian decorative painter. He was very
prolific (at times rather slapdash) and
worked all over Europe.

Perino del Vaga (Piero Buonaccorsi)
1501–47
Florentine painter, active also in Rome,
Genoa and Pisa. He was one of the
principal followers of Raphael and a
leading exponent of Mannerism.

Perugino, Pietro (Pietro Vannucci)
c. 1445–1523
Painter from Perugia, active also in
Florence. His style has a distinctive
sweetness and grace, qualities he passed
on to the young Raphael.

Perugino: *Self-portrait from* **Christ
Giving the Keys to St Peter**, *1481–82,
Rome, Musei Vaticani, Sistine Chapel*

Peruzzi, Baldassare 1481–1536
Sienese architect and painter, active
mainly in Rome. As a painter he is best
known for his elaborate perspective
illusions.

Piazzetta, Giambattista 1683–1754
One of the outstanding Venetian artists
of his period. He was much more serious
and deliberate in approach than most of
his Rococo contemporaries.

Piero di Cosimo 1462–1521
Florentine painter, one of the most
charmingly idiosyncratic artists of his
time. His paintings often have a
captivating, whimsical quality, and he
seems to have been an eccentric
character – according to Vasari he lived
on hard-boiled eggs.

Piero della Francesca 1416?–92
Painter from Borgo San Sepolcro, long
neglected after his death, but now
perhaps the most revered painter of the
early Renaissance. His style is marked by
mathematical beauty of composition,
solemnly graceful figures and marvellous
sensitivity to the effects of light.

Pintoricchio (Bernardino di Betto)
c.1454–1513
Painter from Perugia, active also in Siena
and Rome. He was probably a pupil of
Perugino and his style is similar, although
more sumptuous – well-suited to the
pageant-like secular subjects in which he
excelled.

Piranesi, Giambattista 1720–78
Artist born in Venice but active mainly
in Rome. He is best known today for his
etchings of architectural views, which
greatly influenced Neoclassical
architects.

Pisanello (Antonio Pisano)
c.1395–1455/56
Painter and medallist from Pisa, active in
various parts of northern Italy, mainly as
a court artist. He was an outstanding
exponent of International Gothic,
and a superb observer of naturalistic
details, particularly animals.

Pisano, Andrea a.before 1330–c.1348
Sculptor, goldsmith and architect,
probably from Pisa but unrelated to
Giovanni and Nicola Pisano. He worked
mainly in Florence, especially on the
Duomo and Baptistry. His son and pupil,
Nino (a.1349?–1368), was one of the
earliest sculptors to specialize in life-size
free-standing figures.

Pisano, Nicola a. c.1258–84
Pisan sculptor, originally from Apulia in
southern Italy. He was perhaps the first
artist whose style was decisively formed
by a study of antique art and he stands at
the head of the tradition of Italian
Renaissance sculpture. His son,
Giovanni (a. c.1265–1314), was the
greatest Italian sculptor of his time,
active in Pisa, Siena, Perugia and Pistoia.
He breathed new drama and movement
into Nicola's forms, but his
expressiveness was too personal to find
much of a following.

Pittoni, Giambattista 1687–1767
Venetian painter. His rather sentimental
Rococo style attracted commissions from
the Danish, German and Swedish courts
but he never left Italy.

Pollaiuolo brothers
Florentine painters, sculptors and
goldsmiths. **Antonio** (1431/2–98) and
his brother, **Piero** (1441–96), ran an
important workshop. Antonio was the
more original artist, noted particularly for
his vivid representations of the nude in
action and for his minutely observed
landscape backgrounds.

Pontormo (Jacopo Carucci) 1494–1557
Painter from Pontormo, active mainly in
Florence. He was one of the greatest
Mannerist artists, expressing great depth
of feeling through his tense, elongated
figures and vivid colours.

Pordenone (Giovanni Antonio de'
Sacchis) 1483–1539
Painter from Pordenone in the Friuli,
active mainly in the small towns of the
Veneto. His finest works are his frescoes,
often marked by startling illusionistic
effects in which figures appear to lunge
into the spectator's space.

Poussin, Nicolas 1593/4–1665
French painter, active in Rome for
almost all his career. He was the chief
formulator of the French classical
tradition in painting, his works being
based on a profound study of ancient
literature and art. His paintings were
generally fairly modest in size and
produced for a highly cultivated circle of
private clients.

Pozzo, Fra Andrea 1642–1709
Painter, architect and stage designer, one
of the greatest masters of illusionistic
ceiling decoration. He was a Jesuit lay-
brother and decorated several churches of
the Order. His treatise on perspective
(1693) was influential.

Preda or **Predis brothers**
Milanese painters. **Ambrogio da Preda**
(c.1455–after 1508) and his half-
brother, **Evangelista** (a.1483–after
1490), are remembered chiefly as
assistants to Leonardo da Vinci, although
Ambrogio has some individual substance
as a portraitist.

Preti, Mattia (Il Calabrese) 1613–99
Painter from Calabria, widely travelled
and prolific, active most notably in
Rome, Naples and Malta, where he
settled in 1661. His early easel paintings
are Caravaggesque; his frescoes owe
much to Lanfranco.

Previtali, Andrea a.1502–28
Painter, active in his native Bergamo and
in Venice, where he trained with
Giovanni Bellini. His work is uneven and
eclectic but sometimes very charming.

Primaticcio, Francesco 1504/5–70
Bolognese painter and architect. He
worked with Giulio Romano in Mantua,
then in 1532 went to France, where he
was one of the key figures in the spread of
Mannerism.

Procaccini, Giulio Cesare 1574–1625
Painter and sculptor from Bologna,
active mainly in Milan, where he was one
of the leading artists of the early 17thC.
His father, **Ercole** (1515–95), and his
brother, **Camillo** (c. 1560–1629), were
also painters active in northern Italy.

Queirolo, Francesco 1704–62
Sculptor, born in Genoa and active
mainly in Rome and Naples. His style
derived ultimately from Bernini and he
was a virtuoso technician.
Quercia, Jacopo della 1374/5–1438
The greatest Sienese sculptor of the
15thC. His career was peripatetic; for
much of it he was working at the same
time on more than one commission in
different places. Michelangelo was
influenced by his vigorous, heroic style.

Raphael (Raffaello Sanzio) 1483–1520
Painter and architect in whose works are
found the most complete embodiment of
the ideals of the High Renaissance. For
three centuries after his death he was
almost universally regarded as the
greatest of all painters – the artist who
had expressed the loftiest ideals of
Christianity with the grace and grandeur
of the antique. He had several important
pupils, most notably Giulio Romano, and
his influence was enormous.
Reni, Guido 1575–1642
Bolognese painter, active also in Rome.
His pure, classical style brought him
immense fame and in the 18thC he was
considered by many critics second only to
Raphael. His reputation later suffered
when the work of his many imitators
became confused with his, but he is now
highly esteemed again.
Ribera, Jusepe de (José) **de** (called Lo
Spagnoletto) 1591–1652
Spanish painter, etcher and
draughtsman, all of whose known career
was spent in Italy, especially Naples. His
early works are in a powerful
Caravaggesque style; his late works are
more richly coloured and spiritual.
Ricci, Sebastiano 1659–1734
Venetian decorative painter. He led an
itinerant life, working in England,
Flanders, France and Germany as well as
numerous Italian centers, and his prolific
output is very uneven. His nephew,
Marco (1676–1730), chiefly a landscape
painter, often collaborated with him.
Riccio, Il (Andrea Briosco)
1470/5–1532
Sculptor from Padua. He is best known
for his bronze statuettes, which reproduce
on a small scale the quality of Roman
statuary.

Robbia, Luca della 1400–82
The best-known member of a family of
Florentine sculptors famous for their
coloured terra-cotta reliefs, found as
architectural decoration as well as
independent works. Luca's son,
Giovanni (1469–1529), and his nephew,
Andrea (1435–1525), carried on the
workshop.
Roberti, Ercole de' c. 1450–96
Painter active mainly in Ferrara, where
he succeeded Tura as court painter to the
Este in 1487. His mannered, linear style
is reminiscent of Cossa.
Romanelli, Gianfranco c. 1610–62
Painter and tapestry designer, the chief
pupil of Pietro da Cortona. His style was
sweeter and more classical than his
master's, and his restrained version of
Baroque was influential in France, which
he twice visited.
Romanino, Girolamo c. 1484–after 1559
Painter from Brescia, active in various
parts of northern Italy. His style
combined Venetian colour with the
realism typical of Brescian art.
Romano, Antoniazzo c. 1461–1512
Probably the most noteworthy native
Roman painter of the late 15thC. His
work is not very distinguished compared
with that of his greatest contemporaries,
but he worked on many papal
commissions.
Rosa, Salvator 1615–73
Neapolitan painter and etcher, active
mainly in Rome and best known for the
creation of a new type of wild, rugged
landscape. He was also a poet, actor and
musician and one of the prototypes of the
Romantic concept of the artist.
Rosselli, Cosimo di Lorenzo 1439–1507
Florentine painter. He lacked originality
but his facility and craftsmanship resulted
in many official commissions. He taught
Andrea del Sarto, Fra Bartolommeo and
Piero di Cosimo.
Rossellino, Bernardo 1409–64
Florentine sculptor and architect, one of
the leading artists of his generation. His
sculptural works display a poised and
refined classicism. His brother, **Antonio**
(1427–79), was also a sculptor and is
noted for his portrait busts.
Rosso, Medardo 1858–1928
One of the most original sculptors of his
time. Working chiefly in wax, he caught
the fleeting effects of light and
atmosphere in a manner comparable to
that of the Impressionist painters.
Rosso Fiorentino (Giambattista di
Jacopo) 1495–1540
Florentine painter. His figures are elegant
and self-conscious, but often display
convincingly intense emotion. From
1530 he worked in France, and was
influential in the spread of Mannerism.

Rubens, Sir Peter Paul 1577–1640
The greatest Flemish painter of the
17thC. He was the dominant figure of
Baroque art in northern Europe, but his
style was formed chiefly in Italy, where
he lived 1600–3 and 1604–8, working
mainly in Genoa and Rome. Rubens, in
his turn, influenced many Italian artists.

Sacchi, Andrea 1599–1661
Painter, the chief exponent of classicism
in painting in Rome in the mid17thC. He
was happiest working on a small scale and
was a fine portraitist. Maratta was his
principal pupil.

Salviati, Francesco (Francesco de' Rosso)
1510–63
Florentine Mannerist painter and
tapestry designer, active also in Rome,
Venice and France. His style is rich and
complex and has something of
Parmigianino's elegance.

Sammartino, Giuseppe 1720–93
One of the leading Neapolitan sculptors
of his day, renowned for his virtuoso skill
as a stone carver.

Sansovino, Andrea 1467/70–1529
Florentine sculptor and architect,
working also in Rome and Loreto. His
most important and influential works
were his wall tombs in Santa Maria del
Popolo, Rome.

Sansovino, Jacopo (Jacopo Tatti)
1486–1570
Florentine sculptor and architect, active
mainly in Venice, where he was one of
the most important artists of the 16thC.
He was a pupil of Andrea Sansovino,
whose name he took.

Saraceni, Carlo c. 1580–1620
Venetian-born painter, active chiefly in
Rome. His style was formed on the
examples of Caravaggio and Elsheimer
and when both died in 1610 Saraceni
seems to have taken something of their
market.

Sassetta (Stefano di Giovanni)
1392/1400–50
One of the most important Sienese
painters of the 15thC. He continued the
Sienese tradition of decorative elegance
but was also aware of current Florentine
advances.

Sassoferrato (Giambattista Salvi)
1609–85
Painter, named after his place of birth,
and active mainly in Urbino, Perugia and
Rome. His very sweet, purely drawn
religious works enjoyed great popularity.

Savoldo, Gian Girolamo a. 1508–after
1548
Brescian painter, active mainly in
Venice. He had an individual poetic
sensibility, which comes out particularly
in his nocturnal scenes.

Schiavone, Andrea (Andrea Meldolla)
c. 1510/15–1563
Venetian painter, born in Dalmatia. He
mainly painted small-format
mythological subjects with landscape
backgrounds for private patrons.

Sebastiano del Piombo (Sebastiano
Veneziano) c. 1485–1547
Venetian painter, active mainly in
Rome, where he was a protégé of
Michelangelo. Sebastiano's work
combines the rich colouring of his
Venetian training with Roman grandeur
of form. He painted little after he was
appointed keeper of the papal seals in
1531: they were made of lead (*piombo*),
hence his nickname.

Serpotta, Giacomo 1656–1732
Sicilian sculptor in stucco, in which
medium he was an unsurpassed virtuoso.
He decorated numerous churches in
Palermo with his ravishingly delicate and
often playful work.

Signorelli, Luca a. 1470–1523
Painter from Cortona, active in
Florence, Loreto, Orvieto, Perugia,
Rome and Siena. One of the most
powerful artists of his day, he is
particularly noted for the grandeur and
vigour of his nudes.

Signorelli: *Self-portrait from fresco cycle,*
1499–1505, Orvieto, Duomo

Simone de' Crocifissi c. 1330–99
Bolognese painter, a follower of Vitale da
Bologna. His name derives from the
numerous versions of the ***Crucifixion***
that he painted.

Simone Martini c. 1285–1344
Apart from Duccio, the greatest artist of
the Sienese school. He was highly
esteemed and worked on prestigious
commissions as far apart as Naples and
Avignon. His exquisite gracefulness and
decorative richness influenced French as
well as Italian painters.

Sodoma, Il (Gianantonio Bazzi)
1477–1549
Painter, born in Vercelli, and active
mainly in and around Siena, where with
Beccafumi he was the leading painter of
the day. His style was bizarrely eclectic –
old-fashioned and up-to-date elements
mingling in an often attractive manner.
Solimena, Francesco 1657–1747
Neapolitan painter. He was Giordano's
successor as the unchallenged head of the
Neapolitan school and the most
influential Italian painter between
Maratta and Tiepolo. His works were sent
all over Europe and he taught many of the
leading painters of the next generation.
Spagna, Lo (Giovanni di Pietro) d. 1528
Painter of obscure but presumably
Spanish origin, active mainly in Umbria.
His style derived from Perugino and, to a
lesser extent, Raphael.
Spinello Aretino a. 1385–1410
Painter from Arezzo, possibly a pupil of
Agnolo Gaddi, much influenced by
Giotto. One of the most productive
painters of his time, he filled numerous
churches in Arezzo, Florence, Pisa and
Siena with fresco cycles, often in
collaboration with his son, **Parri
Spinelli**.
Squarcione, Francesco 1397–1468
Paduan painter. Although his life is
obscure, it is clear that his studio helped
to make Padua an important artistic
center. His interest in classical sculpture
was passed on to his pupil, Mantegna.
Stanzione, Massimo 1586–1656
One of the leading Neapolitan painters of
his period. He worked in an impressively
sombre Caravaggesque style, later
modified by Bolognese classicism to such
an extent that he has been called "the
Neapolitan Guido Reni".
Strozzi, Bernardo 1581–1641
The leading Genoese painter of the early
17thC, active also in Venice. His rich
colour and handling were influenced by
Rubens and van Dyck.

Tacco, Pietro 1577–1640
Florentine bronze sculptor,
Giambologna's principal pupil and his
successor as sculptor to the dukes of
Tuscany. He completed several works
Giambologna left unfinished at his
death.
Tanzio da Varallo (Antonio d'Enrico)
1574/80–1635
Painter from Varallo, active mainly there
and in nearby Milan. He probably visited
Rome c. 1610/15, and his style was
considerably influenced by Caravaggio,
although the strange feeling of tension
that pervades much of his work is
personal and distinctive.

Tassi, Agostino c. 1580–1644
Painter, born and mainly active in Rome.
He was one of the leading *quadratura*
specialists of his day, but also produced
small landscapes. Claude was his pupil.
Testa, Pietro 1611–50
Etcher and painter from Lucca, active
mainly in Rome. His work has a bizarre
and romantic quality that places him
temperamentally with artists such as
Castiglione and Mola.
Tibaldi, Pellegrino 1527–96
Painter and architect, one of the leading
Mannerists of the late 16thC. He worked
in Rome, Bologna and Milan, and also in
Spain, where he helped to introduce the
Mannerist style.
Tiepolo, Giambattista 1696–1770
The greatest Italian (and arguably
European) painter of the 18thC and the
last of the great line of fresco decorators.
He worked mainly in his native Venice,
but also in Germany and Spain. His
output was enormous, and he was a
superb etcher and draughtsman as well as
painter. He was assisted in many of his
major fresco cycles by his sons,
Giandomenico (1727–1804) and
Lorenzo (1736–before 1776).
Tino di Camaino c. 1285–1337
Sienese sculptor and architect, active
also in Pisa, Florence and Naples. He was
probably taught by Giovanni Pisano and
his work was highly influential.
Tintoretto, Jacopo (Jacopo Robusti)
1518–94
Venetian painter, with Veronese the
leading artist in the city after Titian's
death. He produced a prodigious amount
of work (most of it still in the place for
which it was painted) in a bold and
dramatic style that often makes use of
strange and vivid light effects.
Titian (Tiziano Vecellio) d. 1576
The greatest Venetian painter and one of
the most celebrated names in the history
of art. He was famed throughout Europe,
the Emperor Charles V and Philip II of
Spain being among his most important
patrons. In every department of painting
he reigned supreme; in particular, he
revolutionized the oil technique, giving
his paint an expressive life of its own. His
influence was enormous.
Torriti, Jacopo a. late 13thC
Mosaic designer, active in Rome. Almost
nothing is known of him, but his work led
to a revival of the mosaic technique.
Traini, Francesco a. 1321–69
The most important Pisan painter of the
late 14thC. His style was heavily
influenced by Sienese artists.
Tura, Cosimo c. 1431–95
The founder and, with Cossa and
Roberti, the leading painter of the 15thC
school of Ferrara, where he became court

painter in 1452. His harsh colouring and hard, knotted forms create a feeling of great emotional tension.

Uccello, Paolo 1396/7–1475
Florentine painter. His virtuoso skill with perspective places him in the scientific current of the Renaissance, but his love of decorative display is typical of International Gothic. His successful combination of these two features produced one of the most attractive and distinctive styles of his generation.

Uccello: *Self-portrait from **The Founders of Florentine Art**, c.1450, Paris, Louvre*

Vasari, Giorgio 1511–74
Painter, architect and writer from Arezzo, working mainly in Florence and Rome. He was an accomplished painter and a fine architect but is best remembered for his *Lives of the Most Eminent Painters, Sculptors and Architects*, the first great work of art history.

Vecchietta (Lorenzo di Pietro) c.1410–80
The most influential Sienese artist of the late 15thC, active as a painter, sculptor, draughtsman and architect. He was a pupil of Sassetta, and his subtle and lively style continued Sienese traditions.

Velazquez (Velásquez), **Diego Rodriguez de Silva y** 1599–1660
The greatest of Spanish painters. He made two trips to Italy (1629–31, 1649–51) and the leading Venetian masters were a major influence on his style, helping to loosen his brushwork. In return, Velazquez's portrait of *Innocent X* had great impact in Italy.

Veronese, Paolo (Paolo Caliari) 1528–88
Painter from Verona, active mainly in Venice, where with Tintoretto he was the leading painter after Titian's death. He was essentially a great decorator, happiest working on a huge scale with scenes of extravagant pomp.

Verrocchio, Andrea del (Andrea di Cione) 1435–88
Florentine sculptor, painter and metal worker. He had the most important studio in Florence in the second half of the 15thC and taught Leonardo da Vinci among others. He has been overshadowed by his famous pupil, but he was a great artist in his own right.

Vitale da Bologna a.1334–61
The most important 14thC Bolognese painter. His colouring is vivid and his compositions are extravagant.

Vittoria, Alessandro 1525–1608
Sculptor, active mainly in Venice, where he was Jacopo Sansovino's pupil and, after the latter's death, the leading sculptor in the city. His prolific output included much monumental work in churches, also medals, small bronzes and portrait busts.

Vivarini family
Family of Venetian painters. **Antonio** (c.1419–76/84) and his brother, **Bartolommeo** (c.1432–99), specialized in carefully composed, highly-finished polyptychs, often working in collaboration. Antonio's son, **Alvise** (c.1445–c.1505), carried on the workshop and painted some perceptive portraits.

Vouet, Simon 1590–1649
The most important French painter of the early 17thC. From 1613–27 he worked in Italy (mainly Rome) and the accomplished eclectic style he took back to France with him was highly influential. He owed his success to hard work and adaptability rather than genius.

Wiligelmo a. late 11thC/early 12thC
Romanesque sculptor, active in Modena. His squat, vigorous figures were widely influential in northern Italy.

Zoppo, Marco Ruggieri 1432–78
Painter and miniaturist, born in Cento and active mainly in Bologna, Venice and Ferrara. He probably trained with Squarcione. His rather harsh linear style is reminiscent of Tura.

Zuccarelli, Francesco 1702–88
Painter of landscapes and mythological works, active mainly in Venice and also in England, where his charming Rococo scenes were very popular.

Zuccaro brothers
Mannerist painters. **Taddeo Zuccaro** (1529–66) and his brother, **Federico** (1540/1–1609), had great reputations and influence in their day, but now seem merely competent. At the peak of his career, Federico was probably the most famous artist in Europe.

GLOSSARY

A selection of the main schools, movements, styles, terms and techniques that appear in this book.

A

Abstract art
Art that does not attempt to represent the appearance of objects real or imaginary, although it may conjure up images for the viewer.

Aisle
Lateral division of a church, flanking the nave or chancel on one or both sides.

Altarpiece
Decorated screen or panel(s) on or behind the altar.

Ambulatory
A continuous aisle around a circular building; an aisle around the apse of a church, originally used for processional purposes.

Antique
The physical remains of the ancient world or, as the expression is more particularly understood in art-historical usage, of Greek and Roman sculpture.

Apse
A semi-circular or polygonal termination to a building, particularly the E end of a church.

Arcade
Range of arches on piers or columns.

Archaic
Pre-Classical Greek art dating from the late 8thC BC to 480BC when the Persians sacked Athens.

Architrave
The lowest part of an entablature; also, more loosely, the moulded frame around a door or window.

Atrium
In Roman houses, an inner courtyard; in early Christian and medieval churches, a colonnaded forecourt.

B

Baldacchino
A canopy over an altar, throne or tomb. It may rise on columns or hang from the ceiling.

Baptistry
Part of a church containing the font for the baptismal rite. It is often a separate building.

Baroque
Term broadly characterizing Western art produced from the beginning of the 17thC to the mid 18thC. Its salient qualities are dynamic movement, overt emotion and self-confident rhetoric. The combination of painting, sculpture and architecture to create an overpowering effect was typical of the Baroque, notably in the work of Bernini, the archetypal Baroque artist.

Basilica
Rectangular Roman civic hall; early Christian church of similar structure.

Bozzetto
Small-scale preparatory model, usually in wax or clay, for a piece of sculpture. The term may also be applied to a painted sketch.

Bucchero ware
A type of Etruscan pottery with a black glaze.

Byzantine art
Art associated with the Eastern Roman Empire, which was founded by the Emperor Constantine in 330 and ended when his capital, Constantinople (formerly called Byzantium), was captured by the Turks in 1453. Byzantine art is characteristically flat and frontal in composition and serious and otherworldly in feeling. Western art produced under its influence is often called Byzantinizing.

C

Campanile
A belltower, usually free-standing.

Canopic vase
A vessel used in Etruscan funeral rites to hold human remains.

Cantoria
A gallery for singers in a church.

Capital
The topmost part of a column or pilaster, often elaborately carved.

Caravaggisti
Term applied to early 17thC painters who adopted features of Caravaggio's style, particularly his emphatic chiaroscuro.

Cartoon
Preliminary, but fully worked-out, drawing to establish the design of a fresco, easel-painting or tapestry.

Caryatid
Carved female figure used as a column.

Cassone
A large chest, either given as a wedding present or used to contain a bride's dowry. *Cassoni* were usually richly decorated, and painted panels from them are now often found as separate pictures.

Cella
Main body of classical temple.

Chancel
Part of church reserved for clergy and containing altar and choir; or, more

generally, the whole of the church E of the nave.

Chiaroscuro
Term, from the Italian for "bright-dark", applied to strongly contrasting light and shade effects in painting.

Choir
Part of church where services are sung, generally in W part of chancel, also used as a synonym for chancel.

Ciborium
An altar canopy; also a liturgical casket for holding the consecrated Host.

Cinquecento
Term, literally the "500s", used of the 16thC, the 1500s, in Italian art.

Cippus
Monumental stone pillar, carved with inscriptions or figures, used in the ancient world to mark a burial place.

Classicism
Term used to describe the qualities of order, clarity and harmony associated with the art of ancient Greece and Rome. In its strictest sense, it refers to the Classical period in Greek art, dating from 480BC to the death of Alexander the Great in 323BC. More loosely, the term is used as the antithesis of Romanticism, denoting art that places adherence to accepted canons of beauty above personal inspiration.

Collage
A picture or design created by sticking pieces of paper, material or other (usually everyday) items onto a flat surface.

Colonnade
Row of columns supporting arches or an entablature.

Colossus
Term that may be applied to any statue appreciably over life-size.

Contrapposto
Italian term used to describe a pose in which the figure maintains balance but twists or turns out of a single plane.

Cope
An ecclesiastical cloak, worn particularly on ceremonial occasions.

Corbel
A bracket or block projecting from a wall to support a roof beam or vault.

Cornice
The topmost part of an entablature; also, more generally, any ornamental moulded projection that crowns or finishes a wall, window or other feature.

Cosmati work
Decorative inlay work using coloured stones and glass, named after the family of 12thC Roman marble-workers who perfected the craft.

Crossing
Space formed by the intersection of the nave, chancel and transepts in a cruciform church.

Crypt
A room beneath the main floor of a church (but not necessarily underground) often used as a burial chamber.

Cupola
A dome, particularly a small, decorative one.

Cusp
The point at which the arcs of two foils meet.

Diptych
A painting or other work of art consisting of two panels or sections, often hinged together.

Divisionism
Alternative term for the technique of Pointillism, developed by French painters such as Seurat. Small dabs of pure colour are applied straight onto the canvas, letting the eye, at the correct viewing distance, mix them optically. The intention is to create an effect of vibrancy. Italian exponents of the technique are known as Divisionisti.

Entablature
In classical architecture, the arrangement of three horizontal bands (architrave, frieze and cornice) between capitals and pediment.

Etruscan art
Art of the Etruscans, the earliest recorded inhabitants of modern-day Tuscany, who were at the height of their power in the 6thC BC. Techniques and styles were borrowed initially from the Greeks of southern Italy but the Etruscans went on to develop a highly individual idiom.

Faïence
A kind of earthenware named after the city of Faenza, still an important center for pottery manufacture.

Fibula
A brooch used to fasten a cloak or tunic at the shoulder.

Figurative art
Painting or sculpture which contains recognizable subjects. The opposite of abstract art.

Fluting
Shallow, vertical grooves on columns or pilasters.

Foil
A small arc in tracery, especially window tracery.

Forum
In Roman architecture, a central space surrounded by public buildings and colonnades.

Fresco
Method of wall painting using water-based paint applied to wet plaster. Paint and plaster fuse as they dry, forming a matt, stable surface.

Frieze
Part of the entablature between architrave and cornice; also, a similar decorative band along the upper part of an internal wall.

Futurism
Italian artistic and literary movement, flourishing 1909–15, which tried to incorporate the dynamism of modern technological society into art.

Genre
Term used to describe paintings of everyday life. In a more general sense, the term describes any distinctive type of painting, such as landscape.

Gesso
Mixture of gypsum and glue applied as a priming to panels to provide a smooth, brilliant white surface for painting.

Gothic
Style of art and architecture prevailing in Europe from the mid 12thC to the 16thC. Gothic is characterized chiefly in terms of architecture, above all by the use of pointed arches, and was assimilated less in Italy than in other parts of Europe.

Graffiti
Scratched or scribbled designs on walls, commonly humorous or obscene.

Greek cross
Cross with arms of equal length.

Grisaille
Painting executed entirely in tones of grey or neutral greyish colours.

Grotesque
Painted or sculpted decoration made up of festoons of tendril-like foliage and scrolled ornament.

Grotto
An artificial cave-like structure used as a garden ornament.

Hellenistic
Post-Classical Greek art dating from 323BC to the late 1stC BC.

High Renaissance See RENAISSANCE.

Hypogeum
An underground chamber, especially one used for burials.

Icon
Image of a saint or other religious figure, particularly applied to panel paintings of the Byzantine and subsequently the Eastern church.

Illusionism
The use of pictorial techniques to create a convincing or even deceptive sensation of real space and form on a two-dimensional surface.

Impasto
Thickly applied paint that creates a textured surface.

Impressionism
Late 19thC movement in painting, originating in France, which sought to produce a spontaneous impression of a scene or object rather than a calculated, detailed portrayal.

Intaglio
Design that is engraved on a hard surface, or the method of producing such a design.

Intarsia
Method of decorating a wooden surface by inlaying it with differently coloured woods and other materials such as ivory and mother-of-pearl.

International Gothic
Style of painting and sculpture that flourished in the late 14thC/early 15thC in most of Europe. Essentially a courtly style, it was characterized by elegance, refinement and a development of interest in secular subjects.

Italiot
Term sometimes used to describe the art of the Greek colonies of Italy.

Jamb
The vertical inside face of a doorway, window or other architectural feature.

Kouros (plural kouroi)
Type of ancient Greek nude male statue. The female equivalent is the *kore* (plural *korai*), which is clothed.

Krater
Ancient Greek vessel, used for mixing wine and water.

L

Latin cross
Cross with three short arms and one long arm.

Lithograph
Print produced from a design drawn or painted onto a limestone block or metal plate.

Loggia
A gallery open on one or more sides. It may be a separate structure, usually in a garden.

Lunette
A semi-circular window or, more generally, any flat, semi-circular panel.

M

Macchiaioli
Group of late 19thC Italian painters, active mainly in Florence, who produced *plein-air* landscapes.

Madonniere
A painter specializing in depictions of the Madonna and Child. The term often refers to anonymous journeymen.

Maestà
Work of art portraying the Madonna and Child enthroned, surrounded by saints or angels.

Majolica
Type of pottery, said to have originated in Majorca (Latin *Majorica*), particularly popular in the Renaissance.

Mandorla
An almond-shaped aura of light surrounding the figure of God, Christ, the Virgin or, less commonly, a saint.

Mannerism
The dominant style in European art from about 1520 to the end of the 16thC. It was characterized by hyper-sophistication and self-consciousness and often has disturbing emotional overtones, marking a reaction from the serene harmony of the High Renaissance.

Marquetry
A pattern formed by inlaid coloured woods, ivory or even shells, referring particularly to furniture.

Metaphysical painting
Short-lived movement in Italian painting founded by de Chirico and Carrà in 1917. It was related to Surrealism in its use of dream imagery and in its desire to express meanings lying beyond physical appearance.

Metope
Block between the triglyphs of an architectural frieze. It may be blank but is often richly carved.

Mithraeum
Temple dedicated to Mithras, a god of sunlight of Persian origin, whose cult was widespread in the Roman Empire. Mithraea were usually artificial underground caves.

Modello
A preparatory painting, drawing or sculpture, generally carried out to show a prospective client how the finished work would look.

Mosaic
Picture or design made by setting small pieces of stone, glass or ceramic materials into cement or plaster. The pieces are called tesserae.

N

Narthex
A porch or vestibule at the W end of a church.

Nave
The western limb of a church or, more specifically, the central space of that area, usually bounded on either side by an aisle.

Necropolis
A cemetery or burial site.

Neoclassicism
Movement dominating European art and architecture in the late 18thC and early 19thC. It was marked by a heroic severity of tone – a reaction against Rococo frivolity – and by a desire for archaeologically correct detail, in part stimulated by the discovery of Herculaneum and Pompeii.

Niello
Black metallic compound used to incise a design on a metal surface.

Nymphaeum
Originally, a cave dedicated to nymphs; later, a term applied to any grotto or building incorporating a fountain and intended as a pleasurable retreat.

O

Obelisk
A square or rectangular free-standing pillar with sides that taper towards a pyramidal top; it was a popular form for monuments.

Oratory
A room or small chapel used for private prayer.

Orthogonal
In perspective, a line apparently at right angles to the picture plane, which if continued far enough meets all other orthogonals at a central vanishing point.

Ottonian art
Art produced in Germany under the Ottonian dynasty (10thC–11thC). It preceded Romanesque.

Painterly
Art term denoting an approach to form which is the opposite of linear. Painterly artists visualize their subject in areas of mass and light and shade.

Pantocrator
Greek term meaning "Almighty", used of Byzantine images of Christ in majesty.

Patera
Shallow dish used in Roman times for sacrificial purposes.

Pediment
A low-pitched triangular gable above an entablature; a similar triangular or segmental feature over a window, doorway or other architectural feature.

Pendentive
One of the concave triangular segments that leads from the angle of two walls to the lower rim of a circular dome.

Perspective
The means by which a sensation of three-dimensional space is created on a flat picture surface, relying on the optical impressions that parallel lines converge as they recede, and that objects become smaller and closer together in the distance.

Piano nobile
The main storey of an Italian house or palace. It is usually raised one storey above ground level.

Pietà
Representation of the Virgin supporting the dead Christ on her lap.

Plein-air
Term used to describe paintings that have been executed out of doors, rather than in a studio. French for "open-air".

Polychrome
Term applied to a work or object (usually a piece of sculpture) that is made or decorated with various colours.

Polyptych
A painting or other work of art consisting of four or more panels or sections, often hinged together.

Pop art
International art movement, at its peak in the 1960s, using objects of popular culture as its theme.

Portico
Covered, often colonnaded, entrance to a building.

Predella
One or more small panels fixed to the bottom of an altarpiece.

Presbytery
The part of a church that contains the main altar.

Putto
Type of chubby, naked child, sometimes winged, first appearing in antique art and found as a common decorative motif in painting and sculpture from the 15thC onwards.

Quadratura
Illusionistic architectural decoration of walls or ceilings, which appears to extend the real architecture of a room into an imaginary space.

Quattrocento
Term, literally the "400s", used of the 15thC, the 1400s, in Italian art.

Relief
Sculpture that projects from, but is still attached to, a background. Classified as high, medium or low relief according to how much the forms project.

Renaissance
Intellectual and artistic movement, inspired by a rediscovery and reinterpretation of classical culture; it originated in 14thC Italy and eventually became the driving force behind the arts throughout much of Europe. The period from c. 1500 to c. 1520 is known as the High Renaissance, when the works of the three great giants – Leonardo, Michelangelo and Raphael – reached a peak of harmony and balance that has ever since been recognized as a touchstone in world art.

Reredos
A screen or wall decoration behind an altar.

Retable
An altarpiece that stands on the back of the altar or on a pedestal behind it.

Rococo
Style characterized by intimacy of scale, asymmetry, lightheartedness and grace, which in the early 18thC superseded the more formal grandeur of the Baroque.

Romanesque
Style of art and architecture prevailing in Europe in the 11thC and 12thC. Romanesque is characterized chiefly in terms of its architecture, which is massive and round-arched.

Romanticism
Artistic and literary movement flourishing in Europe from the late 18thC

to the mid19thC. Romantic art is characterized by the spontaneous expression of the artist's feelings.

Rotunda
Building or room that is circular in plan.

Roundel
Circular panel or medallion.

Sacra conversazione
Term (literally "holy conversation") describing a representation of the Virgin and Child with saints where the figures are united in a single scene rather than occupying the separate compartments of a polyptych.

Sacristy
Room in or attached to a church used for storing sacred vessels and priests' vestments.

Sarcophagus
A stone coffin or chest-shaped tomb, often decorated with sculpture.

Scapigliatura
Literary and artistic movement centered on Milan in the 1860s and 1870s. The term means "dishevelled", and refers to the Bohemian lifestyle of those involved. The Divisionisti owed much to the Scapigliati.

Scuola
A Venetian fraternal society, organized under the auspices of the Church and dedicated to good works.

Seicento
Term, literally the "600s", used of the 17thC, the 1600s, in Italian art.

Sfumato
Term deriving from the Italian for "smoke". It describes the soft, hazy effect produced by the imperceptible blending of colours.

Sinopia
The underdrawing of a fresco, sometimes exposed if a fresco is damaged or carefully removed from the wall for conservation.

Spandrel
The triangular surface or area between two arches or between an arch and a wall.

Stela
An upright stone slab, carved with inscriptions or figures, used for commemorative purposes.

Stucco
Light, malleable plaster reinforced with powdered marble, used for architectural decoration and for sculpture.

Surrealism
Movement in art and literature, originating in France and at its peak in the 1920s and 1930s, that used incongruous juxtapositions of images in an effort to explore the subconscious.

Tabernacle
A canopied niche containing a sculptured figure or other image.

Tempera
Pigment mixed with egg white or yolk, the usual medium with which easel pictures were painted until the 15thC, when it began to be superseded by oil.

Tenebrism
The use of a very dark overall tonality.

Terra cotta
Brownish-red clay used to make pottery and sculpture.

Tessera See MOSAIC.

Tondo
Italian word for "round", used to describe a circular painting or sculpture.

Tracery
Ornamental open-work in Gothic architecture.

Transept
Either of the two projecting arms of a cross-shaped church.

Trecento
Term, literally the "300s", used of the 14thC, the 1300s, in Italian art.

Tribune
In a basilica, apse containing the bishop's throne, or the throne itself.

Triglyph
Stone block in an architectural frieze, decorated with three vertical grooves.

Triptych
A painting or other work of art consisting of three panels or sections, often hinged together.

Triumphal arch
In Roman architecture, a monumental arch built to commemorate a victory.

Trompe l'oeil
Term (French for "deceive the eye") used to describe the application of illusionistic skill to persuade the spectator that a painted object is a real one. *Trompe l'oeil* paintings often have a witty intention, as when a fly is painted on a part of the picture where a real one might alight.

Tumulus
An ancient burial mound.

Tympanum
The space between the flat top of a doorway and the arch above it.

Vault
An arched roof or ceiling.

Volute
A spiral scroll, especially on the capital of a column.

INDEX

PICTURE ACKNOWLEDGMENTS

All photographs for this book were supplied by Scala, Florence, with the exception of the following:

101 – Courtauld Institute of Art (Conway Library), London
121 right, **147, 223, 275, 282, 284** – Mansell Collection, London
190 top left – Nimatallah/Joseph P. Ziolo, Paris
191 center – Professor Gabriele Mandel, Milan
192 center left – Museo Burri, Città di Castello
192 center right and bottom – Galleria Nazionale d'Arte Moderna, Rome
201, 265 – Robert Harding Associates, London
279 – Victoria & Albert Museum, London
280 – Teylers Stichting, Haarlem
287, 289 – Fratelli Alinari, Florence